OXFORD JUNIOR
ENCYCLOPAEDIA

VOLUME VI
FARMING AND FISHERIES

OXFORD JUNIOR ENCYCLOPAEDIA

GENERAL EDITORS
LAURA E. SALT AND ROBERT SINCLAIR
ILLUSTRATIONS EDITOR: HELEN MARY PETTER

VOLUME VI

FARMING AND
FISHERIES

OXFORD UNIVERSITY PRESS

SET IN GREAT BRITAIN
AT THE UNIVERSITY PRESS, OXFORD
AND REPRINTED BY
FERNDALE BOOK COMPANY LTD. LONDON

FIRST EDITION 1952
REPRINTED 1956, 1957

PRINTED IN GREAT BRITAIN

PREFACE

IN authorizing the preparation of this work the Delegates of the Oxford University Press had foremost in mind the need to provide a basic book of reference for school libraries. In form it was to be a genuine encyclopaedia, in treatment and vocabulary suitable for the young reader. To many children (and indeed to many adults) reading is not a natural activity: they do not turn to books for their own sake. But they can be trained to go to books for information which they want for some particular purpose—and thus, very often, to form a habit which will be of lifelong value. Their capacity to read continuously for any length of time being limited, they can absorb knowledge better if they get it in small quantities: therefore they will often read reference books when they may reject the reading of more extended matter. Again, it is probably true to say of such readers that their approach is from the particular to the general, and from the application to the principle, rather than the reverse, that their main interest is in the modern world around them, and that since they are not very good at conceiving things outside their own experience, their capacity for grasping abstract ideas is limited. On the other hand, once their interest is aroused, they will often pursue a subject to remarkable lengths, so long as its development is logical and the treatment avoids dullness.

But such generalizations can easily be overdone: many children using the books will not be of this type. Moreover, it was evident from the first that a project involving so great an amount of work, however exactly it might meet its principal mark, would be fully justified only if it could be of service to a far wider circle of readers. Even for the age-group first in mind, anything like 'writing down to children' must plainly be taboo—but clear exposition and simple language are no bad qualities in writing for any audience. Here, then, it seemed, was the opportunity to provide a work of reference suitable for many readers to whom the large, standard encyclopaedias are too heavy and technical, and the popular alternatives for the most part neither sufficiently complete nor authoritative. The fact that the plan allowed for an exceptionally large proportion of illustrations to text (between one-quarter and one-third of the total space) is an advantage to any reader, since pictures may, in many instances, save whole paragraphs of involved explanation. With these secondary aims well in mind, therefore, the General

Editors have ventured to hope that the encyclopaedia may find usefulness not only among certain younger children, but also among older students in clubs, libraries, and young people's colleges, and even to no small extent among their parents and other adults who may wish for a simple approach to some unfamiliar or forgotten subject.

SCOPE AND EMPHASIS. Within certain limits the OXFORD JUNIOR ENCY-CLOPAEDIA purports to be reasonably comprehensive, though (in common with all general encyclopaedias) not exhaustive. Chief among these limits is that matter already easily available in school text-books is included only so far as its presence is necessary for the proper understanding of the subject under discussion. Thus, although an immense field of history is surveyed, it will be found mainly under headings dealing with its effects, or in the biographies of those who lived to make it. Purely technical or scientific subjects, also, are omitted except when they have some general interest. In natural history and kindred studies the immense variety of forms necessarily led at times either to their treatment by groups or to their omission on purely arbitrary decisions as to which species would, in all probability, never be looked for, or because there was nothing particularly interesting to say of them. In point of general balance the stress is laid rather on the modern world, though due space is given to the factors which have shaped it, no less than to those which are changing it.

ARRANGEMENT. The encyclopaedia is planned to consist of twelve volumes. Each is arranged alphabetically within itself, and each deals with a particular range of related subjects. Within its terms of reference, then, each volume is virtually self-contained, and, owing to the great number of single-line cross-references, can well be used alone. This arrangement, which has several incidental advantages (as of production, in difficult times, and of prompt revision later), arose mainly from one consideration. If articles were to be kept really short—and, in fact, few approach and almost none exceeds 2,000 words—many subjects could be dealt with comprehensively only by referring the reader to other relevant articles—itself a desirable thing to do. It was clearly preferable for these to be under his hand, rather than be dispersed through any of the twelve volumes at the caprice of the alphabet. This the present arrangement achieves to a great extent. If it has led to a small amount of overlapping, that again is not without its advantages.

The cross-references play an indispensable part in the make-up of the encyclopaedia. They are of two kinds: references in the text to further articles amplifying the particular point under review, and references at the end of an article to others taking the whole subject farther. Therefore, a reader looking up any wide subject, such as FORESTRY, and following up its cross-references either in the text or at the end of the article, can discover under what main headwords the subject is treated. These, again, will refer him to any subsidiary articles, as also, in many cases, to those of a complementary nature. Thus he may be guided either from the general to the particular or vice versa. It is believed that the titles of the twelve volumes (see p. xii), in conjunction with their sub-titles, will usually lead the reader straight to the volume containing the information he wants. In selecting headwords, the rules generally followed have been to prefer the familiar, or even the colloquial, reserving the technical alternative for a single-line entry, and to group narrow subjects under a headword of wider scope. Thus, for HORTICULTURE, *see* GARDENING; for BRASSICA, *see* CABBAGE CROPS; for OAK or ASH, *see* TREES, BROADLEAVED; and for FOOT AND MOUTH DISEASE, *see* ANIMAL DISEASES.

L. E. S., R. S.

OXFORD, 1952

LIST OF CONTRIBUTORS

EDITOR

ANNESLEY VOYSEY, B.Sc.

PRINCIPAL CONTRIBUTORS

Agricultural History

C. S. ORWIN, M.A., D.Litt., formerly Director of the Agricultural Economics Research Institute, Oxford.

Farms and Farming

F. FRASER DARLING, D.Sc., Ph.D., N.D.A., F.R.S.E.

JOHN R. ALLEN.

Arable and Grass Crops

H. I. MOORE, M.Sc., Ph.D., N.D.A.

Livestock

F. FRASER DARLING, D.Sc., Ph.D., N.D.A., F.R.S.E. (Cattle, Horses, Sheep).

NOEL L. TINLEY, N.D.A., late Lecturer in Agriculture, Wye College, London University (Pigs).

L. C. TURNILL, late Poultry Lecturer, Kent Farm Institute (Poultry).

Tropical Agriculture

SIR HAROLD TEMPANY, Editor of *World Crops*, formerly Agricultural Advisor to the Colonial Office.

H. L. EDLIN, B.Sc.

Farm Tools and Machinery

H. J. HINE, B.Sc. (Oxon), National Agricultural Advisory Service Unit, National Institute of Agricultural Engineering.

Fruit Growing

NICHOLAS B. BAGENAL, B.A. (Cantab), late of Wye College, University of London.

Forestry

H. L. EDLIN, B.Sc., Publications Officer, Forestry Commission, Author of *British Woodland Trees*.

Fur Hunting and Farming

R. W. HAYMAN, Sen. Experimental Officer, Dept. of Zoology, British Museum (Nat. Hist.).

Gardening

A. H. HOARE, Advisory Aids Officer (Horticulture), National Agricultural Advisory Service, Ministry of Agriculture and Fisheries.

ANTONY HUXLEY, Asst. Ed. of *Amateur Gardening* and *Gardening Illustrated* (Flowers).

Pests and Diseases

A. J. A. WOODCOCK, M.Sc., F.R.E.S.

J. H. P. SANKEY, B.Sc., F.Z.S.

OTHER CONTRIBUTORS

MONTAGU C. ALLWOOD, V.M.H., F.L.S., Foundation Member of British Carnation Society.

A. T. BARNES, F.R.H.S., Vice-President, National Dahlia Society.

BRITISH RABBIT COUNCIL.

DOREEN BROCKHOUSE (Mrs. J. L. BRERETON), Author of *Gardening in Town and Suburb*.

DR. M. BURTON, Deputy Keeper at the British Museum (Natural History).

J. G. CAMPBELL, Grower of Lilies.

N. CATCHPOLE, F.R.H.S., R.H.S. Gold Medallist, Author of *Flowering Shrubs and Small Trees*.

N. LESLIE CAVE, Hon. Treas., Iris Society. Author of *The Iris*.

EDGAR DALE.

MARGARET DIGBY, Sec., Horace Plunkett Foundation.

DULCIE J. EDMONDS.

T. G. EDRIDGE, Horticultural Journalist and Broadcaster.

JOHN EDWARDSON, M.R.C.V.S.

ALAN FRASER, B.Sc., M.D.

G. E. FUSSELL, F.R.Hist.S., Author of *The Old English Farming Books 1523–1793*.

REGINALD GAMBLE, F.R.E.S.

H. V. GARNER, Head of Field Experimentals Section, Rothamsted Experimental Station.

G. H. GARRAD, O.B.E., N.D.A., Late County Agricultural Organizer for Kent.

D. M. GARSTANG, N.D.H., Principal, Studley Horticultural College.

REV. D. GOURLAY THOMAS, Author of *Sweet Peas for Garden and Exhibition*.

D. H. GRIST, Dip.Agric. (Cantab), Author of *An Outline of Malayan Agriculture*.

ZOË, LADY HART DYKE, Lullingstone Silk Farm.

N. P. HARVEY, M.A. (Cantab), Horticultural Writer to Plant Production Ltd., Author of *The Rose in Britain*.

T. H. HAWKINS, M.Sc., M.Ed., F.L.S.

MICHAEL HAWORTH-BOOTH, F.L.S., Author of *Effective Flowering Shrubs* (Collins).

G. P. HIRSCH, M.A. (Oxon.), University Demonstrator and Lecturer in Rural Social Organization, Oxford.

C. T. HOUGHTON, C.B.E., Principal Establishment and Organization Officer, Ministry of Agriculture and Fisheries.

WILL INGWERSON, Author of *The Dianthus*.

F. HOWARD LANCUM, M.B.E., F.L.S., late Advisory Ornithologist to the Ministry of Agriculture.

A. S. McWILLIAM, B.Sc., N.D.A., N.D.D., Author of *Soil Fertility*. (Y.F.C. Booklet.)

G. B. MASEFIELD, M.A., A.I.C.T.A., Lecturer in Colonial Agriculture, Oxford, Author of *A Handbook of Tropical Agriculture*.

B. D. MORETON, B.Sc. Agric. (London). Dept. Ent. (Wye), Agricultural Entomologist.

W. MUIRHEAD.

PROF. J. E. NICHOLS, M.Sc., Ph.D., F.R.S.E.

S. A. PEARCE, F.Inst.A.A., Asst. Curator, Royal Botanical Gardens, Kew.

FRANCES PERRY, Organizer of Agricultural Education, Middlesex.

LOUIS QUINAIN.

PROF. E. J. ROBERTS, M.A., M.Sc., University College, North Wales.

SIR E. JOHN RUSSELL, D.Sc., F.R.S., late Director of Rothamsted Experimental Station.

PATRICK M. SYNGE, M.A., F.L.S., Editor Royal Horticultural Society's Journals and Publications.

E. M. TURNER, M.A., Ph.D., Dept. of Botany, Oxford University.

KATHERINE WARINGTON, D.Sc., Rothamsted Experimental Station.

N. WARREN.

JAMES NOEL WHITE, M.A., F.R.S.A.

W. E. WOOD, Agricultural Journalist.

NORMAN WYMER, Author, Broadcaster, and Photographer.

Assistant Editors—A. T. G. POCOCK, STELLA M. RODWAY, BARBARA WITT.

Assistant Illustrations Editor—GILLIAN AVERY

ACKNOWLEDGEMENTS

THE EDITORS wish to thank all those who have lent photographs or who have given help in selecting material. They especially wish to acknowledge help from the East Malling Research Station; H. J. Hine and the National Institute of Agricultural Engineering; Antony Huxley; and Leonard Hill Ltd. for material from *World Crops*.

COLOUR PLATES

PLAN OF VOLUMES

HOW TO USE THIS BOOK

THIS VOLUME is one of twelve, each on a separate subject, the whole set forming what is called an encyclopaedia, or work from which you can find out almost anything you want to know. (The word comes originally from the Greek *enkuklios*, circular or complete, and *paideia*, education.) Each of the twelve volumes is arranged alphabetically within itself, as twelve dictionaries would be.

The difference between a dictionary and an encyclopaedia is that, while the first gives you no more than the meanings and derivations of words, the second tells you a very great deal more about their subjects. For instance, from a dictionary you could find that HOPS are climbing perennial plants, the flowers of which are used to flavour malt liquors, and you would learn little more; but an encyclopaedia will tell you how hops are grown, how they climb up strings at the rate of 12 to 15 feet in about 7 weeks, how they are picked by bands of hop-pickers from the cities who camp by the hopfields, and how the hops are dried in kilns before being sold to the brewers. Then a dictionary contains nearly every word in the language; but an encyclopaedia deals only with words and subjects about which there is something interesting to be said, beyond their bare meanings. So you should not expect to find every word in an encyclopaedia—every subject is there, but not every word.

To find any subject, you have first to decide in which of the twelve volumes it comes. Each of these has a title as well as a number, and also a list of general subjects to make the title clearer. All these are set out in the Plan of Volumes on the opposite page. Very often you will be able to tell from the title alone which volume contains the information you need; but if not, the list of sub-headings on the plan opposite will help to direct you. For example, if you want to read about people, the way they have lived at different times and places, and the things they have believed and worshipped, you would turn to Volume I. If, however, you want to find out about an animal or plant, you would look it up in Volume II, Natural History. If your subject were something in nature that does not have life—such as the sun, or a particular country or river, or a kind of stone—you would find it in Volume III, with tides, earthquakes, the weather, and many other things. Matters connected with communications of any kind—of people, or goods, or even of ideas—are in Volume IV. So you would look there for languages and printing and broadcasting, as well as for ships and trains and roads. But if it is the engineering side of any of these things that interests you, Volume VIII, Engineering, is the place to look. Business and trade are in Volume VII. Recreations are in Volume IX, which includes games and sports, entertainment, clubs, animal pets, and sporting animals. How we are governed and protected by the State, the law, and the armed forces is told in Volume X. Volume XI deals with almost everything connected with our homes, from the building and furnishing of the house to the clothes and health of those who live in it. The titles of Volumes V and XII, Great Lives and The Arts, explain themselves; and a rather fuller account of the volume you are now reading, on Farming and Fisheries, is given on page xv opposite.

To find your subject in the volume, think of its ordinary name, and then look it up just as though you were using a dictionary—the As on the first page and the Zs (if there are any) on the last. If you cannot find it, try a more general word. For instance, if you want to read about Milking, and cannot find it under that name (as you cannot), try either CATTLE, CARE OF, or DAIRY MACHINERY—either of which will lead you to it. As you read any article, you will probably come across the titles of other articles in some way connected with what you are reading. You will know that they are titles of other articles because they will be printed in capital letters. Either they will be followed by (q.v.) in brackets (this is short for the Latin *quod vide*, and means 'which see'), or else they themselves will be in brackets, with the word *see* in front of them. You can look up these other articles at once if you want to know more about the particular point dealt with, or you can save them up until you have finished the article you are reading. At the end of any article you may find the words '*See also*', followed by one or more titles in small capital letters. If you look these titles up, they will tell you still more about the subject that interests you. These last 'cross-references' are very useful if you want to look up a particularly wide subject (such as ARABLE CROPS or FLOWER GARDENS), because they show you at once the titles of all the main articles dealing with it. You can then decide for yourself which to read.

WHAT YOU WILL FIND IN THIS VOLUME

THIS VOLUME TELLS HOW MEN CULTIVATE AND USE THE PLANTS AND ANIMALS
THAT LIVE ON THE EARTH AND IN THE SEA TO PROVIDE THEMSELVES WITH
FOOD AND OTHER THINGS THEY NEED.

FARMING. For several thousands of years FARM TOOLS have been used in
most parts of the world to cultivate the SOIL and to grow ARABLE CROPS.
Early in AGRICULTURAL HISTORY the PLOUGH was invented, and as time went
on, farmers learnt how to arrange a simple ROTATION OF CROPS in their
fields and how to return to the soil in the form of MANURES and LIME the good
the plants had taken out of it. Man also domesticated for his own use some
of the animals he hunted, and gradually, as he learnt more about the science
of STOCK BREEDING, he evolved the CATTLE, SHEEP, PIGS, HORSES, and other
livestock of the kinds found on farms today. He developed good GRASSLANDS
on which to feed his animals, and by HAYMAKING and, later, by the cultivation of ROOT CROPS and by SILAGE making, he provided food for them through
the winter. In recent years the development of MECHANIZED FARMING has
saved the farmer much hand labour and increased the speed and efficiency
of his work. AGRICULTURAL TRAINING and RESEARCH have also played their
part in getting the best out of the land and reducing the risk of FAMINE.

GARDENING. As well as growing field crops, men and women have for
long cultivated the ground near their homes as VEGETABLE GARDENS and
FLOWER GARDENS, and in these they have grown vegetables such as PEAS,
BEANS, ASPARAGUS, and TOMATOES, and flowers such as ROSES and CHRYS-
ANTHEMUMS. FRUIT GROWING is an important part of gardening, both in
private gardens and in the MARKET GARDENS which provide most of the vegetable food we buy. Gardeners in cool countries build GLASSHOUSES, and grow
in them tender GREENHOUSE PLANTS, such as ORCHIDS and CUCUMBERS, which
need an artificially made atmosphere in which to thrive.

PESTS AND DISEASES. Farmers have had to study the protection of their
crops and livestock from the ravages of PLANT DISEASES and ANIMAL DISEASES,
from the attacks of PARASITIC WORMS, FLY PESTS, APHID PESTS, and many
others. This volume describes how SPRAYING AND DUSTING MACHINES are

used to distribute INSECTICIDES, what VERMIN must be destroyed, and how to recognize and destroy WEEDS.

FORESTRY, FISHERIES, AND FURS. There are riches to be found in the forest, in the seas, and in lands where animals carry rich winter coats. This volume tells about the science of FORESTRY, about the various TREES the forester grows, and about the TIMBER they produce. It describes the important FISHING INDUSTRY and the various FISHING METHODS used all over the world; and the exciting and profitable work of WHALING ships, FUR HUNTING with TRAPS AND SNARES, and the more recent and productive FUR FARMING.

RURAL CRAFTS. Certain crafts are needed in farming, even in these days of machinery. The farmer himself understands HEDGING, DITCHING, and WALLING, and the laying out of field DRAINAGE schemes; other crafts, such as THATCHING, SHOEING, and that of the WHEELWRIGHT, are usually the work of specialists.

FARMING OVER THE WORLD. Farmers' problems vary all the world over. This volume describes the problems of TROPICAL FARMING in hot, wet regions, and also in dry areas where crops cannot be grown without IRRIGATION. It describes the way of life on the CROFTING farms of the Scottish highlands and on the great CATTLE RANCHES of the New World; and it describes new experiments such as CO-OPERATION IN FARMING in many countries and COLLECTIVE FARMING in Soviet Russia.

The words in capitals are the titles of some of the general articles.

A

AFFORESTATION. This means the raising of new forests to provide timber for the future. Sometimes this is done on land where a previous tree crop has been felled, and then it is called reafforestation or replanting. At other times new areas of land, usually moor, heath, or scrub too poor for agriculture, are afforested to increase the total area devoted to timber growing. In Britain, the FORESTRY COMMISSION (q.v.) afforested or replanted a total area of 370,000 acres between 1919 and 1939; and this work of afforestation still goes on.

The first stage is to raise the young trees in forest nurseries ready for planting out. Most forest trees are raised from seed; a few, such as poplars and willows, from cuttings. Most of them take from 2 to 6 years to grow from the seed to the size needed for planting, so the

Forestry Commission

A FOREST NURSERY IN THE SCOTTISH HIGHLANDS

Young larch seedlings are fastened into 'lining-out boards' on the trestles. These are placed in the ploughed furrow and covered with earth at the next bout of the plough. When the earth has been made firm the boards are removed

nursery work must begin well ahead of the actual planting.

The seeds of broadleaved trees vary widely in shape and size, and in their time of ripening. Many seeds, such as acorns and beech nuts, are gathered in autumn from beneath the growing trees. Others, such as the tiny seeds of birch or the stones of wild cherries, must be picked from the tree before the winds scatter them or they are taken by the birds. They are carefully stored, either dry or in moist sand, for one or in some cases two winters, and are then sown in the spring.

The tiny seeds of conifers are hidden within the cones, which open to release them in the spring. Most kinds of cones are collected during the winter, usually from the branches of felled trees, after they have ripened but before the seeds have fallen. When dried in special kilns, the cones open their scales and release their seeds. Some kinds require crushing, but in others the scales as well as the seeds fall freely away; the wings are removed from the seeds, which are then stored till the spring.

In the forest nursery, seed-beds are carefully prepared. The ground is cultivated and made free from weeds, and long beds about 3 feet wide are thrown up some 2 inches above the general ground level and worked till the soil is fine. The seed is sown on these beds, either broadcast or in rows called 'drills'. Before sowing, it is usually soaked in water and often covered with red lead to keep away mice. After sowing, conifer seed is lightly covered with coarse sand or grit. Later on, arrangements are made to shelter with overhead screens the more delicate seedlings, such as spruces, which may suffer from intense sun or severe frost. Hardwood seed is covered with soil, and the seedlings need no protection.

The seedling trees are kept free from weeds so that they do not get choked while they are still very small. They grow on in the nursery for 1, 2, or 3 years, reaching a height of a few inches or a few feet according to species. One lb. of spruce seed may yield 50,000 seedlings; but with larger seeds the numbers are much less, for example, fifty oaks may come from 1 lb. of acorns.

Few seedlings would thrive if they were taken straight out from the seed-bed to the forest. Most need transplanting in the nursery in order to develop their roots. Transplanting is done in autumn, winter, or early spring. The seedlings are lifted from the seed-beds and sorted into grades, and then replanted, or 'lined out', a few inches apart in long straight rows, 6 inches to a foot apart. Here they grow on for a year or more, being weeded throughout the summer months.

When the young trees, now called 'transplants', are from 2 to 6 years old, they are usually big enough for planting out in the new forest. During the planting season, from October to March, they are lifted, sorted, counted, and tied up in bundles. Then they are sent out to the forest area.

Land that is to be afforested must first be made ready. It is often rough waste ground or moorland, sometimes overgrown with scrub and infested with rabbits. First of all, a rabbit-proof fence must be set up around it, and all the rabbits within the fence destroyed—for otherwise they would eat every tree. The rougher scrub growth may then be cleared unless it is needed to shelter the young tree crop. Heather, gorse, and coarse grasses are sometimes burned off to clear the ground for planting. Marshy land must be drained, and the turves cut out when the drains are dry are often used as planting points for spruce trees.

Land that is neither too stony nor too steep, nor obstructed by tree roots, is often ploughed for planting. Powerful tractors, usually with caterpillar tracks, draw specially constructed ploughs, which cut out deep furrows about 5 feet apart. This cultivates the soil and assists drainage; at the same time it marks out the lines for tree planting, provides turves (in the form of furrow slices) for planting spruces, keeps down weeds and undergrowth, and so reduces risk of fire for several years.

After the ground has been prepared, planting begins. This can be done only during the tree's resting period, which is from autumn to early spring. The young trees are carried in canvas planting-bags by the workmen, who mark out the planting positions as the work proceeds. A usual planting distance for most species is 5 feet apart in each direction, and this needs 1,750 trees for each acre of ground. Straight rows are obtained either by following plough furrows or by setting up sighting rods the right distance apart; distances along these rows are measured by the planters with a rod or a tool handle as they walk forward to plant their trees.

With so many trees to plant, the work must be

Gerald J. M. Smith

PLANTING YOUNG BEECH TREES IN THE FOREST OF DEAN BY THE 'NOTCHING' METHOD
The men on the left are making notches with mattocks ready for the trees to be planted

done quickly or it will be too expensive. The usual method, called 'notching', consists of cutting with a spade or mattock two vertical notches in the ground, at right angles to one another, forming a figure L or T. Whilst the notch is held open, the young tree is inserted in the angle of the notches at the correct depth. The ground is then allowed to close again, so that the tree is held firmly in place. Other planting methods are 'pit planting' in carefully dug holes, and 'turf or mound planting' in raised turves, furrow slices, or mounds of earth. But notching is the quickest method, and in favourable ground one man can put in as many as 500 trees in a day.

During their first few summers in the forest, the young trees usually require weeding to prevent their being smothered by quicker-growing plants. The weeding gang, equipped with curved reap hooks or similar tools, works up the rows of trees, cutting back bracken, brambles, and weed growth of all kinds that threatens to overtop and suppress the small trees. This ensures that the trees get their full share of light and air, and are not crushed down in winter by falling vegetation. Weeding continues for 2 or more years, until the leading shoots of the young trees have grown up out of danger.

During these early stages the fences around the plantations must be kept in good order to keep out harmful animals such as rabbits and deer. As the young trees rise above the weed growth, develop their roots in the soil below, and begin to make headway, the plantation is said to become 'established'. Its further progress is described under the heading of FORESTRY.

See also TREES, BROADLEAVED; TREES, CONIFEROUS.

AGRICULTURAL COLLEGES, *see* AGRICULTURAL TRAINING.

AGRICULTURAL HISTORY. 1. EARLY HISTORY. Food is man's first need, and from the times of the earliest historical records the life of the human race has centred on food production. Our first ancestors were not farmers in the sense that the word is understood today, for they did not cultivate the soil and sow seeds, but led a hand-to-mouth existence, finding the food they needed each day by hunting wild animals, gathering berries, and digging up roots (*see* PREHISTORIC MAN, Vol. I). Indeed, there are tribes in some parts of the world even today who still follow a life of this kind, moving slowly round the country they occupy as they eat up the wild

Ashmolean Museum

THE HARVESTER VASE

Cretan stone vase of about 1500 B.C. with a relief of a procession of harvesters

things in it (*see, for example*, ANDAMAN ISLANDERS; PYGMIES; VEDDA, Vol. I).

Sooner or later, however, someone must have caught and tamed some of the young animals which they hunted; sooner or later someone must have thought of collecting the seeds of the plants they used, and sowing them. When the domestication of animals and the cultivation of wild plants had begun, primitive man was able to improve his livestock and crops by the simple process of selecting the best of them and getting rid of the less good ones. How long a period passed before farmers were able to produce flocks and herds such as those Abraham and Lot controlled in the plain of Jordan, or wheat such as was grown in Egypt in the time of Joseph, we do not know; but it must have been a long period of slow development. The type of farming of which we read in the book of Genesis would seem very primitive to us today, but it was far in advance of the hunting stage of man's existence.

Growing crops and to a lesser extent keeping herds meant that a settled communal life was possible or even necessary, either in a farm or homestead or in a larger group as in a village;

and the beginnings of agriculture everywhere seem to be connected with the beginning of such settlements. But as fertilizing the soil was unknown, the land soon became exhausted, and the villages had to be moved to new, unbroken country—a method of agriculture known as 'shifting cultivation', and practised by some primitive peoples even today.

The earliest agriculture we know of seems to have taken place in the Near East (Iraq and Persia) perhaps as long as 6,000 or 8,000 years ago, and in Egypt not much later. In Europe the first evidence of growing crops dates from about 3000 B.C. The earliest farming communities were, as might be expected, in southeastern Europe, where ideas first spread from the civilized countries of the Near East (*see* ANCIENT CIVILIZATIONS, Vol. I). In the lower Danube basin, in Crete, the Aegean Islands, and northern Greece, the first farmers in Europe settled in little villages and learnt the ways of a more secure and settled life. Slowly the knowledge of grain-growing and stock breeding spread across Europe. In Britain the earliest agriculture we know of dates from about 2400 B.C.

2. EARLY BRITAIN. The earliest agricultural settlements in Britain are associated with small cultivated patches, each less than an acre in extent, enclosed by low banks, and hoed with a deer's horn or a hooked stick by man's unaided labour. These cultivated patches were always on the uplands, for the lowlands were covered with forest and swamp, which the farmer could not clear or drain with his simple stone and bone tools (*see* FARM TOOLS, HISTORY OF). Traces of the fields are often shown up clearly by air photographs. In stone country ancient fields can be seen marked out by collapsed stone walls.

The first important advance took place when someone hitched an ox or a pair of oxen to a much stronger, metal pointed, hooked stick, using this extra power to stir the soil more deeply. With this help cultivation was quicker and better, and, after further experiment, the simple point drawn through the ground developed by stages into the PLOUGH (q.v.) as we know it today. In saying this we are not guessing. Just as we can still find communities at every stage of farming from the nomadic tribe to the highly organized and mechanized modern farm, so we can find examples today of every stage in the evolution of the plough, from the crooked stick to the multi-furrow, tractor-drawn implement.

Historians tell us that the long plough fitted with a mouldboard to turn the furrow-slice over, was introduced into Britain by the Romans during their occupation of this country in the first four centuries A.D.

With the introduction of the ox-drawn plough and its extra power, the practice naturally arose of ploughing as long a distance as was practical before turning the ox-team round, and for this the little fields of the earlier system would have been unsuited. Long strips of cultivation lying side by side and without enclosing banks gradually replaced them. The long, narrow strips came to represent a day's work, and the groups of strips, which we can distinguish by air photography, represented the season's work of the community. The strips, in theory at all events, were 220 yards long (that is 1 furlong or furrow-long) and 22 yards wide, this making an area equal to the statute acre (see AGRICULTURAL MEASUREMENTS). In practice, both the length and the width of the strips were determined by

Ashmolean Museum

THE REMAINS OF CELTIC FIELDS ON FYFIELD DOWN, OXFORDSHIRE

This aerial photograph shows up the boundaries between the small fields

soil conditions, whether light land or clay land, by the lie of the land, whether flat or steep, and by other factors. It was exceptional, too, to get as much as an acre of land ploughed in a day.

3. MEDIEVAL FARMING. It must be remembered that farmers right up to modern times were for the most part farming to get food for their families, rather than for sale. It was not until the population of the towns began to increase that farming for profit became general. When land is cultivated to produce crops and livestock for sale, there may be a good deal of variety between one farmer's produce and another's. When men are farming for their own food supply, on the other hand, they will all tend to follow much the same system, for the needs of each, in bread, milk, and meat, are the same. So we find that the medieval farmers and their descendants in a large part of England right up to the 18th century, followed a common system, and this needed a good deal of co-operation and strict obedience by everyone to the regulations governing the use of the land. These were made by common consent in the common interest. On most of the lowlands of Britain there were then no individual farms dotting the countryside, as we see them today. On the contrary, everyone lived in the villages, and the farm-lands around the villages consisted of large areas with no fences or hedges round them, known as the 'open fields'. The chief characteristics of this open-field system were that the land of each man was held, not in blocks but in small strips, scattered throughout the fields; that there was a three-course ROTATION OF CROPS (q.v.) in the fields which everyone had to follow (winter corn, spring corn, and bare fallow); that the stubbles were grazed in common after harvest by the sheep and cattle of all the tenants; that the grassland was grazed in common also; and that this rather complicated system, which might easily involve a good deal of trouble between neighbour and neighbour, was ordered and enforced by the whole body of cultivators, who met periodically in the manor court to draw up the necessary rules and regulations and to appoint twelve of their number (the Jury) to see that these were carried out (see OPEN FIELDS AND ENCLOSURES).

The Open Field System lasted in many parts of England from Saxon times right down to the 18th century; but it gradually broke down, at different times in different places, as opportunity

Musée Condé, Chantilly

SOWING AND HARROWING IN THE MIDDLE AGES

Illustration for October in the Calendar of the *Très Riches Heures du Duc de Berry*, a Flemish manuscript illuminated in 1416

came to farm for a market instead of for one's own family only. The open fields were divided up bit by bit, and enclosed with hedges and fences, and the land was laid out in fields and farms as we see them today. This made it possible for the individual farmers to take advantage of all the new crops, such as turnips and clovers, and the better types of livestock that the AGRICULTURAL IMPROVERS (q.v.) were introducing.

4. MODERN FARMING. Labour-saving machinery and the development of methods of transport have been the main factors in raising the general standard of living in Britain, and in making it possible to maintain a great industrial population. It was the reaper and the threshing-machine that enabled settlers in North America, in the Argentine, and in Australia to develop their great export trade in grain of all kinds, and

particularly in wheat, which began in the last few decades of the 19th century. Without these aids to human labour, the Canadian settler, for example, would have been hard put to it to grow more than enough to feed himself and his family. First with the reaping-machine, followed by the reaper-and-binder, and then the combined harvesting and threshing-machine (*see* HARVESTING), the amount of food grown by each individual farmer has progressively increased, and for a long time Britain was the principal market for the surplus. It was cheaply produced, on cheap land, and cheaply transported. By the 1880's the amount of corn reaching British shores was enough to bring about a drop in British corn prices that was to revolutionize farm practice in this country. For the two preceding generations the price of wheat had averaged something near £3 a quarter; in the 10 years following, this average had fallen by 50%. Whereas during the first half of the 19th century Britain had grown nearly enough corn to meet her needs, she now learnt that she could buy most of what she wanted from overseas for less money than she could grow it at home. The face of the country began to change, and the plough lands of many districts were abandoned to grass; so that where corn crops had met the eye for centuries, grass grazed by sheep and cattle now took their place.

At first the change from cornland to grassland hit landlords and farmers very hard; but gradually they adapted themselves to the new conditions, being helped to do so by the growing demand from the nation for milk, butter, cheese, fresh meat, eggs and poultry, fruit and vegetables. Livestock became the prominent characteristic of British farming rather than corn, and it was a livestock industry maintained on natural herbage (grass) rather than on arable crops grown for animal food.

Agricultural practice has continued to develop on these lines during the present century. The high standard of living of the great industrial population has been made possible in this century by making the best of the food products of the whole world—of the dairy products and the high quality meat and other perishables of Britain and the near-by European countries, and of the bread corn, the supplementary meat, and the animal feeding-stuffs from overseas. The two great wars of this century made it necessary for a time to turn back to corn growing; though after the First World War there was an almost immediate return to pre-war practice, with livestock and its products once more the farmer's principal concern. It remains to be seen what will be the future of agriculture in Britain.

Of recent years there have been further experiments in farming organization aimed at improving the use of both labour and land. One of the most important is the system of COLLECTIVE FARMING (q.v.) carried out in the U.S.S.R. There, all the land belongs to the State. The peasant belongs to a collective farm which is worked to a set plan of production, and he gets a percentage of the produce of the farm according to the amount of work he does during the year. The farm is inspected regularly, and is large enough to make the most use of modern farm machinery. Non-Communist countries have tried to get the advantages of collectivism by CO-OPERATION IN FARMING (q.v.) instead of by compulsion. This attempts to preserve the unit of the small farm and the incentive of the individual owner, and yet to make it possible for him to use expensive modern machinery, and to have the advantage of large-scale marketing.

The development of farming has not proceeded uniformly throughout the world. Even today farming standards vary so much that methods in one place may be hundreds of years in advance of those in another, though both may be within a space of an hour's run in an aeroplane. In one part of the world a peasant population may be seen farming to feed itself, on little plots of ground tilled with the simplest of tools; in another, food production on a very large scale for a great industrial market is going on, aided by the application of every modern invention.

See also LAND OWNERSHIP; RESEARCH IN AGRICULTURE.

AGRICULTURAL IMPROVERS. In the 18th and 19th centuries a combination of circumstances led to great advances in farming practice. At this time Britain was still dependent upon her own farm-lands for the great bulk of her people's food. As the growing town populations increased the demand for food, landlords and farmers had great incentives to try new methods to increase their production, both of crops and livestock. It is difficult to know to whom the credit for very substantial increases in the nation's food supplies should be given, because

By courtesy of the Director of the Science Museum, South Kensington

THE TRIAL OF MCCORMICK'S FIRST REAPING MACHINE IN VIRGINIA, U.S.A., IN 1831

new crops, such as turnips, clover, and grasses, were introduced long before they were adopted by farmers generally (*see* OPEN FIELDS AND ENCLOSURES). The names of Sir Richard Weston (1591–1652) and Andrew Yarranton (1616–84), Viscount Townshend (1674–1738) and Thomas Coke, Earl of Leicester (1752–1842) are memorable for their support in establishing these crops.

The work of the livestock improvers is the easier to describe. In the early part of the 18th century many cattle were still used as draught animals and became beef only in their old age. Now a draught ox needs heavy shoulders with which to pull its load, but the choice cuts of beef come from its loins and hindquarters (*see* CATTLE BREEDS, section 3). Nature, too, designed a cow to give enough milk to rear a calf during a 6 months' summer-grazing season, whereas man needs a surplus of milk all the year round (*see* CATTLE BREEDS, section 2). Here, then, was the challenge to the livestock improvers. One of the earliest and quite the most famous of these was Robert BAKEWELL (q.v. Vol. V), of Dishley Grange in Leicestershire (1725–95). The chief breed of cattle in the Midlands of his day was the Longhorn. Bakewell, and others who used his methods and drew upon his herds, improved the breed out of all knowledge, reducing the great shoulders and heavy bone, and developing the finer parts of the carcass. At the same time, Bakewell turned his attention to the small, coarse-woolled sheep of his day, improving the local breed, the Leicester, both in the quality of its mutton and of its wool. The Longhorn cattle and Leicester sheep upon which Bakewell worked are not numerous today, but his methods inspired those who developed the breeds which have taken their place, and it would be difficult to overestimate his contribution to agricultural progress.

The Shorthorn breed of cattle of County Durham, which in the end displaced the Longhorn, was largely the work of the Colling Brothers of Ketton, near Darlington, who were pupils of Bakewell. In other parts of the country the local breeds, the Sussex, the Hereford, the Norfolk, the Devon, and the Scotch and Welsh breeds, were all taken in hand in the same way, and the various breeds of sheep were likewise improved. COKE of Norfolk (q.v. Vol. V) and Robert Ellman of Glynde in Sussex laid the foundations of the modern Southdown sheep.

The work of the early improvers has gone on right up to the present day; landowners and farmers have continued to improve all classes of livestock, to give us the beef and dairy cattle, the pork and bacon pigs, and the mutton and fine-woolled sheep that have made British farm livestock famous throughout the world.

The improvers also turned their attention to farm implements as well as crops and livestock. For centuries the plough had been almost the only aid to manual work on the farm (*see* FARM TOOLS, HISTORY OF). From the introduction of a horse-drawn hoe in the early 18th century by Jethro Tull, a Berkshire farmer, to the invention of the agricultural tractor, and all the machines that it operates, 200 years later, farm machinery grew more efficient and more elaborate (*see* MECHANIZED FARMING). THRESHING-MACHINES (q.v.), which came into use soon after Waterloo, caused serious disturbances on many farms, for threshing by the flail was the source of steady winter employment, and the farm labourers feared they would lose their work. About the same time there appeared the first efficient reaping-machine—the invention of the Scotsman Patrick Bell, who later became a Presbyterian minister (*see* HARVESTING).

In the 19th century agricultural scientists also took part in this rapid development of farming, which has led to the great increase of farm productivity of today. The German chemist, Justus von Liebig, and in England, Sir John Bennett Lawes, were at work upon problems of plant nutrition. The only MANURES (q.v.) then known to the farmer were organic—such as farmyard manure, bones, and guano from the sea-bird islands of the Pacific. The soil was fed with these, together with lime and marl on heavy land, and clay on sandy land. The most valuable ingredients of the organic fertilizers were the nitrogen, phosphate, and potash compounds that they contained, and Sir John Lawes showed that their supply could be supplemented, and cheaply, from mineral sources. Phosphates in various forms, for example, are part of the components of certain rock formations occurring in great abundance in different parts of the world, which, when suitably treated, will yield a soluble phosphate of high value as a plant food. Sir John established at his home at Rothamsted, in Hertfordshire, an experimental station that has been the leader of scientific RESEARCH IN AGRICULTURE (q.v.) of the world. A waste pro-

Rothamsted Experimental Station

MR. VALENTINE BARFORD AND HIS IMPROVED BAKEWELL LEICESTER SHEEP
Lithograph from an early 19th-century painting by H. Barraud

duct of steel manufacture, basic slag, was found to be another important source of phosphates. Nitrogenous fertilizers are manufactured from the nitrogen in the air (see ARTIFICIAL FERTILIZERS).

The agricultural botanists have discovered the laws controlling the cross-fertilization of plants, and are giving the farmer new and better varieties (see PLANT BREEDING). Animal nutrition is now almost an exact science (see FEEDING (FARM ANIMALS)). Alongside all this work for high production, there has been a great advance in our knowledge of plant and animal health and the control of diseases (see ANIMAL DISEASES; PLANT DISEASES).

See also RESEARCH IN AGRICULTURE.

AGRICULTURAL MEASUREMENTS. A farmer must know how much seed he must sow in a particular field, how much manure or other fertilizers it needs, and what produce he can hope from it. All these things are related to the size of the particular piece of land. So ever since farming took the place of hunting and the gathering of wild grain and berries as the means of livelihood, men have had to devise standard agricultural measurements.

Naturally early man used as his standards of measurement something that he was familiar with by continued use, such as the parts of his own body, the foot, the nail, the finger, the 'span' of the hand, and the 'cubit' or length of the forearm. But these varied so widely that they had to be standardized, and by 1500, the standard yard of 3 feet had become the lawful standard of linear (long) measure This yard could be divided in two ways. The one related to the bodily measure: the cubit was half, the span a quarter, the finger an eighth, and the nail one sixteenth of a yard. The other was based upon the size of a grain of barley: three grains of barley laid end to end lengthwise made 1 inch, 12 inches made a foot, and 36 inches or 3 feet made a yard. These standard measurements can be seen marked out on the north wall of Trafalgar Square in London, and also in Birmingham behind the Town Hall (*see* MEASUREMENT, HISTORY OF, Vol. IV).

Such measurements were effective for measuring distance, but did not help the farmer to estimate either how long it would take him to plough a piece of land or how much seed he would need to sow it. Experience had taught his eye to judge how big a piece of ground could be dug up with a spade or ploughed in a day. The amount of land covered by an average day's ploughing was known as an 'acre', and its original shape was a long narrow rectangle. The long side was as far as the oxen could go without stopping for a rest, a furrow long or 'furlong', legally 220 yards long; the width was the length of four 'rods', goads used by ploughmen to spur on the oxen, legally $5\frac{1}{2}$ yards or $16\frac{1}{2}$ feet long. The original shape of an acre, therefore, was a piece of land ten times as long as it was broad—40 rods in length by 4 rods wide, containing 160 square rods. This in turn was divided into four strips each 1 rod wide and 1 'rood' in area. The first rough measurements of area, therefore, were calculated by the power of oxen to haul a plough a certain distance before they were obliged to stop for breath, coupled with the length of the goad the ploughman used to drive his oxen.

There were other measures used for determining large areas such as the size of a farm-holding or an estate. An 'oxgang' was the area of land that a yoke of oxen could keep ploughed, an area that varied somewhat with the type of soil; and the 'yardland' usually meant 4 oxgangs. These measures, though useful once, are no longer used. Larger areas of farm-land are now always measured in acres, and are rarely referred to in terms of square miles. Men speak of a 300-acre farm or a 3,000-acre estate.

In the last years of the reign of Queen Elizabeth, when both landowners and farmers were becoming more anxious to be sure of the size and situation of their land, an ingenious surveyor, E. Gunter, introduced the use of the 'chain' for land measurement. This chain, which was divided into 100 links, he made equal to 4 rods. This is the same as 22 yards, or the length of a cricket pitch. Ten chains, therefore, equal 40 rods or 220 yards or 1 furlong, and the 'statute' acre that we use today was fixed at 10 square chains. This is a very convenient figure to use when measuring land, and such a chain has been employed ever since Gunter designed it, about 350 years ago.

These measurements were the recognized legal measures of land; but there were local variations caused by local customs of using a longer or shorter rod or oxgoad. In Cheshire, for example, a rod of 8 yards long was used, and in consequence the Cheshire customary acre was much larger than the statute acre—over double in fact. Lancashire, too, had a different acre; and far to the south in Dorset a shorter rod (or 'lug') reduced the size of the customary acre to less than the statute. These local variations, however, in course of time dropped out of use.

Just as all measurements of length and area are based on three barley grains, both dry and liquid weights and measures originated in the size and weight of a grain of wheat. The Imperial (or statute) pound was divided into 7,000 grains, the smallest unit of weight. This standard pound weight is regulated by the weight of a piece of platinum kept in London, and is divided into 16 ozs which are approximately the same as the ounce of Roman times (*see* MEASUREMENT, HISTORY OF, Vol. IV). Many laws were made to regulate measures and weights before these Imperial standards were fixed, and the close relation between the dry and liquid measures had led to a good deal of confusion about them. The measures by volumes, the 'gallon', the 'bushel', and the 'quarter', were originally determined by their relation to weights. In the reign of Edward III it was ordered that 8 lb. of wheat should make a gallon, and since 8 gallons measured a bushel, the bushel contained 64 lb. of wheat. The bushel measure was usually made just over 8 inches deep and of such a diameter that it would hold the right weight of grain—8 lb. to each inch in depth. Another kind of bushel measure, however, known as the 'drum', was much deeper and therefore smaller in diameter. Eight of these bushels make a quarter of approximately 512 lb., and 4 made a sack of approximately 256 lb. Though the weights of the other cereals were less than that of wheat, these dry measures were adopted for them, because it was useful to have a similar measure for all sorts of grain. Nowadays, however, grain is nearly

'STRIKING' A MEASURE OF CORN

Woodcut of 1500. This method of levelling the top of the measure is still used

each stone weighing 14 lb., or a total of 364 lb. The 'tod' was a commonly used measure, and meant 2 stone or 28 lb. The older measure, the 'wey', which varied considerably according to the commodity being measured, was standardized at 182 lb. or half a legal sack of wool. By an Act passed in the reign of Edward I a new cwt. of 112 lb. divided into 8 stones of 14 lb. was introduced, as well as others that included the 'true' cwt. of 100 lb.

Butter and cheese, however, continued to be sold by the old measures—by a stone of 16 lb. instead of 14 lb., and in Suffolk by a wey of 256 lb. instead of 182 lb. Cheese was also sold by the 'firkin' or cask holding about 56 lb., and in Cambridge and Cheshire and elsewhere by the 'long hundred' of 120 lb.—just as eggs are still often sold by the long hundred (120 eggs).

Many other commodities were measured for sale by local customary measures, and most of these were still in use a hundred years ago; some of them still are. A few samples are given below.

A 'bag' of hops in Kent is 2 cwt. 2 quarters.
A 'basket' or 'sieve' of cherries in Kent is 48 lb.
A 'sieve' of apples or potatoes in Kent is a bushel.
A 'pocket' of hops in Kent is 1¼ cwt.
A 'pocket' of wool in Kent is half a sack.
A 'poke' of wool is 1 ton.
A 'bolt' or 'boult' or 'bunch' of oziers is a bundle measuring 42–45 in. round.
A 'bunch' or 'glen' of teazles varies between 10 king heads to 25 heads.
A 'staff' of teazles is 50 bunches or 'glens'.
A 'pack' of teazles is 40 staffs.
A 'load' of hay is 36 trusses of 56 lb. each.
A 'load' of wood is 50 cubic feet.
A 'load' of gravel is 1 cubic yard.
A 'load' of sand is 36 bushels.
A 'load' of straw is about 11½ cwt.

Corn in the field after harvest was sometimes measured by the 'thrave' of 24 sheaves, and straw for thatching by the same measures. Hay was sold by the 'truss' of 56 lb. if old, or of 60 lb. if new and therefore containing more water. Flax was sold by the 'reel' of 2 yards round. These are but a few of endless examples of measurements peculiar to certain commodities or to certain localities, many of which are still in use.

See also Vol. IV: MEASUREMENT, HISTORY OF; COUNTING, HISTORY OF.

always sold by the hundredweight (cwt.) and not by volume at all.

Before the legal enforcement of Imperial standard measures, there were many local variants. In the north of England and in Scotland a 'boll' of grain was a common measure, though a very unsatisfactory one because by custom the boll contained a different quantity in different places, varying from 2 to 6 bushels. The East Anglian 'comb' was more regular, and contained 4 bushels; and there were many other local measures for grain.

Liquid measure was based on 8 lb. of wine, as dry measure was based on 8 lb. of wheat. The Tudor ale gallon and pint were very little different from the present-day gallon and pint. An Imperial gallon of water weighs 10 lb.

The prosperity of agriculture for several centuries depended very largely on its trade in wool, and in some parts upon the sale of butter and cheese. All these articles were sold by weight. The export of wool was so important a business in Plantagenet times and produced so substantial a revenue, that the weight of the 'sack' was carefully regulated. Since the time of Edward III the sack has contained 26 stone,

AGRICULTURAL RESEARCH INSTITUTES, see RESEARCH IN AGRICULTURE.

Rothamsted Experimental Station

THE SMITHFIELD CLUB'S CATTLE EXHIBITION IN 1839

Lithograph by J. W. Giles. The artist exaggerated the size of the cattle to emphasize how much the breeds had been improved

AGRICULTURAL SHOWS. These have become a regular feature of British farming, and of all rural life. Indeed, a large proportion of townspeople enjoy attending an agricultural show even though they have not a professional interest in it. These shows began with competitions between farmers for the best farm animal of its class, but have so grown in size and scope that nowadays a whole day is not long enough for visitors to see all the exhibits, and great shows last 3 days or even a week. The numbers of breeds of stock have multiplied greatly during the past 100 years, so that the number of different classes even in one type of livestock has grown enormously. In addition to competitions for the best CATTLE, HORSES, SHEEP, and PIGS of the various breeds, there may be a section for GOATS, POULTRY, or RABBITS (qq.v.), and there is often an important horticultural section. There may also be horse-jumping competitions, trotting

matches, SHEEP DOG trials (q.v.) and so on. As well as these main events, there are exhibitions of farm machines, many of them in motion, exhibits and demonstrations showing the latest technical advances in such matters as the use of fertilizers, and also trade stands set up by sellers of feeding-stuffs, animal medicines, kitchen equipment, and so on.

The three largest and most important shows are those held in England and Wales by the Royal Agricultural Society of England, in Scotland by the Royal Highland and Agricultural Society of Scotland, and in Wales by the Royal Welsh Agricultural Society. These extend over several days, and attract the best exhibits from all parts of Britain. The 'Royal Show', as the first named is popularly known, was first held at Oxford in 1830, and in spite of the difficulties of transport in those days, attracted exhibits from many parts of England. Since then the Royal

Show has been held at a different centre every year, except when it has been suspended during war. The Society, whose motto is 'Science with Practice', organizes these shows in order to improve British farming, and the object of changing the centre each year is to arouse interest in all parts of the country.

The exhibits of thoroughbred stock are perhaps the most important part of the Royal Show, and farmers come from all over the world to see them. Great Britain has been the leader of live-stock breeding in the world, and the livestock of most other countries has been built up from British stock (*see* STOCK BREEDING). It takes much skill and expense to prepare animals for show. They have to be trained to lead so that they will go round the show-ring, and fed so as to be in the best condition. Thorough grooming is also necessary, and, in the case of sheep, expert trimming of the fleece. In order to grow a good fleece by the time of the show, generally in July, sheep have to be sheared much earlier than in general practice—as early as March, instead of in May or June. In all showing it is not sufficient merely to have an excellent animal, it must be prepared in the right way in order that it may show to the best advantage. The parade of livestock is the high light of the show, when the prize-winning animals of all the cattle breeds parade past the grand stand, bearing their prize cards and rosettes.

At the Royal Show there are whole 'streets' of Farm Machinery (*see* MECHANIZED FARMING) exhibited by the manufacturers, one firm specializing in harvesting machinery, another in tractors, another in stationary engines, and another in milking-machines. At this show a prize is offered as an encouragement to inventors for the best new implement or device. The Agricultural Education exhibit, arranged by the National Agricultural Advisory Service, is a feature at all the larger shows. There are exhibits to show how to increase yields of crops and to breed better and healthier animals. There may be, for example, actual samples of growing wheat plants affected by a disease called Smut, and instructions about prevention. An expert is present to discuss the disease with any farmers wishing to do so. The YOUNG FARMERS' CLUBS (q.v.) also stage exhibits and hold competitions.

Most shows, though not so large as the Royal Show, are run on much the same pattern. The Bath and West and the Royal Counties Shows, the big shows of the south of England, are 4-day events held each year in a different place within the region they cover. The Bath and West covers the whole of the south-west of England and Wales, from Cornwall to Worcester. The

The Times

DAIRY SHORTHORN COWS IN THE JUDGING RING AT THE OXFORDSHIRE SHOW, 1951

Royal Counties visits Hampshire, Berkshire, Surrey, Wiltshire, Dorset, and Sussex. Then there is the Three Counties Show for Hereford, Worcester, and Gloucester. Besides these big shows there are many county and local shows. These, though they draw exhibits from a smaller area, and consequently the standard is less high, yet give rise to quite as keen a competition. Some county shows may be very substantial; the Devon County Show, for instance, occupies 3 days, and the classes for Devon and South Devon cattle, as well as those for Dartmoor and Exmoor ponies, are important features. In the local shows a breed of local importance often receives greater prominence. Thus, in a mountain area, the mountain breed of sheep is probably the most important feature, and a sheepdog trial may also be included.

Because of the danger that good appearance rather than good performance may be awarded the prize at agricultural shows, especially at dairy cattle shows, and that a prize-winning cow, for example, may, in fact, be a poor milker, there are now classes of dairy cattle in the big shows limited to cows that have reached a certain standard of milk yield. In some places the amount of milk, and its butter-fat, are actually measured at the show.

There are a number of special shows dealing with one type of exhibit only. The annual Smithfield Beef Cattle Show is an example of this, as are the International Horse Show and others for horses only (see HORSE SHOWS, Vol. IX), Cruft's International Show and others for dogs (see DOG SHOWS, Vol. IX), and similar special shows for other livestock, such as poultry.

The most important horticultural show is the Chelsea Flower Show, organized by the Royal Horticultural Society, and held in May or June in the gardens of the Chelsea Hospital in London. This show not only has first class exhibits of specimens of all the principal flowering plants, both of garden and greenhouse, but also whole gardens laid out to demonstrate, for example, the use of ROCK PLANTS or FLOWERING SHRUBS, or designs for HERBACEOUS BORDERS or WATER GARDENS (qq.v.). There are also many specialist shows organized by the Royal Horticultural Society, and others such as the Imperial Fruit Show and shows run by the Rose, Alpine, Sweet Pea, and Delphinium Societies.

Apart from these national shows, there are local shows held throughout the country, not only in country places but also in urban districts. These are often run in conjunction with shows of small livestock such as rabbits, guinea-pigs, or poultry, and are closely linked to the ALLOTMENTS movement (q.v.).

See also RESEARCH IN AGRICULTURE.

AGRICULTURAL TRAINING. Agriculture, which is the oldest and most important industry in the world, is a very skilled occupation, and one which requires much knowledge and experience. Nothing can be a substitute for years of experience; but as scientific knowledge becomes greater, the need for special training in the various branches of farming becomes more important. Agricultural training may be undertaken as a preparation for the practical work of farming, for specialist research work, or for some form of organizing or teaching. The student may take a course as short as 3 months at a Farm Institute; he may go for 2 years to an Agricultural College; he may also take a degree at a university with further graduate courses afterwards, involving 3 or 4 years of study, or even more.

1. FARM INSTITUTE COURSES. It is the aim of the Government to have a Farm Institute in every county in England and Wales, and over thirty counties have theirs already. Each Institute is under the control of the County Council, all are residential, and the courses last for 3, 6, or 12 months, depending on the county concerned. The students must, generally, be at least 16 or 17 years old, and they come from all types of schools. Each Institute is provided with a farm, which is managed on up-to-date lines, using modern methods and machinery. Not only do the pupils learn in the class-room, but they also do a certain amount of actual work on the farm, in order to gain experience of good methods. Even if pupils have been brought up on farms, as most of them have, they may not all have had an opportunity at home of seeing every kind of work carried out as it should be, nor of handling modern equipment. They learn to use a milking-machine, for example, in such a way as not to injure the cow, nor carry germs from one cow to another.

The Farm Institute course may be on general agriculture, dairying, poultry, or horticulture. Some Institutes accept both boys and girls; at others summer courses may be provided for girls—mostly on dairying, including butter and

Evening News

STUDENTS LEARNING HOW TO PRUNE TREES AT A FARM
INSTITUTE

which modern farming involves. The syllabus, therefore, includes English, arithmetic, agriculture, agricultural botany, a little agricultural chemistry, animal hygiene, and, of course, practical work. Needless to say, there are social activities, such as debating societies and sports clubs.

2. AGRICULTURAL COLLEGES. There are in England and Wales five Agricultural Colleges where students are trained for a 2-year Diploma course. These are the Harper Adams Agricultural College, Newport, Salop; the Seale Hayne Agricultural College, Newton Abbot, Devon; the Royal Agricultural College, Cirencester; Shuttleworth College, Biggleswade, Bedfordshire; and Studley College, Warwickshire—the last one being for women only. In addition two universities, Nottingham and the University College of Wales at Aberystwyth, provide training for a diploma as well as for a degree. Scotland has no separate Agricultural Colleges, but the universities with agricultural departments (Aberdeen, Edinburgh, and Glasgow) have a college where some students are prepared for a diploma, others for degrees, and some students take both.

A diploma course occupies 2 years, and a degree course a minimum of 3 years. A diploma course is intended to be more practical, requiring less knowledge of the pure sciences such as chemistry, botany, and zoology. Plenty of practical experience in agricultural activities is essential for the diploma. The student need not have passed Matriculation, though a good standard of education, in most cases a School Certificate, is necessary before a boy or girl can get admission to one of the colleges. The diplomas are those awarded by the colleges themselves (some also award certificates of a somewhat lower standard), as well as the following:

National Diploma in Agriculture (N.D.A.).

National Diploma in Dairying (N.D.D.), in Dairy Husbandry (N.D.D.H.), and in Dairy Technology (N.D.D.T.). (These are awarded jointly by the Royal Agricultural Society of England and the Royal Highland and Agricultural Society of Scotland.)

National Diploma in Poultry Husbandry (N.D.P.) (awarded by the National Poultry Diploma Board Ltd.).

National Diploma in Agricultural Engineering (N.D.Agr.E.) (awarded by the Institute of British Agricultural Engineers).

cheese making—and winter courses for boys in agriculture. Since farming varies from county to county, it is only to be expected that the subjects taught vary also. In some counties, like Lincolnshire, crops are of greater importance than animals, while in others, like Cheshire, dairy-farming is of the highest importance. A hill farm in Wales or Scotland is quite different from a lowland farm in the southern counties. At the Institutes pupils are taught to understand the reasons that lie behind farming practice, that is, they learn theory as well as practice. For example, they learn not only that a certain weight of fertilizer may be needed for an acre of ground when under a particular crop, but also what ingredient the fertilizer supplies, how this acts in the soil, whether that ingredient is apt to be washed out of the soil by rain, and so on.

Training at a Farm Institute includes both the science and practice of farming, and some general education. Instruction in English, which was begun in the day schools, is continued at the Institute, and not only widens the pupils' interests later in life, but also teaches them to write good letters, and even, perhaps, to do some public speaking. General arithmetic is also taught, so that the pupils learn to handle money and simple accounts, and also are able to deal with the considerable amount of calculations

Wye College

A PRACTICAL CLASS IN THE BOTANY LABORATORY OF AN AGRICULTURAL COLLEGE

National Diploma in Horticulture (N.D.H.), and various certificates (awarded by the Royal Horticultural Society).

Some colleges group together to offer a diploma, such as the Scottish Diploma of Agriculture; and Nottingham University has a special diploma course of its own.

3. UNIVERSITY DEGREES. Most universities of Great Britain have an agricultural section, which, with the help of the pure science departments, enables the students to take a degree. A student may enter a university at any time after becoming 17 or 18 years of age, and the degree course occupies either 3 or 4 years, a fourth being necessary if a student wishes to specialize in some particular science. Several subjects are studied, some for 1 year only, and others for 2 or more years. Generally speaking, the first year is devoted to the pure sciences, such as chemistry, botany, and zoology, and then the student has to make up his mind as to whether he wishes to take a specialized or general course. If he wishes to specialize and to be, for example, a plant breeder, he will take a specialist course in botany, possibly with agricultural botany; if he wishes to be a soil chemist, chemistry will be selected for the more advanced study; if he wishes to study insect pests, he will specialize in

zoology, so as to become an entomologist. Most of the higher authorities prefer a student to take his advanced examination in a pure rather than in an applied science, and to pursue the applied subjects after his degree. Thus, a student wishing to be a soil chemist would study chemistry for his degree, and would take a graduate course in agricultural chemistry.

The student taking a general agricultural course for his degree will devote less time to pure science than the kind of specialist described above, and will give more attention to the growing of crops and the feeding, management, and breeding of livestock. The application of science to those branches of farming is studied in such subjects as agricultural botany, agricultural chemistry, and agricultural zoology. At least one year's practical farm experience is essential as preliminary training for this type of degree.

4. VETERINARY COURSES. Since the raising of animals and the producton of milk constitutes so very important a part of British farming, the veterinary profession, naturally, has become more and more important. The veterinary surgeon not only helps the farmer to cure diseases of livestock, but, what is now considered more important, to prevent these troubles (*see* ANIMAL DISEASES). To become a veterinary surgeon, it

is necessary to qualify for university admission in the usual way, and to take a degree at the Royal Veterinary College, London, or the universities of Cambridge, Liverpool, or Bristol, or the Royal Dick College at Edinburgh.

Whatever the course of training, it is essential to have had some experience of country life and farm work before going to a farm institute, college, or university. For anyone who has been brought up on a farm, a great deal of this experience comes naturally, and most intending students who live in the country can persuade a farmer to allow them opportunities of learning how things are done. For the town-dweller it is more difficult; but most probably the Educational Authority for the district or the NATIONAL FARMERS' UNION (q.v.) will be able to help.

An apprenticeship scheme of a limited kind is now working in Scotland, and attempts are being made to provide one for England and Wales. The Y.M.C.A. provide opportunities for boys to get farm experience and practical training, and there are a few farm schools such as the Westhall Farm School in Aberdeenshire. Many schools, especially the secondary modern ones, have gardens, keep livestock, and study farms, and this is a great help to those who want to go in for farming or gardening.

In some counties there are part-time evening or day classes in agriculture and horticulture for boys and girls who have recently left school and are working on farms. There are also a few correspondence courses, organized by private firms or occasionally by a Local Education Authority, for those who cannot get to classes, and the National Federation of YOUNG FARMERS' CLUBS (q.v.) provides one for its members. Membership of a club can be helpful to those who are studying agriculture or horticulture.

The work of the estate agent and the land agent includes a certain amount of farming; but these men have to earn separate awards, such as the B.Sc. degree in Estate Management, or membership of the Royal Institution of Chartered Surveyors.

See also RESEARCH IN AGRICULTURE.

ALFALFA (LUCERNE), *see* LEGUMINOUS CROPS.

ALLOTMENTS. An allotment is, strictly speaking, a smallholding of over a quarter of an acre and less than 5 acres; and what we usually call allotments are really 'allotment gardens'.

These are the small, rectangular plots of land, never more than a quarter of an acre each and usually much smaller, that are to be seen on the outskirts of towns and villages, and that are cultivated by the tenants to provide vegetables for themselves and their families. In this article the word 'allotment' is used to mean 'allotment gardens'.

The allotment system began in the early 19th century when certain landowners for the first time provided small areas of land on their farms for the use of their labourers. In some cases the farmers objected because—so they said—this not only reduced the size of their farms but it meant that the labourers could not do justice to the work they were employed to do, especially if the allotments were very large. In 1834, early in the history of allotments, the Poor Law Commissioners declared that these allotments were beneficial provided they did not exceed half an acre, no matter how large a family had to be provided for.

The original purpose of allotments was to help the country labourers at a time when many of them were very poor and found it difficult to get enough to feed their families. Nowadays, however, there are more allotments near towns than elsewhere, and there they provide profitable recreation and opportunities to grow vegetables for those who have small gardens, or live in flats without gardens at all. The area of land under allotments increased considerably during the First and Second World Wars, and the crops produced on them were a valuable contribution to the country's food supply.

Fields of allotments are often owned by the local authority, but in many cases they are owned by an allotment society, which is a co-operative body of the tenants. Since 1908 the local authorities have been bound by law to buy or lease land to satisfy the demand for allotments, and they must provide for allotments in any town-planning scheme. Between the two world wars many societies and federations of allotment holders were formed in order to make local authorities carry out their obligations. Now, through the National Allotments Society Ltd., these societies can negotiate with county and even national bodies. Local societies also benefit their members by buying manures, seeds, and tools in bulk, and by arranging lectures and demonstrations by specialists.

Most well-managed allotments are intensively

COMPOST HEAP	TOOL SHED	SEED BED
TOMATOES	MARROW	RADISH	PARSLEY

A — MISCELLANEOUS CROPS

DWARF PEAS
INTERCROP WITH SPINACH
FOLLOW WITH LEEKS

DWARF BEANS

ONIONS
FOLLOW WITH SPRING CABBAGE

SHALLOTS
BROAD BEANS
INTERCROP & FOLLOW WITH LETTUCE

RUNNER BEANS

B — POTATOES AND ROOTS

PARSNIPS

CARROT

POTATOES (EARLY)
FOLLOW WITH TURNIPS

POTATOES
MAIN CROP

SPINACH BEET

C — WINTER AND SPRING GREENS

CABBAGE (WINTER)

SAVOYS
INTERCROP WITH EARLY CARROTS

BRUSSELS SPROUTS
INTERCROP WITH EARLY BEET

SPROUTING BROCCOLI

KALE

SWEDES

BEET
PRECEDE WITH EARLY PEAS

—30'—

Controller, H.M.S.O.

CROPPING PLAN FOR AN ALLOTMENT

In the second year section C should take the place of A, A of B, and B of C. The following year the order should be B, C, A. to give the correct rotation. The symbols show the number and spacing of rows

cropped with vegetables grown on a three-course rotation (*see* VEGETABLE GARDEN, section 3), and proper digging, cropping, and manuring help to maintain fertility. The standard size of an allotment has come to be regarded as approximately 10 square rods (300 square yards). A 10-rod plot can provide a succession of vegetables that will, with the exception of potatoes, be enough for a family of three.

See also VEGETABLE GARDEN.

ALMONDS, *see* NUTS.

ALPINE HOUSE, *see* ROCK GARDEN PLANTS, section 3.

ALSIKE (CLOVER), *see* LEGUMINOUS CROPS.

ANIMAL BREEDING, *see* STOCK BREEDING.

ANIMAL DISEASES. 1. Most diseases of animals are caused by microscopic living organisms known as BACTERIA, VIRUSES, or FUNGI (qq.v. Vol. II). Other diseases, among them human tropical diseases such as dysentery and sleepy sickness, are caused by some of the thousands of species of PROTOZOA (q.v. Vol. II), and are often spread by insects. These disease-causing organisms or germs are parasites, that is, they live within and at the expense of the body of their victim. Often they can live for a time outside the animal's body—in the soil, in the carcasses of dead animals, in discharges from infected animals, in badly ventilated buildings and sheltered places, in animals which have no symptoms of disease themselves but are 'carriers', and in contaminated food. Thus an animal may pick up infection not only through contact with another infected animal, but also from any or these sources, the germs entering its body in its food, in the air it breathes, or through a wound in its skin. Sometimes a germ is injected into an animal by an insect.

An 'acute' disease produces severe symptoms very quickly; in a 'chronic' disease, the symptoms may be slight and often pass unobserved for a long time until much damage has been done, as in tuberculosis. Many diseases affect only certain kinds of animal, other animals being 'immune' or able to resist the infection. All animals have some natural resistance against disease, and can manufacture in their body substances called 'antibodies', which fight the disease organisms. Young animals, however, and animals in poor condition through under-nourishment or some other cause, have little natural resistance. Some diseases are common to all kinds of animal; others, such as Swine Fever, attack one kind only. Individual animals within a species may be naturally immune from certain diseases; others may become immune after they have suffered from the disease, or have been inoculated with a vaccine or serum. Con-trol methods depend on the disease, but in all cases the best methods are preventive—the provision of good food and healthy surroundings in which the animals build up a good natural resistance; good hygiene; and precautions to pre-vent the introduction of any infected materials to the farm.

2. BACTERIAL DISEASES. All these are infec-tious; some are highly contagious, that is, they are spread when one animal comes into actual contact with another. A healthy animal can often throw off an attack of a few dangerous bacteria, but falls victim to an attack by many. Also an animal may harbour dangerous bacteria but remain unharmed because there is no break in the internal or external membranes, or skins, through which the bacteria can enter its blood-stream. Once such a break occurs, the animal will begin to suffer from the disease. Inside the body the bacteria are attracted to certain tissues (muscle, nerves, or blood) or certain parts or organs, such as the skin or the intestines. There they proceed to multiply, sometimes at a rate of between 15 and 20 million times in 24 hours, and to release poisonous substances which damage or destroy the living cells.

Among the many serious diseases caused by bacteria are several forms of blood-poisoning and acute fevers. Tetanus is a form of blood-poisoning which causes the stiffening of certain muscles, including those of the jaw, and unless an anti-tetanus injection is given, is often fatal. The bacteria live in soil, and enter the body through a skin wound which has come in contact with the soil. One of the worst acute fevers is Anthrax, which attacks all domesticated animals, especially cattle, pigs, and horses, and can also be passed to man. Often the animal dies sud-denly without previous sign of illness, and then the carcass must be disposed of at once so that the disease does not spread, for the spores of the disease can live for a long time outside the animal body, and can resist heat, drying, and

even boiling. Braxy, a disease of young sheep which occurs in cold weather, is characterized by high fever, short illness, and high mortality, and is controlled mainly by means of inoculation. Contagious Foot-rot in sheep is caused by bacteria which live in the soil, and is generally more troublesome on rich, wet land. The foot becomes inflamed and discharges pus, and the horny tissue decays. Regular foot-baths and periodic trimming of hooves are the best pre-ventative (*see* SHEEP SHEARING AND DIPPING). Glanders, a contagious disease of horses, mules, and donkeys, is characterized by swollen glands and the growth of small lumps in certain organs. One chronic form of it, Farcy, attacks the skin, causing swellings and lumps known as 'farcy buds'.

Johne's Disease is a bacterial illness causing wasting and chronic diarrhoea in cattle; B.W.D. (Bacillary White Diarrhoea) is at present an incurable disease of young poultry; Mastitis and Garget are inflammations of the udder in cows and sheep which cause grave loss of milk; and Joint-ill is an illness of young foals, lambs, and calves, caused by bacteria which enter through the umbilical cord before or just after birth. There are, of course, many others. Some can be prevented by inoculation; others, such as B.W.D., can be gradually eliminated by careful blood testing and by the destruction of all diseased animals.

TUBERCULOSIS (q.v. Vol. XI) is a bacterial disease of great importance to the farmer be-cause it attacks dairy cows and, through the infected milk, is passed on to human beings and other animals. It is both infectious and con-tagious: the bacteria can live, often for many years, in dried sputum (matter coughed or spat up by animals) or dung in old farm buildings. Before the Second World War about 40% of the cattle in Britain suffered from it in some degree. It has now been checked in many places, how-ever, mainly by the tuberculin test which helps to detect it in the early stages. All cows which show signs of the disease at the test are removed; a herd which remains free after a series of tests may be recognized as 'attested'. The disease takes several different forms: in tuberculosis of the chest, which causes coughing and wasting, bacteria are found in the sputum; in tuberculosis of the udder they are found in milk; in Tuber-culous Emaciation the animal merely wastes away although it may suffer from no loss of

Paul Popper

AFRICAN LONGHORNED CATTLE SUFFERING FROM RINDERPEST
The sick animals are very thin and their mouths hang open

appetite. In other forms the bacteria can be found in excreta (dung) or in discharges from abscesses or swollen diseased glands.

3. VIRUS DISEASES. Viruses are the smallest known living organisms, invisible under the ordinary microscope. They can live outside the body of a live animal in any suitable harbourage —particularly in the bodies of dead animals; but the longer they remain outside the living body of an animal the weaker becomes their infective power. Extreme heat and some antiseptics kill them; while extreme cold helps some of them to survive. The diseases they cause are all both infectious and contagious, and are particularly liable to be spread by contaminated food. Unlike bacteria, they are often deadly in very small quantities. On entering the body, the virus passes through an incubation period, during which it becomes established in a particular tissue or organ, feeds on the cells, and multiplies at an enormous rate. Before signs of disease appear in an infected animal, it may have infected others. Most virus diseases produce the general symptom of a high fever. Animals which recover from a virus disease are usually permanently immune from that disease afterwards.

Virus diseases spread so rapidly that prevention is of the greatest importance. One of the most important preventives is VACCINATION (q.v. Vol. XI), which inoculates the animal with a modified virus, producing a mild form of the disease and so preventing a serious attack. Since Britain is an island, the strict Government regulations to prevent virus diseases from entering the country by means of live animals, carcases, fodder, and so on can be made really effective, and most of the worst virus diseases have been entirely stamped out or are at least very rare. The most serious virus diseases are notifiable to the police, and the victims are isolated, and in many cases the infected animals are slaughtered at once to prevent the spread of infection. Drugs are of little use against these diseases. In other countries some of the worst virus diseases are the groups known as 'plagues' and 'poxes'. Cattle Plague, or Rinderpest, for example, is a short and often fatal illness, of which the symptoms are high fever and ulcers in the nostrils; and Sheep Pox, Cow Pox, and Fowl Pox are all related to the human SMALLPOX (q.v. Vol. XI). A very serious disease, unknown in Britain except in a quarantine hospital since 1919, is Rabies, which can be passed from dogs to humans, and is then known as Hydrophobia. It is a short, fatal illness, death occurring within a week. Affected animals behave madly at first, swallowing anything which comes their way, such as sticks and stones, and foaming at the mouth, and finally become paralysed and sink into a coma. The disease has such a long incubation period that all dogs imported into Britain have to go through 6 months' quarantine. Dogs can now be almost completely protected by vaccination from the virus disease, Distemper; but for Hardpad, another serious dog disease closely akin to Distemper, no effective preventative has yet been discovered. Hardpad can, however, often be cured in its early stages by an anti-virus injection.

Swine Fever is a disease of young pigs, which may take a chronic or acute form. In chronic cases bleeding occurs, followed by button ulcers in the large intestines; in acute cases the symptoms are high fever, bleeding in many organs, and sudden death. The disease is spread mainly through the food, and through the markets where pigs are bought and sold.

Foot and Mouth is the most contagious disease and one of the most disastrous known in animals. It is in the main a cattle and pig disease, though other cloven footed animals, and even occasionally human beings, may catch it. The germs can be carried from one place to another on the feet of animals, on the boots and clothing of humans, on hay and straw, by birds, in contaminated foodstuffs, and in many other ways. Enormous numbers of cattle, in particular, have had to be slaughtered in order to stamp out epidemics. The symptoms, consisting of fever, excessive saliva, and lameness, appear suddenly, several animals being affected at once. Blisters appear on the tongue, lips, and gums, and on the feet between the toes, or where the hoof and skin are joined. The disease is often fatal to young animals, but adult animals may recover. Any outbreak has to be notified to the police immediately, so that all movement of animals in the district affected can be stopped. Diseased animals have to be slaughtered to prevent the danger of infection.

4. Fungus Diseases. Some of the most devastating Plant Diseases (q.v.) are caused by fungi, but generally speaking fungi cause fewer serious animal diseases than bacteria or viruses, and they also spread less readily. The same general conditions encourage them, especially dampness, darkness, and dirt. Some fungus diseases attack external parts of the body; others internal. The symptoms of external fungus disease are loss of hair, peeling, thickening, and wrinkling of the skin, and sometimes the appearance of lumps and blisters, which may remain local, not greatly upsetting the animal's general health. Some internal fungus diseases cause chronic general illness and even death. Fungus diseases are mainly controlled by setting up the conditions unfavourable to the disease, though antiseptics are also effective. As far as we know now, an animal after recovery from a fungus disease does not become immune, nor can inoculation give immunity.

Ringworm is a well-known external fungus disease which affects young cattle and calves, other domestic animals, and even humans. Circular areas of raised, thick, scabby, and hairless skin appear, usually on the head, neck, and face, especially round the eyes. With cattle, the disease is more common in winter when the animals are kept in houses or a yard, and may clear up quickly in the summer.

Internal fungi cause several serious diseases, among them Epizootic Lymphangitis, a horse

Birmingham Post

AN INSPECTOR DISINFECTING HIS BOOTS ON A FARM WHERE THERE IS AN OUTBREAK OF FOOT-AND-MOUTH DISEASE

disease characterized by swellings on the limbs, and Aspergillosis, a lung disease which attacks horses, sheep, cattle, and poultry. It is the cause of 'brooder pneumonia' in chicks. 'Wooden tongue' with 'Lumpy jaw' (Actinomycosis) is a cattle and pig disease caused by a fungus acting with certain bacteria. The tongue, the bones of the jaw, and the udder develop hard, tumour-like growths which discharge pus. The germ enters by bruises, sometimes even tiny bruises, and treatment is by the use of iodine compounds, and occasionally by operation.

See also HEALTH, FARM ANIMALS; PARASITES; PARASITIC WORMS.

ANIMAL FARMING, TROPICAL. 1.

CATTLE. Most tropical cattle are rather small animals (the West African shorthorns are not much bigger than Shetland ponies) and take a long time to grow to maturity. They are generally hardy, resistant to disease, and able to exist on very scanty fodder. In many tropical countries they are given little or no food except what they get by grazing, which in the dry season is very little, for the making of hay or silage is unknown except where it has been introduced by Europeans. In many districts too many cattle are kept for the grazing available, especially in India, where the Hindus hold cattle to be sacred and will not slaughter them, and in Africa, where many tribes reckon a man's wealth by the number of cattle he owns, and so he is reluctant to part with any of them (see NUER AFRICANS, Vol. I). Overstocking, in fact, has in some places reduced formerly valuable grazing land almost to desert. Housing for cattle is often very primitive; a kraal (the South African name for a cattle enclosure) may consist merely of a circular fence to keep out thieves and marauding animals. Some of the cattle-keeping tribes in Africa, such as the MASAI (q.v. Vol. I) of East Africa, are very brave in defence of their beasts, herdsmen even being known to have speared a lion single-handed. 'Mixed farming' in the European sense is unknown in many parts of the tropics. The nomadic tribes keep the cattle, and the settled farmers grow the crops but keep very little livestock. In consequence, the cultivated areas suffer a good deal from the lack of manure.

The most common breed of cattle in tropical regions is the humped zebu ox, which is native to India. These have also been introduced into Africa, where they are mingled with other types of cattle which have been there longer, such as the longhorns of the Hamitic tribes of East and Central Africa, and the dwarf shorthorns of West Africa. In South America many of the cattle belong to the Andalusian breed brought over by Spanish settlers. Pure-bred cattle of northern European breeds do not thrive in most tropical countries, but they or cross-bred cattle partly descended from them can be kept in highland areas such as Kenya or Southern Rhodesia, or in some islands in the Pacific or West Indies. The water-buffalo is common in Egypt and throughout the Asiatic tropics. As a dairy animal, it gives more milk than the zebu, and for pulling the plough it is stronger, though slower. It is, however, dependent on a daily wallow in water or at least a water shower-bath.

Native tropical cattle do not, as a rule, yield much milk, though the milk of the zebu is richer in cream than that of European cattle, and buffalo milk richer still. The cows will not let down their milk except in the presence of their calves, and so these are allowed to suckle a little at each milking-time. Milking is often done under very dirty conditions, and the milk often watered before it is sold. In some places advisory services have not been able to make improvements in the cleanliness of the milking and in animal feeding. Milk yields have been raised by selective breeding in native herds. In hot countries, instead of making butter and cheese, it is often the custom to boil the cream and to pour off only the pure fat, which is called gee or clarified butter. In a few tropical countries such as Kenya modern dairying methods are used by European settlers and dairy produce is exported. Beef from tropical cattle is generally of poor quality, tough and with little fat, and the hides are often the most valuable product. They are thinner than those from temperate countries, and often of poor quality because of bad flaying and drying on the ground; but the natives are now being taught to dry hides on frames (see HIDES AND SKINS, Vol. VII).

Oxen, still the most important draught animals in the tropics, are used for pulling both carts and ploughs, but as they are generally less powerful than horses, it is usual to use at least two (with one shaft between them) to pull a cart. Four oxen are often used to pull small ploughs on peasant farms. In South Africa a full span of sixteen oxen may be needed to pull a loaded

Public Relations, East African Command

A ZEBU BULL IN AN AFRICAN VILLAGE

wagon or a multi-furrow plough. The oxen usually pull against a yoke fitted over the shoulders in front of the hump, and they are controlled by head-ropes, sometimes passed through a hole bored in the nose. Tropical bulls and bullocks are very docile, although the cows are sometimes rather wild and difficult to milk. Oxen are also used in many countries as pack animals, carrying a load of about 150 lb. slung across their backs; they are sometimes even ridden by their owners (*see* BEASTS OF BURDEN, Vol. IV, section 6).

Everywhere in the tropics the fear of disease is a constant anxiety to cattle-owners. The worst epidemic disease in Asia and Africa is rinderpest (or cattle-plague), but this is now being checked by inoculation. Pleuro-pneumonia, anthrax, and black-quarter are also common, especially as inoculation is not always easy to arrange in time in primitive countries. Redwater in many tropical countries, East Coast fever in eastern tropical Africa, and gall-sickness in Africa and America are diseases carried by ticks, and the group of diseases called 'trypanosomiasis', which are carried by tsetse-flies, make cattle-keeping in some districts impossible. Imported cattle have much less resistance to

these tropical diseases than native cattle, which is one of the difficulties in introducing them to improve local stock (*see* ANIMAL DISEASES and TROPICAL PESTS).

2. GOATS, which are very popular in the tropics, are kept mainly for meat, their milk yield being so little that it is hardly worth milking them. Goat skins, however, are even more valuable than cattle hides; the best tropical goat-skins are used for high-class products such as glacé kid, or for leather book-binding. The goat's habit, however, of browsing on young tree seedlings and pulling up grass by the roots on over-grazed pastures makes it necessary to keep them under proper control and not to allow them into important forest areas.

3. SHEEP. Far fewer sheep than goats are kept in the tropics because they suffer so much from disease. The native sheep of the tropics carries a fleece of hair, not of wool, and a few breeds are almost hairless. However, by crossing with Merinos or other woolled sheep, woolled cross-breeds can be produced which are suitable for some tropical highland areas. Many tropical sheep are fat-tailed, the storage of a reserve of fat in this way helping them to exist during dry seasons when there is little grazing. In general they are less important as a source of meat than goats or cattle.

4. PIGS. There are some good native breeds of pigs in eastern Asia and the Pacific islands—for the Chinese were among the first to develop pigs. In parts of tropical Africa pigs are now slowly spreading into areas where they have not been known before. Pigs of all the European breeds can be kept in the tropics, though the white breeds need protection from sunburn. In some places Europeans have put up bacon factories; but pigs are kept in the tropics mainly for pork. It is difficult to find enough food for them in regions where the peasant farmer can produce only enough grain and root crops to feed his own family.

5. POULTRY. The native fowls of the tropics are small birds that lay few eggs, but they are hardy and can pick up most of their own food. Imported breeds such as Rhode Island Reds, Leghorns, and others do quite well, and cross-breeding with native birds can be successful if the peasant farmers can be persuaded to give the extra food needed by these improved birds for their higher production. The normal fowl diseases are more difficult to control on small peasant farms, and for this reason ducks, which suffer from few diseases, are useful. Ducks of the Muscovy breed are particularly suited to the dry tropics, as they do not need swimming water. Turkeys can be kept in the tropics, but geese are rare; pigeons are kept by some African tribes.

6. OTHER TROPICAL ANIMALS. In the dry tropics camels are reared not only as beasts of burden, but as producers of milk, meat, and hair, the latter being woven locally into rugs or exported (see HAIR TRADE, Vol. VII). Horses, which are unsuited to many tropical countries, are hardly ever used as work animals, though they are kept for riding in some of the drier tropical areas. Donkeys and mules are common in some places as pack animals, mules being used particularly in the American tropics. LLAMAS (q.v. Vol. II) are still used to some extent as pack animals in Peru and Bolivia, and they also provide meat, hides, and wool. Their relatives, the alpaca and the vicuna, provide specially valuable kinds of wool. The ostrich farms of Africa are few in number now that the demand for ostrich feathers has declined. Rabbits thrive quite well in the tropics, and are kept for meat in a few places. Bees are kept to produce beeswax as well as honey, the export of beeswax from some African countries being important. They are usually housed in native hives of poor construction.

The farming in temperate countries of the main animals mentioned here is dealt with in separate articles.

See also TROPICAL AGRICULTURE.

ANIMAL PARASITES, see PARASITES; PARASITIC WORMS.

ANIMAL PESTS, see PESTS AND DISEASES; VERMIN.

ANNUAL PLANTS. An annual is a plant that has only one year's life—it grows from a seed, forms a flower which in turn produces seed, and dies—all within a single year. Many of the farmer's regular crops, such as his grain crops and peas and beans, are annuals, as are many of the gardener's vegetable crops. Many garden flowers are BIENNIALS or PERENNIALS (qq.v.), that is, they live for more than a year or many years, and it is not always easy to make a hard and fast line between them. Annuals may be used in many ways in a garden, for they vary greatly in size and character of growth. SWEET PEAS may grow to 8 feet or more, while some of the EDGING PLANTS (qq.v.), such as alyssum or lobelia, may be only a few inches high.

Annuals or biennials are generally used as BEDDING PLANTS (q.v.), a whole bed or border being generally filled with the same plant; or they are useful for filling odd patches, especially in a HERBACEOUS BORDER (q.v.) where an annual of the required height and colour can be selected to fit the pattern of the border. But wherever they are used, they should be grown in big groups of the same kind of flower in order to get the best effect. It is better to concentrate on a few varieties than to be persuaded by attractive descriptions into buying seeds of a dozen different kinds. Annuals are cheap to grow, and many of them, such as calendula (marigolds) and shirley poppies, will grow on any soil that will make a fine tilth. Others, however, such as sweet peas, need rich, well-prepared soil to nourish their rapid growth and free-flowering habits. Some have special requirements—for instance, mignonettes will not flourish unless the soil contains plenty of lime.

There are hardy, half-hardy, and tender types of annuals. Hardy annuals are those which can be sown out of doors from mid-March to the end of May without any protection. Some, such as cornflower and annual scabious, can be sown in the open in the late autumn to flower in the following spring or early summer, and they will do very well and flower early as long as the winter is not too severe. The soil should be given a fine surface tilth in preparation for sowing. The ideal weather for sowing is a day or two after rain has fallen, when the ground is warm and moist and likely to remain so until the seed has germinated. The seed should be spread thinly and evenly over the area and covered with soil to a depth equal to its own diameter. A gentle raking after the seed has been sprinkled does this quite satisfactorily. Another method is to sow in shallow parallel drills, a good effect being obtained by making the drills for each group of plants run in different directions. The drills should be close together for plants such as scarlet flax which need to be massed, and wider apart for those with a more branching habit of growth.

Thinning is a very important and often neglected operation in the growing of hardy annuals. It should be done twice—when the seedlings are about 2 inches high, and again about a fortnight later when the final results of the sowing and the first thinning can be seen. The gardener must thin with a knowledge of the growing habits of the particular plant to guide him. A shirley poppy, for instance, to do itself real justice, needs about a square foot of space; candytuft about 6 inches square. Crowded plants grow tall, weak, and straggly, and will fall victim to a strong wind or heavy rainstorm.

Half-hardy annuals are those which need some protection during the period of germination and early growth. They should be sown in early spring in seedboxes in cold frames, or preferably even earlier in greenhouses with some heat, and planted out into their permanent positions in late April or May, allowing plenty of space to encourage a branching sturdy growth. Branching asters, for instance, if given space, make big plants. Many medium and tall annuals need some kind of staking, the most satisfactory method being to poke a few twigs into the ground round the plant while they are small, and then to put in bigger twigs as they are required. Heavy single stakes look ugly for plants of slender growth. Watering should not be needed in normal seasons; if it has to be done, it must be done thoroughly—otherwise the roots come up to the surface in search of moisture, instead of striking downwards. If the dead heads are always kept cut off, the plants will continue to give a bright display of colour for a long period.

Tender annuals are those which will not normally flower satisfactorily without the protection of glass for at any rate the greater part of their lives. Some of these, such as petunias, calceolarias, and the lovely butterfly-flowered schizanthus, can be planted out in a protected border once all danger of frost is past, and will flourish in a warm summer. Others, such as cinerarias, always need the protection of glass. Cinerarias and calceolarias, if sown in the late summer, provide lovely house plants in the early spring (see GREENHOUSE PLANTS).

See also BIENNIALS; PERENNIALS.

APHID PESTS (GREENFLY AND OTHER BUGS). There are few plants which do not provide food and shelter for one kind of aphid or another, and these bugs may be a serious nuisance to both farm and garden crops, damaging the plants by sucking their juices. They multiply rapidly, especially in certain years (see APHIS, Vol. II). There are many different kinds of aphids—pests of flowering plants such as ROSES (q.v.), as well as of fruit and vegetables. The usual way of getting rid of them is with a nicotine spray or dust, which may have to be repeated two or three times.

The Hop-damson Aphid (or Hop Fly) spends the winter in the egg stage on the damson and various other plums, and hatches in April. The insects, as all aphids, breed very rapidly, sucking the young leaves of the trees. Towards the end of May winged forms are produced, and these fly on to hops, where they attack the young shoots and leaves.

The Bean Aphid (Blackfly, Dolphin) lays its eggs on the wild spindle plant in the autumn; these hatch colonies of wingless females, which,

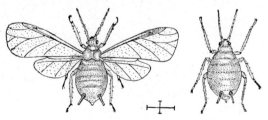

WINGED AND WINGLESS APHIDS (enlarged)

Harold Bastin

GREENFLY ON A ROSEBUD

The black insects are ants and the white objects are skins
shed by the aphids (magnified)

during May, produce winged forms which fly
on to broad beans in early summer; there they
attack the young and soft growing points of the
plants. In gardens, if the top shoots of the beans
are pinched off and a nicotine dust applied to the
plants in warm weather, the beans should escape
the Blackfly. In fields it is best to sow autumn
beans which get beyond the dangerous stage
before the main attack of the bug.

The aphid which attacks cabbages, Brussels
sprouts, swedes, and other related plants lays its
eggs in the autumn, chiefly on Brussels sprouts.
These hatch in April and the young aphids start
to feed on the leaves and later the upper parts of
the plants. Small colonies of adults and young
usually survive the winter as well. From the end
of May the winged forms are produced and go
on to other plants, thus spreading the infestation. Most damage is done towards the end of
summer, the foliage becomes wrinkled, and with
a crop grown for seed the flowers and pods may
be injured. The old stems of Brussels sprouts,
cabbage, and other vegetables which attract
aphids should be cleared away before the middle
of May—that is, before the winged aphids can
arise on them, and so spread the pest. Young
plants can be protected from attack by being
dipped in a nicotine solution before being
planted out.

The eggs of the Leaf-curling Currant Aphid
and other aphids which attack currant or gooseberry bushes hatch in April, and the winged
females eventually produced fly to lettuce and
sow-thistles in June and July. A later brood
return to the currant or gooseberry bushes in
September. The Currant Root Aphid attacks
the underground parts of currant and gooseberry bushes in the summer; the winged forms
appear above ground in the autumn and fly to
the elm, where they lay eggs in the bark to hatch
in the spring. The insects of these generations
cause the leaves of elm trees to curl. A tar-oil
winter wash, where possible, to kill the eggs is
the best protection.

The Mealy Plum Aphid spreads a grey sticky
mass of bugs on the undersides of the leaves,
which may cause a total loss of the crop if they
are not destroyed. The Strawberry Aphid not
only sucks sap from the plants, but helps to
spread the Yellow-edge and Crinkle virus
diseases, as the Raspberry Aphid may spread
Mosaic disease. The several kinds of Apple
Aphid attack leaves, flower-buds, and growing
shoots, leaving twisted leaves and brown wilted
blossoms.

The Woolly Aphis or American Blight is
rather different from other aphid pests, and
unless controlled can ruin the crops of apple-
trees. The aphids excrete a white woolly-looking
substance under which they live in large colonies.
In some years, when the months of May and
June are hot, the attacks may be very severe and
increase in severity; in other years, when the
weather is less suitable, the attack may come
to nothing. Woolly Aphis came to Britain from
the eastern States of the U.S.A. where it is kept
in check by a parasite, *Aphelinus mali*, which eats
the bug. This parasite, however, does not take
kindly to the British climate, though in some
counties colonies of the insect are becoming
acclimatized and the aphid, in consequence, is
disappearing. The pest, however, can be controlled if all patches of the woolly excretion are
at once cleaned off with a brush dipped in a
strong solution of tar-oil. Spraying at high
pressure with a tar-oil wash in the winter or
nicotine in the summer is effective so long as it
is thorough enough to penetrate right through
the clusters of aphids.

Aphids are notifiable by law in the fruit- and

vegetable-growing counties of Bedfordshire, Cambridgeshire, Huntingdonshire, and Hertfordshire.

Some other Bugs (q.v. Vol. II), which live by piercing and sucking the juices of plants, are also serious pests. The Capsid Bug group are among the most troublesome. The Tarnished Plant Bug attacks the leaves of chrysanthemums, potatoes, and other plants all over the world. The Apple Capsid Bug, a bright-green insect, is one of the worst pests in apple orchards. It spends the winter in the egg under the bark of the tree, hatches in the spring, and sucks the sap of the young leaves, shoots, and developing fruit. It is fully grown in July, and soon after disappears, leaving its eggs to hatch the following spring. Besides the apple and other tree fruit, it attacks soft fruit such as black and red currants and gooseberries. Other Capsid Bugs are pests on tea, cotton, and many semi-tropical or tropical crops. Among Scale Insects (q.v. Vol. II) is the Mealy Bug, often to be found on vegetables grown in greenhouses. It has a coat of a mealy, cottony substance, tufts of which adhere to the stems or under the young shoots. The Mussel Scale is a pest on apple and stone-fruit trees, plastering the trunks and branches of neglected trees with 'scales'. The female bug,

having forced her proboscis into the trunk in search of sap, remains fixed, and grows a protective shell under which she lays her eggs; then she dies and disintegrates. The eggs hatch the following May. The pest is easily destroyed by a winter wash of tar-oil.

Greenhouse White-flies (Ghost Fly) are small, white, actively flying, tropical bugs, which in cold climates can only survive in glasshouses. They lay very small greenish-yellow eggs on most Greenhouse Plants (q.v.), especially tomatoes, cucumbers, cinerarias, fuchsias, primulas, and other soft-leaved plants. The flattened green larvae soon become stationary on the leaves, feed by pushing the proboscis into the undersides of the leaves and sucking the sap, and secrete a sticky substance called honeydew, which becomes covered by a dark-coloured fungus. This causes discoloration and puckering of the leaves. White-fly is not easy to get rid of unless the glasshouse can be opened to the winter weather for a short time—which is not generally possible. A very successful method is to introduce into the house a species of Chalcid Fly (q.v. Vol. II), which feeds on the White-fly. These parasites are bred by the Royal Horticultural Society and other institutes, and can be obtained from them and released in the infected house. The effect of the parasite can be seen by the black parasitized scales on the undersides of the leaves. White-fly can be killed by fumigation, either with Tetrachlorethane or Hydrocyanic acid gas; but as both these chemicals are liable to damage certain plants, they are not now much used (*see* Glasshouses). White-fly can be controlled also with DDT smokes or sprays.

See also Pests and Diseases; Spraying.
See also Vol. II: Aphis.

Harold Bastin
WOOLLY APHIS ON APPLE TWIGS

APPLES. This fruit, which has developed from the wild crab-apple, a native of most European countries, has been used for food from very early times. Charred remains of small apples, for example, were found in the excavations of prehistoric Swiss Lake Dwellings (q.v. Vol. I). The apple appears in many ancient legends, though sometimes, as in the garden of Eden story, the name apple is used as a symbol of any fruit to eat. In Britain the usual types cultivated were the green costards and codlins, until in Tudor times varieties of red-skinned pippins were introduced from France. Today the apple

Amateur Gardening

AN ESPALIER APPLE-TREE

is the most widely grown fruit in England and in other countries with a cool climate.

Apples like a medium or heavy loam soil, deep and well-drained, in situations high enough to escape severe late spring frosts, but not greatly exposed to wind from south-west or east. Apple-trees are grown in all forms, but most often as standard, bush, cordon, espalier, and dwarf pyramid. The rootstocks on which the apple is most usually grafted are East Malling IX, II, I, and XVI, according to the size of tree required, though standard trees are also grown on the vigorous crab stocks (*see* FRUIT PROPAGATION). The orchard must be planned with apples of different varieties to secure cross-pollination (*see* FERTILIZATION).

The land must be kept cultivated until the trees bear fruit; but after that, if the trees grow too strongly with little or no fruit, cultivations should cease, and the weeds and grass allowed to grow, until such time as the growth of the trees slows down. If, on the other hand, the trees are stunted with little or no new growth, the ground should be cultivated and kept free from weeds.

The manures most needed are those containing potash; nitrogen only being added when plenty of potash has been given (*see* MANURES).

Winter pruning, which is done only during the season when the tree is not actively growing, consists of removing superfluous branches, and cutting back a limited number of annual shoots in order to keep up a supply of strong young shoot growths every year. Stunted trees should be pruned in winter more severely than strong trees. Summer pruning, which is done when the new shoots are beginning to stiffen, consists of cutting these back to within five or six leaves of their base (*see* PRUNING).

If the trees have set a very heavy crop, better sized apples will be obtained by thinning the clusters of fruit in June to one or two apples only. In some cases, the apples are reduced to one every 8 or 9 inches along each branch. This, however, is only practicable with small trees or trees grown as cordons or espaliers. There is always a risk in thinning too early before the apples have finished their natural dropping.

An apple is ready for picking if it comes away easily when raised on its stalk. The apples must be picked carefully so that they are not bruised into padded baskets or bags, and the same care must be taken when emptying the baskets into storage or market boxes. Under natural storage conditions, such as a cellar with an earth floor, good ventilation, and moist air, early apples keep one or two months (though most are best eaten off the tree), mid-season apples keep to the end of October, late apples until after Christmas, and very late apples until the end of March or even later. All apples keep best when wrapped in oiled wrapping-paper. Apples kept in cold storage will remain sound for 12 months. The apples to be marketed should be graded according to size and packed in standard, non-returnable packages.

The worst diseases of apples are apple-scab fungus (black spot), which covers the leaves and buds with sooty spores, and is best controlled by SPRAYING (q.v.); and apple canker which causes shoots and branches to wither and die, and is controlled only by cutting away and burning all infected parts. Both these diseases are very infectious (*see* PLANT DISEASES, section 2).

The worst insect pests of apple are caterpillars of the winter moth type (*see* BUTTERFLY AND MOTH PESTS). These are best controlled by grease-banding round the trunk before the moth comes up to lay her eggs, or spraying with lead-arsenate or DDT in March to kill the grubs. Other serious pests are aphids of various kinds, red spider, capsid bug, sawfly, codling moth, and blossom weevil (*see* INSECT PESTS).

There are a great many different varieties of excellent apples to choose from when planting an orchard. The private gardener's main concern is to plant varieties which will give him a supply of cooking and dessert apples for as long a period as possible, without too many at one time. Some apples such as Blenheim Orange are excellent dessert apples as well as reasonably good cookers, but the trees are slow coming into

Amateur Gardening

A STANDARD APPLE-TREE

East Malling Research Station

A BUSH APPLE-TREE

East Malling Research Station

A DWARF PYRAMID APPLE-TREE

R. A. Malby

CORDON APPLE-TREES

bearing. Bramley's Seedling, a strong grower which makes a big tree, not only supplies very good cooking apples by late September, but if properly stored keeps well till April, by which time it is very sweet. Both these apples, however, are likely to suffer from scab. Some varieties, such as Crawley Beauty, Royal Jubilee, and Court Penda Plat, which flower late, generally escape frosts.

Recommended apple varieties are:

COOKING

Early: Early Victoria, Grenadier.
Mid-season: Arthur Turner, Rev. W. Wilks.
Late: Lord Derby.
Very Late: Bramley's Seedling, Lane's Prince Albert, Edward VII, Crawley Beauty.

DESSERT

Early: Irish Peach, Beauty of Bath, Epicure.
Mid-season: Miller's Seedling, Saint Everard, Owen Thomas, Premier, Fortune, Exquisite, Worcester Pearmain, James Grieve, Ellison's Orange, Charles Ross, Egremont Russet, Saint Edmund's Russet.
Late: Cox's Orange Pippin, Lord Lambourne, Ribston Pippin.
Very Late: Laxton's Superb, Belle de Boskoop, Orleans Reinette, Heusgen's Golden Reinette, Claygate Pearmain, Rosemary Russet, Pitmaston Pineapple, D'Arcy Spice, Cornish Gillyflower.

Crab-apples are often planted not only because they are useful for jelly-making, but for their decorative value. Siberian crabs, which will grow in almost any soil, are very showy both when in blossom and again when covered with bright scarlet and yellow fruit. Cider apples, which are grown in large orchards in most western counties of England, are not of interest to the private gardener (*see* CIDER-MAKING, Vol. VII).

See also FRUIT-GROWING; FRUIT PROPAGATION.

APRICOTS. These are closely related to PLUMS and PEACHES (qq.v.). They probably originated in Caucasia, and are known to have been cultivated for some 3,000 years B.C. in China, and for many centuries in India, Tibet, and western Asia before they were introduced to Europe in the time of Alexander the Great. The apricot is said to have been brought to Britain from Italy by a French priest who gave it to Henry VIII's gardener. By 1629 a writer describes six sorts as being grown in Britain. The apricot, however, does not like the cold damp climate of

E.N.A.

APRICOTS DRYING IN A CALIFORNIA ORCHARD

Britain, and in most parts will only flourish if grown against a warm south wall. Because it blossoms very early, the frosts of February and March are likely to do damage unless it is well protected.

Apricots need a well-drained, light, rich loam with plenty of lime, for which purpose old mortar rubble is often dug in when the planting holes are prepared. They do not do well on sandy soils. They are generally grown by being grafted on the stock of seedling plum or wild cherry, but can be grown on their own roots by planting an apricot stone. They grow more quickly than peaches, but are shorter lived. In training the tree, the object is to obtain plenty of branches to produce a framework of permanent wood on which fruit spurs will spring (*see* PRUNING). Although the apricot is self-fertile, it is safer to pollinate it by hand by inserting pollen into the flower with a rabbit's tail or camel hair paint brush. The fruit should be thinned, leaving about one fruit to each 4 inches of branch. They suffer from the same types of diseases and pests that attack PEACHES (q.v.).

In Italy and southern France orchards of apricots are grown for drying. The kernels of some kinds are sweet like sweet almonds, though most are bitter. Bokhara dried apricots with sweet kernels are sold all over Russia. There are a number of varieties suitable for growing in Britain, some of which, such as the Breda and the Moorpark, have been well established for a long time—the Breda, for instance, is mentioned in a gardener's dictionary of 1731.

See also FRUIT-GROWING; FRUIT PROPAGATION.

ARABLE CROPS. The term 'arable' is applied to land periodically ploughed, and serves to distinguish it from permanent grass. The crops grown on it, whether for human use or for feeding livestock, are called arable crops.

1. CLIMATE AND SOIL. These are the factors that decide mainly whether agricultural land is to be treated as arable or permanent grass. Under conditions of fairly high rainfall, say 40–60 inches a year, grass grows well, while the cultivation of arable land is difficult, and the crops ripen slowly. So, in the west and north-west of England and in the hilly districts of Wales and Scotland, farming is based on the grazing of permanent pasture (see GRASSLAND). But in the flat country of the Midlands, the rainfall is only about 25–40 inches, whilst in the east and south-east of Great Britain it is 25 inches or even less. Thus, as one travels from west to east, the farming changes from predominantly grass to predominantly arable.

Temperature and hours of sunshine also affect the type of farming. Warm, moist conditions favour the growth of foliage. Hence forage crops (food for horses and cattle) grow well in the west, and livestock and dairying are common systems of farming; while the eastern half of the country is better suited to corn crops, such as wheat, barley, and rye. Farther to the north, where the weather is cooler, oats, swedes, and turnips grow well. Freedom from frost is also important, for this determines the time of sowing in the spring. Thus, in parts of Cornwall and Ayrshire, which are free from early spring frosts, early potatoes and broccoli are paying crops. Generally speaking, coastal regions have a more constant and rather higher temperature than inland areas and districts high above sea-level. Hilly land, therefore, cannot grow the same wide range of crops as can flatter, coastal districts. Fields that lie below the general level of the surrounding country are very subject to frost damage, for here the colder air tends to settle and to turn the hollows into frost pockets. Slopes that face the sun warm up more quickly after winter than those that have a northern aspect; therefore the seeds germinate earlier, and crops grow more quickly. In some parts, notably in Yorkshire and East Anglia, strong winds blow away the light sandy soil, and these 'blowing sands' are particularly troublesome to cultivate (see FARMING DISTRIBUTION).

The choice of crops naturally depends a good deal on the texture of the soil. On heavy land which contains a lot of clay, cultivation is difficult, and the land is often left under grass; but where ploughing is possible, wheat, beans, clovers, and cabbage are grown. On light, sandy land rye, barley, peas, carrots, potatoes, and lupins all do well. On peaty and fen soils sugar-beet, potatoes, celery, and market-garden crops excel. On the medium soils (the loams) practically any crop can be grown, and therefore these soils are very popular and command high rents (see SOILS).

2. CHOICE OF SEED. The selection of seed suited to the soil and other conditions is most important. There are many varieties of each crop, each with its own characteristics. Amongst the cereals, for instance, some are short and others are long in the straw; some ripen early and others late; some are resistant to certain diseases, and others are susceptible. Some potatoes mature early and some late. Some varieties of sugar-beet are much richer in sugar than others. The selected seed must be pure, true to type, and not shrivelled, so that robust seedlings will develop. It must be free from weed seeds and from the spores of fungus diseases. The seed of cereals, sugar-beet, and mangolds are usually dusted with an antiseptic powder as a protection against seed-borne disease.

A farmer generally buys some new seed each year, and saves the rest from his own crops. Many believe that if they use seed grown in districts farther north than their own, the seed will be hardier—though there is little evidence to support this belief. It is much more important to know that the seed was well grown, properly harvested, and of high germination, and for this reason cereal seed from the sunny areas of low rainfall in the eastern counties is preferable. Some crops are grown from seed, which is sown in lines (drills) or broadcast; or sown in a nursery bed and transplanted; others are produced by vegetative methods from tubers, as with a potato crop (see PLANT PROPAGATION).

3. TIME OF SOWING. Wheat, rye, and beans

are most often sown in the autumn, the varieties selected being known as 'winter varieties'. Oats and barley may also be sown then; but since these plants are not as hardy, only winter-hardy varieties sown in well sheltered positions are likely to be successful. Most other crops, such as potatoes, peas, carrots, swedes, sugar-beet, and so on, are sown during the spring, the time varying from March to May. Spring varieties of barley, oats, and wheat are also sown in the new year. Grass and clover mixtures (*see* LEYS) are usually sown in the spring, though occasionally in July or August.

4. CULTIVATION. Different types of soil need different mechanical treatment to bring them to the necessary degree of fineness (or tilth), and one type of tilth does not suit all crops. Potatoes are relatively indifferent to the condition of the tilth and grow well in quite a lumpy soil that would be most unsuitable for a crop such as barley, which is very particular and prefers a fine seed bed. A seed bed is usually prepared first by ploughing to bury all weeds and dead matter, and then by harrowing to break up the furrows. Rollers are also often used during the breaking-down process to crush the clods and give firmness to the tilth. The time that passes between ploughing and harrowing is governed by the type of soil; with heavy clay soils a long period of 'weathering' is needed, to allow the rain and wind, and especially the frost, to break down the soil. The depth of ploughing also varies with the type of soil and the crop to be grown. Cereals need a relatively shallow seed bed, so ploughing is usually only about 4 to 6 inches deep. Beet and potatoes, on the other hand, which like a deep tilth, may need ploughing a foot or more in depth (*see* PLOUGH). Some soils, such as those of the Wolds, for example, are only 3 or 4 inches deep and rest on solid chalk which restricts the depth of cultivation—and in consequence the kind of crop which will flourish there.

Once the crop is sown and the seedlings have appeared, some 'after-cultivations' may be carried out to keep the surface in good order and the weeds in check. Harrows, horse-hoes, and grubbers, which work between the rows of plants, are used for this work (*see* CULTIVATORS). Nowadays there is little hand-hoeing done, except on root crops, and the weeds in cereal crops are controlled by harrowing and, increasingly, by spraying (*see* WEEDS).

5. MANURING. The MANURES (q.v.) used for any one crop depend upon the nature of the crop itself, the nature and condition of the soil, and to a certain extent upon the climate and the season.

Manures are usually applied to an annual crop before the seed is sown, though it is not uncommon to apply a fertilizer which is soluble in the soil (such as nitrate of soda) to a growing crop if it shows signs of needing a 'tonic'. This is known as 'top dressing'. Recent research has shown that the position in which the fertilizer is placed in relation to the seed is important; and combine-drills, that sow fertilizer and seed at the same time, are often nowadays used to place the fertilizer in a narrow band just below the seed. LIME (q.v.) is always applied to the soil separately from the fertilizers.

The organic manures supply foods to nourish the plants, as well as humus (fully decayed vegetable matter) to improve and maintain the condition of the soil. The 'chemical' fertilizers supply plant food only. Both types are used by most farmers, according to crop and soil. A catch crop, that is, one grown quickly between two main crops, may be ploughed green into the soil (a green manure) as a good preparation for many crops on some soils.

6. DISEASES AND PESTS. During the growing season, the crops may be attacked by innumerable PESTS AND DISEASES (q.v.) which, if unchecked, can do immense damage. Good farmers take precautionary measures to prevent an attack, and quick action to restrict it should it develop. The sowing of healthy seed under good conditions is a great help, for a lusty, well-fed plant has a high degree of natural resistance. In serious cases it may be necessary to spray the crop, as in the case of potato blight, black aphis on sugar-beet, or carrot fly (*see* INSECTICIDES). The adoption of a sound ROTATION OF CROPS (q.v.) is a useful precaution.

7. HARVESTING. Apart from market-garden crops, harvest begins, in a normal season, with the cereal crops in July and August, and continues with the root crop: potatoes, carrots, mangolds, sugar-beet and, lastly, swedes. Corn crops must be harvested in fine weather, but this is not necessary with root crops, though when the soil is wet and sticky, the task is more difficult and expensive. Cereals must be stacked until they can be threshed, which gives a further opportunity for them to dry out.

The farmer needs technical skill and a wide

THE REAPERS

The corn is cut with a sickle and bound into sheaves with straw which the woman is twisting. The sheaves are stacked in stooks to dry.

Oil-painting by George Stubbs (1724–1806)

John Topham

DRILLING (right) AND HARROWING (left) A ROW CROP
The fine rolled tilth can be seen on the extreme right

experience of coping with the weather if he is to grow good crops. The many differences in climate, soil, and farming conditions in Britain make it impossible to lay down a fixed set of rules to govern the growing of any particular crop. Even the best arable farmers are constantly changing their methods as their experience grows and conditions change. The different crops grown on arable land are described in separate articles.

See also CULTIVATIONS; SOILS; ROTATION OF CROPS; MANURES; MECHANIZED FARMING.

ARBORETUM, *see* ARBORICULTURE.

ARBORICULTURE. This term means the growing of trees as individuals, and is derived from two Latin words, *arbor* a 'tree', and *cultum* 'cultivated'. FORESTRY (q.v.), on the other hand, is the growth or control of trees in such large numbers that they form a crop.

Individual trees, grown for their beauty of form and the shade and shelter that they provide, are one of the chief features of our gardens and parks, and are given an important place in town planning (*see* ORNAMENTAL TREES). Each tree receives far more attention than is possible in the forest. It is usually grown for several years

in a nursery, to a height of 6 feet or more, before being planted out in a well-prepared and deeply dug position, supported by a stake, and often guarded with a wire cage to keep away animals. Later on it may be pruned to shape, and possibly lopped back when it has grown too large for its position.

Many beautiful trees can be grown where enough care can be given. The present tendency is to prefer those with attractive flowers and fruits, as well as foliage. The more important of these belong to the Rose family of plants, and include flowering cherries (*Prunus*), allies of the pears (*Pyrus*), and varieties of crab-apples (*Malus*).

Old trees that are threatened with death or downfall by the decay of their heartwood or larger branches, may be restored by a form of surgical operation. The decayed material is cut away, all exposed surfaces are disinfected to stop further attack by fungi, and then the holes are filled in with specially prepared cement. The structure of the tree's trunk and branches may also be strengthened with metal struts and stays. This sort of tree surgery is only suitable for preserving valuable specimen trees, and is not applied to trees grown for timber.

A. D. C. Le Sueur

THE BASE OF A TREE REPAIRED WITH CEMENT

An arboretum is a collection of specimen trees grown for their beauty or scientific interest. Well-known examples are to be found at Kew Gardens in Surrey, at Bedgebury in Kent, and at the Royal Botanic Gardens at Edinburgh. Others have been planted in the grounds of large country houses throughout Britain.

These arboretums have been of great value to foresters and gardeners because they have shown which foreign trees would grow, or would not grow, under the various climatic and soil conditions found in different parts of the country. Important conifers such as larch and Douglas fir, and broadleaved trees now familiar to everyone, such as sycamore and horse chestnut, were first grown as rare specimens in these garden collections.

A recent development on these lines is the 'Forest Garden', in which sample plots of many kinds of trees are grown in order to show their possible value for forest planting.

See also TREES, BROADLEAVED; TREES, CONIFEROUS; ORNAMENTAL TREES.

See also Vol. IX: BOTANICAL GARDENS; PARKS AND GARDENS.

ARTICHOKES. The name 'artichoke' is used for three quite different kinds of vegetables. The origin of the name is rather puzzling. It must have been first applied to the globe artichoke from the Italian *articiocco*, for the vegetable has been known in Italy since the time of the Romans. A popular explanation of its use for all three vegetables is that they are plants that choke up the garden.

The so-called Jerusalem artichoke is native to America, and it was introduced into Europe after the European colonization of America in the 16th century. The word 'Jerusalem' has nothing to do with the city, but is a corruption of the Italian *girasole*, a sunflower; the plant is, in fact, a species of sunflower, *Helianthus tuberosus*. The Chinese artichoke is so called because it comes from the Far East. It is sometimes called 'woundwort'.

1. THE GLOBE ARTICHOKE (*Cynara Scolymus*) is a herbaceous perennial plant, which grows up anew each year from the rootstock. The edible part is the large, thistle-like, scaly flower bud, the whole bud being boiled, and the base of the bud and the fleshy part at the base of each scale are eaten. The globe artichoke is probably a native of western Asia and has been cultivated in Europe for centuries. It was popular in Britain during the 17th and 18th centuries, and is eaten a great deal in France. The two usual varieties are Large Green Provence and Large Purple Provence.

The plants are grown as a permanent crop after the manner of rhubarb. They are most easily propagated by vegetative means, that is, by suckers or off-shoots which are taken with as much root as possible from established plants and planted on well-manured soil in the autumn so that they become established before winter (*see* PLANT PROPAGATION). Seed is sown in February or March under glass, and the plants are transplanted in April. The plants grow very large, and need as much space as 5 or 6 feet square each if they are grown on rich soils. They should be generously manured each winter and given an application of a complete fertilizer in the spring.

2. JERUSALEM ARTICHOKE (*Helianthus tuberosus*) is also a herbaceous perennial. Its underground rootstocks have oblong, deeply indented tubers attached to them, which contain a food material called 'inulin', a starch-like carbohydrate. The plant is easy to cultivate and

thrives on the same kind of manuring as is given to potatoes, and on all kinds of soils provided they are not wet. Tubers are planted in the spring (March) 12 inches apart, in rows spaced 3 feet apart. The plants grow so tall that they smother all weed growth, so need little cultivation. The tubers can be lifted and stored in late autumn, or left in the ground and dug as needed.

3. Chinese Artichoke (*Stachys Sieboldii*). The tubers of this Chinese vegetable can be used as a salad, when they resemble radishes, or they can be boiled or fried, when they have a delicate, pleasant flavour. The plant, which is a relative of the wild betony, is quite hardy in Europe. It is a herbaceous perennial, and forms clusters of swollen underground rhizomes (or tubers) late in the season. It is very easy to grow: bits of rhizome are planted in fairly rich soil 12 inches apart, in rows 2 feet apart, from February to April. The rhizomes are taken up when the plants die down in November and are stored in dryish sand for winter use.

4. Cardoon (*Cynara Cardunculus*) resembles the globe artichoke to which it is related, but in this case it is the stem and leaf stalks which are eaten as a vegetable after they have been blanched like celery. The name cardoon comes from the Latin *carduus*, a thistle, referring to the plant's thistle-like flower heads. Cardoon is grown in a similar way to Celery (q.v.), but much more care is needed with the blanching. The blanch-

Amateur Gardening

GLOBE ARTICHOKES
The buds are ready for picking

ing is often done by placing hay or straw closely around the plants or by twisting hay-bands around the stems, instead of by earthing up.

ARTIFICIAL FERTILIZERS. During the 19th century, as the industrial population of Britain increased greatly, there were no longer enough natural fertilizers to grow all the food the people needed. Therefore those essential soil foods had to be found elsewhere and converted into a form available to plants. It was found that the chemical elements, nitrogen, phosphorus, and potassium, essential to the welfare of crops, could be got from ores in the earth, from rocks, or from the air and water, and that they could be prepared in factories as compounds which plants could absorb. The chemical industries produce millions of tons of these artificial manures every year (*see* Chemistry, Industrial, Vol. VII) and they are now used all over the world to supplement organic manures. Their value as fertilizers is a matter of considerable controversy among agricultural experts (*see* Manures, section 3).

1. Nitrogenous Fertilizers. Plants take up their nitrogen (N) from the soil chiefly in the form of a compound called a 'nitrate'. There are several nitrates suitable for this purpose, but the cheapest are sodium nitrate, found in Chile in the form of a crude ore called *Caliche*, and calcium nitrate, which is made by a complicated chemical process requiring very powerful electric furnaces. Nitrogen in the form of nitrate is the quickest acting form of nitrogen for plant growth. It is immediately absorbed by the roots and built up into plant substance, such as plant protein. Any substance that gives rise to nitrate in the soil can also be used as a nitrogenous fertilizer, by far the most important being ammonium sulphate. In the soil the ammonia is rapidly converted into nitrate, one of the many important functions that are carried out by the soil Bacteria (q.v. Vol. II). Therefore, though it was ammonia that was added to the soil, it is nitrate which the plant absorbs. Another important nitrogenous fertilizer, nitro-chalk, contains half its nitrogen in the form of ammonia, and the remaining half as nitrate.

When applied to soils poor in nitrogen these quick-acting fertilizers show their effects in the plant after only a few days. The leaves, formerly yellowish, become fully green, the growth of the leaves and stems is greatly increased, and the crops build up more protein, and so they become a better flesh-forming food for livestock. All crops respond well to nitrogenous fertilizers except those of the clover family, which, by the action of the bacteria in their root nodules, can take their supply of nitrogen gas direct from the air, and need no further nitrate supplies. This 'fixation' of atmospheric nitrogen in the root nodules of LEGUMINOUS CROPS (q.v.) is of the very greatest importance in farming (*see* NITROGEN SUPPLY IN PLANTS, Vol. II).

At the beginning of the present century chemists succeeded in fixing nitrogen from the air on a large scale, using vast amounts of hydro-electric power or coal in the process. The methods have been continuously improved, and now the synthetic production of nitrates and ammonia is a world-wide industry. The nitrogen of the air is combined with oxygen, hydrogen, and other elements and sold to farmers as sulphate of ammonia, nitro-chalk, and other important fertilizers. There is now no possible shortage of these essential helps to growing heavy crops.

Nitrate in solution is easily washed out of the surface soil by heavy rains, so that if the plant is not actively growing and so able to absorb the solution at once, the nitrate finds its way into the lower depths of the soil beyond the reach of plant roots, and is lost to the farm. Ammonia, as such, is kept in the surface soil by combining with the clay and organic matter, but as it gradually becomes transformed into nitrate, the same loss happens. Therefore, in practice nitrogenous fertilizers are used only when a crop is growing in the ground, and since there is nothing left behind after one crop is grown, a fresh dressing has to be given for the next crop.

2. PHOSPHATES. Farmers supplied phosphorus (P) to their crops until a century ago with crushed bone. In this the phosphate is present as calcium phosphate, but this material is so insoluble in the soil water that it is a very slow-acting manure, and often fails to provide enough phosphorus for quickly growing crops. In 1842, however, the great agriculturist and experimenter, Sir John Lawes of Rothamsted, Hertfordshire, perfected his process of dissolving bones and also rocks rich in calcium phosphates with sulphuric acid. Almost all the phosphate contained in the new product, superphosphate, was soluble in water and therefore far more useful to crops. As a result of this important

discovery more superphosphate is now manufactured than any other fertilizer, Great Britain alone making nearly a million tons a year. About 40 years later, in 1884, a second important phosphatic fertilizer appeared. This was the finely ground slag left by the Bessemer process of producing steel from a pig iron made from phosphatic iron ores (*see* IRON AND STEEL, Vol. VIII). The phosphate, though not soluble in water, dissolves fairly readily in soil water, which contains carbon dioxide and thus acts as a very weak acid. Plants can, therefore, take up phosphorus quite easily from basic slag. Bessemer slags are the most soluble and, consequently, the most useful to crops. Basic slag is mainly used on grassland and on arable land that lacks lime and is, therefore, rather acid. Recently, finely ground rock phosphate has been used directly on the land, especially grassland, instead of being made into superphosphate. It is insoluble in water and is only useful on soils short of lime where the acidity helps to dissolve it.

On soils short of available phosphate plants make a poor start, showing a reddish tinge in the leaf; corn crops give poor yields that ripen very late; and the clover in GRASSLAND (q.v.) grows thin and poor. The application of phosphatic fertilizers results in increased yields, and the animals that consume the crops grow stronger bones. The soil has a great power of absorbing and storing phosphate, so that what is not used by the first crop can serve, at least in part, for the crops that follow.

3. POTASH (K = Kalium to avoid confusion with the P used for phosphates). Until 1861 the only potash fertilizer was farmyard manure, but in that year extensive salt-mines were opened at Stassfurt, in Germany, and there both rock salt (sodium chloride) and impure potassium chloride were found. These salts are easily soluble in water, but, like phosphates, the soil retains them for the use of crops. They are particularly valuable for potatoes, sugar-beet, fruit and vegetables generally. Corn crops usually need no added potash. Muriate of potash, crude potassium chloride, is most generally used for agricultural purposes; gardeners and fruit-growers more often use sulphate of potash. Another magnesium and potash fertilizer is 'kainit', which is obtained from natural deposits found in the soil, especially in Germany.

4. COMPOUND OR MIXED FERTILIZERS. The only way of finding out what fertilizers are needed by crops and soils is by direct trial, and large numbers of field experiments have been carried out for this purpose at experimental stations all over the world. The best known, because the oldest, is the Rothamsted Experimental Station begun by Sir John Lawes in 1843, and still the centre of soil and fertilizer research in Britain.

Fertilizers may be used singly, but experience shows that crops more often need two or even three of the constituents (N, P, and K) in certain proportions. Therefore, ready-made compound or mixed fertilizers are purchased in enormous quantities, though the farmer can buy the individual salts and mix them up himself if he prefers. In order that a farmer may know exactly how much plant food he is getting in his fertilizer, it must be sold with a guarantee, giving the percentage of nitrogen (N), phosphoric acid (P_2O_5), and potash (K_2O) in the mixture. For example, sulphate of potash is sold as containing 48% of K_2O.

The 'nutrient ratio' of a compound fertilizer is often expressed in figures: for example, $1:2:1$ indicates that a fertilizer contains twice as much phosphate as nitrogen or potash, whereas $1:2:3$ indicates a fertilizer that contains twice as much phosphate and three times as much potash as nitrogen. The total amounts of plant nutrients in a fertilizer are calculated on the basis of each 100 lb., that is, the percentage. This is called the 'fertilizer analysis' and is also expressed in figures. Thus a $5:10:5$ fertilizer would have 5 units of nitrogen in each 100 lb. (5%), 10 units of phosphoric acid (10%), and 5 units of potash (5%): a total of 20 units.

The vegetable-grower uses compound fertilizers of high analysis, and those containing a total of 20 units or more per cent. of plant nutrient are the most satisfactory for intensive cropping purposes. The National Growmore Fertilizer is an example of a high analysis fertilizer which was specially prepared at the request of the Government for vegetable gardeners during the Second World War. This fertilizer has a $7:7:7$ analysis and therefore $1:1:1$ ratio; it is a suitable general-purpose fertilizer for the vegetable garden.

5. TRACE ELEMENTS. Besides the main elements supplied by artificial fertilizers, some plants need very small amounts of other elements (trace elements) if they are to thrive. Lack of any of these nutrients causes 'deficiency diseases',

Rothamsted Experimental Station

POTATOES ON LAND DEFICIENT IN PHOSPHATE

On the left the ground has been treated with super-phosphate and on the right it has had no fertilizer

and these can be cured by adding small amounts of the missing element to the soil. Zinc deficiency in California affects orange and grapefruit trees; small amounts of manganese must be given on fen soils to prevent 'grey speck' in oats; and the deficiency diseases 'brown heart' in swedes and 'crown rot' in sugar-beet can be cured by adding borax (a compound of the element boron) to the soil.

Fertilizers are usually broadcast uniformly over the surface of the land by mechanical distributors and harrowed into the top soil. A better practice is to drill them in narrow bands quite close to the rows of seeds, using a special machine with delivery spouts which can be set at the necessary depth and distance apart (*see* DRILLS AND DISTRIBUTORS).

See also MANURES; MANURE, FARMYARD; COMPOST HEAP; SOILS.

ARTIFICIAL INSEMINATION, *see* STOCK BREEDING.

ASPARAGUS. Wild asparagus is a sea-shore plant belonging to the same family as LILIES (q.v. Vol. II). It is to be found on most sea-shores in Britain and throughout Europe. Both the Greeks and Romans collected the wild plants to cultivate in their gardens. The name 'asparagus' was originally the Greek name and was adopted by the Romans, later becoming also the English name, though it was corrupted during the Middle Ages to 'sparrow-grass'. The young shoots as they come through the soil in the spring are cut and used as a vegetable.

Amongst the established garden varieties of asparagus are Reading Giant, Palmetto, Argenteuil, and Conover's Colossal. In America, Mary Washington and Martha Washington are varieties developed by crossing Reading Giant with an unknown American variety, and are extensively grown in the U.S.A. because of their resistance to the rust disease. Some market-gardeners specialize in developing their own strains of asparagus, and these are sometimes offered for sale.

Asparagus thrives on a loose though deep sandy soil, such as is to be found in Norfolk and Lancashire, for example. It grows well also on the loamy soils of the Vale of Evesham in Worcestershire. The plant forms a rootstock with long fleshy roots; when once an asparagus bed is established it is left undisturbed for many years. Asparagus beds have been known to remain in a productive condition for over 50 years, but usually the growth becomes rather spindly before this.

Plants for establishing new beds are raised by sowing seed in April in shallow drills 18 inches apart. The next spring, after a year's growth, the rootstocks, which at that stage are called 'crowns', are taken up and replanted in the permanent beds. The crowns are planted in shallow trenches or furrows 15 to 18 inches apart, though if the beds consist only of single rows, a practice becoming more general today, the beds should be at least 4 feet apart.

The beds are well manured each autumn, and fresh soil laid over the surface to keep the developing crowns well covered. In the early spring the surface of the beds is cultivated and moulded up to create a deep fine tilth, and a dressing of salt

Sutton and Sons

ASPARAGUS TIPS GROWING OUT OF THE SOIL

is appreciated by these sea-shore plants. The partly blanched new shoots begin to appear from about mid-April onward according to the season, and are cut for use before they begin to branch out. Asparagus beds are cut for a period of about 6 weeks; after about mid-June the growths are allowed to develop to strengthen the plants for the next season. New beds should not be cut until the plants are in their third season, the first and second years being allowed for development.

The principal pest of asparagus is the Asparagus Beetle (*see* BEETLE PESTS), the grubs of which attack the shoots and foliage. Asparagus Rust is a fungus disease which attacks the foliage (*see* PLANT DISEASES, section 2). Violet Root Rot, which attacks the underground rootstock of the plants, may occur in beds that have been established for some years.

AUBERGINE, *see* EGG-PLANT.

B

BAMBOOS. These are the stiff, hard stems of a group of wild grasses, having the botanical name *Bambusa*, of which there are very many different kinds. They grow wild in tropical Asia where they are also cultivated on a large scale, thriving best in the damp heat of the monsoon climate. Like most GRASSES (q.v. Vol. II), their stems are hollow tubes divided into sections by swollen joints called 'nodes'; and the stems are so large and strong that they can be used for many purposes, such as making huts and furniture. If a hole is bored through the nodes, the large stems can be used as water-pipes, or be made into quivers for arrows, water-vessels, handles, and shafts for spears; the smaller stems can be used as blow-pipes for firing darts at wild animals and birds, and they make useful stakes for supporting garden plants. The young shoots are eaten as a vegetable, like asparagus, in oriental countries, and for this purpose are earthed over to keep them tender. They are also eaten salted, pickled, and preserved in sugar. The inner pulp is used for paper-making in China.

E.N.A.

A BAMBOO GROWING IN KANDY, CEYLON

In the jungles the bamboos form huge clumps, up to 100 feet high and 40 feet thick, and when cut down they grow again very quickly, sometimes as much as one foot in a day. Some kinds are so large that a stem may measure 3 feet round, but this is rare; in general the bamboo is slender and very tall. Often all the bamboos in one district flower at the same time, forming huge tufts of delicate grass-like flowers. The plants, however, flower only about once every 7 years, and after flowering nearly all the clumps die out, to be replaced by seedlings that grow from the countless seeds shed by the bamboo flowers.

See also TROPICAL AGRICULTURE.
See also Vol. II: GRASSES.

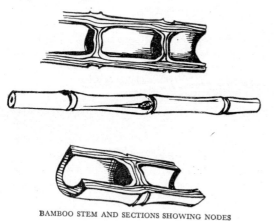

BAMBOO STEM AND SECTIONS SHOWING NODES

BANANAS. These grow on a tree-like plant which is found both wild and cultivated in many tropical countries. In recent years large plantations have been made in Jamaica and in Central and South America. Although essentially tropical, the banana can also be cultivated in such countries as South Africa and Australia. The word 'banana' is of Spanish origin, but the fruit has many native names in different parts of the world. Its botanical name is *Musa*, and an old English name, found in many accounts of voyages and still used in India, is 'plantain'.

Elders and Fyffes, Ltd.

BANANA TREES IN THE WEST INDIES
A bunch carries 6 to 12 'hands', each consisting of 12 to 18 'fingers'

There are many different varieties, each with its distinctive shape, colour, and flavour: among them 'red bananas', 'lady's fingers', 'silk figs', and 'giant figs'. These kinds are not exported, being merely grown on a small scale as a native food crop. The wild bananas to be found in Central America, West and East Africa, and south-east Asia, generally have large seeds: the almost seedless kinds which we know are the result of cultivation. The kinds usually imported to Britain come from Jamaica, the West Indies, and the Canary Islands. Jamaica and Central America produce the 'Gros Michel' banana, and the Canary Islands a very small banana with a very good flavour, which grows on a much smaller plant.

Bananas can be grown only on fertile soil with a warm climate and a steady rainfall the whole year round. They need to be sheltered from the wind. In some places such as southern Jamaica, Colombia, and the Canary Islands, IRRIGATION (q.v.) has been successfully used. When the ground has been cleared for banana planting, it is planted with side shoots or suckers, which are cut off with roots from the base of another banana plant and set about 12 feet apart each way. They soon take root and grow into plants, each of which has a short, stout, underground stem; from this springs a huge shoot that grows to a height of from 6 to 25 feet or more, bearing enormous, ragged, oblong leaves. In the midst of these there arises a small flowering shoot, which develops into a long stalk bearing several clusters of fruit. The plant bears fruit about a year after planting. Each cluster is called a 'hand', as it consists of several bananas spreading out from a central point rather like fingers. When the fruit is gathered, the huge soft green shoot can be cut back, for it dies after bearing one fruit crop. New suckers spring up from its base, forming a clump that gives further crops of fruit for many years.

The bananas imported into Britain are gathered while still green, but begin to ripen and turn yellow during the journey. Those from the Canary Islands usually ripen fully on this fairly short voyage, but when bananas are shipped from more distant countries, the ships need special equipment to keep the green fruit cool and well aired so that it does not ripen too soon. When it reaches Britain, ripening is completed by artificial heat before it is ready for sale.

In some varieties of banana the food reserves are in the form of starch instead of sugar, and the fruits have no sweet taste although they are very nutritious. They have to be cooked by steaming or roasting before they become palatable. These varieties are not exported to Europe, but in some parts of Africa and Asia they form an important article of diet for the native people. Other products of the banana plant are flour and a kind of beer made from the fruit, and tough fibres from the leaves which can be woven into string or rope; the broad leaves themselves are often used as plates or wrappers for foodstuffs.

See also TROPICAL AGRICULTURE.
See also Vol. VII: GREENGROCERY.

BARLEY. This cereal crop is grown principally for malting for beer (*see* MALTING, Vol. VII), or for feeding to livestock. Barley meal is, when available, the main foodstuff in the fattening of pigs. The grain used for malting must be of the best quality—white and starchy, and of high germination. Unlike other cereals, the number of barley varieties is comparatively small: for malting purposes Plumage Archer and Spratt Archer are popular; for feeding purposes, such high yielding varieties as Camton are grown. If their land is suitable, farmers always try to grow a malting sample, for this fetches a higher price than does feeding barley.

To grow a crop of perfect quality great care must be taken over its cultivation and manuring. More important still, however, is a suitable

Plant Breeding Institute, Cambridge

HEADS OF PLUMAGE ARCHER BARLEY

climate. Extremes of hot dry weather, or cold wet weather are undesirable, the ideal being a moderately dry time for sowing, occasional showers during the growing season, and good weather for harvesting. Some of the finest malting barley is grown near the coast, where the moist atmosphere and sea mists have a mellowing effect on the grain. The type of soil is also important, light medium loams being the best. It is difficult to get the fine tilth needed at seeding time in heavy soils, and very light soils are liable to dry out, and the grain then ripens too quickly.

Most barley is sown in the spring, from March to April, though in sheltered districts some is often sown in the autumn, like wheat. Generally speaking, the winter varieties of barley are not suitable for malting, though two new varieties, Pioneer and Prefect, appear to give good results. Autumn sowing relieves the spring work, and since the crops ripen before the spring-sown crops, the harvest is spread out. Also, when spring varieties sown in the autumn are successful, they produce excellent malting grain; but

not being winter hardy, they are often killed by severe weather.

On most farms barley follows a root crop in the ROTATION OF CROPS (q.v.), except when the soil is in such a rich condition that wheat may follow after the roots to use up some of the fertility, and barley can then follow successfully. In these conditions it is quite a good plan to take two crops of barley in succession, the first being used for feeding animals, for which the high fertility is an advantage, and the second for malting.

Barley is grown chiefly in the east and south-east of England, where the climate and many of the soils are particularly suitable. Good samples are also grown in a few sea-coast districts in the south-west.

The seed-bed must be clean and free from weeds, for barley, which has little foliage, cannot compete well with weeds. The soil must be well supplied with lime, and sometimes super-phosphates and perhaps muriate of potash are used. But barley can generally get enough nutrients from the plant food already in the soil. Nitrogenous fertilizers are unsatisfactory for malting barleys because too much nitrogen in the grain produces a somewhat muddy type of beer.

The seed-bed must be ploughed, cultivated, harrowed, and rolled. The ploughing should be finished before the winter in order to allow the frost to take effect upon the soil, the fine frost-mould on the surface being better than any tilth prepared by mechanical means.

To get the best barley for malting, the crop must ripen evenly; therefore, to make the seed germinate evenly it is put in at an even depth ($1-1\frac{1}{2}$ inches), and covered by harrowing and rolling. For this reason broadcast sowing is not satisfactory. The amount of seed sown is 12 stone per acre, with rather heavier seedings for autumn sowing. Additional cultivations after sowing are seldom necessary if the land is free from weeds, though occasionally a light harrowing may be given to check small annual weeds.

Barley is cut when fully ripe, for, unlike wheat, the crop does not mature in the stook. Some showers and heavy dews at this time are welcomed by farmers since they mellow the grain. The stooks are left in the field until they are perfectly dry, when they are carted home and stacked. It is important that in threshing the grains are not injured or 'skinned', for this would spoil their rate of germination. Damaged grain on the malting floor becomes mouldy, and this spoils the flavour of the beer.

The average yield of grain is about 16 cwt. per acre, though crops often yield as much as 25 cwt. or more. The straw left after threshing yields about a ton per acre, and this is usually fed with roots to bullocks when they are up in yards during the winter.

See also ARABLE CROPS; HARVESTING.
See also Vol. VII: MALTING.

BARN MACHINES. There are many crops that have to be prepared in some way before they can be fed to livestock. Therefore an important part of the machinery of the farm consists of fixed equipment inside buildings, or of machines portable enough to be taken out into the field to jobs which are performed in a fixed place.

Grain that is to be processed on the farm for feeding to livestock is usually ground up in a roller mill, a plate mill, or a hammer mill. Roller mills have two rotating cylinders arranged like those on a domestic mangle. The grain that passes between the rollers is not ground to a fine meal but is only kibbled, or crushed, so that it is more easily digested by the cattle. Plate mills

Farmer and Stockbreeder

CRUSHING OATS IN A ROLLER MILL

The mill is driven by a belt from a tractor outside the barn

have two facing steel disks, with grooved surfaces, mounted on a horizontal spindle. In most types one of the two plates remains stationary and the other one revolves against it. The corn is fed into the space between the disks, and the fineness of grinding is regulated by adjusting the width of this space. When they are set close, the meal is very fine; when they are set wide, the effect of the mill is much like that of a roller kibbling mill. Hammer mills work on a different principle: the grain is not crushed between two surfaces, but is hit by rotating hammers. These hammers are attached to a rotor, the revolving part of the machine, which is encased in a steel drum and spins at a very high speed. The outlet from the drum is covered by a sieve, and the grain continues to be pounded until its particles are fine enough to pass through the sieve.

Linseed feed, cotton-seed feed, and other concentrated cattle-foods are often brought to the farm as hard slabs about 2 ft. by 1 ft. by $\frac{3}{4}$ in. thick, and not as a powder or meal. Indeed, it is these slabs which have given to the foods the name of 'cattle cake'. Before they can be fed to the animals they have to be broken up, and a machine is used for this. The cake is put into the top of the machine, vertically, drawn down between two spiked rollers, and broken into small pieces. The machine is called a cake-cracker.

Hay and straw are often chopped up to form chaff to mix with corn and other foods to give them bulk and make them more digestible. Chaff-cutting machines have a trough into which the hay or straw is fed, and toothed rollers which draw it forward towards knives mounted on a rotating flywheel. The length of the pieces of straw or hay produced by the machine can be regulated by altering the relation between the speed of the feed rollers and the rotating knives.

Roots such as swedes and turnips are sometimes sliced or pulped by machine before they are fed to cattle. Some machines have a rotating disk with holes in it, each hole having a concave knife alongside it; others have a rotating drum or barrel with sharp-edged projections upon it. Many of the larger root-cutters have also a rotating cage inside which the roots are shaken about in order to clear off as much dirt as possible before they are sliced.

Most of these food-preparing machines can, in their small sizes, be driven by hand, but this is a slow and laborious way of preparing the

English Electric Co.

A ROOT PULPER DRIVEN BY AN ELECTRIC MOTOR

The circular knife can be seen at the side of the hopper.
The motor also drives a milking machine

food, and most farms of any size have their barns equipped with an engine or electric motors to drive the machinery.

Often several prepared foods are mixed together to form a balanced ration for the stock, that is to say, a ration in which the necessary food elements are present in the correct proportions (*see* FEEDING, FARM ANIMALS). In small quantities the mixing can be done on the barn floor, using a shovel, but when large quantities have to be mixed, a mechanical mixer is used. This is a large round tank with a worm-screw turning round inside it.

There is one machine usually operated in the barn which is not there to deal with the crop, but with the seed. This is the dressing-machine used to coat seed corn with disinfecting powders or liquids to give protection for the plant against seed-borne diseases such as leaf stripe and bunt (*see* PLANT DISEASES). Some machines for coating the seed are of a simple hand-driven type in which a small barrel, pivoted in the middle, is turned over and over; others are large power-driven machines which have a device for accurately measuring out the correct quantity of

disinfectant for a given quantity of seed, and such machines are used on large arable farms.

See also THRESHING-MACHINE.

BARNS AND GRANARIES, *see* FARMSTEAD.

BASKET-MAKING, *see* RURAL CRAFTS. *See also* Vol. VII: BASKET-MAKING.

BEANS, BROAD (*Vicia Faba*). This is a leguminous or pod plant of great antiquity; it was grown by the Egyptians, Greeks, Hebrews, and Romans. It is believed to be a native of Asia or eastern Europe, probably Egypt, but as no wild forms of the species are ever seen at the present time, it is an example of a plant that has been preserved by cultivation. The name is of simple derivation—'broad' referring to the width of the seed, and 'bean' from the Anglo-Saxon *béan*. Other names for this plant are Common bean and (in America) English bean; the Romans called it *faba*, hence the plant's botanical name. Broad beans are grown both as garden and field crops.

1. GARDEN BROAD BEANS. The green unripened seeds of this plant are used as a vegetable —not palatable to everyone because of their rather strong flavour, but very nourishing. They should be eaten when young and tender. There are three main types of broad bean, based on the shape of the pods—the long-podded type, the

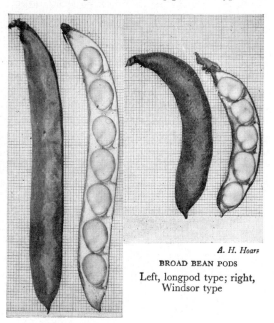

A. H. Hoars

BROAD BEAN PODS

Left, longpod type; right,
Windsor type

Royal Horticultural Society

STAKING BROAD BEANS

Windsor type, and the small or fan-podded type which bears its pods in clusters like a fan. There are many varieties or selections of these types.

Broad beans thrive best on cool loamy soil, and as the plants are fairly hardy, it is customary in Europe to sow part of the crop in the late autumn, using a variety of the longpod type, such as Seville Longpod, and allowing the plants to stand through the winter. Early in the following spring they make new growth, giving a crop of beans usually in June. Seed is sown in late February and March to give crops that mature in July. The rows of beans should be 2 feet apart, and it is customary to sow the seeds 4 to 6 inches apart, in a drill about 2 to $2\frac{1}{2}$ inches deep. The seeds may also be planted by dropping them into holes made with a blunt-ended dibber. Early crops are obtained by sowing under CLOCHES (q.v.) in October or November or in February, in which case the cloches should remain on the plants until April. Seeds sown in frames in January and transplanted to the open land in March also produce early crops.

2. FIELD BEANS. These resemble garden broad beans, except that the seeds are much smaller and less palatable. They are grown mainly as a food for livestock, and are often mixed with oats and crushed for feeding to cattle and horses—hence the common name of horse beans. There are two main varieties, winter and spring beans. Winter beans, sown in the autumn, are capable of withstanding moderately severe weather, and give rather higher yields than the spring sort. Spring beans are sown during March.

The crop does best on heavy land, and in such districts often replaces swedes and turnips in the ROTATION OF CROPS (q.v.). In other districts it may take the place of clover, and on land that has been lying fallow, beans follow wheat after the fallow (or year of rest).

Most farmers try to spare some farmyard manure for their bean crop, which they plough under in the autumn. In addition to this, phosphatic fertilizers are needed, and an application of 10 cwt. of basic slag per acre, or 5 to 6 cwt. of superphosphate, together with 1 cwt. of muriate of potash on the lighter types of soil, is given when the seed is sown (*see* ARTIFICIAL FERTILIZERS).

For autumn-sown beans a fine seed-bed is not needed, for, as with wheat, small clods prevent the soil from caking and give some protection to the seedlings. The seed is generally sown in rows about a foot apart, or even 18 to 27 inches, so that, when the plants come through, horse hoeing between the rows is possible. From $1\frac{1}{2}$ cwt. to $1\frac{3}{4}$ cwt. of seed per acre is used, and this must be placed not less than one inch below the surface. Occasionally the seed is 'ploughed in', which means that it is simply dropped into the bottom of every other furrow as ploughing proceeds and covered by the next furrow which is turned. The crop is then left until the spring, when harrows are used to break down the furrows.

Up to the time of ripening, the pods are soft and green with a white, woolly lining. They then turn black, the soft lining disappears, and the pods become dry and brittle. The crop is cut before it reaches this condition, for otherwise there would be a danger of the pods splitting and the grain being lost. To hasten drying, the cut beans are bound in sheaves and stood up in small stooks. The stems are thick and tough, and need more time to dry out than do the cereal crops. The crop is threshed in the same way as grain, and though the tougher parts are discarded, the straw is used for feeding livestock. An average crop yields about 16 to 20 cwt. of grain per acre with 25 to 30 cwt. of straw.

The black Bean Aphid is the principal pest of broad beans (*see* APHID PESTS). They attack the growing points of the plants, usually as they are coming into flower, and as soon as the pest shows signs of appearing, the top shoots of the bean stems should be pinched out. Field beans have usually got beyond the growing stage before the aphid appears.

BEANS, KIDNEY AND RUNNER. 1. KID-
NEY BEAN. This popular garden vegetable, *Phaseolus vulgaris*, is so called because of the shape of the seed; but it has other names, a common one being the French bean. In France it is known as the *Haricot*, and in North America as the Bush or Snap bean.

The kidney bean is believed to be a native of Central and South America, and was being cultivated by the native Indian population long before Europeans discovered the New World. In Britain it is grown mainly for its green pods, which are used in the same way as runner beans; but in other parts of the world it is grown also for its crop of dry bean seeds. In some countries the bean seeds are eaten green like green peas, and are then called green shell beans. In France the name *flageolet* is used for the green beans, *haricot* for the dry beans, and *haricot vert* for the green pods. Some kinds of this bean are used for canning purposes, and are marketed as the well-known canned baked beans. In the U.S.A. the small white beans are called pea-beans and also navy beans, a name that came into being because originally the U.S.A. naval department took considerable quantities for use on shipboard.

There are several thousand varieties of kidney bean. Some, such as Canadian Wonder, are specially suitable for crops of green pods; others, such as Brown Dutch, are suitable for crops of dry beans; and a few, such as Masterpiece and The Prince, are suitable for all purposes. Some varieties, such as Stringless Refugee and Green Refugee, are classed as stringless because they produce green pods containing no fibre or 'strings', and these are grown in considerable quantities for canning. Another type, such as Golden Waxpod, has yellow pods, also stringless. There are both climbing and dwarf forms of the kidney bean, the climbing forms being most popular on the Continent, and the dwarf or bush bean being mainly grown in Britain. Under glass, however, the climbing form, such as Veitch's Climbing, is preferred.

Kidney beans thrive in sandy loam soils which are well supplied with potash and phosphates, and are not deficient in lime. The seed is sown

Sutton and Sons
KIDNEY BEAN, DWARF TYPE

late, from the end of April onward, because the plants are easily damaged by late frosts. They are set 4 to 6 inches apart in drills 18 to 24 inches apart and $1\frac{1}{2}$ to 2 inches deep, and are thinned to about 10 inches apart. The green pods are ready for use from mid-July onwards. Successional crops are obtained by sowing at fortnightly intervals until mid-July. When a crop of dry beans is wanted, the plants with the pods on are pulled up as soon as they begin to turn yellow, and are then hung up in a shed or greenhouse to dry. When grown on a large scale, the plants are cut, stacked to dry, and then threshed in the same way as peas.

2. RUNNER BEAN. This vegetable, *Phaseolus coccineus*, of which the green pods are eaten, sliced and cooked, is very popular in Britain, though on the Continent and in America the kidney bean is preferred. This bean is a native of sub-tropical Central America, and is still grown throughout both North and South America, largely as a decorative climber, its scarlet flowers being very showy.

Given support, the runner bean will climb by means of its twining shoots to a height of 10 or more feet in a single season. The flowers of different forms are scarlet, white, or both scarlet and white, the white-flowered forms having white seeds and the seeds of the other forms being purplish-pink with black markings. Well known varieties are Scarlet Emperor, Prizewinner, Princeps and Czar, the last-named being a white-seeded variety.

Runner beans are easily damaged by slight frost, and so they are not usually sown until late April or May. Usually a support of stakes, or strings fastened to a post and wire framework, is provided so that the plants can climb. Sometimes, however, especially in market-gardens, runner beans are grown as dwarf bushy plants by pinching out the shoots that the plants produce for climbing; but the plants yield more heavily when they can climb, and the pods are of better quality.

Runner beans succeed best on a rich loamy soil. In the garden it is usually the practice to make a trench 18 inches deep and to put in a dressing of decayed manure or compost before returning sufficient soil to leave only a small depression. Garden fertilizer is dug into the surface soil a week before sowing. The seeds are sown in a double, staggered row, the beans being placed 6 to 9 inches apart. Little is gained by overcrowding the plants.

The plants begin to produce pods about mid-July and continue, so long as the pods are frequently picked, until the early frosts destroy them. This bean is by nature a perennial, and in warm climates the fleshy rootstock persists in the soil and produces new growth in the spring. In Britain, however, the plants rarely live through the winter.

3. LIMA BEAN (*Phaseolus lunatus*), which originated in Peru and is a favourite in the U.S.A., is a perennial twining herb, with small white or violet flowers, usually cultivated as an annual. The pods are flat and curved, and contain several white or mottled seeds. There are numerous varieties, some bush plants and some climbers, some with large and others with small seeds. In tropical or semi-tropical climates, the crop is ripe about 4 months after sowing. Lima beans in the dry state are sold as 'butter beans', and in appearance somewhat resemble haricot beans.

4. PESTS AND DISEASES. Kidney beans are not attacked seriously by any pest; but the fungus disease, Halo Blight, attacks them, and one of the plant viruses, Mosaic, believed to be transmitted through the seed, causes a general weakening of the plants (*see* PLANT DISEASES). Runner beans are often attacked by APHID PESTS (q.v.), especially the blackfly or dolphin fly. The minute Scarlet Runner Thrip also does much damage to the flowers (*see* INSECT PESTS).

BEDDING PLANTS. By 'bedding' is meant the massing of plants, usually ANNUALS or BIENNIALS (qq.v.), of one or more kinds in flower beds. This is a method of planting often used in places where a showy display is needed, as, for instance, in the beds of public parks and around public buildings, or in beds near the house in private gardens. Such beds are usually planted in the autumn with early spring-flowering plants, such as bulbs, polyanthus, and forget-me-not. As soon as these have flowered, they are removed and replaced by summer plants, already well advanced and near the point of flowering. These again are removed when they begin to fade, and a mass of autumn-flowering plants such as dahlias take their place. In this way a continuous display of colour can be kept up from spring to autumn; though much work is needed.

When planning bedding schemes, the height and habits of growth of the plants must be considered so that a massed effect can be obtained without letting the plants be so crowded that they interfere with each other. Tall, rather slender plants such as tulips, fuchsia, heliotrope, or zinnia may be interplanted with low growing

Royal Horticultural Society

RUNNER BEANS STAKED

A mulch is being applied to the surface

Balmain

CARPET BEDDING: THE FLORAL CLOCK IN PRINCES STREET GARDENS, EDINBURGH
This pattern was carried out in low-growing foliage plants for the 1948 Festival of Music and Drama

plants such as candytuft, violas, or French marigold. Bushy plants, on the other hand, such as antirrhinums (snapdragon), calendulas (marigold), dahlias, geraniums, or petunias, do not lend themselves to interplanting but can very effectively be given an edging of dwarf plants such as alyssum, lobelia, or violas (*see* EDGING PLANTS). The massing of dwarf plants over a bed is called 'carpet bedding', and can sometimes be effectively carried out in beds containing permanent plants such as rose bushes.

Harmony and contrasts in colours are most important in bedding schemes. The plants to be grouped together must be selected for their colour as well as for their height and habits of growth. Plants with coloured foliage are useful for bedding. Coleus with their variegated leaves, *Iresine* (Blood Leaf) and *Telanthera* (Joy Weed) with their red and orange-red leaves, and *Cineraria maritima* (the Dusty Miller) with grey leaves are all very effective for this purpose, and low-growing foliage plants, such as *Antennaria* (Cat's Ear), are attractive for carpet bedding.

This kind of planting means a great deal of work in raising, growing on, and replanting. The beds must be dug over between each planting, and the ground must be fed, especially if the soil is light, by the digging in of well-decayed manure. The newly set plants must be watered until they are established. The amount of work involved usually makes this kind of planting impossible in most private gardens, and less ambitious bedding schemes must be adopted. For example, bedding can be carried out with shrubby perennial plants such as bush roses, azaleas, berberis, or spiraea, and these remain in the same bed for many years. If the beds are also planted with spring bulbs and perhaps given a border of some low-growing perennials, such as London pride, pinks, violas, or polyanthus, a good effect can be achieved with much less labour.

Bedding plants, whether permanent or temporary, look best surrounded by grass that is kept mown; and the beds themselves should be of simple shapes.

BEE-KEEPING. The natural home of the honey bee (*Aphis mellifica*) is in a hollow tree, and there she builds her combs. These are used as a food store and as a nursery for the rearing of young bees (*see* BEES, section 3, Vol. II). In the modern beehive man has copied this natural home as far as possible; but, as a foundation for the combs, the hive contains wooden frames fitted with thin sheets of wax. This saves the bees much time, and also allows the combs to be removed for inspection and for extraction of the HONEY (q.v.).

The main part of the hive is the 'brood chamber' in which the bees live throughout the year on large combs, called 'brood combs'. These serve as nurseries in the summer and as food stores in winter. In the summer other chambers containing smaller combs, called 'supers', are placed above the brood chamber, and it is in these that the bees store the honey that is not required by them as food and that the bee-keeper takes for his own use. To prevent the queen laying eggs in the combs of a super, a 'queen excluder' is placed between it and the brood chamber. This is a metal sheet in which are a number of slots large enough for the small worker bees to pass through, but not for the queen bee.

The number of bees in a hive varies according to the time of year. In the summer there may be as many as 80,000, consisting of one queen, several hundreds of drones, and the remainder workers. The whole is called a 'colony', or 'stock'. In the winter there are no drones, and the number of workers is decreased to about 20,000, the others having died off.

The queen is the mother of the colony. In shape she is very different from the worker and the drone, her body being long and pointed, her wings short, and her sting curved and used in fighting other queens but rarely against human beings. Unlike the workers she has no wax pockets and no pollen baskets on her back legs. Her only duty is to lay eggs, and the number she lays depends upon the amount of food fed to her by the workers. In the winter she is fed liberally and may lay as many as 3,000 in a day.

Drones, the largest bees in the colony, are males whose duty it is to fertilize young virgin queens in the spring. They have no sting, no wax pockets, and no pollen baskets. As autumn approaches, they are starved by the workers and turned out of the hive to die.

All the work of the hive is done by the workers, the smallest bees in the colony. They work so hard during the summer that their lives are short—only 6 weeks or so; but in the winter they live for about 6 months. They start to work almost as soon as they are hatched, spending the first 2 weeks of their lives working inside the hive, cleaning out cells, feeding and cleaning the queen, feeding the young grubs, guarding the hive against robber bees and wasps, and, by fanning with their wings, keeping the inside of the hive cool in hot weather. Later, they start work outside the hive, collecting water, bee gum or 'propolis' (a sticky substance from the buds of trees), nectar, and pollen. They also make wax, which appears as tiny scales on the underside of the stomach, for building combs and sealing the filled cells. Like the queen, the workers are females but, except in special circumstances, they do not lay eggs. Their sting is barbed, which prevents its being withdrawn easily, and on their back legs they have pollen baskets in which to carry the pollen they collect from the flowers.

Two kinds of eggs are laid by the queen: one kind develops into a drone, and the other into either a queen or a worker according to the kind of cell in which it is laid and the food fed to it. If the egg is to become a queen, the cell in which it is laid is large and shaped like a peanut hanging downwards from the comb. On the 3rd day the egg hatches into a grub (larva) and is fed on a rich food during the next 5 days. A supply of this food, called 'royal jelly', is then placed in the cell with the grub and, on the 9th day from the laying of the egg, the cell is covered with a capping of wax and pollen. During the next 7 days the larva spins a cocoon and turns into a 'pupa' which, on the 16th day from the laying of the egg, bites through the capping and emerges as a perfect young virgin queen.

The worker cell is much smaller and is six-sided. The worker takes longer to develop than the queen, and finally bites her way through the capping on the 22nd day. Drone cells, also six-sided, are larger than those of the worker, and the capping is dome-shaped. Drones leave the cell on the 25th day after the egg has been laid (*see* METAMORPHOSIS, Vol. II).

Towards the end of January, earlier or later according to the season, the queen starts to lay eggs; and as the flowers begin to bloom in plenty, the egg-laying increases until, towards the middle of May, the hive is crowded with bees. During the early part of this time the bees have been collecting water and pollen to mix with the honey, stored in the cells, to make food for the grubs. In early spring a stock will collect as much as half a pint a day; but when breeding is in full swing, as much as one pint a day will be needed. In collecting nectar and pollen the bees are, unconsciously, carrying out their important work of POLLINATION of flowers (q.v. Vol. II).

At full blossom-time the bees are returning to the hive in thousands, carrying the nectar they have gathered. Thousands of bees are being born daily and the hive becomes overcrowded, a condition that will cause the bees to 'swarm'. This means that the queen and several thousands of the bees will gorge themselves with enough honey to last them several days, and will then leave the hive to find a new home, possibly in the trunk of a tree or in the roof of a building. If they cannot at once find a home, they will cluster together on a branch or on a post until the scouts they have sent out return with news. The whole swarm will then depart.

The colony that has been left will not, however, die out, for in the hive there are still thousands of bees, plenty of food and brood, and also some sealed queen cells. It is from one of these cells that a virgin queen will be born, and her first act will be to sting to death her sister virgins in their cells. Later, usually within 10 days, she will mate with a drone and start to lay eggs, thus becoming in her turn the mother of the colony. But if the bees are very numerous, they may not allow the first virgin to kill her sisters. Instead she will join several thousands of the bees and leave the hive in a second and smaller swarm, or 'cast'. A second or even third cast may follow, but eventually one of the virgins will mate and will remain in the hive to become the mother of a much weakened colony.

The loss of a swarm is a serious matter for the bee-keeper, and he tries to prevent it. He examines the combs in the brood chamber and removes the queen cells, for unless there are queens to leave behind, the bees will rarely swarm. Or he may remove some of the combs

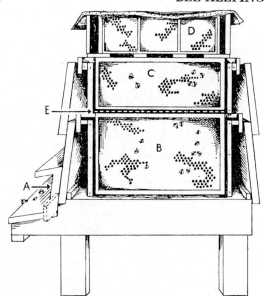

A DOUBLE-WALLED HIVE WITH ONE SIDE REMOVED

A. Entrance to hive. B. Brood frame in brood chamber, in which the eggs are laid and grubs reared. C. Super, in which surplus honey is stored. D. Sections, in which honey is stored to be used in the comb. E. Queen excluder. The air space between the inner and outer walls keeps an even temperature in the hive

and bees to make a small stock, called a 'nucleus', and place these in an empty hive, thus forming a second stock of bees to work for him. Over the brood chamber he places a queen excluder, and above it some extra combs known as 'shallow supers', or small square boxes known as 'sections', in which the bees will store the honey they do not require for themselves. These, at the end of the season, will be removed by the bee-keeper.

As the flowers become less plentiful and less nectar is brought into the hive, so the queen lays fewer eggs, and the number of bees in the hive gradually decreases. Preparations for next winter have already been started, for honey and pollen are stored in the combs in sufficient quantity to last until blossom-time next year. The drones, not being needed, are turned out of the hive. It is at this time that the bee-keeper makes sure that each stock has sufficient winter food. If there is not enough, he feeds sugar syrup, which is ordinary white sugar dissolved in water and fed to the bees in a special feeder. This the bees will store in the cells and seal in the same way as honey. The reserve of honey (or honey plus syrup) that a strong stock needs to last the winter is between 30 and 40 lb.

R. V. Roberts

A SMOKER BEING USED TO QUIETEN BEES SO THAT THE HIVE
CAN BE EXAMINED

As the weather grows colder, the bees fly less often; and finally they cluster on the combs in which their food is stored, remaining there throughout the winter, moving very slowly over the combs as the food is eaten. This state of affairs continues until brood rearing starts once more in mid-January.

The quantity of honey which the bees store, and the quantity they will eat in a year, depends upon the wealth of flowers in the district and upon the season. The average amount of surplus honey over the whole of Britain is estimated at 30 lb. a stock, but a strong stock, given good weather in a good district, might collect in one season as much as 480 lb., of which they would themselves use during the course of the year about 160 lb., leaving a surplus of 320 lb.

Great Britain is not a good country for honey production, mainly because of the shortness of the flowering seasons and the variable weather. In America, Australia, and Russia, where the seasons are more settled, a much heavier average yield is obtained, and occasionally as much as 600 lb. has been given by one stock. In those countries there are many big commercial bee farms, whereas in Britain there are very few. Most British bee-keepers have a few hives in their gardens for a hobby, or keep bees in conjunction with fruit-growing or small-holding.

Bee-keeping can be started by buying a full stock of bees on their combs, or by buying a nucleus, or by buying or catching a swarm. A full stock should produce surplus honey in their first year, if the bee-keeper knows how to manage them. A nucleus is a small stock on four or six combs and, if bought early enough and in a good season, may produce a little surplus honey. The advantage is that as the stock grows in strength, so does the bee-keeper gain experience. If a start is made with a swarm, the bees have to build their own combs on the frames and wax foundation provided by the bee-keeper. They therefore take time to establish themselves, although in a good season they may provide a little surplus honey.

A swarm that has clustered on a branch or on a post can be taken quite easily by shaking or brushing the bees into a box or skep. This is then turned mouth downwards on the ground, and a stone is placed under one edge so that the bees can get air and can fly in and out. In the evening they are shaken out on to a sloping board laid in front of their new hive, or direct on to the frames of wax foundation in the hive.

To work his bees the bee-keeper needs some appliances. He uses a 'veil' fastened to his hat and tucked into his coat to keep the bees from his face. He also needs a 'smoker' in which he burns corrugated paper or old sacking. By pressing the bellows of the smoker, the smoke can be puffed in at the hive entrance and across the combs. This frightens the bees, who gorge themselves with honey and are then less inclined to sting. Another appliance needed is a 'hive tool', or a blunt chisel, with which to prize apart the combs the bees have stuck together with bee gum or propolis collected from the buds of trees.

The bee-keeper's work or 'manipulation' with his bees consists mainly of examining the combs once a week during May, June, and July to destroy any queen cells that may have been formed, and to see that there is plenty of comb space for brood rearing and for honey storage. At intervals during the summer he removes the supers to extract the honey. He also watches for signs of disease, such as Foul Brood, or Acarine Disease (Isle of Wight Disease). In Foul Brood the actual brood (the grubs) is affected and dies, and as it is a very serious disease, the bees must be killed and the combs destroyed by fire. Acarine Disease is caused by a small mite that lives and breeds in the breathing tubes of the bee; but this disease can now be cured by treatment.

See also HONEY AND BEESWAX.
See also Vol. II: BEES.

BEESWAX, *see* HONEY AND BEESWAX.

BEETLE PESTS. 1. BEAN BEETLES (distinct from the Pea and Bean WEEVIL. (q.v.)) are small grey insects variously marked with black and brown. They lay their eggs on the very young pods of peas and beans, and the grubs, when they hatch, bore their way into the pods and into the developing seeds. Here they feed, and then pupate just below the skin of the seed, forming a 'window' which can be clearly seen. When the beetles emerge, they break through the 'windows', leaving behind holes. In large seeds, such as broad beans, the beetles do not as a rule touch a vital part of the seed; but in smaller seeds, such as French beans, the grub often eats through the germ, so that the seed cannot germinate.

2. MUSTARD BEETLES, which are about $\frac{1}{8}$ inch long, rounded, and bright metallic blue, attack plants of the cabbage family, including watercress and mustard and cress. They spend the winter in hedgerows, rough grass, or in decaying stumps of crops which were infested the season before, and come out of hibernation in early summer to infest the crops. At this stage they are too few to do much damage. They lay their eggs in May and June, and then die. When the yellow and black grubs hatch, they feed on the leaves for about 3 weeks and then enter the soil and pupate. About 10 days later, a second and much larger batch of beetles emerges and again attacks the crop. It is this attack which is the most serious. The stalks of infested crops should be burnt, and the land ploughed as soon as possible after harvest. DDT sprays or dusts are effective in destroying the pest in the early part of the season.

3. ASPARAGUS BEETLES are about $\frac{1}{4}$ inch long, and black and yellow with reddish feelers and thorax. They lay brownish eggs, singly or in rows, on the shoots and foliage of asparagus in June. The grub is greyish green with a black head. Both grubs and beetles eat the heads, berries, and foliage of the asparagus.

4. WHITE GRUBS, the grubs of CHAFERS (q.v. Vol. II), are subterranean pests of almost all farm crops from grassland to orchard. As with most underground pests, they do the greatest damage to crops raised on newly ploughed grassland. The Common Cockchafer or May Bug, the Lesser Cockchafer or June Bug, and the Garden Chafer are the most troublesome to English farmers, and the Vine Cutter is a pest in vine-growing lands. The grubs destroy the

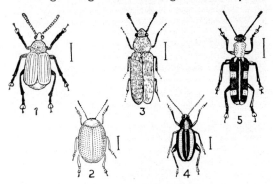

BEETLE PESTS (enlarged)
1. Bean Beetle. 2. Mustard Beetle. 3. Raspberry Beetle. 4. Turnip Flea Beetle. 5. Asparagus Beetle

roots below ground, and the beetles devour the plants, especially the leaves of trees. When they appear, as they do at times, in large numbers, they may strip the trees completely of their foliage. The grubs are a dirty white with greatly enlarged purplish abdomens, powerful jaws, and three pairs of long slender legs. They are helpless when taken out of the ground, but seem to be lively enough when left below. They can be cleared out with a ground dressing of crude naphthalene—2 cwts. to the acre, and on arable and young grassland heavy rolling kills many of the grubs. DDT and BHC sprays or dusts watered or worked into the soil are even more effective controls. In small gardens and allotments handpicking during digging may be sufficient. Moles, rooks, plovers, and gulls eat these grubs voraciously, and so do poultry and pigs.

5. WIREWORMS are the grubs of the Skipjack or Click Beetle (*see* WIREWORM, Vol. II). They live in grassland for 4 or 5 years, feeding on the roots of grasses and other plants. All farm crops grown on freshly ploughed up grassland, except as a rule beans, peas, flax, and linseed, are liable

Rothamsted Experimental Station

AUTUMN-SOWN WHEAT DAMAGED BY WIREWORM

The patch on the left shows the effect of wireworm in the
soil; that on the right had an insecticide drilled into the soil
with the seed

to attack. By constant cultivation of the ground
the grubs are thrown up, and are devoured by
the birds, especially by starlings. In fields very
heavily infested with wireworm 1½–2 cwt. per
acre of BHC wireworm dust should be worked
into the soil, and will persist for 3 years. It cannot, however, be used when root vegetables are
to be grown as it taints them. For cereals a seed
dressing containing gamma BHC is effective.
The danger from wireworm attack is greatest in
spring and autumn, the two main feeding
periods; therefore winter-sown and early spring-
sown corn may escape because the plants will be
far enough forward to resist the attack.

On an allotment or in a garden wireworm
can be destroyed by setting traps. Split Brussels
sprouts' stems or pieces of cut potato or mangold
can be buried in the ground about every 3 feet
as traps to attract the pests. These should be
examined about every 3 days and cleared of
their catch.

6. FLEA BEETLES. Only a few of the many
kinds of flea beetles found in Britain are a
menace to the farmer. These feed on the leaves
of cabbages and related plants such as cauliflower, Brussels sprouts, kale, and turnips, and
occasionally certain of them attack flax, hops,

and potatoes. All are small, but when in large
numbers they may well destroy a whole field
of young seedlings. The kinds that attack
cabbages and turnips are metallic greenish or
blue, or are black with a yellow stripe on each
wing case. All possess considerable powers of
jumping and flight, so that they scatter very
easily. The grubs of some flea beetles feed
on the leaves, others on the roots of the plants;
but few do any appreciable harm, except the
grub of the Cabbage-stem Flea beetle, which
tunnels into the stems of cabbages. The beetles
spend the winter in dirty hedge bottoms,
refuse heaps, haystacks, and such places; the
more this kind of harbourage is removed, the
fewer beetles come through the winter. The
beetles often transfer from wild food plants such
as charlock to the cultivated species, and so the
keeping down of weeds also helps to control
the pest. DDT and BHC dusts will protect the
plants from attack.

7. COLORADO BEETLE. This short, round,
black and yellow beetle, with its plump reddish
grub marked with two rows of black spots, is a
very serious potato pest, and not at all difficult
to identify (*see* COLORADO BEETLE, Vol. II). It
was first discovered in 1823 in the U.S.A. at the
foot of the Rocky Mountains, where it fed on the
Sand-bur or Buffalo-bur, an uncommon wild
relative of the potato. It transferred to the
potatoes planted by settlers, and because of the

Harold Bastin

PART OF A TURNIP LEAF EATEN BY FLEA BEETLES

Two beetles can be seen on the lower part of the leaf

increased supply of food, it increased rapidly in numbers. It is now found everywhere in North America where potatoes are grown, and has crossed the Atlantic on ships and spread over much of western Europe. It has not become established in Britain because of very strict action taken against it. Anyone finding an insect suspected of being a Colorado Beetle or its grub is bound by law to report it at once to the police or the MINISTRY OF AGRICULTURE, for this insect is 'notifiable'. A single specimen should be sent to the Ministry or police in a strong tin with a well-fitting lid. Amateurs should not attempt to collect or destroy any of the insects, since inexpert disturbance of the insects may only cause them to spread, thus increasing the difficulties of spraying and fumigating. Birds will not touch this pest as its taste is very unpleasant.

8. RASPBERRY BEETLES are the most damaging of the pests on RASPBERRIES AND LOGANBERRIES (q.v.). The adult beetle, about $\frac{1}{6}$ inch long and pale brown, is to be found inside the cup of the flower where it lays its eggs. The little white grubs bore into the centre of the ripening fruit where they can be seen when the fruit is picked. A dusting of Derris powder or DDT in early summer, and a Derris spray about 3 weeks later, should clear the raspberries altogether.

Beetle pests are controlled by the use of insecticides such as BHC, DDT, or Derris powder, which are sprayed or dusted on to them. Soil fumigants such as carbon disulphide, used to destroy the pupa, in particular of the Colorado Beetle, are also effective. But as has already been stressed, a well-worked soil which encourages the birds to do their part and the removal of all convenient winter harbourage are important deterrents.

See also PESTS AND DISEASES; WEEVIL PESTS; INSECTICIDES.

See also Vol. II: BEETLES.

BEETROOT. The red beet or beetroot of the garden, the white beetroot (sugar-beet), and the mangold wurzel were all derived from the wild sea-shore plant, *Beta vulgaris*. The beetroot is a biennial plant, developing flowers and seed in the second year. It is a member of the family *Chenopodiaceae* and is remarkable for the colour of its leaves which are generally either reddish-purple or deep purple, though some varieties have green leaves.

Like the carrot and parsnip, the beetroot contains an appreciable amount of carbohydrate in the form of sugar, and so possesses considerable food value. It is popular as an ingredient of mixed salads and as a cold vegetable. The tap-roots, like those of carrots, are variable in shape, and varieties are grouped according to root-shape as Round or Turnip-rooted, Intermediate or Half-Long, and Long. Popular varieties are Crimson Globe, Empire Globe, Detroit, Eclipse, Crimson King, and Crosby's Egyptian of the Round or Turnip-rooted group; Obelisk and Feltham Intermediate of the Intermediate group; and Cheltenham Green Top, Covent Garden Red, Dell's Black-leaved, and Nutting's Select Red of the Long group.

Good quality beetroots need rich soil, and should be grown on soil that was manured either in the autumn or for a preceding crop, and a dressing of complete fertilizer should be cultivated into the soil a week before sowing. The first sowing of a turnip-rooted variety is made in April or early May in drills 12 or 15 inches apart and from 1 to 1$\frac{1}{2}$ inches deep. As the seeds are held in clusters in the original fruit cases, and therefore two or three plants may emerge from a single cluster, it is important not to sow too thickly. If the seed is sown thinly, the seedlings of early crops will need little thinning out, the largest roots being pulled for use as they develop.

Royal Horticultural Society

STORING BEET IN DRY SAND OR PEAT

A barrel is a useful store for a small quantity

The seed of crops for later use and for storage should be sown in late May and in June, any of the three groups, Round, Intermediate, or Long being suitable. The rows should be 18, 20, or 24 inches apart according to the variety chosen, and the seedlings should be thinned out so that the plants are left 6 to 9 inches apart in the rows.

Beetroots are liable to be damaged by severe frosts, and on this account, and because it is more convenient for supplying the house or market, it is customary to lift the roots in November. They are then stored in clamps made in the open (*see* ROOT CROPS, section 2) or in sheds in which they are placed in heaps covered with damp sand, earth, or ashes. The roots 'bleed' easily if roughly handled, and this causes a loss of colour. 'Bleeding' may occur also through the leaf-stalks. Therefore when preparing the roots for storage, they must be handled carefully and the leaves not cut off but twisted off with the hands.

See also SUGAR-BEET.

BIENNIAL PLANTS. A biennial is a plant that grows from seed one year, and produces flower, forms seed, and dies the next year. The foxglove (*Digitalis*) is an example of a true biennial, as are most ROOT CROPS and CABBAGES (qq.v.). Some plants, such as antirrhinums (snapdragons) can be grown either as annuals or biennials, being sown in the spring to flower the same year, or sown in the late summer to flower the following year. Many biennials, such as wallflowers, antirrhinums, and pansies, will continue to flower for several years if they are left in the ground, and produce very fine flowers; but the plants tend to get straggly and badly shaped, and some will be damaged by a severe winter. Because of their bushy, sturdy habits of growth, biennials need little, if any, support from stakes, and are excellent for filling spaces in beds and borders, or for massed effects by themselves. Wallflowers are particularly suitable as BEDDING PLANTS (q.v.) because they flower in April, and in May can be cleared out and replaced by a half-hardy ANNUAL (q.v.).

Biennials should be sown in May, June, or early July in the open or in boxes, and when they are big enough to handle, they should be pricked out into a nursery bed about 4 inches apart, or thinned to that distance. In the autumn they are planted out in the places where they are to flower the following year. They will thrive in most garden soils, provided they do not have to compete with weeds and have a reasonable amount of sun and moisture. Among biennials are many of the best known and most popular garden flowers, such as Canterbury bells, honesty, forget-me-nots, stocks, and sweet williams.

See also ANNUAL PLANTS; PERENNIAL PLANTS.

BINDER, *see* HARVESTING.

BIOLOGICAL CONTROL OF PESTS, *see* PESTS AND DISEASES.

BIRD PESTS, *see* WILD ANIMALS ON THE FARM.

BLACKBERRIES, *see* RASPBERRIES, LOGANBERRIES, AND BLACKBERRIES.

BLACK CURRANTS, *see* CURRANTS AND GOOSEBERRIES.

BLACKFLY, *see* APHID PESTS.

BLIGHT, *see* PLANT DISEASES; APHID PESTS (American Blight).

BONITO (TUNNY) FISHING. The bonito is a large relative of the MACKEREL (q.v. Vol. II) found principally in the Indian and Pacific Oceans, and the Bay of Biscay. The fish is dried and prepared for market, or else canned. In the Maldives (an archipelago of coral-islands near the centre of the Indian Ocean) specially built, long, graceful boats are used for bonito fishing. These are open, except at the stern, where there extends outboard a broad decking, shaped like the outspread wings of a butterfly, from which all the fishing is done. Live bait is carried in a specially constructed well in the hull, through which sea-water circulates.

When a shoal of bonito is sighted, most of the crew stand on the stern platform armed with short rods and lines, on the end of which are bright, barbless hooks. A few of the live-bait are then thrown overboard, and two of the crew splash water over the side with long-handled scoops to make the bonito think they are in the middle of a big shoal of small fish. Bonito are always hungry, and there is an immediate rush to the scene of the anticipated feast, where in their eagerness, they take live bait or bare hook equally blindly, those that make the wrong choice being lifted from the water and swung inboard by the fishermen who are as excited as the fish.

The Japanese use larger boats, but in other respects they fish in exactly the same way, and they also use great floating baskets to store their supplies of live bait.

The French fish for the bonito and albacore (a larger fish of the mackerel family) in the Bay of Biscay, using trim sailing-vessels which come from the southern ports of Brittany. Six long fishing-lines stream out from a long boom projecting from each side of the vessel, and two other lines from the stern. Each line is armed with a double hook, which is usually concealed within a bunch of maize straw and horse-hair. The vessels sail through a shoal of fish at four or five knots, and the hungry fish in mad rushes seize the hooks. They are at once hauled aboard, cleaned, and hung up on a wooden frame amidships, and eventually sent to the canning factory. The canned product is sold under the name of *thon* or tunny.

Off the west coast of the United States, from California southwards, there is an important fishery for the Striped Bonito and the Yellowfin Tunny, also a large relation of the mackerel. Both are marketed ashore as 'tuna'. Powerfully engined boats from 70 to 140 feet long are used, and for fishing in distant waters they are fitted with live-bait tanks, refrigeration, and insulated holds. The fishing gear consists of a stout bamboo pole and a line 6 feet long armed with a barbless hook, which is concealed in a brush of white feathers. The crew hook their fish from the 'rack', a narrow platform, which is hinged outboard on each side. When a shoal of fish is sighted, the engines are slowed, the racks are swung out, and some live bait is thrown into the water. If the fishes are biting, a tornado of hurtling bodies rushes upon the bait. When a fish strikes, the fisherman leans backwards, lifts his prize from the water, and swings it aboard. A deft flick of the rod and line disengages the barbless hook, and the fish is thrown inwards

James Hornell

BONITO FISHERMEN COLLECTING LIVE BAIT OFF MINICOY ISLAND IN THE INDIAN OCEAN
The net for the bait is ready to be lowered. The platforms from which the bonito are caught are at the stern

to fall upon the deck. Without an instant's delay, the lure is returned to the sea ready for the next fish. One man alone is able to land bonitos of a moderate size; but to land the larger kinds, the albacores and the not fully grown tunnies, two men will often work together, using separate rods, playing a joint line. A full-sized tunny may need the united efforts of three or even four men with connected pole-rods to swing it aboard.

See also FISHING INDUSTRY.
See also Vol. II: MACKEREL.

BOTANICAL NAMES. Every kind of plant and animal requires a name, and since Latin has become the universal language of scientists, all scientific names are in Latin or latinized Greek (*see* SCIENTIFIC NAMES, Vol. II). Originally Latin names were written in the form of abbreviated descriptions, which might be six or eight words long. The great Swedish botanist Linnaeus (1707–78) established the two-name or *binomial* system, which is now universally adopted, and is not only concise but flexible. A third name may be added to distinguish even further subdivisions.

Plants and animals are divided into families, which are large groups with certain common features (*see* CLASSIFICATION OF ANIMALS AND PLANTS, Vol. II). Within the family there are sub-groups (called *genus*, pl. *genera*), the members of which have certain features not shared by the rest of the family. The genus is then further divided into *species* (abbr.: *sp.* or *spp.*), which are groups with certain minor features in common. Many species have yet further sub-forms (varieties or races) which differ from each other slightly, though they are not sufficiently distinct to be classed as separate species. Where a variety occurs naturally, it is given a Latin name, but in the case of the many cultivated plants which exist as a result of breeding by gardeners (*see* PLANT BREEDING), these are usually given familiar names in the language of the country of their origin.

This is how the system works. The Sea Lavender belongs to the family *Plumbaginaceae* and the genus *Limonium*. There are many wild species, of which the commonest British one is *Limonium vulgare*. There are also species cultivated for garden display and as EVERLASTING FLOWERS (q.v.), such as *Limonium sinuatum*. There are many varieties of this, such as 'Lavender Queen', a modern selected form.

Where the genus has already been mentioned, it may be abbreviated when repeated. Thus, knowing that *Limonium* is being discussed, we can later write *L. sinuatum* for the particular species; similarly, in talking further about a variety of this species, we can abbreviate to *L. s.* 'Lavender Queen'.

In some cases there have been changes in the Latin names, often because further botanical research has proved them inaccurate. Thus *Limonium* was at one time called *Statice*, a generic name which botanists have abandoned as ambiguous, allotting the different species to the genus *Limonium* or *Armeria* (Thrift). The name 'Statice', however, is still commonly used, for nurserymen, florists, and many gardeners often keep to the old names which are familiar. In this encyclopaedia the names used are botanically up to date, but where a familiar incorrect name exists in common use, as with Statice, it is also generally given.

See also Vol. II: SCIENTIFIC NAMES; CLASSIFICATION OF ANIMALS AND PLANTS.

BOUNDARIES, LAND. From almost the earliest times of man's occupation of the land, boundaries between one ownership and another must have been necessary. Also, as soon as farming developed, some means would be needed for fencing land to hold livestock, both for the protection of the growing crops and for keeping the cattle and sheep from straying.

The earliest boundaries between one piece of land and another, of which we have any knowledge, were banks and ditches. A ditch was dug along the boundary of the piece of land to be enclosed, and the soil thrown up on the inside of it. This produced a barrier of a height double that of the depth of the ditch, for by digging, say, a 3-foot ditch and throwing up the soil on the inside, a 6-foot bank was the result. If our early ancestors decided, then, to erect some sort of a wooden fence—a palisade or piles of brushwood—on top of the bank, as there is evidence that they did, it is obvious that they had formidable defences both against outbreaks of their livestock and against trespass from without. Some of these ditches and banks were very deep and high, and remains of them may be seen in many parts of the country. The largest, no doubt, were for military rather than for agricultural purposes, as, for example, the defences to be seen round Maiden Castle, in Dorset, and round the Iron Age camps all along the chalk downs (*see* EARTHWORKS AND HILL FORTS, Vol. I). Very early, however, in the practice of peaceful pursuits, boundary walls and ditches appear to mark divisions between fields.

In the earliest days of cultivation, the implements at the farmer's command were so simple that the areas he could cultivate and sow were necessarily small. Often, the earliest divisions were no more than low walls formed by dragging the stones off the surface to be tilled and piling them along its boundaries, and many of these remain visible to this day.

As farming developed and became more important, so land became more valuable, and the need for boundaries increased. All boundaries, including walls, banks, or hedges, can, strictly speaking, be called fences for the word comes from 'defence'. In Britain we find that farmers were very clever in making use of whatever suitable materials lay close at hand. Even 100 years ago there was no barbed wire, nor was it possible to send heavy fencing materials long distances by rail or road, and today it still obviously pays to use suitable local materials. So we find that each agricultural district has developed a type of fencing for boundaries of all kinds, and that this depends on the geology of the locality. Thus, the great districts of clay soils, which contain no stone but grow good

Commercial Camera Craft

A RHINE ON KING'S SEDGEMOOR, SOMERSET
The rhines have to be kept clear to assist the drainage of the land

timber in profusion, are marked by hawthorn hedges and fences made of wooden posts and rails; whereas cleft chestnut fences (spile-and-wire) are very common in some sandstone areas where the sweet chestnut grows well. Different districts, however, have developed different methods of making and keeping their hedges, though planting generally follows the same plan. A ditch is dug on the boundary, a low bank thrown up on the inside, and the young hawthorn plants, or 'quicks' as they are called, are planted on top of the bank. This practice has been used for many years to decide disputes between adjoining owners as to where the boundary between them runs, for the law assumes that the ditch and not the hedge is the boundary.

In all the limestone districts, such as the Cotswolds and the Pennine country from Derbyshire to Cumberland, timber is scarce and the winds blow strong. Shelter as well as fencing is needed, and materials for both lie ready to hand in the big stones on, and immediately below, the surface These districts are characterized by boundaries of stone walls, 'dry-walls' as they are called, because they are built without mortar. Like hedging, dry-walling properly executed is

a fine art, and like hedging, too, the practice of it varies from one part of the country to another. A Cotswold waller's technique differs from that of a Yorkshire dalesman's; each would be at a loss if transported to the other's district. (*See* picture, p. 231.)

In some of the western counties, such as Devon and parts of Somerset, where shelter as well as boundaries is needed but suitable stones are less plentiful, banks of the local sandstone collected from the surface, mixed with earth, are built round the fields. They are soon grassed over and hedges of some kind, often of beech, are planted on the top. Every time that the ditches at their foot are dug out, the soil is flung on top of the bank to maintain its height. The hedges are cut and laid periodically, and if properly maintained, this makes a very effective fence.

Still another kind of boundary is met in the fenlands and marshlands. These are ditches which range from the large, artificially constructed rivers of south Lincolnshire, to the small ditches of running water everywhere. In Lincolnshire many of these drains dividing fields and ownerships are called 'delphs'; in Romney

Wolseley Sheep Shearing Machine Co.

AN ELECTRIC FENCE

The cow is taking great care not to touch the wire through which a low intermittent electric current runs

Marsh they are 'wet hedges'; on Sedgemoor they are known as 'rhines'. (The Duke of Monmouth was warned before the battle of Sedgemoor in 1685 to 'beware of the rhine', but not knowing the local word, he remarked that 'the Rhine was a long way off'.)

Today the cheapness and effectiveness of wire fencing on wood or iron posts have brought this type of boundary into all districts, often replacing the traditional forms of boundary fencing. The latest form, and the cheapest of all, consists of a single strand of wire carried a foot or so above the ground for pigs, but higher for cattle, on insulated supports, and connected to a storage electric battery. The electric current passing through the wire gives a sharp but harmless shock to any animal touching it. When properly erected and maintained, it makes an effective fence, particularly useful where a quickly erected temporary fence is needed rather than a permanent boundary.

In many European countries there has been less enclosure of the land into separate fields than in Britain, and the traveller is struck by the lack of fences of any kind, wide areas being farmed without visible boundaries between one man's land and his neighbour's. As the livestock are mostly tethered or kept in stalls rather than in fields, boundaries are not so much needed for this purpose as they are in Britain. In the newer

countries of the world, such as North and South America and Australia, timber fences made of posts and rails split from the growing timber were general in the pioneering days if fences were wanted. Today, galvanized iron wire, either plain or barbed, and strained on wooden posts, is more usual, being cheap to put up and lasting a long time.

See also HEDGING, DITCHING, AND WALLING.

BRASSICA, *see* CABBAGE CROPS.

BREEDING, *see* STOCK BREEDING; PLANT BREEDING.

BROCCOLI, *see* CABBAGE CROPS, GARDEN, section 3 (*d*).

BRUSSELS SPROUTS, *see* CABBAGE CROPS, GARDEN, section 3 (*e*).

BUCKWHEAT (OR BRANK) is a quickly growing crop used mostly for forage and for green manuring (ploughing in), but also for its grain. It is suited to light land, and will often do well on land so poor that even rye would fail. Although it is most generally grown in East Anglia and the Fens, small acreages were at one time grown in most districts—often on the larger estates to provide food for pheasants. It was then left unharvested, and the birds helped themselves. It might be grown more for poultry-food were it not difficult to prevent the wild birds from stripping the plants near harvest time.

The seed is usually sown in May, when the danger of frost is over, about 100 lb. being used per acre. Little cultivation or manuring are needed. If the grain is to be harvested, the crop is cut towards the end of August, usually with a mowing-machine, and is then allowed to become nearly dry before being tied into small bundles by hand. When used as a green manure, the crop is ploughed in before the seed forms. The yield of grain is usually from 10 to 20 cwt. per acre.

BUDDING, *see* FRUIT PROPAGATION.

BUFFALO, *see* ANIMAL FARMING, TROPICAL.

BUG PESTS, *see* APHID PESTS.

BUILDINGS, FARM, *see* FARMSTEAD.

BULBS, CORMS, AND TUBERS. 1. These are all underground STEMS (q.v. Vol. II) which serve as storage organs for plants, and from which grow a great number of well-known garden flowers.

Among such stems is the rhizome, a thickened, root-like organ which produces roots and also buds, as in the flag IRIS (q.v.). A corm is a swollen, solid stem enclosed in papery scales, with roots to hold it down under the soil—as, for example, the crocus and gladiolus. After flowering, one or two new corms form above or beside the original, which finally becomes shrunken and useless. A tuber is like a corm but without the scaly sheath. Tubers vary considerably: for instance, the potato produces several stems from its buds, while the cyclamen has no main stem but produces one set of leaves and flowers direct from the tuber; these are 'stem tubers'. 'Root tubers', however, such as the DAHLIA tuber (q.v.), grow in bunches connected to the crown (the base of the old stem) from which buds spring. If a dahlia tuber is cut off without a bud, it can produce only roots. In the bulb the stem has been reduced to a small, disk-shaped base, around which are packed many thickened scales which are, in fact, modified leaves. The structure is similar to that of a bud. Examples of bulbs are tulips, daffodils, and hyacinths (*see* diagram p. 411, Vol. II).

Plants with these fleshy storage organs—that is, bulbous plants—are different from other PERENNIALS (q.v.) because they have a resting or dormant period during which the majority may be dug up and stored dry. Many bulbs from warm climates require a period of 'baking' in dry soil and hot sun to develop the next season's flowers. On the other hand a few, notably LILIES (q.v.), require some moisture at all times. The dormant phase makes bulbs easy to handle, and hence convenient to the horticultural trade.

2. GARDEN CULTURE. Many of the more commonly grown hardy bulbs flower in spring; some of them, such as snowdrops and aconites, very early in the spring, and this makes them particularly valuable in the garden. The tulip has been bred and grown for nearly 3 centuries, and the daffodil is also an old garden plant.

Tulips and hyacinths are usually 'bedded out' every year and then, after flowering, are lifted and stored. Narcissi (the Latin name for all daffodils, jonquils, and so on) may be treated in the same way, or they may be left to grow naturally in grass or woodland. Most of the small spring bulbs may be left in the ground for many years, until the constant production of offsets, or new young bulbs, causes overcrowding. Then they must be lifted, separated, and replanted.

Amateur Gardening

WHITE DOG'S TOOTH VIOLET, A BULB

Amateur Gardening

SOLOMON'S SEAL, A RHIZOME

Amateur Gardening

MEADOW SAFFRON, A CORM

Amateur Gardening

WINTER ACONITE, A TUBER

In general, bulbs grow best in a well-drained, rather sandy loam. They do not do well in heavy clay soil nor soil which becomes very wet in winter. Dry organic fertilizers prove more satisfactory than animal manure. Bone meal at 4 oz. per square yard and hoof and horn meal at 2 oz. should be worked into the surface soil before planting, and then about half these amounts should be worked in annually in late summer.

Before spring bulbs can be lifted and stored, the leaves must die down completely; otherwise they will not store sufficient nourishment to produce flowers the next year. If the space in which they are growing is needed for the next crop, the bulbs may be carefully dug up with roots and immediately replanted, quite close together, in a spare corner of the garden, or even in a deep box containing soil, to complete their growth. After being lifted, the bulbs should be left in a cool dry place for a few weeks; then the soil should be shaken off, the dead leaves twisted off, and the bulbs placed in boxes in a dry shed until it is time to plant them again. Most spring-flowering bulbs should be planted in August or September, except tulips which can wait till October or November.

The most popular summer-flowering bulbous plants are dahlias and gladioli, both of which are tender and must be lifted each autumn. Gladiolus corms should be planted between March and mid-May, to spread out the flowering season, and lifted when the leaves begin to turn yellow. They should then be hung in bunches in a dry, frost-proof place until the leaves have quite withered and can be cut off, and the corms stored away for the winter.

3. INDOOR BULBS. Spring-flowering bulbs, in particular, are often grown in pots or bowls to flower in the house. Almost every bulbous plant can be grown in a pot, and this is often essential when growing tropical kinds in the greenhouse. Pot culture in the cold greenhouse is also used for many small, early-flowering, hardy bulbs which if grown outside might be too easily damaged by weather.

Bulbs grown under heat may be 'forced' into flower many weeks before their normal time. Though the temperature and the time during which they are forced varies between varieties, the treatment is similar in general. Bulbs for forcing are always planted in soil. After about 8 weeks in the dark, they are brought for 2 or 3 days into a cool greenhouse in a temperature not above 50° to 55° F., in half light, and then given full light and a temperature not above 60° for narcissi, and between 60° and 70° for tulips and hyacinths. During this time they need a lot of water and adequate air humidity to prevent the flowers withering. When the flowers open, the temperature should be lowered slightly.

Bulbs which are required to flower as early as Christmas are specially 'prepared' for forcing. Hyacinths are lifted in June and kept in a temperature of 85° for a few weeks; daffodils are stored in a constant 48° during August and September; and tulips may be treated in the same way, though they do not respond so successfully and, consequently, are not often 'prepared' for forcing.

For more normal culture indoors, bulbs may be grown either in soil in pots, or in bulb fibre in bowls without drainage holes. Glazed bowls are best, as this prevents evaporation at the roots. Bulb fibre is made from 6 parts horticultural peat, 2 parts crushed oyster shell (to keep it open) and 1 part crushed charcoal (to prevent souring). This mixture is nothing but a water carrier and contains almost no nourishment, so that bulbs grown in it will deteriorate and must be planted in the garden the next season.

The fibre, after being thoroughly soaked (a more difficult operation than it sounds), should be put into the bowls damp but not wringing wet. The lower layers should be lightly packed, and those above the bulbs pressed tightly, so that the roots can penetrate easily but the whole is kept firmly fixed in the bowl. Narcissi and hyacinths may have their tops well out of the fibre; tulips and crocuses only the tip; other bulbs need to be slightly covered. If shallow, wide pots are used, there must be good drainage, and a rich, open compost, such as the John Innes No. 2 Compost, is needed (see POTTING).

Once the bulbs are planted, they should have as natural conditions as possible. They must be kept cool to encourage the roots to grow considerably before any top growth appears. They can be placed in a cool cellar or cupboard, but it is better to 'plunge' them in a shallow trench or an open frame outside, under a north-facing wall, where they can remain for 4 or 5 weeks covered with old sifted ashes or peat. Then after being gradually accustomed to full light, they are best in a cold greenhouse or under cloches, or even in a light place in a cool room. Not until the buds are ready to open is it advisable to place them in a warm room for fear the buds may wither. Throughout this time plenty of water is needed. All taller bulbs, when they have made 4 inches growth need the support of twine looped round three or four pieces of cane inserted at the edges of the pot or bowl. Another tie may be needed later just beneath the flowers.

Certain bulbs, such as bunch-flowered narcissi and hyacinths, may be grown in pebbles or gravel kept very wet. Hyacinths are sometimes grown in water alone in 'hyacinth glasses'. None of the smaller bulbs, such as chionodoxa, crocus, muscari, scilla, winter aconite and snowdrop, seem to have sufficient nourishment in themselves to do well except in soil. All these will

John Topham

HOEING A TULIP FIELD NEAR SPALDING, LINCS.
The tulips are being grown for their bulbs

also give better bloom if left outside until January.

Later-flowering bulbs, which are less commonly grown, include bulbous irises and *Gladiolus Colvillei*. Among popular bulbous plants which need a heated greenhouse are arum lily, gloxinia, *Cyclamen persicum*, and lachenalia (see GREENHOUSE PLANTS).

See also Vol. II: STEMS, section 2.

BUTTERFLY AND MOTH PESTS. 1.

BUTTERFLIES. Among the worst vegetable pests are the caterpillars of the Cabbage Butterflies— the familiar Large and Small WHITES (q.v. Vol. II). These butterflies lay their eggs during April and May, and again during July and August, and the caterpillars hatch from 4 to 16 days later according to the weather, and then begin to eat the leaves. The second attack is generally the more severe, and in a long summer there may be a third. It is a curious fact that while whole fields of cabbages are not generally severely attacked, cabbages grown in small gardens may be devoured until nothing is left but a skeleton. Whites attack certain flowering plants as well, in particular the nasturtium.

The Large White usually lays its yellow,

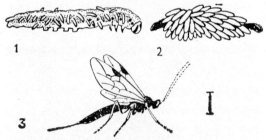

A FLY WHICH IS PARASITIC ON CATERPILLARS (magnified)

1. Caterpillar with fly larvae boring through the skin
2. Cocoons of fly on dead caterpillar
3. The fly which emerges from the cocoons

bottle-shaped eggs in clusters on the undersides of the leaves. Those of the Small White are green and are laid singly. As soon as the butterflies are seen in the garden, the eggs should be searched for and destroyed. The caterpillar of the Large White Butterfly is a conspicuous grey-green, spotted with black and striped with yellow. The caterpillar of the Small White Butterfly is a less conspicuous pale, velvety green, and usually lives singly. In autumn a mass of golden yellow cocoons is sometimes to be seen gathered around a dead or dying caterpillar. These should be left unharmed, for they are the cocoons of a parasitic ICHNEUMON FLY (q.v. Vol. II) which destroys often as many as 90% of the second brood of Large White Butterfly caterpillars each year. If the gardener in the autumn finds chrysalises attached by their tails and by silken girdles to such places as palings and walls, he should destroy them. The best control of the pest is a sprinkling of DDT powder blown on the leaves when the caterpillars are hatched. Derris powder can be used instead, and a spraying of a strong solution of salt and water is very effective.

2. MOTHS. The caterpillars of the Cabbage Moth (see NIGHT-FLYING MOTHS, Vol. II) are often found with those of the Cabbage White. They are brownish-green, and burrow into the hearts of cabbages and cauliflowers, as well as geraniums, dahlias, and many other garden plants. The Cabbage Moth caterpillar generally attacks the autumn crops most severely.

The Diamond-back Moth, a tiny moth about ¼-inch long with diamond-shaped markings on its wings, has a small black-headed green caterpillar which feeds on the lower surface of the leaves of turnips, swedes, cabbages, and related plants such as charlock (field mustard). The

pest is most numerous in southern England, for the moths migrate from the Continent. An attack may be brought to an end by a period of heavy rain, but a serious infestation needs prompt action with an insecticide such as DDT, especially when the small plants have been recently set out.

The Pea Moth lays its eggs on or near the pod, and when the grubs hatch, one or two enter the pod and feed on the developing peas. When fully grown, the small white grub bores out of the pod and goes down into the ground, where it remains in a cocoon until the following summer. The moth emerges about July. Early sowing produces plants sufficiently advanced to avoid the main part of the attack. Spraying or dusting with DDT in the last week of June for early crops, or a week before flowering for later crops, is a good deterrent. All infested pods should be gathered and burnt.

Cutworms, or surface caterpillars, are the caterpillars of the Turnip Moth, Yellow Underwing, Heart and Dart, and other moths (see NIGHT-FLYING MOTHS, Vol. II). They are mostly dark in colour, similar to the soil in which they live, and are marked in various ways with dots and lines. They come out of the soil at night to feed on any garden or field crop, cutting off the plants at the base of the stem, and often eating the leaves as well. Cutworms frequently burrow into turnips and potatoes. These caterpillars are troublesome during the summer months, and even in the winter if the weather is sufficiently mild. In gardens the caterpillars and reddish brown chrysalises should be collected and destroyed when found; poultry are helpful in destroying these pests.

MAGPIE MOTH CATERPILLAR AND CHRYSALIS
The caterpillar is black and white and the chrysalis brown

The caterpillars of moths are among the most serious pests of fruit-trees. The fruit-grower puts grease-bands round the trunks of his trees in the autumn to protect them from the Winter Moth and others of the Geometrid family, such as the March Moth and the Mottled Umber (*see* Loopers, Vol. II). The females of these moths are wingless, and they try to crawl up the tree trunks to lay their eggs in cracks in the bark or on buds. A winter spray is also used to kill the eggs. Those that escape and hatch into green striped caterpillars are sprayed in the spring with arsenate of lead which poisons the leaves, or with DDT or BHC. These are so effective that grease-banding is often omitted. The Magpie Moth, which attacks Currants and Gooseberries (q.v.), is another of the family.

Perhaps the worst pest on Apples (q.v.) and other tree fruits is the Codling Moth, a member of the Tortrix family (*see* Leaf-rollers, Vol. II), which burrows into the heart of the fruit. It is difficult to control, but much can be done by grease-banding, winter washing, and, most effective of all, spraying with arsenate of lead. It is important to keep the trees clear of dead wood which harbours the pests. Other Tortrix pests are the Peach Moth (*see* Peaches), the Light Brown Apple Moth which attacks apple orchards in New Zealand, and the Oak Tortrix Moth which in certain years will defoliate oak-trees almost to the point of killing them. Another group of moth pests are the Clearwings, such as the Currant Clearwing, the caterpillar of which burrows into the stems. The Peach Borer Clearwing, which attacks the tree round the foot, will, if undisturbed, often kill the tree in the course of two or three years.

John Topham

GREASE-BANDING A FRUIT-TREE
The sticky material is being painted on to the paper

There are several other species of moth which give trouble to the fruit-grower, gardener, or forester, such as the Tent Caterpillars of the Lackey Moth (q.v. Vol. II) which attack forest trees in the U.S.A., the larvae of the Goat and Leopard Moths (q.v. Vol. II) which bore into the bark of apple-trees, and the Eyed Hawk Moth and Vapourer (qq.v. Vol. II) which make local attacks on the leaves. The Tobacco Hornworm (a member of the Hawks) is a serious pest on tobacco crops in the U.S.A.

See also Pests and Diseases; Insect Pests; Spraying.
See also Vol. II: Butterflies; Moths; Night-flying Moths; Caterpillar.

C

CABBAGE CROPS, FIELD. These include the true cabbage, the kales, rape, and kohl-rabi. All these can be grown as garden vegetables (*see* Cabbage Crops, Garden) or in the fields for feeding to livestock, in which case they replace roots in the Rotation of Crops (q.v.). The cabbage crops may be eaten on the fields by 'folding' cattle and sheep on them with movable fences (folds), or they may be carted home for feeding to housed cattle. Any that cannot be used fresh are made into Silage (q.v.). As food for cattle they are not likely to flavour the milk, as swedes, turnips, and sugar-beet tops sometimes do.

The cultivation of these crops is much the same as that of roots (*see* Mangolds). The land is generously manured: a good dressing of farm-yard manure ploughed under in the autumn, and as much as 10 cwt. of balanced fertilizer per acre, given just before sowing, is regarded as normal treatment. The large amount of foliage produced by the cabbage crops smothers the weeds, so that the land is left both clean and in rich condition for the following crop. The crop is usually grown in rows and the seed sown in drills; about 4 lb. of seed per acre is needed for most cabbage crops. Sometimes the seed is sown broadcast, in which case more seed per acre is needed; sometimes it is sown in nursery beds, and the plants moved later to the field.

(*a*) *Cabbages.* Several types are grown for farm use, the most common being the 'Ox-heart' type with a conical head, the 'drumhead' type with a large flat-topped head, and the 'savoy' with wrinkled foliage and very high resistance to frost. The drumhead is the most popular for feeding to livestock. The seed is generally sown in a seed-bed, either in March for transplanting in the early summer, or in August for transplanting in October. The best cabbages are often sold for human consumption and the rest used for animal food. In a good climate and rich soil 40 to 50 tons per acre of cabbage may be obtained.

(*b*) *Kale.* This is a sprouting rather than a hearting form of cabbage. The four most popular types are Marrowstem kale (a cross with kohl-rabi); Thousand-headed kale, which carries a great many uncurled leaves much bunched together, and has a good resistance to frost; and Rape kale and Hungry-gap which are hybrid varieties maturing late in the spring and very useful when the other cabbage crops are finished and the spring grass has not yet come. The average yield of kale is 20 to 30 tons per acre.

(*c*) *Rape.* This leafy, juicy plant, which grows from 2 to 3 feet high, is particularly valuable as a food for sheep. It is sown in April, is ready for grazing in July or August, and yields an average of 12 to 15 tons per acre. Rape is sometimes sown broadcast and grown as a catch crop (*see* Arable Crops), and sometimes it is sown thinly (about 2 lb. to the acre) as a nurse crop with grasses and clovers (*see* Leys).

(*d*) *Kohl-Rabi.* This crop is often grown instead of swedes and turnips in districts, such as the eastern counties of Britain, where early sown swedes tend to get mildew and the later ones are destroyed by the turnip flea beetle. Therefore kohl-rabi has earned the name 'the

Eric Guy

SHEEP FOLDED IN A FIELD OF MARROWSTEM KALE
The sheep will eat the crop down to the ground, and will then be moved to another patch

PICKING BROCCOLI IN DECEMBER ON THE SOUTH COAST OF CORNWALL

The Times

Cabbage crops are grown in the fields for human use as well as for animals. The mild climate of the south-west is especially good for them

bulb of dry summers'. Kohl-rabi looks like a small green or purple turnip, but is, in fact, a swollen stem, the whole 'bulb' being above ground. For this reason sheep can eat it all, without waste, on the field—as they cannot do with turnips and swedes which are partly underground. As it stands a fair amount of frost, it can be left growing through much of the winter, being used as it is needed. It can, however, be lifted and stored, like turnips. A good crop yields 20 tons per acre.

See also ARABLE CROPS.

CABBAGE CROPS, GARDEN. 1. KINDS OF CABBAGE.

The various cabbage crops—the true cabbage, cauliflower, broccoli, Brussels sprouts, kale (borecole), savoy, and kohl-rabi—have all been derived from the wild cabbage (*Brassica oleracea*) which grows on sea coast cliffs in Britain and other parts of Europe. There are two other species (*Brassica pekinensis* and *B. chinensis*) which are called Chinese cabbage. Various parts of the different plants are eaten: with the true or 'heading' cabbage it is the compact leafy heads; with the cauliflower and broccoli it is the flower parts; and with the Brussels sprouts and kale it is the leafy buds and shoots that develop on the stems when the plants are fully grown. With the kohl-rabi, on the other hand, the swollen turnip-shaped stem, white, green, or purple, is the edible part. The cabbage crops rank high in importance amongst the garden vegetables because they are rich in vitamins and minerals. They are often called cole crops from the Latin *caulis*, a stem.

There are several kinds of the true cabbage— spring, summer, autumn, and winter cabbages; but there are two main types—those with pointed or conical heads and those with round, flattish heads. There is also a special red, round-headed cabbage used mainly for pickling. The savoy is another distinct kind of very hardy winter cabbage with crinkled leaves, which came originally from Savoy in the Alps. There are different kinds of cauliflower for early summer, late summer, and autumn use, the early ones being the smaller, and also a much hardier winter cauliflower, often called broccoli (from the Italian *broccolo*, a sprout), though it is not a broccoli at all.

The Brussels sprouts, an autumn and winter vegetable originally grown around Brussels in Belgium, has a lengthened main stalk or stem upon which numerous buds, like miniature cabbages, are produced. These 'sprouts' are taken from the stem as they mature.

The kales are large plants which form a profusion of leafy shoots in the spring. Scotch kale or Curly kale has crinkled leaves; Thousand-headed kale produces a great number of leafy

Amateur Gardening

SPRING CABBAGE

Amateur Gardening

SAVOY

Harold Bastin

KOHL-RABI

shoots; Cottager's kale is a common, easily grown variety. These kales are capable of withstanding very severe winter conditions, and so are useful garden crops in times of scarcity.

Kohl-rabi, which is usually sown at intervals to produce a succession of crops, is fairly hardy, and is often left where it grows to be gathered as needed.

The sprouting broccoli, a most delicious and useful vegetable, has three forms—green sprouting, purple sprouting, and white sprouting. The green-sprouting broccoli, very popular in North America and in parts of Europe, especially Italy, is not so much grown in Britain as the purple and white.

2. GENERAL CULTURE. Nearly all the cabbages are transplanted crops, that is, the seed is sown in a seed-bed from which the plants are transplanted, sometimes twice, to their permanent places. In market-gardens a transplanting-machine is used, but in smaller gardens the planting is done by hand. All kinds of cabbages need a fertile soil and plenty of water, loamy soils being best because they hold moisture. Some of the cabbage crops, spring cabbage for ·example, thrive well on land that was manured for the preceding crop. That is why spring cabbage is often planted after potatoes or onions. But if no more manure or compost has been applied, the soil should be given either some other organic fertilizer, such as meat and bone meal or fish manure, or a dressing of a complete artificial fertilizer (*see* MANURES). A complete fertilizer includes phosphate and potash which are necessary nutrients to all cabbages, producing, for one thing, a good colour. Cauliflowers of all kinds and summer cabbage especially need a rich soil, no doubt because a well-manured soil retains the moisture well, even in a summer drought. During dry weather, however, cabbage crops, especially the summer

cauliflower, should be watered—indeed marketgardeners usually irrigate these crops (*see* IRRIGATION). Light top dressings of a quick-acting nitrogen fertilizer, such as nitrate of soda, nitrochalk, potash-nitrate, or soot, applied between the plants and hoed or cultivated into the soil, serve to stimulate growth. Some cabbage crops, such as kale, are 'intercropped', that is, they are planted between the rows of other crops, such as potatoes, to gain time and to make the full use of the land.

Cabbages are attacked by many kinds of pests and diseases. The small Flea-beetles attack the seedlings in the seedbed (*see* BEETLE PESTS), and the caterpillars of the Cabbage White Butterflies and the Cabbage Moth attack the growing crops during the summer time (*see* BUTTERFLY AND MOTH PESTS). The Cabbage Aphid can also become a considerable nuisance (*see* APHID PESTS). The maggots of the Cabbage Root-fly attack the roots of the plants (*see* INSECT PESTS, section 2). The fungus disease, Club-root, usually flourishes most on acid soils; therefore land on which cabbages are grown needs regular dressings of lime. In recent times some of the cabbage crops have been attacked by plant viruses, which are minute disease agents often transmitted from plant to plant by aphids. Nothing can be done to cure plants once they are attacked, and they should be burned to prevent further infection (*see* PLANT DISEASES). The crops will resist disease better and grow more healthily if they are kept free from weeds by constant hoeing, for weeds rob the crops of water and plant foods.

3. CULTURE OF INDIVIDUAL KINDS. (*a*) *Cabbage.* Spring cabbages, which are all of the pointed type, should not be sown until the last week of July; if sown earlier the plants tend to bolt (run to seed). Wheeler's Imperial or Ellam's Early Dwarf are among many good varieties. Transplanting is done during September and October, the plants being placed 15 to 18 inches apart, in rows 18 to 24 inches apart according to the size of the variety.

Summer cabbage seed is sown in March, and autumn cabbage in April. By sowing in February under glass earlier crops can be obtained. The plants are put into their permanent positions in April and May, more space being allowed than for spring cabbage. Nothing is gained by planting this type of cabbage too closely. Leeds Market is a pointed type, and Copenhagen Market a round type.

Winter cabbage seed is sown during April and May, according to district, and transplanted during June and July, even more space being allowed for development. Sometimes winter cabbage is planted 24 inches square. Christmas Drumhead is a well-known variety.

(b) *Red Cabbage.* The seed of red cabbage is usually sown at the same time as spring cabbage —in late July—but transplanting is left until the spring. The seed may be sown in March, like summer cabbage, and transplanted in May. It takes longer to mature than other cabbages and needs as much space as summer cabbage. Red Dutch or Ruby Red are good varieties.

(c) *Cauliflower.* Summer cauliflowers are of the small or medium-sized type known as Northern or Parisian Cauliflower, All The Year Round, Early London, and Snowball being suitable varieties. In order to get a crop by June or July the seed is sown in frames the previous autumn. The seedlings are pricked out in the frame or left until the following March or April. Then they are transplanted on to well prepared land, with a space of about 20 inches between them. Sometimes summer cauliflowers are planted under glass cloches in March to bring them on more quickly.

Autumn cauliflowers, to be ready about September, are sown in seed-beds in April and transplanted during May or June. An earlier crop can be obtained by sowing the seed of a suitable variety, such as Eclipse or Autumn Giant, in frames in March and transplanting in May. The plants grow very large, needing about 30 inches space between them.

Winter cauliflowers or broccoli are hardier, though they cannot withstand severe frost. This kind of cauliflower has been improved considerably in recent years by the introduction of new types from France and by the specialized breeding methods adopted in England. Typical winter cauliflowers suitable for general cultivation in Britain are Veitch's Self-Protecting and Michaelmas White; there is a range of varieties providing cauliflowers for cutting from October to June. Walcheren, an autumn cauliflower, can also serve as an early winter cauliflower in mild districts.

The seed is sown in seed-beds during March and April and transplanted in June or July according to the district. The plants are spaced 2 to 2½ feet square according to the form grown. They do better if fairly close together when fully grown as they then protect each other from cold winds. All cauliflowers, when mature, can be kept for a time in good condition on the plant if the outside leaves are bent over the flowers to protect them from the weather.

(d) *Sprouting Broccoli.* The green-sprouting type is sown during March and transplanted in April or May to provide a crop during late summer and autumn. The purple-sprouting and

Amateur Gardening

BRUSSELS SPROUTS   PURPLE SPROUTING BROCCOLI   PROTECTING CAULIFLOWER WITH A LEAF

white-sprouting types are sown in April and transplanted in June, in order to mature during the spring and early summer of the following year. The plants should be allowed plenty of space, nearly 2 feet square being suitable.

(e) *Brussels Sprouts.* There are dwarf, medium, and tall forms of Brussels sprouts, the sprouts varying in size from very small, called 'buttons', to fairly large or large. The small button sprout is popular in France. Climax is a good example of the dwarf form, Evesham Special or Fillbasket of the medium type, and Bedfordshire Prize or Evesham Giant of the tall type.

The plant needs a long season of growth, therefore seed should be sown as early as possible in the spring, the first sowings often being made under glass and later sowings in open seed-beds. Transplanting should be done not later than early June. The soil needs to be very firm, loose soil being one of the reasons why sprouts sometimes do not grow tight and hard. Brussels sprouts benefit from a double transplanting. At least 30 inches square of space is necessary for full development; in market-gardens a full 3 feet is often given. Brussels sprouts are not at their best for picking until there has been some frost.

See also VEGETABLE GARDEN.

CACAO. Both cocoa and chocolate are made from the fruit of the cacao tree, *Theobroma cacao* (*theobroma* means the 'food of the gods'). This tree is native to South and Central America, and a pleasant drink made from its seeds or beans was well known to the Indians long before the first European settlers arrived. It has now been introduced to most parts of the tropics, and is grown as a crop in the East and West Indies and in Ceylon; but the bulk of the world's supply comes from West Africa, where it is grown by native farmers.

The cacao is a small tree, only about 20 feet high, and thrives only in moist tropical lowlands with a fertile soil. It needs shelter from both the sun and the wind, and this is provided either by leaving some of the original jungle trees standing when the land is cleared, or else by planting other trees, such as kapok, at intervals among the cacao. The young trees are raised from seed in nurseries, being transplanted when a few months old to the new plantations, where they are set about 12 feet apart. Sometimes trees of improved varieties are bud-grafted on to the stumps of poorer ones (*see* PLANT PROPAGATION).

The young trees grow for about 8 years before yielding any fruit, but thereafter continue to bear steadily for many years. They are kept weeded, and are pruned, all suckers being cut away, leaving only the main stem and the principal branches. The leaves of the cacao tree are oval, dark green, and brittle when fully expanded; but when they first open, they are bright red and soft in texture.

A peculiar feature of the flowers is that they are borne directly on the surface of the main stem and the larger branches instead of being set upon the smaller twigs. They are quite small, star-shaped, and red in colour, and appear at intervals during the year, though in most countries there are two main flowering seasons, followed by two major harvests. The flowers give rise to tufts of oval ribbed pods from 6 to 10 inches long, which are green in colour but turn brown when dried. These pods are gathered as they ripen, those on the taller stems being cut down with a hooked knife on a long pole. When cut open they reveal from thirty to forty small seeds, the actual cocoa beans, which are removed by hand.

These beans are made to ferment by being piled in large heaps shielded from the rain with leaves, or stacked in wooden boxes, where they are left for several days. The fermentation aids

CACAO FLOWERS AND BEANS

P. B. Redmayne

DRYING CACAO BEANS IN THE SUN IN WEST AFRICA

the removal of the pulp, and changes the flavour of the beans from a bitter one to the pleasant taste that we associate with chocolate. The beans are then sun-dried on trays, and afterwards packed in bags for export. They contain a fatty substance known as 'cocoa butter', and in the manufacture of cocoa a portion of this is removed; it is added, however, to chocolate, and is also used in medicine and perfumery and in the manufacture of margarine.

About 4 cwt. of prepared beans are obtained from one acre of a good plantation each year, and as the beans ripen continually with very little attention, the crop forms a valuable resource for its owner. Unfortunately the groves are threatened by various diseases, particularly a virus disease known as 'swollen shoot' (*see* PLANT DISEASES), which reduce the crop and may kill the trees; and so far these complaints have proved very hard to remedy.

See also TROPICAL AGRICULTURE; TROPICAL PESTS.
See also Vol. VII: COCOA AND CHOCOLATE.

CACTI (HOTHOUSE). Cacti are succulent plants able to absorb a great deal of water very rapidly and to retain it for long periods. Their round and cylindrical leaves and stems, armed with protective spines, expose the least possible amount of surface to the sun's rays, and so they are able to flourish in very hot, dry climates (*see* CACTUS, Vol. II).

Only those plants that belong to the *Cactaceae* (cactus family) are the true cacti, though there are many other fleshy plants, or succulents, of different families. The true cacti, which are almost entirely natives of America, can be recognized by their habit of developing buds surrounded by a cushion of hairs or spines, called 'areoles'. Familiar species are the *Opuntias* or prickly pears; *Cereus*, some of which flower only at night; *Echinocactus*, or Hedgehog Cactus; *Mamillaria*; and the very beautiful and free flowering *Phyllocactus* and *Epiphyllum*, the stems of which resemble leaves. Most other succulents have less strange flowers than the cacti, but a wider range of highly coloured or waxy leaves (as in *Echeveria*, *Cotyledon*, and *Crassula*) and of strange forms, such as the South African Stone Plants in which the plant is reduced to a small rounded body, closely imitating its surroundings.

Even without a greenhouse, it is quite easy to grow certain cacti and many succulents by putting them in a south or south-west window, provided it is frost-proof and that there are no coal-gas fumes in the room. Most cacti and succulents need a long resting period during the winter, and plenty of water during their growing season; though this habit varies. Winter and

Amateur Gardening

YOUNG PLANTS OF CACTI AND OTHER SUCCULENTS

In the background, *Aporocactus*. Back row, left to right, *Mamillaria, Sedum, Echinocactus*. Centre row, *Echeveria, Cotyledon, Haworthia, Echeveria*. Front row, *Sedum, Cereus, Bryophyllum, Echidnopsis, Kleinia, Opuntia, Crassula*

spring flowering varieties need water before and during their flowering period, and some succulents are better if given water occasionally during the winter, particularly if they are kept in a warm room.

Cacti are propagated by seed, cuttings, and offsets. Cuttings are usually taken between May and September, but can also be taken during the winter if they are first carefully dried off for a week or two before being planted in sharp sand in a warm frame. The cuttings should be kept rather dry until they have rooted and growth has started. Where a large cut has to be made, as in some *Mamillarias*, it is even more important to dry off the cutting before it is planted, and the parent plant should not be given much water until the wound has healed. In certain species of *Mamillaria* and *Leuchtenbergia* the warts may be used, fairly successfully, for propagation if they are carefully dried off. Pure sand, or sand

with a very little leaf-mould, is best for delicate species, but for most cacti the same compost as that for the potted plant is quite suitable.

Succulents are propagated in much the same way, but generally the cuttings can be kept moister. *Stapelia* and its relatives and *Euphorbia* should be dried off for 2 or 3 days before being inserted in sand.

A useful compost for potting cacti and succulents is the following:

2 parts fibrous loam, well rotted,
1 part crushed brick,
1 ,, sharp sand,
1 ,, granulated charcoal,
½ ,, crushed bone or mortar rubble.

This can be varied for different plants. The *Mesembryanthemum* group and succulents with coloured or waxy leaves do better if given rather more sand and less of the richer constituents;

while *Phyllocactus*, some *Stapelias*, and *Echinocactus* prefer a much richer soil.

See also GREENHOUSE PLANTS.

CALVES, *see* CATTLE, CARE OF, sections 5 and 6.

CARDOON, *see* ARTICHOKES.

CARNATIONS AND PINKS. The genus *Dianthus*, to which the carnation, pink, and sweet william belong, is a very extensive one. The name comes from the Greek *dios*, divine, and *anthos*, a flower. The wild species are sometimes cultivated in ROCK GARDENS (q.v.), but the kinds usually grown are the results of intensive breeding. Carnation-growing is a big industry in some places—in the U.S.A. for the florists' trade, and in the south of France for making perfume.

1. VARIETIES. The original wild carnation, or Clove Pink, *Dianthus Caryophyllus*, described by a Greek writer in 300 B.C., was a common wild flower in southern Europe and was cultivated by the Greeks. During the 16th century it became one of the most popular garden flowers in France, Holland, and England, where it was called the gilly-flower (a name also applied to wallflowers and stocks). The modern border carnation is directly developed from it.

By the 18th century there were tender, winter-flowering strains as well as hardy summer-flowering ones, and from the former has been evolved the perpetual flowering carnation (the American or Tree Carnation). This grows to 5 or 6 feet and flowers in mildly heated greenhouses, where, with careful management, it will bloom throughout the year. The perpetual-blooming character was obtained more or less by accident by a French breeder in 1840.

Another race of garden carnations, derived from *D. chinensis* (the Rainbow, India, or China Pink), have flowers like carnations in appearance but the plants are much smaller. They flower all the summer in great profusion, but are usually tender and are treated as half-hardy annuals in Britain.

The garden pink, a flower grown but not much valued in the 15th and 16th centuries, has smaller flowers with a greater range of petal shapes and colour than the carnations. The laced pink, which has petals with 'laced' edges of dark red or maroon shades, was developed

Amateur Gardening

KINDS OF DIANTHUS
Top, Picotee-edge Carnation. Middle, Show Pink.
Bottom, Hybrid Alpine Dianthus

in the 18th century, and since then many strains of pink have been raised by different breeders. Most pinks flourish in a sunny position without special protection.

A modern hybrid race, *Dianthus Allwoodii*, has been produced by crossing the perpetual carnation and the garden pink. These are hardy quick-growing plants which flower from spring to winter. Another hybrid, *D. Allwoodii alpinus*, produced by crossing *D. Allwoodii* and various dwarf alpine species, grows about 6 in. high and flourishes in rockeries or niches in stone walls, flowering from spring to winter.

The sweet william (*D. barbatus*) with clusters of small, variously coloured flowers, is now usually treated as a BIENNIAL (q.v.), since one season's profuse flowering exhausts its vitality. There are also annual sweet williams such as sweet wivelsfield, a cross with *Dianthus Allwoodii*, and these have an extremely wide range of colour and form, and the majority—unlike many recent carnation varieties—are sweet scented.

2. CULTURE. Most species of *Dianthus* grow wild only on European limestone mountains, and carnations and pinks under cultivation also prefer a light soil with very good drainage and plenty of lime. Deep soils do not suit them, but they do well in such situations as cool rock crevices. A sunny and airy situation is best, for the waxy 'bloom' on the foliage of plants exposed to sun and air is their natural defence against pests and diseases.

The average garden soil is too rich and too acid for any *Dianthus*. The acidity can best be counteracted by working limestone chips or old mortar rubble into the soil; and this can also be spread as a 'top dressing' round the base of the growing plants. Burnt earth, used sparingly, is valuable not only for its potash content but also because it lightens and gives drainage to heavy soils.

Border carnations and pinks can be planted 12 to 18 inches apart at any time between autumn and early spring, the earlier the better. Perpetual carnations grown under glass require an average summer temperature of 60° F. and a winter temperature of 50°, never falling below 40°. They need plenty of ventilation.

All carnations and pinks can be propagated by cuttings, but border carnations are best increased by layering, that is, by pegging down pieces of the stems still attached to the parent plant until they take root. Pinks can be grown

satisfactorily from seed, but carnation seed produces a very small proportion of good flowers, and cuttings or layers are much more reliable (*see* PLANT PROPAGATION).

See also ROCK GARDEN.

CARROTS. 1. The fleshy taproots of improved forms of the carrot plant, *Daucus Carota*, which grows wild in Europe, are used as a vegetable. The roots contain carbohydrates, mainly sugar, and, particularly when raw, a large amount of the substance called 'carotene', which, when eaten, is converted by the body into the important accessory food substance known as Vitamin A (*see* VITAMINS, Vol. XI). Carrots, therefore, are a nutritious and valuable food, especially when eaten raw. The name carrot comes from the Latin *carota*, which itself probably came from *caro*, flesh, perhaps because of the fleshy colour of the taproot. Carrots belong to the same family as parsley and parsnips.

There are white, yellow, red, orange, and orange-red varieties of carrot, the white and yellow kinds being grown mainly as food for livestock. The shape of the taproot varies also, some being small and globular, others short and slightly pointed, others half-long or stump-rooted, and others long or very long and tapering. All these carrots have been obtained by selection from the wild carrot, the root of which, in comparison, is quite small. The carrot plant is a biennial, and if not pulled up would produce a flower stalk in the second year. The root is, therefore, not edible after March.

2. FIELD CARROTS. These grow best on deep sandy soils, where the roots can easily develop downwards and sideways, and where the pulling of the crop at harvest is easy. The long-rooted varieties are especially well suited to very deep

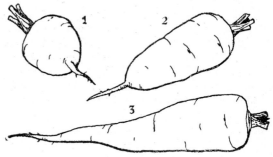

VARIOUS SHAPES OF CARROT
1. Early forcing carrots. 2. Early horn. 3. Long

soils, and the short-rooted varieties to the heavier soils. The rich 'black mould' soil of the fenland district in Cambridgeshire is particularly good for field carrots.

Usually the crop is cultivated and manured in much the same way as turnips and swedes (*see* ROOT CROPS). The feathery leaves have little or no smothering effect upon weeds, so really clean land is necessary. The seed is usually sown on soil which has been manured for the previous crop, for carrots grown on soil too recently manured tend to produce roots with fangs. The soil must be well limed, and a mixture of fertilizers supplying nitrogen, phosphates, and potash should be applied a few days before the seed is sown in March or April. Moisture is also very important for carrots, and the crop often fails in a drought.

About 6 lb. of seed per acre is drilled on a fine seed bed in rows 12 to 20 inches apart. As the seedlings develop, they may be 'singled' or thinned to 4 to 6 inches between plants in the rows. Many farmers, however, fear to single the crop, because the strong smell that comes from bruising the leaves may attract the carrot fly (*see* FLY PESTS). In order to avoid the necessity of thinning, the seed is sown in drills as thinly as possible and the plants are left to develop. During this time the weeds are kept down by hoeing between the rows. Lifting may start in August and carries on into November or even December. In deep, sandy soils it is possible to pull the roots by hand, with little help from the fork. Sometimes the crop is left in the ground over the winter, to be lifted when needed for sale in the following spring. Carrots left in the ground retain their freshness and juiciness much better than those stored in a clamp; but few farmers risk leaving the whole of their crop out for fear of a severe winter. Some farmers have installed equipment for washing the carrots before sale.

On an average, an acre yields about 10 to 12 tons of carrots, but up to 20 tons per acre are sometimes produced. Small and damaged roots unfit for sale are fed to livestock, the crop being particularly valuable for dairy cows because its high content of carotene gives a rich colour to the milk during the winter months.

3. GARDEN CARROTS. In gardens, crops of very early carrots can be grown in FRAMES or under CLOCHES (qq.v.), and main crops for use later in the year and for storage for the winter are sown in the open. Suitable varieties for frame or

Royal Horticultural Society
LIFTING CARROTS WITH A FORK

cloche culture are: French Forcing Horn, Early Gem, and Early English Horn—the last two being also suitable for an early garden crop. These are all short-rooted varieties. For summer crops in the garden, Early Nantes or Chantenay are suitable half-long varieties; and for autumn crops, suitable for storing, the long tapering roots of James's Scarlet Intermediate, St. Valery, and Long Red Surrey are excellent.

In the garden the seed is sown thinly at a depth of about $\frac{1}{2}$ inch in rows spaced 12 inches for early crops and 15 or 18 inches for late crops. In frames the seed is usually sown broadcast, but under cloches, in rows. The plants are thinned to a spacing of from 1 to 4 inches according to the type of carrot grown. Early crops are often hardly thinned at all. In very dry weather, especially in light soils, the carrot crop needs to be well watered.

Late crops of carrots are lifted during October and stored in the open in small clamps covered with soil, or in sand or ashes in a shed where they are protected from frost. The roots shrivel if left exposed to the air.

See also ROOT CROPS.

CARTS, *see* FARM VEHICLES.

CATCH CROPS, *see* ROTATION OF CROPS.

CATERPILLARS, *see* BUTTERFLY AND MOTH PESTS.

CATTLE. In olden days the word 'cattle' was applied to all kinds of farm livestock, and cows and oxen (the bovines) were called 'neat' or black cattle to distinguish them from horses, sheep, and pigs. Today, in Britain at any rate, 'cattle' means only cows, bulls, and bullocks. These are members of the ox tribe, to which bison, buffaloes, yaks, gaurs, and several other wild species also belong (*see* CATTLE, Vol. II).

Domestic cattle provide us with milk (and all that is produced from milk), beef, and hides; in some countries the oxen (bullocks) are used as draught animals as well, just as they were in Britain before they were replaced by horses. In parts of Germany and some other European countries, they are still used in this way. The most famous of all draught cattle are probably the Afrikanders, a breed developed from the cattle of South Africa (*see* BEASTS OF BURDEN, Vol. IV).

Until about the middle of the 15th century, wild cattle roamed in many parts of the forest that covered a large part of Britain, and these were hunted as game. Perhaps the cattle nearest in type to these wild ones are those of the shaggy, long-horned West Highland breed. The earliest

Robert M. Adam

WEST HIGHLAND COW IN SKYE

domesticated cattle, however, were the Celtic or Marsh cattle, which were small (about the size of our modern Kerry), short in the horn, and probably black or red in colour. It is thought likely that they were brought to Britain about 2,000 years B.C. by Neolithic tribes wandering westwards from Europe. Later, the Romans brought their own domestic cattle with them, and these were large, white beasts with a great spread of horn. Then the Saxons and Norsemen came, some bringing red and others dun-coloured, polled (hornless) animals. A few hundred years later, a small number of cattle, of a type that we would describe nowadays as Friesian, were introduced from the Low Countries. The Channel Islands also made a contribution: hence our Jerseys and Guernseys.

Out of this varied mixture of material, cattle of certain recognizable types were produced, some better suited to the hilly country and some to the more fertile plains. And from these different types the breeds as we know them today have eventually come: the Shorthorn, the Red Poll, the Aberdeen Angus, and all the others, each with its record of pedigrees in the form of a herd book. The fixing of the breed characters is the result of careful, painstaking work on the part of British breeders, mainly during the 18th and 19th centuries, and in this work they had the help of two things. Most of the OPEN FIELDS (q.v.) of Britain had been divided up and enclosed by the middle of the 19th century, which was earlier than in many continental countries. Enclosure made easier the controlled breeding of cattle and the cultivation of better crops with which to feed them (*see* AGRICULTURAL IMPROVERS). In addition, the moist and temperate climate of the British Isles encourages the growth of good grass. Without good food it is not possible to breed and maintain better cattle.

This success has led to British stock being the foundation of many of the herds in other parts of the world. In the U.S.A., Argentina, Brazil, Canada, Australia, and other countries, types of Shorthorns, Herefords, and Aberdeen Angus, amongst others, are to be found. Some of the pedigree animals bought for export fetch very high prices: 14,500 guineas were recently paid for each of a pair of Scotch Shorthorns sold to America. A further result of this successful breeding is the cattle parade at the Royal Show (*see* AGRICULTURAL SHOWS), which is the best of its kind in the world.

Useful cattle breeds have also been developed from the native cattle of tropical countries, for these are suited to the climate and are better able to withstand many of the diseases of the tropics to which European cattle are susceptible. The Zebu, the native cattle of India, has a long head with drooping ears and a pendulous dewlap, and a hump on the withers where the animal is able to store fat. These cattle, and crosses of them, are used in many tropical climates, and have been imported into the hotter regions of Australia where European cattle do not prosper. The Nellore, another breed of the same humped type, has been exported to the Gulf of Mexico, Northern Australia, and East Africa (*see* ANIMAL FARMING, TROPICAL). Crosses between many other breeds and British and American cattle are also being experimented with successfully.

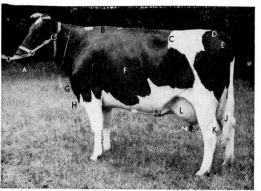

Farmer & Stockbreeder

A BRITISH FRIESIAN COW

A. muzzle; B. withers; C. hook or hip-bone; D. tail head; E. pin-bone; F. barrel; G. dewlap; H. brisket; J. switch; K. hock; L. udder; M. teat; N. milk vein

In Great Britain a young cow is called a heifer, or in the north a quey. She only becomes a cow when she has had her second calf. Calves are heifer calves (females) or bull calves (males), and if a bull calf is not wanted for breeding, he is castrated (*see* STOCK BREEDING), becomes a bullock or steer, and can then be better fattened for beef.

Any cow, whether of dairy, beef, dual-purpose or triple-purpose type (*see* CATTLE BREEDS), will begin to give milk at about the same time as she gives birth to a calf. She may have her first calf when she is about 18 to 20 months old. She gives most milk about a month to 6 weeks after calving, and then gradually less until she goes dry. The time during which she is in milk is called her period of lactation, and on British dairy farms this is about 9 or 10 months. Two or three months after calving she is mated with the bull again and becomes 'in-calf'; she carries her calf for 9 months (the period of gestation), and so, if all has gone well, calves again about a year after her previous calving. Most cows give most milk during the third and fourth lactation, after which there is a gradual decline in yield. A first-rate dairy cow may be kept until she has had ten or a dozen, or even more, calves; but most do not last as long. Single calves at a birth are more common than twins, and more than two at a birth are comparatively rare. The management and care of cattle naturally varies with the purpose for which they are kept, and with the method of calf rearing adopted (*see* CATTLE, CARE OF).

If a farmer has more than a few cows, he may keep a bull to mate with them or make use of artificial insemination. For one or two cows, he may get the use of a neighbour's bull, or he may use artificial insemination. Bulls of different breeds are kept at an artificial insemination station, and their semen, which fertilizes the cows, is distributed to the farms that subscribe to such a scheme, and there injected into the cows. In this way many more cows can be made fertile by fewer bulls, and the A.I. (artificial insemination) stations keep nothing but the very best.

A young bull can be used for breeding (is fit for service) at the age of about 9 months. It is important to handle a bull the right way, gently but firmly, and not to shut him up alone, for otherwise his temper will be spoilt and he will become very dangerous. Even under the best management, however, a bull is not an animal that can be safely played with. Bulls that get good calves should be kept as long as they are fit for service, or until they get too heavy for the cows. When, by results, a bull has been proved to be a good breeder, he is called a proven bull or a proven sire.

In the past, large herds of beef cattle were bred in Britain; but now Britain concentrates much more on dairy farming, and countries such as the western states of the U.S.A. and the South American States, which have a temperate or sub-tropical climate and large stretches of grassland, have become the great cattle producers of the world (*see* CATTLE RANCHES). The U.S.S.R. is a growing cattle country with great possibilities. Of recent years the native

Kalmuck cattle have been crossed with Short-horns to the great improvement of the stock.

See also ANIMAL DISEASES; FEEDING, FARM ANIMALS.
See also Vol. II: CATTLE, WILD.

CATTLE BREEDS. 1. Cattle of some breeds are kept principally to fatten for the butcher: these are known as beef cattle. Some are kept principally to produce milk: these are dairy cattle. Some cattle, however, are bred to produce reasonably good results for either purposes, and these are known as dual-purpose cattle. In some countries cattle are also used as draught animals to draw ploughs and wagons, and can then be described as triple-purpose. When the farmer selects for beef or milk, he is really choosing which way he wishes his cows to turn their food. The whole process of the use of food is called 'metabolism'—the breaking down of food, its digestion, and the building of it up again to form the animal's body. Dairy cows turn a lot of their food into milk and maintain a rather slight body; but the beef cow produces no more milk than is needed to rear her calf, and the rest of her food goes to build a strong skeleton which can carry large muscles (the red meat) and a large amount of fat. Dairy cows, therefore, are finer in bone, thinner in type, lighter in the fore end, and more angular than beef cows.

For the most part cattle breeders have specialized either in beef or dairy breeds, for it is clearly difficult to get the qualities of both at their best in one animal. In some parts of the world, however, it is the custom to breed a type that will provide a good yield of milk and also a good beef carcass.

Farmers do not usually cross one dairy breed with another in order to raise milking capacity: they select perfect specimens within the breed, and keep a herd of pure-bred cows. Occasionally, however, in order to produce more beef, a farmer may cross his dairy cows with a bull of a beef breed, and if this is a Hereford or an Aberdeen Angus, the calves will be of unmistakable appearance: white faced in the first case and polled (hornless) in the second. This 'colour-marks' them, and so prevents the mistake of trying to make the heifers into dairy cows.

Breeders of pedigree beef cattle keep pure breeds; but the producers of fat beasts for beef may use either pure-breds or cross-breds. In a few cases these crosses are of a particularly good type. For example, a white Shorthorn bull crossed with black Galloway or Aberdeen Angus cows produces the famous 'blue-grey', so popular for fattening. Shorthorn bulls are also commonly crossed with Highland cows, and if the cows of this cross are crossed again with an Aberdeen Angus bull, a very hardy, early-maturing beef animal results.

2. DAIRY BREEDS. These cattle have been bred and selected through a long period of years to produce much more milk than is needed to rear a calf. A gallon a day for 5 or 6 months might be enough for the calf—that is, about 170 gallons altogether. But a good dairy cow of to-day has a lactation period of about 10 months, and will yield a total of perhaps 1,000 to 1,200 gallons during this period. Yields as high as 3,000 gallons in one lactation are not unknown. Thus, there is much more milk produced than is needed to rear calves, and it is this surplus that is sold.

(a) *British Friesians.* These are large, black-and-white cattle, and direct descendants of animals imported from Holland. Yields of 2,000 to 3,000 gallons in a lactation are commoner amongst Friesians than amongst other cattle. Friesians in Holland are sometimes red-and-white, and it may have been the red-and-white type which was brought over to England in the 18th century and blended into the Short-horn breed.

(b) *Ayrshires.* As its name implies, this is a Scottish dairy breed, rather fine-boned and with long, upward curving horns, fine at the tip. The cattle are red-and-white or mahogany-and-white, and occasionally even black-and-white, the coloured patches being distinct but not as large or as regular as in the Friesian. The Ayrshire is now popular in many parts of England as well as farther afield in Canada, Scandinavia, and even India. Sweden has made the Ayrshire her national breed of dairy cow (*see* COLOUR PLATE opposite p. 80).

(c) *Kerry.* This is an Irish breed of small black cattle, very hardy and able to live on poor land in windswept places.

(d) *Jerseys.* These are the smaller of the two Channel Island breeds. They range in colour from golden fawn to almost black, and their skin has a distinct yellow colour. Their milk is extremely rich, from 5% to 6% of butter fat being common, as compared with the 3·5% to 4% that is about the average in other breeds.

(e) *Guernseys.* These are the larger of the

Hereford bull   *Hereford Times*

Aberdeen Angus cow   *A. Brown & Co.*

Galloway steer   *Farmer & Stockbreeder*

Welsh cow   *Farmer & Stockbreeder*

Dexter cow   *E. W. Copnall*

Kerry cow   *Sport & General*

BREEDS OF CATTLE

two Channel Island breeds, but are still small compared with Shorthorns or Friesians. They are golden yellow in colour, often with white markings; the skin is very yellow. Guernsey, like Jersey, milk has a high percentage of butter fat, and is usually of a richer yellow colour than the milk of any other British breed. Both Jerseys and Guernseys are widely kept in the south of England, and are common in the United States.

3. BEEF BREEDS. Beef cattle have been specially selected and bred to grow a good carcass and to mature quickly. Wild cattle have strong heavy shoulders, lighter hindquarters and longish legs so that they can fight and move quickly. A good beef beast, on the other hand, lays on fat and muscle evenly all over and has short legs, for the farmer intends that its food should go to building body-weight and as little as possible to be expended in active movement.

The following are the main well-established British beef breeds:

(a) *Beef Shorthorns.* The breed originated in the Teesdale district of Yorkshire, and during the early 18th century was influenced by the newly imported Dutch cows. They became well-known in the mid 18th century as the result of the work of a few farmers who had studied the breeding methods of Robert BAKEWELL (q.v. Vol. V). Some of these farmers concentrated on milking qualities and others on beef qualities, so that gradually there grew up the two types—the Dairy and the Beef Shorthorns. As well as these a Scottish type of beef Shorthorns, mainly the work of Amos Cruikshank (1808–95) in Aberdeenshire, is recognized. These cattle have been exported in large numbers and often at very high prices to the Argentine and other South American countries, and to Canada and the U.S.A. Shorthorns are very adaptable to a variety of conditions, and do well either grazing or kept more intensively. They cross well with native cattle, as has been done, in particular, in the U.S.S.R.

(b) *Herefords.* These handsome cattle are to be found mainly in their own county and in the west of England, though they are also popular abroad. They are deep red in colour with white face and chest, and sometimes with white feet and a white strip running along the top of the neck. They are great grazing cattle and have been much used to stock the ranges of the Americas. The first important improver of the breed was Benjamin Tomkins (1714–89).

(c) *Aberdeen Angus.* These are black in colour and polled. They produce the finest quality beef, and have won the championship at Smithfield (the great beef cattle show) more times than any other breed. The breed comes from the north-east of Scotland, where it is very common. The Aberdeen Angus is small and compact, of rounded form rather than square like the Shorthorn. The 'doddie', as it is called in its own country, is much favoured in beef-producing countries abroad where arable farming has taken the place of the range. The early improvers of this breed were Hugh Watson of Keillour (1769–1865) and William M'Combie of Tillyfour (1805–80).

(d) *Galloways.* This black (occasionally dun), polled breed originated in south-west Scotland and is still mostly found there and in western Ireland. It is a hardy, late-maturing breed, with a heavy coat of woolly hair like that of Highland cattle, and does well in hill country. The 'belted' type has a white middle and black ends.

(e) *Highland Cattle.* This picturesque, long-horned, long-coated breed of cattle, sometimes called Kyloe cattle, is rarely bred outside the Highlands and Islands of Scotland. They are extremely hardy and fitted to a rainy climate, but are the slowest maturing of all British breeds. Attempts to improve them would probably result in making them less hardy. They vary from straw-colour through several shades of red to brindle and black, and are exceptionally docile. Their milk yield is small, but the milk is rich. In Scotland a herd of Highland cattle is always called a 'fold'.

(f) *Sussex.* Oxen of this breed of large beasts were used as draught animals in Sussex until recent times. One Sussex ox is recorded as being 16 hands 2 inches high (1 hand = 4 inches) and weighing 1 ton 15 cwt. 3 qrs. 18 lb. The Sussex has been exported to Africa for both work and grazing, and it stands up well to tropical conditions. Its colour is a deep, rich red.

(g) *North Devons.* These cattle, locally called Red Rubies, are a slightly brighter shade of red than the Sussex cattle. Though mainly kept for beef, a few strains of the breed milk unusually well for cattle of this type.

4. DUAL PURPOSE BREEDS. Many farmers prefer to keep a herd which can be used both for dairy or beef purposes. The heifer calves that show promise can be developed as dairy cows, and the bull calves can be turned into bullocks and fattened.

(*a*) *Dairy Shorthorns*. Despite their name, these are dual-purpose cattle. The breed has a long history of pedigree breeding, and is still very popular because of its dual purpose: the bull calves grow into useful beef bullocks, and such cows as have to be taken out or 'cast' from the dairy herd can also be fattened. Dairy Shorthorns are red, white, red-and-white, and red roan. The breed, besides being found in all parts of England, especially in the north and Midlands, has also been exported to almost every country of the world which has a temperate or subtropical climate.

(*b*) *Welsh Blacks*. These cattle of the mountainous and coastal districts of Wales have horns almost as large and wide-spreading as have Highland cattle. Though mainly kept for fattening on the pastures of the English midlands, where they are called 'Welsh runts', the cows are fairly good milkers.

(*c*) *South Devons*, called locally 'South Hams', are the largest breed of all. The colour is a much lighter red than that of the North Devons, and the cattle are larger boned and less symmetrical.

(*d*) *Dexters*. These cattle are the smallest of all and are black (occasionally red) in colour.

(*e*) *Red Polls*. These are red in colour, and polled. They are popular in many places besides the eastern counties in which they originated.

(*f*) *Lincoln Red Shorthorns*. There are two types of these, one being more 'beefy' than the other, and both being offshoots of the Shorthorns. They are a deep red in colour, and are very common in East Anglia.

The Longhorn and the British White are names for two other breeds of dual-purpose cattle, but herds are now very scarce. The Longhorns are interesting as being the cattle with which the famous Robert Bakewell worked; and the British White are probably the most direct descendants of the once wild cattle of Great Britain.

See also CATTLE; FEEDING, FARM ANIMALS; AGRICULTURAL IMPROVERS; STOCK BREEDING

See also Vol. II: CATTLE, WILD.

See also Vol. VII: DAIRY INDUSTRY; MEAT TRADE.

CATTLE, CARE OF. 1. The management of cattle, especially of dairy animals, is very skilled work. Therefore the cowman has an important job on the farm, and on a large dairy farm is not found doing other work. A dairy cow is a delicate and sensitive creature who will not do her best unless she is rightly handled. The cowman learns to understand and is interested in all her individual likes and dislikes, and she depends on him for the regular daily routine that cows, being creatures of habit, need if they are to do well. All cattle need to be handled very quietly and never to be hurried.

2. COW-HOUSES (byres or shippons). There are several styles of cow-shed, but the following is a usual type. The building is long, with a concrete floor that can easily be washed. It is light and airy and whitewashed. A 5-foot wide causeway runs down the middle with a 2-foot drain on each side. The individual cow-stalls or standings are on the sides, the cows standing with their backs to the central causeway on slightly raised platforms in such a way that most of the manure falls into the drains. The straw, therefore, on the platform is kept comparatively clean and the cow can lie down without getting dirty. A trough of concrete or earthenware at ground level and a hayrack above it at about the height of the cow's nose run the full length of the standings. Each cow is secured in her stall by means of a chain or a metal yoke that encircles her neck. The cows soon get to know their own places in the byre, and when brought in for milking in the evening will usually go automatically to the right stall. Under another system the cows are not brought up to the farm for milking

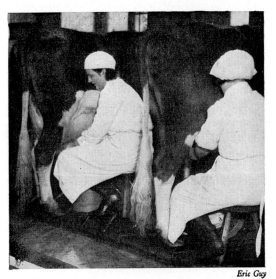

Eric Guy

MILKING COWS BY HAND

but are milked in 'milking-bails' on the field. These movable constructions consist of an open milking-shed and another connecting shed to house the milking-machine. The surrounding fence has an entrance and exit for the cows. Where cows are kept in yards, a 'milking-parlour' is used—that is, a brick or stone building adjoining the yard, generally with stands for four cows at a time.

3. MILKING. Cows are normally milked twice a day, in the early morning and in the evening. Cows with very heavy yields of milk may have to be milked three times a day; but that is not by any means general. The milking hours must be regular, and milking must be done under very clean conditions, not only for the sake of clean milk but also to prevent the spread of disease among the cows (see ANIMAL DISEASES, section 2).

The cows have the hair on their hind quarters clipped short in the autumn so that they are easier to keep clean. They are groomed before milking, and their udders washed. All the milking apparatus is washed, scrubbed, and then scalded or sterilized with steam. The pails are of the covered type, and the milkers wear clean white coats and caps and have scrupulously clean dry hands. Cows are either milked by hand or by a milking machine, the latter being the common method, at least on large dairy farms (see DAIRY MACHINERY). An experienced hand milker can milk eight to ten cows in an hour.

The milker takes his low stool in one hand and his milking-pail in the other. He usually sits on the right-hand side of the cow with his left knee just inside the cow's right hock, the bucket grasped firmly between his knees and his feet tucked back towards the stool. In this position he can protect the bucket, if the cow lifts a hind foot.

The cow has four milking teats which are milked in pairs; the two front ones and then the two hind ones. The milker's right hand holds the far teat and his left hand the near teat. The cow lets her milk down into the teats under stimulus of the action of the milker's fingers. Unless the cow's teats are very small, the milker uses all his fingers to squeeze the teat, at the same time giving it a slight pull towards the bucket. When no more milk comes easily from the teats, the milker 'strips' them, that is, he draws them through the thumb and finger to extract the last drop. This needs to be repeated

several times, for a cow not properly stripped will soon go dry, and these last drops of milk are the richest in butter fat. No one, of course, can learn to milk from a book, but only from practice. A beginner should make his first attempts on a cow near the end of her lactation, for then if the cow goes dry as the result of his inexperienced handling, the loss is less. As soon as the cow is milked, the milk goes from the byre to the dairy, and is passed through a strainer and over a cooler before going into the churn (see DAIRY INDUSTRY, Vol. VII).

A good dairy farmer records the milk yield of his cows on a record sheet in order to find out exactly how much milk each gives. A spring balance graduated in pounds and gallons is, therefore, an essential piece of dairy equipment. A gallon of milk weighs 10·3 lb.—milk being a little heavier than water. This weighing and recording may be done daily or once a week. Yields vary a great deal—from about 500 gallons a year (which is not a good yield) to as much as 2,000–3,000 gallons (which is rare). A herd average of 700 to 1,000 gallons is satisfactory.

4. FEEDING. A cow needs food for maintaining her present condition (her maintenance ration), and food for turning into milk, or in the case of beef cattle, into flesh (her production ration). A dairy cow needs on an average about 3 lb. of 'dry food' daily for each cwt. of bodyweight, and this, in winter when there is but little grass, includes about $3\frac{1}{2}$ lb. of concentrated food (such as oats, cow cake, and bean meal) for each gallon of milk. Thus a 10 cwt. cow giving $3\frac{1}{2}$ gallons of milk a day in January or February might have the following daily diet: 14 lb. of hay; 56 lb. swedes; 14 lb. concentrates. This represents about 30 lb. dry food in all, for all the foods contain some water, and foods such as swedes are largely water. The same cow giving 2 gallons of milk in the autumn, when she is still out at grass, might have: 7 lb. of hay; 30 lb. of kale; $3\frac{1}{2}$ lb. of concentrates. The rest of her food would be taken in the form of about 75 to 80 lb. of grass.

The concentrates might be a mixture of 3 parts crushed oats, 2 parts palm kernel cake, 1 part bean meal, and 1 part cotton cake, with about $1\frac{1}{2}\%$ of bone-forming mineral such as bone meal (calcium phosphate), and a little salt. This might be mixed with about 1 lb. of molasses per cow.

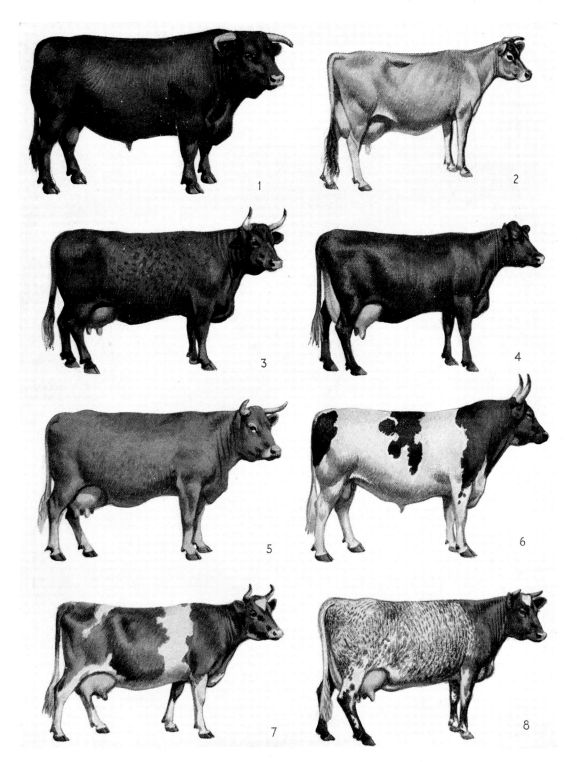

BREEDS OF CATTLE

1. Sussex bull.   2. Jersey cow.   3. Devon cow.   4. Red Poll cow.   5. South Devon cow.   6. Ayrshire bull.
7. Guernsey cow.   8. Dairy Shorthorn cow.

Water-colour by C. F. Tunnicliffe

This general average diet has to be varied, naturally, according to the time of year and the foodstuffs available. Silage, for instance, is often used instead of part of the hay and roots. The food must also be appetizing, and many cows have their likes and dislikes (see FEEDING, FARM ANIMALS). Two feeds a day are usually given, with an additional feed of hay in the evening when the animals are not out at night. Milking cows need a lot of water to drink, and therefore should always have fresh water within reach.

5. CALVING. A cow has her calf about 283 days (that is, just under 9½ months) after mating to the bull, or 'service'. She begins to 'spring', that is, her bag begins to swell, about a fortnight before the birth of the calf. The cowman can gauge fairly accurately the arrival of the calf by the condition of the cartilages or 'gristles' running on either side of the tail to the pin bones. In order to make a passage for the calf between the pin bones these become soft and sink in the middle. The cow is taken from her stall and put in a loose box, with plenty of straw bedding, a week or two before the calf is due to be born. At calving time the cowman keeps an eye on her, and if she is in difficulties he can often help to get the calf's shoulders through by taking its forefeet and pulling them in a downward and outward direction as the cow strains.

There are different methods of managing cow and calf during the first few days of a calf's life. Some cowmen leave the two together for 3 or 4 days, but others take the calf away as soon as it is born, so that the cow never realizes its existence, and therefore does not fret for it. With the first method the cow dries and warms the calf by licking it; with the second, the cowman must rub it down vigorously with straw. In either case the cow is given a restorative oatmeal drink, and ½ hour after calving about ¼ gallon of milk is taken from her. This first milk, the 'colostrum' or 'biestings' is deep yellow or even pink in colour and contains ingredients that are essential to the calf's welfare. About 3 hours later the cow is partly milked again, and this is repeated later. Not until after a day or so should she be milked right out, for if the cow is milked out too soon she may get milk fever, fall down, and lose consciousness. For the first 2 or 3 days after calving she should be lightly fed, but after that she receives a normal milking diet. Her milk yield does not reach its maximum until 4 to 6 weeks after calving.

A. Voysey

FEEDING A CALF

6. CARE OF CALF. Sometimes the calf is allowed to remain with its mother and be suckled by her; but usually with dairy cattle it is removed and brought up by hand. The calf pen to which it is taken is an enclosure some 5 feet square with sides 4 feet high. The first thing to do is to give the calf about a quart of the colostrum, warmed to a temperature of 101° F., in a bucket. This is often a slow business, for the calf's instinct is to turn its head upwards to the udder and suck, and it has to be taught to put its head down into the bucket and drink. The cowman for a time has to use his finger as a sham teat to encourage the calf to take the milk. For the first week the little calf has three or four meals a day, and then it changes to two of about ½ gallon each. If the milk is too cold or too warm, or given in too great quantities, or irregularly, or if the calf pen is dirty and harbours germs, the calf may suffer from 'scouring', a form of diarrhoea. Calves are happier if they have company of their own kind, and even if in separate pens they should have a chance to see each other. After 2 weeks the calf starts on some solid food—some soft hay given, perhaps, in a wide mesh string bag. At 4 weeks it will start drinking water, and after 4 months it can be changed from whole milk to skim milk with some cod-liver oil. About this time, too, if the weather is warm, the calf can go out to grass in the middle of the day. Some calves after the first month are reared on calf meal instead of milk, but they generally do not prosper so well. Bull calves intended for breeding may be suckled until they are just on a year old. Cows of some beef breeds sometimes do not give enough milk to give the bull calf the best start, and he may also have the milk of a second cow. Calves that are reared by their mothers do not need nearly so much care. They can be out with the cows both day and night, even in cold weather. The more they are out, the freer from disease are they likely to be.

7. MANAGEMENT OF BEEF CATTLE. The farmer wants to bring his beef cattle as quickly as possible to a weight at which they can be profitably sold. Methods of doing this vary considerably according to the district and the food available; but the general principles are the same.

The best beef comes from fattened steers and heifers of beef breeds (see CATTLE BREEDS, section 3); but older bulls and cows of all breeds are fattened if they are no longer wanted for dairy or breeding purposes. Calves for fattening are often reared in hilly country and brought to the lowlands in the spring or early summer (see FARMING DISTRIBUTION).

The farmer usually buys 'stores', that is, cattle not yet fattened, from a dealer, and fattens them either on grass or in yards. During the summer it is possible to fatten beasts, at the rate of one beast to the acre, entirely on 'fattening pastures', which carry grass of high quality, or on LEYS (q.v.). If the grass alone is not enough, the beasts are given supplementary rations of starchy foods such as barley, crushed oats, and sugar-beet pulp. Beasts that are not ready by the end of the summer are brought into covered or partly covered yards, where they are fed on hay, straw, roots, silage, corn, and cake. An animal which is doing well should, towards the end, be putting on weight at the rate of about 2 lb. a day.

The management of beef cattle on the big cattle farms of North and South America is described in CATTLE RANCHES (q.v.).

CATTLE RANCHES. The early settlers in North and South America brought with them their cattle from Europe, and at first managed them in enclosed fields as they had been accustomed to do in their homelands. But it was soon found that over large areas of the United States, Mexico, Argentina, and the neighbouring coun-

tries, it was possible to raise great numbers of beef cattle on 'open range', and so cattle ranches were developed. Cattle throve so well on the great open GRASSLANDS (q.v. Vol. III), the prairies of North America and the pampas in South America, that when animals escaped, they formed wild herds which were hunted by both the settlers and the native Indians.

At first the cattle ranchers grazed their stock over unclaimed land; but as time went on, each rancher acquired the ownership of his own ranch, with definite boundaries, and built a ranch house as his headquarters. But as the country was wild and unfenced, the ranchers could hope to keep the herds of cattle safe only by patrolling the country constantly on horseback; therefore every ranch owner employed a staff of skilful riders known as cow-hands or cowboys. Cowboys are called *vaqueros* in Mexico and *gauchos* in South America.

Each rancher marked his own cattle with a brand, that is, an indelible scar, in the shape of a letter of the alphabet or some similar device, which was burnt on the hide of the young calves. From time to time the herds were rounded up and driven to a fenced enclosure near the ranch house, known as a *corral*, where they could be roped with a *lasso* or *lariat* and caught for such purposes as branding. The cowboys were experts at 'cutting out' or separating from the herd just those animals that were needed.

Each ranch owner aimed to keep on his land as large a herd of cows as there was grass to feed, together with enough bulls for breeding purposes. Every year the surplus young males, known as steers, which had reached 2 or 3 years old, were sent to market to be slaughtered for their beef, hides, and other products. The cowboys, working under a 'trail boss', often had to drive the animals over distances of several hundred miles from outlying ranches to the nearest big town or railway. A wagon, driven by the camp cook, carried their stores and provisions. Each day they drove their herds of steers, often a thousand strong, for about 20 miles, allowing them to graze and drink on the way; each night they made camp, with one or two men on patrol to prevent the beasts straying and to look out for attacks by Indians or cattle thieves, known as 'rustlers'. Every cowboy, therefore, carried a revolver or rifle. But though there were risks, the rewards of ranching were great, for a valu-

Ewing Galloway

CUTTING OUT A STEER FROM THE HERD ON A RANCH IN ARIZONA

able herd, from which hundreds of beef cattle could be sold each year, could be built up with very little capital. A big ranch often extended over 100,000 acres—about 150 square miles; but as the animals depended for their food on wild grasses and scrub which are not very nourishing, even these enormous ranches could keep only a few thousand cattle through the winter.

By the end of the 19th century, as cattle increased in value with the growth in population, and as cheap fencing material became available, the ranchers found that it paid them better to fence in their ranges; and there are now very few real open ranges left. Barbed wire fences strung for miles across the country make it possible to control the grazing of the herds with fewer men than were needed in open country, and fewer losses from straying or theft. It is also possible to control the breeding of the herds, and to improve the stock by bringing in selected bulls (*see* STOCK BREEDING). By feeding hay, silage, cottonseed cake, and other kinds of fodder to the herds, larger stocks can be kept through the winter, and steers can be fattened for market more quickly. The coming of railways and motor roads ended the old trailing days, and animals can be brought to the markets rapidly and without loss of weight or condition. Ranch-

ing has now become as highly developed a branch of farming as is cattle farming in other parts of the world (*see* CATTLE, CARE OF). But although the ranches are now based on fixed enclosures or 'paddocks', a good deal of open range grazing still goes on in the summer months, and cowboys, in their picturesque costume of broad-brimmed hat, check shirt, and broad leggings or 'chaps', still ride through the wilder uplands and forests of the western states of the U.S.A. to guard and control their herds. The motor-car, however, is now used a great deal, and very often the cowboy takes his horse the first part of the journey in a horse-box trailer, and rides the last part.

The headquarters of a modern ranch consist of the owner's house—usually a roomy single-story wooden building—living and sleeping quarters for the cow-hands, stables for the horses, and barns for storing cattle fodder and equipment. It is sited in a fertile and accessible part of the range, where there is a good water supply. Close by are the *corrals* or stock yards into which the cattle can be driven, and the 'feed lots' or enclosed pastures in which they are kept for winter feeding or fattening. Often a part of the ranch is cultivated for raising fodder, but most of it remains as natural grazing.

In the early days of open range grazing the

type of cattle needed were hardy animals able to thrive on poor feed in country with limited water supplies. In the 19th century these characteristics were found in the Texas Longhorn, descended from a mixture of Spanish and English strains that run wild in Texas. It has horns with a 6-foot span, and is very tough and active; but compared with modern breeds it is a poor beef producer. Its place has been taken by beef breeds developed in Britain, especially the Hereford, the Shorthorn, and the Aberdeen Angus (*see* CATTLE BREEDS). In the early days cattle took 4 years or more to become beef on the unimproved grasslands of North and South America; but now that lucerne, or alfalfa (*see* LEGUMINOUS CROPS), and other crops have been introduced, and more is known about concentrated feeding (*see* CATTLE, CARE OF), the young steers and heifers are heavy enough to be ready for slaughter by the time they are about 18 months old. Recently American ranchers have introduced the humped Zebu or Brahman cattle from India, as they find that crosses between these and English cattle thrive exceptionally well.

See also CATTLE.

See also Vol. III: GRASSLANDS.

CAULIFLOWERS, *see* CABBAGE CROPS.

CEDAR TREES, *see* TREES, CONIFEROUS; ORNAMENTAL TREES.

CELERY. This popular vegetable can be used raw as a salad or cooked as a hot vegetable. Celery has been developed from the wild celery, *Apium graveolens*, a biennial plant of the carrot family, which is fairly common in marshy places in Britain, generally near the sea-shore. The old name, 'sellery', is probably a corruption of the Greek *selinon*. The Romans cultivated celery but seem to have regarded it as a kind of parsley, hence the generic name *Apium*.

There are three types of cultivated celery—the common or green celery, the stalks of which have to be 'blanched', that is, kept away from the light so that they grow white and tender enough to eat; the yellow-stalked, 'self-blanching' Doré celery of French origin, which does not need to be blanched; and the turnip-rooted celery called celeriac, of which the roots, not the stalks, are eaten. The common celery has many excellent white and red varieties, the outer leaf-stalks of the red showing a reddish coloration.

There are not many varieties of the self-blanching type; Golden Self-blanching is more dwarf in growth than Improved Golden Self-blanching.

Celery is grown for market mainly in fen-land and moss-land districts, for it thrives in a moist fertile soil. In gardens the seeds are sown under glass in February or March and then pricked out into boxes or prepared beds in frames. In May or June, when the seedlings are about 6 inches high, they are transplanted into trenches which are well-manured and 9 inches or so deep. Both single and double (staggered) rows are used, the plants being spaced 6 to 9 inches apart. The celery is blanched by piling up the earth round the stems as the plants grow, beginning when they are about 12 inches high. 'Earthing up' is usually done three or sometimes four times, but before the first earthing, the leaf stalks are loosely tied and wrapped up in brown paper to keep them clean. Common celery is ready for use in September and is available throughout the winter until February. If well earthed up, no protection is needed during the winter: indeed, cold weather is said to improve the quality of celery.

Self-blanching celery is not grown in trenches but in well-manured flat beds, 6 to 10 feet in width. The plants are transplanted 9 to 10 inches apart each way, and when fully grown they have spread so that they have completely filled up the bed. They respond well to a quick-

Royal Horticultural Society

PLANTING OUT CELERY PLANTS IN A TRENCH

acting nitrogenous fertilizer together with water as required. This kind of celery becomes ready for use in August, but does not last long after the winter frosts begin.

Celeriac forms a fleshy rootstock about the size of a large turnip. The leaf-stalks are bitter and cannot be eaten. Celeriac seed is sown in March under glass or April in the open, and the plants are transplanted during May and June in rows 18 inches apart, with the plants spaced 12 to 18 inches in the rows. It is available throughout the winter from October onwards.

The Celery Fly, the maggots of which tunnel in the leaves, is the most serious pest of celery (*see* Fly Pests). The fungus disease, Leaf Spot, attacks the leaves of celery, producing small brown spots and, later, brown dry areas (*see* Plant Diseases). Both Celery Fly and Celery Leaf Spot can be controlled by spraying.

CEREAL CROPS, *see* Barley; Maize; Millet; Oats; Rice; Rye; Wheat.

CHERRIES. This fruit is said to have originated in Asia Minor and to have been brought to Europe by the Romans in 68 B.C. Cherries have been used for centuries not only as dessert fruit but also for making Liqueurs (q.v. Vol. XI) such as Maraschino, Kirsch, and Cherry Brandy. In Britain they are grown especially in the orchards of Kent, in the Home Counties, and in the west midlands. They are grown on a much larger scale in other European countries, in particular Czechoslovakia. There are two main kinds of cherry, sweet and sour.

1. Sweet Cherries. These do best on a really deep, well-drained loam, containing plenty of lime, and do not grow well on clay soils. In orchards they are grown as standard trees in grass, and become very large; in gardens they are sometimes trained as 'fans' on high walls. Their rootstocks are generally wild cherry seedlings, called 'mazards', dug up in the woods, raised from seed, or raised from selected stocks by layering (*see* Fruit Propagation).

Many varieties of sweet cherries cannot fertilize their own fruit, and therefore a single cherry-tree will probably produce no fruit. Cherry orchards must be planned to allow for cross-pollination. As cherry-trees flower early and their prolific blossoming needs a great deal of pollination, the chances of a good crop are much greater if the orchard is protected from the

East Malling Research Station
CHERRY TREES IN BLOSSOM

cold winds that prevent the bees working (*see* Fertilization). The orchard, also, should be on high ground where the April and May frosts, which may damage the blossoms, are less likely to be severe. Where possible, early, mid-season, and late varieties should be planted in groups to save moving the tall picking-ladders more than necessary.

The soil around newly planted trees is kept cultivated for the first 5 or 6 years; but after that grass seeds are sown, and the whole orchard remains under grass. If this is regularly grazed by sheep or geese, the animals' droppings help to feed the soil; if the grass is mown it should be allowed to lie and rot, for this also helps to feed the soil. Cherries benefit from a generous manuring with nitrogen, potash, and phosphates (*see* Artificial Fertilizers). In early years the main branches are pruned in order to make a shapely tree; but, once the framework is formed, only dead or crossing branches are cut out, and this is done after the fruit has been picked. Cherries are picked into sack-lined baskets, and sent to market in 12-lb. chip baskets or cardboard cartons, and in half-bushel baskets.

The chief insect pests of cherries are caterpillars, especially of the Winter moth and Mottled Umber moth which can badly damage whole orchards (*see* BUTTERFLY AND MOTH PESTS). Cherry Black Fly is also a menace (*see* APHID PESTS). Cherry diseases are bacterial canker, brown rot fungus, and silver leaf (*see* PLANT DISEASES).

Among the best varieties of black cherries are Early Rivers; Roundel and Waterloo (mid-season); and Gaucher, Bradbourne Black, and Noble (late). Among the best varieties of white cherries are Elton and Frogmore (early); Kentish Bigarreau (mid-season); and Napoleon and Florence (late).

2. SOUR OR 'RED' CHERRIES. This group includes the Morellos, Kentish and Flemish, and the Duke Cherries. All are mainly used for cooking, bottling, and canning, and for making liqueurs and brandy cherries, and are only sweet enough for eating raw when they are very ripe. They like the same soil conditions as the sweet cherries, and are grafted on the same kinds of rootstocks. They may be grown in the form of a bush or standard, in grass orchards or in plantations. Morellos can be grown in gardens as fan trees trained on a north wall. When harvested, the fruit should be cut from the tree with scissors.

See also FRUIT-GROWING; FRUIT PROPAGATION.

CHICKENS, *see* POULTRY.

CHICORY, *see* SALAD CROPS, section 3.

CHIVES, *see* ONION CROPS.

CHRYSANTHEMUM. 1. FLORIST'S CHRYSANTHEMUM. Under the generic name Chrysanthemum are included several very distinct races of garden plants, most important of which are the 'florist's chrysanthemums' (*C. sinense*). These flowers were highly developed in China and Japan before they were introduced to Europe in the latter half of the 17th century. Since about 1800 new varieties have made their appearance nearly every year. The name comes from two Greek words, *chrysos*, gold, and *anthemon*, flower.

The National Chrysanthemum Society have grouped these different forms of chrysanthemums in twenty-four main sections, the principal division being between indoor varieties, which must be brought into flower under glass, and outdoor varieties, which will flower in the open. The distinction is not always clear, however, for indoor varieties are best grown in the open throughout the summer, and outdoor varieties benefit from the protection of a frame or greenhouse throughout the winter. But these terms refer to the place where the plants will flower and not necessarily where they are to be grown.

Chrysanthemums are grouped according to whether they are grown for exhibition or decoration; according to the relative size of the flowers; whether the petals curve inwards (incurved varieties) or curve outwards (reflexed varieties); and sometimes also by special forms of flower, such as spidery, pompon, anemone-centred, and single.

Chrysanthemums range in colour from white and pale pink to crimson, from pale yellow to orange, and from light bronze to chestnut. There are no blue chrysanthemums, though mauve-pink is common.

They vary in height from about one to 7 feet, and their flowering time lasts from July to January. One or two varieties can even be induced to flower in late spring or early summer. No variety that flowers after 30 September is likely to be satisfactory as an outdoor chrysanthemum in a cool climate such as that of Britain.

Chrysanthemums are normally propagated by cuttings, with the exception of certain single flowered races (Charm chrysanthemums) which are usually raised from seed. New varieties are either obtained from seed or as 'sports' (mutants) from existing varieties (*see* PLANT BREEDING). The chrysanthemum is particularly prone to produce colour sports, which will, as a rule, resemble their parent in every respect except colour. Many valuable new varieties have arisen in this way.

For propagating outdoor chrysanthemums, a few plants of each variety are lifted in the autumn and placed in a greenhouse or frame. Cuttings are then taken from these plants, after which they are discarded. In sheltered places and in the case of some very hardy varieties, such as the Korean chrysanthemums, the plants are allowed to remain outdoors all the winter and are then lifted, split up into small pieces, and replanted in the spring. Cuttings are prepared from young shoots at practically any time of the year, December to March being the most usual

Amateur Gardening

MARGUERITE OR PARIS DAISY   'INCURVED' CHRYSANTHEMUM   ANNUAL CHRYSANTHEMUM

season. The shoot is cut off when 2 or 3 inches in length, the base is cut cleanly through just below a joint, the lower leaves are removed, and the shoot is planted in sandy soil in a greenhouse or propagating frame. A steady temperature of 60° F. will make roots form quickly. When rooted, the cuttings are potted singly and either planted outdoors in late spring or moved into larger pots as necessary. These pots are stood out of doors from late May to late September, when they are brought back into the greenhouse. Pot plants need careful watering throughout.

To get large flowers gardeners often reduce the number of stems formed by each plant, and then disbud the stems so that each stem carries only one flower. To get the very largest flower heads, 8 inches or more in diameter, only one flower to a plant may be allowed; but in general the plant will carry from three to a dozen heads according to the variety and the purpose for which the blooms are grown. When no restriction of flowers is practised, the blooms are borne in sprays.

2. OTHER RACES OF CHRYSANTHEMUMS. As well as these 'florist's chrysanthemums', there are several other species and groups of hybrids grown in the garden, generally as hardy herbaceous PERENNIALS (q.v.). Particularly valuable are the many varieties of *Chrysanthemum maximum* and *C. Leucanthemum*, known by the common names of shasta daisies, moon daisies, and ox-eye daisies. These vary from 2 to 4 feet in height, and have showy white flowers which may be single with a yellow centre, or double and white throughout. They will thrive in any ordinary soil and open

position, and can be increased by dividing the old roots in spring. Most are excellent as cut flowers. Flowers of this species, such as ox-eye daisies and feverfew, are also very troublesome WEEDS (q.v.).

Chrysanthemum rubellum, a species closely related to the florist's chrysanthemums, is a perennial 2½ to 3 feet in height which produces single mauve-pink flowers in July and August. It has been crossed with florist's varieties to give a very hardy, free-flowering type of garden chrysanthemum which may be treated like florist's chrysanthemums of the Korean type. Another useful species is *C. uliginosum*, a hardy perennial growing 5 to 6 feet high and producing single white moon-daisy flowers in September.

Pyrethrums, also, are members of the chrysanthemum group. They are hardy perennials, making a tuft of fine, ferny leaves from which the 2-foot flower stems appear in May and June and sometimes again in August. There are single and double flowered forms in colours ranging from white and pale pink to crimson.

The familiar single white 'marguerite' (*C. frutescens*) used for bedding, window-boxes, hanging baskets, and such purposes, is also a chrysanthemum. It needs greenhouse protection in winter as frost will kill it.

There are also annual chrysanthemums, grown each year from seed, which have single or double flowers, of various colours, often with a strong band of crimson or maroon against a lighter base. They are hardy and may be sown in spring or early autumn where they are to flower, and then thinned to 1 foot apart. Autumn-sown plants will flower in June and July, spring-sown plants in July and August.

See also HERBACEOUS BORDER; GREENHOUSE PLANTS.

CITRUS FRUITS. 1. These include oranges, lemons, grapefruit, limes, citrons, and a number of other less well-known fruits which are cultivated throughout the warmer parts of the world. The original home of the citrus fruits is Asia, where they have been grown since very early times, and from where the various species were introduced into the Mediterranean countries, and then into other parts of the world. They are now grown for export on a large scale in most of the Mediterranean countries, the U.S.A. (especially Florida and California), many of the West Indian islands, Brazil and Argentina, and the Union of South Africa. More citrus fruits are exported than any other fruit, and of course a great quantity is also consumed in the countries where they are grown. Citrus fruits are an important food, and they have also many byproducts, such as oil essences from glands in the rind (see OILS, VEGETABLE, Vol. VII) and pectin, which is extracted from the pith.

Citrus fruits grow for the most part on low trees which, even when mature, do not usually exceed 8 to 15 feet in height. They have smooth, darkish green, shiny leaves, the size and shape of which vary with different species. Citrus fruits have an outer rind of varying thickness and appearance, and an inner juicy pulp containing sugar, citric acid, and other constituents. The juice of citrus fruits is rich in vitamins. Some species, in particular oranges and grapefruit, have been greatly improved by selective breeding.

All species can be grown from seed, but as the flowers are cross-fertilized, it is difficult to ensure that the seedling plants will be true to type. Consequently, in all important producing areas, oranges, grapefruit, and lemons are mainly propagated by budding on to hardy and vigorous stocks, such as sour orange, rough lemon, or pomela (see FRUIT PROPAGATION).

2. ORANGES. The Sweet Orange, *Citrus aurantium*, the most important species of citrus fruit, was introduced into Europe in the 14th century, and from it have been developed such familiar varieties as Jaffa, Valencia, Joppa, Blood, and Washington Navel oranges. The sweet orange grows to greatest perfection in the sub-tropics; it thrives under really tropical conditions but

E. N. A.

AN ORANGE GROVE IN CALIFORNIA

the fruit is often coarse and thick-skinned, especially when the rainfall is high, and remains green even when ripe. It grows best in regions with a moderate rainfall of 30 to 40 inches, and a short mild winter period, as in the Mediterranean region or in Florida or California. In these climates natural rainfall is often supplemented by IRRIGATION (q.v.). Good drainage is essential.

Trees growing in good conditions are planted about 20 feet apart. They begin to bear when about 4 years old and are in their prime at 10 to 12 years. Good orange-trees require little pruning beyond removing superfluous or damaged branches. Potash and phosphoric acid are used as fertilizers. When in full bearing, good trees yield from 400 to 600 fruit a year, though much heavier yields have been reached.

Mandarin or Tangerine oranges, *Citrus nobilis*, are said to have originated in Indo-China. The trees are somewhat smaller and more compact than the sweet orange-trees. The fruit is small and flattened, with a thin rind which separates easily from the pulp, and a very sweet juice. There are a number of varieties, including not only the mandarin or tangerine but also the King orange, the Satsuma orange of Japan, the Nagpur orange of India, and the Tizon orange of the Philippines. They are extensively grown not only in the East but also in parts of the Mediterranean region, in Florida, and elsewhere.

The sour Orange, or Seville Orange, *Citrus*

bigaradia, the best orange for making marmalade, is grown in parts of the Mediterranean region. The fruit is large and yellow, with a bitter flavour. Closely related to it is the Bergamot orange, mainly grown in southern Italy, and used for the production of Oil of Bergamot. The Kumquat is a small, round orange fruit, extensively grown in China and Japan, and used for pickling and preserving.

3. LEMONS. The lemon, *Citrus limon*, is probably a native of India or China, and was introduced into Europe fairly early. It is extensively grown in southern Europe, especially in Spain and Sicily, and, more recently, in California. The fruit, which is very acid, is mainly used for flavouring and for making drinks. The rind yields a valuable oil essence, and is also made into candied lemon peel. The lemon-tree is low-growing, with a tendency to throw out long straggling branches, which need to be cut back to encourage fruit-producing side shoots. It is usually propagated by budding or layering. Like the sweet orange, it does best under sub-tropical or warm temperate conditions, and the fruit is inclined to be coarse and pithy when

grown in the tropics. There are a number of varieties, Eureka, Spanish, and Villa Franca being well-known examples. Lemon juice contains large quantities of citric acid, and in Sicily calcium citrate is made from it. This, and also concentrated lemon juice, are used in making citric acid, though much of the citric acid of commerce is now made from molasses by a fermentation process (*see* ACIDS, Vol. VII).

4. LIMES. The lime, *Citrus acida*, is a small spiny tree grown in all tropical countries for its acid, juicy fruit, which are used in place of lemons. They are considerably smaller than lemons, and vary in shape from egg-shaped to almost round, according to the variety. The juice is richer in citric acid than lemon juice, and from the rind, which is thinner than that of most citric fruits, a valuable oil essence is distilled. Limes are grown commercially in some of the West Indian islands, especially in Trinidad, Jamaica, Dominica, and Montserrat, and also on the Gold Coast of West Africa, where the extraction of lime juice and lime oils are important industries.

5. POMELOS. The pomelo, *Citrus grandis*, also

Paul Popper

AN ORANGE PLANTATION IN PALESTINE

The trees are irrigated by running water into the square basins around each tree

known as shaddock, is the largest of all the citrus fruits. There are many varieties, the largest of which are as big as a man's head, and weigh 10 lb. or more. The fruit has a very thick rind, and the pulp, which is pink to yellow in colour, is variable in quality, usually being sticky and sometimes too acid to be eaten. It is used as a food only in tropical countries where it grows.

6. GRAPEFRUIT. The grapefruit, *Citrus paradisi*, is of uncertain origin, but is probably derived from the Pomelo. Its name may come from the fact that the fruit are borne in clusters like grapes. The grapefruit resembles a large orange in shape, is lemon yellow in colour when ripe, and contains a very juicy pulp, pale yellow or pink in colour. It has a slightly bitter flavour. Of recent years its popularity has enormously increased, and large numbers are exported from California, Florida, South Africa, Palestine, and the West Indies. It is grown in much the same way as the orange, being propagated mainly by budding. A number of improved varieties have been produced, some of which are seedless. Among the most popular are the Marsh Seedless, Triumph, Connor's Prolific, and Pernambuco. The fruit is generally exported whole, but it is also canned, and the juice used for making fruit drinks.

7. CITRON. The citron, *Citrus medica*, was the first of the citrus fruits to be introduced into Europe. It grows on a small tree cultivated widely in the Mediterranean region. The fruit is large and usually round or oval, 4 to 6 inches in diameter. There are many varieties: the 'fingered citron' resembles a man's hand with the fingers bent upwards. The fruit is grown for its thick rind which is preserved in sugar and used in marmalade or as candied peel.

See also TROPICAL FRUITS; OIL-BEARING PLANTS, Section 2.

CLIMBING PLANTS, GARDEN. 1.

The true climbing plants secure themselves to their supports in various ways: by aerial roots that fasten themselves to the surface (ivy and climbing hydrangeas); by leaves that have adhesive disks which grip the wall (virginia creeper); by young growth which, as it grows, twines around its support (honeysuckle, wistaria, and jasmine); by leafstalks which twist round the support (clematis and nasturtiums); by special climbing tendrils (vines and sweet peas); or by thorns which hook themselves to the support (roses and brambles). These climbing devices are more fully described and illustrated in Volume II (*see* CLIMBING PLANTS).

Garden climbers are grown mainly to adorn walls, to grow up pergolas or trellis-work screens, or as scramblers on growing shrubs or trees. Their ornamental value may depend on a comparatively short display of bright and attractive flowers, or a more subdued, all-the-year round decoration of foliage.

The climbing plants themselves may be divided into those that will climb a wall without the need for ties to keep them up; those that will climb and maintain themselves provided that a trellis or network of wires is fixed to the wall; and those that, even with a trellis, require tying-in if they are to remain secure. Wire trellis-work can be made by fixing the wires to staples, or 'vine-eyes', in horizontal lines, in squares, or fanwise from a point at the base.

2. SELF-CLINGING CLIMBERS. To mask an ugly wall or shed, no plants are as efficient or as little trouble as the ivies. The common ivy grows neatly, close to the surface of the wall, and has great vigour; and there are many other varieties with leaves of various sizes and shapes, different shades of green, and markings in silvery-grey, white, yellow, and red. The virginia creepers and 'Japanese ivies' (usually listed under *Ampelopsis*), have much variety in size and pattern of leaves, and many have vivid autumn colours.

Hydrangea petiolaris is a strong-growing, hardy climbing hydrangea with white flowers in June, which grows well on a north wall. A not quite so hardy variety, *H. integerrima*, is an evergreen with smaller white flowers in large clusters, which prefers moist soil and a shady wall. Related to the hydrangea is *Schizophragma hydrangeoides*, which clings by aerial rootlets and whose 'flower' is really a collection of small fertile flowers surrounded by yellowish-white, bract-like, single petals.

None of these climbing plants ordinarily needs any support.

3. CLIMBERS REQUIRING TRELLIS OR TIES. For house walls, the climbing forms of hybrid tea ROSES (q.v.) together with certain hybrids such as 'Mermaid', 'Reve d'Or', and 'William Allen Richardson', are very successful climbers. For open trellises, pergolas, and pillars, the rambler roses are best, hybrid tea climbers being too stiff for such use. The ramblers tend to become diseased if grown close to a wall.

Clematis are best grown on trellis-work affixed to walls, or the more vigorous kinds may be allowed to climb up trees or bushes. The many varieties of large-flowered hybrids range in colours from blue to crimson through pink and mauve. There are also white varieties, and varieties with a coloured bar on white petals. Some have extremely large flowers. The great number of garden clematis include the rampant white, spring flowering *Clematis montana* and its rose-pink variety; *C. tangutica*, with yellow, chinese-lantern flowers and silky seed-heads; *C. Armandii*, an evergreen with masses of small white flowers in spring; and the varieties of *C. texensis*, with red, urn-shaped flowers.

Campsis radicans is the wild, hardy trumpet vine of North America, with small orange-red flowers in late summer, which does well on a warm wall; *C. grandiflora* is less hardy, with huge orange-scarlet flowers which have the disadvantage that they do not open early enough in cool summers. A hardy hybrid of these two species, *C. Tagliabuana*, has the best qualities of both its parents, 'Mme Galen' being the finest variety. Another evergreen trumpet vine, *Bignonia capreolata*, also has orange-red flowers.

The Wistarias, which are better tied in than allowed to twine, grow very rampantly unless pruned annually. The Chinese Wistaria has compact, blue-violet racemes opening all at once in May, whereas the Japanese Wistaria, a still hardier species, has long, slender racemes opening gradually from the base. Both species have white varieties. Another species, *W. venusta*, has white flowers a month later.

The common white sweet-scented summer jasmine (*Jasminum officinale*) needs careful training fanwise to prevent its growing into a tangle. *J. nudiflorum* is the yellow winter-flowering species, and *J. Mesnyi* is an exquisite but less hardy species with large yellow flowers in May.

The honeysuckles grow such thick, strong twining stems, that, if allowed to grow up trees or shrubs, they choke the host-plant by preventing the expansion of its stem. There are evergreen species, such as *Lonicera japonica Halliana* with fragrant cream-coloured flowers; and semi-evergreens, such as the Scarlet Trumpet Honeysuckle (*L. Brownii fuchsioides*) and *L. etrusca* with fragrant cream flowers tinged with purple. *L. tragophylla*, with its large golden-yellow blooms, is a good species for moist, semi-shaded places.

Some flowering climbers will succeed only on

Amateur Gardening

PASSION FLOWER, MORNING GLORY, and CLEMATIS
(*C. texensis*)

Amateur Gardening

CHINESE TRUMPET VINE

warm, sheltered walls—such as a climbing night-shade (*Solanum jasminoides*) with abundant potato-like bluish-purple flowers with yellow centres, and the Passion Flower (*Passiflora caerula*), a vigorous climber with large blue and white flowers of curious design, followed by egg-shaped, orange-coloured fruits. Others are more hardy, such as the Dutchman's Pipe (*Aristolochia Sipho*), a vigorous large-leaved climber with oddly shaped tubular flowers, and *Celastrus articulatus*, which gives a good winter effect with its showy scarlet seeds.

For covering unsightly objects, such as a garden shed, the Russian Vine (*Polygonum Balds-chuanicum*) is a very strong deciduous climber which produces large clusters of small white flowers in late summer. Another rampant climber is a vine, *Vitis Coignetiae*, the huge, shield-shaped leaves of which develop very fine autumn colours. The common hop (*Humulus Lupulus*) is often used for similar purposes, as is its yellow-leaved variety, *aureus*.

The Flame Flower (*Tropaeolum speciosum*), a relative of the nasturtium, has exquisitely shaped red flowers, and once established is magnificent as a scrambler among bushes or on a trellis.

4. ANNUAL CLIMBERS. There are a few truly annual climbers, the best known being the SWEET PEA (q.v.). Morning Glory (*Ipomoea purpurea*), the stinging but beautiful *Caiophora laterita* (usually listed as *Loasa aurantiaca*), and a species of hop, *Humulus japonicus*, grown for its decorative leaves, are all annual climbers. Most of these, commonly grown as half-hardy ANNUALS, are, in fact, tender PERENNIALS (qq.v.), which do best if grown through the winter in a warm greenhouse, for they cannot survive a British winter without protection.

The larger nasturtiums (*Tropaeolum majus*) are in fact climbers, though they usually only scramble along the ground. The Canary Creeper (*T. peregrinum*) has small yellow flowers and delicate lobed leaves. The genus *Ipomoea*, and especially the hybrids from *I. tricolor* (syn. *rubro-coerulea*), produce showy convolvulus-like flowers, large but short-lived, and notably in pale blue and dark red shades.

Two more decorative tender climbers are *Cobaea scandens*, with large green-blue bell-shaped flowers, and the Chilean Glory Flower (*Eccremocarpus scaber*) with clusters of small orange, tubular flowers.

5. CULTIVATION OF WALL AND TREE CLIMBERS. The first essential in growing fine flowering climbers, especially on house walls, is to replace the builders' rubbish and poor lime-ridden soil usually found at the foot of a wall with turf-loam and leaf-mould. The climber should be planted at least 18 inches away from the base of the wall where the soil is generally very dry.

The support provided depends on the type of plant; in most cases the branches are spaced out and tied in the form of a fan. If the plants are to bear large crops of flowers annually, they need regular feeding with a mulch of fallen leaves or rotted dung. Lack of plant food is the usual cause of poor results with climbing roses.

There are varieties of wall plants suitable for growing on walls facing every direction, even east. The warm south or south-west wall is the only place on which sub-tropical climbers such as the passion-flower and solanums will flower successfully.

Tree climbers cannot grow well in the soil at the foot of the supporting tree, for it is usually too dry and full of roots; therefore the climber is better planted a little way from the tree and traincd to grow up a strong post fixed to a low branch of the tree. Alternatively, a bottomless tub of fresh rich soil may be sunk at the foot of the trunk to give the climber a good start.

6. WALL SHRUBS. A number of FLOWERING SHRUBS (q.v.), which are normally grown in the open ground, are also suitable for training against walls, though they are not climbers in the true sense of the word. Some of these are grown in this way mainly because the wall gives protection from frost and wind; these include the blue-flowered *Ceanothus* and the lantern-flowered *Abutilon*. Other shrubs commonly grown against walls are pyracanthas and the various cotoneasters, which have coloured berries in autumn, and the familiar 'japonica' or flowering quince (*Chaenomeles lagenaria*) with its crimson spring flowers. In fact, nearly all shrubs can be trained against a wall if they are given skilful pruning and tying, and they are perhaps easier to deal with in a restricted space than climbers, such as the passion flower, which make a great deal of straggly new growth each year.

See also FLOWER GARDENS.

CLOCHES. The cloche is an exceedingly useful device, like a miniature glasshouse, used in both private and market gardens for covering tender crops to protect them from frost and to advance their growth. It is also used for covering throughout their life crops such as melons and aubergines which normally do not thrive in the open air in cool climates. The word 'cloche' comes from a French word meaning 'bell' or 'bell cover', for the original cloche was bell-shaped.

This type has, however, largely been discarded in favour of the so-called continuous cloche which consists of a series of wire holders each fitted with either two or four panes of glass and called respectively tent and barn cloches. Cloches of these types cover a space of ground up to 23 inches in width. They are set end to end in rows of convenient length; when used on a large scale they are set out in double rows with a narrow pathway between. The ends of the rows are blocked with a piece of glass or board to keep out the draught. When skilfully used, the continuous cloche makes it possible to produce very much earlier crops of vegetables such as lettuces, radishes, carrots, turnips, peas, French beans, sweet corn, tomatoes, vegetable marrows, ridge cucumbers, and cauliflowers. Sweet peas

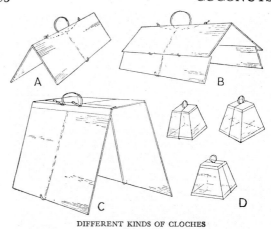

DIFFERENT KINDS OF CLOCHES
A. tent cloche; B. and C. barn cloches; D. hand-lights for individual plants

and other annuals can be sown out-of-doors in the autumn and protected by cloches through the winter, producing flowers much earlier in the summer than if they were sown in the spring. Tender crops such as melons, cucumbers, aubergines, and okra can be grown entirely under cloches especially when electrical soil warming apparatus is installed. Larger types of cloches are also manufactured, and in general these are based on the same principle, that is, panes of glass held in a metal frame. The hand-light, of which the Evesham light is an example, consists of small panes of glass held in a small metal structure; it was once a good deal used, but is now not manufactured to any great extent.

See also FRAMES, GARDEN; GLASSHOUSES.

CLOVERS, *see* LEGUMINOUS CROPS; GRASS-LAND; LEYS.

COCOA BEANS, *see* CACAO.

COCONUTS. In spite of their name these are not true nuts, but stone-fruits or drupes, like walnuts and plums (*see* FRUITS, section 3*b*, Vol. II). They grow on a large palm-tree called *Cocos nucifera*, which is native to the Malay archipelago, but has now been carried to most tropical and sub-tropical regions, growing particularly along the sea-shore. The tree has a tall slender stem, which may reach a height of 50 feet; there are no side branches, and at the top the crown of foliage is made up of enormous leaves each composed of many leaflets, producing a featherlike appearance. Flowering shoots in

Paul Popper

A NATIVE CLIMBING A COCONUT PALM TO PICK THE NUTS
Bunches of coconuts can be seen at the top of the picture

the centre of this group of great leaves produce clusters of coconuts. The coconut that appears in the shops is only the inner seed of the fruit, which, as it grows, is surrounded by a thick layer of fibre and a woody outer skin. This fibre covering, or 'coir', enables the seed to float on water, so that the seeds of trees growing on the coasts of one island may easily be carried to another.

A COCONUT CUT TO SHOW
THE SEED SURROUNDED BY
COIR

Coconut plantations are usually on low-lying level ground, not far from the sea. The land nearly always has to be drained with deep open ditches, and the salt water from high tides is kept out by high dykes. The trees are raised in a nursery from selected nuts still in their outer husk, and these are set on the surface of raised

beds, where they sprout and grow roots. When about 6 months old, they are transplanted and set at a distance of about 30 feet apart each way. The ground between the trees is often planted with a creeping leguminous 'cover crop', which keeps down the weeds. After about 5 years the young trees begin to fruit, and then continue to do so all the year round for 60 years or more. If they are allowed to, the nuts will fall as they ripen, but they are usually gathered every few months by men who use long light poles, with knives at the end to cut away the ripening nuts. Sometimes monkeys are trained to climb the trees and throw the nuts down. The crop is carried to the factory by lorry, light railway, or boat, or by floating the nuts along the ditches.

Coconuts are of great value to the natives of the Pacific Islands and tropical Asia. Every part of the tree has its uses. The wood of the trunk, though not particularly strong, is useful where better timbers are not available; it is called 'porcupine wood', and carvings and furniture are sometimes made from it. The leaves make an excellent thatch, and are even used for the walls of houses. The coir fibre from the husks is woven into ropes and mats or used for brooms and brushes. The white flesh within the nut, called 'copra', is a very good food, rich in oil, and is eaten either fresh or dried. The 'milk' from the centre of the shell is a refreshing drink. In southern India the sap of the flower spike is collected and fermented to form a mildly alcoholic drink called 'toddy', or used as a source of sugar or spirits. The central shoot of the tree makes a delicious vegetable called 'coconut cabbage', but, as the cutting of it kills the tree, this is forbidden by law in many countries. Primitive people use the nut shells as cups or water vessels; charcoal can also be made from the shells—and this is used in the making of gas-masks.

The copra in the coconut is an important source of oil (*see* OILS, VEGETABLE, Vol. VII), and the substance left behind after the nuts have been crushed, known as 'poonac', is a valuable cattle-food. Vast coconut plantations have now been established in Ceylon, Malaya, Indonesia, the Solomon Islands, and other tropical countries.

See also TROPICAL AGRICULTURE; PALM-TREES; OIL-BEARING PLANTS.
See also Vol. VII: COPRA; ROPE-MAKING; BRUSHES.

Norwegian Official Photo.

THE COD FISHING FLEET SETTING OUT FROM LOFOTEN

The motor vessels will be net fishing and the small boats line fishing. The boats start all together when a flag drops

COD FISHING. This northern fishing industry has a very old history. In the Lofoten Islands, off the north-western coast of Norway, cod is still fished in the same way as in early Viking times. In those days fishermen varied the monotony of fishing by making raids on the coast lands of other nations around the North Sea. Today, when the cod gather in the waters round the Lofotens, the mainland fishermen prepare their sharp-ended, canoe-shaped fishing-boats and, equipped very much as were their forefathers 1,000 years ago, steer for the fishing-grounds.

In a normal season the hungry cod are caught in vast numbers by means of the baited lines put out from the boats. These 'great-lines' as they are called, may carry from 1,000 to over 5,000 hooks, each of which is attached to the end of a branch line or 'snood' given off at regular intervals from the main line. The snoods are coiled up in baskets or trays, with the hooks arranged round the edges, so that the lines can be shot quickly without getting entangled. When the fishermen take their catch ashore, the fish are split open, gutted and cleaned, and all blood is carefully washed away. They are then sprinkled with salt, and laid out on the bare rocks to dry in the sun and wind. Every night, or whenever there is possibility of rain, the drying fish are built into circular piles, the top being protected by a conical capping of woven willow wands.

Cod are also fished by trawlers which scour the bottom of the sea with their bag-nets (*see* TRAWLING). Fleets of British trawlers from Grimsby and Hull steam to the rich northern fishing-grounds to join in the cod fishery. On the DOGGER BANK (q.v.) they mingle with fishing-boats from Denmark and Holland, and other North Sea countries.

On the other side of the Atlantic are the rich cod resources of the Newfoundland Banks, which the Basques and the fisherfolk of Brittany began to exploit shortly after Cabot discovered Newfoundland in 1497. This 'Banks Fishery', as it is called, is still the scene of intense activity during the fishing season, and is the meeting-place, among others, of a large fleet of boats called *Terreneuves* from St. Malo, and other fishing ports on the north coast of France. With them are many fishing-boats from the American fishing-port of Gloucester, the home of more than 6,000 deep-sea fishermen. The dried cod furnished by this fishery is exported in great quantity to the Mediterranean countries.

See also Vol. II: COD.

COFFEE. Coffee beans, from which the drink is made, are the seeds of several kinds of *coffea* trees that are cultivated throughout the tropics. The tree is believed originally to have been a native of Abyssinia, and the best quality and most widely grown coffee, the Arabica, has been cultivated in Arabia for thousands of years. Coffee has been introduced into the other parts of Africa, and other tropical countries. It is now

Brazilian Warrant Co.

A COFFEE PLANTATION IN BRAZIL

In the foreground are coffee bushes and beyond the coffee is spread out to dry in the sun

an important crop in South America, especially Brazil, which has a large Arabica crop and is one of the world's biggest producers. It is also grown in the East and West Indies, India, East and West Africa, and Ceylon. Next to Arabica the most widely cultivated kind of coffee is Robusta, which is hardier than Arabica. The terms 'hard' and 'mild' which are used in the coffee trade refer to the methods of preparation rather than to the kind of coffee.

Coffee-trees are raised from seeds, selected from the best-yielding trees, and with the pulp of the fruit but not the husks removed. They require a very warm climate, with no frost or drought, and a well-drained soil. The seeds are sown in nursery beds, and the young plants are transplanted after a year to the plantations, where they are set about 10 feet apart. The trees themselves are small and shrubby, from 10 to 20 feet high, with stout, oval, glossy, and evergreen leaves. As they grow they are pruned to

COFFEE BERRIES AND FLOWERS

shape. This is specially important with Arabica coffee, as the berries are borne on the young wood, and are more prolific if they are severely pruned. In some countries coffee-trees are all kept down to a height of about 5 feet to make picking easier. Often shade trees are grown to protect the coffee from strong sunlight. After about 2 years coffee-trees bear clusters of white flowers at intervals throughout the year, and from these develop juicy fruits, known as 'cherries', which they resemble, each containing two coffee-beans protected by hard husks. The tree does not give a full crop until it is about 6 years old, and after 14 years or so it generally begins to bear less.

The fruits ripen more or less continually throughout the year, and are gathered by hand. On small plantations the 'cherries' are often dried in the sun, and then the dry pulp and husks removed with simple hand-operated machinery; but most coffee now goes to a factory. There, the soft pulp that surrounds the beans is loosened and then washed away by machinery, and the beans are dried in the sun and separated from the husks. The green beans have to be roasted dark brown and ground into a powder before coffee can be made; but the more freshly roasted the beans, the better the coffee.

See also TROPICAL AGRICULTURE; TROPICAL PESTS.

COLLECTIVE FARMING. The purpose of collective farming, which is mainly confined to the U.S.S.R., is to bring peasant farmers to a better system of farming and living. All the peasants in the village are formed into one group, and their holdings are brought together to make one large farm, instead of several hundred small strips and patches of land. The farm may be 1,500 or more acres divided into some five or six fields. This makes it possible to plough by tractors and to harvest by combines instead of by hand; and this saving of labour means that children's work is no longer required as it used to be, and they can go to school.

The method was developed in the U.S.S.R. after the Revolution of 1917. At first, no private property other than personal belongings and certain money savings was allowed, all land and means of production being taken over by the State. Peasants entering the Collective had to give up their land, their farm implements, seeds, and livestock: all were reduced to one level. Each farm was set a programme or 'Plan' of production which it had to fulfil. This very rigid organization has now been relaxed a little, though the principle is the same. The members elect a Committee, and the Communist Party (called 'The Party' because only one is permitted) approves a chairman. This Committee discusses how best the 'Plan' can be carried out, and divides the workers into groups, called 'brigades', allotting so much work to each brigade and appointing to each a 'brigadier' to see that the work is done. No wages are paid to anyone, but each task is priced at so many 'labour days', and when it is accomplished, the worker has these 'days' credited to him in the farm books. At the end of the year the farm produce is divided up: the government takes its share, so does the farm and village, and whatever is left, which may be 30% to 50% of the total, according to the yield, is divided among the workers in proportion to the number of their 'labour days' during the year.

On an average a worker might obtain as his year's earnings about 2 to 4 cwt. of grain, 10 cwt. to 1 ton of potatoes, 2 to 8 cwt. of hay, and about £2 or £3 worth of roubles in cash. But some workers are quicker than others, and can get through enough work to earn them two or even three 'labour days' in the course of one working day. Those who earn 600 or even 700 'labour days' in a year instead of the average 200, are greatly respected, and earn a special title 'Stakhanovite', after Stakhanov, a coal-miner who popularized the idea.

The workers can do what they like with their share of the produce: either eat it, or sell it to the farm, or to the Co-operative Society (entirely different from a British Co-operative Society), or they can take it to one of the peasant markets and sell it for whatever price they can obtain. Actually the peasants eat a good deal of it; and during the year, while they are waiting for the harvest, they often have to borrow grain from the farm, which, of course, they must pay back.

Besides the big collective fields, each household has a piece of land to itself, varying from about ½ acre to 2 acres or more according to the district, on which the householder can grow what he likes. Here the peasant can grow vegetables, and keep poultry, pigs, or a cow, the produce belonging entirely to the house. These allotments were not part of the original scheme, but were introduced later to satisfy the peasants' passionate desire for a piece of land of their own. The land actually belongs to the State, but the householder can use it as he likes, and this satisfies him. The peasants also do a certain amount of other work besides farming—making roads or clearing forests—for which they are paid separately.

The Collective farmers thus live partly on the food they grow and partly on the money they earn, and these come from three sources: (1) the Collective farm (mainly food, some of which they can sell, and some money); (2) work done outside the farm on roads, forests, &c. (mainly money); (3) their own allotments (mainly food). The standard of living is much simpler than in England: the houses are much smaller, and the diet more limited—chiefly black bread, millet, porridge, and vegetable soup, with very little meat. The women work in the fields just as hard as the men, there being no work, however heavy or difficult, they will not undertake. The young children are left at the crèche while the mothers work.

The advantages of the method are that the large farming units can afford to use modern farm implements and so release men from the land to work in factories; better varieties of crops can be grown, better fertilizers and cropping systems used, and better animals bred. On many Collective farms a cottage is fitted up as a little museum where the workers can see speci-

Planet News

COLLECTIVE FARMERS EXAMINING THE QUALITY OF SEED GRAIN

On the left is the Brigade Leader who has been made a Hero of Socialist Labour for his good work on the farm

mens of insect pests, fungus diseases, and other things that interest and instruct them, and where simple examinations of soils and plants can be made. Periodically an expert adviser comes from the large Agricultural College to look round the farm and help in any difficulty; he uses this cottage as his centre. As all losses, due to whatever cause, are borne by the workers, they are naturally anxious to obtain all help possible for avoiding them. Collective farms need not buy the tractors and combines; they can hire them, along with teams of skilled workers from the Machine and Tractor Stations, and pay for them in grain or other produce.

Trouble has periodically arisen because the peasants preferred to work on their own allotments rather than on the Collective farm, finding it more profitable; and in consequence laws have had to be passed compelling them to work on the farm for a certain number of days each year. Collectivization has undoubtedly resulted in improvements in Russian farming, and the crop yields are now up to about one-third of those in Great Britain. But it does depend very largely on the right of the State to compel its workers.

Outside of the U.S.S.R. and its subordinate countries collective farming is practised only to a very small extent. Some Collectives have been set up in Palestine by Jews who are 'ideological Communists'; also there are some Collective farms elsewhere; but nowhere are they so systematically developed as in the U.S.S.R. A few unsuccessful experiments have been tried in England, and no non-Communist government has adopted the method; the elements of compulsion and the practice of punishing heavily all who fail to obey the Party instructions made it unacceptable. These countries prefer the western method of Co-operation in Farming (q.v.).

See also Vol. I: RUSSIANS.
See also Vol. X: COMMUNISM.

COLORADO BEETLE, *see* BEETLE PESTS, section 7.

COMBINE HARVESTING, *see* HARVESTING (GRAIN).

COMPOST HEAP. Weeds, vegetable waste, straw, grass cuttings, bracken, and similar plant materials found on farms and in gardens all contain organic matter (matter which has come from living things) and useful amounts of nitrogen, phosphate, and potash. If returned to the soil, they put back these nourishing materials, and are to that extent to be regarded as MANURES (q.v.). Experience has shown that their effect is improved if they are allowed to rot down in a heap before they are applied. Compost heaps in which vegetable wastes have been mixed with lime or even with soil have been a feature of farming since very early days. These old-style composts require time to mature, and at least 2 years is usually allowed. If the heaps are turned over and well mixed after the first few months, a better and more uniform product is obtained in a shorter time. Many gardeners have a succession of compost heaps, perhaps three—one ready for use, one half matured, and one being prepared.

In recent years much scientific work has been carried out on the composting process, and now the preparation of composts has been made more rapid (a matter of months instead of years) and more certain. The essential needs for speedy rotting are a correct amount of air, moisture, active nitrogen compounds, and some chalk or lime to prevent the mass from becoming acid. On farms straw is the chief basis for composts, and the necessary nitrogen is provided in the form of sulphate of ammonia or sometimes of sewage sludge. A large quantity of water is needed to saturate the straw. The product when mature looks rather like well-rotted farmyard manure but, of course, it lacks some of the valuable ingredients of good dung (*see* MANURE, FARMYARD).

In gardens green weeds and vegetable wastes are used, and these are easier to rot down than ripe straw. Autumn leaves are better composted separately. It is important not to allow the roots of pernicious weeds, such as couch grass or convolvulus, to get into the compost heap. It is usual to spread the various materials in layers, sandwich fashion. The layers containing the vegetable refuse are the deeper (6 to 9 inches deep) and the alternating layers, which contain materials for assisting decomposition, are much thinner (from $\frac{1}{2}$ to 2 inches thick according to the substances used). Sometimes water or liquid manure is added while the heap is being made, though it must not be made too wet. To protect the heap from rain it is often covered with a layer of soil, or a wooden or metal sheeting is placed over it, though with an air space between. The materials used for hastening decomposition (accelerators) are sulphate of ammonia (the most commonly used one), nitro-chalk, or proprietary compounds and extracts. The Indore process (vegetable matter+animal manure+soil+chalk) is one that is followed by some growers.

Composts are valuable for improving the working properties of soils, but they seldom contain sufficient plant food for successions of heavy crops, and they should in most cases be supplemented with ARTIFICIAL FERTILIZERS (q.v.). Where artificial fertilizers are the principal manures used, compost is needed as well to provide the humus which the fertilizers are without, and which is an essential ingredient of SOILS (q.v.).

See also MANURES.

CONIFERS, *see* TREES, CONIFEROUS; ORNAMENTAL TREES.

CONSERVATORIES, *see* GLASSHOUSES.

CO-OPERATION IN FARMING. When men first learnt to farm, they grew food and materials for clothing for themselves and their families. In modern times the farmer sells most of what he produces to shopkeepers, wholesale traders, or manufacturers, and uses the money he earns to provide for his own needs. He also has to spend money on his farm, buying tools and machinery, seeds, feeding-stuffs for his animals, the animals themselves, fertilizers, and other things. As animals and even plants take a long time to grow, the farmer usually has to spend fairly large sums for many months or years before he can expect to earn anything by selling his produce. In the past, and in some countries to this day, traders have taken advantage of the farmer's difficulties. If he could not pay cash for what he needed, the traders allowed him to get into debt; and in order to pay off his debt, he had to sell his harvest to the trader at a low price. Sometimes the trader was an actual money-lender as well.

An early attempt to do away with this evil system was made in Germany about 1850 when a Rhineland burgomaster, Raiffeisen, persuaded the small farmers to form village co-operative loan and savings banks. A farmer could then borrow from the bank of which he was himself a member, knowing that he would only have to pay a small interest on the money. He could buy his seeds or tools for cash from the trader, and afterwards sell his crop to whomever would pay the best price. Later the members found that if they put through a large order for seeds or fertilizers for the whole village at the same time, they could get them cheaper and often of better quality. From this discovery grew co-operative trading societies with offices, warehouses, and mills in the country towns. Sometimes these also sold household goods to the farmer's wife.

The co-operative loan and savings banks were a great success, and were copied not only in nearly all European countries but also in India, many British colonies, and elsewhere. In Britain there are no village co-operative banks, for British farmers were much less worried by money-lenders. Co-operative trading societies have, however, grown and flourished. They supply the farmer with everything he needs (except livestock) to carry on his farm. They often manufacture as well, give services such as grass or grain drying, and market the farmer's produce, especially grain and potatoes.

A century ago the farm milk was made into butter and cheese in the farm-house. Then machinery was invented which made it cleaner, more convenient, and more economical to carry

The Field

A LAND SETTLEMENT ESTATE NEAR WOODBRIDGE, SUFFOLK

The estate is divided into small holdings which are farmed individually. Seed and plants are supplied and the produce is marketed co-operatively

out this process in small factories in the village. Later came mechanical weighing, grading, and packing, especially of eggs and fruit, which again could be done more efficiently in a factory. In most countries these factories, creameries, canneries, and packing stations are owned by co-operative groups of farmers. They not only process but also sell the product, often for export. The movement started in Denmark about 1882, and in Ireland under the influence of Sir Horace Plunkett a few years later. It flourishes today all through western Europe, North America, and the British Dominions, and is spreading to Asia and the tropical countries.

Besides co-operative banking, supply, and marketing there are a number of valuable services such as the loan of machinery, breeding stations for pedigree animals, water supplies, telephones, or medical aid for the farmer and his family which can be provided co-operatively. In some cases farmers even join their land together and work it as one big co-operative farm.

A co-operative society is not the same thing as a commercial company and comes under a different law. The important rules in a co-operative are (a) any one of good character may join, (b) every member makes about the same contribution to the funds needed to run the society,

(c) the co-operative is run by a committee elected by all the members, each of whom has one vote only, (d) if there are any profits at the end of the year they are distributed in proportion to the use each member has made of the co-operative. (For instance if he has sent in eggs worth £50 he will be paid for them as they are received, but he may get an extra 50 shillings at the end of the year.)

Because all the members of co-operatives have equal standing and no one is trying to get the better of his neighbour, and because co-operatives are usually small and all the members know one another, they work in a friendly, family atmosphere. In the more backward countries they give the peasant farmer a chance to learn to conduct his own affairs, to contribute helpfully in meetings, and to understand business. They can also improve his farming by giving him good advice as well as better implements and improved seeds. Village or other local co-operatives are usually linked up in national unions and central banking or trading societies which they themselves have built up. These national centres carry on import and export business, watch over the local societies to see that they are properly run, and speak on their behalf to governments.

Some of the figures are difficult to get, but it is believed that there are over 60 million farmers throughout the world who are members of co-operative societies. Great Britain is an industrial country, but in England alone there were in 1950 nearly 200,000 farmers belonging to co-operative societies, and their business with the societies during the year was calculated to be worth about £50 million. They have their own central organizations, the Agricultural Co-operative Association in England and the Welsh and Scottish Agricultural Organization Societies. Those societies that sell the farmer his supplies and buy his grain are the most numerous; then come egg-packing stations, fruit and vegetable marketing societies, and societies selling wool and other livestock products. Grass-dryers and machinery pools are new ideas, which may become important. In British colonial territories it is government policy to introduce co-operation so as to bring greater prosperity and self-reliance to the peasants of Africa and Asia and to increase their output.

See also Agricultural History; Collective Farming. See also Vol. VII: Co-operative Societies.

COPPICE. If a broadleaved tree is cut down at ground level, the root in many species will throw up a number of smaller stems. If these in their turn are cut back, another crop of new shoots appears, and so on, year after year, indefinitely. Woods grown in this way are known as coppices or copses, from the French *couper*, to cut. But, in fact, many woods now known as copses contain nothing but big timber, for the name frequently persists after the method of forestry has changed.

In former times coppices were of great value to the countryside, for they produced fencing material, firewood, poles for many uses, wattles for wattle-and-daub walls of buildings, and bark for tanning. Oak, ash, beech, birch, horn-beam, and alder were all grown in this way. Nowadays, only three kinds are important: hazel for hurdles, bean rods, thatch spars, and such uses; sweet chestnut for hop poles and cleft fencing; and willows or withies for basketry (*see* Rural Crafts).

Many coppices are split up into small blocks by rides (wide paths). The correct way to manage a coppice is to fell these blocks in turn, only one or two each year, so that by the time the last is felled, the first ones are ready for cutting again. The length of the rotation varies with the type of tree. Hazel takes from 7 to 10 years to reach the stage of cutting; sweet chestnut 12 to 15 years; oak 20 years; whereas willow takes only one year. When scattered timber trees are allowed to grow up amongst the coppice, the wood is called 'coppice with standards'.

Pollarding is a similar method of growing small brushwood, but differs from coppicing in that the trees are cut back at a height of about 6 feet, instead of at ground level. Pollarded willows are grown by the sides of streams in many counties, where their roots help to keep up the banks. The brushwood is cut every 2 or 3 years and used for much the same purposes as coppice material.

See also Forestry; Trees, Broadleaved.

CORDON, *see* Pruning, section 2.

CORMS, *see* Bulbs, Corms, and Tubers.

CORN, *see* Oats; Maize; Wheat; Barley; Rye.

COTTON. The raw cotton from which thread and cloth are made consists of the fibres that grow on the seeds of the cotton plant, which is grown in many warm countries on the fringes of the tropics. The principal cotton-growing

Rural Industries Bureau

CLEAVERS PREPARING CLEFT FENCING PALES IN A CHESTNUT COPPICE IN WEST SUSSEX

U.S. Information Service

PICKING COTTON ON A PLANTATION IN MISSISSIPPI

There are many varieties of the cotton plant, all types belonging to the genus *Gossypium*. Cotton, though really a shrubby perennial, is grown as an annual, that is, planted afresh every year, as this method is easier and gives a heavier crop. Fertile soil with abundant moisture is needed: many of the best plantations are in river valleys where the land can be irrigated. There must also be plenty of sunshine, and a growing period of about 220 days free from frost. Cotton grows best in a tropical or sub-tropical climate. In countries north of the Equator the seed is sown about April in thoroughly cultivated and clean land. Sometimes the land is dug into ridges, about $3\frac{1}{2}$ feet apart, which are allowed to weather before the cotton seed is sown. The seed is then sown on the ridges by hand, or more generally by mechanical drills. If flat ground is used, the seed is sown in rows 3 or 4 feet apart. About one bushel of seed is needed to each acre of ground, four or five seeds being set together about $\frac{3}{4}$ inch deep. When the young plants are a few inches high, they are thinned out to about 1 foot apart, and the spaces between the rows are hoed to keep them free from weeds. Then the cotton plants grow rapidly into little bushes about 5 feet high, covered with red, white, or yellow flowers shaped like those of the garden hollyhock. The bushes are usually pruned to keep their growth in check.

About August the flowers give place to the

countries are the Southern States of North America, Egypt and the Sudan, India, Brazil, and China, and a large proportion of the world's cotton comes from the 'cotton belt' of the U.S.A. Some is also grown in Europe, and in Australia, but only in very small quantities. The cotton plant, and the secrets of cotton manufacture, were introduced into Europe by Mohammedan invaders in the 7th century and onwards. A Moorish writer of the 12th century wrote on cotton cultivation, and mentioned Sicily as a place where the plant was being grown, and in the 14th century, Granada and Barcelona were manufacturing centres.

The quality of cotton is judged by the length of the fibres: the finest quality is Sea Island, so called because it was originally grown in the West Indies and in the islands off the coast of Florida. It is still grown there, though nowadays it is grown also in the coastal belt of the mainland, particularly in the States of Georgia and Florida. Next in quality to Sea Island is the highest grade of Egyptian cotton, called Sakellaridis. American upland cottons come next, of which there are nine grades, Long Stapled Uplands, the best grade, being hardly inferior to the Egyptian Sakellaridis. Cotton from India and other parts of Asia has a shorter fibre and cannot be used for the finer fabrics (*see* COTTON MANUFACTURE, Vol. VII).

FLOWERS AND BOLLS OF THE COTTON PLANT

seed pods, or 'bolls', which open as they ripen, revealing the white tufts of cotton attached to the seeds within them. At this time of year the fields are a beautiful sight, the patches of white showing brilliantly against the green bushes. The picking of the cotton crop is a long, slow job, for it is generally done by hand, mostly by women carrying large baskets to receive the tufts as they pick them from each open boll. Each picker gathers about 100 lb. of cotton a day; but as the crop does not all ripen at once, two or three pickings are needed. Picking-machines have been invented, but are not so successful as hand picking because of the need to select the ripe bolls from the unripe ones. Each acre of a cotton plantation yields from 100 to 500 lb. of cotton each season.

Cotton is a greedy crop that can rarely be grown for 2 years in succession on the same piece of ground. It is best grown in rotation, the ground being well manured and vegetables grown between two crops of cotton to restore fertility to the soil (see ROTATION OF CROPS). Cotton is attacked by various PESTS AND DISEASES (q.v.), among the most serious being the Boll-weevil, the Cotton-stainer, and the Cotton Aphis (see TROPICAL PESTS).

After being picked, the cotton is 'ginned', that is, the fibres are separated from the seeds, a process which is usually performed on the actual cotton fields, but sometimes in a factory. It is then sent to the cotton mills for spinning into thread. The seeds which remain are rich in oil, minerals, and protein (see OILS, VEGETABLE, Vol. VII). After part of the oil has been pressed out of them, the material that remains is made into cotton-seed cake, a valuable FOOD (q.v.) for farm livestock. It is also useful as a fertilizer, supplying humus and much of the mineral food that the cotton plants drew from the soil (see MANURES).

See also Vol. VII: COTTON MANUFACTURE.

COWS, see CATTLE.

COWMAN, see CATTLE, CARE OF.

COWSHEDS, see CATTLE, CARE OF; FARM-STEAD.

CRAB AND LOBSTER FISHING. Crabs and lobsters are caught in large numbers in traps called 'pots', baited with pieces of fish. The commonest lobster-pot, the one generally used in Cornwall, has a flat bottom and rounded sides and is made of wicker-work. The only opening is through a funnel at the top through which the lobster can enter but cannot get out again, and so is caught in the trap. The trap has a door at one side for removing the catch. On the north-east coast of England, lobster traps are called 'creels' or 'creeves'. A creeve has the shape of a half cylinder with a flat bottom and a top supported by three or four half-hoops; it is covered with stout cord or wire netting. In one or both sides a non-return funnel is fitted. A lobster-pot

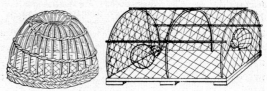

A CORNISH LOBSTER-POT AND A NORTH-EASTERN 'CREEL'

of a French pattern is made of netting held open by three cylinder-shaped hoops, and has a funnel at each end.

Lobster and crab pots may be set singly or as a fleet. In a fleet the pots are attached to a rope at intervals of about 60 to 80 feet, the number of pots varying according to the means and energy of the fisherman. The depth at which the pots are laid and the distance offshore at which they are set vary greatly, both depending on the fisherman's knowledge of where the lobsters and crabs are most likely to be found. Usually, they are not set more than 8 or 10 fathoms deep. The pots are generally set at low tide and, if weather permits, the fisherman visits them the following day to remove the catch and renew the bait—pieces of fish tied (or hung) inside the trap. Lobsters prefer the bait to be stale and smelling high; but crabs like their food fresh. The fisheries are carried on practically all the year round; but they depend, of course, on reasonably fine weather.

Crabs are sometimes caught in hoop-nets made by lacing the mouth of a shallow bag-net to a ring made of willow or stout iron wire. Across the mouth are two strings, and the bait is tied on at the middle. The fisherman lowers his baited net and, when he feels a tremor in the line, he hauls it up so quickly that the crab has not time to escape.

As well as the fisheries in the seas around the British Isles, there are large fisheries for the

Spiny Lobster or Crawfish off the Cape of Good Hope and off the east coast of Siberia, north of Japan. Vast numbers of large, blue-clawed Swimming-crabs are caught in the Mediterranean off the delta of the Nile.

See also Vol. II: CRAB; LOBSTER.

CRAFTS, RURAL, see RURAL CRAFTS.

CRESS, see SALAD CROPS, section 5; WATERCRESS.

CROFTING. This word is applied to the farm life of the small farmers of the Highlands and Islands of Scotland. Crofting means a subsistence style of farming, in which the crofter works a small area of land, about 2–10 acres, to grow his own food. He may or may not have a common grazing right for a certain number of sheep and cattle on the hills surrounding the crofting 'township' or group of holdings. In some ways crofting is a survival of a way of living common in many parts of England in medieval times. A crofter today, however, owns his cottage and buildings, and rents the land with absolute security of tenure so long as he does not misuse the land. He is also able at his death to leave the tenancy of his croft to his heirs. If he wishes at any time to leave the croft and go elsewhere, the landlord is compelled to pay him the value of the cottage and buildings as assessed by the Scottish Land Court, which makes a visit of inspection. The position of crofters was once not nearly so secure; but the Crofters' Act of 1886 established these fair and favourable conditions.

The individual holdings are rarely fenced, and the arable land of the whole township is often laid open for grazing from November till the following spring. This means that all the crofters must grow more or less the same crops; no-one can grow winter forage crops, such as kale; and any attempt at individual improvement of agriculture is scarcely possible (see OPEN FIELDS AND ENCLOSURES). A crofter may have 4 or 5 cattle in all, 20 to 100 sheep, and one strong pony which he may share with a neighbour. His crops are oats and potatoes, the oats being fed to the cattle in the straw (unthreshed) and the potatoes shared between the family and the cows. Some barley is grown in the Outer Hebrides as

Robert M. Adam

CROFTS ON THE ISLE OF SANDAY ORKNEYS

bread corn. It is scarcely possible to make a living from a croft in these days, and most crofters are fishermen, sailors, or weavers as well, and, apart from the spring cultivations, most of the farm work is done by the women. The men usually look after the sheep but the women deal with the cows.

The crofting areas of Scotland are generally remote from railways and points of communication, and the land is mostly rather poor and rocky, so that crofting means a simple, even primitive, way of life. A similar system is to be found in the west of Ireland, though peasant ownership of the land is being fostered by the Irish Government.

CROPS, *see* ARABLE CROPS; VEGETABLE GARDEN.

CUCUMBER. The cucumber plant, *Cucumis sativus*, is a trailing vine-like annual which has been cultivated in gardens for thousands of years. It was known to the ancient Greeks, Egyptians, and Romans; it was introduced into China about 2,000 years ago. The name cucumber, originally *cucumer*, comes from the Latin. Cucumbers are grown throughout the world for the sake of their green succulent fruits which are eaten raw. The gherkin, a type of small cucumber, is used for pickling.

Like the tomato, the cucumber is a native of warm climates, and in Britain has to be grown with some protection, generally in heated glass-houses—special types of low span-roofed glasshouses, heated with hot-water pipes. The plants which like a temperature of 70° to 80° F. and a very moist atmosphere, are trained on a wire trellis close to the glass roof so that the long fruits hang down beneath. The cucumber plant is monoecious, that is, the male and female organs are carried on separate flowers *on the same plant*. Seedless fruits, however, are formed without fertilization of the female flowers, and these are better shaped than the fertilized fruits, and the plants will bear more fruits if none of them is fertilized by the male flowers. Gardeners therefore, except when growing for seed, try to prevent the fertilization of female flowers on plants grown under glass by removing the male flowers and by excluding all pollinating insects.

A hardy type of cucumber, known as the ridge cucumber, is grown in Britain in the open. The

Amateur Gardening

CUCUMBERS GROWING IN A GREENHOUSE

They are grown in turfy loam, manure containing plenty of straw, bonemeal, and lime

plants are raised under glass from seed sown in pots and boxes, and the seedlings are transplanted in the open usually in June when there is no risk of frost. They should be placed about 2 feet apart, in rows 4 feet apart, to give room for their free-branching and spreading type of growth. Cucumbers need rich soil and plenty of water during dry weather. The seed can be sown in the open during late May and June, but this gives rather late fruit.

Varieties of cucumber suitable for frame and cloche culture also are available, and are grown much like the outdoor kinds. In general the varieties commonly grown in Britain are: Telegraph and Butcher's Disease Resister (in glasshouses); Conqueror (in frames); Bedfordshire Prize Ridge, Stockwood Ridge, and Cheltenham Long Ridge (outdoors).

See also GLASSHOUSES; FRAMES; GOURD VEGETABLES.

CULTIVATIONS. Man first became a farmer when he got the idea of settling down on a piece of land and breaking up the soil in order to grow a crop of his own choosing (*see* AGRICULTURAL HISTORY). The first kind of cultivation was a mere breaking of the surface of the soil, and many primitive races do no more than that even

Royal Horticultural Society

CULTIVATING A SEED-BED

After the ground has been dug, it is hoed or lightly forked to allow the soil to dry. It is then trodden down to make it firm and raked to make a fine tilth and to remove stones

today. The action of ploughing, in which the soil is turned over, is a development of this simple idea, and is probably about 2,000 years old in Britain, and very much older in the ancient civilizations of the Near East and China (*see* FARM TOOLS, HISTORY OF). Nowadays ploughing, or in the garden digging, is the first and main process in the cultivation of the soil among advanced peoples.

In general, cultivation is designed to prepare the soil for sowing seed, so that the plants shall have a good chance of growing to the stage at which they are harvested. There is, however, more in it than this, and as our knowledge grows, we understand better what happens in the soil when it is cultivated. This knowledge helps a farmer to be a better cultivator. He has to learn about the effects of weather—rain, frost, wind, and sun—and he must understand the effects of previous crops, and the influence of animals on the soil, as, for instance, when he folds sheep on it before ploughing for a crop of corn. He must understand the important work done by EARTHWORMS (q.v.) in the soil, and the need for adequate supplies of LIME (q.v.) and humus, especially in clay soils. These matters are dealt with more fully in the article SOILS (q.v.).

For most crops it is necessary to drain wet land before it can be cultivated at all. This

DRAINAGE (q.v.) in itself tends to reduce the sourness of the soil, and as the water goes out of it, air goes in. Air is a great sweetener of soil, and plant poisons (such as sulphides) react with the oxygen of the air and are made harmless. Now when the land is ploughed, the top layer of the soil is so broken up that much more air enters it, and the cultivations that follow ploughing help to keep the soil well aired, thus maintaining those conditions that suit plants best. The most obvious results of cultivation are seen in the physical characteristics of soil. For example, heavy clays are broken into fine crumbs, loam comes down to a granular state, and very light soils can be made to hold more firmly together.

Different crops need different types of cultivations. The general routine for cereals is ploughing, disking or cultivating, harrowing, sowing, lighter harrowing, and rolling. POTATOES (q.v.) are planted in rows drawn by a ridging-plough with a double mould-board. After planting, the ridges are split with the ridging-plough and the tubers thus covered in the rows. Turnips and swedes in some parts of the country are sown on ridges too; elsewhere they are sown on the flat (*see* ROOT CROPS). Grass seed requires a particularly fine tilth and very clean ground (*see* GRASSLAND). 'Tilth' is the top inch or two of soil in which seed is sown. In a fine tilth the particles of soil are smaller than in a coarse tilth. Lumpy,

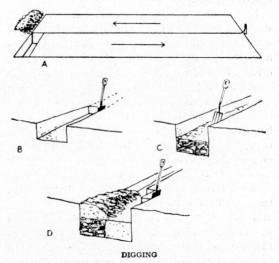

DIGGING

A. The plot to be dug. It is divided into two and digging starts at one end, working up one half and down the other. The earth taken out of the first trench is used to fill in the last. B. Digging the first spit, two spits wide. C. Digging the second spit. D. The earth from the second trench is thrown into the first

loose, firm, and other words are all used to describe a seed-bed, and refer to the kind of tilth that has been produced by cultivators and the weather.

Cultivation among growing crops is practically all done with the idea of killing WEEDS (q.v.) or preventing their growing. There are both hand and horse-hoes for this purpose, as well as hoes attached to the tractor's tool-bar, and these are kept busy most of the summer (*see* CULTIVATORS). Sometimes a farmer cultivates a piece of ground during the whole of the spring and summer merely to clean it for a future crop such as wheat. This is called 'bare fallowing'. He ploughs and cultivates, waits till the weeds germinate, and then ploughs and cultivates again to kill them. After the next germination of weeds he cultivates and harrows again, taking advantage of all the dry weather he can get. A crop taken after a bare fallow is usually a heavy one.

Cultivations in the garden follow the same principles as those on the farm. Digging takes the place of ploughing, and is mainly done in winter and early spring, when MANURES (q.v.) may be dug in.

Digging in the garden is carried out with fork or spade; if the soil is easy to work the spade is more efficient. The ground may be dug one, two, or occasionally three spits (spade-depths) deep, and the less fertile soil at the bottom of the trench is loosened but not brought to the surface. If the ground is to be 'double dug', a trench is dug two spits deep, and the soil from the top spit is wheeled to the other end of the plot, to be turned into the final trench. The digging then proceeds as shown in the diagram. Single digging or digging three spits deep (trenching) is done in just the same way.

The depth of cultivation depends on the condition of the soil and the type of sub-soil, as well as the type of plants to be grown and the time and labour available. The deeper the soil is dug the deeper plant roots can penetrate; but this is less important with most vegetables and herbaceous plants than with trees and shrubs. Usually an initial double-digging will be sufficient for several years, with an annual single-digging in the years between.

Just as the plough turns up ground and leaves a large area of soil exposed to the air, so in the garden, particularly on heavy soils, ridging may be done to expose as much soil as possible to the beneficial breaking-down action of the weather. Before seed sowing, the ground is brought to a fine tilth by raking; this corresponds to harrowing. Sometimes rolling is needed on light soils to firm the surface, but it is a mistake to imagine that rolling will also consolidate the subsoil or have much effect on making the surface truly level. The gardener should, therefore, complete the winter cultivations several months before seed sowing or planting is done, for then the whole depth of soil is given time to settle.

Summer cultivations among growing crops follow farm practice, the only difference being that hoeing is generally a manual operation. Well-worked soil allows summer rain to be used to the best advantage, and prevents the soil from baking hard in hot weather.

See also ARABLE CROPS; SOILS; WEEDS; PLOUGH; CULTIVATORS; DRAINAGE; LIME; MANURES

CULTIVATORS. After ploughing, much of the breaking down of the ridges of earth, or 'furrow slices', into smooth soil suitable for a seed-bed takes place naturally by the action of sun, rain, and frost; but mechanical cultivators are used to hasten and control the process. Heavy implements with strong, deep tines or prongs break the furrow slices; then harrows, which are merely light cultivators, break up the clods into the fine crumbs needed for a seed-bed.

Heavy cultivators are made on a wheeled frame which can be towed by a tractor, or they are mounted on a frame attached directly to the tractor. Cultivating needs a very heavy pull, and horses are now rarely used for the work. When a separate trailed cultivator is used, the stems for the tines are on a frame which can be lifted to bring the tines out of work. The lifting device is worked by a cord as in the case of a trailed PLOUGH (q.v.).

Harrows are of many kinds, varying according to their purpose and to the power available for pulling them, and also according to local custom. Some have small, closely set tines for the final preparation of the extremely fine seed-bed needed for some market-garden crops, a kind of seed-bed called an 'onion bed'. Some harrows, called chain harrows, have each tine set at the corner of a link of a square chain, thus forming an implement that is flexible enough to follow the lie of uneven land. Other harrows have their tine points mounted at the end of a semi-circular spring, which keeps the tine vibrating as it passes through the soil.

Bristol Tractors Ltd.

A HEAVY CULTIVATOR WITH RIGID TINES MOUNTED DIRECTLY
ON A TRACKED TRACTOR

The tines are forced deep into the soil

Eric Guy

DISK-HARROWING A SEED-BED

The axles carrying the disks are set at an angle to the
line of travel so that the disks shall bite into the soil.

There is also quite a different kind of tool, sometimes called a cultivator and sometimes a harrow, which has saucer-shaped disks, about 18 inches in diameter, instead of fixed tines. These disks have sharp edges and stand on end, like wheels, being mounted along axles with spacers, about 6 inches wide, between them. Four or six of the axles are mounted on a tractor-drawn frame.

Rolls, or rollers, are cultivation implements used to crush clods and level the land. They are also used to press the soil particles tightly round a seed or a young plant. Some rolls are smooth cylinders; others have ridged cylinders made up of many separate wheels, running on an axle, each wheel with a prominent rim which bites into the soil. These ridged rolls are often called Cambridge rolls because they first came into use in Cambridgeshire, or ring rolls because each section or wheel is like a ring. They have a better cultivating effect than have the smooth rollers. A Crosskill roller is like a ring roller except that in place of the knife-like rim each section carries strong spikes.

Rotary cultivators and gyrotillers, in which the tines rotate around an axis, are very powerful cultivators which can work at a greater depth than the implements so far described. The

Eric Guy

CAMBRIDGE ROLLS PREPARING A SEED-BED FOR SUGAR-BEET

gyrotiller cultivates to a depth of 18 inches or so but does not turn the soil over as does a plough. The rotary cultivator penetrates less deeply.

Another kind of mechanical cultivator, called an inter-row cultivator or hoe, does part of the work that used to be done by hand hoeing. When plants have been set in evenly spaced rows, it is possible to draw a hoe, pulled by horse or tractor, along the rows, so that it disturbs and cultivates the soil between the rows without damaging the plants. This cultivation helps to keep down the weeds and lets air into the soil.

See also MECHANIZED FARMING; CULTIVATIONS; ARABLE CROPS.

CURRANTS AND GOOSEBERRIES. These
are cultivated varieties of plants belonging to the species *Ribes*, which are natives of most temperate European countries. Gooseberries may have been so named because a sauce of the fruit was often served with roast goose, or the word may be a corruption of gross-berry or gorse-berry.

All these fruits have much the same habits, with one important exception. Black currants and gooseberries carry their fruit 'trusses' or clusters along the whole length of the young shoots, so that to get a big crop, plenty of long, strong new shoots are needed. Red and white currants, on the other hand, carry most of their fruit trusses at the bottom of the young shoots, so that a great many short new shoots are needed, and the tree has to develop an open framework which will allow the sun to get in to ripen the fruit. This calls for quite different treatment in PRUNING (q.v.).

With black currants, a few old shoots are cut out clean from the base every year, leaving room for the strong growth of new wood. Black currants are grown as a 'stool', that is, a number of young shoots grow from the ground instead of from a short 'leg' or stem, as with red currants. Gooseberries can be treated almost exactly the same as black currants, being grown from a stool from which new strong shoots are encouraged to spring. The shoots must, however, be more widely spaced than those of black currants, because otherwise the thorns make picking impossible. Dessert gooseberries are often grown on a short stem with a permanent framework of branches from which the young shoots grow out,

the main extension growths being tipped and the side growths cut to three or four buds. Red currants which are grown as open-centred bushes, rather like apple or pear trees, are pruned heavily (*see* Fig. 1). In the winter pruning, half the growth that was made in the previous summer is cut away from each of the eight or so main branches, and all side shoots are cut to two buds (about ½ inch). Then in June or early July all strong young shoots are cut back to the fifth or sixth leaf from the base to let in the sun and to ripen the fruit. Gooseberries and red currants are also grown on walls as cordons. (*See* PRUNING, section 2.)

Currants and gooseberries will grow satisfactorily in most soils so long as they receive enough manure. Black currants can get all they want from well-rotted farmyard manure, for their principal need is nitrogen. If farmyard manure is not available, they should have compost reinforced with organic fertilizers such as bone meal. They do not need lime. Gooseberries, on the other hand, are most dependent on potash. They soon show lack of potash in the condition of the leaves which begin to show brown margins (*see* MANURES). Although all plants should be kept clean of weeds with the hoe the ground round the base of the plants should never be dug for fear that the surface roots be disturbed and the plant loosened. It is usual to market the fruit in 4-lb., 6-lb., or 12-lb. chip (very thin wood) baskets or in cardboard cartons.

There are several serious pests and diseases which attack and may destroy currants and gooseberries. The Big-bud Mite is perhaps the most serious black-currant pest. Thousands of these microscopic mites inhabit a single bud, making it swell. The pest can sometimes be checked in the very early stages if the swollen buds are picked off and burnt; otherwise the trees must be given a lime-sulphur spray (*see* FRUIT SPRAYING). Along with Big-bud often comes the devastating black-currant virus disease Reversion. This may start on a single spray, altering the shape and appearance of the leaves (*see* Fig. 2.), but soon spreads to the whole tree. The disease is incurable, and the plant must be dug up and burnt (*see* PLANT DISEASES). Red currants do not suffer from Big-bud or Reversion, but are attacked by Aphis, the Capsid bug, and the caterpillars of the Currant Clearwing Moth and Currant Sawfly (*see* INSECT PESTS). The

East Malling Research Station

FIG. I. A RED CURRANT BEFORE AND AFTER WINTER PRUNING

About twelve main spurs, all growing away from the centre, form the framework of the tree. All other shoots are cut right back to one or two buds—the buds which will bear next year's fruit

fungus, Coral Spot, often attacks old or neglected trees. The larva of the Gooseberry Sawfly will in some years completely strip the leaves of the trees, unless they are treated with Derris powder or with an arsenate of lead spray. The Gooseberry Mildew, a fungus disease which produces a white fungus-like patch on the berry, is dealt with by spraying, generally with lime-sulphur (*see* PLANT DISEASES), and by cutting out and burning all infected shoots.

The most popular early black currant, and one which produces the largest fruit is Boskoop

East Malling Research Station

FIG. 2. REVERSION DISEASE IN BLACK CURRANTS

The left-hand diseased shoot has produced a lot of smaller, narrower leaves and no fruit. The right-hand healthy shoot is maturing a good crop of fruit

Giant, though Mendip Cross and Wellington are heavier croppers. A good mid-season variety is Seabrook's Black—perhaps the best to plant where one variety only can be grown. Of late varieties Baldwin grows very well where the soil is rich, and Malvern's Cross produces the latest blackcurrants. Fay's Prolific is an excellent early red currant, and Laxton's No. 1 a later variety; while Versailles is a good white currant. Gooseberries are not grown commercially as much as they were in the 19th century. There are, however, a number of excellent varieties, though some popular ones, such as Leveller, will not stand lime-sulphur spraying. Lancashire Lad (red), Whinham's Industry (red), Keepsake (green), Leveller (yellow), and Whitesmith (White) are five good varieties to plant.

See also FRUIT-GROWING; FRUIT PROPAGATION.

CUTTINGS, *see* FRUIT PROPAGATION; PLANT PROPAGATION.

CUTTLEFISH FISHING, *see* OCTOPUS, CUTTLEFISH, AND SQUID FISHING.

CUTWORMS, *see* BUTTERFLY AND MOTH PESTS.

CYPRESS, *see* TREES, CONIFEROUS; ORNAMENTAL TREES.

D

DAHLIA. This half-hardy, herbaceous, tuberous-rooted perennial belongs to the same family as the daisy (*Compositae*). The flower was named in honour of the Swedish botanical explorer D. Andreas Dahl. The dahlia, in both single and semi-double forms and various colours, originated in Mexico, and was known to the Aztecs as *acocotli* and *cocoxochitl* from a word meaning tubes or water-pipes, because of the plant's hollow stems. It was first illustrated by Francisco Hernandez for a book describing the plants, animals, and minerals of Mexico, published in Rome in 1651.

The first dahlias grown in Europe were grown in Madrid from seed sent in 1789 from Mexico.

Dahlias were introduced to Britain around 1800. There were about ten original Mexican species, several of which have contributed to the development of the modern dahlia. Most important is *Dahlia pinnata*, which varies so much that it is itself probably a natural hybrid.

The dahlia is now one of the most important garden flowers, and special dahlia shows are held as well as large exhibits in general Flower Shows. In 1805 its real development began with the appearance of several semi-double 'decorative' types, that is, flowers with several sets of broad and pointed petals. In 1817 a purple fully-double decorative dahlia was imported from France. Between 1820 and 1830 the most popular dahlias were the 'ball' varieties, from which in 1836 there first appeared the 'show' and 'fancy' types, fully-double, almost globular flowers with short petals with incurving edges. Anemone-flowered forms, flowers with an outer ring of flat petals and an inner mass of tubular florets, were introduced in 1830; in 1850 the little 'show' type, called pompons or lilliputs, arrived from Germany. The 'cactus' has been developed from a long-petalled scarlet flower, with curved or twisted petal edges, which was introduced in 1818. The first 'collarette' and 'star' varieties, flowers with one or more sets of flat outer petals, and either a 'collar' of very

DECORATIVE DAHLIA

Amateur Gardening

CACTUS DAHLIA

R. A. Malby

COLLARETTE DAHLIA   *Amateur Gardening*

POMPON DAHLIA   *Amateur Gardening*

ANEMONE-FLOWERED DAHLIA

small inner petals or a central disk, came from France. The modern dahlia has a tremendous range of form and colour, and its size varies from giant decoratives nearly a foot across to 1-inch pompons.

Dahlias grow well in most types of soil. They can be obtained as green plants grown from cuttings struck from February onwards, or as pot roots, that is plants which have been grown in 3-inch pots during the previous season. Moreover the tubers of an old plant can be divided, if care is taken that each division contains a bud; the buds arise on the 'crown' or base of the old stem (*see* BULBS, CORMS, AND TUBERS). Dahlias can be grown quite easily from seed, being treated as half-hardy ANNUALS (q.v.), but only the small single and semi-double varieties are satisfactorily produced by this method; other mixed seed usually produces nondescript flowers.

In the south of England green plants can be planted out of doors during the first week in May, but in the north this is best delayed until early June, when the danger of late frosts is over. Old divided tubers and pot roots can be planted 4 to 6 inches deep, during the middle of April, but they do better if they start growth in shallow boxes of soil, and are planted out later. Each dahlia should be given one strong stake, the larger ones three stakes, with string loops at 18-inch intervals.

The dahlia will flourish in a sunny or semi-shaded position, but tends to 'draw' (grow straggly) if too near high walls or trees. When in full growth, it needs plenty of water and a mulch of strawy manure or compost up to 6 inches deep spread around the plants to keep in the moisture. The dead heads of the plants must be cut off regularly in order to stimulate further flowering.

The foliage turns black at the first severe autumn frost, and then the stems should be cut down to 6 inches and the tubers carefully dug up. Any damaged part of a tuber should be cut away and dusted with lime. After the tubers have dried for a few days, and all soil has been removed, they should be stored in a dry, frost-proof place until the spring.

See also BULBS, CORMS, AND TUBERS; DAISY FAMILY.

DAIRY CATTLE, *see* CATTLE BREEDS.

DAIRY FARMING, *see* CATTLE, CARE OF. *See also* Vol. VII: DAIRY INDUSTRY.

DAIRY MACHINERY. Milking-machines, milk coolers, and steam sterilizing equipment help greatly in the production of a plentiful supply of clean milk. Hand milking is one of the most irksome jobs of the farm, and it is very difficult to prevent milk going sour without the help of coolers and sterilizers.

The milking-machine imitates the calf when suckled by a cow, and subjects the teats to both squeezing and suction (*see* CATTLE, CARE OF, section 2). On to each teat is fixed a rubber-lined metal cup, in which there is an air space between the rubber and the cup. This space is partly exhausted of air about fifty times a minute. At the same time there is a continuous suction on the inner side of the rubber liner, and this acts on the teat of the cow. When the air is drawn out of the space between the liner and the metal cup, there is no firm pressure against the teat; but as soon as air is admitted again to the space between the rubber and the cup, the rubber presses against the teat and squeezes it. This alternate squeezing and relaxing, together with the suction at the outlet of the teat, acts like the sucking and the pressure of the calf's mouth, and causes the milk to flow out of the udder and along a pipe into a bucket. In some milking-machines there are no buckets, and the milk is conveyed through a long pipe from cowshed to milk-room, and is delivered direct on to the cooler.

The vacuum needed for working the machine is provided by a small suction pump driven by either a petrol engine or an electric motor.

The milk from the cow is warm, and it has to be cooled quickly to prevent its going sour before it can be distributed and used. Where plenty of really cold water is available, a simple cooler is used; in this the milk is cooled by being poured over copper tubes through which the cold water flows. To cool milk to a lower temperature than is possible by water, and to provide COLD STORAGE (q.v. Vol. VII), mechanical chemical refrigerators are used.

All dairy utensils have to be kept perfectly clean and sterilized. The parts of the milking-machine and other equipment have to be sterilized with chemicals or with steam, as well as being brushed, scrubbed, and washed. The steam, raised in wood or coal burning, oil-fired, or electrically heated boilers, is blown through the milking-machine teat-cups and pipes. The rest of the equipment is placed in a sterilizing chest that is then filled with steam. Any bacteria are killed by the heat.

Mechanical milk separators separate the cream from the milk much more quickly and thoroughly than can be done by hand skimming. The separator works centrifugally. Cream is lighter in weight than the rest of the milk. Therefore, when the whole milk is rotated at a high speed in a spinning bowl, the heavier skim milk moves towards the outside of the bowl and forces the lighter cream towards the centre. The skim milk is drawn off the outer edge of the

Eric Guy

COWS BEING MILKED BY MACHINE

The vacuum pipe leads to the milk bucket and from there milk and vacuum pipes lead to the cup fixed to each teat

bowl through one spout, and the cream is drawn from the centre through another. The bowl is a composite vessel made of many saucer-shaped disks with spaces between them into which the milk is drawn. The bearings supporting the bowl have to be very accurately made, for, on small separating-machines, the bowl rotates at more than 6,000 revolutions a minute.

Where milk is bottled on farms for sale locally instead of being taken away in bulk to a milk distributor, machines are sometimes used for filling and sealing the bottles. Mechanical bottle-washers also are used; these consist essentially of mechanically driven rotary brushes kept wet by continuous jets of water.

See also Vol. VII: DAIRY INDUSTRY.

DAISY FAMILY. The plant family *Compositae* deserves special mention because it is the largest among flowering plants, containing nearly 800 genera, and producing a very large proportion of our garden flowers.

The family is distinguished from most others by the collection of many small flowers (florets) into a single head surrounded by a ring of bracts, so that the whole looks like one flower. Some members of this family have the whole head composed of tubular florets, some of which may be longer than others, as in the common cornflower (*see* Fig. 1); others have heads composed entirely of florets with tiny tubes at the bottom containing the stamens and stigma, and long, narrow, flat, petal-like pieces growing from one side of the tubes, as in the dandelion. This type of floret is not found in any other family. Yet others, such as the daisy, *Bellis perennis*, have a central disk of tubular florets and an outer ray of florets of the dandelion type (*see* Fig. 2). In many of the daisy family, in the dandelion, for example, the calyx of each floret is replaced by hairs or small scales which remain attached to the seed and, by bearing it aloft in the slightest wind, carry it away from the parent plant (*see* SEEDS, Vol. II).

Among the important garden flowers in this family are the DAHLIAS, CHRYSANTHEMUMS, many EVERLASTING FLOWERS (qq.v.), marigolds, zinnias, globe thistles, the autumn-flowering michaelmas daisies, and the long-flowering gaillardias. The well-known alpine edelweiss is of the daisy family (*see* ALPINE PLANTS, Vol. II). The sunflower is sometimes grown as a crop plant for the oil in the seeds (*see* OIL-BEARING

Crown Copyright reserve

FIG. 1. CORNFLOWER.   FIG. 2. MARIGOLD (DAISY TYPE)

PLANTS), as well as in the garden. Vegetables include lettuce and chicory (*see* SALAD CROPS), scorzonera (*see* SEAKALE), cardoon, and both globe and Jerusalem ARTICHOKES (q.v.). Many members of the daisy family are weeds, such as thistles and hawkweeds. One genus, *Senecio*, which includes weeds such as the ragwort and some exotic shrubs, has interesting representatives among succulent plants (*see* CACTI).

DAMSONS, *see* PLUMS AND DAMSONS.

DATE PALMS. The Date Palm-tree, *Phoenix dactylifera*, grows wild in the deserts of Asia Minor, and is cultivated in the hot, dry parts of North Africa, Arabia, Iraq, India, and in some parts of America. It can grow with less water than any other food plant, and, though it grows

E. O. Hoppé

CLUSTERS OF DATES ON A PALM IN EGYPT

Paul Popper

LOADING A BARGE WITH DATES IN PERSIA

in these hot, dry countries, it can survive a fairly low temperature. It must, of course, have a certain amount of water at its roots, and so is usually grown only in the oases, which are patches of land watered by springs, streams, or wells. As few plants will grow in these hot, dry regions, the date palms are highly prized by their owners, many of whom count their wealth by the number of trees that they own. Date-trees are given a great deal of attention, and the groves are often enclosed within high walls of mud or stone.

The date palm is a tall tree with a slender ribbed stem without side branches, bearing at its tip a cluster of huge feathery leaves. It can be grown from seed, but it is more usually raised from offshoots that grow out from the base of the trunk; in this way the growers make certain of cultivating the right variety of date. The offshoots are planted about 15 feet apart and begin to bear fruit about 7 years later. The trees often grow to a height of as much as 100 feet, and continue to bear fruit for centuries. Date-trees bear flowers of one sex only, either male or female, and it is only the female trees that bear fruit. Therefore growers propagate

only as many male trees as are needed for fertilization. In order to ensure a full crop of fruit the growers climb the trees during the flowering season to carry pollen by hand from the male trees to the female ones.

When the dates first form, they are green in colour, but towards the end of the summer they ripen to yellow, brown, or red, according to variety, becoming juicy, sweet, and delicious. Those that are shipped to England have been dried in the sun in order to preserve them. The Arabs eat great quantities of both fresh and dried dates, and also feed them to their camels. The seeds are ground up to form a meal that is also used as camel food.

See also PALM-TREES.
See also Vol. II: DESERT PLANTS.

DELPHINIUM. These very beautiful garden plants have been developed from species found growing naturally in many parts of the northern hemisphere, by careful selection of particularly good forms and by cross-breeding. Few reliable records exist of the work of early plant breeders, and in consequence it is only possible to guess the

Amateur Gardening

DELPHINIUM

The two spikes are from the same plant. The one with
white centres to the flowers is a 'sport'

history of garden delphiniums by their resemblance to some of the wild plants.

There are three principal garden races: (1) perennial delphiniums with long spikes of flower, (2) perennial delphiniums with short freely branched spikes or loose clusters of flowers, and (3) annual delphiniums or 'larkspurs' which may be either freely branched, sometimes called 'bouquet larkspur', or relatively erect and unbranched, the 'rocket larkspurs'. There are at least 300 species of delphinium, a few of which are grown in gardens and may have been used by breeders, but most of which are wild flowers, of botanical interest only.

The perennial, long-spiked delphiniums have been most highly developed by gardeners. There are hundreds of varieties in cultivation, and the number is constantly increasing. Colours range from pure white and palest mauve to deep blue and purple, and there are also some allied varieties with pink flowers, first obtained by a

Dutch nursery garden firm called Ruys, **by** hybridizing garden delphiniums of this group with a red-flowered species named *Delphinium nudicaule*. The long-spiked delphiniums range in height from about 3 to 8 feet, and there is considerable variation in the size and form of individual flowers. Some are fully double, some single, but the majority of the popular garden varieties have semi-double flowers with an 'eye' which may be white, brown, or black.

The perennial delphiniums with flowers, both single and semi-double, in small, freely branched spikes are generally referred to as Belladonna delphiniums, but these have not been as highly developed as the long-spiked type, and there **are** far fewer varieties.

All these perennial delphiniums flower in June and July, and in favourable years throw up further flower spurs in the autumn. They thrive in any ordinary garden soil and reasonably open position. They are hardy, but suffer badly in winter in water-logged soil. Some varieties tend to be short-lived and must be renewed from seed **or** cuttings every few years. The seed loses its germinating powers quickly and should be sown in late summer as soon as harvested or, at latest, the following spring. It will germinate outdoors, but germinates better in an unheated frame or greenhouse. Seedlings usually give some flowers in their first year, but are not at their best until the second year. They often vary considerably in form and colour from their parents. In consequence, the most successful varieties are propagated by cuttings of young shoots taken in March or April from near the crown of the plant and inserted in sandy soil in a frame or greenhouse. Such cuttings will often produce flowers in late summer but, like seedlings, **are** not at their best until the second year.

The annual larkspurs have a wider colour range, including shades of pink and red, as well as white, mauve, lavender, blue, and purple. They are raised annually from seed, which may be sown outdoors in March, April, or September where the plants are to grow. Seedlings should be thinned or transplanted so that they are about 1 foot apart. Those sown in September will flower in June and July, those sown in spring in July and August.

See also HERBACEOUS BORDER.

DISEASES, *see* PESTS AND DISEASES; ANIMAL DISEASES; PLANT DISEASES.

DISTEMPER, *see* ANIMAL DISEASES, section 2. *See also* Vol. IX: DOGS, CARE OF.

DISTRIBUTORS, *see* DRILLS AND DISTRIBUTORS.

DITCHING, *see* HEDGING, DITCHING, AND WALLING.

DOGGER BANK. This great sand-bank, the most prolific fishing-ground in the British seas, is about 170 miles long and 65 miles wide. It is a submerged plateau, nearly at the centre of the North Sea, almost midway between the Yorkshire coast and that of Denmark. The bottom is composed of long stretches of smooth sand or of a mixture of sand and shells, which is ideal ground for TRAWLING (q.v.). On and in its sands live a multitude of shell-fish, such as the small scallops which fishermen call 'queens', various small clams and razor-fish, whelks and other small molluscs, starfish, crabs, and worms, which are the food of the larger fish.

An examination of the stomach contents of the various fishes caught on the Bank shows that the cod lives chiefly on crustaceans—swimming crabs, hermit-crabs, prawns, and shrimps—and also eats small fishes and worms. The haddock is not a fastidious feeder but prefers a diet made up chiefly of small shell-fish, with a fairly large percentage of crabs, worms, small starfishes, and sea-urchins. The plaice's chief food is small bivalve shell-fish, but they also feed on worms, small sea-urchins, starfishes, crabs, prawns, and shrimps. Soles are more discriminating, sea-worms being their favourite food.

The first fishermen to work the Dogger area were the Dutch, who were attracted by the large numbers of cod. The name 'Dogger' is a Dutch word meaning a 'cod-fishing boat'. This rich fishing ground is now fished by the fleets of most North Sea countries, and when fish are present in great numbers the scene is one of lively activity. Conspicuous among the crowd of boats are the clean-lined steel trawlers from Grimsby and Hull, pushing their way cautiously along while their huge trawls scour the bottom for any lurking fishes. Mingling with these, and giving a warning signal from the mast-head, are scores of trim motor boats, mostly hailing from Esbjerb and other Danish ports. The majority are busy shooting and hauling their favourite encircling net, the *snurrevaad* or Danish seine (*see*

FISHING METHODS). In contrast to these neat Danish double-ended craft are the bluff, heavily built Dutch boats, painted in gay colours. When the fishermen are satisfied with their catch, they draw in their fishing-gear and thread a devious way through the tangle of boats and nets still at work. Once free, they steam at full speed on the homeward run.

See also FISHING INDUSTRY; COD FISHING; TRAWLING.

DOGS, WORKING, *see* SHEEP DOGS. *See also* Vol. IX: DOGS.

DONKEYS AND MULES. The donkey and its relative the mule, both members of the horse family, are two valuable working animals on farms, particularly in certain parts of the world, and on smallholdings. They are strong, hardy, and inexpensive to keep. They can stand the climate in tropical and sub-tropical countries, and, being sure-footed and able to feed on rough pasturage, are valuable BEASTS OF BURDEN (q.v. Vol. IV) in mountainous regions. Donkeys are much used on the farms in Ireland.

The domestic donkey, which is descended from the wild Ass (q.v. Vol. II), is only about 12 hands (1 hand = 4 inches) at the shoulder—about the size of a small pony; though there are some larger breeds. For its size, however, it is as strong as a horse, and though slower and more obstinate, it can work as hard. It can eat much coarser food than a horse, and thrives well on weeds, thistles, and many wild plants which are poisonous or distasteful to other animals. It can even drink brackish water. Donkeys are used mainly as pack animals, or to draw light carts, though on some farms they may also be used to lead the herd of cows, as there is a traditional belief that this prevents abortion amongst the cows. This belief may have arisen because the donkey eats certain weeds which otherwise might have poisoned the cows.

The mule is descended from a male donkey or 'jackass', and a female horse or mare. It inherits quality from its father and size from its mother; therefore it is hardy and can withstand heat like a donkey, but is more useful as a working animal because it is larger and more powerful. Mules are used in the warmer parts of the U.S.A. and in Central and South America, as well as in Mediterranean countries, and are valuable not only on small farms but as pack and draught animals on cotton and sugar planta-

R. J. Salt

A MULE TEAM DRAWING A COMBINE HARVESTER IN CALIFORNIA ABOUT 1900

tions, in lumber camps, and in mines. In the great wheat regions of North America the earliest combine harvesters used to be drawn by teams of twenty-five or more mules harnessed four or five abreast and driven by one man sitting high on the harvester and directing his team by word of mouth and by one rein attached to the front outside right animal.

Being a hybrid—a cross between two different kinds of animal—the mule rarely breeds. In the cotton belt of the U.S.A. particularly fine mules are bred from purebred jackasses and mares.

The hinny is also a hybrid, being descended from a male horse or stallion, and a female donkey. It is smaller and therefore less useful than the mule, and so is not usually bred deliberately. It can stand the heat, however, and is used to some extent by small farmers and peasants in tropical and semi-tropical countries. Like donkeys and mules, it can endure a hard life and subsist on poor and scanty food.

See also Vol. IV: BEASTS OF BURDEN.

DRAINAGE, LAND. No normal crops grow well in land that is waterlogged, for the water has taken the place of the air in the soil and is suffocating the roots of the plants. A great deal of land has natural drainage that carries away surplus water; the land is on a slope or has a porous subsoil through which the water drains. But low-lying land, and land with a clay subsoil, may be so waterlogged that it is useless for

agriculture altogether, or at least it floods during wet seasons. Most land with a heavy soil needs some sort of artificial drainage to keep it in good condition in the winter.

Many large LAND RECLAMATION schemes (q.v. Vol. VIII) have been carried out to drain swamps and marshes and to bring many thousands of acres into cultivation. Such schemes have played an important part in the history of Holland; and the Pontine Marshes in Italy, huge areas in the Mississippi basin in the U.S.A., the Fens district in eastern England, and many other areas have been so reclaimed. This article, however, is concerned not with the reclamation of land for farming, but with the drainage carried out by the individual farmer for a particular field or group of fields in order to keep good land in condition.

The earliest and simplest drainage consists of open furrows, drawn with a plough down the slope and leading to a ditch at the bottom. These are called water furrows. Underground drainage of fields is mentioned for the first time in the 15th century, and drain tiles came into common use towards the end of the 18th century. These were U-shaped, made of clay, and placed upside down on flat tiles to make a channel. By the middle of the 19th century they were being replaced by clay pipes.

Today the farmer drains his fields by ditches, by mole drains, and by pipe drains. The ditches or dykes (*see* HEDGING, WALLING, AND DITCHING) run round the outside of the fields and serve to carry away the water brought to them by the mole and pipe drains.

Mole drains, so called because they form a passage through the earth rather like that of a mole, are cheaper and quicker to make than a pipe drain, but do not last as long. The 'mole', a bullet-shaped piece of metal 2 inches in diameter fixed to a vertical, knife-like coulter, is drawn through the soil by a tractor at a depth of 15 to 20 inches, leaving a little tunnel behind it. If the drain has to be cut below grassland, a disk coulter is also fitted to the mole plough to cut a passage through the turf for the main coulter. Mole draining is most satisfactory and will last for several years in fairly heavy land that is free from stones; in lighter land the moles soon cave in.

Pipe drains, well laid, will last a lifetime and often longer. Unglazed, earthenware pipes are generally used, and are laid in trenches (afterwards filled in) at a depth of 2 to 4 feet, and about 12 to 40 feet apart: the heavier the land the more shallow and the closer together must be the drains. The main drains may be about 5 to 8 inches in diameter, and the branch ones 2½ or 3 inches: it depends upon circumstances. The mains empty into ditches at 'outfalls', and these need occasional inspection lest they get blocked. The pipes are laid end to end without cement, so that the soil water can enter through the joints as well as through the walls of the pipes themselves. The trenches in which the pipes are laid must be dug so that there is an uninterrupted fall from end to end. This needs great skill on the part of those laying the pipes. There are nowadays machines to dig the trenches, and the working of these also demands skill, though of a rather different kind.

In 1861 the first Land Drainage Act was passed, and this set up Internal Drainage Boards to organize drainage systems on a larger scale, each Board being responsible for a defined area. The Land Drainage Act of 1930 set up Catchment Boards to control individual rivers and groups of rivers (see WATER SUPPLY, Vol. VIII). This act also empowers the government to make contributions to private drainage schemes, and to organize the supply of machinery and materials for such schemes.

See also IRRIGATION.

See also Vol. VIII: LAND RECLAMATION; WATER SUPPLY.

DRILLS AND DISTRIBUTORS.

Nearly all seeds are planted in rows, and the machine for opening a furrow or 'trough' in the earth, dropping in the seed, and then covering up the trough, is called a 'drill' (see picture, p. 33). Some drills have a knife like the coulter of a plough, and some a disk to open the furrow. In some the seeds are picked out of a box by cups on the edge of a revolving wheel, which is geared to the land wheels of the drill, and each cupful is emptied down a tube to fall into the trough. The speed of rotation of the cup wheels can be adjusted in relation to the speed of the drill as it moves over the field; this alters the frequency with which the little cups are emptied into the trough, and therefore alters the amount of seed put in on each acre. In other kinds of drill there are no cup wheels; the seed is forced into the tubes by fluted rollers.

In all kinds of drills the seed is carried in a long narrow box, called a 'hopper', fastened across the frame of the drill. Some corn drills are constructed so as to sow a small amount of powdered fertilizer with each seed. Such drills, called combine drills, have two compartments

Farmer and Stockbreeder

A MOLE DRAINER DRAWN BY CATERPILLAR TRACTOR

in the hopper, one for seed and one for the fertilizer.

ARTIFICIAL FERTILIZERS (q.v.) may, however, be applied to the land separately from the seed, and for this purpose machines called distributors are used. The distributor has a hopper rather like the hopper of a seed drill, and the fertilizer falls out of the bottom of this at a measured rate, and is evenly spread by the machine as it travels over the field. In some kinds of distributor the powder falls through slots in moving plates which form the floor of the hopper; in others, the powder falls on to horizontal spinning disks which whirl the fertilizer out in a cloud.

Farmyard manure is sometimes loaded mechanically from cowsheds and cattle yards on to special tractor-drawn trailers. The floor of the body of such a trailer is an endless conveyor which is put into gear when the outfit gets to the field where the manure is to be spread. Thus the manure is moved slowly towards the open back of the trailer, where it falls on to revolving paddles which break it up and scatter it over the land.

Young plants, as well as seeds, can be set in the soil mechanically by machines, which are called 'transplanters'. One such machine for the transplanting of young seedlings has seats for four operators, who take the tiny plants from a box carried on the machine and place them between the machine's rubber-covered iron fingers. The mechanical fingers grip them, carry them down to the soil, and place them in a trough cut by a coulter on the front of the machine. A specially shaped wheel, mounted behind, then closes the trough and presses the soil round the roots of the newly set plants.

Most machines for planting potatoes are, like the machines for transplanting seedlings, not entirely automatic, but are 'human assisted'. The seed potatoes are fed into cups by operators who ride on the machine. Some of these machines plant the potatoes 'on the flat' by opening out a narrow trough or furrow in which the seed is set. Others drop the seed potatoes into the wider and deeper furrows made by a 'bouting' or 'ridging' plough body—a body that has two mould-boards, one set on either side of a single share. When the potatoes have been set in the furrows, they are covered by 'splitting back the ridges', that is to say, each ridge is split in the middle to form a new furrow, and the soil from the old ridges falls to either side, forming a new ridge and covering the POTATOES (q.v.).

See also MECHANIZED FARMING.

DUCKS. The domestic breeds of ducks, with the exception of the Muscovy Duck, are thought to be all descended from the wild Mallard (*see* DUCKS, Vol. II). As was the case with the fowl, ducks were first kept in Britain to provide meat rather than eggs. These 'table' breeds, such as the Aylesbury, Pekin, and Rouen, are large birds which lay very few eggs—only 30 to 60 in a year. In 1850, however, a breed called the Indian Runner was imported from Java and Malaya, and these are very good layers indeed —laying 150 to 200 eggs in a year, and sometimes as many as 300. Then in about 1900, a new breed, the Khaki Campbell, the product of a cross between the Mallard, Rouen, and the Indian Runner, was introduced. There are also a great many breeds of very prettily coloured ducks that are often to be seen on the lakes of gardens and parks. These are kept solely because they are ornamental.

Ducks are very hardy creatures and easy to look after. They like to have water for a swim, but can live, lay, and breed quite well without it. The table duck grows very quickly and will reach a weight of about 6 lb. at 10 weeks old; a chicken would take twice as long. The Khaki Campbell and the Runners will lay as many eggs as, or more than, a fowl, and all ducks are cheaper to feed than hens for they will forage a great deal for themselves if given free range.

N.I.A.E.

POTATO PLANTER

The machine cuts three rows of furrows to receive the potatoes, which are dropped from the revolving trays at the back. The furrows are then split back to cover the potatoes. Men or girls seated at the back keep the trays supplied

KHAKI CAMPBELL DRAKE

KHAKI CAMPBELL DUCK

A. Ric

WHITE RUNNER DUCK

AYLESBURY DRAKE

MUSCOVY DRAKE

Their eggs are also a little bigger. Ducks lay all or nearly all their eggs in the early morning, whereas a hen may lay at any time during the day. On leaving their nests both ducks and geese cover their eggs with straw or other litter, an instinct to protect them from discovery. In a breeding flock the proportion of ducks to drakes is about 4 to 1 with the table breeds, and 6 or 8 to 1 with the laying breeds.

In the coloured breeds, such as the Khaki Campbells, Rouens, and the ornamental breeds, the drake is gayer in colour than the duck, and in all the breeds, except the Muscovy, the drake, when fully grown, has two or three curly feathers in his tail. The voices of the two sexes are also different, for the duck has a loud 'quack' and the drake makes a hoarse, hissing sound. This difference can be noticed from the time the birds are about 6 weeks old.

The Muscovy duck is often thought to be a goose, but is probably a species of duck. It grazes grass like the goose; the drake has no curled feathers in its tail; the eggs take 36 days to hatch, which is longer than either duck or goose eggs; and it is a great flier, sometimes making its nest in trees in a most unducklike manner. In Australia it is popular as a table bird, but in Britain it is kept mainly as an ornamental water-fowl.

See also POULTRY.

See also Vol. II: DUCKS (wild species).

E

EARTHWORMS. It has long been known that earthworms play an important part in the work of the farmer and the gardener. There are a great many kinds or species of earthworm; they live in the moist upper layers of soil all over the world, except where the climate is very cold, or where the soil is dry, as, for example, in deserts. Their outer skins, through which they breathe, need to be kept moist all the time. They feed mostly on the decaying remains of plants and other dead matter which they find either in the soil or on its surface. They emerge, principally at night time, and pull into their burrows any leaves or grasses they can find on the surface of the ground. They may eat large quantities of soil with their food, including sand grains which serve to grind the food in their gizzards, and at least two species excrete this soil in the form of worm-casts, the little piles of mould which are often seen on the surface of the ground near the burrows, especially after rain (*see* WORM, section 2, Vol. II).

Gilbert WHITE (q.v. Vol. V), the naturalist, was the first to write about the important work of earthworms. He noticed how they improved the soil and helped the growth of vegetation by 'boring, perforating, and loosening the soil, and rendering it pervious to rains and the fibres of plants by drawing straws and the stalks of leaves and twigs into it; and most of all by throwing up such infinite numbers of lumps of soil called wormcasts, which, being their excrement, is a fine manure for grain and grass.' In these ways earthworms improve the physical condition of the soil.

Later, the biologist Charles DARWIN (q.v. Vol. V) carried out a careful study over a period of 40 years, of earthworms and their work. In his book, *The Formation of Vegetable Mould by the Action of Earthworms*, Darwin tells us how he calculated that each acre of land contained from 25,000 to 53,000 earthworms, and that these worms could bring to the surface of each acre from 10 to 18 tons of new fresh mould every year. Since Darwin's day it has been discovered that earthworm populations vary a great deal, and that some types of soil may have a population as high as 2 or 3 millions per acre.

Where the soil is stony, earth-worms can be used to increase the proportion of top-soil by causing the stones to sink. This is based on another observation recorded by Darwin; he had noticed that a stony field had been changed into a good pasture field during the course of time entirely by the action of earthworms. Earthworms of certain types are now even being bred, specially for this purpose, in boxes and beds filled with compost, and their eggs are sold to farmers to place in the fields they wish to improve, though whether the earthworms that are added to the natural population will find enough food is another matter. The worms of artificial cultures have, of course, to be fed with suitable material so that they can increase and

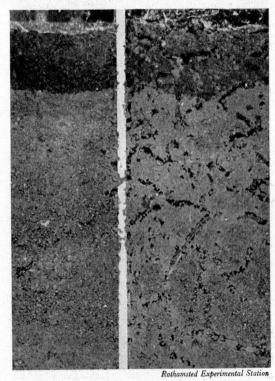

Rothamsted Experimental Station

SECTIONS OF SOILS WITH EARTHWORMS (RIGHT) AND WITHOUT (LEFT)

Amateur Gardening

THE USE OF EDGING PLANTS IN A BORDER
White alyssum alternates with dark blue lobelia

multiply on their own. This earthworm culture has developed mainly in North America.

See also CULTIVATIONS; MANURES; SOILS.

EDGING PLANTS. A flower-bed or herbaceous border is often given a more finished appearance by an edging, which can be made of bricks, tiles, concrete, or wood, or can take the form of a grass verge, or may be composed of certain low-growing, compact plants.

The most permanent edging plants are low-growing evergreen shrubs, such as dwarf lavenders, lavender cotton (*Santolina*), and box, which must be regularly clipped to make them keep their compact shape. A number of herbaceous perennial plants make good edges. Some of these form mats of foliage which persist in winter, such as the familiar arabis, aubrietia, and snow-in-summer (*Cerastium*). Other good 'edgers' are those forming tufts such as thrift (*Armeria*), or rosettes as in London Pride (*Saxifraga umbrosa*). Plants which grow very fast, such as Creeping Jenny (*Lysimachia Nummularia*), are difficult to control, and so better avoided.

Annual or perennial plants which flower profusely in the summer make showy edgings. Perennials such as double daisies and forget-me-nots are apt to die out in a wet or cold winter, but pinks will survive. The brilliant blue annual lobelia continues to flower over a long season.

Any fairly low plant may be used as an edging so long as it continues to look neat and shapely throughout the year, as well as producing a show of colour. In some cases, however, especially for beds filled with BEDDING PLANTS (q.v.), only a summer display is needed. Naturally the annual or tender edging plants are more trouble than perennials, but such plants are on the whole far gayer during the most important garden season, and a considerable variety can be achieved. On the other hand, a neat edging of garden pinks, for example, is always pleasing whether in flower or not, so long as the plants have had the dead heads cut off.

EDUCATION, AGRICULTURAL, *see* AGRICULTURAL TRAINING.

EEL FISHING. Both the young eels, called elvers, and the full-grown adult eels are fished for. A vast number of tiny elvers arrive in the Severn and other western rivers of Britain in early spring, and are caught with fine-meshed nets. Full-grown eels are caught by spearing, angling with thorn-hooks, barbed steel hooks, and gorges (solid objects swallowed by the fish), and sometimes by 'bobbing' with threaded worms. To make a 'bob', forty or fifty worms are threaded on a bunch of worsted thread, and this bob is tied to a short line and flicked up and down till an eel bites. The eel's teeth become so

James Hornell

WEIR FOR TRAPPING EELS AT COMACCHIO, ITALY

like creatures that can be serious pests of certain crops. They spend part of their lives within the host plants and part of their lives free in the soil or in water. They are so small that they cannot be seen properly without a lens.

1. POTATO-ROOT EELWORM. This pest is whitish and about $\frac{1}{25}$ inch long, and feeds inside the roots of POTATOES and TOMATOES (qq.v.), causing serious loss or even complete failure of the crop. It is one of the worst pests in allotments and gardens and on the farms in potato-growing districts such as Lincolnshire. An attack first shows as a patch of stunted plants in the potato field or bed; this patch increases in size year by year for as long as potatoes are grown in the same ground. Towards the end of the summer the female eelworms turn into little white, rounded bodies called 'cysts', somewhat smaller than a pin's head, which can be seen stuck to the roots of infested plants. Later, these cysts turn brown and drop off into the soil. In each one there are between 150 and 600 eggs, and these hatch into young eelworms again only if their food plant (tomatoes or potatoes) is close by. They have been known to live for as much as 6 years before hatching. Eelworms easily spread from place to place, for the cysts may be carried from infected ground in soil sticking to boots, tools, or cartwheels. There is no known chemical cure for this pest, and the only way of controlling it is to grow potatoes in the same ground not more often than once in every 3 years, and even less often if the land is badly infested. All other vegetables except tomatoes can, however, be grown, as the potato-root eelworm does not attack them.

2. ROOT KNOT EELWORM. This tiny pear-shaped eelworm, which is only just visible to the naked eye, causes the swollen and galled appearance of the roots of TOMATOES, CUCUMBERS, and sometimes LETTUCES (qq.v.) grown under glass. Each female lays up to a thousand eggs, and the young become mature in about 4 weeks. They live in the galls on the roots of

entangled in the wool that it can usually be caught if the line is jerked smartly up.

Eels are also caught in traps. In Lincolnshire, these are made of closely woven wicker-work and shaped like huge soda-water bottles. In other places sleeve-shaped bags are often used. The simplest trap of all is a sack with a piece of drain-pipe fitted into the mouth, filled with straw and baited with offal. The dark opening of the pipe tempts the eels, and the catch is often very large.

Nets are also used. In Lincolnshire a small-mesh 'seine' or encircling net is thrown around any spot where eels are known to be plentiful. When the seine is hauled, the eels are herded into the tail end.

To catch eels on a large scale, weirs are often constructed, the most famous of which are those of Comacchio in Italy. These weirs are gigantic traps placed at points where the drainage from the marshes empties into a river. The traps are v-shaped mazes with very thick walls of tightly packed straw, supported on beams sunk deep into the ground. At the apex is a narrow entrance into a heart-shaped pound or trap. Periodically the fishermen clear the pounds with big dip-nets, and carry the catch to the factory, where the eels are prepared for market.

See also Vol. II: EELS.

EELWORMS. These are microscopic, worm-

the plants and also in the soil, where they can survive for some time. The foliage of infected plants fades, especially on the lower parts, and the upper leaves wilt in sunshine. Control is very difficult. As a temporary measure, a layer of peat about 1 inch thick can be placed round the plant, in which the plant may make new roots. The best control is by sterilization of the soil by steam or by a chemical when the ground is clear of crops.

3. Beet Eelworm (Beet Sickness). The Beet Eelworm has a similar structure and life-history to its relative the Potato-root Eelworm. It attacks sugar-beet and red beet, mangolds, spinach, radish, and a wide variety of plants of the cabbage tribe (*Cruciferae*). The rootlets are eaten by the eelworms, but the plant often produces other rootlets to make up for those damaged by the pest; the result is a thin beet covered with many fine rootlets. The plant also develops yellowish outer leaves and many small green inner leaves. The cysts contain a large number of eggs, some of which hatch each year no matter what crop is grown, though if no suitable food-plant is available, they die.

The only effective control is a system of rotation whereby the crops likely to be attacked are planted only once in every 3 or more years. Land already infested must be given a rest from these crops for 4 or more years, according to the severity of the infection. Care should be taken not to spread soil and plants contaminated with

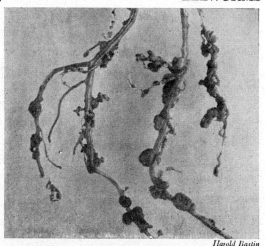

Harold Bastin

GALLS ON CUCUMBER ROOTS MADE BY ROOT KNOT EELWORMS
(ENLARGED)

the cysts on to uninfested land. By the Sugar Beet Eelworm Order, 1943, of the Ministry of Agriculture (q.v.) the following crops are not allowed to be grown in infested land without a licence: sugar-beet, mangold, red beet, spinach, cabbage, kale, cauliflower, broccoli, Brussels sprouts, turnip, swede, mustard, cress, radish, kohl-rabi, and rape.

4. Chrysanthemum or Strawberry Eelworm. This attacks many plants, the chrysanthemum and strawberry being the most important. It gets into the leaves through the stomata (breathing pores), and travels from plant to plant when the leaves touch. Part of its life is spent in the thin film of water that surrounds the particles of the soil. It can also live in a dried up condition, coiled up like a watch spring, for 3 years. The leaves of a plant which has been attacked develop pale yellowish patches, which later become dark brown, and the petals may be dwarfed or the bud destroyed before it opens. In a severe attack the leaves may fall from the stem.

The eelworm on chrysanthemums can be checked by weekly sprays of nicotine through the summer; but a complete cure can only be achieved by the 'warm water treatment'. After flowering, the stems are cut back and the whole plant is lifted, washed clear of soil, and then immersed for a period of 5 minutes in water kept at a temperature of 115° F. Then the plant is cooled in cold water and replanted in sterilized soil. Later, cuttings are taken and planted in soil free of the pest.

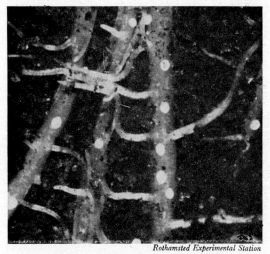

Rothamsted Experimental Station

POTATO-ROOT EELWORM CYSTS ON POTATO ROOTS

The round objects are the cysts (enlarged) in which the female eelworms have produced eggs

5. STEM AND BULB EELWORM. This eelworm attacks a great many wild and cultivated plants, some of which may pass on the infestation to other types of plants.

The existence of 'biological races' or strains of eelworm is beginning to be understood, though no differences in their appearance have yet been detected. For example, there is a 'race' of Stem Eelworm, known as the 'oat-onion race', which attacks oats, onions, beans, parsnips, rhubarb, strawberries, and various weeds such as chickweed, sandwort, scarlet pimpernel, and cleavers —but not other farm crops. The 'red clover race' attacks red clover, alsike clover, kidney vetch, and also to a small extent white clover, and is one of the causes of 'clover sickness'; but it hardly ever touches sainfoin, lucerne, or trefoil. Other races attack lucerne and white clover; another attacks narcissus but not tulip, and another attacks tulip. The eelworm can at least be discouraged if the land is kept entirely clear of host plants, including weeds, for at least 12 months. The main control is by a ROTATION OF CROPS (q.v.), by planting immune crops or resistant varieties, and by the chemical treatment of the seed. Bulbs, when dormant, and also strawberry runners can be given the 'warm water treatment'.

See also PESTS AND DISEASES.

EGG-PLANT (AUBERGINE). The fruits of the egg-plant or 'garden egg', *Solanum Melongena*, are used as a vegetable, being sliced and fried or stuffed and cooked. Aubergine is the French name; the name 'egg-plant' arose because some varieties have white, egg-like fruits. The egg plant is an erect, branching, annual plant of which there are three distinct types, bearing white, black, and purple fruits respectively; the black and purple varieties, which have longer and more pear-shaped fruits, are the most commonly cultivated.

The egg-plant needs a high temperature and so cannot be grown in the open in Britain. It has, however, been cultivated successfully under CLOCHES (q.v.), but usually thrives most satisfactorily in a glasshouse where a uniform temperature not lower than 65° F. can be kept day and night.

The egg-plant, when grown under glass, is cultivated much like the TOMATO (q.v.), except that it needs rather more warmth and humidity. The seeds are usually sown in seed-boxes or on

Sutton and Sons Ltd.

EGG-PLANT WITH FLOWERS AND FRUIT

a hot-bed in March (not earlier), and the seedlings pricked out into boxes, and later transplanted. The plants are grown to maturity either in large (16-inch) pots or in prepared beds in the glasshouse. They need a lot of water to encourage them to grow freely. They should not be planted out under cloches until mid-May or early June, and even then they do better with some form of heating—electric soil warming or a hot-bed—to assist the ordinary warmth of the cloche.

In warm countries egg-plants are planted in the open in well manured soil as soon as the temperature is above 65° F. The plants are spaced 24 to 30 inches apart in rows from 3 to 4 feet apart; a wider spacing is required by stronger varieties and on rich soils.

The fruits, which need careful handling, are gathered when mature, but before the seeds are fully developed.

ENCLOSURES, *see* OPEN FIELDS AND ENCLOSURES.

ENDIVE, *see* SALAD CROPS, section 2.

EROSION, *see* Vol. III: Soil Erosion.

ESPALIER, *see* Pruning, section 2.

ESPARTO GRASS, *see* Fibre Crops. *See also* Vol. VII: Paper-making.

EVERGREENS, *see* Flowering Shrubs; Ornamental Trees; Garden Hedges.

EVERLASTING FLOWERS. A number of plants produce papery flowers which, when dried, will last for a long time. Most of these belong to the *Compositae* or Daisy Family (q.v.); in these the brightly coloured papery parts of the flowers are actually petal-like bracts. Perhaps the most satisfactory everlastings are *Xeranthemum*, the Mediterranean Immortelle, and *Helichrysum*. Others are *Hemipterum* (which seedsmen call both *Acroclinium* and *Rhodanthe*), *Ammobium*, and some species of *Anaphalis* and *Antennaria*, the last two having small woolly flowers.

Other everlasting flowers, not of the daisy family, include the common wild sea lavender and its relations, and various annual species, called statice, in many colours. *Gomphrena globosa* has rather less papery flowers, somewhat like clover heads, white, red, or violet. Two plants which are grown for the value of their dried seed pods are honesty (*Lunaria*) with flat, oval, satin-white pods, and the Cape gooseberry or Chinese lantern plant (*Physalis Alkekengi*) which bears its seed within the red or orange calyx which becomes inflated and bladder-like. Most of these plants are Annuals (q.v.) or can be grown as such, and are easy to grow, if given plenty of room to branch and grow strong.

Everlasting flowers should be cut in dry, sunny weather, and hung in small bunches upside down in a dry, airy place. The daisy kinds should be cut before they are fully open,

Amateur Gardening

EVERLASTING FLOWERS

Statice, helichrysum, honesty, chinese lanterns, and the seed pods of the flag iris

and the leaves should be removed from the stems. Statice and everlasting seed pods should be cut when fully mature, and treated in the same way. They may be used when the stems are quite stiff and dry. The flowering kinds do not always produce stems strong enough to support the heads, and sometimes need strengthening with florist's wire.

Though not strictly 'everlastings', wild grasses, teasels, and bulrushes also dry well, and can be used for dry decorations, together with berries, pine cones, dried hydrangea flower-heads, and old man's beard. Some of these, as well as Butcher's Broom (*Ruscus*) and magnolia leaves, are much used by florists, and are often artificially coloured.

See also Vol. VII: Flower Trade.

F

FAMINE. This may occur whenever the course of a normal year's farming is interrupted by such catastrophes as floods, drought, earthquakes, and the ravages of pests and war. Any one of these may cause crop failures that bring starvation to the people, especially in those countries where a large proportion of the population lives at 'subsistence' level, that is, with little or no reserves of food or money.

Because of their climatic conditions some countries are more likely to experience crop failures than others. In India, where four-fifths of the people are farmers, the crops very largely depend upon the MONSOON rains (q.v. Vol. III). If these come too soon, they prevent planting; if they come too late or fail altogether, there is widespread drought. In addition there are cyclones that may destroy the crops before harvest. (*See* HURRICANES, Vol. III.)

The Indian peasant to a large extent still farms only five or six strips of land, widely separated from each other, amounting in all to 2 or 3 acres, and from this and the common pasture he supports his family. He still uses the primitive farming methods of his forefathers, and, since he has no reserves to fall back on, a bad season means disaster (*see* INDIANS, VILLAGE LIFE, Vol. I). The Bengali word for famine is *durviksha*, meaning 'difficult to beg', and the first sign of a food shortage anywhere is the movement of beggars away from those areas where there is most want.

In 1943 the province of Bengal experienced one of the worst famines on record, due to a combination of factors. The 1942 winter rice crop had failed from drought, and in 1941 and 1942 there were cyclones over the delta lands known as the 'granary of Bengal', which destroyed in the latter year 1½ million tons of rice, and reduced the population to starvation level.

At the same time the normal supply of rice from Burma was cut off by the Japanese occupation, the supply of wheat from the northern parts of India was seriously affected by the flooding of the Damodar river, and the movement of relief supplies was handicapped by the lack of small boats which had been called in by the government through fear of a Japanese invasion.

The government Famine Relief Organization set up food centres in the towns, and, later, relief was taken to the villages where those who had not crowded to the towns were living on whatever roots and herbs they could collect. By the end of 1943, when the autumn crop was harvested, distress had been relieved slightly; but months of starvation had destroyed what little resistance to disease the poorer peasants had, and of the 1½ million deaths more were due to the epidemics of cholera and malaria than to actual starvation.

In 1950 a series of EARTHQUAKES (q.v. Vol. III) in Assam in north India affected 20,000 square miles in the Brahmaputra valley, destroying roads and bridges, and causing landslips and blockages. Many rivers were entirely blocked for several days, and when the headwaters forced a way through, rice fields and tea plantations were washed away and cattle drowned. Half a million people were made homeless, and some 100,000 lost their lives in the floods. The sending of food supplies to Assam so seriously strained India's very slender resources that the government determined to build up a central reserve of grain ready to meet any sudden shortage in a particular area, and also to embark on a long term plan to increase food production.

In northern China the Hwang-Ho, or YELLOW RIVER (q.v. Vol. III), is known as 'China's Sorrow' because of its tendency to flood the fertile and densely peopled plain. The Chinese farmer, like the Indian peasant, lives on the poverty line, existing on a meagre diet of wheatcakes and vegetables if he lives in the north or of rice if he lives in the south. With no reserves to tide him over a bad season, he faces starvation if his crops fail. Should the Yellow River overflow and flood the great plain, then distress occurs on a large scale.

The control of this river by means of dykes and embankments is essential. In 1938 a Chinese general, in an attempt to stop the advance of a Japanese force, blew up a dyke. The result was disastrous. The whole of the Yellow River poured through the gap and flooded 3 million acres of land, drowning 400,000 people. There were a million refugees of whom an enormous number died from lack of food and from epidemics. It was to meet such a disaster as this that the International Famine Relief Committee was set up, and UNRRA (United Nations Relief and Rehabilitation Administration) organized.

By 1945 the breach in the river's embankment was finally repaired and the river turned back into its old course. The refugees then began slowly returning to their homes. UNRRA observers reported the amazing way in which a family of refugees would make straight for a piece of land they declared was their own, and start to dig to uncover a well or buried household goods which they had left behind them. Temporary camps were set up to provide food and shelter, and the land was gradually brought back into production.

In many parts of the world famines have been caused by LOCUSTS (q.v.). Early settlers in North America and Australia had to fight them in their hordes; in parts of South America a plague of locusts still means disaster; in India, Central Asia, and China too, locusts are also a danger; but it is in Africa and the Middle East that the damage they do is most widespread and serious. Three thousand years ago the prophet Joel described how 'the land is as the garden of Eden before them, and behind them a desolate wilderness'. In 125 B.C. 800,000 people are said to have died of famine in Cyrenaica, a fertile Roman province, because locusts ate their crops.

In 1928 there was a plague of locusts in French West Africa, and during the next few years flying swarms invaded every country from Guinea to the Cape, destroying immense areas of crops. In Tanganyika alone over three-quarters of all the native crops were destroyed in one year. Some swarms took days to pass, and the Africans fought them desperately, digging trenches in their path, lighting fires, making smoke-screens, and beating the insects with branches. When all else failed, they resorted to the banging of drums, casting magic spells, and sacrificing goats to their gods. Poison bait finally checked the plague. Famine was only averted by immediate relief from outside, and in Kenya alone £250,000 was spent on locust control and famine relief. The Anti-Locust Research Centre has now been established, and groups of trained men are sent out to locust infested areas to locate breeding centres and to destroy the swarms.

Bad crops and shortages of food are sometimes caused in countries with a cool, moist climate by lack of sunshine and too much rain, for these conditions encourage plant diseases. It was a series of poor harvests that caused the famine in England in 1586, and led to the beginning of the POOR LAW System (q.v. Vol. X).

The great Irish famine of 1846 was caused by the potato blight (*see* PLANT DISEASES, section 2). Of the 8 million people in Ireland at least half were dependent on the potato for food. When the blight appeared two years running and crops failed, famine affected not only the poor labourer who had no reserves to fall back on, but also the small farmer who kept cattle and corn to pay the rent and grew potatoes to feed his family. Starving people died by the roadside on their way to the towns, and those who reached the overcrowded towns developed famine fever. Altogether about 1 million people died.

By 1848 the famine had been checked, for the 1847 harvest was a good one; but during the famine years thousands of people emigrated overseas, chiefly to America. Emigration continued until the end of the century, so that by 1911 Ireland's population had declined to 4¾ millions, in spite of a high birth-rate.

Acts of war not only destroy the standing crops but prevent the sowing of next year's crops. After the Second World War, thousands of European refugees, whose country had been devastated, were fed and given shelter by such voluntary organizations as the Oxford Famine Relief Committee and the Friends' Relief Service, and UNRRA sent food supplies to Greece and Holland.

It is now recognized that the problem of preventing famine is an international one. The United Nations Food and Agriculture Organization has, therefore, proposed the creation of reserves of basic foodstuffs for use in time of famine in any country; and it has suggested that money should be advanced through the International Bank for the development and conservation of natural resources, the development of new lands, and the use of new farming methods.

See also Vol. X: UNITED NATIONS ORGANIZATION.

FARM ANIMALS, *see* CATTLE; HORSES; PIGS; POULTRY; SHEEP; ANIMAL FARMING, TROPICAL.

FARM BUILDINGS, *see* FARMSTEAD.

FARM COTTAGES. Farm workers may live
either in cottages on the farm itself or in cottages
or houses in a nearby village or town. In the
first case the occupation without rent of a cottage
on the farm may form part of the farm-workers'
wages. They have what is called a 'service
tenancy'—that is, they occupy his cottage as long
as they are working for the farmer; when they
leave his service they have to leave his cottage
as well.

This is called the 'tied-cottage' system (*see*
LAND OWNERSHIP, section 2 c). It has several
advantages and disadvantages. The advantages
are that a farm worker, when he accepts a job,
is sure of some kind of a home, and one situated
conveniently near to his job, a matter of special
importance when his work is the care of livestock.
The great disadvantage is that, should he lose his
job, he also loses his home, and when there is a
shortage of houses, this is a very serious matter.
Also, in a tied-cottage, he is never away from his
work and the sight of his work, and is, perhaps,
too constantly under his master's eye.

When a farm worker, on the other hand, rents
a house or cottage unconnected with the farm,
he has a private life separate from his work;
when off duty he is really off duty. Also he can
change his job without the certainty of losing
his home.

Perhaps advantage and disadvantage are
fairly equal on farms with a convenient village
nearby. But in more remote districts, particularly
in hill country, the nearest village may be too far
away to enable the farm worker to do his work
properly. For example, after a fall of snow he
may be quite unable to reach the stock for
which he is responsible. In such cases the tied-
cottage system seems the only practical one, in
spite of all its social drawbacks.

But whether housed under one system or the
other, the farm worker's views (and still more
the farm worker's wife's views) have changed
considerably within recent years as to what
comfort and convenience a farm cottage should
provide. Some of the old farm cottages in the
country are very picturesque, but many of them
are still without the proper amenities of civilized
life. There is often no light except lamps or
candles, no bathroom, no indoor sanitation, and
nothing to cook food on except an open grate.
These farm cottages are not unfairly called
'rural slums', though the country cottage has at
least this advantage over the town slum—it has
plenty of fresh air and space round it, and often
has lovely surroundings.

The modern farm worker very reasonably
wants a cottage that, in essentials, is no different
from that which the town industrial worker
wants. He wants a small house, probably of not
more than four rooms, if possible detached from
other houses, and with indoor water and sanitation, a bathroom, and a labour-saving kitchen.
He wants his house to be not too far from public
transport, so that his wife can go shopping and
his children to school; and he wants a small
garden. His views on these matters are so
firmly fixed that unless they are largely met, he
will not accept a job on a farm, but will try to
get work in a town instead. The proper housing
of the farm worker is, therefore, essential to the
prosperity of agriculture. Most married farm
workers would prefer a really good cottage and
a smaller wage to an out-
of-date cottage and more
money.

When houses are very
scarce, as after the Second
World War, this problem of
housing farm workers pro-
perly is no easy matter, and
is most difficult on remote
farms in the country where
public services such as water,
gas, and electricity may not
exist. Many farm cottages
can, however, be moder-
nized to some extent; and
though such modernization

16TH-CENTURY FARM COTTAGES IN SUSSEX

may cost a good deal of money—more, possibly, than was spent originally on building the cottage—reconstruction may be cheaper and more immediately possible than the erection of an entirely new cottage.

Probably, however, more and more farm workers and their families will come to live in housing estates, going and coming from their farm work by motor transport. There are disadvantages to this arrangement, especially for farms with a large proportion of livestock; but it is, in fact, no more difficult or expensive to take a man from a village to work on a farm than to take his children from the farm to the village school.

The farm cottage of the past, with its thatched roof and roses above the door, is in many places being inhabited, not by farm workers at all, but by artists and others who enjoy its charm and beauty, and can afford to add a certain amount of modern convenience.

See also FARM LABOUR; FARM-HOUSES; LAND OWNERSHIP.

FARMERS' UNIONS, see NATIONAL FARMERS' UNION; FARM LABOUR.

FARM-HOUSES. The main fault of most farm-houses is that for modern times they are too big. In other respects, when in repair, the best of them are splendid homes. In parts of England there are farm-houses dating from Elizabethan or Jacobean times, many of which were not built as farm-houses in the first instance, but were originally the homes of the smaller squires and country gentlemen. In the 17th and 18th centuries some of these squires built larger and more splendid country houses, and the original manor house often became the house of the farmer of one of the estate farms. Again, in the 18th century, when many of the smaller estates were absorbed by larger estates, the small squire often became the large farmer, and his manor house the farm-house. In this sense many old farm-houses have seen better days. Other ancient farm-houses were converted out of old

John Topham

MODERN FARM COTTAGES AT CHARING, KENT

monastic buildings at the time of the Reformation when the monasteries were closed. There are many such in the county of Kent, where the farm kitchen may show evidence that pilgrims, riding to Canterbury, came there for food and shelter.

Most farm-houses, being old—some of them, at least in part, very old—were built by local craftsmen of local materials. In Anglo-Saxon times they were built of wood, and later of local stone and of locally made brick (see HOUSES, HISTORY OF, Vol. XI).

Although many of these old farm-houses are too big for convenience today, in former times the farm-house needed to be big. Most farmers had large families, and all farmers on farms of any size had several servants. Much skilled work—cheese and butter making, spinning and weaving, bread-baking, and bacon-curing—were carried on within the farm-house. The house was none too big for all the people and busy indoor activities it contained. A vivid account of an early 19th century farm-house and the life within it is given in George Eliot's *Adam Bede.* Mrs. Poyser of the Hall Farm bought no butter and bread, nor bacon and cheese. The ale was home-brewed. Enough home-spun linen was made not only to supply the large household but also to set up her nieces when they married. The large red brick home-place housed quite a community of people. Not only three generations of Poysers lived there, but also the two servant girls, Nancy and Molly, and

The Times

A FARM-HOUSE IN THE LAKE DISTRICT
The low buildings, built of local stone, are sheltered from
the wind by trees

Alick the shepherd and Tim the ploughman.
The unmarried farm workers lived as a matter of
course in the house of their master. They often
lived, and indeed still do in some places, in a
'bothy', a one-roomed hut on the farm, coming
to the house for their meals.

The size of the farm-house remains the same
today, but the busy community life within has
altogether changed. Farmers' families are much
smaller; in place of many servants the farmer's

Topical Press

THE MANOR FARM HOUSE, KENCOT, OXON.
Built in the 17th century when the Cotswold sheep farmers
were prosperous

wife very likely has no servant at all, or only a
daily servant; there is no spinning nor weaving,
rarely cheese-making or bread-baking; even the
butter and bacon are often bought in a shop.
For the modern farmer's wife, without the help
of servants, has often enough to do to keep a big
house clean and to cook big meals in an inconvenient, out-of-date kitchen, generally without
the conveniences which help the town housewife.
The provision of domestic labour-saving equipment is often made difficult because of the lack
of electricity and gas. Much, however, can often
be done to modernize the old farm-houses: an
unused downstairs living-room may perhaps be
converted into a modern kitchen, and the old
kitchen premises be used for storage purposes.
A small bedroom can, perhaps, be converted
into a bathroom. And public services such as
water, drainage, gas, and electricity, are reaching
farther out into the country.

The modern farmer, like his wife, has new
difficulties to contend with. In the old days a
farmer had very little paper work to do. The
writing of an occasional cheque or receipt was
about all the book-keeping he was compelled
to do. But today, he must keep accounts to
satisfy the tax-collector. He has, by law, to make
many returns for the information of Government
Departments; he must fill up forms on a variety
of subjects; he has all the complications of his
men's pay and insurance to see to. For all this
he needs a good office which is not the living-
room. The installation of a telephone, even
though often unduly expensive in country places,
will soon pay for itself by saving journeys by car.

In these and other ways the old farm-house
may be changed to suit modern conditions, while
still retaining the solid worth and beauty of its
architecture.

See also Vol. XI: HOUSES, HISTORY OF.

FARMING DISTRIBUTION. The kind of
farming being done at any one place is not a
matter of chance. It depends on climate, soil,
slope, communications, and the needs of those
who use the farm produce. To understand
why the various kinds of farming occur as they
do one needs to study a physical map, a geolo-
gical map, a rainfall and temperature map, and
one showing road and rail communications to
the towns. The geographer, geologist, and biologist sometimes use the term 'Highland Britain'
in referring to the area north-westward of a line

Aerofilms

DEREHAM, NORFOLK
A half-timbered farm-house thatched with Norfolk reeds

drawn from Dorset to Northumberland. This is a very rough division indicating that the hillier, wetter areas are to north and west, and that for the most part the older rocks are also on that side of the line. The mountainous parts of Cornwall, Devon, Wales, the Pennine Chain, and Scotland are all in the 'Highland' region; the vales and plains of the Midlands, the chalk hills, 'wolds' or 'downs' of southern England and north Yorkshire, and the dry flat plain of East Anglia are to the east and south of the imaginary line. One can say, very roughly, that north-west of this line are the livestock-raising and mainly grassy parts of the country, and south-east of it are mainly the arable parts—in other words, that stock rearing needs plenty of water and is not upset by rough country, and that cereal grains are most easily grown in a fairly dry climate and on smooth land surfaces. The east side of Scotland really belongs to the 'Lowland' side of Britain, because it also enjoys a dry climate and deep soils on moderate slopes.

There are many exceptions to this broad division; for example, there is an arable area on the red soil of south Devon, another on the flat plain of western Lancashire, and another on the seaward edge of southern Ayrshire. They are examples of special conditions of red, easily drained, or 'early' soils in places where late frosts are infrequent, and the main arable crop is the potato, which needs plenty of moisture

and a more even climate than is common to the south-east. If we take wheat as the typical cereal grain, we find that it needs a warm, dry summer to ripen it, and is indifferent to hard frosts in winter and spring, when little of the crop is showing above ground.

One of the main difficulties in 'Highland Britain' is to grow and harvest enough winter keep for the great number of animals which can be grazed there in summer. On the other hand, the arable 'lowland' side grows far more animal foods than is needed for the animals it can keep in summer. Therefore, there is a constant and well-ordered traffic of young cattle and sheep from northern and western Britain to eastern and southern Britain. The lowland farmer, by wintering cattle and sheep and using up arable by-products, is able to give his land more farm-yard manure, of which he never has enough to replace all that the arable crops take out of the soil. This 'store cattle' trade includes Welsh Blacks from the Welsh hills, North Devons from the Exmoor region, Herefords from the grass farms of the Marches, Galloways from the southern uplands of Scotland, and Highlanders from the north-western islands and mountains. The hardy 'Highland' sheep gain a good deal by leaving their poorer conditions for a period and enjoying the richer conditions of the south and east.

Such arable land as is to be found in the

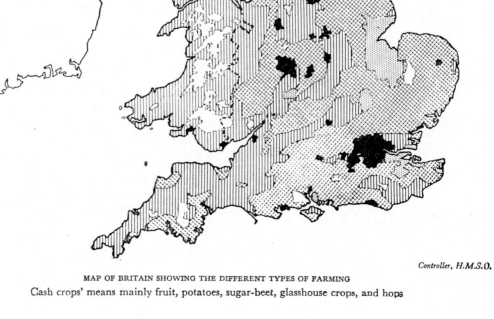

MAINLY DAIRYING,
REARING AND GRAZING

MIXED OR MAINLY
ARABLE FARMING

MARKET GARDENING
AND CASH CROPS

MOUNTAINS
HEATH AND MOOR

URBAN AREAS

Controller, H.M.S.O.

MAP OF BRITAIN SHOWING THE DIFFERENT TYPES OF FARMING
'Cash crops' means mainly fruit, potatoes, sugar-beet, glasshouse crops, and hops

stock-raising districts is devoted to raising winter keep for the breeding stock; and as ROTATION OF CROPS (q.v.) is a necessary principle in arable agriculture, even the mainly cereal-growing areas will grow some crops, such as swedes and kale, specially designed to be converted by animals into manure.

Limestone or chalk areas are particularly good for animal farming. Thus the carboniferous limestone regions of Derbyshire, north Yorkshire, and Westmorland are essentially stock-breeding and horse-growing regions. The chalk hills, such as the Chilterns and the Sussex Downs, are also excellent for stock, but in the past they have tended to be short of water, so that more sheep than cattle have been raised there, and these are farmed in conjunction with the arable cultivation of the lower slopes. A 'sheep and corn farm' is a very common expression in the chalk areas. Now that the water supplies are better, more cattle are to be found on the downs.

The character of the soil often decides the type of farming. There are areas of heavy clay in the Midlands and Sussex, for example, which are difficult to cultivate, so that such places, which grow some of the best grass in Britain, become summer pasturage for fattening cattle and sheep. Areas liable to flooding, such as the Somerset moors, parts of the fens, and stretches of river valleys, tend to become mainly summer pasturage,

Proximity to large centres of population also has an important influence on the type of farming. Thus we find milk being produced all over the country, even from such poor land as the southern Pennine Chain, where the acid soil and cold climate would indicate the farming of only the hardiest kinds of sheep. Improved roads and motor transport have also helped to bring country of that kind into dairy farming for the industrial populations of Yorkshire and Lancashire. Again, such thickly populated centres need a lot of market-garden produce, so that any nearby flat, easily worked land tends to be given up to growing vegetable crops. Such influences are often greater even than those of climate and geology.

See also ARABLE CROPS; CATTLE; SHEEP; MARKET-GARDENING.

FARM INSTITUTES, *see* AGRICULTURAL TRAINING.

FARM LABOUR. As soon as early man passed out of the wandering stage and began to settle down in one place, he provided for himself and his family by tilling the soil to grow plants, and by keeping animals so that he could have milk, meat, and clothing (*see* AGRICULTURAL HISTORY). He had nothing but his own hard work to depend on, and even so a spell of bad weather at the seed-sowing time or at harvest might mean famine in the next year. Everyone laboured on the land in those early days; and even today it is estimated that about 80% of the population of the world (say four people out of five) are working at farming of one kind or another. Most of them are producing food, but some of them are growing the plants that give us raw materials for manufactured goods, such as cotton or rubber.

By far the greatest number of farm workers are peasants, that is, men whose farms are very small—some perhaps having only a few acres, others up to 30 or 40 acres. All of them are engaged in growing the food they need, with only such labour as their wives and children are able to give. If they can grow more than they want themselves, the surplus is sold to give them money to buy a few other things. Peasant farmers may be the owners of the land they farm, or they may hire it from a landowner and pay him rent, but the characteristic which all of them have in common is that they work their little farms entirely with family labour and without hired men. The life involves long hours of work, often in return for a very scanty living. The farms are too small, and the peasants are too poor to employ the farm machinery that would lighten their toil and give them larger returns for their labour.

The peasant type of farmer is still found over a large part of the world. Peasant farming is the general rule in France, Germany, the countries of northern Europe, and all through central Europe, as well as in the greater part of Asia. In the New World, in Canada and the United States, for example, and in Australia and New Zealand, many of the farms are each worked by a family, though these family farmers differ from the peasant farmers in that their holdings are much larger and they cultivate them with machinery instead of by hand. These farmers differ also from the peasants in that their first object is to grow things that they can sell on the market, instead of farming mainly to feed themselves. Thus, while the Flemish peasant on a

C. S. Orwin

BROADCASTING SEED
The sower uses both hands in a rhythmic motion, flinging
the seed evenly over the ground

few acres of land is growing vegetables, keeping a cow or two for milk, some rabbits for meat, and chickens for eggs and poultry, almost all of which is consumed by the family, the Canadian farmer on 160 acres or more, while no doubt supplying himself with some of these things, is also growing, with the aid of tractors and harvesting machinery, a large quantity of corn to sell for export to industrial countries like Britain. He differs also from the peasants of the Old World in that he will employ labour to help him at the busy seasons of harvesting and threshing his corn.

Thus, most of the world is farmed by family farmers of one kind or another, without hired labour except at certain seasons; yet all over the world there are now also large districts in which the farmers occupy big farms, some of them very big indeed, on which they themselves work only as managers, and rely upon hired men, who are paid wages, for the manual labour needed on the land. These farms are of many types. In North and South America, for example, farms running into thousands of acres are producing mainly cereal crops (wheat, barley, oats, or maize) for export, and everyone has read of the great American cattle ranches with their cowboys, and of the great sheep stations in Australia and New

Zealand. These need men permanently for the regular work of the year, though some of them, such as the big Australian sheep-farmers, depend at shearing time upon travelling labour gangs which move from one station to another to clip the wool. In the tropics, too, still another form of labour organization is found, for in India, Ceylon, Malaya, Java, and some other countries, we find what is called 'plantation' farming, where people produce one crop only: tea, sugar, coffee, or rubber, with the aid of low paid native labour. In the old days many of these plantations were worked by slaves.

In Britain, as in other countries, the small farmer, cultivating his land and breeding live-stock mainly to supply the wants of his own family, was the rule almost up to modern times. This farming to supply the home is called 'subsistence farming'. The growth of the big towns, however, with their large populations depending upon other people to grow food for them, made the development of 'commercial farming' necessary. Under this system subsistence farming gave place to a type of farming the main object of which is to supply the market.

This new kind of more productive farming, which developed during the 18th and 19th centuries, was possible only if the farms were worked in much larger units; and so the peasant holdings were gradually absorbed into the larger commercial farms. The process, of course, reduced the number of independent farmers to those who tended to be the more enterprising and successful ones. The others who no longer had land of their own became workers for wages. So we find in Britain today that the prevailing system of agricultural labour is wage-labour. Instead of most of the workers occupying land themselves, there are in Britain about twice as many farm workers as farmers, and before the use of machinery had so materially reduced the work on farms, this proportion was higher still.

This change from a rural community of peasant farmers to one of larger farmers and hired workers was not easily made. The man who occupied 30 or 40 acres of land may have had to work very hard for a not very large return, and when the seasons were unkind and harvests bad, life was difficult for him. But there was always a living of some kind for himself and his family, better in some years than in others, but never failing him altogether. When these men had to give up their land to work for wages, they lost this security, for there were no trade unions in the 18th century to protect their interests. They were dependent on what they could buy, not on what they could grow; and as their wages were daily wages which stopped when they were not working, a week of bad weather might mean that a man earned nothing at all. The history of farm wages and of farm workers in the early part of the 19th century is a story of poverty and want that makes unpleasant reading today when the attitude of employers towards their workers is very different. The government took no part in protecting their rights; poor relief and the workhouse were then the only assistance that the farm worker could expect, the former very inadequate, the latter involving the break-up of the family. All through Queen Victoria's reign farm wages rose, but only slightly; and on the whole the workers' standard of living, the houses they lived in, and the hours of work which they had to do compared very badly with that of workers doing work of equal skill in other industries.

This state of affairs led to an attempt by Joseph Arch, in 1872, to organize agricultural labourers in a union of their own, so that they could demand better conditions (see TRADE UNION HISTORY, Vol. VII). Arch was a Warwickshire farm labourer and champion hedge-layer of England. He was a natural orator, and his efforts met with considerable success. It was unfortunate for his Agricultural Labourers' Union that, when it looked like becoming firmly established, farming in Britain entered upon a long period of low prices, so that the farmers, having less money to spend, had to employ fewer men. The men they stood off first were Union men, and in a short time the Union had lost almost all its members. In the end, however, Arch's work helped the farm labourer, and today the National Union of Agricultural Workers is a vigorous trade union.

The two World Wars did a great deal to improve the status of the farm labourer. The vital need to grow more home food in Britain put the farm workers in a better position to demand better conditions—not only higher wages, but security of employment and better houses and hours of work.

In 1917 the Government set up the Agricultural Wages Board, on which both employers and workers are represented, with powers to fix the rates of pay for all ages and classes of farm workers,

REPAIRING A TRACTOR
Eric Guy
Some knowledge of engineering is now necessary for farm workers

to decide the hours of labour and the rates of pay for overtime, to award holidays with pay, and generally to control and regulate the conditions of employment on the land.

See also MINISTRY OF AGRICULTURE; NATIONAL FARMERS' UNION; OPEN FIELDS AND ENCLOSURES; COLLECTIVE FARMING.

See also Vol. VII: LABOUR; TRADE UNIONS.

FARM MACHINES, *see* MECHANIZED FARMING.

FARMSTEAD, PLANNING OF. Any landscape of farming country is studded with homesteads or farm steadings—that is, farm-houses and other farm buildings. Their size and type depends upon the size and type of farm. The farmstead of a large arable farm, say of 500–1,000 acres, may have almost as many buildings as a small village. First, there is the farmer's house —probably a substantial building of brick or stone, set in its own grounds, often with a high-walled garden, sometimes with a short avenue of trees (see FARM-HOUSES). In some parts of Britain there are rows of cottages for the farm workers belonging to the farm, although in many districts the farm workers rent cottages in nearby villages unconnected with the farm (see FARM COTTAGES). Then there are the stables and byres to house the farm animals, sheds to shelter the implements and machinery, and barns for the hay, straw, roots, and grain.

In a new country where farm lands are being laid out for the first time it is possible to plan on paper what type of farm buildings are most suitable to the farm and how they can best be arranged. Naturally, the details of the plan will vary with the size and type of farm, and with the district's climate. In a mild, kindly climate, shelter for livestock and machinery may be quite simple and inexpensive and yet suffice. A dairy farm will need quite different buildings from those of a principally grain-growing or sheep-raising farm. And in all cases the farm buildings must be in proportion to the size and fertility of the farm. Nevertheless, there are certain general principles that apply to the design of all farm buildings.

When building costs are high, the erection of the most suitable buildings may cost more than the land could ever repay, and some more simple type of building must suffice. The main cost of building is the cost of skilled labour, and the simpler the design of the buildings, the more of the building work can the farmer and his men do themselves.

Farm buildings should be easily adaptable, so that as farm practice changes, the buildings can be altered to serve a new purpose. A good example of the type of building which has become an encumbrance as the result of change in farming practice is the unsightly tall chimney, like those of factories, to be seen on some farms. These were erected to drive threshing machinery by steam power in the days when this invention was new. But today oil fuel, the internal-combustion engine, and the electric motor have made them useless. Some of the elaborate and expensive model dairy byres of the 20th century are already becoming outdated.

The layout of a farm must be carefully planned beforehand, to prevent such mistakes as gateways that are too narrow for modern implements, or doors that open in an inconvenient way. There is always a lot of traffic coming and going about a farm, and all this traffic begins, ends, or passes through the farmsteading, so that good roads, leading to and through a farm, are important. Nearness to a main road with regular bus service is of increasing advantage, particularly in securing reliable and contented labour; but the main road should never, if it can be avoided, pass through a farm.

There is no question concerned with farm buildings on which opinion has changed so rapidly within recent years as that of suitable housing for animals. The original purpose of housing for domestic animals was to protect them from bad weather—in Britain, chiefly from cold and wet in winter. Consequently the old-fashioned dairy byre or pig stye was a warm and cosy place, but also often very dirty, ill-lit, and stuffy. Largely in the attempt to wipe out tuberculosis in dairy cattle, a new type of building appeared, which could be kept much cleaner. It was built mainly of concrete, with metal in place of wooden fittings. The new byres were well-lit and well-ventilated, and with little labour could be swilled out by hoses several times a day, and disinfected should disease occur. Piggeries of the same type were built. But these byres and piggeries were often cold, damp, and draughty, so that in spite of their clean condition, the animals were not comfortable in them, and therefore did not prosper. Another disadvantage of these elaborate model byres and piggeries is that they are too permanent to be shifted to fresh ground—whereas it is now realized that a change to fresh ground is often of great importance in maintaining health and controlling ANIMAL DISEASES (q.v.). Consequently experiments are always being made to discover the most healthy methods of housing CATTLE, PIGS, and POULTRY (qq.v.).

The idea of movable housing has found a wide use in poultry and pig keeping, the elaborate and fixed poultry houses and equipment being now seldom seen. In most up-to-date poultry farms all equipment, particularly chicken rearing equipment, is kept simple, in small units, and freely movable from field to field (see POULTRY, CARE OF, section 1). As it appeared that young pigs, in particular, throve better when scampering around a dirty old farm steading than when in model concrete piggeries, the movable farrowing hut for sows has become increasingly popular, and seems to give much better results (see PIGS, CARE OF, section 1).

When designing and planning farm buildings, one of the first considerations is the water-supply. Plenty of good water is absolutely essential for modern dairying—and dairying is now by far the most important and profitable branch of farming in most parts of Britain. Water on farms may come from the wells or other sources on the farm, or by connexion to a town's or

Eric Guy

TURNERS COURT FARM, OXFORDSHIRE

In the centre is the barn, behind it a silo tower, and to the left a Dutch barn. On the right are the cowsheds and dairy, and in front of the barn on the left is a yard to hold the cows. The photograph was taken in the late afternoon when the horses were returning from work

village's public supply. Generally a public water supply is by far the most satisfactory, for local water supplies, usually sufficient during winter, are apt to fail in a dry summer, and so disorganize the whole working of a farm.

In Britain the opportunity for designing new farm buildings is rare, and the problem is to make the best use of what is available. Usually the buildings are already on the farm; sometimes they have been there for centuries. The most striking feature of many English farmsteads is still the immense corn barn where, in the old days, the corn, loose or in sheaves, was taken to be threshed out by flails on the barn floor. Some of these barns are many centuries old; but, of course, corn is hardly ever threshed by flail in these days. Unless these barns are to be merely picturesque and perhaps inconvenient antiquities, some new use must, by improvisation, be found for them. On several farms they are found suitable for housing the grain driers used in connexion with the combine-harvester, the most modern of all machines for HARVESTING grain crops (q.v.).

Improvisation should never be undertaken in a hasty way. On all matters connected with farm buildings it is wise to think twice before making a change, and many times before buying new equipment.

See also AGRICULTURAL HISTORY; MECHANIZED FARMING.

FARM TOOLS, HISTORY OF.

Scraps of stone and bone provide the earliest knowledge we possess about farming tools. Over a long period of time, early man got into the way of encouraging the growth of certain plants suitable for food and then of actually planting and rearing them instead of depending only on wild plants (see AGRICULTURAL HISTORY). Fragments of prehistoric tools, dug up by archaeologists, are sometimes like those used by very primitive tribes today. Early wooden tools, of course, have rotted long ago, but sharp stones or pieces of bone, which have clearly been attached to a wooden handle, have been found.

The simplest tool known among primitive people is a branch of a tree, sharpened to a point for digging or for cutting a furrow. Sometimes a stick is used weighted with a stone collar to help it to penetrate the soil. A hoe for scratching the ground would be made from a deer's antler or from a piece of stick with a stone blade

fastened on to it. For cutting the grasses and corn at harvest time a sickle was devised very early in the history of arable farming. A row of toothed flint flakes was set along a groove cut in a stick.

Flails and fans were used for threshing the seeds out of the grasses and cereals, and a stone quern or rubbing-mill for grinding the grain into a rough whole-meal flour. This quern consisted of a saddle-shaped block of stone and a smaller stone which was pushed to and fro over the saddle to crush the grains (see FLOUR-MILLING, Vol. VII). Clay pots were made for storing the grain and flour, for carrying water, and for use in milking (see PREHISTORIC POTTERY, Vol. I).

Simple tools and vessels such as these, made of stone, wood, bone, and earthenware, were the only equipment of the earliest farmers. They gradually came into use during the New Stone Age. The animal-drawn plough, the invention which had such great influence on man's history, was not invented until the Bronze Age, when men first learnt how to use metals (see PREHISTORIC TOOLS AND WEAPONS, Vol. I).

The ancient Egyptians had a well-shaped, animal-drawn, digging implement which had some of the features of a plough. The early Greeks had only rough implements fashioned from the boughs of trees. In Rome the ploughs were at first made entirely of wood, but later the wearing parts were tipped with iron to lengthen their life. Some of the ploughs mentioned in the early books of the Bible evidently had metal in their construction, for they needed the work of a smith. In the Old Testament (I Sam., ch. xiii) we read how the Philistines,

British Museum

EGYPTIAN TOMB MODEL OF A DIGGING IMPLEMENT, ABOUT 2000 B.C.

The wooden stick had no cutting edge and was dragged through the soil by the oxen

Bodleian Library

British Museum

CUTTING CORN WITH A SICKLE AND THRESHING WITH FLAILS IN THE 14TH CENTURY
The man with the sickle has a hooked stick in his left hand to hold the corn as he cuts it. (Bodl. MS. 264 and B.M. Roy. MS. 2 B. VII)

after they had conquered the Israelites, banned smiths throughout all the land of Israel lest the Hebrews should make stockpiles of armaments of swords and spears. So the Israelites had to go 'down to the Philistines, to sharpen every man his share, and his coulter, and his axe, and his mattock'.

If the word 'coulter' here means a plough coulter, then the reference indicates that the plough had advanced well beyond the primitive digging stick by about the 10th century B.C. in the Near East. It must have had a knife for making a vertical cut in the soil as well as a share for the horizontal cut. It is unlikely, however, that the ploughs of this time had a curved mouldboard for inverting the slice of soil cut by the share and the coulter. The first plough known to turn the soil over and bury the surface vegetation beneath the furrow slice was the Saxon plough, a very good implement. The idea of turning over the soil, may, nevertheless, have occurred in other countries. Indeed, it is so difficult to trace the history of the plough and to find by what route the invention passed from one country to another that one is inclined to think that the invention must have taken place in more than one country. It must have been developed independently in several parts of the world, by people of different races who had no connexion with each other. Chinese tradition, for example, attributes the invention of the plough to the legendry Emperor Shen Nung, the 'divine husbandman', some time before 2500 B.C. Such a legend at least indicates that the plough has been known for so long in China that

it is not easy to see how the origins in China and Egypt can be connected.

In Britain the plough by the end of the 18th century had taken the form in which we know it now, although improvements in detail have been going on ever since. One great improvement has been that the coulter and share have been made easily detachable and replaceable. Another improvement has been in the wearing quality of the share (*see* PLOUGH).

Ploughing is really mechanized digging; this took many centuries to perfect; the mechanization of the other field operations started very much later, but has developed very quickly.

Robert M. Adam

A CROFTER USING A CASCHROM IN THE HEBRIDES
A caschrom is in effect a hand plough. The metal blade is forced below the turf and then twisted to turn the soil

Percy Simms

PLOUGHING WITH OXEN IN THE COTSWOLDS EARLY IN THE 20TH CENTURY

The next step forward in mechanizing harvest work was the addition in 1879 of a binder and twine knotter to the reaping-machine. The resulting machine, the reaper and binder, left on the field a ready-tied sheaf, neatly bound with twine. Then, quite recently, progress in corn harvesting methods took a great step forward with the development of the combine harvester, which, when driven over a field of standing corn, collects the threshed grain into a tank or leaves it in bags lying on the stubble (*see* HARVESTING).

Haymaking, too, has been revolutionized in very recent times. The mower, the hay-loader, the elevator, the sweep, the tractor-drawn pneumatic-tired trailer, and the pick-up baler are all of them new inventions (*see* HAYMAKING). The mechanical harvesting of potatoes and sugar-beet, so recently begun, has now reached a stage at which potatoes can be dug, cleaned, sorted, and bagged automatically, and sugar-beet can be topped, cleaned, and loaded into trailers.

One of the great concerns of the farmer from very early times has been the matter of traction which until the last century depended on some draught animal or other. The horse was little used on the farm until about the 17th century. Oxen were the most common draught animals on the farms of Europe, including Britain—though as early as the 12th century Walter of Henley is recorded to have recommended one horse in front of two oxen as a team for ploughing. Animals were also used for driving stationary barn machinery such as chaff cutters and mills for making flour; though WATER POWER and WIND POWER (q.v. Vol. VIII) have been used for such purposes since very early times. The coming of the steam traction and winding engine, then the motor tractor, and later electric power brought such boundless power to farm operations that new and complex machines which could never have been operated by animal power began to appear. Steam power enabled the threshing-machine to replace the flail. Electric power brought the possibility of labour-saving

Towed CULTIVATORS (q.v.) for breaking down ploughed land into a seedbed were not used before the 19th century, but they are now to be found on nearly every farm. In earlier times pickaxes or mattocks were used to break up any very large clods of soil in a field. In Britain seed was broadcast by hand until the beginning of the 18th century, when the first mechanical instrument for sowing seeds in rows was introduced by Jethro Tull. The sowing of seed in this way had the great advantage that the growing plants were in rows, and therefore a horse hoe could be drawn between the rows to kill the weeds without damaging the plants (*see* DRILLS AND DISTRIBUTORS).

The most recent, and the quickest development of farm tools has been in the harvesting of corn and grass and of root crops. Right up to the beginning of the 19th century, all corn was cut by scythe or sickle, collected into bundles by hand, and tied into sheaves. Many workers were needed to cut and bind even a small field of corn. Then, in 1828, Patrick Bell, a Scottish Presbyterian minister, devised the reaper. This machine cut the corn by means of a knife bar with triangular sections which moved backwards and forwards in contact with the stationary knife plates, and cut the corn like a row of giant scissors. It also had a bunching device which caused the corn to be deposited in bundles on the ground. It was much easier to pick up these bundles and tie them into sheaves for stooking than it had been to collect corn that had been cut by sickle or scythe. At about the same time the THRESHING-MACHINE (q.v.) was beginning to take something of its present form.

machines to the milking-shed and the dairy (*see* DAIRY MACHINERY) and to the barn (*see* BARN MACHINES), and even brought a convenient source of heat for such purposes as the artificial drying of grain. Complex modern machinery is generally made in large factories by methods almost like the mass-production methods of motor-car factories. This means that designs are standarized so that there are far fewer variations and local types than there were in the days when local WHEELWRIGHTS (q.v.) and blacksmiths made implements. At the beginning of the 20th century nearly every county had its own particular design of plough thought to be peculiarly suitable, indeed essential, for the soil and other conditions of the neighbourhood; but now ploughs of the same design are mass-produced and sold all over the country, almost irrespective of soil conditions, variations occurring only according to the purpose for which the ploughs are to be used. This local variation in type applied to barn and dairy utensils as much as it did to field cultivation implements. In some counties milking-stools had three legs; in others they had four. The wooden pails, which succeeded the pottery vessels used by the earliest farmers, were made in many types and of many different woods. In Gloucestershire pails were made of oak strips bound with ash hoops, while Wiltshire pails were of oak but were bound with iron hoops. The modern milking-machine pail is of a standard factory design, and varies little from county to county.

See also HAND TOOLS; POWER FOR FARMING.

FARM VEHICLES. Much of the power used on farms is used for transport. Seed and manure have to be carted to the field; crops have to be carried away at harvest time; milk has to be taken every day to the roadway to be collected by motor lorry. Well-designed wagons, carts, and trailers are therefore needed. Many four-wheeled harvest wagons, made long before tractors were invented, are still in use now, though some have been converted for use with

Crown Copyright

MODEL OF A SUSSEX WAGON

The design of wagons varies in different parts of the country. From an exhibit in the Science Museum, South Kensington

tractors by removing the shafts and fitting a drawbar in their place. Sometimes the large iron-tired, wooden-spoked wheels are replaced by pneumatic-tired wheels—the pneumatic tire being one of the greatest benefits that modern invention has brought to the farmer. Iron-tired wheels, however large their diameter and however broad their rims, sink into soft soil, making the vehicle very heavy to move; but pneumatic tires, being flexible, distribute the load over a larger area of contact with the ground, making the weight at any one point smaller, so that the wheel sinks in less readily.

Two-wheeled carts (sometimes called 'tumbrils') are chiefly used for moving farm-yard manure and carting roots, and four-wheeled wagons for harvesting corn and hay and for bulky and heavy loads which are to be trans-

Eric Guy

TWO-WHEELED CARTS BEING LOADED WITH MANURE

Harry Ferguson Ltd.

A TRACTOR TRAILER
The trailer can be tipped up by hydraulic power supplied by the tractor

ported long distances and therefore need more than one horse. A heavily laden two-wheeled cart puts great strain on the back of the horse in the shafts, and this strain cannot be relieved by a second horse. A two-wheeled cart, however, can be built as a tipping vehicle, a design which is not possible for a four-wheeled wagon. The body of such carts is generally carried on a secondary axle so that it can be tipped backwards to pitch a load in a heap on to the ground, leaving the main frame and the shafts, axle, and wheels undisturbed. On the other hand, a four-wheeled vehicle is often much more convenient in a harvest field. A loaded wagon can be left standing while the horse is working on another wagon, or can even be left overnight, whereas a two-wheeled cart has to be propped up if the horse is taken out of the shafts. The capacity of both carts and wagons for light bulky material such as newly made hay or sheaves of corn can be increased by fixing inclined rails called 'raves' or ladders at each end. In East Anglia and the East Midlands a cart is used which can be converted to a four-wheeled wagon by adding two wheels on a fore-carriage. This is called a pomfrey or morphry or a hermaphrodite (*see* picture, Vol. I, p. 78).

Tractor trailers are mostly two-wheeled and all have pneumatic-tired wheels. Many have auto-matic tipping devices, often operated by the hydraulic system of the tractor. Some can be tipped at will in any one of three directions, the load being discharged out of the back of the trailer or on either side. The drawbars are designed to take the pull direct from the axle of the wheels and not through the bodywork which would not be strong enough to stand the pull in very soft sticky soil. Tractor trailers are usually loaded with the greater part of the weight forward of the axle, as this, by adding weight to the rear of the tractor, helps the grip of the tractor driving wheels in difficult conditions. Some trailers have the axle well towards the rear of the trailer in order to achieve this weight distribution, the tractor and trailer then really becoming a six-wheeled lorry. Four-wheeled trailers and converted wagons are used chiefly for harvest work and for carting manures.

Motor lorries are used both on the fields and on the roads. Many farms have rough roadways built as near as possible to each field, so that the lorry can collect the produce almost straight from the field where the crop was grown and take it to the town or railway station.

In summer, lorries with tires that have good deep-tread patterns can drive right on to the fields, particularly where there is stubble to hold the soil in place. Many farmers use lorries on the cornfields to carry away the grain emptied from the tank-bins of the combine-harvester. For this purpose the body of the lorry, or indeed the body of any trailers used for this purpose, have to be lined with metal, or carefully patched with pieces of wood, to make it grain-tight.

Motor vans are also used on farms to carry supplies of fuel and oil to the tractors working in the field; and the farmer himself often uses a van or old motor-car to go the round of his fields. It used to be said that the best manure for a field was the footprint of the farmer; it might now be said that the best manure is the tread mark of the farmer's motor. The small four-wheeled vehicles developed as jeeps for use in military operations can run on to farm fields even in the winter. In fact they can go almost wherever a man on horseback could go, and almost wherever a man could walk. They have taken the place of the farmer's hack or his trap and cob (see HORSES, Vol. IX).

See also WHEELWRIGHT; POWER FOR FARMING.
See also Vol. IV: CARTS AND WAGONS.

FEATHER HUNTING AND FARMING. 1. A bird's FEATHERS (q.v. Vol. II) consist of the long, stiff, external or contour feathers and the small, soft, down feathers. There is a wide variety in texture, colour, and size; and these have been put to use by man in many different ways, industrial, domestic, and ornamental.

The use of feathers for ornament dates back to very early days. Until modern times they figured more in men's costumes than women's, and it was only during the reign of Henry VIII that feathers first appeared in women's bonnets. During the late 19th century the craze for feathers and plumes reached fantastic proportions, women wearing whole wings and even the stuffed bodies of birds as decoration. Now this type of ornament has gone out of fashion. Many birds, therefore, especially birds of paradise which at one time were nearly exterminated, are beginning to increase again in numbers (see COSTUME, HISTORY OF, Vol. XI).

Until the steel pen took its place, the quill pen was the common writing instrument. It was made for preference from the main wing feathers of the goose, although the feathers of the swan, crow, eagle, and owl were also used for this purpose. Quills are still used for holding artists' sable or camel-hair brushes. Feathers are also used to make brushes—those of the domestic

fowl for the cheaper kinds, and the soft plumes of the rhea or South American ostrich for the better kinds. Down is used for filling quilts, pillows, and cushions and for making feather beds. Goose is most commonly used, but the very finest quality comes from the Eider DUCK (q.v. Vol. II), from which has come our word 'eider-down', meaning a quilt.

The strangest use of feathers occurs in the island of Santa Cruz in the Pacific, where the red feathers of the HONEY-EATER bird (q.v. Vol. II) are used as a medium of exchange or standard of value (see PRIMITIVE MONEY, Vol. VII). Spiral coils of bark or fibre are closely bound with overlapping rows of these feathers, and the man who possesses a number of these objects is reckoned as a man of wealth. It is believed that the art of making them has now nearly died out.

2. FEATHER HUNTING. Among the birds most eagerly hunted in the past to satisfy the demands of the plume trade were the white EGRET of America, Africa, and India (whose plumes were traded as 'osprey' or 'aigrette'), the Great Crested GREBE of Europe and North America, the Adjutant STORK of India (whose plumes

A BIRD OF PARADISE

Coloured engraving from François Levaillant's *Histoire Naturelle des Oiseaux de Paradis*, 1806

E. O. Hoppé

AN OSTRICH ON A FARM IN SOUTH AFRICA DISPLAYING ITS FEATHERS

were known as 'Marabou'), and above all the OSTRICH and the BIRDS OF PARADISE of the New Guinea region (qq.v. Vol. II).

The plume hunters were often ruthless in their methods. Colony after colony of white egrets was wiped out by the hunters, who lay in wait at the nesting season and shot the old birds, leaving the young to die of starvation and exposure. Immediate profit was their sole concern, and no attention was given to the need for maintaining breeding stocks. If it had not been for international action which was taken to protect them, as well as a decline in demand, many plume-bearing birds would have been exterminated.

Ostriches in Africa were generally shot with guns, either from a hide near the nest, or after a mounted chase. Although faster than an average horse, the ostrich has a habit of running on a set course. Mounted men, therefore, stationed at previously arranged points, had a good chance of getting near enough for a shot. Africans sometimes surrounded a troop of these birds from a distance, and closing in gradually, often succeeded in spearing a number of them. This, however, was a risky method, for the ostrich's kick can easily kill a man. The aboriginal Bushmen in Africa, disguising themselves in ostrich skins, stalked the birds, and then shot them with poisoned arrows. It was, however, the man with the horse and gun who killed most ostriches.

The naturalist and explorer, Alfred Wallace, has described the methods used by the native

hunters in the Aru Islands, near New Guinea, to take birds of paradise. The splendid male birds, whose skins have for hundreds of years formed a valuable article of trade in that part of the world, assemble during the breeding season in large numbers in the tops of tall trees. Here they display in rivalry their magnificent plumage. The hunters build leafy hides in these trees, and taking their positions before daylight, wait for the birds to arrive. Then they shoot the birds with arrows capped with blunt wooden knobs to avoid breaking the skin. The stunned birds fall to the ground and are retrieved by hunters waiting below.

In parts of New Guinea there are various local practices. Hunters who are not skilled with the bow prefer to set snares or nets on the branches and operate them from a hide-out. Some species of birds of paradise use display sites near or actually on the ground, and the hunter who knows the birds' habits is the one most likely to succeed. At the height of the boom in paradise plumage, early in the present century, hundreds of Malay and other traders fitted out small expeditions into the interior of New Guinea, taking with them goods to exchange for the skins. From the native villages selected as bases, Papuan hunters went out daily throughout the season, and although no females or young birds were taken, the annual toll amounted to scores of thousands of skins. Fortunately, complete protection has now been given to these birds, and they are becoming common again in many parts.

3. FEATHER FARMING. Until 1870 the ostrich-plume trade relied entirely on feathers from birds killed wild; but in that year, stimulated by the high prices then being paid for plumes (£5. 11s. 7d. per lb.), and because wild birds were becoming rare, ostrich farming began in South Africa. It spread so rapidly that, 5 years later, 32,000 birds were being reared, and by 1904 the total was 357,790 birds. By that time the price for plumes had dropped to £2. 5s. per lb., each adult bird providing about 1½ lb. of plumes a year. A good pair of breeding birds often sold for £200 to £300, and the value of single birds was from £5 to £10 each.

In the early days of ostrich farming, the eggs were hatched in incubators, and the young birds were reared artificially; but this method led to outbreaks of disease, and later the birds were allowed to hatch and rear their young naturally. The eggs, in clutches of 12 to 16, hatched in 6 weeks, both parents taking turns by day and night with the incubation.

There were two types of ostrich farm. On one, the birds were grazed on irrigated fields of lucerne, at five birds to the acre—an expensive method which yielded the finest quality plumes. On the other, the birds found their own natural food on large ranches of 2,000 to 3,000 acres, allowing 10 to 20 acres per bird. The chief drawback to this system was that the birds tended to become wild and unmanageable. The success of ostrich farming depends upon fashion, and when ostrich feathers became less fashionable, somewhere about 1910, ostrich farming suddenly collapsed, and the farmers suffered heavy losses.

At one time GEESE (q.v.) were farmed on a large scale in Great Britain and other European countries as much for their down and quills as for food. The quills were plucked once a year, and the down was stripped from the living birds several times between spring and autumn. This barbarous practice has been abandoned now for many years; but geese are still farmed for their down, especially in eastern Europe and along the banks of the Danube.

The collection of the high-quality down of the eider duck in Norway and Iceland almost ranks as farming, for although the birds are wild creatures, they become confiding enough to nest near houses and in artificial nesting places. The down, about a handful each time, and some of the eggs are removed from the nests several times during the season to encourage the duck to produce more; and finally enough eggs are left to maintain the necessary numbers. There is no truth in the old story that when the duck has used up all her own down, the drake lines the nest with his.

FEEDING (FARM ANIMALS). Imagine a dairy cow, a fattening bullock, and a sheep grazing in the same grass field. All are eating the same food. If it is a good grass field, all are eating a mixture made up mainly of rye-grass and wild white clover. Yet the uses made of the food eaten are very different. The dairy cow 'converts' grass and clover into milk, the bullock converts them into beef, the sheep into mutton and wool. To take another example. If a dairy cow, a fattening pig, and a laying hen eat the same mixture of grains, the compositions of their food are identical; but the cow turns the grain

into milk, the pig turns it into pork, and the hen turns it into eggs.

These two examples illustrate the main reason for the use of domestic animals on farms. They convert food such as grass, which man cannot eat, into the milk and meat that man eats or into the wool that he wears. Or they may convert food that man can eat, such as grain, into still more valuable foods such as bacon and eggs, or, in the case of horses, into useful work.

Each, however, needs part of the food it eats to maintain its own life, and the amount needed to do this is called its 'maintenance requirement' or its 'maintenance ration'. (Sometimes a maintenance ration is all that is needed, as, for example, where a fully grown bullock is being kept lean during winter for later fattening on summer grass.)

But if a domestic animal is to be of any use to mankind, then at some stage in its life it must produce a surplus, and to do this it must receive more food than its mere maintenance ration. This extra food is called the animals' 'production requirement', and the food added to its maintenance ration is called the 'production ration'. The quantity fed depends upon how much the animal is producing. A cow that is giving 6 gallons of milk a day, for example, needs a bigger production ration than one giving only 2 gallons. To feed her less than her full production requirement is to waste a good cow, and to feed her more may be to waste good food. A hen that lays 200 eggs in a year needs a much bigger production ration than one laying only 100 eggs, and the same principle holds for all farm animals, whether they give milk, meat, eggs, wool, or anything else.

If a high-producing animal is to give as much as it possibly can, it must have enough room inside to hold all the necessary food, and it must also have a good digestion. In a dairy cow, as in other animals, there is only a limited space in which the food taken in can be held during digestion, and the food must, therefore, not be too bulky.

Farm animals may be divided into two main classes, according to the type of food that they can best use. Animals that are RUMINANTS (q.v. Vol. II) (cattle, sheep, and goats), make the best possible use of the bulky vegetable foodstuffs that we ourselves can only partly digest or, in some cases, find completely indigestible. These bulky foods, commonly called roughages, include

Eric Guy

MEASURING A RATION OF PIG NUTS

The quantities of each ingredient are weighed so that
each pig gets what it needs

such foods as grass, hay, and straw which cattle
and sheep can digest and make good use of
owing to their power of rumination. The
roughage (hay, for example) when first swallowed, passes into a large compartment or
paunch, called the 'rumen', where the hay is
stored and ferments. At intervals, when the cow
or sheep is at rest, this partly fermented hay is
brought back into the mouth, chewed again in
a leisurely manner (a process commonly referred
to as 'chewing the cud') and then swallowed
once more. After being thoroughly broken up
by repeated chewing in the mouth and by
fermentation in the rumen, the hay, when
swallowed for the second time, by-passes the
rumen and passes almost directly into the true
stomach, where digestion is completed in much
the same way as in non-ruminant animals. Ruminants therefore convert foodstuffs such as grass
and hay, which are useless as human food, into
such things as meat and milk, which are of the
greatest importance in feeding human beings.

Rumination being a leisurely business, a very
productive animal, such as a high yielding dairy

cow or a rapidly fattening lamb, may not be
able to digest the bulky foods fast enough to
satisfy its needs. They must, therefore, be fed
partly on less bulky and more concentrated
foodstuffs, such as oilcakes or grain.

Although the horse has not got a rumen and
is, therefore, not a ruminant animal, it is still
able to digest roughage, such as hay or grass,
because of the development and enlargement of
the large intestine in the bowel—where fermentation of roughage takes place.

In pigs and poultry the digestive apparatus,
as well as the process of digestion, is much more
simple and direct than in ruminants or horses.
The special digestive organ of the fowl—the
'gizzard'—is used for the grinding of grain and
not for the fermentation of roughage. It is true
that both pigs and poultry eat a certain quantity
of grass and other green food, which do them
good, but neither can live on roughage alone.
Indeed, if we want to get a pig to grow very
quickly into pork or bacon, and make a good
hen lay as many eggs as she possibly can, we
feed both on large quantities of grain in one form
or another, and we give them very little else.
Therefore, when harvests fail, or grain is scarce
as in times of war when nearly all of it is needed
for human consumption, the country's stock of
pigs and poultry has to be reduced, and bacon
and eggs become rare luxuries.

Wheat and rice are the two most important
grain foods for human beings; and when there
is plenty of both to be had, the most easily
digestible part of the grain is extracted as flour
and most of the less digestible fraction—often
called 'millers' offals'—is fed to poultry and pigs.
When grain is scarce, the extraction rate of flour
may be raised, which means that more of the
offals are left in the flour, the flour becomes
darker in consequence, and there are fewer offals
to feed to farm animals. That is why a rise in the
extraction rate of flour means fewer eggs and less
bacon.

In much the same way, the oilcakes, so
widely used as concentrated foods for the high
producing farm animals, are by-products of
other useful industries. Cotton-cake, for example,
is a by-product of the cotton and vegetable oils
industries. Domestic animals, therefore, are
useful not only because they turn foods useless
to man into some of the most valuable human
foods, but also do the same to some factory by-
products, which might otherwise be wasted.

Dung and urine from animals is also a valuable manure for the land (*see* MANURE, FARMYARD).

Domestic animals are not, however, merely machines converting material that is useless into that which is useful. If the best use is to be made of them, they need more kindly consideration and understanding than a tractor or a motor-car. An animal will give of its best only when gently handled, with careful attention given to its comfort and health. That is why, with the same animals and with the same food, one stock-man will get better results than another. A skilful cattleman, for example, will not merely weigh out and distribute food. He will study the individual appetite and taste of each beast under his care. In the feeding of animals, therefore, scientific accuracy alone is not enough. For real success there must be something of that unfailing thoughtfulness and care that a good mother devotes to her child.

See also FOODS (FARM ANIMALS).

FENCES, *see* BOUNDARIES, LAND; HEDGING, DITCHING, AND WALLING; HURDLE-MAKING.

FERNS (GARDEN AND GREENHOUSE). Hardy ferns are not difficult to cultivate; their chief needs are shade, shelter, and much moisture. The majority favour shady, damp positions, and a few will thrive in such out of the way places as old walls, down mouths of wells, in snug rock crevices beneath the dripping waterfall, or even in the water itself. As pot plants they are useful, for they will keep in good condition for several weeks in a hot, stuffy room, so long as they are given a period of recuperation afterwards.

Ferns propagate by means of spores, found beneath the small brown 'scales' on the backs of the fronds (*see* FERNS, Vol. II). These are usually sown in autumn or early in the spring in a warm house; those of the Royal Fern (*Osmunda regalis*) need to be sown as soon as they are ripe, but most spores will keep their vitality for years. The spores are sown in much the same way as the seeds of flowering plants, in compost composed of sharp silver sand, sifted loam, and sifted leaf-mould in equal parts, with a sprinkling of finely powdered charcoal. A thorough watering is essential before sowing; and after sowing, the pans should be stood in trays of water to keep them constantly damp. The soil should be an inch or two beneath the rim of the pot, and a piece of glass placed over the top to conserve the moist, humid atmosphere in which the spores will germinate most easily. Germination may take days, weeks, or months. The first growth to appear, the 'prothallus', looks something like a green scale, and bears the male and female organs (*see* picture, p. 142, Vol. II). The fusion of these organs results in the true seedling fern. When the young plants are large enough to be handled, they must be pricked out into other pans, and moved when they become overcrowded into small pots. Growing ferns from spores is a slow

Amateur Gardening

MAIDENHAIR AND SPLEENWORT FERNS

HARE'S FOOT FERN

but interesting business, particularly as ferns are in the habit of producing 'breaks'—that is, varieties from the parent plant. Lady Ferns and Hart's Tongue especially produce these breaks.

Pot ferns in houses should be kept just moist during the winter rest period; they must be protected from frosts, but should not be encouraged in any way to grow. When the spring comes, they need more moisture, but not too moist an atmosphere. The plants need plenty of light, but not glare: if necessary they should be covered from strong sunlight. Ferns such as *Adiantum cuneatum* and *A. Capillus-Veneris* (the maidenhairs), *Davallia canariensis* (Hare's Foot), *Asplenium bulbiferum* (Spleenwort), *Cheilanthes elegans* (the Lace Fern), and *Nephrolepis exaltata* are popular varieties for growing in houses. During the growing season these plants must not be allowed to dry out.

PTERIS SERRULATA CRISTATA FERN, A POPULAR HOUSE FERN

Among the most beautiful of the hardy ferns is the American Hardy Maidenhair (*Adiantum pedatum*), which grows 18 inches to 2 feet high, and bears its drooping fronds on glistening black stems. It is advisable to cover the crown with a light covering of leaves during severe weather. The Lady Ferns (*Athyrium*), which produce a large number of varieties, are adaptable but flourish best where the ground is constantly moist. The Ostrich Feather Fern (*Struthiopteris germanica*) is a fine-looking plant, 3 to 4 feet high, with spreading pale green fronds arranged in a circle like a shuttlecock. Harts' Tongues and the *Polypodium* are other well known ferns which are neither difficult to obtain nor hard to grow.

FERRETS, *see* VERMIN. *See also* Vol. IX: FERRETING.

FERTILIZATION. In order to produce FRUITS (q.v. Vol. II) and seeds the blossoms must be fertilized. The word to 'fertilize', when used in this sense, means to make productive by pollination (*see* REPRODUCTION IN PLANTS, Vol. II, sections 5 and 6). Pollination takes place when the pollen grains containing the male reproductive cells are brought from the anthers of the flower to the female pistil by insects, by wind, or by water. When a pollen grain arrives on the stigma of the pistil, it begins to germinate like a seed, but instead of sending out a root the pollen grain pushes out a thin tube that grows downwards through what is known as the style of the flower until it gets to the lowest part—the ovule. When all this has taken place, the ovule begins to grow into a seed, and the ovary, or part that contains the ovules, begins to swell up and finally becomes the fruit (*see* FRUITS, Vol. II, section 3). The apple blossom usually has ten ovules, and in order to get a perfect apple with ten perfect seeds or pips, ten pollen grains have to arrive on the stigma, and push pollen tubes down the style into the ovules. Stone fruit and nuts, on the other hand, have only one ovule.

With some plants the stamen, the male organ bearing the pollen, is in a different flower from the pistil, the female organ bearing the stigma and ovary. This is the case with catkin-bearing plants such as walnuts and cob nuts (*see* NUTS), and also with VEGETABLE MARROWS, MELONS, and CUCUMBERS (qq.v.). The former depend largely on wind fertilization; the latter can be easily hand fertilized if the male flower is picked

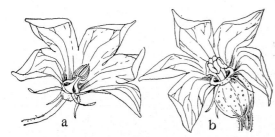

FIG. 1. VEGETABLE MARROW FLOWERS: (*a*) MALE, (*b*) FEMALE
Petals have been removed to display the centres

and the pollen-covered anther pressed on to the stigma of the female flower (*see* Fig. 1). Most plants depend for pollination mainly on insects, especially bees. Some very early-flowering fruit trees, such as peaches and apricots, may not attract enough insects in a cold sunless spring, and some assistance with hand fertilizing is needed. This is easily done by dabbing pollen with a rabbit's tail or soft paint brush into the freshly opened blossoms. Fruit trees and other plants grown under glass, and therefore not easily accessible to insects, need such treatment. It is possible, also, to do the work of insects or wind with a spray.

With some plants, such as currants and gooseberries, the pollen grains from any one plant will pollinate the blossoms on that plant; and these are known as fully self-fertile or self-pollinating. But with most of the tree fruits, in particular, full crops cannot be got unless pollen grains are brought from other varieties of the fruit. This is called cross-fertilization or cross-pollination, and the plants are self-sterile. All sweet cherries and some apples are fully self-sterile and depend entirely on cross-pollination. For this reason fruit-growers have to arrange their trees in the orchard or plantation in such

a way that different varieties of the same fruit are near enough to each other for insects to carry pollen grains from one to the other, when they visit the blossoms looking for nectar. This is what we mean when we speak of planning an orchard to allow for cross-pollination. If, for instance, we are planting an orchard of Cox's Orange apples, which need another variety such as James Grieve to effect pollination, we must plant at least one in nine of the second variety to ensure successful cross-pollination (*see* Fig. 2).

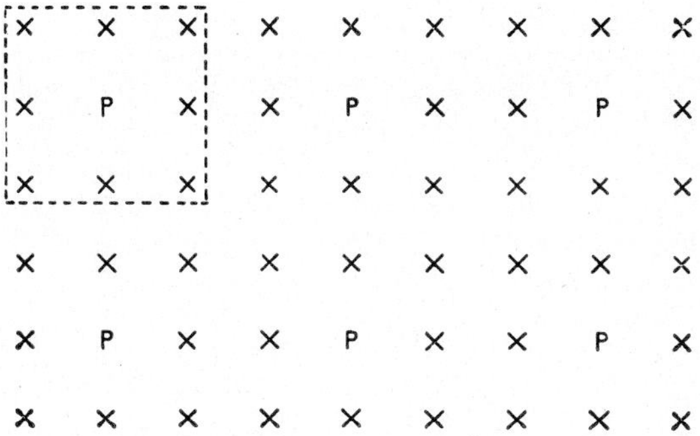

With some fruits fertilization is made more difficult because some of the best sorts, as for instance Cox's Orange Pippin apple, Doyenne de Comice pear, River's Early cherry, and Coe's Golden Drop plum, are very particular which pollen grains they will have to pollinate their blossoms. As a result of experiments made by the John Innes Horticultural Institution, it is now possible to get lists of the most suitable 'cross-pollinating' varieties for each of the well-known varieties of fruits. These varieties must, of course, have the same times of flowering. In a small garden, where there is not room to plant a pollinating tree, fertilization can often be effected by placing trusses of the blossom of a suitable pollinator among the branches of the self-sterile tree on a sunny day when insects are busy. But this is only practical on a small scale. Interesting experiments are now being carried on in breeding self-fertile varieties of these at present self-sterile plants (*see* PLANT BREEDING).

See also Vol. II: REPRODUCTION IN PLANTS.

FERTILIZERS, *see* MANURES; ARTIFICIAL FERTILIZERS.

FEUDAL SYSTEM, *see* LAND OWNERSHIP. *See also* Vol. X: FEUDAL SYSTEM.

FIBRE CROPS. These include many different kinds of plants, some of which are of great commercial importance, though others are important only in the countries where they are grown. The most valuable are such crops as COTTON (q.v.) and flax, which yield long, strong fibres suitable for spinning to make fabrics. Vegetable fibres are also used for rope-making, paper-making, stuffing upholstery and mattresses, packings, and other purposes.

1. FLAX is a fibre crop cultivated in temperate countries. In Great Britain it is grown only 'on contract', that is to say, a farmer agrees to grow

FIG. 2. A METHOD OF PLANTING FRUIT TREES WITH ONE POLLINATOR (P) TO EIGHT TREES OF THE MAIN VARIETY (X)

the crop for a flax factory at a certain price. The factory supplies the seed and, where necessary, advice on the cultivation and manuring of the crop.

Flax and LINSEED (q.v.) both come from the same blue-flowered species, *Linum usitatissimum*, flax being grown for the fibres in its stems, and linseed for its seeds. Varieties grown for flax, therefore, are sown thickly so that the plants grow tall and unbranched, for the fibres in the stems must be, as with almost all fibre crops, as long and unbroken as possible. The yield of seed from a crop of flax is of minor importance, the average being only about 4 cwt. per acre.

Flax is grown in much the same way as linseed, though even more care must be taken to keep it free from weeds, since these spoil the crop when it goes through the machines at the factory. Officials from the factory generally inspect the land for its suitability before the seed is sown, and if the farmer fails to keep out harmful weeds such as thistles, the factory may refuse the flax or pay a reduced price.

In order to obtain as long fibres as possible, flax is always pulled up by the roots, and not cut. Pulling-machines, which also tie the crop into sheaves or 'beets', like a binder, are sent out by the factory to the farms. When hand pulling, one worker covers only about one-sixth of an acre in a day, but a pulling machine averages 5 acres pulled and tied. The beets are stooked immediately, and are left in the field until perfectly dry. They are then carted and stacked near a good road, from where the factory can collect them as they want them at any time during the winter (*see* LINEN INDUSTRY, Vol. VII).

An average yield of flax is 2 to 2½ tons per acre. The factory keeps the seed, but the farmer can buy, if he wishes, the chaff for feeding.

2. JUTE. This crop has been grown since earliest times in Bengal, which is still the chief centre of production, for labour is cheap there and the climate very suitable. Jute is an annual plant, growing to a height of from 5 to 10 feet. The seed is sown thickly to encourage the plants to grow tall without forming side branches. When the clusters of small yellowish flowers fade, the crop is harvested, the plants being cut at ground level, tied into bundles, and allowed to wilt. The fibre is extracted by being soaked, or 'retted' (*see* JUTE INDUSTRY, Vol. VII).

3. RAMIE (*Boehmeria nivea*), known also as Rhea or Chinagrass and cultivated in the Far East, is a fibre plant closely related to the ordinary stinging-nettle and growing in much the same way, though it has no sting. Ramie has a perennial root system from which every year stems develop, growing to a height of from 4 to 8 feet. The plant bears very small greenish-brown flowers arranged closely along the stem, and leaves with silvery under-sides. It grows rapidly, producing from two to four crops a year. When ripe, the stems are cut down and the outer part stripped off. These strippings contain bark, fibre, and a quantity of very adhesive gum, which is removed by steeping the strippings in hot caustic soda. Then the fibre is washed and dried. Ramie fibre varies in quality, the best quality being used as a substitute for linen, the coarser for making ropes, nets, and canvas.

4. SISAL (*Agave sisaliana*) is widely grown in East Africa, Indonesia, and Haiti. It has a short stout stem, bearing a number of very stiff, blue-green leaves, up to 6 feet in length, terminating in a tough spine. The plant is raised from 'bulbils' (buds in the axils of the leaves which contain a store of food for starting the new plant), or from basal suckers. About a thousand plants go to an acre, and about 18 months to 2 years after planting the farmer begins to cut the lower leaves, and continues to do so for about 6 years. He may gather each year about 1½ tons of fibre

Indian Jute Mills Assn.

CUTTING A FIELD OF JUTE

Ewing Galloway

A SISAL PLANTATION IN MEXICO

per acre. After the spines and prickles are removed, the stems are scraped by a special machine to remove the waste material from the fibre, which is then dried, and used among other things for rope-making.

Henequen (*Agave fourcroydes*) and Mauritius Hemp are somewhat similar plants producing fibre of rather inferior quality, mainly used for binder twine and for ropes.

5. HEMP (*Cannabis sativa*) is an annual plant related to the stinging nettle, which is a native of India and Persia, and has been cultivated for its fibre in China since very early times. In western Europe it was grown up to the Middle Ages for its seed, which was used for food. It has slender stems growing about 8 feet high. The male and female flowers are produced on separate plants, the male providing the better fibre. The process of manufacture is much the same as with flax and jute.

There are other 'hemp' crops which are not true hemps. Manila hemp (*Musa textilis*), or abaca, is a tall species of BANANA (q.v.) native to the Philippines, where it is grown for its fibre, the fruit being of no value. The plant is grown from suckers. The stem is cut down at 2 or 3 years, when the plant is about to flower, and the fibre

is obtained from the outer portion of each leaf stem, which is stripped off in a 'ribbon'. The ribbon is then held against the edge of a knife and pulled across it, a scraping process which removes everything except the fibre. The cleaned fibre is then dried.

Manila fibre is very resistant to the action of sea water and is therefore used for marine cordage, and other purposes where great strength and durability are required (*see* ROPE-MAKING, Vol. VII).

6. KAPOK. The cotton-woolly floss known as kapok is obtained from the seed pods of trees which grow in wet tropical countries, especially Java. Kapok trees are tall, bearing horizontal branches, which have no leaves during the fruiting season. When the seed pods are ripe they split open, releasing the floss and seed. The pods are collected before they split, and the floss is separated from the seed by machinery. It is used in industry as a stuffing material, where its buoyancy and water-resisting capacity make it suitable for life-saving apparatus, among other things. Its fibre is too short and brittle for spinning (*see* KAPOK, Vol. VII).

7. SUNN HEMP (*Crotalaria juncea*) is mainly grown in India, not only for its fibre but also for ploughing back into the land as a green manure. It is an annual crop which grows to a height of 5 to 10 feet. The fibre in the stems is separated by being soaked or 'retted'. It is used for making ropes and for oakum.

8. OTHER FIBRES. Fibre is obtained from the husk of the COCONUT (q.v.) which produces coir, used in making mats, brooms, brushes, and ropes, and as a filler in upholstery. The leaves of the PINEAPPLE (q.v.) yield a very fine fibre which can be woven into cloth. Fibres are also obtained from the leaves of most of the palms of both wet and dry tropics, one of the most important being the fibre from the dwarf palm (*Chamaerops humilis*), grown in Algeria, which is used as a 'filler' in upholstery. Raffia comes from the leaves of a palm grown in Madagascar and Japan; Panama hats are made from the fibre obtained from a palm grown in Central America. Fibrous tissue of the leaf stalks of many kinds of palms which remain after the softer portions have decayed are used in appreciable quantities for rope-making. Some of the grasses are suitable for the extraction of fibre. Cereal straws are used for hats and mats, and in Asia for sandals. Esparto grass (*Stipa tenacissima*) from Algeria has long been used for making ropes, sandals, baskets, and bags, and in the manufacture of paper. Many other tropical plants yield fibre materials suitable for PAPER-MAKING (q.v. Vol. VII).

See also Vol. VII: ROPE-MAKING; LINEN INDUSTRY; JUTE INDUSTRY; KAPOK; PAPER-MAKING.

FIGS. These are natives of most sub-tropical countries. There are many varieties of both white and black figs, some growing into large trees and others growing as creeping and trailing shrubs. Figs were probably introduced to Britain by the Romans, but were re-introduced from the continent in medieval times: Thomas à Becket planted a fig garden in the 12th century, and Cardinal Pole planted figs at Lambeth in 1555. They are cultivated throughout southern Europe and the Southern States of the U.S.A. Great numbers are dried, especially in Mediterranean countries such as Greece. They form an important item in the staple diet of the peasants of these countries, for their rich sugar content makes them, like dates, good sustaining food.

In Britain figs can be made to fruit successfully in the southern and western counties, especially if they are trained fanwise up a protected south wall where the maximum amount of sun-heat can reach the fruit. Unlike most fruit trees they do not need deep rich soil, for this results in rank growth and no fruiting. They fruit best where they have a very restricted root area—no more than 2 feet deep and approximately 16 sq. feet of surface area. Where a special bed is being made for a fig tree, the foundation should be of brick or slabs of stone which allow drainage but discourage tap root growth. The side roots should be confined by stone or brick walls. The soil should be mixed with mortar rubble. The tree needs to be pruned severely; suckers are cut out, and only as many long shoots allowed to grow as there is room to space them widely on the wall (*see* PRUNING).

Figs have an unusual method of fruiting. A fruiting shoot will bear large figs on its lower part, very small figs farther up, and embryo figs towards the top, all at the same time. The large figs on the older wood are the only ones likely to ripen in Britain; but in hotter countries the small figs on the new wood will produce a second or third crop. In Britain these small figs should be removed since they take strength from the tree; but as the embryo figs are next year's crop, they should be left and, if possible, should be given some protection through the winter.

Amateur Gardening

RIPE FIGS AND THE SMALL SECOND CROP FIGS WHICH WILL NOT MATURE IN THE BRITISH CLIMATE

AN EGYPTIAN NOBLE AND HIS FAMILY SPEARING FISH AND FOWLING

Painting from the tomb of Menne, Thebes, 1420-1411 B.C. (N. M. Davies: *Ancient Egyptian Paintings*, Oriental Institute, University of Chicago)

FIRS, *see* TREES, CONIFEROUS.

FISHING, HISTORY OF. One of the first things that men learnt to do in order to get food was to catch fish. Fishing came long before farming (*see* PREHISTORIC MAN, Vol. I). One of the earliest, simplest methods was to use a thing called a 'gorge', which was a piece of bone or a tough stick, tapered at each end, with a hole in the middle for attaching a line. Bait was put on the gorge, which, when the fish swallowed it and pulled on the line, jammed crosswise in the fish's throat. Even today, in the Fiji Islands, fish are caught this way, the bait used being the tip of an octopus arm.

The fishing hook was a great improvement on the gorge. First, a twig with a strong thorn, and bait to hide the thorn, were used. Next, hooks were made of bone, tortoise-shell, or flint. Metal hooks were, of course, not used until people had discovered metals and learnt how to use them.

Nets rot and leave no remains, but perforated stones, believed to be net-sinkers, suggest that nets were used in very early times. Ancient Egyptian paintings and tomb models prove that they were used in Egypt hundreds of years before

Christ. A model of two reed canoes from a Theban tomb, for instance, shows the canoes towing a bag-net between them in much the same way as the Italian *paranzella* trawlers can still be seen fishing outside Port Said. The ancient Egyptians also used two-pronged spears when fishing in the marshes.

Probably the oldest illustrations of men catching fish by hook and line are to be found in the Assyrian sculptured panels, now in the British Museum. The ancient Assyrians used short rods and lines, and the line, instead of being wound on a reel or a frame, was fixed to the top of the rod—a 'tight line', as it is called. From these early times until the 19th century A.D. there was very little change in fishing methods. Local improvements were probably used wherever there were clever fishermen, but no records remain. Early in the 19th century, however, the beam trawl was invented (*see* TRAWLING). When British fishermen began to trawl with this device, they were able to tow bag-nets on the bottom of the sea, using single vessels instead of pairs as had been the practice until then.

With the introduction of steam and motor power, great changes were made in the fishing industry. When the marine steam-engine was perfected, steam fishing-boats were used more and more instead of the slow-sailing older types. The building of a network of railways and the invention of refrigerators made it possible to distribute the fish rapidly to inland towns and to keep it in good condition. Consequently there was a much greater demand for fish (*see* FISH TRADE, Vol. VII). Money flowed freely into the fishing industry, making it possible to build larger and more weatherly boats, and encouraging the invention of more powerful fishing-gear so that larger catches could be made (*see* FISHING METHODS).

FISHING INDUSTRY. 1. BRITISH FISHERIES. The herring fishery was among the first of the important industries to be developed in Britain, and has been of national importance from a very early date. In the Middle Ages the centre of the herring fishing industry was Yarmouth, and the town was given privileges in recognition of its enterprise and of the aid which its ships rendered to the State in time of war. Every year at the end of September a fair was held at Yarmouth, attended by merchants from all over England and the Continent. They traded their wares, and bought the cured herrings which had accumulated towards the end of the fishing season. Fishing-boats, called 'buses', from many far-off posts took part in the fishery. Another herring-fishing port of first-class importance is Lowestoft on the east coast (*see* HERRING FISHERY).

Northwards from Yarmouth, the next great fishing-ports are Grimsby and Hull, now the

James Hornell

A HASTINGS LUGGER BEING RUN DOWN THE BEACH INTO THE SEA

This boat uses an otter trawl

chief centres of the east-coast steam and motor-driven trawling industry. From these ports fleets of trawlers sail either to the DOGGER BANK (q.v.) or northwards to Bear Island off Spitzbergen, or to the rich CODFISHING grounds (q.v.) off the Faeroe Islands and Iceland.

Between Lowestoft and the Thames estuary there are many minor fishing-ports—homes of fleets of fishing-craft which range from small shrimpers to deep-sea trawlers. Oyster dredgers are numerous, particularly on the Essex coast and at Whitstable, from which come the finest oysters of British seas. OYSTER FISHING (q.v.) is a very old industry. In fact, during the Roman occupation of Britain these Thames oysters were very highly prized, and some were probably sent to Rome.

All along the south coast there are large numbers of small ports, mostly ill-provided with modern harbour installations, which send out small sailing-craft to fish near the coast. Formerly, they were generally rigged as luggers, like those which can be seen at Hastings; but today motor power has largely taken the place of sail. These boats are engaged mostly in trawling for the flat-fishes (plaice and soles) which abound in Rye Bay; in the herring season they take part in drift-netting.

In the extreme west Plymouth fits out a good-sized fleet of trawling smacks. Some boats engage in hooking, while others fish for herring and mackerel with drift-nets. The neighbouring harbour of Brixham claims to have introduced beam-trawling, and TRAWLING (q.v.) is still the main occupation of its fishing community.

The busiest fishing-ports of the west coast and the Irish Sea are Milford Haven and Fleetwood. Of less importance are Dublin, and the Manx ports of Peel, Ramsey, and Castletown. Milford Haven and Fleetwood send some of the largest and best-equipped of modern trawlers to far-distant waters, some going to the coast of Morocco to fish hake, others to Iceland and the Far North, bringing back fine catches of fish such as cod, turbot, and haddock. Many of the smaller vessels are drifters, fishing for herring and mackerel.

There is little deep-sea fishing off Ireland apart from the fleets engaged in the herring and mackerel fisheries. On the wild western coast the industry is greatly handicapped because the Irish have not invested in power-driven fishing craft necessary for large-scale operations in distant waters. This is partly due

PORTUGUESE SARDINE FISHERS BRINGING IN THEIR BOAT

Paul Popper

to innate conservatism, and partly to the poverty of the fishing community. The fisherfolk still cling to their flimsy currachs, made of a wicker or lath framework and covered with tarred canvas, which they allege to be actually safer than wooden-hulled boats: and indeed they do stand up to seas which even the Norwegian cod-fishers would consider hazardous (*see* CANOE, Vol. IV).

Except for a few large ports, mostly on the east coast, Scottish fishing-stations are generally small and widely scattered. The most important methods employed are drift-netting and line fishing for cod, whiting, ling, and other white-fish. The main fishing-ports of the east coast are Aberdeen, Leith, and Newhaven, but there are many smaller ones. These fishing-stations rely for their prosperity mostly on the herring fishery which takes place between July and September. There is also long-line fishing for white-fish, as well as seining (fishing with encircling nets) for sprats. Oysters are dredged, and whalers, fitted out at Leith, work in the Antarctic Seas (*see* WHALING). Trawlers from Aberdeen fish mainly in the Far North, from the Faroes to Iceland and the White Sea, and to Bear Island off Spitzbergen. Its fish quays are a wonderful scene of activity when a number of boats arrive together with full catches.

To the north there are rich fishing-grounds in the Moray Firth. The Findon cure, a method of smoking fish which produces finnan haddocks, is an important source of wealth. The land-locked waters of Scapa Flow afford some good fishing-ground for herrings and some line fish. In the northern section of the group the principal fishing is by lines for white-fish of various kinds.

On the west coast Stornoway in the Outer Hebrides is a convenient centre from which to operate drift-nets for herrings in the Minch— the waters between the Hebrides and the mainland. May to July is the earliest local season in Scotland for starting the herring fishery. In years when it is possible to open the season on 1st May there are great rejoicings and local celebrations. The farther south the later in the year is the herring season—in the English Channel it does not begin until November.

South of the Hebrides, in the Clyde area, there is a wonderfully rich herring fishery in Loch Fyne; these herrings, of unusually fine quality, are caught mostly by the ring-net, a kind of seine (or encircling net) shot from boats instead of from the beach. Off the coast of Ayr and Galloway and in the Solway Firth there is fishing in inshore waters by small craft—shrimping, line fishing for cod, and trawling for flounders.

2. EUROPEAN FISHERIES. On the Continent

fishing is of prime importance to all countries with long or rich seaboards—the Scandinavian countries, Holland, France, Portugal, and Italy in particular.

The best known Portuguese fishery is for sardines, which rivals the French fishers of Brittany. In Italy fishing with trawls is still done by an ancient method—the trawl-net being towed by two sailing (or motor) trawlers, which are sailed abreast of one another at an equal speed. Hundreds work in pairs in this manner in the Adriatic, and also off the Nile delta, landing their catches at Port Said. These boats catch large numbers of small red mullets and excellent swimming crabs.

Fishing is of very great importance in France, which has coasts fronting both the Atlantic and the Mediterranean. Sardines are caught off the coast of Brittany, and in the Bay of Biscay there is a large fishery for the BONITO (q.v.), the flesh of which is canned under the name of *thon* or tunny. Oyster fishing, or rather oyster-farming, employs a large number of workers at the two great centres of Auray and Arcachon. Besides these fisheries, trawling on a grand scale is operated by vessels which are often larger than the average British trawler.

The Basques were the pioneers of the cod fishery on the Newfoundland Banks; but today St. Malo and other seaports in Brittany are the main centres. They use boats called *Terre-neuvas*, each of which carries twelve flat-bottomed 'doreys', built so as to fit inside one another. When on the Banks, two men set out in each dorey, taking with them a supply of baited lines, together with a supply of food, since they may be held up by fog. It is a dangerous calling, and many men have lost their lives.

Off the West African coast a most valuable fishery is operated by the Spaniards in Levrier Bay, south of Cape Blanco, where, at one particular season, fleets of Spanish schooners catch immense numbers of the big corvinas in large-meshed nets, and salt them down aboard the vessels. When the fishermen return home, usually to Las Palmas in the Canary Islands, the fish are washed and dried in the sun on the rocks, and sold in the market under the name of *baccalão*.

3. ASIATIC FISHERIES. In Asia the glamour of the PEARL-FISHING (q.v.) of the Persian Gulf, Ceylon, and India overshadows the unspectacular coastal fisheries which provide the people with food. In spite of poor boats and fishing-gear, these are carried on as busily as in Europe.

In India little attention is given to deep-sea fishing except for the bonito and FLYING FISH (q.v.) fisheries. For coastal fishing they use dug-out canoes, catamarans, and small sailing-vessels which are neither large enough nor well enough equipped to secure large catches. The fishes of the Indian coasts are varied, ranging from small mackerel and sardines to swordfish, bonito, and sharks.

In the Malay areas the favourite fishing devices are basket-work traps of many shapes, the staked fishing-weir, lines with baited lures and hooks, and the lure, which is sometimes carried over the sea by means of a kite (*see* KITE FISHING).

The Chinese have many ingenious devices for capturing fish in their rivers, including the use of cormorants and otters. The cormorants are trained to fish either from the bank or from a raft. They usually wear rings round their necks which prevents their swallowing fish above a certain size. After capturing its prey, each bird is hauled back to its owner by a line tied to a girdle around its body. The fisherman then forces the bird to disgorge the fish. Otters are also trained to bring back their prey to their owners, until they receive permission to hunt for themselves.

In Japan the fishing industry ranks next to agriculture in providing food for millions of the population. The major fisheries are for the bonito, which they smoke and dry, and for the giant spider crab, which is caught in the trawl in great quantities off the coast of Saghalien. There are few fishes which the Japanese disdain to eat: the octopus and the cuttle-fish are delicacies, the shark's flesh is pounded up and sold by weight, shell-fish of every kind are made use of, and even the bonito's intestines are prepared for sale. Oysters, clams, and many other shell-fish are cultivated.

4. THE FISHERIES OF OCEANIA. The native peoples of the Pacific Islands have been for generations skilled fishermen, for fish was and is their main supply of food and source of wealth (*see* PACIFIC ISLANDERS, Vol. I). In the South Seas today there are fisheries for a variety of large fish, including the bonito, albacore, and several species of flying fish. In addition, a seasonal fishery for a marine worm, the palolo, is an event awaited with eagerness by the people of Fiji, Samoa, and many other islands, where this is considered a great delicacy. When the breeding season arrives, the natives flock to the outer side of the reef, either wading over its jagged surface or paddling there in small canoes. They scoop up the clotted masses of palolo worms in long-handled scoop-nets.

Australian and New Zealand fishermen use British fishing methods—the trawl, the seine, the drift-net, and lines with baited hooks.

5. AMERICAN FISHERIES. Both in Canada and the United States the fisheries are highly organized, and receive considerable government support. The same fishing methods are used as in the British Isles. The Newfoundland Grand Banks, one of the chief fishing-grounds of the world, provide mainly cod, but also hake, halibut, and herrings.

Fish canneries are situated on the Californian coast, on the banks of the salmon rivers in Alaska and British Columbia, and on some of the western rivers of the Unites States (*see* SALMON FISHING). Fishes of the sardine and herring types are canned, and also the abalone, a large species of shell-fish of which the Chinese are specially fond. Other important fisheries, for bonito, albacore, and tunny, are all carried on off the coast of California.

Off the eastern coast and in the Great Lakes there is a great variety of fishes of good table quality, in particular the shad, a member of the herring family. What cannot be sold as human food goes to factories to be transformed into food for cattle, pigs, and fowls; and the remnants are made into valuable MANURES (q.v.).

Fishing as a sport is described in Volume IX.

See also Vol. VII: FISH TRADE.

FISHING METHODS. The three main methods of fishing today are by nets, by traps, and by hooks and lines.

1. NET FISHING. This is on the whole much the most important fishing method, and varies considerably according to the type of net used.

(*a*) *Seine nets.* Seining is fishing with an encircling net, the net being operated in various ways to catch different kinds of fish. The beach seine method, which consists in shooting the net in a semicircle, is generally used on sandy and sloping beaches to capture fish which have come near to the shore—mackerel, herrings, sprats, sand-eels, and others. It is also used to capture river salmon in places where the river broadens into a quiet pool with a sandy beach at one side. The beach-seine is a single net attached at each end to a long rope by means of a cork-line which floats and a leaded-line which sinks. The rope

James Hornell

HAULING IN A BEACH SEINE NET AT PORT SAID
The other end of the net is being hauled in further along the beach to the right

is secured on shore, and the fishermen take the net on board a small boat and shoot it out in a large semicircle. The men ashore then haul in the two ends by means of the rope, bringing in the net with all the fish that have been encircled. The ring-net is a seine which is shot and hauled from a boat instead of being operated from a beach, and is used, in particular, in Loch Fyne to catch the fine herrings of those waters. The purse-seine is another encircling net much used by Cornish fishermen for catching pilchards. When this net has encircled a shoal of fish, a running rope draws its lower edge together to form a bowl-shaped trap or purse, and then the net is gradually hauled and the fish ladled into the boat. The *snurrevaad* or Danish seine, which is now used a great deal on the Dogger Bank, is pivoted upon an anchored buoy, and can be shot in a full circle.

(*b*) *Bag-nets*. TRAWLING (q.v.), or towing a bag-net over the bottom of the sea to catch bottom-living fish, is a very old method of fishing which can be traced back to the ancient Egyptians. Italian and Spanish fishermen still trawl much as the Egyptians used to by towing their net between two boats. The Italians call this net a *paranzella* net, and the Spaniards a *pareja* net. The bag-net, however, is now generally towed by a single vessel. British fishermen have long trawled in this way, using first a 'beam trawl' and now, mainly, the 'otter trawl'. With either of these a special device keeps the mouth of the net open, so that two towing-boats are unnecessary. Large steam trawlers are used in the seas around the British Isles.

The finest example in Britain of an anchored bag-net is the 'stow-net' used on the East Coast. It is a very large and long bag-net, with the wide mouth kept open in a tide-way by bridle-ropes, which lead to heavy anchors securely bedded in the bottom of the sea. At the turn of the tide, any fish caught in the bag are taken out by the crew of the boat working the net. In India an even larger net of the same type is operated off the coast of Kathiawar to catch the maigre or Jew-fish, a big fish not unlike the salmon in shape, and also the delicate little fish called 'Bombay duck'.

(*c*) *Drift-nets, Gill-nets, Trammel-nets*. These are the nets mainly used for catching surface-swimming fish by entangling them in their meshes.

The drift-net is so called because it is not anchored, but drifts with the tide or current. Off the British Isles it is used to catch herrings, mackerel, and sprats, and also salmon, the meshes of the net varying according to the size of the fish to be caught. When the fish try to pass through the nets, they are caught just behind the head where the body begins to grow larger. Drift-net fishing vessels are either sailing craft, usually rigged as luggers, or small steam or motor-propelled boats. Each boat carries a number of nets attached to a long headline, and this is shot from the boat as it moves slowly forward. When all the nets are overboard the drifter lies to, with a small sail set on the after or mizzen-mast so that she can lie head to the wind, keeping the headline of her nets stretched as she drifts slowly backwards, dragging the fleet of nets after her. Drift-nets are usually set at sunset, and the fishermen wait through the night until daybreak to haul in the nets and disentangle the fish caught in the meshes.

A moored gill-net is used in Scotland in sheltered bays and in some deep-water coastal lochs to catch herrings. It catches the fish in the same way as the drift-net, but it is moored by an anchor or a heavy stone at each end, and buoyed along the headline so as to keep it vertical. It is left untended during the night and hauled soon after daybreak.

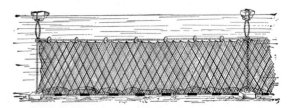

A TRAMMEL NET

A trammel-net consists of three vertical curtains of net: the middle one is of small mesh and set slack; the outer ones are of very coarse mesh and are stretched. When a fish strikes the nets, it pushes part of the middle net through one of the meshes of the outer nets, forming a pocket or bag within which it is caught. Trammel-nets are used on beaches where there is a considerable fall of tide, to catch any kind of fish that may be about, and are set usually in the area bounded by high and low water levels.

(*d*) *Dip-nets*. These are used to scoop up fish, principally in China, where they catch various kinds of estuary and river fishes. Small ones,

The manner of their fishing.

AMERICAN INDIANS OF THE 16TH CENTURY, NETTING, SPEARING,
AND TRAPPING FISH

Water-colour by John White (working 1585–93)

called hoop-nets, are used to catch large prawns, crabs, and small fishes.

(e) *Cast-nets* are circular nets weighted round the margin and with a retrieving line at the centre. The net is operated by one man, who throws it in such a way that it opens like a parachute and then settles in the water, capturing any fish that are below it. Cast nets are generally used from the beach for catching bass, mullet, smelts, and all fish that come inshore to feed. For sardine fishing in Malabar, however, the net is thrown from a canoe.

(f) *Fyke Nets.* These are a series of net funnels, the mouths of which are kept open by hoops. They are specially used to catch eels.

2. TRAPS. Stake-nets or fishing-weirs are frequently used as small fish traps. The many varieties all consist essentially of fences made of stout netting or of brushwood frames supported upon strong stakes. The stakes, generally arranged in the form of a V, induce the fish to swim towards the apex, where it passes through a narrow opening and finds itself in a trap from which escape is impossible. Many stake-nets are kept in repair and in position the whole year. They are set in shallow water and usually go dry at low tide. The fisherman visits the trap as the tide recedes, and captures the trapped fish which are splashing about in the last pools of water. The staked keddle net, used on the south coast of Kent and Sussex, is a typical example of these permanent fishing weirs. Sometimes the stakes are dispensed with, and the walls of netting are pegged to the ground, while the headlines of the net are buoyed up by large corks and held in

A CHINESE DIP-NET

position by rope guys. These floating keddles are used mainly during the mackerel season. Salmon on their journey up-stream to the spawn-beds are caught in special weirs in which the opening at the apex of the V-shaped palisade is blocked by a large bag-net, which the fisherman hauls up immediately he feels a vibration in it. (*see* SALMON FISHING).

The old type of small cage-trap is not much used by British fishermen except for catching lobsters and crabs, and sometimes eels. Cage-traps of many shapes are, however, still used elsewhere, particularly in the Mediterranean. The Italians, who are very fond of this kind of fishing, bait the traps with crabs and fish of little value, and visit them daily to clear the catch and to renew the bait.

3. HOOKS AND LINES. Fishing with lines armed with many hooks is still a common way of catching fish, especially cod and haddock. The lines, or 'hookers', used by the larger boats are often miles long and are armed with hundreds and even thousands of hooks. The 'small lines' for haddock are usually baited by the womenfolk ashore and arranged on wooden or basket-work trays. The 'great lines' for cod are, however, baited with herrings on board the boats. Each hook is attached to the outer end of a branch line or 'snood', given off at regular intervals from the main line. The fishermen search for a good fishing-ground, and then remain there, allowing their boat to drift slowly with the current while they shoot and haul their lines.

A troll line is a baited line towed behind a moving boat. The line often carries a lure to attract fishes to the hook concealed in the bait. Trolling is mainly carried on for fish of the mackerel family—for mackerel itself in home waters, for the giant seer in the seas around Ceylon, and for the bonito and its relatives on the high

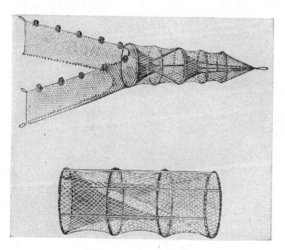

TWO KINDS OF FISH TRAP

seas. A great variety of bait is used. For mackerel, live bait is put on the hooks, the small
fish being fixed so cunningly that it remains
alive. The silvery body of a sand-eel or a
piece of squid flesh, the daintiest titbit that can
be offered to a fish, may also be used. Sometimes a bright metal object shaped like the bowl
of a spoon is used, or a gaudy feather, or some
bright white object will entice many fish to snap

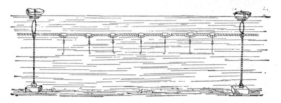

A LONG LINE ANCHORED TO THE SEA BOTTOM

at the hook—a fact well known to tropical
fishermen, who often tempt the Ceylon seer with
the white flesh of a coconut or a tuft of white
feathers.

Many kinds of fish are caught on ground lines
—long lines to which short branch lines or
snoods are attached. These are usually sunk on
the sea bottom and moored by stones or anchors.
The most usual fish caught are whiting, pollack,
haddock, cod, sea-bream, gurnard, conger, bass,
plaice, and dabs.

Jigging is fishing by means of hooks attached
to the end of a pole or to a short line hung from
a fishing-rod. The fish are foul-hooked, that is,
hooked in any part of the body.

These are the main fishing methods of today;
but there are many others used in various parts
of the world for particular kinds of catch—for
instance, KITE FISHING (q.v.) for the garfish,
HARPOONING (q.v.) for swordfish and sharks, and
the use of the sucker fish in TURTLE FISHING
(q.v.).

See also FISHING INDUSTRY.
See also Vol. II: FISHES.

FISH SHOOTING (BLOWGUNS AND BOWS AND
ARROWS). Blowguns are used by the natives for
shooting fish in the streams of Travancore,
Cochin, and southern Malabar in south India,
in Borneo, and in the Amazon region of South
America. Fish shooting is, in fact, a popular
native sport.

The commonest form of Indian blowgun is a
hollow reed, as nearly straight as possible. The

barrels are often decorated with lacquered
designs in yellow, scarlet, and black. The blowgun of Borneo is a long, wooden weapon, from
5 to 6 feet long, the barrel of which is often
elaborately ornamented with a fine tin inlaid
pattern. For a mouthpiece the simplest kinds
have merely a disk of coconut shell; but the best
have mouthpieces of turned brass or of lacquered
wood. The darts vary considerably in form. In
the simplest kind, used by jungle tribes in
Travancore, the shaft is a thin bamboo splint,
sharpened at the end, with a wad of cotton cloth,
a mop-head of threads, or a tapered cylinder of
pith tied to the butt end. A more elaborate dart
has the form of a miniature harpoon: a single-
barbed steel head fits loosely on one end of the
shaft and is connected to it by a long thin length
of twine. All these darts are propelled by violent
blowing through the gun's mouthpiece, and the
fish are shot when they chance to come up near
the surface. As the sport is limited to small
streams, it is usually fairly easy to retrieve the
wounded fish.

In several parts of the world fish are killed
with arrows shot from an ordinary stringed bow
or a cross-bow. The stringed bow is used by
hunter fishermen in the interior of Africa, and on
the backwaters and streams of south India, South
America, and Borneo. The cross-bow was introduced into India and the Malay Archipelago by
the early Portuguese adventurers, who very
likely found the natives using ordinary bows
and arrows and imitated them with their cross-
bows. The natives in their turn imitated the

James Hornell

SHOOTING FISH WITH A CROSS-BOW AND HARPOON IN SOUTH
INDIA

new weapon, and the cross-bow is quite commonly used today for shooting fish in the inland waters of south India and Burma, and also by the wild hill tribes from the borders of India and Burma.

FLAX, see FIBRE CROPS.

FLEAS, see FLY PESTS. *See also* Vol. II: FLEA.

FLOWER GARDENS. The gay, well-cared-for flower gardens to be found, not only round the houses of the wealthy but by many cottages, are a characteristic of the English countryside. Even those whose houses have no gardens often cultivate an ALLOTMENT, or at least WINDOW-BOXES (qq.v.). It is not usual to find a quite uncared for patch of garden.

The choice and preparation of site, the treatment of SOIL, the use of MANURES, and protections against PESTS AND DISEASES, are in general the same as in the VEGETABLE GARDEN (qq.v.). Flowering plants, however, do not in the main need so rich a soil as do the successive crops of vegetables; though it is important to prepare the soil well and to give it plenty of humus, because much of the flower garden is planted up permanently, and can therefore only be cultivated on the surface. Flower gardens also need much less watering than vegetable gardens, and the deep-rooted herbaceous plants and flowering shrubs hardly ever need watering at all, especially if a mulch has been applied when the top-soil was still full of moisture. A mulch consists of a layer of peat, well-rotted compost, or even lawn mowings, spread on the soil surface several inches deep, and perhaps added to at intervals during the season. This conserves moisture in the soil by preventing evaporation, and also makes it less necessary to hoe.

English gardens have developed from a wide variety of designs popular at different periods in the past (*see* GARDENING, HISTORY OF). Nowadays most gardens have to be designed with an eye to economy in money and labour. The vast formal schemes of BEDDING PLANTS (q.v.), so popular with the Victorians, are now seen mainly in public parks (*see* PARKS AND GARDENS, Vol. IX). In most private gardens HERBACEOUS BORDERS, filled with hardy perennial plants which remain where they are planted for several years, and FLOWERING SHRUBS (qq.v.) which need the least amount of attention, are the main-

stay of the garden. In the larger gardens ORNAMENTAL TREES and 'wild gardens', where large long-lived plants can grow with the minimum attention, are playing a large part. This does not mean that there is no place in the modern garden for ANNUALS, BIENNIALS, and the shorter-lived or more exacting PERENNIALS (qq.v.), but the area devoted to them is likely to be confined to small beds and borders, generally near the house.

The most popular garden flowers are ROSES, CHRYSANTHEMUMS, DAHLIAS, SWEET PEAS, CARNATIONS and certain BULBS, CORMS, AND TUBERS (qq.v.) such as gladioli. Dahlias and gladioli are often grown in spite of the fact that both are tender and have to be lifted from the ground annually; the chrysanthemum also needs a good deal of attention, and so does the sweet pea, which is an annual. Other popular flowers in British gardens are DELPHINIUMS, LILIES, IRISES (qq.v.) and bedding plants such as wallflowers and geraniums (*Pelargonium*). As a group, the DAISY FAMILY (q.v.) (Michaelmas daisies, asters, chrysanthemums, gaillardias, and others) is by far the most common in the herbaceous border. Bulbs such as hyacinths, tulips, and daffodils are widely used for spring display.

Almost every English garden has a LAWN (q.v.), the green expanse of which, if well kept, adds a great deal to the effect of the flower beds and trees around it. Such well-matured lawns are rarely found in continental gardens. The main feature of the large landscape garden is an expanse of turf, often ending in a meadow, a wild garden, or ornamental woodland.

The ROCK GARDEN and WATER GARDEN (qq.v.) are both popular features, and both introduce variety into the layout and provide quite different groups of plants for the garden. In small gardens the rock or water garden is usually formal in design, but in larger gardens an attempt is often made to imitate nature, and a natural stream or pool may be built into the design. The larger the scale, the more likely 'natural' effects are to succeed. GARDEN HEDGES and GARDEN PATHS (qq.v.) are not only useful but also often ornamental. During the 20th century a great many beautiful plants from other countries have been introduced to our gardens, many of which flourish without difficulty, though others, such as rhododendrons and other PEAT-LOVING PLANTS (q.v.) need special conditions.

The lines of a house are generally straight and

Homes and Gardens

A GARDEN IN SUMMER: THE MILL HOUSE, OCKHAM

regular, and some formality of design round a house is usually the most effective: to bring the wild garden, for example, right up to the windows is not usually a success. Besides, the relatively few flower beds of the modern garden should be near the house where they will show best and be most appreciated. The rectangular lines of the house can often be softened by the growing of CLIMBING PLANTS (q.v.) on the walls and by planting small, compact ornamental trees and shrubs near the house. In the small town garden, especially, which is usually a rectangular area bounded by walls or fences, the top-heavy effect of the house walls and the shut-in effect of the side walls can be reduced by the use of climbers and wall shrubs.

In the small garden, even more than in the large garden, simplicity of design always pays: too many complications in the form of tiny beds, small pools, rockeries, paths that lead nowhere, and garden ornaments, only give a confused and restless effect. The small garden may encourage the gardener to specialize, and indeed some gardeners today are almost fanatical in their devotion to one genus or group of plants. There are many national societies for these plants, and these hold shows which increase the interest. Another result of specialization has been a great advance in PLANT BREEDING (q.v.). Some flowers, including most of those previously mentioned, have been improved so that they barely resemble their ancestors, though others are still virtually the original wild species.

See also VEGETABLE GARDEN; GARDENING, HISTORY OF. See also Vol. XII: LANDSCAPE ART.

FLOWERING SHRUBS. The definition of a shrub is, broadly, a woody plant that never grows taller than about 15 feet and produces many stems from the base, rather than a single trunk. The distinction between a large shrub and a small tree is often vague; the same species may grow in the one form or the other, according to circumstances and training—the lilac being an example.

Flowering shrubs are popular for many

reasons. They have the great advantage that once planted they give a good show of flower, year after year, with the minimum labour and cost. Most of them are easy to grow, and kinds can be found that suit different soils and situations. By making a wise selection it is possible to have a show of flowers, foliage, or berries the whole year round. There is a great variety of size—from the dense-growing kinds of heath (*Erica*) and almost prostrate kinds of rock-rose (*Cistus*) to the large *Buddleia* and *Garrya* which are almost trees. Flowering shrubs can be selected, therefore, which are suitable for large or small gardens and for almost any situation. They are often planted as windbreaks or as screens to block out kitchen gardens, sheds and fences, neighbouring houses, or any unsightly objects. They make an effective background for herbaceous perennials, annuals, bulbs, and other plants, and provide some shade and shelter for the garden generally. In large gardens the skilful planting of shrubs is an important part of the design, for they can be made to accentuate the effect of distance, or may help to guide the eye to some object of attraction such as a garden ornament or distant view.

At certain periods as, for example, the beginning of this century, flowering shrubs were not much planted, for formality was the keynote of design in gardens and took the form of terraces and regularly shaped lawns, with formal beds and clipped hedges. The few shrubs available at the beginning of the century, many of them drab evergreens such as laurels and privets, were usually found where little else would grow.

After the First World War three factors increased the popularity of shrubs. In the first place the activities of the great botanical explorers during the previous 50 years resulted in the appearance of many new and beautiful flowering shrubs capable of withstanding a temperate climate, and hybrids were also raised in nurseries. Next, people had less money to spend on garden upkeep, and shrubs produce a show for the least expenditure of labour. Lastly, the earlier fashion for straight lines and formality in garden design was gradually giving way to gardens of more natural appearance, and shrubs were ideal for this type of design.

Today flowering shrubs are more popular than ever, and borders consisting entirely of shrubs are often planted. New varieties continue to be produced at reasonable cost, and with their help gardens both permanently attractive and labour saving can be maintained.

Among the kinds which are often grown are many varieties of berberis (showy both in blossoms and berries), brooms (*Cytisus*), camellia (now considered much more hardy than hitherto), heaths (*Erica*), magnolia, ROSES (q.v.), many wild species of which grow as large shrubs with beauty of foliage, flower, and fruit, and various viburnums which include the well-known guelder rose or snowball tree (*Viburnum Opulus*) and laurustinus (*V. Tinus*), as well as several newer species, some of which are very fragrant.

The planting of permanent plants, such as shrubs, is a part of the design of the whole garden. Some knowledge of the ultimate size and habit of growth of each specimen is essential if they are to be arranged and grouped to the best advantage. There is as much variation in rate of growth and habit as in ultimate size. When shrubs are grouped in clumps, they must be planted so as to allow room for growth, so that when their maximum size is reached, they can show their proper shape.

The 'mixed border', which includes both shrubs and other hardy flowering plants, is now one of the most popular forms of planting. This border is arranged with a framework of shrubs, the remaining areas being planted with herbaceous perennials, bulbs, annuals, and biennials. As the shrubs must be spaced with a view to their ultimate size, there are at first large spaces to be filled with other plants.

The border is most effective if it is planted, not in straight lines, but in graceful curves and sweeps, with here and there taller plants brought forward to the front, and drifts of lower growing plants going well back into the bed. Standard specimens of the smaller ORNAMENTAL TREES (q.v.) are also sometimes included. This arrangement has the advantage that it provides sheltered bays with protection from frost and wind, and some shade for those plants that need it. It also gives a background of varied and attractive shrub foliage, which increases the beauty and colour of the plants in front.

Some shrubs, such as the mock orange (*Philadelphus*), lilac (*Syringa*), and buddleia, are grown primarily for their flower, though often for their scent as well. Others, such as *Viburnum fragrans* and the winter sweet (*Chimonanthus praecox*) are grown principally for their scent. Berberis, cotoneaster, and pyracantha have brilliantly coloured berries in autumn and winter, and sometimes leaves that show beautiful colours in the autumn. The snowberry (*Symphoricarpos*) and spindle (*Euonymus*) are also grown for their fruits. The evergreen *Garrya elliptica* has huge catkins in winter. Some species of osier willow (*Salix*) and dogwood (*Cornus*) are cut down to the ground each season to encourage them to grow young stems which become brightly coloured in winter. Some shrubs are primarily used for GARDEN HEDGES (q.v.).

Many shrubs, of course, combine several of these qualities. *Cornus Kousa* for example, though not easy to grow, has beautiful flowers, fruits, and autumn leaf colour. Most of the azalea group of rhododendrons have beauty of flower in May and June, and intense autumn leaf colour. *Choisya ternata*, the Mexican orange, has fragrant flowers and aromatic, evergreen leaves.

There are also shrubs, such as some varieties of holly and privet, that have attractive gold and silver variegation on the leaves, and there are also many striking silvery or grey-leaved shrubs which make an attractive colour contrast in a border, such as *Senecio laxifolius* and *Santolina Chamaecyparissus* (Lavender Cotton).

Most catalogues divide shrubs into two main sections: deciduous shrubs which lose their foliage during winter, and evergreens which retain their foliage at all seasons. A reasonable proportion of both kinds are needed to give balance of effect in winter. In another group are the climbing shrubs (*see* CLIMBING PLANTS, section 6). Azaleas, botanically included with rhododendrons (the largest of all shrub families, embracing thousands of species and varieties), and heaths are sometimes listed separately by specialists (*see* PEAT-LOVING PLANTS).

Most shrubs are deep-rooted plants. Borders for their reception should be thoroughly dug, preferably to a depth of 2 feet. Where the surface soil is shallow, the subsoil must be retained in its original position, though well broken up. Evergreens are preferably planted in October and November or in April and early May; deciduous shrubs may be planted at any time between November and March, that is to say, after leaf fall, but before growth starts. No shrubs should be planted during frosty weather and cold winds, or when the soil is very wet. Shrubs should always be planted very firmly, and the taller ones often need stakes.

Manure is not as a rule necessary except in the poorest soils, and then it must be well decayed. A top dressing (or mulch) 3 to 4 inches deep of leaf-mould, peat, or well-rotted garden compost, placed around the stem above the root area, after planting, and also during dry weather acts as a tonic and prevents the drying of the roots.

Almost all evergreen and many deciduous shrubs need no PRUNING (q.v.). There are some, however, which must be pruned annually if they are to maintain full vigour and beauty. The pruning of these depends on whether they flower on this year's or last year's growth of wood.

According to the type of shrub, one or more of the following methods of propagation are used: division, seeds, cuttings, layers, budding, and grafting (*see* PLANT PROPAGATION).

See also ORNAMENTAL TREES.

FLOWER SHOWS, *see* AGRICULTURAL SHOWS.

FLYING FISH FISHING. Off the east coast of south India, north of Palk Strait, a great flying fish fishery is carried on each year at the spawning season from the end of May to the middle of July.

To catch these fish very large rafts, called catamarans, are used. A flying fish catamaran is made up of seven great logs of a specially light wood, roped securely together, with a triangular sail hoisted on each of the two stumpy masts. A crew of seven men, taking advantage of the morning land-wind, set sail early for the fishing-ground, which is far out to sea, just beyond the shoreward margin of deep water, and easily recognized by the intense indigo blue of the water.

Flying fish spawn by twining their strings of eggs in and out of the branches of any floating weeds which they find adrift in the sea. The fishermen, knowing this habit, take with them as fishing-gear several bunches of little salt-marsh bushes, each tied to the end of a long cord. As soon as they locate a shoal of flying fish, they put their little bushes into the sea and let them float away to the full extent of the cords. The flying fish, seeking shelter for their eggs, eagerly gather round, and begin to lay their eggs among the branches. The fishermen then begin very cautiously to pull the bushes towards their log raft. The fishes follow, sheltering under the bushes from the fierce heat of the sun; and when within reach, are scooped up on to the raft by

James Hornell

A CATAMARAN OFF NEGAPATAM, SOUTH INDIA

Bundles of bushes are ready to be put into the water to attract the flying fish

means of hand nets stretched between two long sticks. When the fish are plentiful and do not take fright, the men can gather in an hour as many as the raft can carry. They then set sail for home, and spread the fish on the sands to dry before shipping them to the markets of Arakan and Burma.

In the Polynesian islands of the Pacific, when flying fish are about, the natives attract them inshore with lighted torches made of palm leaves. As soon as the fish have come close enough, they are dipped out with long handled scoop-nets.

See also FISHING INDUSTRY, section **3.**
See also Vol. II: FLYING-FISHES.

FLY PESTS. Some of the worst pests to the farmer and gardener are certain species of two-winged FLIES (q.v. Vol. II), the maggots of which may be PARASITES on animals (q.v.) or may do great damage to a variety of plants.

The Celery Fly, a pest of both celery and parsnips, is a little insect with brilliant green eyes, a brown body, and mottled wings, which it keeps at right angles to its body as it walks rapidly about. The fly first appears between April and May, and lays its eggs on the under-

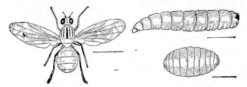

CELERY FLY, LARVA, AND PUPA (enlarged)

sides of the celery leaves. The maggot, when hatched, bores into the leaf, making brownish tunnels. When fully grown the maggots escape to the ground, where they pupate. The flies, when they emerge, come up above ground between July and August and start the cycle of attack again. The fully grown maggots of this second brood also go underground to pupate and remain there throughout the winter. The damaged leaves which harbour the grubs should be handpicked and destroyed.

The Onion Fly, Cabbage Root Fly, and Mangel Fly are all similar to small HOUSE-FLIES (q.v. Vol. II). They spend the winter in the ground as pupae. The Onion Fly begins to emerge in May, and three generations are produced during the course of the summer. The eggs are laid on the ground near the seedling onion plants, and the maggots bore into the roots. The Mangel Fly, a pest of spinach and beet, also produces three broods. It lays its eggs on the undersides of the leaves, in which the maggots form tunnels. The Carrot Fly, which has two broods, lays its eggs in clusters in cracks in the ground, and the maggots bore into the carrots. All these pests can be much discouraged if the soil round the plants is kept very firm so that the maggots cannot make an easy entrance.

Most MIDGES and MOSQUITOES (q.v. Vol. II) are pests at the adult stage, the females being bloodsuckers both of humans and also of many animals. In some equatorial regions it is not possible to keep domestic cattle because of the attacks of mosquitoes (*see* TROPICAL PESTS). The Pear Midge, a very troublesome pest to pear-growers, is a tiny fly which lays its eggs in the open blossom of the pear. When the maggots hatch, they make their way to the centre of the fruitlet, which for a time seems to develop quicker than unaffected fruitlets. In late June or early July the affected fruit falls off, and the maggots enter the soil and pupate. They sometimes stay in the cocoon for two winters, and emerge as midges in the spring. All obviously affected fruit should be picked off and

Harold Bastin

LARVAE OF PEAR MIDGE IN A YOUNG PEAR

burnt. A DDT spray at the white bud stage or a nicotine spray into the open flowers should kill the hatching maggots.

The FLEA (q.v. Vol. II), which is generally classified as a wingless fly, is a pest which sucks the blood of the warm-blooded animals, that is, of birds and mammals. The flea lives as a parasite on the body of its host; as a larva, however, it lives on refuse matter and is a scavenger. Fleas are of many different kinds, some living only on one or two kinds of animal. The Common Flea, *Pulex irritans*, lives mainly on man and on the badger, but is also known to infest foxes and other animals. Some fleas will use an alternative host (generally an animal that associates with the original host); the Rabbit Flea, for instance, will leave a rabbit and attach itself to a cat which is hunting rabbits, and the Rat Flea will leave the rat and attach itself to man.

There are several other parasites among the

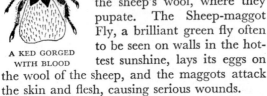

two-winged flies. The KED (q.v. Vol. II), for instance, is a bloodsucker upon sheep. It does not lay eggs, but drops its maggots one at a time among the sheep's wool, where they pupate. The Sheep-maggot Fly, a brilliant green fly often to be seen on walls in the hot-

A KED GORGED
WITH BLOOD

test sunshine, lays its eggs on the wool of the sheep, and the maggots attack the skin and flesh, causing serious wounds.

Many of the maggots of the two-winged flies attack sheep, cattle, and horses by entering their bodies. The Sheep Nostril Fly, for instance, drops its maggots or its eggs into the nostril of the sheep, and the maggots travel upwards inside the nostril, doing great harm. When fully grown, they come down again and fall upon the ground, where they pupate. Warble Flies lay

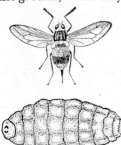

their eggs on the legs of cattle in hot summer weather from May to August. The maggots bore into the animal and travel about, causing the swellings known as 'warbles', which appear in March to June of the following year upon the backs of the cattle, causing

WARBLE FLY AND LARVA
(ENLARGED)

BOT FLY (NATURAL SIZE)

great irritation and also damaging the hide. The Bot Fly lays its eggs in masses upon the hair of horses' legs. The horse licks the place, and the warmth, moisture, and friction cause the eggs to hatch, and the maggots are carried into the mouth. They collect in clusters in the stomach, attaching themselves to the stomach-walls.

In controlling flies it is important to see that places where they are likely to breed are cleaned out, and that manure heaps and middens are not placed close to cow-sheds, pig-sties, or stables.

See also PESTS AND DISEASES; INSECT PESTS.

FOODS (FARM ANIMALS). In mixed farming some of the land is used for growing food for the farm animals, though the proportion of land used in this way varies from farm to farm. Nowadays, grass is the most important animal food grown, and it is grazed mainly by cattle, horses, and sheep. Grass, however, varies a great deal in quality. Good grass may be made of a mixture of rye-grass and wild white clover; the worst grass may be little better than weeds (*see* GRASSES and GRASSLAND).

In some countries (the North Island of New Zealand, for example) grass grows throughout most of the year; but in Britain it makes so little growth during the cold winter months that, if the livestock were dependent on grass alone, all except the hardiest breeds of sheep would starve. In the summer, however, there is usually more grass than the animals can eat, so some of this abundance is preserved for use in winter. Grass is cut and either dried in sunshine for HAY-MAKING (q.v.), or packed while green into a silo to make SILAGE (q.v.), or heated in ovens at controlled temperatures to make dried grass (*see* GRASS-DRYING). In this way it is possible to feed cattle and sheep almost entirely on the produce of grass fields alone, and this practice is becoming more common because grass is the cheapest food for animals that the soil and climate of many countries can provide.

But grass varies in its chemical composition at different seasons of the year. In spring and early summer grass is fresh and leafy with no flower head or stem. Consequently, it contains a great deal of water and digestible protein and very little fibre (that rather hard and indigestible form of carbohydrate which only RUMINANTS (q.v. Vol. II) and horses can properly make use of). If grass is cut when short and young it will, apart from a loss of water, have a similar chemical composition no matter how it is preserved; but it is very difficult to make satisfactory hay until the grass has become partially dry, stemmy, and mature, whereas silage and dried grass can be preserved while their protein content is much higher and their fibre content less. These may, therefore, be better than hay for animals that are growing rapidly or are in milk, and therefore need much protein.

In the past, when cattle and sheep were grown slowly to full size before they were fattened, and when smaller winter milk yields were expected of the dairy cow, two other winter foods, grown on the farm land, were more widely used. These foods—still grown today—are roots and straw.

ROOT CROPS (q.v.)—turnips, swedes, mangolds, sugar-beet—contain as much water as young grass, though they contain far less protein. Most of their dry substance is made up of carbohydrate. In sugar-beet much of this stored carbohydrate is in the form of sugar, which is extracted at the sugar-beet factory for human use. The carbohydrate in all roots is readily digestible and is very useful in fattening, because when carbohydrate is fed to farm animals they can convert it into fat. Roots alone, however, do not contain enough protein to form a satisfactory winter diet for growing animals or milking cows.

Straw is never grown specially as an animal food, but is a by-product of grain growing. On mixed farms it is used for the animals partly as a foodstuff and partly for bedding and to make farmyard manure. Wheat straw is useless as a food; but oat straw, particularly when grown in cool, moist climates, and to a lesser extent barley straw, may be sufficiently digestible to be used in the fattening of mature cattle and the maintenance of horses.

Both roots and oat straw are carbohydrate foods which are of value in maintaining fully grown animals or in fattening them. They are, however, very bulky, and animals have to eat a lot of them to get enough nourishment. Besides, neither alone nor in combination do they contain enough protein to make young animals grow quickly or to support full milk production.

They must be supplemented by more concentrated, less bulky foods, and by foods rich in protein. These 'concentrates' are either home-grown corn, beans, and peas, or specially rich protein foods prepared from oil-bearing seeds from which the bulk of the oil has been extracted. Two of the best-known are linseed cake or meal, prepared from linseed, and cotton-seed cake or meal, prepared from cotton-seed. When first introduced into farm practice, these made it possible for the farmer to get his stock fat at an earlier age and to keep up the production of milk throughout the winter. Roots and hay, or roots and good oat straw, with a protein concentrate added, is often called a balanced ration, because the protein in the concentrate balances the carbohydrate in the roots and hay.

Now, grass in summer and grass preserved in some way for use in winter may form a satisfactory diet for CATTLE and SHEEP and, to a less degree, for HORSES (qq.v.). That is because both cattle and sheep, being ruminants, can fully digest the cellulose and fibre which enclose the minute cells of which plants are composed. But PIGS and POULTRY (qq.v.) cannot do this nearly so well, and cannot, therefore, be fed on the produce of grass alone.

In order to produce a satisfactory bacon pig, it is necessary for the pig to grow rapidly and

Eric Guy

FEEDING SOWS IN A YARD

The Times

THE MIDDAY MEAL ON A FARM IN WILTSHIRE
Horses are slow eaters and must be given time to eat their oats and chaff

to lay on abundant lean meat while it is fattening, and this needs special food. Before the Second World War it was a common practice to feed pigs on barley, wheat, and maize products for carbohydrate, and fish meal for protein (*see* PIGS, CARE OF). None of this was produced on the farm, the grain being imported and the sea providing the fish. Much the same practice was followed in feeding poultry. Nowadays, since so much less is being imported, more of their food must be grown on the farm. This has a good many advantages; one of them is the freedom it gives the farmer to change his style of farming to suit conditions—for example, he can grow corn and market it either indirectly by turning it into bacon and eggs, or directly by selling it in the grain market.

There are also other foods, needed in much smaller amounts, but nevertheless of equal importance. There are, first, the mineral foods, of which calcium and phosphorus are, perhaps, the most important because together, in the form of calcium phosphate, they form the greater part of an animal's bones. Without them, no animal can keep alive for long; but fortunately there is enough of both in the crops grown on a properly manured farm. Clover, for example, either fresh or in hay, contains plenty of both; and cattle, horses, and sheep seldom need a mineral supple-

ment on cultivated land, though they may do so on natural pastures of poor quality, particularly in South Africa, where phosphate deficiency is common on the Veldt. Under certain conditions pigs may need a mineral supplement, and poultry always need extra lime in the form of shell grit if they are to keep healthy and lay hardshelled eggs.

There are other mineral elements which in various parts of the world are present in too small an amount in the soil or in the vegetation to meet the needs of farm animals. Two interesting examples are iodine and cobalt. A lack of these elements is indicated by the diseases— 'deficiency diseases' they are called—that result. Thus, if there is too little iodine in the food of sheep, their lambs are born with swollen necks, and if sows go short of iodine, the young pigs may be born dead and hairless. Cobalt deficiency is shown in sheep by their becoming anaemic and ceasing to grow. Quite minute additions of iodine or cobalt, respectively, will prevent these deficiency diseases from occurring.

Then there are the vitamins, known by the letters of the alphabet—for example, vitamins A, B, and C. If there is not enough of these in an animal's diet—and very small quantities will do —other deficiency diseases may occur. The danger is greatest when animals are kept in

Eric Guy

FEEDING COWS ON KALE IN WINTER WHEN THERE IS NOT ENOUGH GRASS
The kale is spread out in a line across the field so that the cows can reach it easily

confinement and not given much fresh food; and wherever possible they should be given occasional access to the soil and natural vegetation. For example, young pigs that are subject to anaemia caused by iron deficiency do much better if they are allowed to run out on the grass and root in the soil. There they get the iron they need, and possibly other elements the importance of which is not yet recognized. Similarly, poultry, especially young poultry, thrive better if allowed to range over pasture, picking at clover and eating insects. Variety of food is good for all farm animals and is a safeguard against these deficiency diseases.

Water is a food that all farm animals need. None can live without it, though it must be remembered that many farm foods, particularly young grass and roots, contain a great deal of water in themselves and thus reduce the need for the animals to drink. But when dry food, such as withered grass, hay, straw, concentrates, or grain form the main part of the food, all farm animals must be allowed to drink plenty of fresh water.

Farm animals can be fed on a much greater variety of foods than is generally supposed. Sheep, for example, are usually fed on grass, but they can, if necessary, be kept alive on very strange rations. Flocks on occasion have been maintained in droughts or storms on such unusual

sheep foods as potatoes or fallen apples. Sheep in some of our northern islands get much of their living from sea-weed. Pigs, as is well known, will eat a great variety of foods. and can be fattened, too, on refuse alone.

The foods fed to farm animals can be classified into (a) Roughages, (b) Succulents, and (c) Concentrates.

(a) Roughages contain a high percentage of fibre. They include such foods as hay, straw, and mature grass. All animals need a certain proportion of roughage in their diet, and ruminants, in particular, can convert roughages. which would otherwise be merely wasted, into meat and milk.

(b) Succulent foods contain a high proportion of water. They include such foods as roots, silage, cabbages, and young grass. The dry matter contained in succulent foods is usually of an easily digestible nature, which is one reason for their value in stock feeding.

(c) Concentrates contain a high proportion of dry matter, either of protein or carbohydrate, or of both. Unlike roughages, the dry matter of concentrates is easily digestible without preliminary fermentation. Consequently, they can be used by non-ruminant animals, such as pigs and poultry, as thoroughly as by ruminants, such as cattle and sheep. They may be protein con-

Eric Guy

FEEDING POULTRY

The man will scatter grain from the bag on his shoulders
for the birds to pick up

centrates such as linseed cake, or carbohydrate concentrates such as maize.

A practical point of some importance is the mechanical effect of the different foods in maintaining a healthy bowel action. For example, succulent foods fed alone, particularly to sheep, may cause looseness of the bowels and therefore unformed dung (the animal is then said to 'scour'). Roughages, on the contrary, may constipate. A combination of succulent food and roughage, as in a ration of hay fed with turnips, will produce a steady normal bowel action that may make all the difference to the health of the animal.

The actual amounts of food needed by animals, and the balance between carbohydrates, fat, and protein that suits them, vary according to the type of animal and the purposes for which it is kept. In books and pamphlets the results of chemical analyses of feeding-stuffs are often given to several decimal places, and this gives an impression of great accuracy. The actual methods of analysis by which the results are obtained, and by which an animal's needs are measured, are, however, relatively crude. Consequently, farm animals must never be fed according to the book alone, but attention paid also to the practical experience of feeders, and the results of trials that have been observed and handed down over many generations.

See also FEEDING (FARM ANIMALS)
See also Vol. II: NUTRITION OF ANIMALS.

FOOT AND MOUTH DISEASE, *see* ANIMAL DISEASES, section 3.

FOREST FIRES. These are a serious danger, especially with coniferous forests. In dry weather a stray spark, a neglected camp fire, a match, or a cigarette end, may start a blaze that quickly gets out of control. The flames rise from the undergrowth and, especially if there is a wind, quickly involve trees of all sizes over a wide area, destroying them all, both young and old. In the vast coniferous forests of northern Europe and America, tracts of forest covering many square miles have been destroyed, involving homesteads and causing loss of life. In a high wind the blaze spreads rapidly, sometimes advancing faster than a man can run, and producing a terrific heat.

Foresters, therefore, have developed many methods of reducing the risk of fire and fighting it should it occur. If the fire can be discovered while it is still small, a few men can probably put it out. But if it gets as much as a few hours start, it may have spread so widely that thousands of fire fighters cannot control it. Fire towers at good look-out points are manned day and night throughout the dangerous dry seasons, and are linked by telephone with a central control room. The whole forest is mapped so that, as soon as smoke is seen, the fire watchers on each of the towers can report its direction, giving the compass bearing, and enable the fire controller at headquarters to plot these directions on his map and thus fix the site of the fire.

Fire parties are rushed out without delay, equipped with beaters, axes for cutting broad lanes, called 'fire-breaks', through the undergrowth, and water-pumps worked by hand or driven by motors. The men may have to fight a grim, arduous battle for hours or even days. Often the fire can only be held with the aid of some natural obstacle, such as a lake, river, or hill-crest. Sometimes a change in the weather may save the situation. The fire-party leaders take advantage of every change in the ground, the weather, or the nature of the forest growth, to beat out the blazing front of the fire. Sometimes it is necessary to start a counter fire to check the main fire. A controlled fire is lit in the path of the main one, and allowed to burn a strip so wide that the main fire cannot cross it, and thus, having nothing to burn, dies out.

Aeroplane patrols are sometimes used for fire

spotting, and experiments have been made in dropping men by parachute to deal rapidly with small fires in remote places. Another use of the aeroplane in fighting the vast fires which occur in some countries, is as a control station. A forest officer flying above the blaze has a good view of its extent and rate of spread. He can send back information by wireless to his head-quarters, so that help can be sent to the points where it will do most good.

In Britain, where the climate is moister and large blocks of coniferous forests are few and far between, the fires are less spectacular. But enormous damage is done each year in young plantations by small fires. This is very serious, because the lost growth can never be replaced, even though the burnt areas may be replanted. In consequence, notices are put up in forest areas warning people to be careful about fire, and telling them what to do if a fire starts. The Forestry Commission has developed special means for restricting fire losses. Wide fire-breaks are left unplanted and often ploughed up to prevent fires spreading. Fire brooms are pro-vided along roadsides, ready to beat out fires in case of need. The foresters are constantly on the alert, ready to send out men, tools, and water supplies as soon as a fire is reported.

The simplest way to put out fires in young plantations is to beat down the edge of the blaze with brooms or beating tools; a branch of a fir-tree, a birch broom, or a spade, are all excellent beaters. If the fire has not got a strong hold, a small party, working steadily along the edge of the fire, can usually head it off and prevent its spreading. But the work is hot and tiring, and there can scarcely be too many helpers to share it. Prompt action by everyone who sees the fire may save large areas of future forest, and preserve a valuable store of timber.

FORESTRY. This is the craft and science of raising, tending, and using tree crops for the service of man. Forests are usually grown for the supply of TIMBER (q.v.), though they serve other useful purposes such as holding water supplies in the hills and saving the soil from damage by sudden rainstorms and floods (*see* SOIL EROSION, Vol. III).

The great forests of North America, northern Europe, and the tropics, are mainly of natural growth (*see* FORESTS, Vol. III). They therefore contain trees of many kinds, ages, and sizes.

Illustrated

A FIRE-FIGHTING LORRY USED BY THE FORESTRY COMMISSION IN EAST ANGLIA

Forestry Commission

A 60-FOOT FIRE TOWER IN THE NEW FOREST

The watcher on the top of this tower can overlook many miles of forest and report a fire immediately by telephone

Forestry Commission

TEN-YEAR-OLD POPLARS IN BAGLEY WOOD, OXFORD
The wood has been thinned once

The foresters who tend them have to protect them from damage and arrange the felling of timber so that it is not cut faster than it grows. For as the old trees are cut down, seedlings spring up naturally to replace them.

But nearly all British forests are made up of plantations, that is, woods planted by man. In each plantation the trees are of the same age and more or less the same size. Often they are all of the same kind, though mixed plantations are also made by planting two or more kinds of trees together. In a large forest or woodland estate the ages of the different plantations vary, so that the forester has to look after trees of all sizes from young plants a few feet high, recently planted out, to mature timber trees over a 100 years old and a 100 feet tall. He looks upon his forest as a crop, part of which ripens every year, whilst the rest grows steadily in size and value.

To the forester his woods are never the same for two seasons together. As his crops grow, they need tending in different ways at various stages. At first, the young trees, planted in rows about 5 feet apart, are so small that the bracken, brambles, and other plants tend to smother them. So they have to be 'brushed', that is, weeded **each summer** with **sharp curved** tools called

reap hooks and staff hooks, until they rise safely above the weed growth.

A few years later, when the trees have reached a height of 10 or 12 feet and are interlacing their branches to form a thicket, it may be necessary to cut away with bill hooks the tall woody weeds and climbers that threaten to outgrow the tree crop. Then, some 15 years after planting, the upper branches begin to close over and form a canopy of green foliage, whilst the older branches below them die off from lack of light. In the case of coniferous trees these lower branches are cut away with a small curved saw —an operation known as 'brashing'. This enables the forester to enter his woods to study their growth, mark trees for thinning, and get the felled trees carried out easily by his woodmen; it also reduces the risk of fires spreading through the trees (*see* FOREST FIRES), and keeps the timber free from knots which make it hard to work.

The plantation has then reached the thinning stage; the forester controls its growth by thinning out the trees as they increase in size at regular intervals of from 3 to 10 years. The number of trees growing on each acre is gradually reduced from about 1,750 to 200 or less. But those that are left grow steadily in height and increase the volume of timber, whilst those that are removed are used for fence stakes, pit props for coal-mining, and poles of all kinds. Thus, the forest makes some return at an early age, and continues to do so steadily for many years as the plantation grows. Selecting trees for thinning-out needs great skill if the right number of good ones are to be left to grow on and form straight timber for the final crop.

The felling of the final timber crop is made when the trees are between 60 and 150 years, or even older, the age varying with the kind of tree and the type of ground. When felled, the trees will be about 80 to 100 feet tall on good soil, and each acre of ground will produce several thousand cubic feet of timber. The trees might live much longer, but their timber would not greatly improve, and so it pays to fell them when they become mature (*see* TIMBER FELLING). A year or two later a fresh crop of young trees will be planted to replace it (*see* AFFORESTATION).

The trees that are most widely grown in modern British plantations belong to the coniferous group, as the greatest demands are for SOFTWOODS (q.v. Vol. VII) and the pit-props that these produce in large quantities at an early age. The seven most important kinds are the Scots and Corsican pines, European and Japanese larches, Norway and Sitka spruces, and Douglas firs (see Trees, Coniferous). Many other conifers are grown on a smaller scale. Each needs tending in its own way, and this needs careful study and brings variety to the forester's daily work. Of broadleaved trees, the oak, ash, beech, birch, and sycamore are widely grown as timber crops (see Hardwoods, Vol. VII), whilst many foresters have to look after coppice crops of hazel, sweet chestnut, and willow (see Trees, Broadleaved).

In managing and controlling his forest the forester aims, as a rule, to have different parts of his woods ready for felling at different times, if possible in a continuous sequence, so that there is a steady return from the timber sold to cover the outlay on replanting and other forest operations and to show a steady annual profit.

Large forests are best managed according to a plan, laying down the work to be done for 10 or more years ahead. First of all the forest is mapped, various colours being used to show the different kinds of trees at various stages of their growth. With the help of this map the woods are divided into small blocks, each some 20 to 30 acres in extent, called 'compartments'. These correspond to the farmer's fields, forming divisions for purposes of management. The simplest plans are based on the areas occupied by tree crops of various ages. For example, if the trees grow to an age of 100 years before felling, then 1% of the area might be cut down each year; and if the same amount of ground were replanted, the losses would continually be made good. In making the working plan the oldest woods would naturally be selected for the first fellings, and gradually a forest would be built up in which there was an equal area of ground under trees of every age from 1 to 100 years.

More advanced plans are based on the volume of timber within the forest, and the rate at which this volume is increasing each year, the eventual aim being to cut the timber as fast as it is replaced by the natural growth of the remaining trees. Forecasts of future timber yields are usually based on 'yield tables', which record the rate of growth of actual measured plantations. They show the probable timber production of each kind of tree at various ages on different qualities of soil. With their aid the forester can estimate the most profitable age for cutting down

Forestry Commission

SPRUCE PLANTATIONS IN THORNTHWAITE FOREST IN THE LAKE DISTRICT

In the foreground a space has been cleared for cutting up and stacking logs

his tree crop. The age to which the crop is grown is known as the 'rotation'. The shortest rotations, of a few years only, are used for some Coppice Crops (q.v.), and coniferous trees are sometimes grown on rotations as short as 20 years in order to produce pit-props. For bigger saw-mill timber, on the other hand, rotations vary from 60 years for pines and larches on favourable soils to 120 or even 200 years for oak; in tropical countries more rapid growth leads to shorter rotations (see Timber).

The measurement of timber crops is fairly simple in Britain, for good maps are available. Sample plots are selected in the woods of each age and species, and the trees growing on them are measured; then the volume of growing timber for the whole of each compartment can be calculated, and the total for the whole forest ascertained (see Timber Measurement). Abroad, where the vast forests are often completely unmapped, the area of land under trees is often discovered by aerial photography. Foresters can identify the kinds and qualities of their tree crops from an examination of aerial photographs aided by their knowledge of the ground and the measurement of sample strips.

If he knows the extent of his forests, their volume, and rate of growth, the forester can

Robert M. Adam

GLEN MORE NATIONAL FOREST PARK IN SPRING

Glen More, at the foot of the Cairngorms, was originally a natural pine forest which was acquired by the Forestry Commission in 1923. Its timber has been used for centuries. The Scots Pines in the foreground are about 200 years old

forecast their ability to produce timber and to show profits. Where they have been artificially planted, he has to allow for the long gap between the investment of the money and its return, but this too has been reduced to a matter of mathematics, and forest management has become an exact science.

An important side of the forester's work is the preparation of poles and timber for sale. He has to know how each kind will be used, the correct size to which to cut it, the best time of year to prepare it, how to bring it out from the woods quickly and cheaply, and the right prices and purchasers for it when it is ready. In this way he manages his tree crops so that they show a profit to their owners, whilst at the same time providing timber and smaller produce for the many uses of modern civilization.

The forester has also to control the wild life within the woods so that it does little damage to his tree crops or to neighbouring farms and game preserves (*see* VERMIN). Many animals and birds, however, may be tolerated or even encouraged in the forests, which form a sanctuary for game and rare plants and animals of many kinds (*see* WILD ANIMALS ON THE FARM). Forest trees give a welcome shelter to the farmer's crops and stock, whilst their varied outlines enrich the landscape of the countryside.

See also AFFORESTATION; TIMBER; LOGGING; TREES, BROADLEAVED; TREES, CONIFEROUS.

See also Vol. VII: TIMBER INDUSTRY.

FORESTRY COMMISSION. This is the state forest authority for Great Britain, established by the Forestry Act of 1919 with powers to develop state-owned and private forests. Its main work has been the creation of a great national forest estate, made up of forests in different parts of Great Britain, which by 1950 covered over $1\frac{1}{2}$ million acres. By 1950 some 600,000 acres were actually carrying tree crops. These are planned to meet a proportion of the present and future timber needs of Britain, particularly in the event of war when the importing of timber is difficult or impossible.

The Forestry Commission also assists private foresters by cash grants for tree-planting and with technical advice; and it issues the licences that are needed before woods can be felled. It carries out research work in the main branches of forestry, and undertakes the technical education of foresters. It has developed large nurseries for raising forest trees, as well as means for preparing and marketing poles and timber from the forests in its charge. Many of its workers live on smallholdings, dividing their time between forestry and farming according to the season of the year; others live in the new forest villages built especially for them.

Amongst the largest of the Commission's own forests are the New Forest of Hampshire, the Forest of Dean in Gloucestershire, Thetford Chase in East Anglia, and Allerston on the Scarborough moors in the North Riding of Yorkshire. Farther north there is a large new forest at Kielder on the borders of Northumberland and Roxburgh, and the numerous Scottish forests include Inverliver in Argyll and others as far afield as Sutherland and the Isle of Skye. Other large forests have been formed in the mountains of north Wales, such as Gwydyr Forest in the Conway valley of Caernarvonshire, and in south Wales there are many smaller forests. The land selected for new afforestation is of little value for agriculture, being largely moorland and waste. Existing woodlands have also been taken over and brought under systematic management by the Commission.

An interesting aspect of the Forestry Commission's work has been the development of Britain's first National Forest Parks. One of the best known is the Argyll National Forest Park near Loch Goil; here 54,000 acres of Highland country, intersected by sea lochs, have been devoted partly to commercial forestry and partly to other rural uses in a way that enables naturalists and holiday makers to use this wide tract of countryside for study or recreation. The Glen Trool Park occupies 110,000 acres of hill country, broken up by many lochs and rivers, in the Galloway uplands of south-west Scotland; and the Glen More Park in Inverness-shire rises from the sandy beaches of Loch Morlich to the snow-clad heights of the Cairngorms, over 4,000 feet above sea-level. In England a new park has been formed at Hardknott in the Lake District, while the ancient Forest of Dean and the New Forest are managed by the Commission in such

a way that their scenery and attractiveness to country lovers are preserved. In Wales the forests around Snowdon form a National Forest Park amidst the mountains.

The Forestry Commission has made plans for the establishment of a total area of 5 million acres of useful forests, which when fully grown would supply one-third of Britain's timber requirements (*see* TIMBER INDUSTRY, Vol. VII).

See also FORESTRY; AFFORESTATION.

FOWLS, *see* POULTRY.

FOXES, *see* VERMIN; FUR FARMING. *See also* Vol. II: Fox.

FRAMES, GARDEN. Several types of garden cold frames are used for the raising of plants and the growing of early crops of various kinds. They are used also for growing such crops as cucumbers and melons which do not thrive in the open air in Britain. Frames are usually movable structures, made of wood, metal, or concrete, oblong in shape, and about 1 foot high at the back and 8 or 9 inches at the front. They are covered with 'lights' (frames containing glass). The frames are placed in such a way that the lights tilt towards the south to gather all the sun warmth possible.

The Dutch light consists of an unpainted wooden sash or frame with grooves into which a single large pane of glass, about 56 inches by $28\frac{3}{4}$ inches, is inserted. This admits the maximum amount of light and, being in one piece, cannot leak, though it is easily broken. The French light is 53 inches long by 51 inches wide and is fitted with three metal sash-bars. They are light to handle and are much used on frames covering hot-beds. The old English garden frame consists of a large and rather deep frame or 'box' about 6 feet long and either 4, 8, or 12 feet in width. One, two, or three wooden lights, each 6 feet by 4 feet and fitted with sash-bars, are used with sliding bars. The disadvantage of the old English light is that it is heavy to manipulate. The lights of the French and Dutch types are lifted clear of the frames for working, but those of the old English type are arranged to slide up and down. For market-gardening the Dutch and French types of light are most popular; but there is another type of English light, somewhat resembling the French light, which is used sometimes in market-gardens in

Horticultural Photo Supply

PICKING LETTUCES GROWN UNDER DUTCH LIGHTS

Horticultural Photo Supply

FRENCH LIGHTS

place of the French light. All types are useful in the home garden for various purposes.

A more permanent type of frame, the pit frame, is often heated with one or two hot-water pipes attached to the walls on the inside. The pit frame is generally sunk a little below the surface of the ground to help conserve the heat. It is usually built of brick or concrete and is $2\frac{1}{2}$ to $3\frac{1}{2}$ feet deep at the back and $1\frac{1}{2}$ to $2\frac{1}{2}$ feet at the front. Pit frames are often built several together and are placed abutting on to the glasshouse so that the same heating system will serve both with the least waste of heat. Frames are particularly suitable for the use of electric soil-heating equipment. The pits are very useful for housing pot plants when they are not in flower, for propagating tender plants to be used for bedding, and for forcing certain vegetables such as seakale and rhubarb.

See also GLASSHOUSES; CLOCHES.

FRUIT-GROWING. 1. TYPES OF TREE AND BUSH. In Great Britain apples, cherries, bullace plums, sloes, blackberries, raspberries, and gooseberries are all natural wild plants of the country, and these and many others can be successfully grown in the open if the fruit-grower gives them help in the form of manuring, pruning, spraying, and cultivations. Such fruits are known as hardy fruits, to distinguish them from sub-tropical and tropical fruits, which are natives of warmer climates, and all to a greater or less degree tender. Some of the tender fruits, for instance, bananas, oranges, lemons, pineapples,

and melons, can be grown in Great Britain and other northern countries in glasshouses, frames, or pits, where they are supplied with heat and large quantities of water, thus artificially producing the conditions to which they are accustomed in their native lands. Others, such as figs and peaches, can be grown out of doors in protected and sunny situations. In countries of very low rainfall, and in places where the annual rainfall is unevenly distributed throughout the year, fruit growing is only possible where the supply of water can be increased by artificial IRRIGATION (q.v.).

The terms 'top', 'tree', and 'hard' are used for those fruits, such as apples, pears, plums, and cherries, that have a firm flesh and that grow into tall trees. The low-growing, soft-fleshed fruits are known as 'bottom', 'bush', or 'soft' fruits. Soft fruit bushes do not usually continue to bear good crops after 10 years because as they get older they are prone to disease; so that it is only profitable to grow soft fruits for market under the best conditions. Where the soil is deep enough, apples, pears, plums, and cherries can usually be depended on to grow and eventually to crop. There is, however, a wide difference in the times they take to come into cropping, and in the kind of fruit they give; and success depends upon the skill in choosing the best varieties and the right sort of rootstock to plant, as well as in the treatment of the growing plants.

2. PLANNING AND PLANTING. Hardy fruits can be made to grow in most soils and climates, provided enough time and money are spent on them. But anyone who has to earn his living from fruit-growing has to choose the right place to plant his stock. In a small garden apple-trees can be grown successfully on a very stiff clay soil if the ground is made suitable by draining, deep digging, and by adding lime and long strawed farm-yard manure; very light sandy or gravelly soils may be improved on a small scale by digging in short-strawed farm-yard manure, and artificial fertilizers. But it would be unwise to plant any large acreage of such soils with fruit, because too much money would have to be spent on it before it could grow good trees. Again, whilst it might be worth planting a few fruit trees in a very low-lying, sheltered situation, where frost damage to blossom might be expected, and to make arrangements to raise the temperature on frosty spring nights with orchard-heaters, such a site could never be recommended for a fruit farm.

Therefore, when choosing a site for a fruit farm, there are many considerations. The soil should be a medium loam (*see* Soils) and as deep as possible. For tree fruits at least 3 feet of good soil before reaching the sub-soil of clay, sand, gravel, or rock is desirable; soft fruits need, on the whole, less depth of soil. Fruit trees need plenty of sunlight. High land is better than low because there is less danger from spring frosts, but if there is still higher land immediately near, there is still danger from cold air drifting down. Trees must not be exposed to the full force of gales from the south-west in autumn and winter, or to east winds in April and May; so some form of wind-break is desirable, such as a tall hedge.

The orchard should not be on a very steep slope because of the danger of Soil Erosion (q.v. Vol. III), and because of the difficulty of picking the fruit. There should be a good supply of water, not very hard, that can be relied upon not to give out before the spraying season finishes at the end of June. There should be a good road or track from the site to the farm buildings; and, lastly, the site should not be so remote that it is impossible to get labour, or difficult to get the fruit away to market. For example, supposing strawberries were to grow well and crop heavily half way up Mount Snowdon, strawberry-growing there could never be a paying proposition because of the expense of picking and marketing the fruit.

Having decided on the kinds of fruit most likely to do well in the district, and on the varieties and rootstocks that are most suitable,

the next step is to plan the lay-out of the orchards or plantations ready for planting. For this we need a rough plan on squared paper showing the dimensions of each field, so that the position of every tree can be plotted, allowing for roadways where needed. Having decided on the scheme of planting, we must then fix the proportion of each type of fruit tree, where each type is to go, and how far apart the trees are to be planted. Then we can calculate how many trees of each kind and variety must be ordered from the nurseryman.

Trees should be ordered well in advance, and if possible inspected while growing in the nursery. When they are delivered in the autumn or early winter, their straw coverings are taken off and all the roots well covered with soil. As soon as conditions are favourable, the trees are planted very firmly, supported with stakes, and protected by netting, if necessary, from rabbits; they are then pruned and sprayed with a winter wash to keep down pests. If the ground is much trodden, a plough or disk harrow is run up between the tree rows to break up the hard surface and let the air into the soil.

3. CULTIVATING AND SPRAYING. In the spring, as soon as the ground is dry enough, the cultivator is drawn over the plantation to break up the large lumps and level the surface soil to a uniform 'crumb'. From then onwards the soil should be stirred at intervals by horse-drawn or tractor-drawn hoes to prevent weeds from growing and the soil from caking down during the hot summer months. Routine spring and early summer SPRAYING (q.v.) must be carried out each season. In the autumn the plough again lays the furrows up and down the slope of the ground in order to provide natural drainage for the winter rain and snow. If the orchard needs a potash fertilizer, this can be broadcast all over the field or thrown in circles round each tree before ploughing begins. If nitrogen manures are needed, they are given in the spring before the first cultivations.

Winter PRUNING (q.v.) may be started as soon as the leaves have fallen, and should be finished as early as possible in the winter. After the pruning and winter washing, the routine work in the orchard is finished for the season.

The winter is the time for such jobs as repairing the wire fencing and the hedges and ditches, renewing tile drains, and overhauling, repairing, and painting the machinery, tools, and such equipment as orchard boxes and ladders. When spring comes and the buds start to swell, the spring and summer programme of spraying and cultivation begins. In grass orchards, unless cattle or sheep are brought in to graze the grass, it will need mowing. The cut grass is left to rot, and so to supply humus to the soil.

When the fruit has formed, it may be necessary to thin some varieties of apples and plums; but with the majority of kinds this thinning is done by a natural fall of immature fruit, and in any case time should be left for this natural fall to take place.

4. FRUIT PICKING. When the trees have grown too large to be picked from ground level, light portable steps or ladders are needed. For really tall old cherry trees, special fruit-picking ladders are used, perhaps 40 or 50 feet long, which require great skill in manoeuvring. There must be suitable picking-bags, buckets, boxes, or baskets to hold the gathered fruit. With apples and pears, these are usually emptied gently into wooden orchard boxes, which are carried into the packing-shed to be properly packed for market. Most other fruits are picked straight into the packages in which they are sent to market, jam factory, or cannery. The important thing is to have everything ready and organized well before it is time to begin picking, so that when the job actually begins there need be no delay. All fruit should be picked only when it is dry.

It is essential to handle the fruit, especially soft fruit, with extreme care. Very often, when soft fruits, such as strawberries, raspberries, gooseberries, and currants, are being picked, the weather turns hot. Then the filled baskets must be placed in the shade out of the glare of the sun. On many fruit farms there are skeleton frameworks of small huts scattered about the plantations, which at picking time are covered over with tarpaulins to form a shelter for the picked fruit. The foreman is generally at one of these shelters, covering over each basket, and labelling each with the address of the fruit salesman to whom the fruit is to be sent.

5. SORTING, PACKING, AND MARKETING. From time to time the baskets or boxes will be carried by a cart or trailer to the packing shed, where they will be prepared for dispatch by road or rail. Apples and pears have to be sorted before being stored or marketed. The best fruits are usually sorted into different sizes by a GRADING MACHINE (q.v.), and then packed into special boxes lined with good quality paper in such a way that the fruit is not damaged by being shaken about. Inferior grades of fruit may be sent to market in packages of different sizes and materials, from round 'sieve' or 'half-sieve' baskets to chip baskets and cardboard cartons. The chips and cartons are provided by the grower himself and given away with the fruit; the more solid containers are provided by the fruit salesman, and hired out to the grower at a fixed charge.

Fruit is sent by road or rail to a big wholesale market, or to shops in a local town. In either case it is usual either to pay a fruit salesman to sell it from his stall in the market or to sell it outright to a wholesale fruit merchant. In the first case the salesman acts purely as an agent. In the second case the fruit is sold to the wholesale merchant outright at an agreed price, and he in turn sells it to a retailer.

6. THE SKILL OF FRUIT-GROWING. The first part of the business of fruit-growing, the planning and planting, the ploughing and hoeing in early years, is much like other kinds of farming. The specialist's skill comes in when the trees or bushes come into bearing, for it is then that he starts interfering with nature on a big scale. Nature is only concerned with the production of seed, and not, as is the fruit-grower, in the size and quality of the fruit. The fruit-grower, therefore, makes the tree grow into some special shape that nature never intended, in order to provide a strong enough scaffolding to carry large crops. He has to induce it to keep growing far more new shoots than is natural. Then he has to keep a balance between the growth of new wood and the production of fruit. Too much pruning, for instance, may make the tree develop a forest of wood shoots; and so he may have to check growth by leaving off pruning altogether, or by giving up cultivations and letting the ground go down to weeds, or by a combination of both.

The skilled fruit-grower knows what to look for in the trees, and understands what sort of condition they are in—what are the symptoms of a healthy tree and of a sick tree, of a tree that is growing too much or not enough. He recognizes these symptoms by such things as size and colour of the leaf, by the colour of the bark and twigs, and by the size, colour, and skin texture of the fruit. All this needs observation and experience. As well as this he must know how to deal with the number of PESTS AND DISEASES (q.v.) that may attack the trees at certain times, often causing serious damage and possibly resulting in a complete loss of crop. It is easy to understand that fruit-growing is one of the most interesting as well as one of the most difficult branches of farming. The culture of the different kinds of both soft and tree fruits is described in separate articles.

FRUIT PROPAGATION.

Propagation of plants means the multiplying of specimens so as to keep up a supply of new plants (*see* PLANT PROPAGATION). The place where the plants are propagated is called the 'nursery'. There are two distinct systems of plant propagation. New plants can be raised from ripened seed; or they can be raised from the vegetative or growing parts of the old plant, for example, runners or cuttings—and this is called 'vegetative propagation' (*see* REPRODUCTION IN PLANTS, Vol. II).

To raise fruit plants from seed, ripened seeds which have matured for some time in sand in a cool temperature are sown in the ordinary way in pans, trays, or pots. In course of time they germinate and send out roots and shoots. Propagation by seed, although it may produce great numbers of new plants, has the disadvantage that there is no guarantee that any one of the seedlings will bear an exact resemblance to the parent plant. For instance, one seedling out of those grown from the seeds of a strawberry might by chance turn out to produce especially large and juicy fruit. But if seeds from this fine strawberry were sown with the idea of repeating the plant, it is quite possible that not one of the resulting seedlings would reproduce the qualities of its fine parent. Plants, however, reproduced by vegetative propagation can be depended upon to resemble in every way the parent plant or 'clone' from which they were raised. We could, therefore, reproduce

one very fine strawberry plant by raising new plants from its runners.

It is important to remember this difference when we come to consider the question of rootstocks on which fruit-trees are grafted. Grafting, which is the practice of making one variety of tree or shrub grow on the roots of another, is a much quicker way of getting a fruit tree, especially the finer fruiting varieties, to reach the stage of bearing fruit than by growing it on its own roots. But if fruit trees, or indeed flowering trees such as ROSES (q.v.), are to be grafted or budded (another form of grafting) there must be a stock plant of some kind on which to graft them—and such plants are called the 'rootstock'.

The rootstock must belong to the same botanical species as the plant to be grafted on it. Pears, for instance, are often grafted on to quince rootstock, but could not be grafted on to crab-apple—a common stock for grafting apples. Grafting takes place in the spring when the sap is rising. It consists of cutting the top off the stock and fitting the graft on in such a position that after a time the two grow together and become one plant (*see* Fig. 1). The edges of the join are covered with wax to hold the two cut surfaces

East Malling Research Station

HOW THE ROOTSTOCK AFFECTS THE GROWTH OF TREES

The large tree is a Cox grafted on the vigorous growing rootstock M.XII, and the small one in the left foreground is a Cox on the dwarfing M.IX rootstock

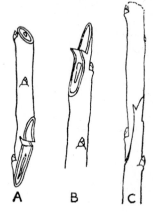

FIG. I. WHIP AND TONGUE GRAFTING

A. Scion; B. Rootstock; C. Graft before it is tied and waxed. This is the commonest kind of grafting

closely together so that the sap, flowing through the tree, knits the two parts in the same way as a piece of bone can be grafted by a surgeon on to his patient's limb. The graft is a twig or shoot, called the 'scion', cut off in winter when the sap is not rising, from a tree of the variety to be propagated, and heled into the soil until time for grafting. The stock is a young rooted tree with a stem about ½ inch in diameter, that has been planted in the nursery the winter before. As soon as the two parts have grown together, probably in 2 or 3 weeks, the top or 'terminal' buds burst and grow out into shoots. By the autumn we have what is called a 'maiden' tree all ready for planting out.

Budding is done in summer. A bud, growing in the axil of a leaf, is removed, together with a small shield of bark, from a shoot of a tree of the desired variety, and inserted in a slit made in the bark of the rootstock. The whole is then bound round with raffia or rubber strips until the new bud and rootstock have grown together (see Fig. 2).

Experiments have shown that the natural character of the rootstock on which a fruit tree is grafted has very important effects upon the way in which the tree grows and crops. A dwarfing apple rootstock, for instance, will cause the grafted tree to remain quite small all its life, whilst a vigorous stock will make a very big tree. For some purposes a small tree, for other purposes a large tree, may be more suitable; so that several kinds of rootstocks are needed.

Rootstocks can be propagated from seed, but, as already explained, we cannot know for certain whether rootstocks from such seedlings are likely to be vigorous or not in their effect on the tree.

For that reason rootstocks also are best raised by vegetative propagation. This is done in two ways: by 'stools' and by 'layers'. The stool consists of a single rooted stock which, after one season's growth, is cut down to ground level. The following summer it grows shoots and, as they grow, earth is heaped up round them into a mound or 'stool', covering the base of the young shoots. These, finding themselves underground, send out roots, so that in the autumn the soil can be scraped away from the mound and the rooted stocks cut off from the parent stool and planted out in the nursery (see Fig. 3). The stooling method is used mainly for apple and quince rootstocks.

When a stock is to be 'layered', it is planted at an angle of 45°, and left to grow in this way for one season. The next season, before the end of February, it is pegged down and covered with about an inch of soil (see Fig. 4). In the spring the young shoots break through, and as they grow, earth is heaped around their base, so that they also grow roots. In the autumn all except one are cut off and planted out in the nursery, the one being left for pegging down in the following February. The main differences between stooling and layering are that stools are planted upright, layers at an angle; stools are left bare of earth until the first earthing up begins in early summer; layers are pegged down and given a light earthing before any growth starts in the spring.

CURRANTS AND GOOSEBERRIES (q.v.) are raised from what are called 'hardwood cuttings', that is, from shoots that grew during the summer and are cut off from the bush in early autumn as soon as the leaf has fallen. These shoots are cut into

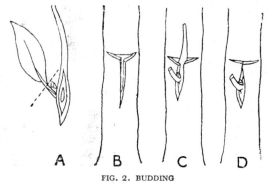

FIG. 2. BUDDING

A. The bud shield; B. The stock with 'T' cut to receive bud; C. The bud in place; D. The bud trimmed and ready for tying

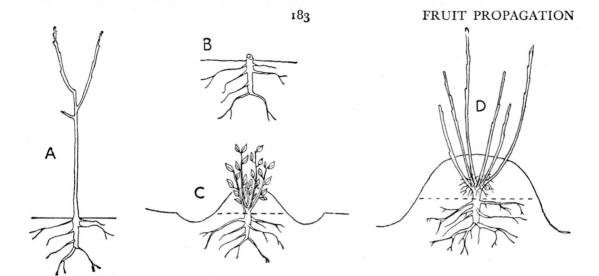

FIG. 3. STOOLING

A. Rootstock; *B.* Rootstock cut down one year after planting; *C.* Stool earthed in early summer; *D.* Rooted shoots on the stool in winter

lengths of from 12 to 15 inches, and pushed into the ground to a depth of 5 to 6 inches. On the part that is buried roots form, and from the part that is not buried the buds break in the spring and grow out to form the currant or gooseberry bush.

STRAWBERRIES (q.v.) are propagated from 'runners', so-called because they appear to be running away from the parent plant on a long horizontal stalk, known as a 'stolon'. A number of these stolons grow out from the parent plant in the course of the summer, and at intervals of from 12 to 15 inches there appear rosettes of small leaves. If at these points the stolon is anchored to the ground by a stone or a peg, roots will soon grow to form a new strawberry plant, 'maiden', or 'runner'. Runners are taken only from healthy and vigorous parent plants.

RASPBERRIES (q.v.) are raised from 'suckers' or 'spawn', that is, the young canes that grow up from round the base of the fruiting canes. These are dug up in winter, each with a good clump of roots attached, and planted out in the new positions they are to occupy in the plantation. Raspberries can also be raised from 'root cuttings' obtained by chopping downwards with a sharp spade round the base of a fruiting plant and bringing up pieces of root between $\frac{1}{4}$ and $\frac{1}{2}$ inch in diameter. These are cut into lengths of 2 to 3 inches and laid in a shallow trench a few inches apart, covered over with soil, and well trodden in.

LOGANBERRIES and BLACKBERRIES (q.v.) can be raised either by a method known as 'tip rooting' or from 'leaf-bud cuttings'. Both loganberries and blackberries send out very long shoots or canes during the summer; one of these is bent down and its tip or growing point is pegged down with a wooden or wire peg just below the surface of the soil. The buried tip then sends out roots, and the end bud on the cane

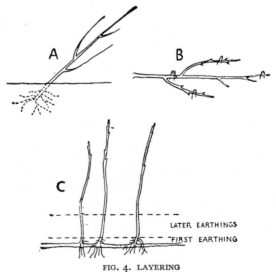

FIG. 4. LAYERING

A. Rootstock planted at an angle of 45°; *B.* Rootstock pegged down one year after planting; *C.* Rooted shoots on the stock one year later

(Figs. 1–4 by courtesy of the Imperial Bureau of Horticulture

pushes out into a shoot that grows straight upwards to form the new young plant. In the following spring the buried cane is cut off about 9 inches back from the tip and planted out in a nursery for one more season before it is ready for its permanent quarters.

Leaf-bud cuttings are made by cutting off a leaf and bud just behind where the leaf-stalk joins the stem, taking care not to injure the bud, and putting it into a cold frame in sandy soil, so that the bud and leaf-stalk are just below the surface of the soil, while the upper surface of the leaf remains exposed to the light. The glass top is then put on the frame, which is kept shaded from the sunlight. When roots form, the top of the frame is gradually opened and removed altogether in about 2 months' time. In the following spring the rooted cuttings are transplanted to the nursery for a season before being planted out.

Maiden trees and young bushes that are being grown in the nursery must not be left to take care of themselves. As they are planted close together in rows, the roots need all the moisture they can get to keep the plants growing through a dry season; therefore the hoe must be kept going between the rows to kill weeds which might otherwise rob the young plants. Protection from wind may be necessary, especially for fast-growing maiden fruit trees and for vigorous young red currants and gooseberries. Also, insect pests are just as fond of young trees and bushes as they are of older ones, and there is just as much need to keep them sprayed (*see* FRUIT SPRAYING).

See also FRUIT-GROWING; PLANT PROPAGATION.

See also Vol. II: GROWTH OF PLANTS; REPRODUCTION IN PLANTS.

FRUIT SPRAYING.

FRUIT SPRAYING. A certain amount of spraying and dusting is necessary to protect fruit trees from PESTS AND DISEASES (q.v.). Sprays may be used in the winter, when the trees are dormant, to kill the eggs of the pests and remove moss and lichen; or they may be used in the spring to poison the leaves on which the pest feeds; or they may be used at a later stage to kill directly the active insects. Certain sprays must be used before the leaves and buds unfold, for otherwise they would harm them. Others if used too late, might poison the fruit. Certain sprays cannot be used on some varieties of fruit; for example, lime-sulphur may do harm to Blenheim

Orange and some other apple-trees and to certain gooseberries. A knowledge of the behaviour of the pest is also necessary: for instance, the red spider mite mostly keeps to the under sides of leaves and may well escape the spray unless the sprayer remembers this fact; certain pests burrow into the stem or fruit-bud where no spray can reach them, and they must therefore be caught at an earlier stage in their growth; the black currant big-bud mite can be most effectively attacked at the time when the bud is opening and the mites are on the move. In all cases spraying should be used to prevent rather than cure severe attacks of pests and diseases. If the pest or disease is allowed to get a very strong hold before being attacked, it may be difficult or impossible to check it, at any rate before it has seriously weakened the tree and spoilt a season's fruit. The fruit-grower must keep a careful watch and be quick to recognize the early stages of an attack.

Certain recognized sprays are used for different purposes. The most commonly used winter washes are tar-oil emulsion and DNC petroleum oil emulsion, and these control aphids, moss and lichen, and destroy the eggs of the winter moth and red spider. In the spring a lime-sulphur spray or Bordeaux mixture controls scab in apples and pears, peach leaf-curl fungus, big-bud mite, red spider, gooseberry mildew, and other fungus diseases and pests. The spray may have to be repeated once or twice in May and June. A lead arsenate spray in early May controls biting pests such as the tortrix and winter moth caterpillars in apples and pears, and in late June the codling moth. A nicotine spray on a warm day in May or June kills sucking insects such as aphids, apple sawfly, and capsids. A dusting of derris powder on a still day also destroys the sucking type of pest, and a dusting of DDT is deathly to caterpillars and weevils. There are, of course, many other insecticides, but those described above, if used thoroughly and in time, should control the usual pests and diseases. The quantities to be used are always given on the makers' packets or tins. Arsenate of lead and nicotine are highly poisonous, and must therefore be treated with great respect. They must be clearly labelled and always kept locked up.

Plenty of clean and preferably soft water is needed for spraying. If an orchard of large trees is to be sprayed, a machine with sufficient pres-

John Topham

SPRAYING FRUIT TREES WITH AN OIL SPRAY IN WINTER

sure to send a spray well over the top of the tree is needed. This can be driven by its own motor or by the power-take-off from a tractor. In commercial orchards it is sometimes necessary to give seven or eight sprayings in the course of the year, so efficient SPRAYING MACHINES (q.v.) which give enough power and can be easily taken to pieces for cleaning, are essential. Spraying in gardens, except for very big trees, can be perfectly well carried out with much simpler apparatus. A watering-can with a fine rose can be used for strawberries or potatoes. A stirrup pump is a very efficient sprayer, and a great deal can be done on a small scale with a garden syringe. Dustings with such insecticides as derris and DDT can be given with a flit gun or with a small hand-bellows.

See also FRUIT-GROWING; VEGETABLE GARDEN; PESTS AND DISEASES; INSECT PESTS; PLANT DISEASES; INSECTICIDES; SPRAYING AND DUSTING MACHINES.

FUMIGATION, *see* INSECTICIDES.

FUNGUS DISEASES, *see* ANIMAL DISEASES, section 4; PLANT DISEASES, section 2.

FUR FARMING. 1. This means the raising of fur animals in captivity for their pelts. During the past 50 years fur farming has increased a great deal, but though we may look on it as a modern venture, the practice of raising animals for their pelts has a long history. For many centuries the Chinese have bred sheep, goats, and dogs for this purpose, while the karakul sheep of Central Asia has been bred in enormous numbers for the production of the lamb-skin known to the fur trade as karakul.

When the most valuable fur-bearing animals began to get scarce as the result of greatly intensified FUR HUNTING (q.v.), people began to consider the possibility of raising the animals in captivity. At first, for various reasons, experiments with most animals failed. Fur farmers have, however, been completely successful in breeding the silver fox, blue fox, and mink, and the high value of these pelts makes such farming very profitable. It is quite possible that, when more is known about the problems of breeding and rearing, many more types of animal may be farmed as successfully.

The animal-lover must welcome the practice of farming in place of trapping the fur animals. The farmed fox or mink lives a healthy life under good conditions, and when the time comes to take the pelt, death is swift and painless. The pelt is only taken when in prime condition. In trapping, on the other hand, as well as the undoubted suffering inflicted on the trapped animal, there is much waste, for the catch will always include a proportion of young animals, breeding females, and others with their coats in poor condition.

In some cases a species, without being moved from its natural home or enclosed in a fence, has been 'farmed' in the sense that its numbers have been increased by controlling local conditions, increasing the food supply, and limiting the annual kill. The best examples of this free farming are the musk-rat of North America and the blue fox of Alaska.

2. SILVER FOX. By far the most important farmed fur is silver fox in all its varieties. Fifty years ago, only small numbers of these beautiful black pelts with the silvery overhairs came on to the markets, and these were all trapped in the north of the American continent or in north Russia and Siberia. There, they occurred as occasional sports or varieties of the common red fox, in the proportion of about two silvers to a hundred reds. Today more than 90% of the world's silver fox production is from farms.

E.N.A.

A SILVER FOX FARM ON PRINCE EDWARD ISLAND, CANADA

Before silver foxes were farmed on any large scale the prices of the skins rose until, in 1910, a fine skin fetched £540. Such prices stimulated the attempts in Canada to raise the animals in captivity. In 1894 a pair of captured silver foxes produced a litter on a farm on Prince Edward Island. By 1900 the first farmed pelts were offered on the London market. Soon, fox farms sprang up all over the more suitable districts of Canada and the U.S.A., as well as in northern Europe. Many beginners lost their capital through lack of experience, but in spite of this the industry expanded rapidly. Canada exported 120,405 farmed pelts in 1935, accounting for 31% of the Dominion's raw fur crop for the year, while in the U.S.A. farmed fox formed 20% of the year's fur crop. Beginning with one pair in 1913 Norway is now the third largest producer in the world: she sold 103,604 pelts in the 1934–5 season. In the British Isles 3,000 silver foxes were raised in 1932. With this great increase in production, prices dropped rapidly, until in 1933 a good skin fetched about £25. Outstanding new types known as platinum and white-face have since been developed. The large amount of white in these very beautiful pelts gives them a unique appearance and makes them rather more valuable.

For the production of the best quality fur, silver foxes need a climate with a fairly heavy rainfall and a long cold winter. Most farms are in the northern part of the U.S.A., and the two largest, in Wisconsin, each house some 7,600 breeding pairs. Many others are quite small. Fox farms can often successfully occupy land otherwise unfit for cultivation, so long as it is well-drained. Some trees for shade are an advantage. The animals are normally housed in pairs in wire netting pens, the walls being 9 or 10 feet high, with an inward overhang at the top to prevent escape. If the pens are of the crate type, totally enclosed by the wire netting, they need be only 6 feet high. Wooden kennels or dens are provided for shelter. The pens are separated from each other to prevent the spread of disease or fights through the wire between the male foxes. A stout guard fence surrounds the whole farm, serving the double purpose of preventing the escape of animals and of keeping away dogs and other intruders. An essential to the large farm is the watch-tower, which must be high enough to enable the staff to supervise the whole ranch and watch the behaviour of the animals, especially during the breeding season, without disturbing them.

The best diet, fed twice daily, includes a large proportion of cooked cereals and vegetables, mixed with ground cooked meat. Milk and eggs, when these are available, are added to the diet of the vixens (female foxes) when they have whelped and are suckling their cubs. Offal, such as heads and entrails of rabbits, is best avoided because of PARASITIC WORMS (q.v.). Cleanliness of the food and the feeding-vessels is a very important factor in checking disease.

February and March is the mating season, and the young, averaging four to a litter, are born 51 or 52 days later. During this period absolute quiet is essential. The cubs are taken from the vixen at about 8 weeks old, and an average of two per litter reach maturity. A vixen may continue breeding for 8 or 9 years, beginning at the age of 18 months.

The pelts of the silver fox are at their prime during December and January, and may be taken at any age, once maturity is reached. The skinning and treatment of the pelts is described under FUR TRADE (q.v. Vol. VII). At one time, dealers considered farmed pelts to be inferior to those from the wild animals, but now first class farmed pelts command as high a price as any.

3. BLUE FOX. Another well-established branch of fox farming is the raising of blue foxes in Alaska and Norway. These are a colour phase of the arctic or white fox, which remains slaty-blue in winter instead of turning white. Their natural home is the coastal areas of Arctic and sub-Arctic regions, and, during the past 30 years, they have been farmed successfully on the numerous small islands along the south coasts of Alaska, and to a lesser extent in Norway. In this type of fur farming, the animals are turned out on small islands and live in a natural condition, except that they are fed by the rancher (fish being the main food). When the pelts are prime, the animals are caught in small trap-houses scattered over the island. The breeding habits of the blue fox are much like those of the other foxes, though the litters are usually larger.

4. MINK. Second only in importance to silver fox is mink, a ferret-like animal with a sleek dark brown fur, noted for its hard wearing qualities. Mink farming was first attempted in the U.S.A. at the end of the 19th century, but it did not become well established for some 40–50 years. The top price for best pelts in 1944 was £6 each. Recently breeders have produced new varieties, the so-called mutation minks. At the New York 1945 sales such new forms as Silverblue, Blue Frost (the names indicate the

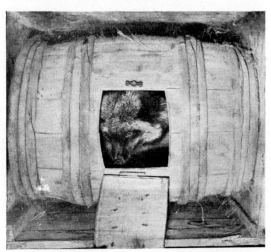

Canadian National Film Board
A BREEDING 'DEN' ON A SILVER FOX FARM
The barrel prevents the pups from getting cold, for if they try to get away from the mother they will roll back to her

colours) and Royal Kohinoor (white fur with black guard hairs) were in great demand. Blue Frost skins averaged £11 each, the top price being as much as £26; Royal Kohinoor skins reached a maximum of £43, and Silverblues £53. It takes sixty or more large skins to make a full-length fur coat.

Mink are farmed on much the same lines as the other flesh-eating fur bearers. They are more economical to rear than foxes, being smaller, they need less food and smaller enclosures. Also they are more prolific.

5. OTHER FARMED ANIMALS. (*a*) *Nutria.* In South America the farming of nutria (trade name for the Coypu, a large beaver-like rodent found in that country) has made some progress, and some nutria farms have been started both in the U.S.A. and in Europe. The fur, however, is not of high value. In many cases animals have escaped from insufficiently fenced farms and have thrived in the wild state. In Norfolk several hundreds were killed on the Broads during and after the war years.

(*b*) *Musk-Rat* (Musquash). Reckoned in terms of numbers and total value this is the most important of all fur animals today, although the best skins in 1944 fetched no more than 3s. to 5s. each. Attempts to farm this animal in pens, however, have met with little success; but by encouraging the growth of the water vegetation on which it feeds, and limiting the annual kill to reasonable proportions, free farming of the musk-rat in its native marshes in the U.S.A. has been most successful. In some years as many as 14 million pelts have reached the market. The Russians have imported musk-rats, and encouraged them to populate the extensive marshes on their western borders, for the benefit of the fur industry. Escapes of musk-rats from farms in Britain have caused considerable damage (*see* VOLE, Vol. II).

(*c*) *Chinchilla.* Not many years ago chinchilla was the most expensive and exclusive of all furs. During the boom year in the fur business of 1920 a chinchilla wrap, containing over 200 of these exquisitely soft and silky skins, was valued at £10,000. Yet only 20 years earlier hundreds of thousands of the skins had been exported yearly from Chile and Peru at very low prices, to be used for trimming or children's muffs and stoles. Excessive trapping so reduced the supply that, by 1918, the trade was entirely banned in an attempt to save the chinchilla from extermination.

In 1923 an American succeeded in transporting to California eighteen live chinchillas; and from this small beginning a large population has been reared in the U.S.A., and high profits have been made by the sale of breeding pairs at £200 or more per pair. The value of the pelts has now, however, dropped a great deal, since today there is little demand for a fur with such poor durability as chinchilla. In 1944, 3,315 farmed pelts realized only £3. 10s. each.

(d) *Rabbit.* By no means least in importance are the numerous fur breeds of the domestic rabbit. These are the small man's speciality, and many of the pelts reaching the trade come from backyards and small holdings (*see* RABBIT-KEEPING). Varieties such as the Chinchilla rabbit, Blue Beveren, Havana, Blacks, Whites, and the velvet-coated Rex are all in good demand. Typical wholesale prices for cured pelts in 1943 were; chinchilla 92s., blue 11s. 3d. to 31s., whites 28s. 6d. to 50s. a dozen. The low cost of rearing rabbits ensures them a prominent place among the cheaper furs.

See also FUR HUNTING.
See also VOL. II: FOX; WEASEL; COYPU; CHINCHILLA.

FUR HUNTING. The hunting of wild animals for their pelts, as the skins of the fur bearers are called, must have been going on ever since people took to wearing clothes to keep themselves warm. We know little of how these first fur garments were treated to preserve them and make them supple enough for wear, though among the PREHISTORIC TOOLS AND WEAPONS (q.v. Vol. I) left behind by people of the Stone Age have been found scrapers obviously used for working on skins.

In some primitive communities furs have long been used for exchange, and they have played an important part in TRADE (q.v. Vol. VII). Today the world's fur trade is a very large and highly organized business, with an annual turnover amounting to many million pounds. From the trapper to the skin dresser, the garment maker and the sales-woman, the industry employs many thousands of workers (*see* FUR TRADE, Vol. VII).

In the history of the northern countries, where most of the more valuable furs come from (for only in lands of severe winters do animals develop thick and rich winter coats), the hope of making money quickly from new sources of fur supply has been an important motive for exploring new lands. This has happened especially in the northern regions of the North American continent, where the pioneer was the fur trader, bartering the white man's goods for the abundant BEAVER, FOX, OTTER, MARTEN, SQUIRREL, and MINK skins (qq.v. Vol. II) trapped by the Indians. The history of the development of Canada is bound up with the history of the famous HUDSON'S BAY COMPANY (q.v. Vol. VII), who sent their agents to establish trading posts wherever Indians or Eskimoes were to be found. In the early days of the Company, skins were frequently used as a medium of exchange instead of money—a pound weight of beaver skin, for instance, was reckoned as worth roughly 8s. in trade.

In course of time, as the growing demand for furs became more and more difficult to satisfy, professional white trappers took up the work and began to explore new regions solely for their furs. These men, a tough and hardy race of pioneers, invaded the forests of the north with their snow-shoes, their guns, and their traps, built themselves log cabins for the winter, and set lines of traps limited only by the amount of gear they could transport and the distance they could cover. Frequently these trap lines were so long that 2 or 3 days were needed to cover them; but in the intensely cold and dry climate of the far north the frozen skins did not deteriorate if the animals were left some time in the traps.

Such intensive trapping meant that after a few years the natural supply of animals began to fall off; so the trappers moved on, found fresh hunting-grounds, and at the same time added greatly to our knowledge of the new countries. In the wake of the trappers came more trading posts to supply their needs and buy their winter catches; and so the settlements grew.

Throughout the history of hunting for fur, TRAPS AND SNARES (q.v.) in some form or other have always proved more effective than weapons, whether spears, clubs, bows, or guns. Among primitive peoples the art of trapping has often reached a high level, the ingenuity displayed by some tribes in devising snares and traps being remarkable. Young children learn the technique at a very early age by trapping and snaring rats, mice, and small birds, in preparation for the time when they will make a living as hunters. The snare, one of the simplest types of traps, has always been popular; it is usually set unbaited on a game trail, or is placed at gaps in a prepared

SEALING IN SIBERIA
Sealers, with ropes and gaffs (spears), leave the ship on arrival at the Arctic sealing grounds

fence or hedge in bush or forest, or on logs forming natural bridges over streams. The second most common native trap, particularly in the northern countries, is the deadfall, a trap consisting of weighted logs held by a support so arranged that when the animal tries to reach the bait it displaces the support and is killed by the crushing weight of the logs. These traps were used by many of the early white hunters in the north.

With the introduction of the white man's steel traps, the older types have tended to fall into disuse. The metal trap, used either baited or unbaited, and made in a great variety of forms and sizes for every kind of animal, is so easy to carry and set and so effective that its use is world-wide. But it has the overwhelming drawback, from the humanitarian point of view, that it holds the suffering animal alive until such time as the trapper makes his rounds. Because of its cruelty there has been much agitation to make its use illegal.

Before the discovery of America, Russian Siberia was the most important source of furs; but as the supply was limited, the sable and ermine reaching western Europe in the Middle Ages were mainly reserved for royalty and the nobility at the courts (*see* Furs, Vol. XI). With the opening up of North America, a hitherto untapped source of supply was rapidly exploited. The tundras of the far north, the forests, mountains, prairies, swamps and rivers of Canada

SEALERS APPROACHING THE SEALS ON PAN ICE IN SIBERIA

and the United States all contributed their quota of fur. The pelts of mink, marten, otter, red, blue, and silver fox, beaver, musquash, and many others poured in to the fur markets of the world, of which London for many years was the biggest. For some time past the U.S.A., including Alaska, has been the world's largest producer of fur, and the average amount paid out annually to the trapper and fur-farmer for their products has been over £12 million. To many farmers in the U.S.A. the trapping or hunting of fur in the autumn and winter is a highly profitable sideline, sometimes giving higher cash returns than do farm crops.

In some districts and for some types of animals the most effective way of taking furs is the hunt, particularly trailing with hounds. In the southern states of the U.S.A. by far the greater number of OPOSSUMS and RACCOONS (qq.v. Vol. II) are taken by this method, moonlit autumn nights being specially favourable for the hunter. The hunted animal takes to a tree to escape the hounds and is then shot by the hunter. In Australia the kangaroo hunters rely on the rifle, either riding the kangaroo down on horseback on the plains or waiting for them at water-holes.

Seal skins are taken on a very large scale by a method which cannot be classed as trapping or hunting. After the mating season at the great breeding stations on the Pribilov and other islands of the Bering Sea in the North Pacific, thousands of skins are obtained by clubbing the bachelor male seals on land. This slaughter is strictly controlled by the United States authorities under an international control agreement signed in 1911. Before that date there was so much indiscriminate killing of seals of all ages and both sexes at sea by sealing parties in schooners, that there was real danger that the seals in this area would soon be exterminated.

The islands in the seas separating Alaska from Kamchatka in the extreme north of Russia still provide the great bulk of seal fur; and before the international control agreement, as many as 220,000 skins from this part of the world might be offered at one sale in London. Since the control was instituted, about 60,000 a year are taken from the main herd on the Pribilov Islands, without disturbing the breeding stock. In 1942 during the Second World War no killing took place, because the Japanese had occupied the Aleutian Islands near by; but the next year an American sealing expedition under government control visited the Pribilovs and came back with the enormous total of 170,000 skins (see SEAL, Vol. II). In the early days the sea otter, one of the most valuable furs ever known, was to be found in these waters, but it was so severely hunted that its numbers are greatly reduced, and only a very small number now reach the fur markets (see OTTER, Vol. II).

Australia and South America are much less important fur areas than the northern districts. During the middle of the 19th century the fur resources of Australia were thoroughly explored. Great numbers of skins of animals such as KANGAROOS, WALLABIES, OPOSSUMS, KOALAS (traded under the name of wombat) (qq.v. Vol. II), and other less well-known animals, have been exported every year, as well as large numbers of rabbit skins which are so important to the less expensive side of the fur trade. These animals are now beginning to become scarce.

From South America come furs of much less value but still filling a useful place on the market. Perhaps the best known is ocelot, a handsome, short-haired, striped and blotched wild CAT, and nutria, the fur of the water-loving COYPU, a beaver-like rodent. At the present time the famed CHINCHILLA (qq.v. Vol. II), a beautiful rabbit-like rodent with a squirrel-like tail and incredibly soft grey fur, is hardly to be found in the wild state, although 40 years ago hundreds of thousands of skins were sent out of Chile annually. Today FUR FARMING (q.v.) in California and elsewhere in the United States has saved the chinchilla from extinction, though the market for furs of such softness and delicacy is always likely to be limited.

See also TRAPS AND SNARES.
See also Vol. VII: FUR TRADE; HUDSON'S BAY COMPANY.

G

GARDEN, *see* FLOWER GARDEN; VEGETABLE GARDEN; GARDENING, HISTORY OF.

GARDEN HEDGES. These are used as garden boundaries, as wind-breaks, and also for decoration. Formal, clipped hedges as well as informal ones can serve these purposes. Formal hedges can be made from evergreen shrubs such as box, bush, honeysuckle, lonicera, cypress, holly, privet, pyracantha, and yew (both green and golden), or from deciduous shrubs such as beech, cherry-plum, hawthorn, and hornbeam. These are all hardy plants which will grow well in towns as well as in the country. Informal

hedges can be made from shrubs that will not stand heavy clipping, such as *Berberis stenophylla* (burning bush), lavender, rosemary, tree heaths, and veronica (evergreens), and also from lilac and roses and, in warm coastal districts, fuchsia and the grey-green, feathery-leaved shrub called tamarisk. Hedges can also be made of cut-leaved blackberry and Japanese wineberry if some support is given (*see* FLOWERING SHRUBS).

In choosing hedge-plants the type of soil in which they are to grow must be taken into consideration. Bush honeysuckle, hornbeam, and lilac suit heavy soils; holly, lavender, rosemary, and tamarisk do well on light soils; and beech, box, and yew like a chalky soil. Deciduous shrubs should be planted in open weather between October and March; evergreens are best planted in September or October or in late April or May. The ground should be well prepared. A strip 3 to 5 feet wide should be deeply dug and if necessary drained; poor soil should be enriched with rotted manure or compost, and bone meal and wood ash dug into the top spit. It is best to plant into damp soil, and the plants should be very firmly set. The spacing depends, naturally, upon habits of growth and size of the plants. Most hedge-plants should be planted in a single row about 15 to 18 inches

Amateur Gardening

A FORMAL GARDEN WITH BOX EDGINGS AND HEDGES AND CLIPPED TREES AT LUTON HOO, BEDFORDSHIRE

apart; beech, hornbeam, and privet need to be a little closer, and bushy plants like cypress, holly, and lilac may need wider spacing. If a thick boundary hedge is required, the shrubs should be planted in double alternating rows, the rows being 9 to 12 inches apart. A hedge should be planted well away (2 to 3 feet) from any boundary wall or fence.

The young plants may need to be watered until they are established and must be kept clear of weeds. If the hedge is being planted in a windy situation, some wind protection will be necessary at first, to prevent the plants from being 'wind-rocked' and worked loose in the ground.

A hedge must be trained to grow thick at the base, and this is done by correct pruning. Plants of a naturally leggy growth, such as lonicera or privet, ought to be cut down as low as 6 inches from the ground at planting to encourage them to throw out side-shoots; other plants, such as cherry-plum, hornbeam, and sometimes also beech and hawthorn, need this severe pruning after a year's growth. Most evergreens, however, only need to have their side shoots and long, thin leading shoots shortened after 2 years'

growth. When well established, all hedges need regular pruning according to their rate of growth in order to curb over-vigorous side-shoots and to encourage an even height.

The pruning of formal hedges, especially in the early stages, is a skilled craft. The pruner has to keep in mind the shape that he wants his fully grown hedge to take, and then to maintain it. Many evergreen shrubs, in particular box and yew, can be made to take the most fanciful shapes: the art of this kind of trimming is called TOPIARY (q.v.). A smart effect can be achieved by trimming the hedge to an even, flat top and sharp, vertical side-lines. The secret of success is in keeping the growth thick at the base. A simple rectangular shape with sharp right-angled corners as in Fig. A looks handsome, but is the most difficult shape to maintain well. The thickness of the hedge should be about 18 inches to 2 feet, and the top should be absolutely flat along the whole length of the hedge. A hedge with a wider base and slanting side lines has the advantage that the lower growth is not shaded by the upper (Fig. B). Fig. C shows a suitable shape for a boundary hedge, planted in a double row. If the hedge is in an exposed place so that it often has to withstand strong winds or heavy snow, shapes as shown in Figs. D and E are practical. Most evergreens except conifers are best pruned in the spring; many, such as box and privet, need pruning several times through the summer. Conifers (cypress and yew) and deciduous shrubs should be pruned in July.

In places where there is a considerable extent of trimmed hedge, electric hedge-cutters are often used. Large-leaved evergreens are best trimmed with secateurs so that as few leaves as possible need be cut. The ordinary shears can do all other jobs.

See also FLOWERING SHRUBS.

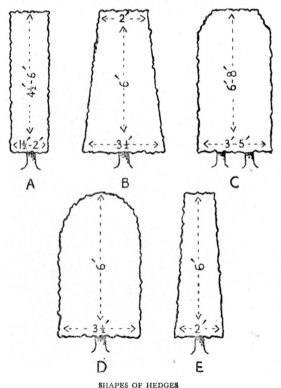

A   B   C

D   E

SHAPES OF HEDGES

GARDENING, HISTORY OF. **1.** ANCIENT TIMES. The history of gardening begins very early, perhaps before 2500 B.C., when Egypt and Babylon were great kingdoms. Its development through the ages has not been a matter of chance, but has depended upon the ways in which people lived. We may find in it, therefore, a record of civilizations; and as the ANCIENT CIVILIZATIONS (q.v. Vol. I) of which we have most knowledge first arose in the Nile Valley and in Mesopotamia, its beginnings may be looked for there. Gardens, however, are not lasting like

AN EGYPTIAN GARDEN WITH A POOL SURROUNDED BY FRUIT TREES, PALMS, SYCAMORE, PAPYRUS, AND OTHER SHRUBS
The goddess of the sycamore is seen with her offerings on the right. Painting from a tomb at Thebes, about 1420–1375 B.C.
From N. M. Davies: *Ancient Egyptian Paintings*, Oriental Institute, University of Chicago

great buildings, and their early history has to be pieced together from the art, literature, and records of ancient times. From wall paintings in tombs and hieroglyphic pictures we know that the Egyptians made walled gardens with orchards of vines and figs, avenues of date-palms, acacias, and tamarisks, vegetable and flower-beds, artificial canals, and pools covered with blue lotus lilies and fringed with the native papyrus reed. We see men pruning and training fruit trees, watering with buckets, using sickles, rakes, and forks, arranging pot plants and growing, among other vegetables, peas, beans, radishes, onions, and lettuce. The lotus, which covered every stream and at the time of the Nile flooding changed the country into a field of flowers, was first among many other flowers. The rich soil, hot sun, and the Nile waters provided the conditions for this skilful and beautiful gardening in the narrow river valley (*see* EGYPTIAN CIVILIZATION, Vol. I).

Mesopotamia, watered by the Tigris and Euphrates rivers, where the ASSYRIAN and BABYLONIAN civilizations arose (qq.v. Vol. I), had nothing to equal the Egyptian gardens. Assyria to the north was a semi-forested region in which war-like kings built fortress-palaces surrounded by great hunting parks. Babylonia had many towns and people supported by the elaborate irrigation of the Babylonian plain, formerly an uninhabitable swamp. Wheat, barley, and apple and date orchards covered the country, and gardens made on town walls must have looked like hanging gardens from the plain. The 'Hanging Gardens' of the city of Babylon became famous as one of the seven wonders of the ancient world. Later on, the tradition of garden-parks spread to the neighbouring country of Persia, where many sweet-scented flowers, especially roses, were cultivated. Gardens were also developed in India, where the Moguls made famous gardens as settings for their palaces and temples.

The history of Chinese gardens begins before 2000 B.C., and flowers, shrubs, and trees, cultivated for centuries in China, were introduced into Europe in the 18th and 19th centuries—chrysanthemums, for instance, many roses, lilies, peonies, primulas, wistaria, peaches, and cherries. Marco Polo, the 13th-century Venetian traveller, returned with detailed descriptions of these Chinese gardens. The characteristic Chinese garden design was based on miniature reproduction of natural landscapes. Mountains, rocks, streams, and trees were all faithfully reproduced in miniature, for the Chinese had discovered the art of growing diminutive trees which were exact models of the forest giants. These exquisite garden creations were not, however, only copies of landscapes, for every twig and stone had some symbolic meaning to those who designed them (see CHINESE CIVILIZATION, Vol. I).

2. EUROPEAN GARDENS. (*a*) *Greece and Rome.* The Greek way of life was very different from that of older civilizations, and gardening changed to suit new conditions. The country was infertile compared with alluvial river valleys; but we know from Homer's *Odyssey* how vigorously the people farmed, tended herds, and planted

Royal Horticultural Society

GARDENING IN THE EARLY 16TH CENTURY
From the title-page of one of the first printed books on gardening, published in 1530

orchards. Greek literature is full of the beauty of trees and wild flowers. Temples were built in groves of planes and oaks which were never pruned or cut down. The crowded cities had few private gardens, but public gardens were much used. Philosophers walked and talked there with their pupils and sat under shady trees. Later, philosophers, such as Plato and Epicurus, bought land and made gardens which they left to their schools. Aristotle taught in a famous garden. After the wars with Persia Greeks returning to Athens told about wonderful oriental gardens and Egyptian flowers; but the Greeks did not attempt to copy gardening ideas unsuited to their country-side and to their habits of life (see GREEK CIVILIZATION, Vol. I).

Gardening, as well as agriculture, flourished in the Roman Empire. At first, public-spirited Romans beautified the cities with public gardens in the Greek fashion, but, as wealth increased, the luxury-loving Romans made elaborate private gardens around their town and country villas. One of them, Lucullus, who brought the cherry from the east, made the first 'princely garden', which became typical of Roman gardening. Cicero, Plutarch, and Pliny wrote accounts of their many gardens, which abounded in fountains, marble-edged pools, sculpture, colonnades, pergolas, elaborately clipped box trees, avenues of plane trees wide enough for chariots to hurtle along, cypress groves, rose gardens, formal flower-beds, orchard terraces, vineyards, myrtles, olive and laurel groves. Flowers were grown in nurseries for decorations, and hot-houses of a kind are mentioned in the 1st century A.D. (see ROMAN CIVILIZATION, Vol. I).

(*b*) *The Middle Ages.* After the fall of the Roman Empire, gardening was kept alive by the monks, who cultivated farms, orchards, and gardens around their monasteries. Gradually, as more peaceful conditions prevailed in the 12th and 13th centuries, interest in gardening revived. The return of crusaders from the east and the spread of Arab civilization into Spain brought fresh ideas of gardening. Medieval gardens were small and gay, with smooth turf seats against walls, little paths, fountains, flower-beds, and arbours. Pictures of them may be seen in illustrated manuscripts such as *The Romance of the Rose* in the British Museum.

(*c*) *The Renaissance and Italian Gardens.* In Italy during the 14th and 15th centuries the old medieval way of life began to break up, and the

Bodleian Library

A LATE 16TH-CENTURY DUTCH FORMAL GARDEN

great revival of learning brought about a revival of interest in the classic past of Greece and Rome. Wealthy independent princes became patrons of the arts. They built villas with gardens designed and adorned by famous artists and architects. Water, shady trees, and marble were used profusely to give coolness, and to harmonize with the buildings and the surrounding landscape. Cascades, fountains, grottoes, terraces, sculpture, garden theatres, tall cypresses, and spreading trees helped to produce some of the most beautiful gardens ever made. Public gardens were also revived in Italian Renaissance cities (*see* RENAISSANCE, Vol. I).

(*d*) *French Gardens.* The famous French gardener, Le Nôtre (1613–1700), gardener to Louis XIV for 40 years, made gardens which were architectural and formal in the 'grand manner', suited to the magnificent houses built by the noblemen of that period. The VERSAILLES gardens (q.v. Vol. XII) are typical of his work— miles of radiating avenues, great sheets of water,

immense parterres and orangeries set among regularly spaced plantations of trees. Ninety-five sculptors decorated the gardens with statuary. Le Nôtre and his pupils designed gardens in every country of Europe, and established a formal tradition which dominated garden design for half a century.

(*e*) *Dutch Gardens.* By the end of the 15th century the Dutch had a European reputation for flower cultivation. Their gardens were small, neat, and formal, with little canals, small clipped trees, and tulips in orderly rows. Some of the earliest BOTANICAL GARDENS (q.v. Vol. IX) were made in Holland.

(*f*) *Moorish Gardens.* The MOORS (q.v. Vol. I), between the 8th and 15th centuries, were the garden-makers of Spain. They irrigated the dry country-side so that agriculture and gardening flourished together. Moorish gardens were linked architecturally with the houses by means of patios, or garden courtyards, through which small canals of water ran. The high walls covered with climbing plants, the fountains, flowering trees, and arbours provided much-needed shade and coolness.

3. ENGLISH GARDENS. With the establishment of great estates and the increased magnificence of Court life in Tudor times, gardening developed rapidly in England. About 1520 Cardinal Wolsey designed the Hampton Court gardens, and Henry VIII continued his work. Some of the Tudor character of the gardens still remains in the Pond Garden and the Maze. A maze consists of paths between high hedges leading to a centre, but with so many false turns that the visitor easily loses his way. Elizabethan gardens were laid out on a geometric plan, each part divided from the next by walls and hedges. They had knotted beds of flowers, bowling and archery greens, covered walks and entwined lime alleys, labyrinths or mazes, low terraces overlooking sunk gardens, galleries, and clipped shrubs (*see* TOPIARY). Beyond the garden there was sometimes a little wood or wilderness, and inside the walled gardens artificial 'mounts' were made from which to view the surrounding country-side. Examples of Tudor garden design can still be

seen at Compton Wynyates in Warwickshire, Montacute in Somerset, and Wilton House in Wiltshire.

During the 17th century many new foreign plants were introduced, and in 1621 the first botanical garden was made at Oxford where it still flourishes. After the restoration of Charles II continental ideas again dominated English gardening. Many of Le Nôtre's pupils came to England to design gardens and parks in the French manner. Lawns were substituted for the little beds with box edges and intricate scroll-work shapes. Long avenues were planted radiating from large formal gardens. But in England the excessive formality of French gardens was avoided, and many lovely gardens belong to this period. The Dutch formal garden, in which the garden was subdivided into many small units, also had its influence on English design.

Formality in garden design continued until the beginning of the 18th century, when new ideas in philosophy, literature, and art led to the ROMANTIC MOVEMENT (q.v. Vol. XII). ROUSSEAU (1712–78) (q.v. Vol. V), whose influence on this period was great, was a romantic believer in 'nature', and painted a glowing picture of an imaginary 'natural' garden which he set on the shores of Lake Geneva. The late 18th century had little use for the ways of life and thought of the period which produced the grand formal gardens of Le Nôtre. Painters and poets, too, sought the 'natural' and the picturesque, and despised formal patterns and artificiality of any kind. Violent changes in garden design were one of the ways in which the new ideas were reflected. In a short space of time garden walls disappeared and landscape parks designed like romantic pictures with trees in groups, winding streams, pools, and open views ending in classic temples became the fashion. English literature of the period is full of descriptions of the new passion for picturesque garden-making. At first, the owners of the gardens and parks themselves supervised the changes, but later, professional designers were employed everywhere. The most famous was Lancelot Brown (1715–83), who later became known as Capability Brown because he never failed to find capabilities for landscaping in any garden he advised upon. Although he destroyed many fine formal gardens and avenues, nevertheless he made beautiful parks with large placid lakes, thick plantations of trees, wide expanses of turf, and landscapes

P. Hart

A MOORISH GARDEN IN GRANADA
A small canal runs through the middle of the garden

THE 18TH-CENTURY FRENCH GARDEN AT CHATSWORTH, DERBYSHIRE

controlled into a gentle informality. Many trees were planted through the English country-side at this time. Repton (1752–1818) succeeded Brown and was the last of the great landscape designers. The passion for 'landscaping' spread to France, where 'Le Jardin à l'Anglaise' became the fashion.

The 19th century saw the introduction of many more new plants brought from China and the Far East, and improved methods of cultivation made it possible to grow more flowers. Many of these were not hardy in English climatic conditions, so that conservatories and glasshouses became the fashion. The Industrial Revolution brought money to people some of whom had no interest in garden and landscape design, and no idea of the beauties that were possible. They employed gardeners to fill innumerable beds with half-hardy plants and to make 'carpet' beds of tender foliage plants. The lovely uses of hardy old English perennials were forgotten, except in cottage gardens and the unchanged gardens of the smaller country houses.

At the beginning of the 20th century notable gardeners such as William Robinson and Gertrude Jekyll laboured to bring back the use of hardy flowering plants and so to break down the uninspired formality of much Victorian gardening. Many architects, too, began to study garden design and to understand the beauty of the old architectural type of garden. They realized how it could be combined with the best influences of the landscape school which suits the English country-side so well. We are still in the midst of this period of garden history. The other main development of the 20th century has been the small garden, often specializing in one particular type of plant.

See also FLOWER GARDENS; VEGETABLE GARDEN.
See also Vol. XII: LANDSCAPE ART.

GARDEN PATHS. In any but the smallest gardens, well-planned paths are necessary so that people can move about the garden conveniently, both to enjoy it and to work in it. As paths, once laid down, are permanent, they must be planned in relation to the whole lay-out of the garden, before any construction is done. In general, the fewer paths the better; they should have a definite purpose, and not result in small, awkward areas of garden; and they should themselves play a part in the design of the garden.

The minimum width of a path should be 2 feet, and in big gardens some central paths of 4 to 6 feet wide are desirable. All paths should have a foundation of solid but porous rubble, well pounded down. If there is any doubt about drainage, as on heavy soils, tile drains should be laid in the rubble. Water freezing under a path will break up the surface, whatever it is, and lack of drainage will waterlog the path in wet weather.

The surface material of the path may be asphalt, gravel, ashes, bricks, concrete, or stone slabs.

Asphalt, though hard-wearing, is too unsightly to be suitable in an ornamental garden, though

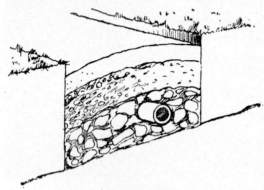

SECTION THROUGH AN ASPHALT PATH

A layer of drainage material is placed at the bottom, and a drain-pipe provided if necessary; then a layer of small rubble and finally the asphalt. The camber prevents water collecting on the path

it is useful in less showy places. A layer of $\frac{1}{2}$ to 1 inch thick should be laid. Gravel is much more attractive to look at, but has the disadvantages that it easily becomes infested with weeds, and also tends to cling to muddy boots and get carried away. A depth of 2 inches of gravel should be laid, and this should be wetted and rolled as laid. It is best laid on a layer of clay and the path 'wet-rolled' until it is really hard. Ashes are not very satisfactory path material, since they are easily kicked up in dry weather, and stick to boots in wet. They are useful, however, for quickly made service paths in the vegetable garden, for instance, which can easily be resurfaced as more ashes become available. The cinders should be sifted, and the fine material rolled in on top of the coarse.

Bricks may be laid in various attractive patterns, bedded either in sand or ashes, and the cracks between filled with sand. A more permanent though more expensive path can be made by setting the bricks in cement. Brick paths are apt to be rather slippery in wet weather.

Concrete, though not very decorative, is cheap, long-lasting, and easily laid. One part of fresh cement should be well mixed with 3 or 4 parts ballast (fairly coarse gravel or stone chips) and 2 parts sand; water should then be gradually added and stirred in until the whole mixture is wet but fairly stiff. The concrete layer should be at least 3 inches deep. The path may be coloured by mixing special powder colours into the uppermost layer of concrete.

Stone of pre-cast concrete slabs, either rectangular or 'crazy', are probably, apart from brick paths, the most decorative path material. They may either be bedded in concrete or, where less wear is expected, in sand or ashes, like bricks. In either case little pockets of soil may be made here and there, and suitable creeping plants inserted, a device often used in crazy paving.

Slabs of stone or concrete may also be placed in a lawn, just below the grass surface, about 18 to 24 inches apart, in places where the 'path' will not have very much use. This is useful and attractive beside a herbaceous border or around a pool. Turf paths may also be 'reinforced' with such slabs to prevent their becoming worn, or in wet weather very muddy.

The problem of keeping paths clear of WEEDS (q.v.) faces all gardeners. Decorative paths in which pockets are left for creeping plants or with borders of EDGING PLANTS (q.v.), must be weeded by hand. The more utilitarian paths of the vegetable garden can be poisoned with a

Amateur Gardening

A CRAZY-PAVING PATH IN A GARDEN AT BECKENHAM, KENT

A. Rice

EMBDEN GANDER   CHINESE GEESE   TOULOUSE GANDER

weed killer such as sodium chlorate. If the path has an edging of brick or concrete, this prevents the garden soil from spreading on to the path and makes it easier to poison without injuring the garden plants.

See also GARDEN HEDGES; GARDENING, HISTORY OF.

GARDEN PESTS, *see* PESTS AND DISEASES.

GARDEN TOOLS, *see* HAND TOOLS.

GARLIC, *see* ONION CROPS.

GEESE. Geese have been domesticated for longer than any of the other kinds of poultry. The Egyptians kept them 4,000 years ago; they are mentioned in Sanskrit writings; and they are said to have given the alarm that saved Rome from capture by the Gauls in 365 B.C. Their feathers provided quill Pens until the steel nib was invented, and as long ago as 2,000 years they were praised for providing feathers for bed-making.

Unlike chickens and turkeys they are natives of Britain, all the known domestic breeds being descended from the wild Grey Lag goose. They are also the most hardy of all our types of poultry, and are therefore very easy to keep. They need only a very simple shed for shelter, and, except in winter or during a very dry summer, they can live largely on grass. Five or six geese eat as much as a sheep, and their grazing can much improve a pasture. When there is not enough grass, they can be given cabbages, chopped up turnips or swedes, potatoes either raw or cooked, and perhaps a little corn.

Geese are kept mainly for their table qualities (that is, for eating), so that, although their eggs are very tasty, these are generally reserved for hatching. Geese of most breeds lay only about thirty eggs a year, the exception being the Chinese or Swan goose which sometimes lays as many as 140 eggs. A breeding pen or 'set' usually consists of one gander and three geese. A goose will cover about fifteen eggs, and these take 30 to 31 days to hatch. The gander is the only male bird of domestic poultry that concerns himself with the welfare of his family. He will protect them fiercely. He will not mate with a goose until he has been long enough with her to get to know her—perhaps 4 to 6 weeks.

There are a number of breeds of geese, the best known being the Toulouse, a very large, grey bird, and the Embden, a large, white bird with sky-blue eyes. The Chinese or Swan goose is smaller, with a long snake-like neck and a knob on the top of its beak. There are both fawn and white varieties. The Roman goose is small and white; the Sebastopol goose is white with curly feathers. An 'auto-sexing' breed (that is, one where the male and female goslings have a different colour pattern when hatched, and so can be easily told apart) is found in the west of England and also in Canada. The ganders are white and the geese grey with white heads. They are called Pilgrim Geese in Canada, which suggests that they were taken to the American continent by the Pilgrim Fathers.

Compared with most birds, geese live to a great age, 20 years being not uncommon. Although geese are waterfowl they can live quite well without swimming water, and on most

Amateur Gardening

FIG. 1. METAL-FRAMED LEAN-TO GLASSHOUSE

Amateur Gardening

FIG. 2. THREE-QUARTER SPAN GLASSHOUSE

farms never see a pond or river. But, like ducks, their eggs are more likely to be fertile if the geese have access to water.

See also POULTRY.
See also Vol. II: GEESE (WILD).

GERANIUMS, *see* BEDDING PLANTS; HOUSE-PLANTS.

GLADIOLI, *see* BULBS, CORMS, AND TUBERS.

GLASSHOUSES. 1. These can be used for forcing ordinary English garden plants to make them flower or fruit out of season. They can also be used to get early germination of seeds and to bring on young half-hardy plants which can be moved into the garden as soon as the weather allows. Also, tropical plants unsuited to the English climate can be provided in glasshouses with an artificially made climate in which they will flourish. The term glasshouses includes the little lean-to unheated greenhouse to be found in a great number of English gardens, the elaborate system of hot-houses belonging to large estates, public parks, or botanical gardens where one house may be devoted to a single type of plant, and the acres of glass belonging to large market-gardens, often called glasshouse nurseries.

2. TYPES OF GLASSHOUSE. There are three main types—lean-to houses, three-quarter span houses, and full-span houses. The lean-to type is built against a wall facing south or south-east, and is used most often for early fruit, such as vines, peaches, figs, or tomatoes, which can be grown up against the wall (Fig. 1). The three-

quarter span type is also built against a wall but has a more elaborate framework, as can be seen in Fig. 2. These are the most common ones in small private gardens, and are often used as unheated greenhouses. The glasshouses of market-gardens are usually of the third type—the full-span—where generally a number of spans are built together to form a block or range that can be heated from one source of heat. The full-span houses can be of two types—the vinery type for low-built houses, and the aeroplane type for high-built houses (Figs. 3 and 4). The aeroplane type is used for plants needing the maximum amount of light and air, such as carnations, tomatoes, and chrysanthemums.

3. GLASSHOUSE CONSTRUCTION. (*a*) *Building.* The house should be situated on a level piece of ground on a site that gets the maximum amount of sunlight. The foundations and solid walls are made of brick or concrete. The framework is usually of wood, though aluminium, various alloys of steel, and reinforced concrete are also used. Prefabricated types of greenhouses of these materials, built in sections and easily put up, can be obtained. The wood and metal are painted to preserve them. Large panes of glass are better than small ones as they admit more light, but they are also more expensive. English glass (21 oz. grade) is the best, but Dutch light glass (24 oz. grade), which is rather thicker, is used a great deal. Glasshouses in which pot plants are grown, such as conservatories, must be fitted with shelves or staging, set at the height of the walls so that the plants can get the full benefit of the light from the glass roof and walls. The ideal staging is made of corrugated iron or asbestos sheeting, supported on wooden or brick

FIG. 3. VINERY TYPE OF GLASSHOUSE   *McCann*

uprights. The staging is covered with an inch or two of gravel which absorbs the moisture when the plants are sprayed with water, and keeps the pots moist and cool. In a general-purposes glasshouse there should be at least one high shelf under the glass roof where boxes of seedlings can be put near the light so that they may grow stocky and strong. Glasshouses in which crops such as tomatoes or vines are planted do not need any staging.

(b) *Heating.* Some houses need only enough heat to keep out the frost in winter; others must keep a hot, moist, even temperature throughout the year; it all depends upon the type of plants grown. Where there are a number of glass-houses, a succession of different temperatures from cold to tropical can be kept in different houses. For effective general use a minimum air temperature of 55° F. should be maintained. The most common form of heating is by means of a boiler and pipes through which hot water is circulated, the number of pipes varying according to the amount of heat required. Usually the boiler is at the lowest level, and often sunk a few feet below ground. The flow pipes are attached to it at the top, and are on an ascending slope, and convey the hottest water outwards; the return pipes, continuing the circuit, gradually descend until they return to the lower part of the boiler, bringing back the cooled water for reheating. Some large glass-house nurseries heat the water by steam, which is generated in a steam boiler, and then taken to the house in narrow, well-lagged pipes, and forced into the pipes that convey the water. The cooled water is returned to the boiler to be reconverted into steam. Where this steam is available, it can also be used for soil sterilization (*see* POTTING).

Glasshouses are also heated by electricity, but this, though efficient, is expensive, and is usually only used for small houses. It has the advantage that a thermostat will automatically keep the temperature at a given level without wasting current. Special oil lamps are also useful for keeping the frost out of small houses. The lamps can be fitted with pipes for radiating the heat.

Electric soil heating cable is being increasingly used in FRAMES (q.v.) outside and in propagating cases within the greenhouse. This is like the wire of an electric fire except that it only becomes warm. It may either be run directly off the

John Topham

FIG. 4. GLASSHOUSES OF AEROPLANE TYPE UNDER CONSTRUCTION

The spans are supported by concrete posts with a partition wall running down the centre of the group

mains, when it must be carefully insulated, or through a transformer, when it operates at 4 or 6 volts and need not be insulated. The spacing of the cable and the depth at which it is buried depend on the plants concerned and their stage of growth; makers usually give suitable advice with their products. Electric soil heating produces a bottom heat which promotes rapid root growth, and is especially effective for quick germination and rooting of cuttings (*see* PLANT PROPAGATION).

(*c*) *Ventilation.* The glasshouse must have enough fresh air so that the temperature and atmospheric moisture can be regulated. Uncontrolled ventilation reduces the moisture in the house and causes a fall in the temperature. All glasshouses need ventilators along the top, and generally there are also others built into the brickwork at the bottom of the house. Side ventilators or windows that open are also desirable for all except very hot houses. Ventilators should be opened a little at a time when the temperature is rising, and closed again gradually before the temperature has fallen far. Plants are very sensitive to draught, and the ventilators on the leeward side only should be opened, especially when there is a north or east wind.

Atmospheric moisture is quite as important to the plant as water at the roots, and most greenhouse plants die quickly if the air becomes dry. The usual fate of the florist's cyclamen in the living room is an example. During hot weather, it is necessary to create moisture in the air by thoroughly wetting the floor and walls of the greenhouse several times a day; most plants also appreciate direct syringing of the foliage with a fine spray. During rainy weather the opening of the ventilators is often sufficient, and in cold weather too much air dampness may be actually harmful unless the greenhouse is kept warm. Ventilation and damping go together, and the right amounts according to inside and outside conditions can only be learnt by experience, though the principles are simple.

4. LIGHT AND SHADE. Plants cannot grow properly without plenty of light; and as glass, even when kept clean, only transmits about 90% of the light, the plants may easily suffer from too little light during the short days of winter, and in consequence grow 'drawn' and 'leggy'. Experimental work is being done in Britain, America, and Russia on 'overhead irradiation', that is, the use of electricity supplied in special lamps of long, tubular shape to add to the time of natural sunlight (*see* PLANTS, SCIENTIFIC CONTROL). Tender plants may, however, be wilted and scorched by too strong a sun, and some houses are therefore fitted with blinds on rollers that can be raised and lowered as needed. A cheaper method of providing shade is to give the glass roof of the house a thin wash of lime or distemper during a hot spell of weather.

5. WATER-SUPPLY. If possible the glasshouse should be fitted with an inside water tank so that the water used on the plants is of the same temperature as the house. The rainwater that falls on the roof of the house, and possibly on neighbouring roofs too, should be caught in the gutters and run through a pipe into this tank, for rainwater is much better for plants than 'tap' water. If there is no tank, however, the tap

water should be drawn and kept standing in cans for some hours in the house before being used.

6. HOT-HOUSES AND SPECIAL HOUSES. (*a*) *Stove house.* This is the hottest kind of glasshouse, used for tropical plants that need a temperature between 65° and 85° F. (*see* GREENHOUSE PLANTS.) The type of house used is generally a three-quarter span or full-span vinery type, and the house is often partly sunk below the level of the ground in order to conserve the heat better. There are at least six rows of pipes, and the house is ventilated by a few top ventilators. A brick, concrete, or tiled path runs down the middle of the house. Inside the roof is a roller blind for shade in the summer and for protection at night in the winter.

(*b*) *Propagating house.* This is used for producing new plants from seeds or cuttings, the temperature depending upon the type of plant that is being propagated. The most convenient type of house is a low, narrow, full-span type with a staging 3 foot wide on each side of a central path. The hot-water pipes are usually run under the staging so as to provide bottom heat for the propagation frames on the staging. In warm houses the water tank should have a hot-water pipe running through it.

(*c*) *Orchid house.* If a great variety of ORCHIDS (q.v.) are to be grown, at least three houses, each providing a different temperature, will be needed. The cool house should have a temperature of 50° to 60° F., the intermediate house 60° to 70°, and the tropical or warm house 70°. A soft-water tank inside each house is essential, for this not only provides water at the right temperature for the plants but also helps to keep the atmosphere moist. Low, narrow, full-span houses with top and bottom ventilators are best. Each house must have roller blinds for shade. In addition to the slatted staging upon which the pots are stood, there should be a dummy staging a few inches below, covered with shingle and kept damp.

(*d*) *Alpine house.* This house needs little or no heat, but it must have plenty of light. It is used for the growing and display of alpine and ROCK-GARDEN PLANTS (q.v.), particularly those that cannot stand the wet of an English winter. A narrow full-span house with top and bottom ventilators and a central path with slatted staging on each side is most suitable.

See also GREENHOUSE PLANTS; FRAMES, GARDEN; CLOCHES,

GOATS. Goats are kept for the sake of their milk, or for meat, or in some cases for their hair (*see* HAIR TRADE, Vol. VII). The GOAT (q.v. Vol. II) is naturally a mountain animal. It is hardy, can do well on poor pasturage, and can stand a fairly hot climate. Goats, therefore, are suitable animals for Mediterranean countries such as Greece, Cyprus, and Malta, where they are kept in large numbers and are the main source of milk. The goats that give most milk, however, are found in temperate countries, such as those of northern Europe and North America, though in these countries they do not seriously compete with cows as dairy animals. In Britain there are about 150,000 goats, kept mostly in small herds to supply milk to the household.

There are three Swiss breeds, the Saanen, the Toggenburg, and the Alpine, and one Eastern breed, the Nubian. These have been imported into Britain and crossed with the one remaining native breed, the Old English. Thus we have the British Saanen, the British Toggenburg, the British Alpine, and the Anglo-Nubian. There is also in Britain the Anglo-Nubian Swiss, which is the result of selective crossing between various native and imported goats to develop size, stamina, and milk yield. Individuals of the breed vary a good deal in appearance, though most generally resemble the Swiss breeds.

The goat has a coat of coarse hair, usually quite short, but very long in the case of the Angora goat, a native of Turkey, which is bred for its hair. Most males and many females of all breeds have beards, and many goats carry hair-covered growths on each side of the neck called 'tassels', or sometimes 'doddles' or 'wattles'. Most breeds were originally horned, but breeders, finding horns a nuisance, have tried to breed them out. They may still appear, however, even on kids of hornless parents. By treating the horn buds with caustic potash or some such substance when the kids are 3 days old, the horns can be prevented from developing. This is known as 'disbudding'.

A young goat is called a 'kid'; a male yearling is a 'buckling'; a female yearling, a 'goatling'. An adult male (over 2 years) is called a 'buck' or a 'billy', a female being a 'nanny'. The female goat is 'on heat', or 'in season', that is ready for mating, at intervals of 3 weeks during the mating season (September to February). Usually she is not mated until she is about 18 months old, though sometimes rather earlier if she is very

BRITISH SAANEN NANNY

BRITISH TOGGENBURG GOATLING

BRITISH ALPINE BILLY

Horace Hall

ANGLO-NUBIAN NANNY

well-grown. Too early mating may retard her growth. It is usual to breed from the females once a year, mating them 7 or 8 months after the previous kidding. If, however, the goat is not mated again at once, she may continue to give milk for 2 years or even longer. A Stud Goat scheme has been organized by the Ministry of Agriculture and the British Goat Society, so that for a small fee smallholders can mate their nannies to billy goats of good strain which are kept specially for breeding.

The kids are born about 5 months after mating, generally about March or April. There are usually one or two at a birth, though triplets and quadruplets are not uncommon. The average weight of a new-born kid is about 8 lb. The male kids are generally either destroyed at birth or killed for meat at 6 to 10 weeks old, only the best being kept for breeding. Many goat-breeders 'hand-rear' their kids, bottle-feeding them from birth, or from about the 4th day, drawing off the milk from the mother. If, however, the kids are being reared by the goat, they may be weaned at 2 or 3 months, though they do better if they are fed by their mother until they are 6 months old. When weaning them, the milk should be gradually reduced and replaced by skim milk and cod-liver oil, or calf meal. The weaning should not be completed until the kid is at least 3 months old.

Normally goats should be milked twice a day, at fixed times, preferably 12 hours apart. The method of milking is the same as for a cow (*see* CATTLE, CARE OF). Goats' milk is whiter and different in taste from cows' milk. It has smaller fat globules, which makes it not so suitable for butter-making, but good for cheese-making. It is easily digestible for the same reason. A good milker gives from 6 to 8 pints a day when her yield is highest, and may total about 200 gallons in a year; a moderate milker gives from 80 to 120 gallons a year. The British and Swiss breeds are the best milkers, though 'strain' (that is, the qualities of the direct ancestors) is of great importance, as milking qualities are inherited, often through the male parent.

At night and in bad weather, goats are generally kept in a goat-house At other times they may be on 'free-range', running loose in a grass paddock, when they get plenty of fresh air and exercise, and can find a considerable amount of their food by grazing and browsing. As they are good jumpers fencing them is often a problem, and electric fencing is sometimes the best solution. When free range is not possible, goats may be 'herded'—taken out to browse on the roadsides, woodlands, and waste land. They usually soon learn to follow their owner about and to keep within call. Frequently, goats are kept tethered, either with a chain and pin, or, if there is enough room, with a chain threaded on a wire stretched along the ground. This allows the goat a greater range. If a tethering pin is used, it has to be moved several times a day. Some kind of shelter must be provided unless the goat is to be brought indoors when the weather is bad. The goat must be tethered well out of reach of trees; otherwise it will strip the bark off and kill them.

Sometimes goats are kept 'intensively', that is, stall-fed, living indoors with only a yard for exercise, and having their food brought to them. In all cases the goat-house must be dry, well-ventilated, and free from draughts, and wheat straw, hay, or bracken bedding can be used. The milking goats can be tied up in stalls or kept in loose-boxes as the younger goats are. If a billy is kept, he is generally housed away from the milking goats, as he has a rather strong smell, which may taint the milk.

A goat is a RUMINANT (q.v. Vol. II), that is, it chews the cud. It can eat coarser food than a cow can, browsing rather than grazing. Besides grass it likes rough vegetation such as roadside weeds, hedge trimmings, brambles, gorse, and the leaves and shoots of many trees. It can also eat vegetables such as mangolds, cabbages, and kale, and hay made from grass and clover, lucerne, or sainfoin. Although goats on free range or tethered can find much of their own bulk food in summer, they need a supply of hay and roots as well in winter.

In addition, milking goats and the goatlings and bucklings need a certain proportion of concentrated food such as grain, cake, or special ready-made mixtures that are rich in protein and starch (*see* FOODS, FARM ANIMAL). Concentrated food is usually fed at the rate of about 5 ounces for each pound of milk the goat gives, and it is given in two feeds, one at each milking. Household scraps, such as stale bread dried in the oven, can take the place of some of the starchy concentrated food, and older goats can be given carrot tops, the outer leaves of cabbages and cauliflowers, pea and bean haulm, Brussels sprouts stalks split lengthwise, and cooked potato peelings. Goats are also fond of dried nettles and dandelion leaves, and ripe, dried acorns and chestnuts may be fed in limited quantities to adult goats. A goat when kidding needs plenty of laxative food—green stuff or bran mashes, for example.

Goats, though very hardy creatures, have, of course, their troubles, one of the commonest being PARASITIC WORMS (q.v.). A good deal can be done to prevent infection by frequent changes of pasture land and regular disinfection of the goat house; but when it does occur, the goats should be 'drenched' with a liquid medicine. 'Scour', a kind of diarrhoea, attacks goats if they eat wet or too juicy grass, or kids if they take milk too quickly or at the wrong temperature. The white of an egg given in a tablespoonful of water instead of one of the feeds should cure a kid. Goats browse so freely that poisoning is not uncommon, especially from rhododendron leaves, or from yew, laurel, box, laburnum, ivy, ragwort, or wild clematis. A vet should be sent for in a case of poisoning, but in the meantime a large teaspoonful of bicarbonate of soda in a tablespoonful of melted lard is an effective first aid.

To prevent disease and injury to the feet, the horn of the hoof should be trimmed about once a month. Running on hard ground helps to keep the feet in good condition.

See also ANIMAL FARMING, TROPICAL, section 3.
See also Vol. II: GOAT.

GOOSEBERRIES, *see* CURRANTS AND GOOSEBERRIES.

GOURD VEGETABLES. These include the marrow, the pumpkin, and the squash, and all, like the CUCUMBER (q.v.), belong to the family *Cucurbitaceae.*

1. MARROW. The large, oblong, smooth-skinned fruits of *Cucurbita Pepo*, a trailing vine-like annual plant, have long been used in the unripe condition as a vegetable, and have been called marrows because of their soft flesh. It is difficult to separate clearly the different kinds of squashes, marrows, and pumpkins on a botanical basis. The marrow, however, belongs mainly to European gardens and the squash mainly to American. Bush varieties have now been produced, and both these and the trailing kinds have long fruits which are green, white, striped, or variegated.

The marrow is easy to grow, its chief requirements being a rich soil, warmth, and moisture. The trailing type is often grown in odd corners of the vegetable garden, on old compost or manure heaps or allowed to climb over a fence or garden shed. The bush type, however, is grown in rows, the plants being spaced about 4 feet apart. Marrows are raised from seed sown in pots or boxes under glass during April and May. As they are tender and easily damaged by frost, they are not usually planted in the open until late May or June. Generally the first autumn frost kills the plants. The fruits are cut when still immature, that is, before the outer rind begins to harden; though they are sometimes allowed to mature and then hung in some frost-proof place for use in the winter. Very young marrows, cut when they are only 3 or 4 inches long and cooked whole in their skins, make a delicious vegetable.

2. PUMPKIN. The large yellow fruits, often 50 lb. or more in weight, of some varieties of *Cucurbita Pepo* and *C. moschata* are used as a winter vegetable, being preferred by some people to stored marrow. In Elizabethan days the name was pumpion—a name still occasionally heard in some parts of England. The pumpkin is grown much like the vegetable marrow, requiring a well-manured soil and plenty of water throughout the growing season. It should not be grown on manure heaps, but on the garden land. It needs a good deal of space for development. The fruits are left on the plants until the autumn, when they are removed to a dry, cool, but frost-proof store. Under suitable conditions the pumpkins will keep in good condition for several months.

3. SQUASH. Some kinds of summer marrows and pumpkins, *C. Pepo*, are known as summer squashes, but squashes are mainly the fruits of *C. maxima*. The squash is a popular vegetable in the United States. There are both summer and winter squashes, the former being used fresh like marrows and the latter being stored when mature for winter use. The most popular squashes are those of the Hubbard group. Squashes are grown just like marrows.

See also CUCUMBERS.

GRADING-MACHINES. Some farm crops, particularly those crops that are sold off the farm instead of being consumed by the farm's own livestock, have to be sorted into different sizes. Potatoes are sorted into large ones sold for eating, called 'ware', medium sized ones to be used for seed, and the smallest ones, the 'chats', to be used for feeding to pigs and other livestock. Fruit going to market, especially apples, is graded so that each box sold shall

Sutton & Sons

VARIOUS KINDS OF EDIBLE AND ORNAMENTAL MARROWS

Farmer & Stockbreeder

POTATOES BEING FED ON TO A SORTER

This machine has two riddles, one above the other, which shake to and fro. The largest potatoes travel to the end and fall into the sack on the right. Smaller ones fall through the upper mesh to the lower riddle and travel to the sack on the left. The very small potatoes pass through both riddles and out by the spout into the bucket

can be graded in them without being broken. The slope of the floors of the passages is so gentle that the eggs roll along them only very slowly. No machine has yet been invented to sort the very soft fruits, like strawberries and raspberries, without spoiling them; nor are there any machines for sorting fruit according to its quality. There is, however, a most ingenious adaptation of the selenium cell, or 'electric eye' (*see* VALVES, THERMIONIC, Vol. VIII), which sorts out red ripe tomatoes from green unripe ones. Damaged and misshapen fruit has to be picked out by hand; but this can be done much more conveniently when the fruit is passing along the conveyor of a sorting-machine than when it is in a heap.

contain fruit all of about the same size, and fruit for canning, such as plums, is sorted so that the contents of a tin shall be uniform.

Potatoes are sorted by being shaken through sieves. In some machines the sieves are in the form of a rotating wire cage; in others the sieves or riddles are flat, but are sloping and are kept shaking by a power-driven wheel. Brussels sprouts also are sorted by sieve, and if the sprouts are firm and compact, the leaves take no damage from the wires. When the sieve method is used for grading fruit, the wire of the riddle is coated with rubber, or a rubber mat with accurately cut holes is used instead of the wire sieve.

Apples and pears are often graded by weight instead of by size. The fruit travels along a conveyor over weight-balanced trap-doors; as each fruit comes over a trap-door which its weight will open, it falls through into a padded box. The trap-doors which will open only under heavier pressure are at the beginning of the travel of the conveyor, and those opening to lighter pressure are towards the end of the travel. Machines working on this principle, but usually constructed in the form of a rotating turntable, are made with so delicate an action that eggs

Corn is graded for size. Stationary threshers have rotary screens to sort the grains into 'tailings corn', 'seconds corn', and the biggest and best, 'head corn'. Combine harvesters have no graders, and if it is necessary for the crop to be sorted for size, this must be done in the barn or granary, in a machine which usually combines a rotary screen with a winnowing fan to clean the grain.

See also BARN MACHINES.

GRAFTING, *see* FRUIT PROPAGATION.

GRAIN DRYING, *see* HARVESTING (GRAIN).

GRAPEFRUIT, *see* CITRUS FRUITS.

GRAPES. Grapes are the fruits of several kinds of climbing plants called vines, the best known of which has the scientific name of *Vitis vinifera*, meaning the 'wine-giving vine'. This is native to the countries bordering the Mediterranean Sea, where it has been cultivated for thousands of years. It was an important crop in the days of the ancient Greeks and the Romans, and the latter probably introduced it to Britain. In medieval Britain, especially in Worcestershire and Gloucestershire, vineyards were quite common, and the monasteries were the great wine-makers. But after the dissolution of the monasteries by Henry VIII vine-growing began to die out.

Nowadays, grapes are grown as an outdoor crop not only in the Mediterranean countries but also in central Europe, southern Germany, California and other parts of the U.S.A., South Africa, and Western Australia. Grapes are also the source of currants, raisins, and sultanas, which are important products in many countries, especially in Greece and Asia Minor. To prepare these, grapes of special varieties are left on their vines until very ripe, and are then dried in the sun. Grapes thrive best in countries with a warm and sunny summer season, and although they are hardy, it is generally found that the climate of England does not provide a long enough warm ripening season for the fruit to mature fully, except in favourable situations.

Grape vines are grown as a rule from cuttings, each about 1 foot long, which are first 'struck' (made to form roots) in a nursery bed, and then transplanted to the vineyards. In many parts of Europe it is necessary to graft the choicer kinds of grapes on to the roots of American vines. This is done because their own roots would be attacked and killed by a tiny insect called the vine-louse, or *Phylloxera*, which was introduced into Europe from America, quite accidentally, about the year 1880. This pest, however, does little or no damage to the roots of the American kinds. Attempts to introduce European varieties of grapes into America have generally failed because of the *Phylloxera*.

The vineyards in which the grape vines are grown are formed on light and well-drained soil, often on hill-sides so steep that the ground has to be built up into terraces. Newly planted vines take 3 years to come into bearing, but after that they continue to yield fruit each autumn for very many years. In its prime a single vine may produce 20 lb. or more of fruit. They are planted in rows about 8 feet apart, leaving 6 feet between the plants in each row.

Supports have to be provided, and the young vines are often trained on trellises of wire, about 6 feet high, supported on wooden poles. In parts of Italy they are sometimes trained on the living stems of small elm, maple, and mulberry trees. The vines are pruned hard to encourage the growth of the young wood on which the grapes are borne. In winter their long, thin, woody stems are leafless, but in the spring the broad-lobed green leaves appear, followed by curved tendrils with which the vines cling to their supports. Later come clusters of small greenish flowers, and from these the grapes develop in heavy, green or purple, hanging clusters that ripen about September in countries north of the Equator. Vines are sometimes grown as standards without supports. The canes are cut back to short stubs on a short, stocky trunk each year after harvest, and from buds on these the new wood grows, bearing fruit near the trunk.

Once the vineyard has been established, its care consists of weeding, manuring, pruning, and training, and the gathering of the annual crop or 'vintage'. Many helpers, both men and women, are needed to pick the clusters of grapes and to carry them to the ox-carts or lorries that convey them to the wine presses. Dry and sunny weather is needed for a good vintage, and rain may ruin the crop or make it unfit for the finer kinds of wine. The precious juice must be pressed from the grapes a few hours after they are gathered.

Although the character of the wine is decided by the vintner, its quality depends on the variety of grape used, the soil of the vineyard, and the weather during the growing season. Wines of the highest quality are only produced in certain seasons, known as 'vintage years' (*see* WINE-TRADE, Vol. VII).

Dessert grapes, for eating as fresh fruit, are grown on a large scale in southern Europe and the United States of America. In Britain they are raised in greenhouses known as 'vineries'. Some of these vineries are very old—indeed some vines over 400 years old are recorded. A famous vine at Kippen in Stirlingshire, Scotland, is reported to be the largest vine on record. Its main stem is 46 inches in circumference and the vine stretches 300 feet in width. It has been known to yield 3,000 bunches in a season. The famous vine at Hampton Court, which is about 180 years old, is also very large. Vines grown in Britain, whether out of doors on a south wall or under glass, are usually trained to spread in horizontal branches from a strong vertical central stem, much as a wall pear is trained. Sometimes they are grown from four vertical branches. Black Hamburgh, the variety of the Hampton Court vine, is a good outside black grape, and

A HERBACEOUS BORDER AT THE WICK, HYDE HEATH, BUCKS., IN LATE JULY

Oil-painting by Beryl Sinclair

E. O. Hoppé

VINEYARDS IN TERRACES ON THE BANKS OF THE RHINE
In the foreground are vines trained on sticks and planted in terraces similar to those on the opposite bank of the river

Royal Muscadine is, perhaps, the best outside white grape.

Beside *Phylloxera*, grapes suffer from that common pest of wall fruit, the Red Spider mite, which is best prevented by a derris spray, and also by syringing the undersides of the leaves with water and giving plenty of water to the roots. Bordeaux mixture was first used on vines in the vicinity of Bordeaux in France. Vines also are attacked by the fungus disease Powdery Mildew.

See also FRUIT-GROWING; FRUIT SPRAYING; PRUNING.
See also Vol. VII: WINE-TRADE.

GRASS-DRYING. In recent years grass, instead of being made into hay in the fields, is sometimes carried green and dried artificially by hot air in a drier. Fresh young grass contains as much as 80% of water and must be dried until no more than 8% of moisture remains. This is a reliable way of preserving grass for winter forage, for it is independent of weather conditions yet, unlike SILAGE (q.v.), does not alter the chemical make-up of the plant. In this way, also,

it is possible to preserve young grass that is too short to be made into hay by normal means, and which has a much higher feeding value than grass cut at the flowering stage. In fact, dried grass is so rich a food that it can take the place of cakes and meals in the winter feeding of livestock (*see* FEEDING, FARM ANIMALS).

The short, damp grass, cut when it is only a few inches high, is not as easy to gather from the field as hay. It can, however, be collected with a special kind of sweep, called a buck-rake, with tines set close together, which is attached to the rear of the tractor instead of the front. A special kind of wagon loader is used to load the green grass on to the wagon to take it to the drier.

All hay-driers, though they differ in design, work on the principle that hot air from a coke or oil-fired furnace is drawn through the wet grass until it is sufficiently dry. The dried grass must be much drier than hay so that its bulk may be packed under pressure into tight bales, or ground into a meal and packed in bags, without the danger of its going mouldy or fermenting.

Farmer & Stockbreeder

GRASS BEING FORKED ON TO THE CONVEYOR OF A GRASS DRIER

On the right is the oil-burning furnace. Hot air blown through the grass on the conveyor dries it as it passes slowly through the machine

The wet grass is put into large ovens, either packed into trays with perforated bottoms through which the hot air can pass, or drawn through the oven on an endless belt, or cascaded inside a revolving drum in which the hot air circulates. Drying usually takes about 30 minutes if the grass is not wet from rain or dew, and the average output from most driers is about 3 to 4 cwt. of dried grass per working hour.

Unfortunately grass-drying furnaces are at present so expensive that the cost per ton of grass is very high. Grass-driers, therefore, are used only where there is a large acreage of grass for drying. In some districts farmers can take their grass to central drying-plants; but the transporting of heavy wet grass to the drying plant is so expensive that most farmers still use the simpler and cheaper process of haymaking to preserve large quantities of grass for the winter.

See also GRASSLAND; HAYMAKING.

GRASSES. At first sight all the grasses seem much alike, except when they are in flower. Some, however, make early growth in the spring, whilst others remain dormant for several weeks longer; some are very leafy, others stalky; some recover rapidly from cutting or grazing, others do not; some are long lived, whilst others die out after the first or second year's growth;

some grow only in tufts, others creep along the ground or through the soil; some prefer damp soils and others dry; some grow best on a deep soil, and some prefer a shallow one. The usefulness of any particular piece of grassland, therefore, depends upon the plants of which it is composed, and when it is sown down to grass, great care must be taken to select a suitable mixture of grass and clover seeds. After that, the quality of the turf obtained depends upon the farmer's skill (*see* GRASSLAND).

When grasses are in flower they are not difficult to recognize, but as they are in flower only for a short time each year, and in a grazing field may never flower at all, it is necessary to be able to identify them from their leaf and stem characteristics.

Italian ryegrass, which lives only for 1 or 2 years, and Perennial ryegrass which is much longer lived, are both tufted plants with bright shiny leaves and red bases to the shoots. Perennial ryegrass has a distinctly folded leaf blade, whereas Italian ryegrass, which is the larger and more tufted plant, is rolled (*see* Figs. 1 and 2).

Cocksfoot has a characteristically folded leaf with very flat stems, and just behind the leaf sheath is a piece of white skin called a 'ligule'. Most grasses have ligules, but that of cocksfoot is particularly noticeable. The foliage is a bluish-green, and the plant starts growing in the spring, soon after the ryegrasses which are the earliest of the grasses (*see* Fig. 3).

Timothy, on the other hand, is a late grass and takes a longer time to develop. It is a light green plant with a short, rolled leaf blade, broadest at the point of junction with the stem sheath; and the base of the stem is swollen, like a bulb, and is coloured chocolate-brown (*see* Fig. 4).

Many farmers also use such grasses as rough-stalked and smooth-stalked meadow grass and crested dogstail, which are low-growing grasses of special value for providing a close turf.

Rough-stalked meadow grass is used for moist rich soils; smooth-stalked meadow grass for dry, sandy, and poor soils; and crested dogstail for the more heavy, clay soils (*see* Fig. 5).

Within these different species of grasses are strains with different habits of growth. Some strains produce more leaf than others; some are earlier in the season; some have a prostrate habit of growth well suited to grazing; whilst others are upright and better adapted for mowing and making into hay; their length of life varies considerably too. The seedsman has classified these strains into two big groups, commercial strains and those called indigenous, pedigree, or bred strains. Grasses of the commercial strains are generally rather more stemmy than the indigenous strains, they are not so long lived, nor are they likely to be quite so green during the winter. They are valuable for the fact that they begin growing about a fortnight earlier in the spring, and their seed is much cheaper to buy. To get the good points of both, many farmers now include a proportion of both types in their grass mixtures. The Aberystwyth strains are now very much used, especially for LEY farming (q.v.).

Quite apart from differences in structure, grasses vary in the kind of soil they prefer. Cocksfoot, for example, resists drought and prefers the lighter types of soil, whereas timothy thrives best under heavy clay land conditions. The ryegrasses are less particular and are found on many types of soil, although perennial ryegrass tends to die out after 3 or 4 years on poor, light land, especially if the rainfall is low (under 30 inches a year). In fact, when grown on poor soils all the better grasses tend to die out, and inferior and coarser species, such as bent grass, Yorkshire fog, and the brome grasses, take their place.

Other grasses of a medium quality are likely to be found in many grasslands, among which are the oat grasses, meadow foxtail, and sheep's and meadow fescue. The poorer grasses tend to turn brown in the winter because their leaves cannot withstand the frost, instead of remaining 'winter green' as do the better varieties. Some grasses, however, such as the bromes, which do not make useful pasture in Britain, are valued highly in other countries with a different climate.

See also GRASSLAND; LEYS; HAYMAKING; SILAGE; LEGUMINOUS CROPS.

Harold Bastin

1. ITALIAN RYEGRASS   2. PERENNIAL RYEGRASS   3. COCKSFOOT   4. TIMOTHY   5. CRESTED DOGSTAIL

The Times

ROUGH GRAZING IN THE PENNINES: SHEPHERDS BRINGING DOWN THEIR FLOCK FROM THE HILLS

GRASSLAND. In Great Britain grassland is used not only for grazing but also for the production of hay and dried grass (*see* HAYMAKING) and SILAGE (q.v.), all of which go to feed the farmer's livestock. A field of 'grass' contains a large number of plants—the true grasses, the clovers, and many other miscellaneous plants such as ribgrass, dandelions, and daisies. The proportion in which the grasses, clovers, and weeds are present in any particular field varies a great deal, depending upon the soil, the climate, and the farmer's management. In MOORLAND areas (q.v. Vol. III) the grassland is generally short, rather brown, and hungry-looking, whereas on the banks of rivers where the soil is seldom short of moisture, the grass usually grows green and lush. Near large industrial cities the grassland invariably looks dirty. The acid fumes from the smoking chimney stacks settle upon the soil and in time make it acid; this tends to kill out the good grasses, which are replaced by inferior ones and worthless weeds (*see* GRASSES).

Grasslands may be classified according to whether they are (i) natural, (ii) semi-natural, or (iii) cultivated.

Among the natural grasslands are the hill grazings which are composed of moor mat grass,

bent grass, and fine-leaved fescues intermingled with such plants as heather, bracken, and sedges, the actual proportion of each varying with the altitude, type of soil, and rainfall. Moorland grazings have a low feeding value suitable only for sheep, ponies, and hardy cattle. On the sandy heathlands, common to parts of southern and eastern England, the soil is hungry and lacking in humus, and can only support unproductive plants, and these 'swards' (the farmer's term for turf) are composed in the main of the coarse 'bent grass'. (The origin of this ancient name is uncertain.) Such land has too poor a feeding value to be suitable for farming, though it can be made to grow a close, short turf suitable for golf, racing, and other sports. Another type of natural grassland, the Downs, contains a high proportion of the better grasses, such as ryegrass, crested dogstail, and fine-leaved fescues, together with many leguminous plants such as vetches, and these rolling stretches of grassland provide some of the sweetest natural grazing for livestock.

The prairies of America and Canada, the veldt or savannahs of Africa, the pampas or campos of South America, and the steppes of Russia also provide tracts of natural grassland that feed large numbers of horses, cattle, and

GRASSLAND ON THE DUTCH POLDER

J. G. Van Agtmaal

sheep. The plants that form these grasslands vary in each country, but a number of grasses found in British pastures are also found in other countries, though sometimes under different names. Kentucky blue grass, which is the same as our smooth-stalked meadow grass, is common in America, and cocksfoot and wild white clover are quite common in Australia. The striking difference, however, is the relatively low feeding value of the herbage in some of these areas, especially in semi-arid regions, which accounts for the small numbers of livestock that graze on it and the unrestricted grazing which the animals are allowed compared with the fenced and well tended enclosures of Britain (*see* GRASSLANDS, Vol. III).

Semi-natural grasslands include the many natural swards that have been improved far beyond their original state by the farmer's efforts in manuring and cultivation. Good examples are the 'fattening pastures' of the Midlands and Northumberland and the marsh-lands of Kent, Yorkshire, Lincolnshire, and East Anglia. Not only can these grasslands carry a large 'head' (number) of stock, but both grazing cattle and sheep fatten to a point fit for the butcher on the grass alone, without the need for additional food. (The term 'pasture' is used for land grazed by livestock, in order to distinguish it from the land mown for hay, which is called 'meadow'.) Pastures of this type are largely composed of perennial ryegrass, cocksfoot, and timothy, with a considerable proportion of wild white clover. The improvement has been brought about by the generous use of fertilizers, in some cases by draining, and by the skilful way in which the farmer has allowed his stock to graze. Continuous grazing throughout the season with a large number of animals promotes the spread of wild white clover; undergrazing with only a few animals brings about coarseness of the grasses which in turn will crowd out the clovers; and too early grazing in the spring may so punish the early grasses that they are weakened and may die out. To keep grassland in good condition a farmer must adjust the numbers of animals in each field according to the growth of grass. ARTIFICIAL FERTILIZERS (q.v.) containing phosphate, such as basic slag, are used regularly and generously, and on soils not naturally supplied with LIME (q.v.), this very important plant food is given in addition.

The practice of ploughing up the grassland from time to time is growing, and this cultivated or rotation grassland is likely to be the most important in the future. The idea of treating grass as a crop, and not simply as a natural occurrence, is not new. The system of 'alternate husbandry', whereby cultivated grassland, or LEYS (q.v.) as it is called, is ploughed periodically for arable cropping, has been practised in the north of England and in Scotland for generations. This way of treating grassland, which is called 'ley farming', became much more common during the Second World War. Temporary grass as distinct from permanent grass is usually a richer crop. Soil which is periodically ploughed up is less likely to harbour parasitic diseases harmful to crops or livestock than permanent pastures. Also ploughed up grassland generally grows other crops well and economically, for the fertility from the dung and urine of the grazing animals is stored under the grass, the clover which is in all good leys has enriched the soil with nitrogen, and the fibrous rootlets and turf, when ploughed in, add humus to the soil. Ley farming, however, is not possible everywhere. Some soils, especially clay soils, are difficult to plough and cultivate; arable land needs more labour and machinery than may be available; and under a system that involves stock farming, each field must be both fenced and supplied with water, and this is not always practicable.

The grazing of grassland each year and the removal of hay crops means a loss of plant food from the soil in the form of milk, wool, flesh, hides, or fodder, and this plant food must be returned to the soil in some way. So, on the best farms, grass is treated as any other crop and receives periodic applications of lime, phosphates, potash, and nitrogen, which are the essential plant foods (*see* MANURES). In addition, most farmers harrow their grass fields every autumn or winter to comb out any dead herbage, to spread the animal droppings, and to break the surface of the soil so that the air and water, lime, and fertilizers can reach the roots. Also, if possible, they apply a dressing of farmyard manure to grassland from which they intend to take a crop of hay the following summer.

Like any other crop, grass cannot withstand stagnant water, and so the fields must be well drained, and the ditches maintained in good working order to carry away the surplus water. Grassland also benefits from a good rolling in the early spring to make the soil firm and counteract the effects of the winter frosts which tend to break up the surface.

See also GRASSES; LEYS; HAYMAKING; SILAGE.
See also Vol. III: GRASSLANDS.

GREENFLY, *see* APHID PESTS.

The Times

SHEEP PASTURING ON THE SOUTH DOWNS

GREENHOUSE PLANTS. The greenhouse is usually devoted to the cultivation and display of plants that are not hardy, or whose display is improved by the protection of glass (*see* GLASS-HOUSES). The earliest record of 'glass' protection is by the Romans, who are said to have dug pits, heated by rotting manure or hot-air flues and covered with panes of mica, in which they grew grapes and possibly other tender plants.

Oranges were the first plants to be grown under glass above ground; there are records dated 1619 of a movable structure of wooden frames and glass that was used to protect orange-trees in a garden in the German town of Heidelberg. From this developed the 'orangery', with large glass windows and usually a solid roof—very popular in the 17th and 18th centuries. The orangery was heated sometimes by a slow fire in a pit in the floor, sometimes by furnaces under the floor, or by hot air flues under the floor and in the walls. Before long vines also were forced in such houses, and pineapples were grown by nurserymen in special low pit houses.

Vines and other fruit-trees were also grown on walls protected by glass—at first (about 1700) merely panes set in wooden frames which were placed in position in cold weather; but about 30 years later these panes were set in permanent brickwork to form the other wall of a long narrow 'house', with a sharply sloping tiled roof and glass ends. This is the ancestor of the modern 'lean-to' greenhouse. Later, glass roofs were adopted when it was found that snow did not damage them; and finally full-span houses, with glass on both sides, came into being. The use of metal in greenhouse construction was developed by Sir Joseph Paxton at Chatsworth in 1838, and was used in the great Palm House at Kew Botanical Gardens, about 1850.

Steam heating was first used in 1788, and hot-water pipes in 1827. Once the latter had been made to work efficiently, about 1838, they were almost universally adopted. This development vastly increased the range of plants which could be grown, for it made it possible to provide a moist heat.

In the early days of greenhouses, bulbs—especially hyacinths—pelargoniums (geraniums), myrtles, ferns, fuchsias, primulas, bouvardias, cinerarias, and a species of everlasting flower (*Helipterum*) were much grown, together with roses and arum lilies for cutting.

As early as 1822 nurserymen were sending

Amateur Gardening

A COLLECTION OF HOT-HOUSE PLANTS CULTIVATED FOR THEIR DECORATIVE FOLIAGE
Hot-water pipes run beneath the gravel-covered staging on which the plants stand

pot-plants, grapes, pineapples, and strawberries grown in greenhouses to Covent Garden Market, and from that time on greenhouses have been important in the nursery and market-garden trades. Tomatoes, grapes, peaches, strawberries, melons, and cucumbers are the most important hot-house fruit crops today, and many varieties of pot-plants, such as cyclamens (*see* HOUSE-PLANTS), and cut flowers such as CHRYSANTHE-MUMS and CARNATIONS (qq.v.) are grown, as well as specialists' plants such as ORCHIDS and CACTI (qq.v.). MUSHROOMS and forced RHUBARB (qq.v.) are also sometimes grown in heated greenhouses, though more often in dark heated sheds.

In the 19th century, more than today, greenhouses formed a most important auxiliary of private gardens, and often housed valuable collections of exotic plants. Nowadays, heated greenhouses cost too much for most private gardeners to maintain, and it is mainly in BOTANICAL GARDENS (q.v. Vol. IX) and public gardens that decorative plants needing any considerable amount of artificial heat are grown in any quantity.

THE PALM HOUSE AT CHATSWORTH, BUILT BY JOSEPH PAXTON (NOW DEMOLISHED)

begonia are grown mainly for their ornamental foliage; others for the beauty of their flowers, particularly the various winter-flowering begonias of the Gloire de Lorraine type and other hybrid forms, which need a good deal of skill and attention to grow to perfection. If a visit is paid to Kew, or other large public gardens, during the winter months, these begonias will be found growing in quantities, not only in pots on the greenhouse staging, but also in baskets suspended from the roof.

There are, of course, types of begonia that may be grown without a lot of heat and with less attention. Of these the large-flowered tuberous type with either single or double blooms is the most popular class grown today, either by amateur gardeners or by professionals. Certain varieties of the fibrous-rooted begonia (*B. semperflorens*), although half-hardy and much used as summer BEDDING PLANTS (q.v.), can be grown for winter and spring flowering in the greenhouse, provided a minimum temperature of 50° F. can be given them.

Climbing plants were a special feature in the stove or warm greenhouse and conservatories of the 19th century, and are still to be seen in the conservatories of public gardens. They generally occupy permanent positions in beds of well-prepared soil with ample drainage, often at the base of a pillar or wall where the trailing growth is trained to wires or trellis. The evergreen white stephanotis, the yellow allamandas, the scarlet or crimson clerodendrons, the orange and red gloriosas, and certain species of passion flowers and convolvulus are outstanding among the 'hot-house' climbers. For cooler conditions in the conservatory the purple bougainvilleas, white jasmines, blue plumbagos, and many others are useful climbers.

No greenhouse would be complete without FERNS (q.v.) of some kind, and at one time they received much attention, being allocated special quarters, or ferneries, such as may be seen today at Kew. Many ferns need warm conditions to

To keep greenhouses and conservatories with a constant display of flowering plants, it is necessary to grow, not only large batches of plants in pots and other receptacles, but a great variety of different kinds. Many of them can be grown to perfection only with the aid of much artificial heat, and many need special conditions of moisture. In such gardens as Kew, therefore, specially constructed greenhouses are devoted to the culture of ORCHIDS, tropical WATER-GARDEN Plants, and PALM-TREES (qq.v.).

The 'stove' or very warm greenhouse is heated to maintain a high temperature and humid atmosphere. It is often a low house built over a hotbed, originally made from fermenting waste materials from tanneries, in which the pots were plunged. In this type of greenhouse are cultivated rare exotic 'stove' plants from tropical countries, such as many of the highly coloured ornamental foliaged plants, and flowering plants, such as the Flamingo Plant (*Anthurium*), a 19th-century favourite with brilliant coloured arum-like flowers. The sweetly scented white gardenias and Amazon lilies (*Eucharis*) and the flamboyant orange or red West Indian jasmine (*Ixora*) were other favourites, demanding a good deal of skilled care in their culture.

Begonias have always been popular greenhouse plants. Some species and varieties of

grow successfully, but there are quite a number that may be grown without much heat or even under comparatively cool conditions. Two plants commonly grown and generally called ferns are not true ferns, but are really flowering plants related to the LILIES (q.v.). There are *Asparagus plumosus* and *A. Sprengeri*, both commonly called Asparagus Fern, and grown for the value of their foliage among other plants in the greenhouse and for cutting.

The many kinds of amaryllis (*Hippeastrum*), a genus of bulbous plants producing large trumpet-shaped flowers in early spring, and the scarlet, orange, or yellow clivias, a related South African genus, are very popular for their fine brilliant flowers. They are not very difficult to grow, and do not need much heat.

The winter-flowering poinsettia (*Euphorbia pulcherrima*) is still grown for its brilliantly coloured scarlet bracts or 'floral leaves'. The 'Red-hot Cat's-tail' (*Acalypha hispida*) used also to be a great favourite but is not often seen now except in botanic gardens. To these must be added the well-known arum lily (*Richardia africana*), the white and crimson Scarborough lily (*Vallota purpurea*), the many-coloured streptocarpus, and the rich velvety gloxinia. The Flame Nettle or coleus, of which the varieties of *C. Blumei* are grown also for their flowers, are popular foliage plants.

Because of the cost of maintaining stove plants, the demand today tends to be for cool or cold greenhouse plants rather than hothouse plants. Present-day conditions have led to the discovery that quite a number of plants, once thought to need a great deal of artificial heat, can be grown successfully under much cooler treatment. A few examples are gloxinias, streptocarpus, various begonias, arum lilies, coleus, and poinsettias.

Annual plants raised from seeds sown either during autumn or spring provide excellent material for spring and summer displays, whilst bulbous plants, such as freesias, African corn lilies (*Ixias*), bugle lilies (*Watsonias*), and montbretias (*Tritonias*), all natives of South Africa, can be grown to provide successional displays. Many hardy BULBS (q.v.) are forced in pots to provide greenhouse winter display, and some FLOWERING SHRUBS (q.v.) can also be successfully forced under glass, though some artificial heat is necessary for the best results. Lilacs, magnolias, the prunus group (peach, almond, and Japanese cherry), flowering crab-apple, forsythias, azaleas,

and spiraeas are all suitable if enough space can be allowed for them to do themselves justice.

Camellias, although now known to be perfectly hardy, were once the occupants of the warm greenhouse. They are excellent evergreens for planting out in a permanent position in a cool conservatory, or for pot culture. Other shrubby plants include the South African heaths (*Erica*), and several kinds of Australian plants, such as the Australian Native Rose (*Boronia*), the Bottlebrush (*Callistemon*), and the Australian heath (*Epacris*). All these may be grown under quite cool conditions.

There are many varieties and types of fuchsia, a great favourite for many years, which, in addition to its usefulness as a pot plant, is also an excellent 'climber' for pillars or roof, provided the strong growing varieties are chosen.

Cyclamens, calceolarias, cinerarias, primulas, CARNATIONS, and CHRYSANTHEMUMS (qq.v.) are popular greenhouse plants, so well known that they hardly need description. They are all suitable for the amateur who has a small, slightly heated greenhouse. The cacti and succulents are also popular coolhouse plants, but their culture is specialized, and they are better grown separately and not associated with other plants. This is also true of Alpine and ROCK-GARDEN PLANTS (q.v.) grown in cold 'Alpine' houses.

The plants mentioned in this article are only, of course, a few examples of the wide variety of greenhouse plants once grown or grown today.

See also GLASSHOUSES.

See also Vol. II: TROPICAL JUNGLE.

GREEN MANURES, *see* MANURES, section **2.**

GROUNDNUTS. These, sometimes known as peanuts, monkey-nuts, or earth-nuts, are the fruit of a small trailing leguminous plant called *Arachis hypogaea*, an annual with egg-shaped leaves and yellow flowers. After flowering, the end of the flower-stalk bends downwards of its own accord and forces the young seed pods into the ground, where they ripen, and from where they are dug out at harvest time. Groundnuts are not really nuts at all, but crinkled pods about 1 inch long, containing two or more round seeds covered with a brownish red skin.

The plant probably originated in Brazil, but is now grown in most tropical countries, and is particularly important in India, Burma, West and East Africa, and the warmer parts of

Crown Copyright Reserve

A GROUNDNUT PLANT BEING LIFTED OUT OF THE GROUND

America. India is the largest producer, the total annual production being about 3 million tons, less of which is now exported as more is consumed inside the country. The crop is mainly grown by smallholders using hand methods; but in recent years it has also been grown on a large scale by mechanical methods, especially in America, which is the second largest producer. Efforts to develop mechanical production are also being made in East and West Africa.

Groundnuts grow best on light, friable (easily crumbled) soils, which the flower-stalks can easily penetrate, and they need a moderate rainfall of from 30 to 40 inches a year: they do not flourish in a wet climate. They are grown from shelled seed sown 9 inches apart, in rows 2 to 2½ feet apart, about 50 lb. of seed being needed to plant 1 acre. The crop takes from 4 to 5 months to mature. The crop is harvested mainly by hand, though mechanical harvesters are used on large plantations. Yields of unshelled 'nuts' per acre vary from about 600 to 1,500 lb. They are usually shelled before they are exported. There are several kinds, 'Spanish' and 'Virginia' being among the best. The crop is not subject to many diseases, the most important being rosette disease caused by a virus spread by aphids (*see* PLANT DISEASES).

Groundnuts are the most important of the oil seeds (*see* OIL-BEARING PLANTS). The oil is used in cooking, as a table oil, and for making margarine and soap (*see* OILS, VEGETABLE, Vol. VII). After the oil has been extracted, the pressed cake, which is very rich in protein, makes a valuable cattle food. Groundnuts are also a useful food for human beings, and can be used in soups, curries, confectionery, or as dessert.

GUAVAS, *see* TROPICAL FRUITS.

United Africa Co.

HARVESTING GROUNDNUTS IN TANGANYIKA

SPECKLED GUINEA-FOWL

A. Rice

GUINEA-FOWL. The common guinea-fowl, or galeeny, is a native of West Africa, where it is still to be found in the wild state. It is a small bird of an average weight of about 3½ lb., grey in colour with white spots.

As table birds guinea-fowls are marketed in February and March, a time when game is out of season and before the spring chicken is ready. The hens begin laying about March, and will lay 100 or so eggs each during the season. They much prefer finding nests for themselves in nettles or brushwood to accepting the nests provided for them. When breeding guinea-fowls, the eggs are generally set under hens or occasionally in incubators. The eggs take 28 days to hatch. Guinea-fowls are usually kept on free range on farms and get much of their own food from insects, weeds, and so on. Sometimes they have a share of the food given to the other poultry.

Cocks and hens cannot be easily told apart except by their voice, for it is only the hen that makes the characteristic cry, which sounds something like: 'Come back! Come back!'

Guinea-fowls, like geese, are good watch-dogs, and will let you know when strangers are about. A farmer who kept both guinea-fowls and Chinese geese (the best alarmists of all geese) said that his dogs never troubled to bark at strangers, but left it to the birds to announce them.

See also POULTRY.
See also Vol. II: GUINEA-FOWL (WILD).

GUINEA-PIGS, or CAVIES (q.v. Vol. II), are bred for exhibition or to be kept as PETS (q.v. Vol. IX), or to be used as laboratory animals in scientific experiments.

It is a common practice for people who breed guinea-pigs for exhibition to sell those animals that are useless for show to the laboratories. To be of use these must generally weigh more than 8 oz.; white or cream are preferred to coloured animals, and the smooth to rough-coated type. The demand, and therefore the price, varies a good deal, but the average price paid in 1950 was between 35s. and 40s. a dozen. Most of the animals are sold to dealers or through the Laboratory Animals Bureau of the Medical Research Council, although some large-scale breeders have direct contracts with hospitals and laboratories.

Usually three sows and one boar are kept together in a pen about 3 by 2 feet, and each sow will, on the average, rear two litters with three or four young ones in each, in a year. The gestation period, the period between mating and the birth of the young ones, is 70 days, more than twice as long as with rabbits. The feeding of cavies is very much the same as that of rabbits. The common diseases include various respiratory infections, 'guinea-pig plague' or paratyphoid, and tuberculosis. These can usually be prevented by clean conditions, though cure is almost impossible.

See also Vol. II: CAVY.

H

HAND TOOLS. Although machines are being used more and more for work on the land (*see* MECHANIZED FARMING), there are still a great many jobs of the farm, forest, and garden that are done by hand with simple tools. This is usually because better or quicker results are got by handwork, or because no machine has yet been invented to do the job: grafting a fruit-tree, shaking up the bedding in a loose-box, or laying a hedge all have to be done by hand. Sometimes

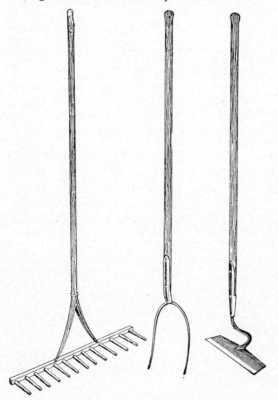

FIG. 1. SOME HAND TOOLS USED ON THE FARM
A hay rake, pitchfork, and swan-necked hoe

the machine is too expensive to use in the particular circumstance: for example, it would not pay to buy a potato lifter to lift the potatoes in a small garden, and so they are dug by hand with a fork.

It is important to know how to use tools in the right way so that the job can be done quickly and well with the least fatigue and without spoiling the tool. The best ways to learn to use a tool are by watching a skilled craftsman at work, and by practice. A skilled workman can swing a hook, a curved knife much used on the farm for jobs such as clearing nettles, for hours at a stretch because he grips the handle in such a way that the right proportion of each stroke comes by movement of the wrist, and the right proportion by movement of the arm. Quite large loads of hay can be lifted with a two-pronged fork without any strain if the fork is manipulated correctly so that the principle of leverage (*see* LEVER, Vol. VIII) is brought into action. Swinging a sharp axe with rhythm and precision can take much of the monotonous hard work out of tree-felling.

Tools must be looked after properly just as machines must. The toolshed of a good gardener is a most orderly place in which every tool has its place. Tools must be cleaned and dried after use, and at intervals they must be greased to prevent their rusting. All tools with edges, such as hooks, scythes, and topping knives, must be kept sharp, and shears and clippers must also be set to make them cut true. Cutting tools are sharpened on a grindstone or whetstone, or by close-toothed files.

Garden tools consist of spades, shovels, forks, rakes, various kinds of hoes, shears and secateurs, trowels, and small hand forks (*see* Fig. 2). On the farm two-pronged and four-pronged forks are used for jobs such as pitching hay or straw or handling manure; hooks and scythes are for cutting weeds and odd patches of grass or opening a way in a corn field for the harvesting-machine. A variety of knives is used, such as hay knives for cutting hay from the rick and topping knives for cutting off the tops of sugar-beet roots, before they are carted off the field (*see* picture, p. 432).

The hedger and ditcher, the thatcher, the forester, and other rural craftsmen all have the special hand tools of their craft (*see* RURAL CRAFTS).

Scything needs considerable skill. The long

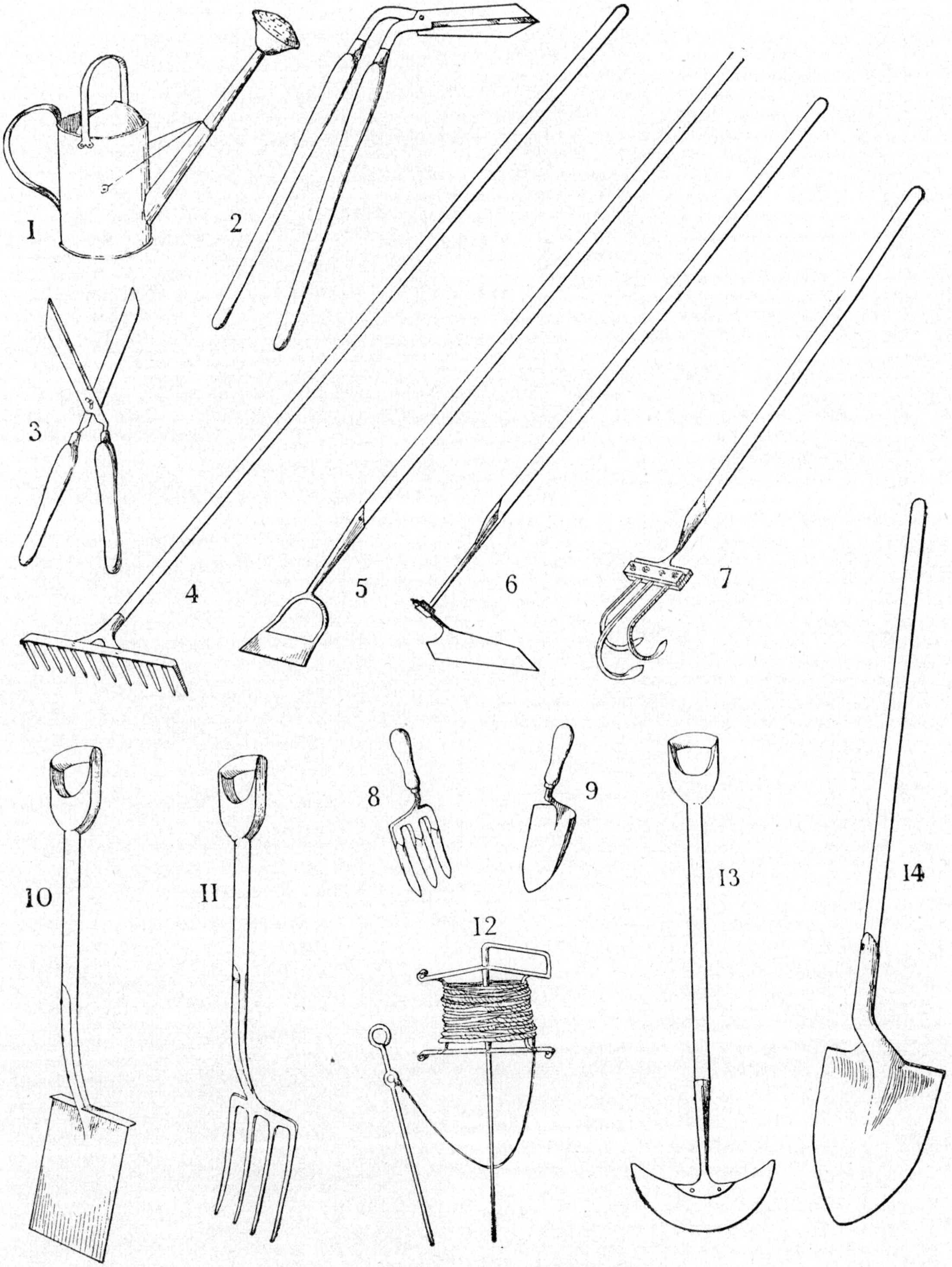

FIG. 2. HAND TOOLS USED IN THE GARDEN

1. Watering-can. 2. Long-handled edging shears. 3. Grass shears. 4. Rake. 5. Dutch hoe. 6. Draw hoe. 7. Three-pronged cultivator. 8. Hand weeding fork. 9. Hand trowel. 10. Spade. 11. Digging fork. 12. Garden line and pins. 13. Edging iron or 'half moon'. 14. Trenching spade

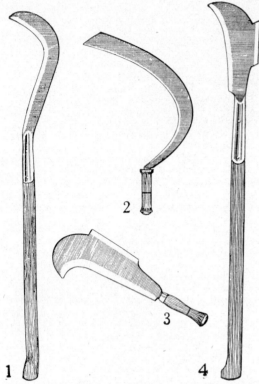

FIG. 3. HOOKS USED IN VARIOUS PARTS OF THE COUNTRY

1. Brushing hook. 2. Bagging hook. 3. Bill-hook.
4. Slasher bill-hook. 1, 3, and 4 are hedging tools and 2
is used for cutting nettles, &c.

sweeping movements possible with a scythe make the mowing of grass or the cutting of corn with this tool much quicker and less tiring than with a hook, because the operator can use both hands and does not have to bend his back. An experienced workman can scythe an acre of grass in a day.

The distinction between a hand tool and a machine is not very easy to define. Generally if a tool has moving parts it is called a machine. Machines, even some that we look upon as automatic, need skill in their use, often quite as great as that needed for hand tools; both skill and experience are needed to use buck-rakes properly, and to get the best results from combine harvesters. Machines such as lawn-mowing machines need human power to push and steer them, and even the motor lawn-mower must be guided by hand. Although on the whole gardeners use only hand operated tools, in market-gardens and large private gardens small motor-driven cultivators, generally with two wheels and handles like a horse-drawn plough, are used for breaking the soil into a seed-bed and hoeing between rows of plants.

See also FARM TOOLS, HISTORY OF.

HARICOT BEANS, *see* BEANS, KIDNEY AND RUNNER.

HARPOONING. A harpoon, a barbed spear with a long line attached, has been used for catching whales and also large fish for many hundreds of years. The Basque fishermen of the coasts of France and Spain used the word 'harpoon' for the weapon with which they hunted whales during the Middle Ages.

Although in modern whaling the hand-thrown harpoon has been superseded by the harpoon-gun, it is still used in native fisheries in the Pacific Islands and Indian Ocean. The people of New Guinea use harpoons for capturing turtles, and sometimes sharks and the huge ray-fishes. The fisherman paddles out to sea in a small boat, and when he has succeeded in harpooning his victim, he tries to exhaust it as quickly as possible, so that he can land it. To do this, he threads on his line, between the harpoon and the boat, a disk of wood, sometimes called a 'retarder', and shaped according to the fancy of the maker. Sometimes it is carved into a rude representation of the great Ox-ray fish, with two horn-like projections jutting out from the front of the head; sometimes it is merely a circular disk, carved on one side with some fantastic pattern; sometimes it is shaped in imitation of the outspread tail of a fish. The retarder acts like a powerful brake, and helps to tire out the victim in its attempts to escape.

James Hornell

HARPOONING THE SWORD-FISH
The fisherman is playing a model of a bonito to lure the sword-fish within reach

Norwegian Official Photograph

SHOOTING THE HARPOON ON A WHALING SHIP

When the animal is nearly exhausted, the fisherman, judging it safe to approach, paddles alongside and spears it to death, or, in the case of a turtle, takes it in tow.

Harpooning the sword-fish is an important local industry in the Laccadive Islands of the Indian Ocean. The bait used for attracting the sword-fish is either a live flying fish, or a black and white wooden imitation of one, about 12 inches long, on the end of a short rod and line. Each fisherman uses one distinctive design for all his lures. When there are sword-fish about, the fishermen put to sea in elegantly modelled boats. One of the crew stands at the prow, holding a long harpoon in his right hand and the rod and line in his left. If he is using an imitation fish, he makes it leap and skip on the waves like a living flying fish. When a sword-fish sees the lure, it makes a rush to seize it. The harpooner has to act swiftly, because if he misses his mark he will not get a second chance. Once the fish is alarmed, it will seek safety in flight.

In 1865 Svend Foyn, a Norwegian, invented a successful harpoon-firing gun that carried a line heavy enough to secure the biggest whale. The harpoon-gun was mounted in the bows of a small steamboat, ready to shoot as soon as a whale should come within reach. The whale, when struck by the barbed harpoon, could not shake or wriggle it off, and so made away at a considerable speed, towing the boat as it went. The aim of the captain of the boat's crew was then to shorten the line and approach the whale close enough to wound it mortally. The great danger was that the whale might dive; and, to counter this, one of the boat's crew, axe in hand, was told off to cut the line at the last possible moment. If the boat's crew were fairly fortunate,

the whale would be 'played' for a long time, as a fisherman plays a fish, and it would eventually become exhausted enough to be approached and killed.

The perfected harpoon-gun of today is accurately sighted, has a bore of $3\frac{1}{2}$ inches, and fires a 6-foot harpoon weighing 1 cwt. This harpoon has an explosive head with a delay fuse. Even after the extensive damage done to it by this weapon, a whale will live for some time unless by chance a really vital spot has been hit. A line is still attached to the harpoon as in earlier days, although it is now made fast to power-winches aboard the vessel. Whales have still to be 'played' for a considerable time. Experiments have recently been made with electric harpoons, which electrocute the whale, and these may eventually replace the weapon with an explosive head.

See also FISHING METHODS; WHALING.
See also Vol. II: SHARKS; TURTLES; WHALES.
See also Vol. IX: BIG-GAME FISHING.

HARROW, *see* CULTIVATORS.

HARVESTING (GRAIN). In Britain corn is usually cut either by reaper-and-binder or by combine-harvester. The reaper-and-binder cuts the corn with a cutter bar in much the same way as grass is cut by a mower. The cut corn falls on to a conveyor—a moving canvas belt which carries the corn to a platform where the machine packs it into bunches. When the bunch reaches a certain size, it ties it automatically with twine. The knot having been tied, the twine is cut from the main supply, and the tied bundle, called a sheaf, is thrown out on to the field (*see* picture, p. 297). In some hill farms where there is little arable land, as on Exmoor, the old-fashioned reaper is still sometimes used, and the sheaves are bound by hand.

The sheaves have to be stood upright in groups over the field so that they shall dry before the corn is carted away to be built into a stack to await threshing. Building the sheaves into these groups, called stooks, has to be done by hand, and the loading of the sheaves on to the carts and wagons is also usually done by hand, with pitchforks.

Nowadays grain is often gathered by the combine-harvester, especially on large farms. The corn is allowed to continue growing until it is very ripe and dry, and then it is cut and

A COMBINE HARVESTER HARVESTING WHEAT

The threshed grain is poured into bags at the top of the machine and the straw is thrown out behind

threshed by one complicated power-driven machine as it travels over the field. The stage of standing the cut corn in stooks on the field is omitted. A form of combine-harvester was used in America before the days of the petrol engine. It was drawn by a large team of mules—perhaps twenty-five or thirty of them—and the turning of its large wheels provided the power for all the operations carried out by a modern harvester, the bags of grain being dropped out and collected by a following wagon.

The conveyor mechanism of a combine-harvester is sometimes a canvas belt, as in the reaper-and-binder, but is often a revolving screw-shaped shank which forces the cut corn along the giant thread of the screw and delivers it into the mouth of a threshing-drum. The threshed grain pours out either into bags which, when full, are thrown out on the field in batches, or into a large tank which can be discharged into bins carried on carts, trailers, or lorries. The straw and chaff left after threshing are dropped out in a long line or swath behind the combine-harvester, often to be picked up from the ground by a pick-up baler, a machine which packs it into bales.

Combine-harvested grain is not as dry as grain threshed out from a stack, because it has missed the period of drying in stooks which generally lasts several days, and also the weeks or months of slow drying in the stack. Usually, therefore, in a country where harvest time is often moist, as it is in Britain, the grain has to be dried artificially by heat to bring it down to about 14% moisture, when it can be safely stored.

There are several kinds of equipment for drying grain. In continuous grain-drying machines the damp grain is elevated to the top of a tower, and is then allowed to trickle slowly downwards inside the tower, meeting a rising current of hot air. The dried grain falls out at the bottom of the tower, and is then cooled by a blast of cold air before being taken away to store. Another kind of drier, the platform drier for bagged grain, consists of a large platform in which are openings about 1 foot by 2 feet, each fitted with a metal grid, on which is laid a bag of damp grain. Hot air from a small furnace, usually oil-fired, is driven by a fan up through these openings, through the bags (which are made of open textured material) and so through the grain. The third method of treatment is a combined drying and storing method. The damp grain is put into a bin with a porous or perforated floor, through which warm air is forced, and the grain slowly dries from the bottom upwards. Electrical heating is generally used for this ventilated bin method of drying grain. Grain drying and storing call for much conveying of the grain from one part of the barn to another, and pneumatic conveyors which force the grain through a tube by air pressure are often used, and so are mechanical conveyors, which consist of endless belts fitted with pockets or buckets to pick up and carry the grain.

In the U.S.A. elaborate mechanical 'corn pickers' attached to tractors are used to harvest the large fields of 'corn' (*see* MAIZE), and these tow a wagon into which the harvested maize is dropped by the picker.

See also WHEAT; OATS; BARLEY; RYE; THRESHING-MACHINE; MECHANIZED FARMING; Colour Plate opposite p. 32.

HAYMAKING. Grass is an ideal food for most livestock, and grazing is the cheapest way of feeding them, since they can then help themselves to it. But grass is not available throughout the year, and provision has therefore to be made for preserving the surplus of the summer grass for use in winter. By good grassland management and the use of better-quality GRASSES (q.v.), it is now possible to provide fresh grass for livestock for at least a month longer than was possible in the days of our grandfathers. Even if there were enough fresh grass, however, animals could probably not graze all the year round because the weather in many places would be too severe for them, and they would also damage heavy land by treading it when wet.

Hay is by far the most important food for the winter feeding of cattle, sheep, and horses. It can be obtained from permanent meadows or from temporary LEYS (q.v.). The term 'meadow' is usually applied to grassland from which a hay crop is removed, and the hay is called 'meadow hay'. A seeds ley provides seeds hay or fodder.

Haymaking depends on the principle that grass can be stored safely without going mouldy when the moisture content, which is about 80% when it is fresh, has been reduced to about 15%. The way hay is made in Great Britain differs in small details from county to county, the actual sequence of operations and the manner in which they are carried out being determined by the

summer rainfall. In dry districts the process is quick and simple, the hay being cut, turned, cocked, and carried within about 3 days. In areas of high rainfall, say over 45 inches a year, however, haymaking can be a prolonged operation causing much anxiety, for every time that the grass is wetted after cutting it loses some of its feeding value.

In general the hay is cut when the majority of the grasses are in flower. The grass is cut by a mowing-machine with a cutter bar about 5 feet wide, which has about twenty-two triangular knives moving to-and-fro over stationary plates (ledger plates). The cut grass falls behind the cutter bar on to the ground, where it lies in a ridge or swath. At the far end of the cutter bar there is a wooden board which directs the grass inwards, so that the swath falls clear of the standing crop. Some mowing-machines are horse-drawn, some are tractor-drawn, and some are directly attached to a tractor.

When the grass is cut it has to be cured, that is, dried into hay before it can be safely stored in a rick. The action of sun and air in drying the grass is hastened if the grass is turned over instead of being left closely packed in the swath;

Eric Guy

MOWING GRASS FOR HAY

The knives on the horizontal cutter bar are driven by the wheels of the machine, which are ridged to help them grip the ground

The Times

HAYMAKING IN HAMPSHIRE

A sweep on the front of the tractor is pushing the hay up to the elevator. The elevator is raised as the rick grows higher

and machines, known as haymakers, do this work. Some of these haymakers are violent in their action, and some are gentle. The tedder is a violent machine with revolving bars, which stir up the swaths and throw the grass well into the air. The swath-turner-and-side-delivery-rake is a gentle machine which can be set merely to turn the swath over onto dry ground so that the underside receives some air and sun, or it can be set to throw two swaths of dried hay into one, ready to be carried (a 'windrow'). The hay is often gathered into heaped up piles, called hay-cocks, ready for carrying. Sometimes the cocks are built on tripods which keep it off the damp ground and allow the wind to blow through it. In Norway and Sweden small quantities are dried by being hung on wires.

Very often a hay-loader is used to pick up the swaths of dry hay and to load them on to a wagon to be carried away to the rick. The hay-loader, which is towed immediately behind a wagon, is a machine with prongs on an endless belt that pick the hay off the ground and carry it over the back of the wagon to deposit it on top of the load. There a man with a pitchfork levels it out so that the wagon is loaded evenly. If a hay-loader is not used, the hay is pitched on to the wagon by hand.

Another way of collecting the hay in a field is by a 'sweep', which is a set of large horizontal wooden teeth or tines fixed in front of a tractor or of a motor-car or lorry. The hay is pushed along the ground instead of being picked up. This method is very quick and needs little labour, but it can be used only on flat fields and in places where the rick is to be built actually in the field where the grass has been grown. Wagons can take the hay along lanes and roads to the place where it is convenient to build the rick.

When the wagon or sweep delivers the hay at the bottom of the rick, some kind of elevator is generally used for lifting it on to the rick. Some-times the elevator is a grapple fork working on a derrick something like the grabs for loading ships; more often it is an endless moving chain with spikes to carry the hay, working in an inclined trough.

Some hay is made not in ricks but in small bales, about 18 inches wide, 2 feet deep, and 3 feet long, and weighing about 80 lb. These bales are then built into stacks. When the time comes to use the hay for feeding cattle, the bales can be carried to the cattle as whole parcels, instead of the feed having to be cut out of the rick with a hay-knife. Sometimes the hay is swept to

BALING HAY IN SURREY

The Times

On the right a side-delivery rake gathers the hay ready for the pick-up baler on the left to compress it into bales

stationary machines called 'balers', placed usually near the centre of the field; but often automatic pick-up balers are used which move across the field, picking up the hay from the ground, baling it, and tossing out the bales on to the field. Pick-up balers generally use twine for tying the bales; stationary machines generally use wire.

Occasionally it may be possible to take two crops of hay in one season, but usually the 'aftermath' or 'eddish', as the second growth is called, is left for grazing or is cut for Silage (q.v.) or drying.

See also Grass-drying; Grassland.

HEALTH (FARM ANIMALS).

A stockman can tell by many signs if the animals under his care are well or not. Some of these indications are common to all animals.

If an animal is not ready for its regular meals, in spite of the food being good, then all is not well. On the other hand, if it always seems ravenously hungry and remains thin, in spite of good and regular meals, then also there is something the matter with it (*see* Feeding, Farm Animals). If a ruminant (a cow, sheep, or goat, for example) stops chewing the cud for a long time, that is a sign that something is wrong. If

the dung of the animal is more liquid or more solid than normal, its digestion is probably upset in some way; the colour of the dung, however, varies according to its food and is not necessarily an indication of health. The temperature, rate of pulse, and rate of breathing are normal in the healthy animal; and for the different kinds of animals there are different normals. A dog's normal temperature, for example, is 101° (compared with 98.4°, the normal for a human being); that of cattle is 101–102°; that of sheep is 104°.

A healthy animal has bright, clear eyes, and the bases of its ears (and also horns of those animals that have them) feel slightly warm to the touch. The noses of cattle, goats, and pigs, as well as dogs, are moist when they are well, and there is no discharge either from the nostrils or from the eyes. The skin of cattle, goats, and horses should be loose on their ribs, and not 'hide-bound'. These animals, and also rabbits, have dense coats which, when the animals are healthy, shine and feel glossy. They are not, however, always smooth, for cold weather makes the hairs rise, and healthy cattle, for example, lick their coats and make them look rough. The opposite of a glossy coat is a harsh and 'staring' one. Pigs can to a certain extent be judged this way too, the skin of an unhealthy pig being scurfy.

A bird's feathers should also look glossy, though the moult, which they all go through, affects their appearance. When a bird goes sick, its comb and wattles lose their colour, but as this also tends to disappear in a bird that has laid a lot of eggs, all the signs must be considered together.

An animal shows its health by its general attitude. A sick animal stands about and mopes, and may try to get away by itself and hide. A healthy one, on the other hand, is alert, moves about freely, and if it is young it often wants to play. If cattle and sheep, especially calves and lambs, stretch themselves when they get up from lying down, that may be taken as a sign that all is well with them.

See also ANIMAL DISEASES; CATTLE, CARE OF; GOATS; HORSES, CARE OF; PIGS, CARE OF; POULTRY, CARE OF; RABBIT-KEEPING; SHEEP.

HEATHS, see PEAT-LOVING PLANTS.

HEDGING, DITCHING, AND WALLING.
As the old 'open-field' system of agriculture gave way to the marvellous pattern of enclosed fields, which is now a characteristic feature of the British landscape (see OPEN FIELDS AND ENCLOSURES), barriers to divide one field from another became important. These are of three main kinds—hedges, ditches (or dykes), and dry-stone walls; the walls are found in the hillier

C. S. Orwin

PUTTING IN THE STAKES OF A LAID HEDGE

districts where there is good stone near the surface, the ditches in flat land which needs drainage, and the hedges, with or without ditches beside them, over the rest of the good farming land. A fourth type of barrier, the fence (post and rails, post and wire, and others) is also much used, especially in the newer countries of the world; and lately the electrified wire fence has been introduced, though this is usually a temporary form of fencing.

1. HEDGES. Hawthorn, also known as white-thorn or quick, is much the most commonly used hedgerow plant; but here and there hedges of blackthorn or sloe have been planted. Many other kinds of tree have been planted locally, or have found their way into hedgerows as chance seedlings; but few except the thorns are robust and prickly enough to resist cattle. The young hawthorn trees for making a new hedge are raised in a nursery, from seed extracted from berries which have been stored in a pit for 18 months. When the seedlings are 2 or 3 years old, and 2 or 3 feet high, they are transplanted, during winter or spring, to the line of the new hedge, being set about 1 foot apart. For the first few years they must be protected against animals by a temporary fence of hurdles or wire. Then they grow stout and strong enough to be 'cut and laid'. If they were left alone, they would grow into tall flowering hawthorn trees; but instead the hedger cuts certain of the branches halfway through with his billhook, and lays them slanting along the line of the hedge, weaving them in and out of the standing stems. This work, known in some districts as 'pleaching', forms a sturdy barrier of interwoven living stems, for the laid branches continue to grow and become firmly interlaced with the upright ones. To give a young hedge more strength, however, stakes are driven in at intervals of 3 feet or so, and their tops are joined together with long thin rods of hazel, which are cunningly inter-twined to form a strong top layer. This part of the work is called 'ethering' or 'heathering' and the hazel rods are known as 'ethers' (see Fig. 1).

After a young hedge has been built up in this way it continues to grow tall, and if left alone would soon become gappy at the bottom, allow-ing farm animals to get through. So every few years the hedger comes round, usually during the winter months, wearing his stout leather gloves and wielding his billhook. First he trims away all the unwanted, thin, top branches, and

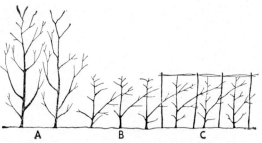

FIG. I. LAYING A HEDGE

A. Before cutting. *B.* Cut and laid. *C.* Staked and 'ethered'

then he picks out stout yet pliable stems to lay slantwise as before, especially across any gaps that are forming; but unless these gaps are large, he will not always need to put in more stakes or ethers. In this way the hedge is brought down to its original height of about 4 feet, and kept thick and sound near ground level. The details of the work vary a little in different districts. Many hedgers leave occasional sapling trees uncut; these grow bigger to form the hedgerow timber that is often useful for farm repairs. Hedges are valued as shelter for live-stock, and they are the homes of many useful insect-eating birds, besides a wealth of beautiful wild flowers (*see* HEDGEROWS, Vol. II). Indeed, in some places where hedges have been replaced with fences, the field crops are suffering from lack of birds.

2. DITCHES. These serve a twofold purpose: to act as field boundaries, and to drain the land. In many districts they are combined with hedges; when the ditch is dug, the earth is raised to form a bank, and hawthorn seedlings are planted on the top. The actual legal boundary is nearly always along the farther edge of the ditch, the man on the 'hedge' side owning both the hedge and the ditch. In the fen country around the Wash and certain other estuaries, no hedges are planted, and the deep ditches are the sole boundary; often they are linked together to form an elaborate drainage system, and different names are used for the main and branch ditches. In Romney Marsh the main dykes are called sewers.

In most kinds of soil ditches are dug with an ordinary garden spade. The line of the ditch is marked out on the ground with pegs and string, and a wooden gauge, or 'template', is made in the same shape as the cross-section of the ditch (*see* Fig. 2). This is always wider at the top than

at the bottom, the slope or 'batter' in the sides of the ditch enabling the sides to remain firm, without falling in. A ditch 4 feet deep and 3 feet wide at the top, for instance, should only be about 1 foot wide at the bottom. It is very important to site the line of the ditch so that it has a steady fall from one end to another, leading the water away to a good outlet such as a stream. The line may be fixed with SURVEYING INSTRUMENTS (q.v. Vol. VIII); but most of our ditches were, in fact, laid out by eye, by men who knew the ground so well that they could judge how the water would flow. Sometimes simple rods, shaped like a letter T and known as 'boning rods', are used to help the workers to 'sight' the line of the ditch so as to keep it straight and with an even fall. The downward slope of the ditch, from one end to the other, must not be too steep or the running water will wash away the

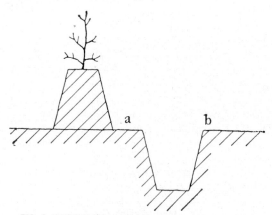

FIG. 2. SECTION OF A DITCH, BANK, AND HEDGE

a. Berm. *b.* Boundary of land belonging to the owner of the hedge

bottom, and the sides will fall in. The fall should be between 1 and 3 feet in every 100. The earth taken from the ditch, called the 'spoil', must be piled well back from the edge, leaving a flat ledge a foot or more wide, called a 'berm'.

In Essex and other counties with a heavy clay soil, a peculiar narrow spade with a curved blade, called a 'graft' is used in ditching. In peaty areas, particularly in Scotland and the north of England, a special 'rutting spade', with a triangular blade shaped like a hay-knife, is used to cut the sides of the future ditch; then the same tool is driven in across the ditch at intervals of about a foot. In this way the peat is broken up into slices, which are lifted out with a special bent fork called a 'hack' or 'drag'. Then the bottom of the ditch is made smooth with a shovel. Special ditch-digging machines are now often used to do this work.

After some years, a ditch tends to become choked with mud and weeds, and so it has to be cleaned out. Most of the work is done with the spade and shovel, but to remove the finer, water-logged mud and silt, special tools called 'scoops' are often required; they have a rounded blade to hold the mud, and some, called 'push' scoops, are pushed away from the user, while others, the 'pull' scoops, are drawn towards him. Ditches are often fed by systems of tile drainage, mole drainage, or open drains, and on most soils they play an essential part in making the land fit for agriculture or forestry (*see* DRAINAGE, LAND).

3. DRY-STONE WALLS. The walls used by farmers as field boundaries are usually built without mortar, and so they are known as 'dry-stone' walls or, in Scotland, 'dykes'. They are found mainly in upland districts where rock comes close to the surface, making it difficult or impossible to divide the fields with hedges or ditches. The kind of stone used varies according to the local stone of the district. The most striking and easily recognized stone is the white limestone which occurs in parts of Derbyshire and Yorkshire; another kind of limestone which is soft brown in colour is used along the Cotswold Hills, which stretch across the English Midlands. Various kinds of sandstone, grey or brown in colour, are used elsewhere, as well as slate and granite. But whatever rock is chosen, it is usually obtained from a quarry, as the surface stone is nearly always too soft and weathered to make a good wall.

The secret of making a sound stone wall that will stand without mortared joints lies in 'building it double'. That is to say, there are two distinct sets of stones, one on each side, and as the wall gets narrower towards the top, these two faces are able to support one another. The 'waller' starts work by marking out the line of the new wall with strings; he also makes a wooden gauge or 'template' to show the required height and also the widths, both top and bottom. A wall 5 feet high needs a width of at least 2 feet at the base, narrowing to 14 inches at the top. Then he prepares the foundations by digging away the turf along the line of the wall, enabling the stones to rest on solid soil. Meanwhile the stone from the quarry is laid in loose heaps along the course that the wall is to follow.

Next the waller picks out the largest and heaviest stones to use as foundations, one or two spreading across the wall's full width. On this base he builds up the sides of the wall with selected stones; as these are irregular in size, he fills up the centre with smaller stones. About one-third of the way up, he arranges a layer of large, long stones called 'throughbonds' because they run right across the wall from one side to the other, binding it together. The wall is then carried up to its full height, using smaller stones as the two sides approach each other. Finally, the top layer is put on, only one row thick; it consists of the 'coping stones', which are usually set on edge and give the wall a firm and finished appearance; sometimes this top layer is set in mortar (*see* Fig. 3).

Wallers usually work in pairs, as some stones are too heavy for one man to lift. The skill lies in so arranging the stones that their weight binds them firmly together, so that they will stand for scores of years. The skilled waller can tell at a glance just where any stone will fit in, and

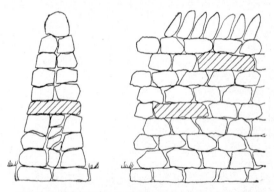

FIG. 3. SECTION AND ELEVATION OF A DRY-STONE WALL
The shaded stones are the 'throughbonds' or 'throughs'

wastes no time handling stones unnecessarily. Anyone climbing across a stone wall should test the stones carefully first; a fall of stone can be dangerous, as well as causing troublesome repairs for the farmer.

In some districts with a peaty soil, where no good stone is available and hedges will not grow easily, the fields are divided by turf walls or banks, built up like a stone wall, but consisting of square pieces of turf, like tiles, about 3 inches thick. A bank 3 feet high should be 3 feet wide at the base, tapering to only about one foot wide

Eric Guy

BUILDING A DRY-STONE WALL IN THE COTSWOLDS

at the top. A hedge of gorse, or a low wire fence, is set along the top to prevent animals getting through, and the heather grows out naturally from its sides. Such banks, which last indefinitely, are very common in east Dorset.

See also RURAL CRAFTS; BOUNDARIES; DRAINAGE, LAND.

HEDGES, *see* GARDEN HEDGES; HEDGING, DITCHING, AND WALLING; BOUNDARIES, LAND.

HEMP, *see* FIBRE CROPS.

HERBACEOUS BORDER. A collection of herbaceous plants can be grown together in such a way as to provide colour and variety throughout the growing season. Herbaceous plants are PERENNIALS (q.v.) which die down above ground every year, although their roots remain alive below ground; thus, herbaceous borders have nothing to show during the winter months, but, at the first hint of spring, a variety of young growth thrusts itself up as the different plants become active once more. From the time of first flowering until late autumn, a well-planned border should give continuous colour (*see* Colour Plate opposite p. 208).

1. CHOOSING A SITE. Although any site can be used, the most satisfactory place in a small garden for a mixed, all-season border is at right angles to the house windows, so that people normally look along the border and not directly at it. The prettiest effects are thus obtained, and any gaps are less noticeable. In bigger gardens several borders can be made to give different effects: for example, there may be a border with a western aspect, which looks particularly beautiful in the long rays of the setting sun; a spring border, which is planned to look at its best early in the year; an autumn border in which there are varieties of such flowers as michaelmas daisies and chrysanthemums; or borders in which one colour predominates (blue, purple, pink, or white borders).

The border should be neither too long nor too short for its width, but should have pleasant proportions that fit the garden as a whole. The background is also important, and in old gardens it may be possible to use distant trees, a wall, an orchard, a rose pergola, or a well-grown hedge. In new gardens a background may have to be planned and made as part of the work of making the border. Quickly growing hedges such as lonicera or a line of trained fruit trees can be planted; hurdles or a trellis, especially of the small square kind with climbers trained on it, can be very effective, and can give a town garden a country effect.

2. PREPARING THE SOIL. The soil should be free from weeds, especially the perennial kinds, and should be well prepared, and rich. A good loam is best, but practically any type of soil can be made suitable. It should be dug two spits deep, and humus should be added in the form of farmyard MANURE or COMPOST (qq.v.). A light soil needs to be enriched with plenty of farmyard manure; a heavy soil needs lightening with humus and also with coarse sand. The soil must be allowed to settle again before the border is planted.

3. PLANNING THE BORDER. The majority of plants in the border should be herbaceous. These can be raised from seed, or bought as young plants from a nursery, or obtained as small rooted pieces from friends' gardens, or reproduced by division, layers, and cuttings, from plants already established in the border (*see* PLANT PROPAGATION).

In addition to the herbaceous plants, ANNUALS, BIENNIALS, other kinds of PERENNIALS and BULBS (qq.v.) are useful to fill up spaces and to get colour all through the year. Annuals such as calendulas (marigolds), larkspurs, and china asters are all easily grown from seed. Pansies,

Amateur Gardening

A HERBACEOUS BORDER AT ERIDGE CASTLE IN KENT

wallflowers, and antirrhinums (snapdragons) are popular biennials; and tender perennials such as dahlias and pentstemons or small shrubs such as lavender can all find a place. Bulbs and corms, not only of the spring-flowering kinds, but summer lilies and autumn gladioli, can fit into the plan. Rock plants, such as arabis, aubrietia, and pinks, can be planted in front of the border (*see* EDGING PLANTS).

Having decided what kind of border is wanted —whether a mixed, all-season border (the easiest and most usual), or a special border of any kind—we can make a list of the plants available, and then draw a plan of the border to scale on paper, and allot places to the various plants, arranging them in clumps rather than scattered individually. A clump may need as few as three or as many as ten or more plants according to the nature of the plants and the size of the border. The shape of the groups is important. 'Drift shapes', that is to say, long and fairly narrow shapes, are most effective because they fit into each other. The heights of the groups must be considered carefully so that the border shall not appear as a series of steps:

tall groups may be allowed to come forward at intervals, and low plants to go well back. A certain amount of repetition of groups of the same kind of plant is good to look at. For example, a bold clump of delphiniums might be repeated at fairly regular intervals along a border: other plants, both big and small, can be planted effectively on this principle.

The habits and needs of the various plants must be studied when planning. For example, phlox and michaelmas daisies need moisture; irises need all the sun they can get and a warm soil; rock plants must have sun and good drainage; pansies and aquilegias (columbines) flourish in semi-shade. Other points to remember are the times at which the different plants will flower and the kind of foliage they have— whether bushy, delicate, spiky, feathery, or solid. In planning a herbaceous border the secret of success is to think of the whole plant, not the flowers only.

4. PLANTING. Suitable weather in late autumn or early spring must be chosen for planting. The border should be marked with stakes to correspond to the paper plan. The plants for a

section of the border should be spread out to correspond with the plan, and then planted where they lie. They must be planted firmly and well watered in. The clumps ought to be plainly labelled, and the trodden soil lightly forked over.

5. CARE OF THE BORDER. In early spring the ground should be lightly forked to break up winter clods; and spaces should be filled up with annuals and biennials. As the summer progresses the border must be kept clean by periodical weeding and light forking or hoeing. As the plants grow they must be staked and tied up. Regular cutting off of dead-heads is important. Many herbaceous plants, such as lupins and delphiniums, will throw up good second blooms in the autumn if the summer flower spurs have been properly cut down as soon as they are faded. For this reason free picking of herbaceous plants does good. The autumn is the time for carrying out major changes: clumps can be lifted and divided if necessary, and rearrangements made. In late autumn all dead tops should be cut down close to the base, and the plants and the ground tidied up for the winter. No litter should be left to provide shelter for hibernating pests.

Borders may be 'lifted' completely every 5 or 6 years, the plants 'heled in' out of the way, and the ground double dug, manured, and replanted; or individual clumps may be lifted as they grow old, divided, and replanted, until the whole border has been renewed.

See also FLOWER GARDENS.

HERBS, GARDEN. 1. Certain plants with strongly flavoured or aromatic (sweet smelling) leaves are grown in the garden for use in the kitchen for such purposes as sauces, stuffings, flavouring, and decoration. The flavour or scent is due in most cases to an oil in the leaves. In old days more kinds of herbs were used than nowadays, and it was quite common to find a special herb garden as well as the kitchen garden, where medicinal herbs and herbs for flavouring were grown. Nowadays there are only four common kinds of kitchen herbs—mint, parsley, sage, and thyme; though fennel, tarragon, sweet marjoram, and savory are still to be found. The flavour of new potatoes and green peas is greatly improved by the addition of a few sprigs of fresh mint, and mint sauce is served with lamb. Parsley, sage, fennel, and thyme are used for sauces and mixed herb stuffings. Sweet marjoram, savory, and thyme are used for flavourings, and tarragon is used for making a kind of vinegar. All these are quite easy to grow.

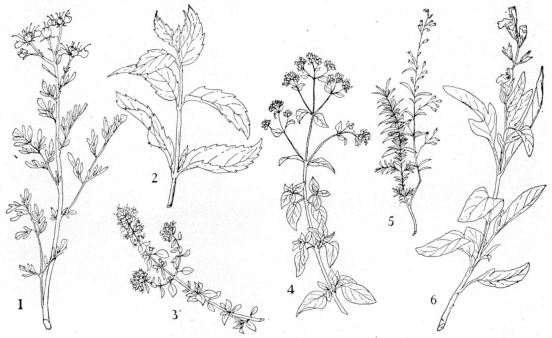

1. RUE.   2. MINT.   3. THYME.   4. MARJORAM.   5. SAVORY.   6. SAGE

2. MINT. The garden mint (*Mentha viridis*), commonly known as spearmint, is a plant probably native to eastern countries and not indigenous to Europe. A near relative, peppermint (*M. piperita*), is grown for its oil, which is the peppermint of commerce. Spearmint is a perennial herbaceous plant which sends up fresh shoots every spring from slender rhizomes. It is propagated by removing shoots with a little root growth from the parent stock in the spring, and transplanting them in a prepared piece of ground. As the mint bed will remain undisturbed for several seasons, it should be manured when the new bed is made. If the rhizomes are lifted in January and forced in a prepared bed under glass or in a heated frame, early supplies can be obtained.

3. PARSLEY (*Petroselinum crispum*). Has finely divided, bright green, scented leaves, probably more used than those of any other kitchen herb, and no garden is complete without it. It is a biennial plant which should be grown afresh from seed each year. The seed should be sown in June or July in order that the plants, after being thinned out, should give a supply of parsley during the autumn and winter and the following early summer. Flower stems are produced in June, but if these are removed, the plants will continue to provide parsley until the new sowings take their place. The native home of parsley is quite unknown. The English name, originally 'perselye', is a corruption of an old French word. The Romans regarded celery as a kind of parsley also, and used the same name, *selinon*, for it.

4. SAGE. The common garden sage is a small hardy shrub, *Salvia officinalis*, which is a native of southern Europe and belongs to the same family (*Labiatae*) as thyme, mint, marjoram, and lavender. It thrives best on rather poor gravelly soils containing plenty of lime, and needs an open sunny position. Sage is propagated either by cuttings which are rooted in a frame and transplanted, or by dividing an old bush into pieces, each with a little root. The plants remain undisturbed for a number of years. The leaves may be dried for winter use by being placed in a slow oven. This makes certain of a winter supply, for in a severe winter the bushes lose their leaves.

5. THYME. The common garden thyme (*Thymus vulgaris*) is a close relative of the wild or shepherd's thyme, and also of a highly scented variegated variety which is a popular plant for rock gardens. The garden thyme is a small, hardy, shrubby plant, of dense compact growth, which is propagated and grown in the same way as sage.

See also OIL-BEARING PLANTS; SPICE CROPS.
See also Vol. XI: FLAVOURINGS.

HERRING FISHERY. This was the earliest organized British fishery, being already of considerable importance in the Middle Ages (*see* FISHING, HISTORY OF). The ports of Yarmouth and Lowestoft in East Anglia have always been its most important bases. Besides the fisheries around the British coasts, herrings are fished on a large scale along the coasts of Norway, Denmark, and the Baltic countries, as well as in the White Sea of Russia, and on the eastern and western coasts of North America, extending even into Japanese waters and into the Behring Strait. In warmer seas, such as the Mediterranean, the herring is not found. The British fishing season begins off the northern Scottish coast, usually between May and July, for the shoals leave deep water and approach the coasts at an earlier date in northern than in southern latitudes.

Herrings are usually caught in drift-nets, although trawl-nets may sometimes be used (*see* TRAWLING). The drift-nets are great lengths of net which hang vertically in the water like a curtain. Originally the nets were of hemp, and were made by hand, but today, they are generally of cotton and made by machine. The size

The Times

HERRING BOATS AT LOWESTOFT
A drifter returning with a morning catch passes another outward bound

The Times

HAULING IN A NET ON A YARMOUTH HERRING DRIFTER

of the meshes depends on the size of the fishes to be caught, that for herrings being just large enough to let the head but not the shoulders pass through. The fish, having got its head through, is unable to withdraw, for when it tries to do so the edges of the gill-covers open out and catch on the sides of the mesh. The separate lengths of the nets are tied end to end to form a 'fleet,' which may be up to 3 miles long.

Small sailing-craft and steam and motor boats are used in the herring fishery. The boats usually set their nets at sunset and haul them at dawn. As each net comes over the rail to be emptied on the deck, its meshes sparkle with the silvery bellies of the herrings and the glint from myriads of detached scales. The fish are shaken out of the nets, and stored below in broken ice. When all the nets are in, a course is set for home.

The curing of herrings for the home and foreign market employs many hands. The principal cures are salted herrings, kippers, which are slightly salted herrings which have been split and gutted and then smoked, and bloaters, which are ungutted herrings, salted and dried.

See also FISHING METHODS.
See also Vol. II: HERRING.

HISTORY, AGRICULTURAL, *see* AGRICULTURAL HISTORY.

HONEY AND BEESWAX. Honey is made from a sweet liquid, called 'nectar', that is to be found in flowers. The bee collects this nectar by sucking it up with her hairy tongue into the honey sac inside her body. On her return to the hive she disgorges the nectar into the cells (*see* BEE-KEEPING). When freshly gathered the honey contains a great deal of water; but, during the flight home and after it has been put into the cells, it undergoes a number of changes during which a great deal of the water is evaporated. This process is called 'ripening'. When the honey is ripe, the cells are sealed over with a capping of wax, and when all the combs in a 'super', or wooden frame, are sealed in this way, they are ready to be removed from the hive and the honey extracted. If sections are used, these are removed and sold, when full.

To clear the bees from a super in order to extract the honey, a special appliance, a 'clearer board', is placed between the super and the brood chamber. This allows the bees to pass down into the brood chamber but prevents their returning. Within a few hours, when the combs

R. V. Roberts

A HONEY EXTRACTOR

The combs are revolved to extract the honey which is
drawn off through a tap at the bottom

are clear of bees, they are removed from the hive
and carried to the beekeeper's workshop. Here
the wax cappings are removed with a hot, sharp
knife, and the combs are placed in an extracting
machine that whirls them round and round and
flings out the honey. The combs are then
returned to the hive to be refilled by the bees,
or are packed away for the winter, according to
the time of year. From the extractor the honey
passes into a straining tank, which removes the
small particles of wax, and is then allowed to
stand for a few hours so that the air bubbles that
have got into it during the extracting may rise
to the surface and escape. It is then put into
bottles or tins ready for sale.

Honey may vary in colour from water white to
nearly black, according to the kind of flower
from which the nectar was gathered, and according to the nature of the soil on which the plant
was growing. For example, honey from the
limes is of a greenish colour, honey from sainfoin
is a bright lemon, while honey from ling heather
is a dark amber, and is jelly-like and cannot be
extracted from the combs in an ordinary extractor. Honey varies also for the same reasons in
aroma and flavour. The aroma generally
reminds one of the flower, but the flavour does
not—for instance, hawthorn honey has a rich

nutty flavour, while fruit honey, on the other
hand, has a very definite 'plum' flavour.

With the exception of ling honey, most types
of honey will 'granulate' and set hard, a natural
process which shows that the honey was properly
'ripe' when taken from the hive for extraction.
It can be made to return to its liquid state by
standing the container in warm water.

Honey in sections (in the honeycomb) is more
difficult and expensive to produce than is
extracted honey, for it needs a good district and
special management of the bees; and as the wax
comb itself is also sold and eaten, the bees have
to build a new comb, which takes time and uses
up honey.

Bees produce beeswax, as well as honey, which
they need to build combs and to seal with cappings the cells containing honey. To produce
beeswax the bees gorge themselves with honey,
or with honey substitutes provided by the bee-
keeper, and then hang quietly together in a
cluster. In about 24 hours small scales of wax
appear in the wax pockets on the undersides of
their abdomens. The bees chew the wax scales
until they are ready for use.

Bee-keepers extract this wax from the combs
and melt it down into wax cakes by various
methods—by steam wax extractors when large
quantities are involved or, with small quantities,
by melting it in a double saucepan, straining it
through a cloth into a soaped basin standing in
hot water, and then allowing it to cool. The
cake of wax can then be easily removed.

See also BEE-KEEPING.

HOPS. The hop is a perennial, herbaceous,
climbing plant, which dies down to the level of
the ground every autumn. On good soil hop
gardens (or hop yards: never hop fields) may
last from 30 to 50 years, but a few plants die each
year and have to be replaced. The normal life
of a hop plant is about 15 years.

Each plant forms what is called a 'hill', the
number of 'hills' per acre varying between 800
and 1,600, according to the vigour of the variety
and the nature of the soil: 1,000 hills per acre is
about the average. The gangways between the
rows of hills vary from 6 to 10 feet, and are known
as 'alleys'.

The stem or 'bine' of the hop plant is too weak
to stand erect by itself, so it climbs up anything
that is within reach. At one time hops were
always trained up poles—two, three, or four

poles to every hill—and these had to be pulled out of the ground at hop-picking time so that the crop could be picked. They were then stacked in the field for the winter and put up again every spring. Nowadays this method is seldom seen, the more modern way being to erect fewer but permanent and stouter poles, 13 to 16 feet high and about 20 feet apart, and to join their tops with strong galvanized wire. Close to each hill is fixed a wooden stump or wire screw peg, and every spring from two to four strings of coconut fibre are stretched from the stump or peg upwards and outwards to the permanent wires. There are other methods of stringing hops, but the principle is the same in all cases.

When the hops begin to grow in the spring, they are trained up these strings, two or three 'bines' or stems to each string, and they climb very rapidly up the strings until they reach the top wire. They start growth from the ground level about 1 May, and 50 days later, by the 3rd week in June, they have grown 12 to 15 feet to the top wire. They then form side growth in preparation for the cones or hops to form in late July and early August. The hops eventually ripen for picking in late August and September.

Hops need a great deal of cultivation, and as they have to make so much growth, they need very liberal manuring. A normal dressing is 15 tons of farmyard manure and 10 to 20 cwt. of chemical fertilizers per acre each year. Large quantities of waste organic manures such as shoddy (wool waste), cloth clippings, hair waste, rabbit waste, feather waste, sprats and other waste fish are used on hop gardens (*see* MANURES, section 3).

In the past the yield of hops fluctuated enormously from year to year because no effective way was known of controlling the various PESTS AND DISEASES (q.v.) which attack the crop. There was an old rhyme:

> First the flea, and then the fly,
> Then the mould—and then they die!

In some years the crop was a complete failure and the hops were never picked. Today a complete failure of the crop is very exceptional. The yield is double what it used to be, and between 12 and 14 cwt. of hops per acre is an average crop. Pests and diseases are controlled by a very elaborate and expensive programme of spraying and dusting.

Hop-picking is still done almost everywhere by hand, though a few of the larger growers are trying out hop-picking machines. Sooner or later the hop-picking machine will, probably, be so much improved that it will supplant hand-picking almost entirely. Hop-picking generally starts about the end of August and lasts about a month. Men, women, and children all help, and the local schools close down. When there is a large acreage of hops and not enough pickers in the locality, 'foreign pickers', from the poorer parts of London and other large towns, come down to help. Some come by road in lorries; others in special hop-pickers' trains. The whole family comes, including babies in prams and young children in push carts. They bring such furniture as they want for the little one-roomed hopper huts in which they live on the farm during the picking season. In old days the conditions under which the hop-pickers lived were very bad, and these were not improved by the very rough nature of the people themselves. Now, conditions are quite different. Under the local by-laws, a cook-house, sanitary conveniences, and a good water supply have to be provided to serve each group of hopper huts, though many families in fact do their cooking on a camp fire outside their hut. Sunday is a visiting day when

The Times

HOP-PICKING IN KENT

The hops are cut down from the top wires to be picked

By permission of the Controller, H.M.S.O.

A HOP GARDEN IN KENT. THE OASTS ARE AT THE LEFT OF THE BUILDINGS

many of the pickers' friends and relations come down in motor coaches to pay them a visit.

The hops are picked into either a canvas bin or a basket, and two or three times each day the picked hops are measured with a bushel measure. The pickers are paid at an agreed rate per bushel, the price varying from garden to garden and from season to season according to whether the hops are large or small.

The hops are then taken in 'green-bags' or 'pokes' from the garden to the oast to be dried. The hop oast contains storage space, one or more kilns, and a cooling-floor. The old-fashioned hop kiln is very similar to the kiln of a malt house—the hops are spread on an open floor, covered with a close-mesh, horse-hair net, under which is an open fire, so that the heat rises through the hops and out through the cowl surmounting the high roof of the kiln. Only smokeless fuel—charcoal or best anthracite coal—can be burnt because smoke fumes injure the hops. The modern kilns are fitted with closed furnaces or are heated by oil-burners. In these the hot air from the furnace is driven through the layer of hops by a rotary fan, the force of the air being under strict control. Any sort of cheap fuel can be used in the closed furnace as the smoke goes up the chimney instead of through the hops. The

new system of drying has no need for a tall conical roof, and so the picturesque old-fashioned hop oasts, which were a feature of the landscape in Kent, Sussex, Hereford, Worcester, and the other hop-growing counties, are being replaced by ugly squat buildings, often with a nearly flat roof and louvre ventilators.

When the hops have been dried, cooled, and packed in strong canvas bags called 'pockets' (each weighing about $1\frac{1}{2}$ cwt.), they are taken over by the Hops Marketing Board and sold by them to the brewers.

See also Vol. VII: BEER BREWING.

HORSERADISH. The thick rootstock of the horseradish, *Cochlearia armoracea*, has long been used for making a sauce to serve with roast beef, and the plant is therefore one of the permanent crops in many vegetable gardens. It belongs to the cabbage family, and is easily propagated by planting pieces of root 6 to 8 inches long. These root cuttings are set in sand and then transplanted in the spring, 9 to 12 inches apart in rows. Usually horseradish is dug up as required, but the rootstocks can be lifted and stored in sand or ashes. It is a crop which must be kept in its place, for it can quickly spread and become a weed very difficult to get rid of.

HORSES (FARM). The horse was domesticated several thousand years ago and was used for hunting and for war (*see* HORSES, Vol. IX). By the time of the Roman Empire the horse had become an important means of transport (*see* HORSE TRANSPORT, Vol. IV), though for the slow, heavy work of the farm the ox was used over most of the known world (*see* BEASTS OF BURDEN, Vol. IV). In Britain in the Middle Ages oxen were still the principle draught animals, though horses were beginning to be used. By the early 19th century horses had almost entirely replaced oxen on British farms, though oxen are still used in parts of Europe. In parts of Britain and the U.S.A. horses themselves have now been largely superseded by the Tractor (*see* POWER FOR FARMING).

Some of the native wild horses of Britain were of the strong, heavy type that has helped to produce the heavy work horses of today. This heavy type of British native horse was much admired by Julius Caesar, and he started an export trade in horses from Britain that is still active today. Centuries of selective breeding, and improvement in farming conditions generally, have been necessary to produce horses of the size of the modern Shire and Clydesdale. English kings and governments played their part in this improvement. In particular, King John, Edward II, Edward III, and Henry VIII all passed laws limiting the use of small and inferior stallions (male breeding horses), prohibiting the export of the best animals needed for breeding in Britain, and encouraging the importation of special stallions from the Continent. Powerful horses were needed to carry the weight of a knight in armour. At the present time all stallions registered for breeding must, by law, have a certificate of soundness.

A male horse is known as a colt foal during its first year of life, a colt until it is 3 years old, and then a stallion or an 'entire' horse if it is being kept for breeding, or a gelding if it has been castrated (an operation usually performed at one year old). A gelding, which cannot breed, is usually more easy to manage than a stallion. A female horse is called a filly foal for the first year, then a filly till she produces her first foal, and after that a mare. A horse will normally live to about 30 years, but it is usually past regular farm work by the time it is 20, and so is not kept any longer. Horses working in towns do not last so long, for town work is much more

trying on their legs and feet. Horses of the Suffolk Punch breed are particularly long-lived —indeed, one Suffolk mare is recorded as having bred regularly until she was 37 years old.

There are four principal breeds of heavy farm horses in Britain, three of them British and one French.

1. SHIRES. The Shire is the biggest and heaviest type of horse in the world. Few stallions are below 16·2 hands at the shoulder, and they are often over 17 hands. (1 hand = 4 inches.) They weigh nearly a ton. They carry a good deal of 'feather', that is, long hair from the back of the knee and hock joints down to the heel. They have a tendency sometimes to grow too much coarse feather on the lower leg, and this is generally a sign of poor quality bone. It also makes it difficult to keep the horse's legs and feet clean. They are rather slow animals, but they are generally very sweet-tempered and easy to manage. In England there are more Shires than horses of any other breed, but there is very little export trade in them. There is no distinctive colour, though bays and browns are the most common, and blacks, greys, and chestnuts much less common.

2. CLYDESDALES. These are the draught horses of Scotland and the north of England. They have not the long history that the Shires have, and do not appear as a definite type until the 18th century. They tend to be higher in the withers than Shires, but are not as heavy in bone

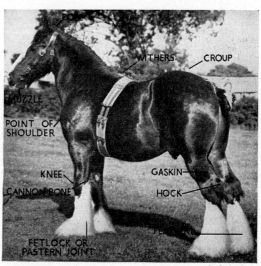

G. S. McCann

A SHIRE STALLION, SHOWING THE POINTS

CLYDESDALE

SUFFOLK PUNCH

Sport & General

PERCHERON

and body. They have longer legs and are quicker movers, and have therefore proved more popular in countries such as Canada where large areas have to be ploughed as quickly as possible after the snow has melted. A Clydesdale can often keep up a walking speed of 5 miles an hour. The bone of a good Clydesdale is of beautiful quality, and it carries a finer and not so abundant feather as the Shire. However, it has not, perhaps quite as equable a temper. A less well-bred Clydesdale has often rather flat ribs and a poor middle, and tends to stand with its hind legs too close together. As a rule they have more white about them, especially on their faces and legs, than most Shires. Blacks, browns, and bays are common colours. Many people very much favour a cross between these two breeds. A Clydesdale stallion and a Shire mare will be likely to produce a foal with the better qualities of both breeds.

3. SUFFOLK PUNCHES. These are thick, massive, clean-legged (that is, no feather) draught horses, bred in East Anglia and not found to any great extent elsewhere. They are not as tall as either of the other breeds, but their well-knit bodies make them very strong and hardy. They are chestnut in colour—generally a light chestnut. Their outstanding characteristics are their steady docile natures, and their long working lives.

4. PERCHERONS. This French breed from the district of La Perche in Normandy has become popular in Britain since 1918, and is the most popular draught breed in the United States. They are clean-legged, very thick-set animals, usually grey but sometimes nearly black in colour. Percherons are horses of much spirit and will trot well, an action which is not good for heavy horses in general. Probably this capacity to move actively is a legacy from their earlier history when these horses were the kind used in the heavy coaches of the French postal system.

Some kinds of small pony-like draught horses are also often used on farms, especially farms in hilly rough country where the fields are small, and the Shires and Clydesdales would be unsuitable. Such pony-horses often do a great variety of jobs on the farm, being often ridden and driven to market, as well as doing the more usual draught work. Welsh cobs, Dales ponies, and Highland Garrons are all useful little horses of great hardiness and staying power, and easier to keep in winter time than the bigger horses. Crosses between the Shire and some types of cob

A TEAM OF HORSES DRAWING A TIMBER WAGON
The Times
Immense strength is needed to draw the heavy load through soft mud

are also bred for farm work; they are usually intermediate in size between the two parents.

See also Vol. II: Horse (Wild).
See also Vol. IV: Horse Transport.
See also Vol. IX: Horses; Horse-racing; Horse Shows; Riding.

HORSES, CARE OF. The horses on a farm work in such close relationship with their masters that the skill and understanding with which they are handled are very important. No other animal on the farm except the Sheep Dog (q.v.) depends so much on good training for its efficiency. Horses are generally docile and willing creatures who co-operate intelligently in carrying out their tasks, and an old, experienced horse plays a considerable part in the training of a young horse.

1. Breaking and Training. Farm horses in Britain are 'broken-in' or trained for work at the age of 2 years, but this first season's work is a light one. The young horse is brought in from grass, where it will have spent its early life, and accustomed to the bit, an important stage in its training. The first bit used is a wooden one, thicker than the usual nickel or steel bit, and has three small metal 'keys' hanging from the middle and resting on the horse's tongue. A rein

from each side of the bit is fastened to the top of a surcingle or waistband which surrounds the girth. The young horse is then turned loose in a small paddock or left in a loose box for a few hours. A daily repetition of this treatment toughens the gums or 'bars' where the bit rests. If a horse is driven without this preliminary toughening, the bars may be wounded, and when they heal will be covered with hard scar tissue, making the horse's mouth insensitive to the reins. 'Hard-mouthed' horses are difficult to control, and are the result of bad handling.

A young farm horse usually does its first work in chain harness, a steady, experienced horse in front of him and another in the shafts of the cart behind him. Farm horses now have so long a tradition of work that they appear to inherit an instinct for it, and do not prance about for long when put into a team. The youngster is then tried with an older horse as one of a pair in ploughing, or one of three abreast in a cultivator, learning from the driver and from its own companions all those words of control which are better than reins in horsemastership. Work between shafts comes a year later. This is rather a critical moment in breaking in: the noise of the wheels immediately behind and the possible sight of the shafts can be frightening things, and

FIG. 1. CART GEAR (BACK HORSE) AND CHAIN GEAR (FRONT HORSE)

for quite a long time it is usually unwise to leave a young horse to stand alone with no one at his head. At 4 years old the horse should be completely reliable and capable of all work. Then after another year of steady and varied labour on the land, many horses are sold from farms to work in the towns.

2. SHOEING AND HARNESS. A young horse is first shod when he is first brought in for training. Until then his hooves have been allowed to spread naturally, with no more than an occasional paring to keep the shape right. The farmer needs to understand the principles of good SHOEING (q.v.), though the actual work is done by a farrier.

British farm horse harness is of three kinds: cart gears (Fig. 1), plough gears (Fig. 2), and chain gears; but some parts of the harness are common to all three. All horses wear bridles when in work, for on the bridle depends control of the animal through the bit and reins. Then comes the large padded 'collar' that takes all the pull, or traction, on the horse's shoulders. The collar must fit well, or the horse will soon have sore shoulders, which are often difficult to heal and may lead to jibbing (sudden refusal to pull). The 'hames' are shaped metal or wooden additions to the collar, and when buckled in position take the chains of whatever gears are being used. The cart gear has a heavy saddle which buckles to the collar in front and carries a 'britchin' or 'breeching' behind. This part of

the harness goes round the back of the horse's thighs and is attached to the saddle by a strap, and to the shafts by short chains. This part of the harness enables the horse to back the cart. A girth strap secures the saddle in position, but is not drawn tight as with a riding saddle. The cart saddle has a transverse iron-lined groove over the back to take the chain 'backband' (or 'ridger') which extends from shaft to shaft. A broad leather 'bellyband' prevents the cart tipping backwards.

Chain gear, or trace harness, is used for the front horse when two are driven 'in tandem'. It has a broad strap running along the back of the horse from shoulder to tail, buckling to the collar in front and ending in a 'crupper', a loop which passes under the tail. A broad back-band of leather rests over the middle of the horse's back

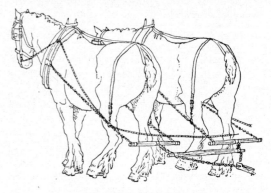

FIG. 2. PLOUGH GEAR

and carries the chains, which are fastened on the hame hooks on the collar in front and are attached behind to the large rings below the front of the cart shafts. Between the chains on the near and off (left and right) sides of the horse, and just behind his tail, a wooden 'stretcher' is fixed to keep the chains apart and prevent their chafing his flanks.

Plough gear is generally simpler than chain gear; it has a transverse backband supporting the chains, and sometimes a loose bellyband. The chains go to the hames on the collar in front and to the 'swingle-tree' behind—the swingle-tree being a crossbar pivoted in the middle, to the ends of which traces are fastened and so yoke the plough team to the plough. Plough chains are lighter in weight than those of chain gears. When two horses are worked in a vehicle fitted with a pole, plough gear is generally used, with the addition of two strong broad straps threaded

FIG. 3. HARNESS FOR TWO HORSES IN A VEHICLE WITH A POLE

through the throats of the collars and supporting the two ends of the pole's cross-bar (*see* Fig. 3).

Breast-harness, which has no collar, is used in the U.S.A., Canada, and some other countries.

Horses at work should wear a rope or webbing halter as well as a bridle, and should always be tied up by this halter—never by the bridle. In the stable the horse wears a leather headstall or a neck strap, the rope of which runs through a ring fixed on the edge of the manger, and is secured by a square of light wood on the end (*see* Fig. 4).

3. FEEDING. A horse has a small stomach, and should be given only a little food at a time. A large quantity in the manger will probably turn the horse against his food, and if this is left in the corners of the manger, it will go sour, put

FIG. 4. HORSE WITH NECK STRAP IN STABLE

the horse off his next feed, and start digestive troubles. Unlike the cow, which can pack away a lot of food in her immense rumen and chew the cud at leisure, the horse needs to feed often. Thus, the good horseman carries a nosebag of food and slips it over the horse's head whenever there are a few spare moments. The order of drinking and feeding is also important: the horse should be watered before he is fed, not after, or the feed may swell and give the animal great discomfort. But a heated, sweating horse should not be allowed to drink a lot of cold water until he is cool.

The staple feed of stabled farm horses in Britain is oats and hay. The oats are crushed and mixed with chopped hay, the mixture being damped down with a little water, to which a small quantity of salt and sometimes treacle (molasses) have been added. The chopped hay is mixed with the crushed oats to make the horse chew his food slowly. A horse likes a lump of rock salt in the manger, and this does him good. Long hay is also given in fair quantity, especially last thing at night. Dusty or poorly got hay is bad for a horse's digestion and his wind (breathing). Farm horses usually spend the summer on grass, and the spell on natural green food is very good for them. When they are not at grass, they should be given a few swedes. A Shire horse on medium work and not out to grass needs about 16 lb. crushed oats, 16 lb. hay, and some 10 lb. swedes daily. This can be varied by a laxative bran mash on Saturday evening and only 10 lb. oats on Sunday when the horse is not working. Extra work needs extra food: less work, less food.

4. GROOMING. This is an important part of

SHIRES AND THOROUGHBRED HORSES WITH THEIR FOALS

Farmer & Stockbreeder

the horse's daily routine. When he is kept in the stable, it is the only way in which his skin can be kept clean and healthy. A horse must be able to sweat properly if he is to keep healthy. He also breathes through his skin, as well as through the nostrils, and so the pores of the skin must not be blocked up. The curry comb is used first to remove the dirt that resists brushing. The stiff dandy brush follows, the horseman working from head to tail and being careful not to overlook the parts between the front legs, under the belly, and inside the hind legs. Passing the hands over the skin after using curry comb and dandy brush tells one immediately whether all the dirt has been removed. Grooming may be finished by a rub over with a wisp of hay and a smooth cloth, and by combing out forelock, mane, and tail. Grooming is a form of massage and most stimulating to the horse, quite apart from its value in keeping him clean. A small sponge can be kept for cleaning the corners of the eyes and nostrils, and the dock. A healthy horse has a sheen to his coat, and his skin should be loose enough for a fold to be taken up easily with the finger and thumb.

If the horse is to live out during the winter, he must be allowed to grow his full winter coat. But if kept in the stable, the farm horse is clipped trace-high (that is, legs and belly) in the late autumn—otherwise his thick coat will make him sweat too much when he is working.

5. MARE AND FOAL. A mare is generally mated to the stallion in the spring or early summer, and gives birth to her foal about 11 months afterwards. The foal then has the warm months of the summer in which to grow, and is sufficiently well grown and hardy to be able to pass the following winter out-of-doors.

When the foal is due, the mare is put into a scrupulously cleaned, disinfected loose box, and bedded down with plenty of clean straw. In a dirty stable the germs of the foal disease, 'joint-ill', may enter through the break in the umbilical cord at birth. When the birth is near, the mare stops eating and begins to whisk her tail and become restless. Most mares are best left by themselves over the birth, for the presence of humans may excite them. The horseman, however, keeps a watch in case the mare needs help. An excitable mare should be secured by her neckstrap, so that the horseman, or, if necessary, the veterinary surgeon, can enter the box in case of trouble.

When birth is complete, the end of the umbilical cord should be tied with iodine-soaked tape, about 1½ inches from the foal's navel, and the foal lifted and put near the mare's head. She will then lick it all over, and this both dries it and massages it into activity. In about half-an-hour, when the foal gets on its legs, it should be guided to the mare's udder and encouraged to suck. In the meantime, the horseman, having cleared away the afterbirth (the membranes in which the foal was enclosed before birth), will prepare a stimulating oatmeal drink for the mare. Then he will supply her with plenty of water and hay, and leave her undisturbed. For several days she will need no oats, though she might have a bran mash every evening.

In about 2 days, if the weather is good, the mare and foal can go out to grass during the day, and after a week they can be out altogether. The foal is weaned at 6 months, and then the mare returns to work, the foal remaining out all winter with an open shed for shelter. From the time the foal is about 2 months, it should get accustomed to being handled, to wearing a halter, and being led. This will make it more used to control when the time for serious training arrives.

HORTICULTURAL SHOWS, *see* AGRICULTURAL SHOWS.

HOTHOUSE PLANTS, *see* GREENHOUSE PLANTS.

HOUSE-PLANTS. 1. In parts of the U.S.A. and in the Scandinavian countries in particular, where there are comparatively few outside gardens, many plants are grown more or less permanently in dwelling houses. The fairly constant house temperatures maintained with central heating and air conditioning in these countries are favourable to house-plants. In Britain, however, where almost every householder has a garden or allotment, less attention is paid to keeping permanent house-plants.

2. POT PLANTS. There is a big trade in certain pot plants in Britain, notably cyclamens, primulas, solanums ('Winter Cherries'), and azaleas. Most of these plants, being tender and having been reared in a warm, humid greenhouse, suffer a good deal from the change to the average living-room, which is usually hot and stuffy in the evening and cold during the night. The humidity of the average warm greenhouse is about 80%; that of a living-room 25%, which resembles a desert to a cyclamen. The hotter the room the more moisture does a plant need in the

air around it, so that pot plants are more likely to keep alive for a reasonable time in a room which never becomes very hot: too cool is better than too hot. Some air moisture may be produced by surrounding the pot with damp sphagnum moss or standing it on a block of wood in a bowl of water. Water at the roots should only be given when the soil is almost dry, and should not collect round the pot. Gas fumes in the air are usually fatal.

Other plants which are raised in greenhouses for indoor culture include pelargoniums ('geraniums'), begonias, fuchsia, and chrysanthemums, as well as bulbs such as narcissi and tulips. These last better than the popular pot-plants, mainly because the conditions in the room are more like those in which they were reared.

3. PERMANENT HOUSE-PLANTS. There are a number of plants, chiefly from arid, sub-tropical regions, which will stand the poor cultural conditions of a living-room for a long time. Most of these will not flower in such situations, but are grown for the interest of their form and leaves. The Victorians often grew palms, aspidistras, and some kinds of fern in the house, but these are no longer very popular.

For well-lit, sunny windows, CACTI (q.v.) and other succulents are undoubtedly the most successful, and there is a wide selection of varieties.

A VICTORIAN ROOM WITH PALMS AND OTHER PLANTS

Not all varieties will thrive, but those commonly offered for sale by florists should succeed.

Another family of valuable house-plants, of which many varieties are cultivated in America, is the *Bromeliaceae* (to which the pineapple belongs). The leaves and flowers are of curious form and brilliant colour. These are tolerant of drought and some shade, but need a minimum night temperature of 50° F. *Sansevieria*, the Snake Plant, has striped or mottled, sword-shaped leaves rising vertically from the soil. *Sparmannia africana* has large pale green leaves, and needs a light position. The India-rubber plant, *Ficus elastica*, and its relative *F. lyrata*, the Fiddle-leaf Fig, are both popular hardy house-plants.

Indoor climbing plants include *Ficus pumila*, varieties of ivy (*Hedera helix*), species of *Cissus* (Grape-Ivy), and *Philodendron*, which will grow in deep shade. *Hoya carnosa*, the Wax-plant, may even bloom well indoors. Smaller, hanging plants are the Wandering Jew (either *Tradescantia fluminensis* or *Zebrina pendula*), which has variegated leaves.

There are many other plants which can be grown permanently indoors with a little care, but those mentioned are among the most suitable.

The plants are best placed close to a window with a south-easterly aspect. Otherwise they need much the same treatment as do the tender pot plants, but are not so dependent on humidity. They benefit from frequent mist-spraying with an insecticide sprayer, and if possible should have a weekly syringing all over, which can best be done by putting the plants on their side in the bath. This treatment is the most effective against that worst pest of indoor plants, the red spider mite (see MITE AND TICK PESTS). It is important not to wet the flowers nor to get too much water on hairy leaved plants. The soil must not be made very damp.

House-plants will thrive in well-drained pots and in John Innes compost (*see* POTTING). It is best to arrange the pots in trays with a false bottom through which surplus moisture can drain, and fitted with a plug to let out the excess.

See also WINDOW-BOXES.

HUMUS, *see* SOILS; COMPOST HEAP.

HUNTING, *see* FUR HUNTING.

HURDLE-MAKING. There are two principal types of hurdles—the bar hurdle (Fig. 1), and the wattle hurdle (Fig. 2). Names for them vary in different parts of the country. Hurdles are used in various ways as temporary fencing.

The craft of the bar hurdle-maker or 'cleaver' depends almost entirely on manual skill, only a few simple tools being used to prepare the poles and make the hurdle. Hazel, ash, chestnut, and sometimes oak are the timbers used. The hurdle-maker uses an axe and a draw-knife for shaping the poles, and a froe or bill-hook for 'cleaving'. His workshop is often a primitive shelter in a clearing in the wood. The special skill of hurdle-making lies in the cleaving, which is the process of splitting the timber along the grain. The split follows the grain so that the wood retains its natural strength and pliability. In hurdles used for penning pigs and bullocks, in particular, strength is of the first importance.

Hurdles and wooden gates and palings are all constructed from timber grown in COPPICES (q.v.), which are woodlands where trees of a dozen or more years' growth are cut down to the base and then allowed to put out a number of shoots which grow up into long, straight poles. These are usually cut when 12 to 16 feet long, and then barked and trimmed with the draw-knife The hurdle is then constructed by morticing the cross-bars into the uprights and bracing it by a vertical and two diagonal bars nailed

Norman Wymer

FIG. 1. MAKING A BAR HURDLE
The parts are fastened together on a frame the same shape as the hurdle

Rural Industries Bureau

FIG. 2. HURDLE-MAKER FINISHING THE FINAL ROD OF A WATTLE HURDLE
He is making an unusually high hurdle

to the frame, as shown in Fig. 1. The morticing is often done with a special tool called the 'twivil', with which the mortices are cut and the loose wood picked out.

Chestnut hurdles and fencing are still made by hundreds of craftsmen in the counties of Kent, Surrey, and Sussex. Chestnut is not only easy to cleave, but also has a natural resistance to decay because the proportion of heart-wood to sap-wood is very high (*see* TIMBER). This makes chestnut very suitable for stakes which are to be driven into the ground. The natural resistance is increased by placing the stakes in boiling creosote and leaving them to soak while the liquid cools, so that the creosote penetrates deeply into the wood. Coppiced chestnut grows into stout poles in about 12 years.

Wattle hurdles, used principally for penning sheep, are made from cleft hazel rods woven tightly between a series of hazel stakes, which are held in a pierced wooden base until the hurdle is finished. Although no nails, cord, or wire is used, the wattle hurdle provides a strong and efficient wind-break, and so light that the shepherd can carry a number of them on a pole which he passes through the hole left in the centre of each hurdle. Nowadays such wattle hurdles are sometimes also used as wind-breaks in the garden.

See also RURAL CRAFTS; COPPICE.

I

IMPLEMENTS, *see* FARM TOOLS, HISTORY OF.

INDIAN CORN, *see* MAIZE.

INHERITANCE, *see* STOCK BREEDING.

INSECTICIDES. These, as their name suggests, are substances used to kill insects, though they are also used against other pests, such as mites and slugs. They act either as stomach poisons, killing the pests through the food they eat—mostly the leaves of plants; or as contact poisons, destroying the waxy skin that protects an insect from drying up, or entering its body and damaging it inside. Most contact poisons are also stomach poisons, and must not be used on a crop that is soon to be harvested; though others cease to be poisonous after a short while and can be used on fruit and vegetables within a few days of picking. All contact poisons must be applied very thoroughly, with the aim of hitting as many of the pests as possible.

1. TYPES OF INSECTICIDES. 'Stomach poisons', that is, those that kill only if swallowed, are of two kinds: those that leave a deposit on the surface of the plant, and kill only those pests that swallow fragments of the fruit or foliage; and those that are absorbed by the roots or leaves and enter the plant's system (systemic insecticides). These latter kill also those pests, such as aphids and red spider mites, which suck the sap of plants but do not eat the surface. Lead arsenate, sprayed on to fruit trees to poison caterpillars eating the leaves, and Paris Green, an arsenical substance mixed with bran to form a poison bait to destroy leather jackets and cutworms, are examples of the former insecticide; and Shradan (*Bis-dimethylamino-phosphonous-anhydride*) is an example of the latter—a quite recent discovery.

'Contact insecticides' can be divided into three main groups according to what they are made of:

(1) Substances obtained from plants:

(*a*) Nicotine is a nerve poison extracted from tobacco, and is used against such insects as aphids and thrips. It evaporates very quickly and so must be applied thoroughly, under the leaves as well as on top, so as to hit as many of the insects as possible. In its concentrated form it is highly poisonous and can penetrate the human skin. It must be handled with great care.

(*b*) Derris is obtained from the roots of the *Derris* and *Lonchocarpus* plants, and is used in far eastern countries for POISON FISHING (q.v.). It is useful against aphids, red spider mites, wasps' nests, and such caterpillars as those of white butterflies and saw-flies. It is harmless to humans, and is only effective for a day or so.

(*c*) Pyrethrum is another nerve poison, and is dissolved from the flowers of a species of *Pyrethrum* plant. It, too, has only a short life, and is chiefly used in fly sprays and louse powders.

(2) Substances made by the chemist in his laboratory and not occurring naturally:

(*a*) HETP (*hexa-ethyl-tetra-phosphate*) is a mixture of which the chief poisonous part is TEPP (*tetra-ethyl-pyro-phosphate*). Both these are several times as poisonous as nicotine, and will kill aphids, thrips, springtails, woodlice, and some mites. In water they soon change to harmless substances, and so can be used on fruit and vegetables up to 2 days from picking. Parathion or E. 605 (*diethyl-nitrophenyl-thiophosphate*) is also highly poisonous, and so persistent that it must not be used within a month of harvesting a crop. There are few insects and mites it will not kill, so friend and foe alike are destroyed. These three insecticidies are organic substances containing phosphorus, and are so dangerous to the user that they should not be handled without expert instruction in precautions.

(*b*) DDT (*dichloro-diphenyl-trichlorethane*) and BHC (*benzene hexa-chloride*) can penetrate the insect's skin and slowly bring about paralysis and death. They do not dissolve in water, and persist for several weeks. As dusts and powders they are reasonably safe to use, but in concentrated solutions they are dangerous and need careful handling. DDT readily kills beetles and their grubs, butterflies and moths and their caterpillars, thrips, flies, lice, earwigs, and capsid bugs, but not red spider mites. BHC kills most of the insects which fall to DDT and also aphids

Pest Control Ltd.

HELICOPTER SPRAYING POTATOES IN NORMANDY TO CONTROL THE COLORADO BEETLE

and some mites, and has proved valuable against wireworms.

(*c*) Azobenzene is used only against greenhouse red spider mite, usually in the form of smoke.

(*d*) Metaldehyde is mixed with bran as a poison bait for slugs and snails.

(3) Substances obtained from coal tar and petroleum oils:

Tar oils are egg-killers (ovicides) and are sprayed on to fruit trees in winter to destroy the eggs of aphids and apple and pear suckers. Petroleum oil is used in a similar way against the eggs of Capsid bugs, winter moth, and red spider mite; it is usually combined with DNOC (*dinitro-ortho-cresol*), another product of coal tar, which kills aphid eggs, thus making a general purpose spray. A refined petroleum oil, known as white oil or summer petroleum, can be used on the foliage of some fruit trees for red spider mite.

2. APPLICATION OF INSECTICIDES. Insecticides are generally applied by spraying or dusting.

(*a*) Spraying usually gives the most complete 'cover' of the plant to be treated. For this purpose the insecticide is mixed with water, or if it will not do this, it is made as a wettable powder which forms a cloudy suspension in water, or as a liquid which will make a milky-looking emulsion in water. Most insecticides are diluted to one part in 1,000 to 10,000 of water. A substance known as a 'spreader' is usually included to enable the mixture to wet the leaves more thoroughly.

(*b*) Dusting can be very effective and is convenient where quantities of water are not easily available. The insecticides are mixed with a powder such as lime or gypsum to enable them to be broadcast or put through a dusting-machine. Dusts generally do not stick to foliage so well as sprays, and are best used when there is little wind.

(*c*) Fumigation. In enclosed spaces such as granaries and glasshouses some insecticides can be introduced as gases, such as nicotine by burning tobacco 'shreds', and hydrocyanic acid. DDT, BHC, Azobenzene, and Parathion are also made in smoke generators or 'bombs', which, when lit and burned, give off clouds of smoke laden with particles of the poison. There is also an apparatus for blowing solutions through a fine muzzle under high pressure, producing a cloud of extremely minute droplets.

Chemicals for fumigating soil, such as carbon bisulphide, are sometimes used, especially in GLASSHOUSES (q.v.).

As well as being able to kill insects, an insecticide must, of course, be a chemical that can safely be put on to plants without causing any injury to them. Most of those that have been mentioned can be used on a wide range of plants at any stage of growth, but there are exceptions which the grower needs to remember. For example, DDT and BHC will seriously damage plants of the cucumber and melon family, and tomatoes do not like HETP. BHC is absorbed by some plants and gives them an unpleasant flavour, so consequently cannot be used as an insecticide in soil in which certain root vegetables are to be grown. The tar and petroleum oils injure foliage but do not harm fruit-trees when they are in a dormant condition, so are valuable as winter sprays against the eggs of several fruit pests.

Some insects have shown the ability to develop resistance to the constant use of some insecticides —for example, house flies to DDT—and in such cases changes in the insecticide programme have to be made.

See also PESTS AND DISEASES; INSECT PESTS.
See also Vol II: INSECTS.

INSECT PESTS. Not all INSECTS (q.v. Vol II) are harmful. Some, especially bees and butterflies and moths, perform an essential service in pollinating the flowers so that they become fertilized and produce fruit. Others prey on harmful insects: the ICHNEUMON FLY, for example, is a parasite on the caterpillars of the Cabbage White Butterfly as well as many other insect pests, and the LADYBIRD preys on Greenfly (aphids). Some insects, also, help to keep down unwanted plants: the Cochineal SCALE INSECT feeds on the Cactus plant, a serious menace in many tropical countries, and it, together with *Cactoblastis Cactorum* from America, has prevented the Prickly Pear Cactus from overrunning vast areas of fertile country in Australia. Many butterfly caterpillars, such as those of the subfamily VANESSINAE, feed on harmful weeds such as nettles and thistles. Other insects are useful scavengers: the burying BEETLES, for instance, will bury a rotting carcase in the ground, and

STAG BEETLES (qq.v. Vol. II) help to clear forests of decayed wood.

Generally, however, it is as pests that we are concerned with insects on the farm and in the garden, for most of the pests that do harm to growing crops, to stored produce, and to livestock are insects. They do harm, however, not only by eating crops or biting animals, but also by spreading diseases both among plants and animals. One species of the APHID PESTS (q.v.), for instance, spreads Mosaic disease in raspberries, and the louse (*see* PARASITES) spreads typhus fever, and the mosquito (*see* FLY PESTS) spreads malaria and yellow fever from man to man.

The majority of insects are pests while in the larva (grub) stage—the stage in which insects make their growth. The caterpillars of many moths and of the Cabbage White Butterflies (*see* BUTTERFLY AND MOTH PESTS) are among the most harmful of all insects; and the caterpillars of the SAWFLY (q.v. Vol. II) are pests of corn, of

GOOSEBERRY SAWFLY AND LARVA (ENLARGED)

fruit such as apples, currants, and gooseberries, of turnips, and of young pine-trees. A severe attack of Sawflies will strip the trees entirely of their leaves unless action, such as spraying with arsenate of lead, has been taken against them. BEETLE and WEEVIL PESTS (qq.v.) not only do damage as grubs, but, unlike many other insect pests, are also destructive as adults, for they feed on the leaves of plants. Another insect destructive in the adult stage is the Thrip or Thunderfly, which damages many kinds of crops, particularly

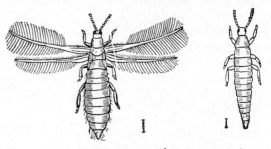

ADULT AND IMMATURE THRIPS (MUCH ENLARGED)

peas and beans, of which it attacks flowers, pods, and leaves.

ANTS (q.v. Vol. II) are very bad gardeners. They collect and carry away seed, they loosen the soil round the roots of plants, they swarm over Greenfly-infested plants carrying the aphids to other plants, and they are most troublesome in frames and greenhouses where they loosen the seedlings in boxes and pots and so kill them. A BHC dust, powdered on the ants and then carried back by the insects themselves into their nests, is effective. The nests should also be destroyed by pouring on boiling water, preferably mixed with 2 oz. of borax per gallon.

EARWIGS (q.v. Vol. II) are active at night when they will eat the leaves and flowers of certain plants, especially hops and dahlias. During the day they creep into any convenient crevice to take shelter. If a flowerpot is filled loosely with straw and put over the top of the stake supporting the plants, the earwigs will take shelter there and can then be shaken out and killed. Poisoned baits can also be used, and DDT and BHC dusts are useful against them.

See also APHID PESTS; BEETLE PESTS; BUTTERFLY AND MOTH PESTS; FLY PESTS; MITE AND TICK PESTS; PARASITES; TROPICAL PESTS; WEEVIL PESTS; INSECTICIDES.

IRISES. 1. These form a large group of generally hardy plants of great variety, some growing from bulbs, and a much larger number from rhizomes (see STEMS, Section 2, Vol. II). Irises are natives of the Northern Hemisphere, none being found south of the Equator. All have six segments to the flower; the three upper ones are called 'standards', the lower ones 'falls'. The rhizome irises can be divided into the bearded (pogon) and beardless (apogon) kinds. The 'beard' is formed of a multitude of hairs growing on the upper part of the falls. There is also a small group of irises with crests instead of beards. The bulbous irises include the well-known Dutch, Spanish, and English irises. Some irises like very moist conditions, and some are definitely WATER PLANTS (q.v. Vol. II).

2. BEARDED IRISES. These are the most important from the gardener's point of view. There are dwarf, intermediate, and tall bearded irises, the latter being the showiest. The modern sorts, which originated from natives of eastern Europe and Asia Minor, have been developed by inter-crossing for many years. Their colours include white, all shades of yellow to orange, all

Amateur Gardening

A BEARDED IRIS

shades of blue, violet, and purple, pink, brown-red, red-purple, and blends of yellow with other colours. In height they range from 2 to over 4 feet, and they flower at the end of May and beginning of June.

They need firm planting in a sunny position in good rich soil, very well drained. The rhizome, after the iris has been planted, should lie level with the surface of the soil. After 3 or 4 years, unless the plants are lifted and divided, they will become congested and cease to bloom. Only the healthy rhizomes round the outside of the clump should be replanted. Flower stems should be cut off flush with the rhizome after the blooming season, and dead leaves removed in late autumn.

Dwarf bearded irises flower in April and require the same treatment as the tall ones. They flower very freely, and the blooms are large in proportion to the short stems. Intermediate irises, raised by crossing the tall and dwarf types, flower at a season in between the others.

In Palestine, Asia Minor, and Turkestan are found the Oncocyclus and Regelia irises. The first have flowers of most wonderful colours, but are difficult to grow without the conditions of their native land, where they have a short

Amateur Gardening

A BEARDLESS IRIS, 'I. STYLOSA'   A JAPANESE IRIS, 'I. KAEMPFER'

growing season and a long period of baking by the sun. The Regelias, not quite so striking in appearance, are rather easier to cultivate.

3. CRESTED IRISES (EVANSIAS). These include some pretty species, especially the very dwarf-growing lilac, white, and orange *cristata* from the U.S.A. and the lilac pink *gracilipes* from Japan. These need a cool, fairly shady position, *gracilipes* requiring moisture as well. The petals of most of the Evansias are delightfully frilled.

4. BEARDLESS IRISES. This very large section has two main divisions—the Siberian irises and the Spurias—and many smaller ones. The 'Siberian' irises (they are actually European) have grassy leaves and slender stems bearing rather small flowers of white, yellow, blue, violet, or purple. There are many hybrid sibiricas useful for the border where they will grow well in rich soil. *I. Forrestii* and *I. Wilsonii* are of medium height and bear yellow flowers, and *I. chrysographes* has violet purple flowers with golden veins.

The Spurias (natives of Europe, Asia Minor, and Kashmir) have broader leaves and must be grown in full sun. *I. ochroleuca* is white and yellow and has a giant form fully 6 feet tall; and there

are several named hybrids of blue Spurias. *I. graminea* and *I. Sintenisii* are dwarf Spurias, the former with greengage-scented flowers of red-purple and violet nestling among the tall leaves, and the latter with many narrow-petalled violet blooms.

Oregon and California have some particularly pleasant late spring-flowering species of varied colours, including the beautiful but not very robust, apricot-yellow *I. innominata*. All members of this section have sparse, wiry roots, difficult to transplant, and are best grown from seed in peat and leaf-mould. Other varieties of beardless irises come from western America, including *I. longipetala*, with handsome white flowers veined with violet.

One of the most useful of all irises is *I. unguicularis* (or *stylosa*), a native of North Africa, which flowers during mild spells throughout the winter. It has delicate lavender flowers, and there is a white form. It should be planted at the foot of a sunny wall in poor soil, and the scented blooms pulled, not cut, in bud.

5. MOISTURE-LOVING IRISES. Besides the common yellow water flag, *I. Pseudacorus*, there are other irises, especially the so-called Japanese irises, that flourish in moist places. *I. laevigata* of gleaming blue will grow well in a pond, while the reddish-purple and yellow *I. Kaempferi*, and the purple American *I. versicolor* grow well in rich, marshy, acid soil. Some forms of *I. Kaempferi* have enormous flowers, often beautifully marked, which appear in July. They are among the most striking of irises.

6. BULBOUS IRISES. Those irises that grow from bulbs can be divided into three sections: the early spring-flowering *reticulatas*, so called because the bulbs are cased in netted fibres, the Junos which in growth resemble miniature sweet corn, and the Dutch, Spanish, and English irises. The loveliest of the very early spring iris is *histrioides* with shining blue flowers marked with yellow and white, that appear before the leaves. It is followed by *reticulata*, of which there are pale blue and deep purple forms. They need good, well-drained soil and a sheltered position, though their flowers withstand frost surprisingly well. They should be planted in August. A black fungus disease sometimes plays havoc with them, and any bulbs spotted with black should be destroyed.

Among the Junos are dwarf kinds such as the lilac purple and yellow *alata*, and rather taller kinds such as the white and yellow *bucharica*, the latter being the easier to grow. All have bulbs to which are attached spindly roots, which must remain intact if the plants are to thrive.

The Spanish irises of commerce are hybrids from the wild *I. Xiphium*; the Dutch are hybrids between this and similar irises. Both have been greatly improved of late. They like well-drained warm soil, and should be planted in October. English irises (hybrids from *I. Xiphioides*), on the other hand, require a cool, moist position, and should be planted in September.

The three main diseases of rhizome irises are rhizome rot, scorch, and leaf-spot. Scorch, which is the most serious, turns the leaves of infected plants bright russet-brown so that they look as though they have been scorched. There is no treatment, and the infected plants should be burnt. Rhizome rot attacks the rhizome at the base of the leaves, which sometimes give warning of the disease by turning an unhealthy yellow or brown. If taken in time, rot can be cured by cutting away all the soft part of the rhizome until firm white tissue is reached, and leaving the cut surface exposed to the air for a week. Leaf-spot appears in autumn as brown

Amateur Gardening

A BULBOUS IRIS, 'I. RETICULATA'

spots on the leaves which gradually widen and may kill the foliage. It is not serious, and if the leaves are cut down to a few inches from the ground and the prunings burnt, the plants do not seem to suffer very much.

See also BULBS, CORMS, AND TUBERS.

IRRIGATION. This word comes from the Latin *rigare* 'to water', and means the artificial watering of crops. Plants take in a great deal of water through their roots, and if the rainfall cannot satisfy their needs, crops must be irrigated. More than half the earth's cultivated surface would be useless for agriculture were it not for irrigation. In regions where the rainfall is less than 10 inches a year, crops depend almost entirely on artificial watering. In some other parts irrigation is needed during the hot season only. The amount of water which has to be artificially supplied depends, however, not only on the rainfall of the country, but also on the nature of the soil and the crop to be grown. Rice, for instance, requires well over twice as much water as wheat or cotton, since it needs to grow in water.

Irrigation was used thousands of years ago in lands lying in river valleys, and quite com-

Paul Popper

'FURROW' IRRIGATION IN A COTTON FIELD IN OKLAHOMA

plicated systems were developed during the ancient civilizations of Egypt, Assyria, Babylonia, China, and India, as well as later in Greece and Rome. These early systems developed in a natural way from the annual overflowing of the river banks, for crops could be planted where the waters had subsided. The Egyptians, who were probably the earliest irrigators, learnt, however, to control the flood water of the Nile, distributing it with canals and ditches in much the same way as flood irrigation, as it is called, is carried out today. Flat land near a river is divided by banks into small compartments, with little channels running into them. When the river floods, the water is let into these basins of low land through sluice gates and allowed to collect there to a depth of several feet. It remains there, often for several weeks, until the river floods have gone down, when it is allowed to run back into the river. Crops are then sown broadcast on the damp land. In some

countries, such as South Africa, Egypt, and parts of America, whole areas of land are flooded for short periods of time.

The majority of large irrigation schemes are carried out by damming up a river to create a large artificial lake, and then releasing the water thus held back into one or more large canals, from which it is distributed on to the land by a network of small channels and still smaller streamlets. The land is divided up into nearly rectangular blocks, so that the water channels are straight and therefore as short as possible. Even so, a great deal of water is lost by soaking through the banks and by evaporation; indeed, even on good schemes the loss may sometimes be as much as a half.

In dry regions, where irrigation of all crops is necessary, the soil often contains harmful salts which dissolve in the irrigation water and tend to collect in low-lying places, killing the surrounding plants. Some crops, such as rice and sugar-beet, are better able than others to resist these harmful salts, but even these are unlikely to be able to grow in hollows where poisonous alkalis (sodium carbonate and sodium bicarbonate) have collected. There must, therefore, be a good DRAINAGE system (q.v.) to carry surplus water away as well as to bring it on to the land, and much skill and experience are needed in judging how much water to release at any one time. Generally speaking, a crop needs more water while it is growing rapidly than while it is fruiting and ripening. In every large irrigated region there should be an experimental station where investigations are made to determine the best times to irrigate and the right quantities of water to use, and where tests can be made to determine the amounts of salts in the soil.

'In most irrigation schemes water is more plentiful at one season of the year than at another, and economy is effected by a system of 'rotations', some of the small canals being closed in turn for part of the time. Reservoirs are often built where the canals start so that the flow of water into the canals can be controlled and kept equal throughout the year.

Some of the largest and best irrigation schemes are in India, Egypt, and the United States. India has now the world's most extensive irrigation systems, and these have greatly reduced the risk of famine in India. The LLOYD BARRAGE (q.v. Vol. VIII), at Sukkur on the River Indus in north-west India, is the world's largest dam (see picture, Vol. III, p. 233): it is nearly a mile long, and seven canals are connected with it, irrigating some $5\frac{1}{2}$ million acres of otherwise desert land. Seventy million acres of land in India are already under irrigation, and still more irrigation schemes are projected. Egypt depends for her agriculture upon the irrigation schemes of the valley of the NILE (q.v. Vol. III), beyond which lies barren desert. The waters of the Nile are controlled by the great ASWAN DAM (q.v. Vol. VIII) and a series of barrages, and are lifted into the irrigation canals by power pumps, or in many places by much more primitive methods. Primitive water-lifts, such as the shadouf (a bucket and pulley), the water wheel operated by oxen, and the foot pump, are used also in many tropical countries.

In the United States of America large areas have been put under irrigation since the passing of the Reclamation Act of 1902, by which the government undertook to build dams and canals,

the farmers paying for the water they receive. The building of the BOULDER DAM (q.v. Vol. VIII) on the Colorado river and the Roosevelt Dam in Arizona has made it possible to irrigate large areas in the western states, and huge dams have been built to control the flooding of the Tennessee river. In Australia important irrigation works have been established on the Murray and the Murrumbidgee rivers in New South Wales and Victoria. Most of these schemes are combined with the making of electricity by machinery driven by WATER POWER (q.v. Vol. VIII).

Where there is no large river, irrigating water is often obtained from wells. This, like canal irrigation, has been practised from the earliest times. By the modern method a metal tube with holes in the sides is sunk into the ground. The water flows through the holes into the tube, and is then pumped out into the distributing channels. Well irrigation is much used in the Ganges Plain of northern India. The water flows first into small basins from which the women can fetch it for household use, then into larger basins where they may do their washing, then into still larger ones where the men and boys bathe, then finally, out on to the land. Well irrigation has the advantage that control is easy, for each pump serves only a small area and it is possible to cut off the supply by simply stopping the pump. Unlike the canal system it can be used in hilly country.

'Furrow irrigation' is used for field crops, the water being run along furrows suitably spaced in the field. 'Basin irrigation' is often preferred for fruit crops. In orange plantations in Palestine, for instance, a low earth wall is made round each tree, as far out as the roots extend, and water is run into the basin which this forms. A small inner earthen wall is built round the tree a few inches from the trunk to protect it from the water, as direct contact might cause disease (see picture, p. 89).

Spray irrigation is a method of distributing the water over small areas, such as market-gardens. By this method water is sprayed over the plants like rain. It is economical of water, has no bad effects on the soil, and the washing of the leaves benefits the plants. It is often carried out on lawns by means of sprinklers.

In recent years remarkable experiments in cloud control have been carried out in America, the object being by scientific methods to make

Sigmund Pumps Ltd.

ROTARY RAINERS WATERING THE SOIL IN A MARKET GARDEN BEFORE A CROP IS PLANTED

rain fall from the clouds when and where it is needed. Scientists have discovered that if 'dry ice' (solid carbon dioxide) is dropped by aircraft through suitable clouds, snow will fall, melting into rain as it comes through warmer air. Silver iodide crystals have been found to serve the same purpose as dry ice, and they are carried up into the clouds by the smoke from portable generators burning coke saturated in silver iodide. The generators are placed to windward of the clouds. This method, known as 'seeding' the clouds, has already been used to some extent in New York to help to fill the city reservoirs.

The 'weather controllers' also hope to discover how to control clouds so that low cloud can be kept over fields to protect crops against spring frosts, and so that storm clouds can be dissolved into gentle rain rather than into violent hail storms which damage the crops. Irrigation by cloud control is still in an experimental stage, and even when it becomes a practical matter, it will probably be limited in its scope Over regions as hot and dry as the Sahara, for instance, where there is little potential moisture in the clouds, it is not likely to be successful.

See also Vol. VIII: DAMS; IRRIGATION WORKS.

J K

JUTE, *see* FIBRE CROPS. *See also* Vol VII: JUTE INDUSTRY.

KALE, *see* CABBAGE CROPS, FIELD.

KAPOK, *see* FIBRE CROPS. *See also* Vol. VII: KAPOK.

KITE FISHING. Fishing with a kite is a method used for catching the garfish or greenbone in the Malay Archipelago and in the Melanesian Islands in the Pacific. The fisherman baits his line, about a quarter of a mile long, with an attractive bait, and then attaches it to a kite, which he flies so that the bait hangs just above the surface of the water. The kite is made of the leaves of a forest fern or from strips of palm leaf skewered together. The bait may be a small fish

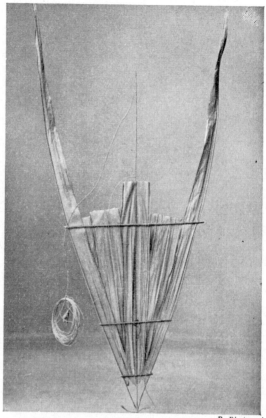

B. Blackwood

A FISHING KITE MADE OF PALM LEAVES FROM THE SOLOMON
ISLANDS

or a prawn, but very often it is a tassel of the web threads made by a big jungle spider. The fisherman makes the bait or tassel lure dance over the water, so that it looks to the pursuing fish just like a live prawn leaping out of the water.

When the garfish sees the bait or lure dancing along close to the surface of the water, it rushes forward to seize it. Its jaws, which form a spear-like beak and are armed with sharp teeth, become entangled either in the threads of the lure, or, if a bait is used, in a running noose made in the line. It is then hauled alongside the fisherman's canoe and lifted aboard.

The garfish is the only type of fish which can be caught in this way.

See also FISHING INDUSTRY, section 3.
See also Vol. II: GARFISH.

KOHL RABI, *see* CABBAGE CROPS.

James Hornell

THE METHOD OF KITE FISHING IN THE SOLOMON ISLANDS

L

LABOUR, FARM, see FARM LABOUR.

LAMBING, see SHEEP; SHEPHERD.

LAND OWNERSHIP. 1. HISTORY. Strictly speaking, all the land of England belongs to the king. This dates from 1066 when England was conquered by William, Duke of Normandy. The Conqueror made grants of land to his followers, but instead of being given outright, the land was granted as a 'feud' or 'fee' in return for special services rendered to the king. These landlords themselves made grants of land on the same terms to tenants. The 'tenure' or holding of land under the FEUDAL SYSTEM (q.v. Vol. X) was of two kinds, free tenure and unfree tenure.

Most tenants held land either by 'chivalry' (mainly military service), or by 'socage' which involved giving of service or payment of rent. All free tenants had to take an oath of 'fealty'— that is, a promise of loyalty to their lord. This system of land tenure had been the custom on the Continent for a long time, though William made some changes when he introduced it to England.

Those tenants holding their land by chivalry began to pay a sum of money, called 'scutage', instead of providing military service for the king; and by the end of the 13th century this kind of military service had practically ceased to exist. In 1660 all tenure by chivalry was converted into tenure by socage. A tenant by socage held his land in return for certain agricultural work, but more and more the practice of paying a money rent instead of work came in.

In the ordinary manor in the Middle Ages, in addition to the 'freeholders' or those who held their land by free tenure, there were the 'villeins', or those who held their land by unfree tenure. The villein had the use of his land in return for a considerable amount of labour on his lord's land. The villein was bound to his land and might not go elsewhere if he wished; but he had certain rights, such as the right to graze his animals on the common land, and he could claim the lord's protection. Although, in theory, his holding was dependent on the will of his lord, in fact, the villein could apply to his lord's court, the manor court, which dealt with him according to the custom of the manor.

After the Black Death the shortage of labour made it impossible for the manorial system to carry on. Lords began to accept rent in place of labour, for they began to turn to sheep farming instead of arable farming. The new terms of the villeins' holdings were then recorded in the rolls of the manor court, and the villeins came to be called 'copyholders', those holding by copy of the court roll. The gradual fall in the value of money in the 16th century made these various fixed money payments of little value; and in course of time the freeholders came into undisputed possession of their land. Copyhold remained a form of holding land, existing side by side with freehold, right up to the present century, when the Property Act of 1922 abolished copyhold tenure. Now all land is held by freehold tenure of the king.

2. TENANCY TODAY. (*a*) *Tenant from year to year.* Most of the farm lands of England today, and a great deal of house property, is held by an annual tenancy. The owner grants the tenant the occupation of the property for a term of one year from its commencement, and this tenancy, in common law, continues from one year to the next, and so on, until ended by 6 months' notice to quit given by either party. This notice must expire on a day corresponding with the date of the commencement of the tenancy. Thus, a man who enters upon the occupation of land or buildings upon, say, 25 March, can quit after the first year only on notice given or received before or on the following or any subsequent 29 September. This requirement of 6 months' notice may be varied by express stipulation in the contract of tenancy or by statute. The landlord and tenant of a farm worker's cottage may, for instance, agree to, say, 3 months' notice given by either, and nowadays under the Agricultural Holdings Act a farmer, wishing to give up his farm, must give his landlord 12 months' notice of his intention to quit. In all such cases, however, the notice, whatever its length, must take effect at the end of a year of the tenancy.

(*b*) *Lessee for a term of years.* Another form of tenancy is the lease for a term of years. Sometimes the tenant may need security of tenure for a period longer than one year; for instance, the man who hires land with the intention of opening up a gravel pit or a slate quarry needs time for developing and exploiting these resources. The lease for a term of years is also common when building development is intended.

At one time it was a common practice for farmers to have leasehold tenure of their farms, the term of an agricultural lease being generally 21 years. A great deal of the land of England has been brought under cultivation by the joint enterprise of landlord and tenant. In such cases land was let at low rentals for the early years of the lease, during which both parties were laying out capital, the landlord in works such as buildings of all kinds, the tenant in land reclamation by fencing, draining, and so forth; and there were provisions for an increase in rent in the later years of the lease, during which the landlord expected to receive interest on his outlay, and the tenant would be drawing profits on his. When the work of making new farms was more or less complete, and rural England had settled down, say by the middle of the 19th century, to its present agricultural equipment, the 21 years' agricultural lease at a fixed rent continued to be a favourite form of tenure, as giving the tenant security to farm and time to plan his work and life. The agricultural depression and slumps in prices of the 80's and 90's, however, showed the dangers of the leasehold tenancy. The farmer might find himself under contract to pay a rent for the unexpired term of years which was about twice as much as the land could earn at the lower level of prices. From that time onwards farmers in general have preferred the annual tenancy, which leaves them free to quit at one year's notice if things are going badly with them or if they wish to move from any other cause. At the same time, under the Agricultural Holdings Act, they enjoy a very large measure of security should they wish to stay indefinitely; for the landlord cannot now as a rule turn the tenant out of an agricultural holding without paying him adequate compensation for the disturbance of his tenancy, unless he can be proved a bad farmer or unless he fails to pay his rent.

The purpose of any contract of tenancy is, of course, to define the terms upon which the landlord grants his property for the use of the tenant.

Each party contracts (promises or undertakes) to do and not to do certain things. Thus, the contract says whether the repair of farm-house, cottages, and buildings is to be done by the landlord or by the tenant. It decides whether the landlord or tenant is to have the right of shooting game over the farm; who is responsible for maintaining gates, fences, roads, and ditches, and so forth. At one time it stipulated how the land was to be cropped and manured to prevent impoverishment of the soil; but in most counties or districts there is now a well defined practice in these matters, which has grown up between landlord and tenant in the course of time. This is so well known to everybody in the locality that a contract of tenancy, instead of setting out in detail how the land is to be used, usually will merely stipulate that the tenant shall 'farm according to the custom of the country and the rules of good husbandry'.

(*c*) *Service tenant.* Another form of tenancy of considerable importance, especially in agriculture, which is neither a tenancy from year to year, nor one for a term of years, is described as an Occupational or Service Tenancy. It occurs where an employer includes the occupation of a house or cottage as part of the contract of service. Thus, the resident agent of an agricultural estate may occupy a house rent free during the time that he continues in the estate owner's employment, and a farm worker may hold a cottage on a 'service' tenancy because he is required to live in a particular cottage for the proper performance of his work. This is the well-known 'tied cottage' system, which makes the tenant a trespasser if he continues in occupation after his employment has ceased. It has been the subject of more controversy in connexion with the farm worker's contract of service than any other condition of it. The recent Rent Restriction Acts have done much to protect this class of tenant from being unreasonably ejected, even if his contract of employment has been terminated. But for the farmer it is still argued that he cannot get labour unless he can offer accommodation, so that any man quitting his employ, or being dismissed from it, should forthwith surrender his house to his successor. The farm worker's case is that the fear of losing his home puts him at a disadvantage in all his relations with his employer (*see* FARM COTTAGES).

At the beginning of the present century about 90% of the agricultural land in the country was held under the landlord-and-tenant system. In recent years, however, a great many tenants have purchased their farms from the landlords, and now it is estimated that about two-thirds of the agricultural land is occupied by tenant-farmers, while about one-third is farmed by men who own their land.

See also AGRICULTURAL HISTORY.

LAND RECLAMATION, *see* DRAINAGE, LAND. *See also* Vol. VIII.

LANDSCAPE GARDENING, *see* Vol. XII: LANDSCAPE ART.

LARCH TREES, *see* TREES, CONIFEROUS.

LAVENDER, *see* OIL-BEARING PLANTS, section 2.

LAWNS. The word 'lawn' originally meant a woodland glade. In the 18th century it meant the undulating sweeps of meadow which, together with groups of trees, formed the landscape garden (*see* GARDENING, HISTORY OF). Until 1831, when the lawnmower was invented, the scythe was the only means of trimming grass. After this, however, formal lawns became more and more popular, and now almost every garden contains a lawn, which is an essential part of the design.

Much research has been made into the choice of grasses for use in lawns. Cheap seed mixtures contain perennial rye grass (*Lolium perenne*),

Amateur Gardening
LAYING TURVES TO REPAIR A LAWN

which is suitable for lawns receiving hard wear, but is coarse. Turf obtained from sea marshes is often used for very fine lawns such as for bowling greens, but it is expensive and deteriorates rapidly unless it receives constant specialized attention.

While special conditions (for instance, a very shady site) demand special seed mixtures, it has been found that a mixture of 7 parts by weight of Chewing's Fescue (*Festuca rubra fallax*) and 3 parts New Zealand Browntop or Bent (*Agrostis tenuis*) is the most generally satisfactory. The more vigorous fescue covers the area quickly and 'nurses' the weaker but better-quality browntop, which in time replaces it. Natural turf is often used for making lawns, but unless very good meadow turf is obtained, mainly composed of bent with few weeds, seeding is more satisfactory in the long run.

Since a lawn is usually made to last many years, trouble in preparing the site properly is fully worth while. Deep digging is essential. Heavy soils should be improved by adding gritty material such as coarse sand or sifted ashes, and they may need drainage systems to prevent waterlogging. All kinds of soil should, if possible, have rotted manure or other organic matter worked in; otherwise a dressing of balanced fertilizer should be applied before the turf is laid or the seed sown. The ground must settle naturally, and then be rolled or trodden, and raked into a fine tilth or crumby surface ready for turfing or seeding.

Seeding takes place either between mid-August and mid-September or between mid-March and April, in mild, moist weather. The seed is 'broadcast' evenly over the surface, and then raked in very lightly or covered with a sprinkling of fine soil. An expert can obtain good results with only ⅛ oz. of seed per square yard, but 1 to 2 oz. per square yard is the more usual quantity. The young grass is cut with a sharp mower when 2 inches high, the cutters being set high enough to remove ½ inch only.

If turves are used, they must all be of the same thickness, and laid staggered like rows of bricks in a wall, so that they 'bind' well. They may be lightly mowed after 10 days. Any spell of mild weather between September and April is suitable for turfing.

The upkeep of a lawn consists in regular mowing and application of fertilizers during the growing season. A lawn needs a dressing of a

Amateur Gardening

THE LAWN AT SUTTON PLACE, SURREY

suitable lawn fertilizer in the spring, and during the summer a monthly dressing of sulphate of ammonia, ¼ to ½ oz. per square yard, mixed with soil or sand to prevent scorching. In the autumn a dressing of pure coarse sand, up to 2 lb. per square yard, is good on heavy soils, or the same quantity of 2 parts loam, 1 part sand, and 1 part well-rotted manure or compost, finely sieved, on other soils. In addition, an application of 6 parts bonemeal and 1 part sulphate of potash, at 3 oz. per square yard, may be given.

Most common lawn weeds may be kept down by a mixture of 3 parts sulphate of ammonia, 1 part sulphate of iron, and 20 parts soil or sand, at 4 oz. per square yard, used instead of the monthly dressing of plain ammonium sulphate. There are other selective weedkillers, that is, weedkillers that kill only the harmful weeds and not the useful grasses.

Aromatic lawns are sometimes grown, using such common, sweet-smelling herbs as Chamomile (*Anthemis nobilis*) or various thymes (*Thymus Serpyllum* varieties) instead of the ordinary grass mixtures.

See also Grasses.

LEEKS, *see* Onion Crops, section 5.

LEGUMINOUS CROPS. These pod-bearing plants of the *Leguminosae* or pea family are grown either for their pods and seeds or for their foliage as fodder for animals. The Latin word *puls* meant a pottage made of such seeds, and so these crops are sometimes known as the pulse crops. They are a useful protein food both for humans and animals. Among those grown for their seeds are Peas, Beans, and Lentils, and a great number of tropical and sub-tropical crops such as Groundnuts and Soya Beans which are important not only as protein foods but also as Oil-Bearing Plants (qq.v.). This article, however, is concerned with those crops grown in temperate climates for fodder: for grazing, for cutting and feeding at once, for Haymaking, or for making into Silage (qq.v.).

Leguminous crops have the capacity to draw nitrogen from the air, which is converted by bacteria into a form which the plant can absorb and store (*see* Nitrogen Supply in Plants, Vol. II). But though they need no nitrogen fertilizer, these crops need phosphate and potash, and, with the exception of Lupins (q.v.), a soil well

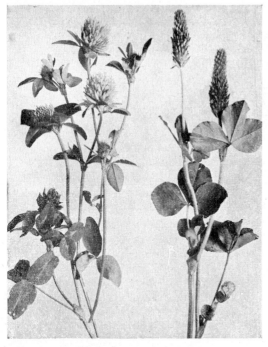

RED CLOVER AND TRIFOLIUM

Harold Bastin

COMMON VETCH

supplied with lime (*see* MANURES). They must be sown in weed-free soil, especially if the crop is to be left growing for several years, as they can easily become smothered. All hay crops of the clover family require careful harvesting to avoid breaking the leaves, which are the most valuable part of the plant.

Of the clovers common in grassland there are two red-flowered types and two white ones.

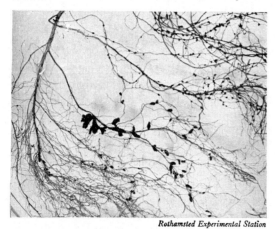

Rothamsted Experimental Station

CLOVER ROOTS WITH NODULES CONTAINING BACTERIA WHICH ABSORB AND STORE NITROGEN

Broad red clover and Dutch white clover are short lived; late-flowering red clover persists for 3 to 4 years; whereas wild white clover is a true perennial which, owing to its small-leaved, spreading habit of growth, under favourable conditions soon covers the ground. Another clover that is sometimes grown in mixtures is alsike, which compares in size with the red clovers but has pinkish flowers and hairless leaves. This plant is hardier than the other clovers and less sensitive to soil conditions; it is, therefore, frequently included in mixtures as a safeguard against failures. Ladino or giant white clover is very popular in parts of the U.S.A., but not much grown in Britain. Sometimes the small, yellow suckling clover is to be found, but most farmers consider it a second-rate plant and do not usually sow it.

Plant breeders have recently done much work in developing strains of clovers with particular characteristics such as late or early flowering or special vigour of growth. The Aberystwyth S 100 and the New Zealand certified white clover are very vigorous strains of the wild white clover and are much used for LEYS (q.v.) which are to last for more than 2 years. They seed and spread so rapidly that they soon knit the grass into turf.

Trifolium or crimson clover is a rather taller clover crop often grown in southern England as a catch crop following another crop. It is sown in the autumn following a cereal, and grazed by sheep the following May and June. By sowing early, medium, and late strains, and a late white flowered variety, it is possible to get a sequence of growth that will last the sheep a considerable time. The land is not ploughed, as the seed needs an exceptionally firm seed-bed: when the crop follows corn, the stubble is merely harrowed across before receiving the seed. About 20 to 24 lb. of seed is sown per acre. Trifolium does not make good hay as the mature flower heads, being very hairy, make the dried crop indigestible.

Vetches (or tares) are grown in all parts of Britain, being suited to many soils and climates. Because of its reliability, the crop is a favourite for silage making, for which it is generally grown mixed with oats and peas or beans. Winter vetches are sown during September or October, and the spring variety during February or March. Grown as a catch crop, the seed is sown about June—following, say, early potatoes. The crop is usually cut for seed when the pods are nicely formed, but when wanted for feeding fresh it is mown as required. A mixed crop of vetches and cereals will give about 8 tons per acre of silage, or about 3 tons of hay. When grown alone for seed production, about 12 to 18 cwt. per acre of seed is obtained. Mixed with oats, the grain makes useful protein food for cattle and sheep.

Lucerne is much grown in America and Canada, where it is called 'alfalfa'. The crop is particularly valuable for growing on the drier types of soils because the plants are so deep rooted that they can find water in the driest of summers. Lucerne, therefore, often provides keep for livestock when other green crops, including the grass, have failed. Most of the seed sown in England comes from France (Provence variety) or from Canada (Grimm variety), although a small quantity is home produced. The seed can be sown in spring or late summer. Some farmers prefer to sow it alone, others mix it with grasses, such as cocksfoot and perennial ryegrass, which help to keep the weeds in check. When sown alone it is often drilled in rows about a foot apart, wide enough to allow hoeing between the rows to be carried out each year. When the crop is sown in the spring, a cereal, such as barley, may be used as a 'nurse' crop,

in the same way that the seeds mixture is sown in the Norfolk 4-Course rotation (see ROTATION OF CROPS). In this case, the barley seed is first drilled, harrowed in, and rolled, and then the lucerne is sown. By the time that the barley is harvested, the lucerne seedlings should be well established in the stubble.

In order that the lucerne may become deeply rooted as quickly as possible, it should not be grazed until the following year. Moreover, neither grazing nor mowing should be so close that the crowns of the plants, from which the new growth springs, are damaged. The total yield of green fodder is about 20 tons per acre each year, cut three times during the season.

When lucerne remains growing for several years—and 6 years is not unusual—it is necessary to feed the crop by an occasional application of phosphate and potash and, when it can be spared, a light dressing of farmyard manure.

Sainfoin, like lucerne, does well in dry districts and warm dry seasons, and is a favourite crop on the downlands of southern England on which to graze sheep. The hay is also greatly valued by breeders of thoroughbred horses. There are two

Harold Bastin

LUCERNE   SAINFOIN

types of sainfoin: Common Sainfoin, a perennial plant, may last for several seasons, and can be grazed as well as made into hay, and Giant Sainfoin, which lasts only for about 2 years, is used mainly for hay.

The seed is generally sown between February and May in rows about 7 inches apart, and placed about one inch deep. If sown in the husk ('unmilled'), about 100 lb. per acre is sown; but if milled seed, which germinates better, is sown, only 56 lb. per acre is needed. Occasionally sainfoin is included in mixtures of grass and clover seeds. For hay, the crop is cut as soon as flowering begins, the average yield being about 30 cwt. per acre. When a seed crop is taken, from 5 to 6 cwt. per acre of unmilled seed is obtained.

See also ARABLE CROPS.

LEMONS, see CITRUS FRUITS.

LENTILS are the seeds of *Lens esculenta*, a soft hairy herb cultivated in sub-tropical and tropical countries. It is a LEGUMINOUS CROP (q.v.), related to the vetch, growing to a height of from 6 to 18 inches, and bearing small leaves and pale blue flowers. The pods, which are less than an inch long, hold about two seeds each. There are several kinds: French lentils are grey and flat, and the Egyptian and Indian kinds are round and orange-red in colour. The crop grows best on clay loams or fertile black soils; in the East it is sometimes grown to follow rice in the ROTATION OF CROPS (q.v.). Sowing generally takes place from October to December and harvesting from February to April.

The lentil plant originated in the Mediterranean countries, and has been grown in the Middle East from very early times. The red pottage of lentils, the 'mess of pottage' for which Esau sold his birthright in the Biblical story, was probably made from the red Egyptian lentil. Lentils are now an important food crop in Asia, particularly in Bengal and other parts of India, where the young pods are sometimes eaten as a vegetable, the stem and foliage used to feed animals, and the seeds, called *dhal*, made into a thick sauce. In European countries lentils are used in soup, and in Roman Catholic countries are sometimes made into meal to be eaten on fast days.

LETTUCE, see SALAD CROPS, section 1.

LEYS. In a great many crop rotations a 'ley', or mixed grass and clover crop of varying duration, is included (see ROTATION OF CROPS). This crop is generally referred to as the seeds ley, or just 'seeds', and is usually sown in the same field as a cereal crop, which is then called the 'nurse' or 'cover' crop. For instance, in the four-course system of farming, the sequence of crops is roots, barley, seeds, wheat; and in this case the barley acts as the nurse crop for the grass and clover mixture. The seeds mixture is sown in the spring with the nurse crop; therefore both begin growing together, and while the corn is growing, the grasses and clovers are getting established.

Moreover, the nurse crop shelters the tender seedlings of grass and clover from the summer sun and the drying winds. When the barley has been harvested, the lower growing seeds are flourishing in the stubble, and so the livestock can begin grazing right away. Thus there is no loss of time, for by the following season the ley has grown enough grass to feed plenty of grazing beasts or to yield a good crop of hay, whichever the farmer needs.

Many farmers, however, do not use a nurse crop, but sow the seeds mixtures alone so as to get grass for grazing as rapidly as possible without having to wait for the nurse crop to be harvested. To protect the seedlings from drought it is necessary either to sow very early in the spring so that the plants become well established before there is any danger of drought, or to delay sowing until late summer or early autumn when the hottest and driest part of the season is over. When sown in this way leys can often be used for grazing some 6 weeks later. As a rule farmers prefer to graze a ley in its first season, and to delay taking a hay crop until the next year, so that the seedlings have time to become strong plants before undergoing the strain of yielding a large crop of hay. Grazing takes energy from the plants, but fertility is returned through the droppings and urine of the animals, and the nibbling of small grass and clover plants serves as a form of pruning which causes them to send out side shoots, or 'tillers'. This 'tillering' makes the turf thick, so that it covers the ground, retains moisture, and keeps out weeds.

When a farmer nowadays needs to bring back old and exhausted grassland to good condition as quickly as possible, he generally re-seeds it direct. He ploughs the land to bury the old turf, fertilizes it suitably, and then harrows the

Eric Guy

SOWING A LEY IN SPRING ON CORN PLANTED THE PREVIOUS AUTUMN

Grass and clover seeds are broadcast from the seed box. The guide stick helps the sower to cover the ground evenly

furrows to prepare a seed-bed and sows the seeds mixture. As soon as the young plants are about 4 inches high, grazing can begin.

'Seeds' mixture for a 1-year ley

Broad red clover .	. 12 lb. per acre	
Italian rye grass .	. 12 lb.	,,
Total	. 24 lb. per acre	

'Seeds' mixture for a long ley, or permanent grass

Late-flowering red clover	3 lb. per acre	
Perennial rye grass .	. 10 lb.	,,
Cocksfoot . .	. 6 lb.	,,
Timothy . .	. 4 lb.	,,
White clover (Wild white and S 100) .	. 1 lb.	,,
Total	. 24 lb. per acre	

See also GRASSLAND; GRASSES; HAYMAKING.

LICE, *see* PARASITES. *See also* Vol. II: LOUSE.

LILAC, *see* FLOWERING SHRUBS.

LILIES. This large genus of bulbous plants belongs to the natural order *Liliaceae*, of which there are a great many wild species (*see* LILIES, Vol. II). Lilies are among the oldest known cultivated plants. Ancient Greek and Roman writers praised the beauty of what may have been *Lilium candidum*, known today as the Madonna Lily or June Lily; and even earlier, the Cretans and Assyrians included such a plant in their architectural designs. The Early Church chose this lily as the emblem of various saints, and later it came to be particularly associated with the Virgin Mary. Herbalists used all parts of it in making their drugs. Early in the 17th century other lilies besides the Madonna Lily were being grown in English gardens, among these being the European Scarlet Lily (*L. chalcedonicum*) and Pompone Lily (*L. pomponium*), the yellow Pyrenees Lily (*L. pyrenaicum*), and the American *L. canadense*.

Since then, especially in the 20th century, the species cultivated have increased enormously, and in particular, numbers of Asiatic lilies have been discovered. For many centuries lilies have been cultivated in various parts of Asia for their bulbs which were used for food. The Tiger Lily, in particular, is still cultivated for this purpose in China and Japan.

The bulb of a lily is made up of a central core

surrounded by a mass of scales, modified leaves, which feed the stem until the roots have developed sufficiently to take over that work. Some lilies are described as 'stem-rooting' because in addition to the roots sent out by the bulb, further roots develop on the stem above the bulb. In some species the bulbs live for several years, others renew their bulbs annually. Most American lilies develop their new bulbs on a short underground stem, and in the course of years a group may have moved an appreciable distance from its original site.

The majority of lilies are quite easy to grow, and need little beyond plenty of moisture and good drainage. An ideal position for them is a south-facing slope sheltered from wind, and with light porous soil. Heavy clay soils need to be lightened by the digging in of leaf-mould, sand, and gravel. Some Asiatic lilies find British winters too wet and need protection from the moisture.

With one or two exceptions, notably the Madonna Lily and the Giant Lily (*L. giganteum*), both of which should be planted with the tips of the bulbs not more than one inch below the soil, most lily bulbs should be planted at three times their own depth. Thus a bulb 3 inches high is planted with its base 9 inches below ground level. This rule has to be varied in certain circumstances; for instance, on heavy soils it is better to plant shallow and give a good mulch in spring. Stem-rooters should be planted more deeply than bulb-rooters which produce roots only from below the bulb. The bulb should be planted on, and surrounded by, coarse sand, the greatest care being taken to avoid damaging the roots, as these are vitally important. A little sand and fine soil should be worked in among the roots, but without pushing the bulb down upon them. It is a good plan to put a small stake near each bulb to mark its position and also to preserve a place among the roots in which a larger stake can, if necessary, be inserted later, without risk of damaging the bulbs.

Well-rotted farmyard manure, but never fresh manure, can be placed not less than 6 inches below the bulbs, and well-rotted leaf-mould or compost may be used freely, both in the soil and also as a thick mulch round the base of the plant to preserve the moisture. If possible, it is best to plant in autumn. With few exceptions, lilies like to have their heads in full sun, but their lower parts should be shaded by other plants so that they do not get too dry. In very hot weather it is important to see that the plants get enough moisture.

Lilies can be propagated in several ways. Those which produce seeds are best increased by that means, for plants grown from seed will be free from virus disease, and when planted out will receive little or no check to growth. Lilies can also be increased from scales removed from the bulbs, from underground bulblets, and from 'bulbils' which some species produce on the stem above ground. Grown from seeds, many kinds, such as Regale Lilies, will flower within 2 years from the time of sowing.

Lilies suffer from very few PLANT DISEASES (q.v.), those most likely to be met with being Botrytis and Mosaic. Botrytis is caused by the fungus *Botrytis elliptica*. The disease shows itself by the appearance of brown spots on the leaves which spread rapidly, killing the leaves and affecting the stems, buds, and flowers. The spores are wind-borne, and so the disease spreads quickly if it is not dealt with by picking off and burning the affected leaves and spraying the plants with Bordeaux mixture. The Madonna Lily is especially susceptible to attack by Botrytis. Mosaic, a virus disease which causes mottling and distortion of leaves and buds, will eventually kill the plant, for there is no known cure. All affected plants should be lifted and burned immediately the disease has been recognized.

Slugs, leather-jackets, wireworms, and millepedes all cause damage to the bulbs (*see* PESTS AND DISEASES). APHID PESTS (q.v.) are an even more serious menace, especially as they help to spread the Mosaic disease. Aphids should be kept down by spraying with a suitable insecticide at the first sign of attack.

Most lilies dislike lime, and consequently are suitable for planting among rhododendrons and other shrubs which enjoy acid soils. This is particularly true of the magnificent *L. auratum*, which produces its great scented flowers of white, crimson, and gold in late summer.

Lilies vary greatly in size, colour, and form of flowers as well as in height. Many, also, have deliciously scented flowers. In form lilies range from the dainty purple Turk's Caps of *L. Martagon* and the bell-like yellow and red flowers of *L. canadense*, to the huge white, yellow, and purple bowl-shaped blossoms of *L. auratum* and the immense yellow and brown trumpets of *L. sulphureum*. In height they may range from the

TURK'S CAP LILY   'LILIUM CANADENSE'

Both these are small-flowered lilies

Amateur Gardening

GIANT LILY   A HYBRID OF 'LILIUM AURATUM'

Two of the largest lilies

pink *L. rubellum*, less than 2 feet high, to the great Giant Lily, which may tower up to 12 feet.

Groups of Madonna or June Lilies, with their lovely spurs of white, strongly scented flowers, are very suitably placed in the HERBACEOUS BORDER (q.v.), as are also the white, gold, and purple Regale Lilies, and the orange, red, and black Tiger Lilies. In a herbaceous border it is easy to place them among plants which will give them the shade that they need round the lower part of the plant. Where space permits, a border in which lilies take the chief place is very effective in any garden, and by careful selection a succession of flowers can be ensured from early June until October. Such a border should be carpeted with low growing plants and shrubs, and the lilies should be planted in groups, each of one kind.

The Giant Lily can look very striking if planted freely in a light, open, ornamental woodland. Each bulb, however, only flowers once, taking about 5 years to reach that stage, and having flowered, it dies away leaving numerous bulblets which must be transplanted to keep up the succession. An annual succession of flowers can be obtained if groups of bulbs of different ages are planted. The very graceful *L. canadense*, which flowers in July and August, is also ideal for woodland plantings.

Some lilies, particularly the American species, the orange and crimson Swamp Lily (*L. superbum*) and *L. Parryi*, are especially suitable for planting on the banks of a pond or stream. The banks must be high enough to ensure that the bulbs are several inches above the highest water level.

Many varieties of lilies make excellent pot plants and can be forced into bloom early in a cool greenhouse. Some are too delicate to grow out of doors in Britain and must have greenhouse protection all the year. The graceful white *L. Harrisii*, which grows wild on Table Mountain in South Africa, is very suitable for greenhouse culture, needing a temperature of 55° to 65° F. There are many hybrid lilies of great beauty, and often of greater stamina than their parents, that are worthy of inclusion in any collection.

See also BULBS, CORMS, AND TUBERS.
See also Vol. II: LILIES.

LIMA BEANS, *see* BEANS, KIDNEY AND RUNNER.

LIME. This term refers to compounds of calcium that are put on the land in order to supply the plants with a necessary food to prevent the soil being sour (or acid), and to make heavy (clay) soils easier to cultivate and to work down to a seed-bed. Lime has been applied to land since prehistoric times. Farmers of the past knew no chemistry, but they learnt by experience the value of using lime. They got good results even though they did not know what lay behind it all.

Calcium carbonate occurs in nature in the form of chalk and of limestone. Large stretches of the south and east of England lie on a deep bed of chalk, others in the west are limestone, and in the north of England are great areas of carboniferous limestone. In all these areas there are kilns for burning the chalk or limestone to make quicklime. This very old practice of burning to

Rothamsted Experimental Station

THE OLD METHOD OF 'CHALKING FROM PITS' IN HERTFORDSHIRE

Chalk was dug from the subsoil and spread on the fields, producing a practically permanent improvement in the topsoil

Rothamsted Experimental Station

APPLYING LIME TO A FIELD WITH A DISTRIBUTOR

get quicklime is a chemical process: calcium carbonate is turned into calcium oxide. The farmer and the builder buy quicklime and 'slake' it, that is, expose it to the air, which is another chemical process resulting in the production of calcium hydroxide. Quicklime weighs little more than half the weight of the limestone that went into the kiln, the other part having been burnt away and gone up the chimney in the form of gases. When exposed to the air the quicklime takes up moisture rapidly from the air, and so becomes calcium hydroxide. Even in this form it does not remain for long, but gradually takes up carbon di-oxide from the air, and finishes up as calcium carbonate once more.

The calcium carbonate, which is the result of this chain of chemical reactions, is quite different in physical texture from the original limestone: it is an exceedingly fine white powder, easily dissolved by the water in the soil, and can be used by plants as food. Quicklime, on the other hand, is a powerful poison to plants and cannot, therefore, act as a plant food until it comes back to the state of calcium carbonate again.

Lime burning is expensive, and for agricultural purposes it is becoming more usual to crush the limestone and grind it to a fine powder. This physical process is cheaper than the chain of chemical ones; but whereas a farmer bought one ton of quicklime in the old days and allowed it to slake on the land, he must now buy almost 2 tons of good limestone to get the same value.

In farming it is reckoned that an acre of crops takes, on the average, about half a ton of calcium carbonate a year out of the soil. In practice, the farmer generally applies a dressing of 2 tons to the acre every 4 or 5 years, though many market gardeners prefer smaller dressings at more frequent intervals—say, half a ton of burnt lime every year.

Lime is needed on pastures if the animals reared on them are to grow well, for the compound of lime and phosphorus, known as tricalcic phosphate, makes up a large part of their bones. Thus, ground bone made into a fine powder and called 'steamed bone flour' (the steam treatment removes the fats) is a most valuable fertilizer. Local farmers also use waste lime from the sugar-beet factories, which is in the form of calcium carbonate.

Lime tends to sink in the soil and should as a general rule be applied on the surface after ploughing. The fact that lime quickly washes downwards in the soil accounts for what may seem the extraordinary condition of a soil overlying limestone rock being short of lime. The best north-country limestone farmers were accustomed to give occasional fairly heavy dressings of lime to their land long before the science of the practice was understood.

A serious shortage of lime in the soil of large tracts of country, such as in the Highlands of Scotland, makes it impossible to graze a large number of animals on the land. If plenty of lime were present, there would be a great increase in the clovers and better grasses (see GRASSLAND).

Chemical name	Common names	Equivalent value
Calcium carbonate	Limestone; Ground Limestone; Chalk; Carbonate of Lime.	100
Calcium oxide	Burnt Lime; Quick-lime; Ground Lime.	56
Calcium hydroxide	Slaked Lime; Hydrated Lime.	74

See also MANURES.
See also Vol. III: LIMESTONE.

LINSEED. This plant is grown both for the oil-bearing seed and the fibre, which is used for making linen. In the former case it is called linseed, and in the latter, flax (see FIBRE CROPS).

For seed, a warm climate and moderate rainfall are needed; so in Britain the crop is confined mainly to the drier eastern and south-eastern counties, where the medium loam soils are ideal. For many years 'Plate' linseed, originating from the River Plate region of the Argentine, was the variety grown; but recently it has been found that the North American varieties, Redwing, Royal, and Bison, are better suited to English conditions.

Linseed often follows wheat in the ROTATION OF CROPS (q.v.), and is sometimes used as a nurse crop for the grass and clover LEYS (q.v.). It is an excellent nurse crop, as its light foliage does not smother the clover and grass seedlings; but for this reason, unless it is sown in clean land, it can itself get quickly smothered by weeds. Neither wireworms nor rabbits generally touch the crop, so that where these pests are prevalent a good crop of linseed can often be secured when other crops would be ruined.

After autumn ploughing the land is usually left in the furrow over winter to weather; then in late February or early March a fine seed-bed is prepared with the harrow, and a moderate dressing of phosphates and a little potash applied. The seed is sown as soon as soil and weather conditions are suitable, from March onwards, 60–80 lb. of seed per acre being needed. Little further attention is given to the crop until harvest. It is ready to harvest when most of the seed is shiny and pale brown in colour; the less mature seeds will ripen while the sheaves are stooked in the field. If left until it is fully ripe, a lot of the seed will shell out and be lost. The crop is usually cut with a binder. The straw is extremely tough and hard on the cutting knives.

When the crop is grown on a large scale, the seed is sold to merchants for the extraction of the valuable linseed oil, the residue being pressed into cakes and used for cattle food. Farmers who grow only a small acreage, on the other hand, use the seed for feeding direct. It can be crushed in the grinding mill and mixed with oats for feeding, or it can be boiled to make linseed porridge. Linseed chaff (the outer parts of the 'bolls', or fruits, left after threshing) is a valuable feeding-stuff, especially for sheep. In America the straw is used for making paper. About ½ ton of seed per acre and 8 to 9 cwt. of chaff are obtained from an average crop in Great Britain.

LIVESTOCK, see CATTLE; GOATS; HORSES; PIGS; SHEEP; ANIMAL FARMING, TROPICAL.

LOBSTER FISHING, see CRAB AND LOBSTER FISHING.

LOCUSTS. These insects, which are closely related to GRASSHOPPERS (q.v. Vol. II), have been from time to time the cause of terrible devastations: swarms of locusts can, in a few hours, strip vast areas of green and fertile country of all signs of vegetation. Locusts are occasional or periodic pests. In one year a district may be quite free from them; in the next they may descend out of the sky in enormous swarms, and devour all the vegetation before them. Then, after this heavy invasion is over, they may not reappear for 10 or 14 years. Now that more is known of the way of life of this insect, these periodic invasions are better understood and, consequently, more controllable.

Locusts exist in two forms, or 'phases', so different from each other in both appearance and habits that the phases were thought to be distinct species, until it was found that the off-spring of insects in one phase developed into insects of the other. The phases are called the gregarious (or swarming) phase and the solitary phase. In the gregarious phase the immature locusts, known as 'hoppers', are strikingly coloured, and the adults do not breed until after they have carried out a long migration. In the

Anti-Locust Research Centre

A LOCUST SCOUT IN THE SUDAN DESERT LAYING BAIT ROUND
A BAND OF YOUNG DESERT LOCUSTS

The bait is a mixture of bran and poison

fewer regions; and never in western Europe. There are regions around the Caspian Sea, across tropical Africa, in Madagascar, the Malay Archipelago, and in Australia, from which invasions of the Migratory Locust occur. The most destructive locust is the Old World Desert Locust, found over nearly the whole of Africa and south-western Asia. This is the insect referred to many times in the Bible, and which caused such devastation in Palestine in 1928 and in many places in Africa until 1931 (*see* FAMINE).

Scientists now know the regions in which the gregarious phase of locusts may occur, and can even sometimes tell in advance when an outbreak will take place; and so action can be taken to meet the attack. By modern methods of dusting and spraying, carried out if need be by aeroplane, the hoppers can often be destroyed on a large scale before they have done much damage. DDT insecticide has proved particularly effective. It is also often possible to alter the crops grown in the regions where the solitary locusts breed, so as to prevent the periodic enormous increases in numbers and the start of a migration.

See also PESTS AND DISEASES; TROPICAL PESTS; FAMINE.
See also Vol. II: GRASSHOPPER AND LOCUST; MIGRATION.

solitary phase the hoppers vary in colour and usually tone with their surroundings, and the adults are able to breed at once. During the period between two successive outbreaks the locust is present only in the solitary phase, when it is harmless. When an outbreak occurs, the locusts appear in dense swarms and set out upon a long MIGRATION (q.v. Vol. II)—for what purpose is not known—during which they cause terrible devastation. The gregarious phase is brought on by great increases in numbers, and this is due to an unusual abundance in certain favourable seasons of suitable food. When the locusts in a district are few, they will remain in the harmless solitary phase. Interesting experiments have been carried out with locusts in captivity, when they have been converted from one phase to another by changing their living conditions and supply of food.

There are five species of migrating locusts found in the Old World, and two in America. The most widely distributed is the insect called the Migratory Locust, which in its solitary phase is found as far west as Belgium, as far east as Japan, and as far south as New Zealand. Outbreaks of the gregarious phase occur today in

LOGANBERRIES, *see* RASPBERRIES, LOGANBERRIES, AND BLACKBERRIES.

LOGGING. In countries with vast timber forests and great rivers, such as Russia and Canada, logs are hauled from where the trees have been felled to the nearest waterway, and are then floated downstream. Smooth lakes are crossed by building the logs into rafts which can be towed by tug-boats. Much of the felling is done in winter, when the frozen ground makes haulage easy; and sledges are then sometimes used. But the floating must wait for the spring thaw to free the ice-bound rivers.

On their journey down the river from the forest to the sawmill the logs are controlled by skilled men called lumberjacks. There is always the risk of a 'jam', caused by logs striking rocks or other obstacles and piling up on each other so as to dam the river. Clearing a jam is difficult and highly dangerous work, for the men go out over the mass of floating logs to reach the place where the obstruction has occurred.

The sawmill is often placed well downstream, beside a small lake or wide stretch of the river, where the current runs more slowly. A 'log pond' is formed by dividing off a section of the water with a wooden boom. The logs, as they come downstream, are steered within this boom and stored until needed for sawing. Then they are guided to a mechanical elevator, working on the endless belt principle, which lifts them bodily up a sloping gangway into the mill, where they are sawn into planks.

Timber haulage is an expensive operation. In fact, it may cost more to take a log to the mill than it did to grow the tree. Many methods are used in different countries. In Burma, Siam, and parts of India, elephants are trained for the work and become very skilful in hauling and piling teak. In Malaya, water-buffaloes are often employed for hauling, especially in marshy ground, and oxen are used in many parts of the world.

Light railways are often built to serve highly productive forest areas. The Americans have devised overhead ropeways for hauling in huge logs to these temporary railways, by the process known as 'skidding'. The main ropes are secured to the tops of the tallest trees available, and their erection, or 'rigging', is a highly skilled and dangerous task. A steam-engine, mounted on a truck which can travel along the railway, hauls in the running ropes to which the logs are secured. When the logs reach the railway, they are loaded on to flat rail-cars.

In hilly country logs can be dispatched down-hill on 'timber slides'—trough-shaped runways built of wood, running steeply downhill, and lubricated by a constant stream of water. Slides usually end above a lake or river, so that the tree falls into the water and its speed is checked without damage to the timber.

'Timber Bobs' or 'Big Wheels' are two-wheeled bogies that are used in some places to support one end of a log, or even the whole of it, above the ground, so that it can be easily hauled by horses. Special types have been designed for use with tractors, and some of these run on cater-pillar tracks. Another useful device, when the ground is too soft for a direct pull, is to attach a winch to a tractor anchored to the ground, and to wind in the log with the power-driven winch.

See also FORESTRY; LUMBER CAMPS.

LUCERNE, *see* LEGUMINOUS CROPS.

LUMBER CAMPS. In North America the areas where big timber grows are often remote from towns and settlements, and the lumbermen or 'lumberjacks' have to build their own camps out in the wilds. Early in the 19th century most of these camps were on the Atlantic seaboard, in the forests of Maine and Quebec. As the timber was cleared, the lumbermen moved westwards to the region of the Great Lakes. Now they are mostly working in the Pacific Coast zone, amidst the mighty Douglas firs and western pines of Oregon and British Columbia (*see* TREES, CONIFEROUS). Each camp is put up by a timber company which has bought the standing timber on a tract of forest that may cover many square miles. The site chosen is usually in the heart of woods, beside a river, road, or railway that will carry the logs or the lumber away to distant ports and towns. Often a sawmill is built beside the camp to convert the round logs to planks and beams before shipment.

Life in the camps is hard and rough, and appeals only to hardy men willing to spend months away from civilization. They live together in huts built of round logs or sawn boards, and sleep on wooden bunks. Their clothing, too, is rough but serviceable and picturesque; their thick woollen shirts, patterned in broad checks, enable them to work out of doors in all but the roughest weather; and their heavy boots, studded with nails to give a grip on the slippery bark of wet logs, save their feet from injury in the rough undergrowth. Most of the loggers are experts in some particular branch of the lumbering trade—fellers who bring down great 200-foot stems to the cry of 'Timber!'; riggers who put up high wire cables to haul the logs away; tractor drivers, sawyers, and water-men who guide the timber down the swift rivers to the sea. All are tough, strong, and muscular, and the coming of modern machinery has given them more scope for their skill, ability, and hardihood. The timber firms find it most profit-able to work out their timber stands (that is, clear the areas selected) at a rapid rate, and pay high wages to men who can fell and haul away the forest giants, weighing several tons apiece, at top speed despite hardships and danger.

Every camp has its cookhouse, where cooks prepare ample and excellent meals for the hungry loggers. Good food, supplied at low prices, is a feature of all lumber camps; but by a curious tradition the meals are always eaten in silence. Most camps have a store where tools, clothes, tobacco, and other necessities can be

J. J. Lynx

LOGGING IN NORTHERN QUEBEC
Powerful tractors haul the felled timber to the power saw in a 'timber bob'

J. J. Lynx

MOVING A CANADIAN LUMBER CAMP TO A NEW SITE
The huts are drawn through the snow on skids by tractors

bought. The men serve under foremen, whose discipline is rough and ready though usually fair. There is a good fellowship amongst them, for they live together for months on end and have to make their own amusements. They play card games, spin long yarns, and sing old songs of the trails that have been passed on from one gang to another since the lumbering trade first began.

It is a rover's life, for as soon as the stand of timber has been felled, the whole camp is struck and moved to a fresh site which may lie many miles away across the forested hills. As transport, settlement, and planned forestry reach out into the wilds, there is less need for these shifting mills and camps. But for many years to come they will be needed to win timber from the remote backwoods, and bold spirits still take up the calling of the wandering lumberjack.

See also LOGGING; TIMBER FELLING.

LUPINS, FIELD. These are grown mainly for 'green manure' to be ploughed in to the soil again, but also for their seeds which are used in feeding sheep. Lupins will grow on poor, light land in the east of England, where it is difficult to get the usual farm crops to flourish. The crop can, for instance, grow on sandy land that is short of lime. Since lupins, like other leguminous crops, take in nitrogen from the air, they form a valuable green manure which puts the soil into a condition to grow more difficult crops afterwards. But when the crop is being used for this purpose, it should have generous lime and fertilizers to produce heavy growth, so that, when ploughed in, it will provide plenty of humus for the soil. White, yellow, and blue flowered varieties are grown, the blue lupin being the most common. The seed is usually sown in April, though sometimes as late as August. When the crop is grown for seed, it is sown in drills in rows 20 inches apart, 90 lb. per acre being used; otherwise it is broadcast, using 120 lb. per acre.

When grown for seed, the crop is cut with a mowing-machine and tied into sheaves by hand, for the pods are so hard and have such sharp spines that they would wear out the elevating canvasses if a binder were used. About 12 to 18 cwt. of seed is obtained from an acre of land. The seed can be fed to sheep at about $\frac{1}{4}$ lb. per head per day; but they must be brought to it gradually, as lupin seed can be poisonous to most animals at all times and to sheep unaccustomed to it.

Recently, a sweet variety of lupin has been introduced from the Continent, which continental farmers have found to be a valuable crop for light soils. The seed forms a food rich in protein, and appears to be safe for all livestock and, since it is not bitter, more palatable than the other varieties.

Lupins are also a very popular garden perennial plant, and many lovely colours, white, pink, yellow, blue, mauve, and purple, have been produced by plant breeders.

See also LEGUMINOUS CROPS.

M

MACHINERY, FARM, *see* MECHANIZED FARMING.

MACKEREL FISHING, *see* FISHING INDUSTRY.

MAIZE. Maize, *Zea mays*, is one of the principle grain crops of tropical and sub-tropical countries. It is a native of Mexico, and had been cultivated by the American Indians long before the coming of the Europeans: hence it is often called 'Indian corn'. (The word 'corn' in America always means maize.) It has now been introduced to all parts of the world which have a suitable climate, and early strains have been developed that will ripen as far north as Germany. Much of it is grown in small plots by peasant cultivators, especially in the tropics, but in North and South America, Australia, and South and East Africa, it is grown on an extensive scale by farmers using up-to-date methods and machinery. In South Africa, where it is a particularly important crop, it is known as 'mealies'.

Maize is an annual grass and must have fertile, well-cultivated soil, and a growing season of at least 85 days free from frost, against which it has little resistance. In the tropics maize may be sown at nearly any time of the year, but elsewhere it is sown in late spring. The seeds are generally set two or three together about 2 feet apart, in rows 3 feet apart. If hand sown, only about 4 lb. per acre of seed is needed; but machine-sowing is more extravagant. Throughout the growing season, maize requires little attention apart from weeding. The seedlings grow quickly, forming a handsome erect plant from 6 to 10 feet high. The male and female flowers are carried in separate clusters on the same plant. The male ones called the 'tassels' grow near the top of the stem, and are long and feathery; the female ones grow lower down, forming long green oval structures, enclosed in a leafy sheath from the tip of which protrudes a tuft of white stigmas, known as the 'silk' Pollination is effected by the wind.

From 3 to 6 months after the crop is sown, the corn, in a suitable climate, ripens. The large, wedge-shaped grains are set in rows round a cylindrical 'cob' or swollen stalk, the whole being enclosed in the broad sheath or 'husk'. As a rule the corn is yellow in colour, but it may be white, red, purple, blue, or black, according to the variety grown. The whole cob is gathered, usually by hand, although in America elaborate machines are used for harvesting. The cobs are then dried, and the husks removed; often the corn is stored on the cob to be removed during a slack period in the winter. The shelling is often done by hand, but hand-driven or power-driven machines are used in many countries. The yield of shelled grain varies from 1 to 2 tons per acre.

Ripe maize has many uses. The whole grain is fed to farm animals, especially to pigs and poultry, enormous quantities being at one time

International News Photo

PICKING RIPE MAIZE IN AMERICA

The male flowers are at the head of the stalks and the cobs develop from the female flowers lower down the stem

Eric Guy

HARVESTING MAIZE FOR FODDER IN HAMPSHIRE

exported to Britain from North America and the Argentine. It also forms the basis of many prepared animal foods. Peasant cultivators make a coarse flour by pounding the grain in mortars, or using hand-driven grinding machines; sometimes the whole grain is boiled and eaten. It is also roasted to make 'pop corn', or is specially prepared as 'corn flakes', which are eaten as a breakfast cereal. In America, and to a growing extent in Europe, 'sweet corn' or 'corn on the cob' is used as a vegetable (*see* SWEET CORN). The ripe, starchy grain is also used industrially as a source of starch and alcohol. Different varieties of maize are grown for these various purposes, or to suit particular soils or climates.

The cobs from which the grain has been removed are used for cattle feeding in America, together with more concentrated food; and the whole crop is often grown purely as a silage crop, being harvested before the grain ripens.

In England maize is grown only on a limited scale and almost always for feeding green to cattle or for silage. Because it is very resistant to drought, it is a useful crop in the southern and eastern counties of England, where the grass often dries up towards the end of the summer, and some alternative green crop is needed. Recently varieties have been found that will ripen in Britain if there is a long enough period of hot sun in the ripening phase.

Maize is most often grown on part of the root land (*see* ROTATION OF CROPS), but sometimes the crop is grown for a number of years in succession on a suitable patch of land near the farm buildings, where, when ready for cutting, it is handy for feeding to the livestock.

As maize grows quickly, the soil must be in 'good heart' and generously fed with farmyard manure and fertilizers—perhaps as much as 20 tons per acre of farmyard manure applied in the autumn, and 5 to 6 cwt. per acre of balanced fertilizer in May, just before the seed is sown. Deep rich loams are ideal, and when such soils are found in favourable climates, very big yields can be obtained. About 56 lb. of seed (far more than is needed for a grain crop) per acre is sown in rows 20 inches apart to allow for hoeing during the growing season. Rooks can be very destructive to the crop, once they discover it, so a watch must be kept while the plants are small.

Cutting begins when the pastures are drying up, usually about mid-August, and continues until frost damages the crop. Any portion of the crop that is not needed for feeding green may be cut, chopped, and made into SILAGE (q.v.). The crop is best for this purpose when the cobs have formed but the grain is still quite soft. About 20 to 25 tons per acre of green maize is obtained from an average crop, but 35 tons or more is not uncommon under very good conditions.

See also SWEET CORN; TROPICAL AGRICULTURE.

MANGE, *see* MITE AND TICK PESTS.

MANGOLDS, *see* ROOT CROPS.

MANGOES, *see* TROPICAL FRUITS.

MANURE, FARMYARD (DUNG). This is the most important soil improver in all countries where livestock are kept. Strictly speaking, it is a mixture of the excreta of animals (dung and urine) and the straw that is used for bedding. However, when the droppings go direct to the land, as when animals graze or are folded, they are also a valued means of maintaining fertility.

The foods fed to livestock (such as hay, straw, roots, corn, and oil cakes) all contain varying amounts of the important plant foods, nitrogen, phosphate, and potash (*see* MANURES). Some of the nitrogen and phosphate are retained by the animal to make flesh and bone, and a little of the potash is also used; but the balance appears in the solid and liquid excreta, the dung and the urine. These are mixed with the bedding, usually straw, which absorbs liquids and thus keeps the animals dry and comfortable. The liquid manure contains most of the active, quick-acting nitrogen and potash excreted by the animal, while the solid excreta contains the less available nitrogen compounds that have resisted digestion by the animal, and almost the whole of the phosphate not needed by the animal. The straw itself contains only a small amount of nitrogen and phosphate, but a useful quantity of readily soluble potash.

From the point of view of feeding the plant, the liquid manure is by far the most valuable part of farmyard manure, and the value of the manure depends very largely on how much of this liquid is retained by the straw bedding. Fresh farmyard manure is 'long', which means that the straw is still tough and, although soaked with liquid manure, appears to be little changed. A brisk FERMENTATION (q.v. Vol. II), however, soon sets in, the mass heats up, about half of the straw is burnt away, and part of the nitrogen is usually lost in the air in the form of ammonia. The part of the straw that has resisted decay takes on a dark brown colour and becomes brittle. In farmers' language the dung is now 'short'. If manure made by well-fed animals is dug in when very fresh, it gives off so much ammonia in the soil that the young plants may be damaged. The remedy is either to apply it some weeks before sowing the seed, or to air the

Eric Guy

FARMYARD MANURE READY TO BE SPREAD ON A FIELD

manure well before applying it in order to release the excess of ammonia.

The quality of dung as a fertilizer depends on several factors. Generous feeding with oil cakes, complete absorption of the liquid manure, and shelter from the weather give a rich manure. Poor feeding, not enough litter (bedding), and exposure to rain lead to great waste of plant food and therefore to a poor manure. It is not surprising, therefore, that the quantity of plant food and dry matter in farmyard manure varies greatly. About three-quarters of an average mixed sample is water, up to 20% is organic matter, and 5% is mineral ash. Poultry manure is often used by gardeners and allotment holders. As a fertilizer it is relatively rich in nitrogen and phosphate, but poor in potash. Therefore it needs to be supplemented by muriate of potash to make a satisfactory dressing for most vegetable crops. The actual quantity of nitrogen per ton depends on the amount of moisture, grit, and straw present, but it ranges from 4% in a good dry sample to $1\frac{1}{2}$% in a poor one.

Farmyard manure suits all crops and soils. In general, the long manure is applied to heavy soils in autumn, and the short to light soils in spring. It is a 'complete' fertilizer, and the humus in it has a good effect on the texture of the soil and its power to retain water. The full effect of the application of farmyard manure upon a crop is often delayed, for it takes some time for the more resistant materials in it to become soluble and available. The effect, therefore, of a dressing of dung may continue for two or three successive crops. Few farms can provide enough dung to manure each field more than once in 4 or 5 years, and the amount used is generally from 10 to 15 tons per acre, usually given to the root crops but occasionally to wheat, beans, or grass to be mown for hay. Farmers, therefore, find it necessary to use suitable dressings of chemical fertilizers as well as dung, especially when growing root or vegetable crops.

MANURES (FERTILIZERS). **1.** These are substances added to the SOILS (q.v.) in order to make up for the plant food used up by crops, or to provide poor soils with the plant food not present to start with. Their purpose, therefore, is to keep the land fit to grow good crops. Fields without manures will grow smaller and smaller crops, till finally it is no longer profitable to grow them at all. The roots of growing crops suck up from the soil a number of substances in the dissolved state. There are many of these substances, but most soils can supply enough of most of them without any outside help. There are some substances, however, that are needed in relatively large amounts and quickly become used up under the feeding action of crops. The four most important are the soluble compounds of the elements nitrogen, phosphorus, potassium, and calcium, and are known as nitrogen, phosphate, potash, and lime. Shortage of lime is so important and has so many special effects on soils and plants that it has been dealt with separately (*see* LIME). Here we shall consider the action of the materials that provide the three elements: nitrogen, phosphate, and potash (kalium), or to give them their accepted symbols N, P, and K.

Farmyard manures and compost not only provide these plant foods but have other useful effects on the soil as well. They make it crumble more easily when it is cultivated, and help it to hold water, so that the seeds sprout quickly, and the young plants find a good supply of moisture for their growth. Such manures consist largely of plant and animal remains, that is, they are rich in organic matter and supply the soil with humus. They are therefore called organic manures. Those that supply plant food only are usually rather simple inorganic or mineral salts, and are commonly known as chemical or artificial fertilizers. These inorganic fertilizers cannot completely replace the organic manures, but they can supplement them by providing more plant food.

2. ORGANIC MANURES. All organic manures contain nitrogen, most of them phosphate, and a few contain potash as well. The nitrogenous compounds in organic manures are chemically much more complicated than in the inorganic nitrogenous fertilizers, and are not as a rule immediately useful to the crop. They are broken down into a more simple form in the soil by several types of BACTERIA (q.v. Vol. II), their final stages being ammonia and nitrate. As this process takes time, the organic manures are not so active or 'forcing' in their effects as are the nitrogenous chemical fertilizers; but though their action is slow, it is steady and sustained, and may last to some extent even over a period of years. This type of behaviour has advantages for certain crops, particularly for horticultural crops that must never be allowed to be checked in growth. Organic manures are easy to use and suit all

THE EFFECT OF DIFFERENT CHEMICALS ON RADISHES

Rothamsted Experimental Station

These plants, which were all sown on the same date, received (1) nitrogen only, (2) nitrogen and phosphate, (3) nitrogen, phosphate, and a small quantity of potassium, (4) nitrogen, phosphate, and a large quantity of potassium

crops, whereas to use artificial fertilizers to the best advantage needs more special knowledge. On the other hand, the organic manures are more expensive, and certain important farm crops such as potatoes and sugar-beet need more plant food than can easily be provided in the form of organics alone.

By far the most important organic manure is farmyard manure or dung, which is made on every farm that has animals. It is not only an excellent method of returning straw to the land, but it also saves much of the nitrogen, phosphate, and potash contained in the home-grown and purchased cakes and meals fed to livestock. It contains all the plant foods. On many farms it is by far the most important potash manure; therefore, root crops, which particularly need potash, benefit greatly from dung. Dung can, however, be badly spoilt by careless storage (*see* MANURE, FARMYARD).

Other bulky organic manures made on the farm are COMPOSTS (q.v.) and green manures. Waste straw, weeds, and any other plant remains rotted down in a heap make a compost that has certain of the soil-improving properties of dung, but rather less fertilizing value. Green manures are quick-growing crops, such as mustard, rye, lupins, or tares, that are grown on the land and then ploughed in when fully grown to give the

soil a useful addition of humus, together with the nitrogen, phosphate, and potash contained in the plant substance.

Close to big towns farmers can obtain sludge from the sewage works and town refuse collected from dustbins. Both are useful organic manures, and can often be bought for little more than the cost of cartage. Their important constituent is nitrogen, but they contain almost no potash. Near the sea-coast, seaweed is a very valuable nitrogen and potash manure.

Gardeners pay high prices for certain concentrated organic manures from the animal industries. Dried blood, hoof-and-horn, shoddy (wool-waste from the wool mills), and the like, are all excellent materials for providing a steady supply of nitrogen for special garden crops. Dried blood and hoof-and-horn are valuable by-products of the slaughter houses, particularly in beef-cattle countries such as the Argentine. Fish meal and meat meal, made from fish and meat waste too coarse or damaged to be used as animal foods, are sold as manures containing nitrogen and phosphates.

In the rainless islands off the coast of Peru, ancient deposits of sea-bird manure, called guano, are found, and were first shipped to England in 1840 for use on farms. Nowadays, the limited supplies are generally used for garden crops. Guano contains little potash, but it is a useful nitrogen and phosphate fertilizer.

3. ARTIFICIAL FERTILIZERS. Fertilizers made by chemical means in factories were first introduced about the middle of the 19th century as the result of experimental work at research institutes, in particular that of Sir John Lawes at Rothamsted (*see* RESEARCH IN AGRICULTURE). Such fertilizers aim to supply the soil with all the necessary mineral nutrients, in particular nitrogen, phosphates, and potash, derived from other sources than plant and animal organisms. It was discovered that mineral salts containing these nutrients could be extracted from inorganic sources, such as mineral ores in the earth, rocks, and the air itself (a very good source of nitrogen). These can be prepared quite cheaply in enormous quantities in factories and are easy to apply to the soil (*see* ARTIFICIAL FERTILIZERS). The value and also the dangers of using these chemical fertilizers as supplements to organic manures are very much disputed among agriculturists, and there is a strong school of thought which holds that artificial fertilizers, being without the germ of life, only force artificial results from the soil without really restoring to it the virtue which has been taken out of it. This school declares that the agriculture of a country should be so balanced that, in fact, there is enough farmyard manure, together with compost, green manures, and other organic manures, to provide all that the fields require. Whether this line of argument is right or not, everyone will agree that without humus the soil will deteriorate, as it will lack the organic substances which, apart from their food value, are necessary to keep right the structure of the soil (*see* SOILS).

See also SOILS; MANURE, FARMYARD; COMPOST HEAP; LIME; ARTIFICIAL FERTILIZERS.

MAPLE TREE. Maples belong to the genus *Acer* (as also does the sycamore), a group of trees of which almost all have sugar in their sap. In the Sugar Maples of North America, especially Canada, this sugar is produced in sufficient quantities to make its extraction a valuable industry. The Sugar Maples need a cold temperate climate as this encourages an abundant flow of sap, and they prefer a wet soil—the Red Maples, for instance, grow well in swamps.

The sugar-bearing sap is collected in the spring by tapping the trees—that is, by boring small holes in the trunk and fitting the holes with spouts

E.N.A.

COLLECTING MAPLE SAP IN QUEBEC PROVINCE, CANADA

A can into which the sap runs can be seen on the tree on the left

which carry the sap to buckets tied to the trunk below the holes. The buckets are periodically emptied and the sap taken to the refinery to be converted into maple syrup or maple sugar (*see* SUGAR REFINING, Vol. VII). About 3 lb. of sugar is produced annually from a good tree.

Maple trees, especially Japanese Maples, are also often planted as ORNAMENTAL TREES (q.v.). They grow quickly and to a symmetrical shape, and they produce beautiful autumn colouring. Some varieties are also lovely in the spring, their opening buds being a brilliant red; and others, such as the Hard or Rock Maple, yield valuable timbers (*see* HARDWOODS, section 2 (*l*), Vol. VII).

See also TREES, BROADLEAVED.

MARKET-GARDENING. The market-gardener who grows fruit, vegetables, and flowers in order to make a living follows the same general principles of culture as does the private gardener; but he grows crops on a much larger scale, generally concentrating on those crops for which there is a good regular demand at a price which brings him a reasonable return. The general principles of planning, planting, and cultivating a vegetable garden or a fruit orchard are described in VEGETABLE GARDEN and FRUIT-GROWING (qq.v.), and the culture of particular fruits, flowers, and vegetables is described under the names of the principal crops.

Most market-gardeners find that the crops which command the best prices and the most certain market are those which can be sold out of season—early strawberries or tomatoes, Christmas pears, new potatoes and garden peas for Whitsun. Therefore GLASSHOUSES, FRAMES, and CLOCHES (qq.v.) are an important part of market-garden equipment. These are used not only for forcing crops to maturity ahead of their normal season, and growing tender crops such as melons, cucumbers, and winter chrysanthemums, but also for PLANT PROPAGATION (q.v.) so that well-advanced young plants are ready for planting out of doors as soon as the weather allows.

Not all flowers are suitable for marketing, especially for passing through a wholesale market. The flowers must be of the kind that can stand up to the handling and transport necessary before they finally reach the consumer. Thus, flowers such as chrysanthemums, carnations, and narcissus are easier to market than such delicate flowers as larkspur and sweet-peas; and short-lived flowers such as poppies are useless for anything but local sales. Some flowers, roses for example, are always picked and packed as buds,

for they travel better that way. Certain old and well-tried favourites, such as roses, sweet-peas, and violets, always find a market, and there is a steady demand from florists for certain white flowers. On the other hand, some flowers become temporarily fashionable, very often because their colour is in vogue that year, but soon lose their popularity. This selling side of his business is as important to the market-gardener as his actual gardening skill. He has to reconcile the likely demands of the market with the possibilities of his soil and the type of skilled labour he can get. The growing of many flowers under glass, such as specimen chrysanthemums, roses, and carnations, demands skilled labour of a highly specialized kind. Gluts are likely to occur during the summer months, so that large acreages of ordinary flowers, even though these may be comparatively easy and cheap to grow, may bring in little profit. Equally, it is unsafe to grow on a large scale what may be called novelties, that is, flowers to which the average buyer is unaccustomed, even though the price obtained for them may be tempting. Flowers, however, which can be brought to perfection at a season such as Christmas are very likely to be profitable.

The vegetable and fruit-grower also has to consider his probable market in deciding what to grow. It is of no use for him to produce a very large supply of lettuces, for instance, if these all

A LARGE MARKET GARDEN

Fox Photos

The site is flat and has been cleared of trees. To the right is the pumping house for the irrigation, with compost heaps beside it. Irrigation pipes run across the beds

mature at a time when lettuces are a glut in the market. If, however, he can produce lettuces slightly out of season, early or very late, he can be sure of a market and a profitable price. Large quantities of early apples and pears which will not keep may be difficult to dispose of at a profit, whereas a later-keeping variety, which can be stored until fruit is becoming scarce, is much more profitable.

A standard of grading and packing, known as the 'National Mark', used to be applied to many fruits and vegetables, but this scheme came to an end at the beginning of the Second World War. Growers, however, when sending produce to the larger markets or wholesalers, should use the recognized standard market boxes or crates which are often provided by the wholesaler on a credit system. In order to secure a fair price for the produce, it is important to grade it uniformly and to pack it securely. The Ministry of Agriculture has issued as a guide to growers a list of National Recommended Grades for most fruit and vegetables.

The majority of growers now use the non-returnable type of container, which is of less durable material but is not expected to last so long. For example, for many years the wholesalers at Covent Garden and similar markets have used for tomatoes a 12-lb. returnable wicker basket known as a 'strike'; but with the coming of the National Mark, wooden non-returnable boxes became more popular, and even growers who did not use this mark tended to market their tomatoes in boxes, chips, or cardboard baskets.

Where produce is sold through the wholesale markets, it is sent to a commission AGENT (q.v. Vol. VII) who acts as the middleman between producer and retailer, generally taking a percentage of the price obtained to pay for his services. This, with the freight and packing costs, must be deducted before the grower can arrive at an accurate estimate of the real selling price of his crop. Smaller growers who sell direct to retail shops or to their own customers, or in the local markets, do not have all these costs.

In some districts co-operative marketing is practised. Growers, by combining with each other and sending their produce to a central packing station in the district, can have it properly sorted and sent to the best market. The manager of such a station is in constant touch with all the markets, large and small, and is able to send the different packages to the places where they are most likely to sell successfully. He can also advise growers not only about methods of packing and grading but also about the types of crops that will pay them best to grow.

See also MARKET-TOWNS; VEGETABLE GARDEN; FRUIT-GROWING.

See also Vol. VII: GREENGROCERY; MARKET.

MARKET-TOWNS. Many towns, some large and some small, are called market-towns. They are important to the country people of the surrounding district because a market is held in each of them on a certain day in the week. To that market the farmers bring their horses, cattle, and other produce for sale; and at the market they can buy the things they need for their farms and for their households.

There have been markets of some kind for a very long time, but not before there were people with goods to sell and others who wished to buy. Farmers have no need for a market until they can raise more corn and cattle than their families need to eat; and even when the farmer has something to sell, a market is no good to him until there are people in villages and towns who have neither crops nor cattle and must buy the things they eat. Therefore markets begin after the occupations of the people have become a little specialized.

Markets are now held once a week in the market-town, but in their beginnings they were much less frequent. There were several reasons for this. First, the country people had goods to sell only at certain times—cattle and sheep in the autumn when they were fat off the pastures; wool about midsummer when the flocks were shorn; fat geese at Martinmas; some wheat after harvest. Secondly, the roads were bad and travelling took a long time. So it became the custom to fix one or a few days in the year when a market or fair would be held in a certain town, and all the farmers of the district and the merchants from the towns could meet there to buy and sell (see TRADE FAIRS, Vol. VII).

The farmers, having sold and been paid for their farm produce, would take the opportunity to buy the things that they and their families needed; and that brought other merchants to the market. STREET ENTERTAINERS (q.v. Vol. IX) went there too—jugglers, tumblers, musicians, and ballad sellers. It was a grand mixture of business and pleasure.

As time went by, and the farmers had more

Rothamsted Experimental Station

THE MAY SHEEP FAIR, BOSTON, LINCS.
19th-century lithograph after George Northouse

and more to sell, and the towns grew in size and wanted more and more to buy, frequent markets became necessary. It was now possible to hold these because better roads and, later, railways made travel much easier.

This weekly market was usually held in the middle of the little town, in the High Street or the wide market place. Some country towns, such as Thame in Oxfordshire, still hold their weekly market in the wide main street. Sellers brought their cattle and horses, penned or haltered them, and stood by them, waiting for a buyer. The buyers walked round, saw what was in the market, and decided what price to offer. The making of the bargain often took all day, and the price a farmer got depended on his skill in the delicate art of bargaining. The sale of horses and cattle was only a part of the business done. In some corner of the market the people who made butter and cheese and kept chickens laid out their produce and traded with the town people and with the merchants who were buying to sell in the big cities. In some old market-towns there are still the stone halls with open sides where the butter was sold by the yard and the women sold their eggs and cheeses. The millers and grain merchants, the maltsters and brewers, also attended the market to buy wheat and barley from the farmers. Indeed, nearly all the farmers and those they did business with were there. These weekly markets were not unlike the great fairs of the earlier times, with this difference—that many of the merchants who used to travel from fair to fair, selling their goods to the farmers, had settled down in the town and become the draper and grocer whom we know today.

Another important change came when sales began to be conducted by AUCTION (q.v. Vol. VII). Instead of each seller standing by his

The Times

A CATTLE MARKET AT BASINGSTOKE
The auctioneer is standing on the right

beast and making his own bargain, he handed his beast to the auctioneer who proceeded to sell it by auction. This is the practice with many goods today. The auctioneer stands on a high place where he can see everybody. The animal is led before him where everybody can see it, and the auctioneer asks how much anyone will offer him for it. Whoever offers the highest price gets the animal. This is better for the farmers than the old system of each man making his own bargain. If many buyers are anxious to buy cattle, they offer more and more, bidding against each other; and so the farmer gets a better price.

The market held in the open can be pleasant in summer, but it is often very uncomfortable in winter for beasts and men. Some auctioneers provide shelter for both by building a mart—a covered sale-ring and covered standings for the beasts. This is the rule in Scotland where the weather is much colder than in the south of England.

There have, however, been more changes in very recent years. The trade in horses has greatly declined since horses are now so much less used on farms. Cattle and in some places sheep and

pigs are more than ever the chief part of the market. The cattle business is divided into three parts—the store trade, that is, in young cattle ready to be fattened for the butcher; the fat trade, that is, in cattle ready for the butcher; and the trade in dairy animals. The sales of fat cattle used to be the great excitement because the prices there decided whether the farmer had made money or lost it during a year's work in feeding the young beasts he had bought the year before. During and after the Second World War, however, the trade in fat cattle came under the control of the Ministry of Food who bought all the cattle offered in the market (see BULK PURCHASE, Vol. VII). When there is only one buyer there cannot be an auction; instead, the Ministry of Food paid fixed prices according to the quality of the animal, and officials called graders assessed the quality of each fat beast. Eggs, too, were no longer sold by private bargain; they were taken by the Ministry of Food at fixed prices.

The market hardly plays as important a part in country life as it used to. Country people have motor-cars, bus services, telephones, and newspapers and magazines full of advertisements. They need not buy everything in their local market-town. Many thousands of them go to the real modern fairs such as the Royal Show and the Royal Highland Show, and order their machinery from the merchants there (*see* AGRICULTURAL SHOWS). They need not go to the market-town to sell their barley: they may send the merchant a sample in an envelope and make the deal by telephone. The women need not go to town to do the week's shopping, for the merchants drive up to the door in their vans. But in spite of these changes, the market and the market-town are still important.

The people in the market-place on market-day are not all farmers; quite often the farmers are in a minority. There are the people to whom the farmer sells—grain and potato merchants. There are the many more people from whom the farmer buys—the men who sell tractors, oil, machinery, cattle food, poultry food, fire extinguishers, paint, drain tiles, sheep dip, fertilizers, insecticides, and patent medicines. There may be the people who do work for the farmers —agricultural contractors who undertake to plough a field or harvest a crop or dig a mile of drains. There may be another and a very important person—the agricultural adviser for the district. He is a government servant trained in agricultural science, whose job is to help farmers in applying the latest scientific discoveries to their flocks and fields. It may seem that few people pay attention to the auctioneer and many stand about, gossiping in twos and threes. But the gossip may be serious business about the buying of a tractor or the correct fertilizer to apply to a difficult field. Those conversations at market may save the writing of many letters— a job that farmers greatly dislike.

It is not only on market-days that the market-town serves the farmers. It has the bank which handles his money, and the lawyer who advises him. It has the agricultural engineer who sells him machines and keeps his tractors in repair. It is the centre of the farming in the district, and farming is made a much more pleasant and efficient business when there is a good market-town.

See also Vol. VII, Colour Plate, p. 384.
See also Vol. IX: FAIRS.

MARROWS, *see* GOURD VEGETABLES.

MEASUREMENTS, AGRICULTURAL, *see* AGRICULTURAL MEASUREMENTS.

MECHANIZED FARMING. Most farm implements and machines carry out more quickly and cheaply, and sometimes more pleasantly, jobs traditionally done by hand or by simple tools drawn by animals. Tractor ploughs do just the same work as horse ploughs; reapers and binders do the work men used to do with scythes; threshing-machines have replaced flails. These inventions have not directly enabled the farmer to do any particular job better than his forefathers but to do it more quickly. Speed is of importance if it helps the farmer to beat the weather, for many of the most important farming operations have only a short season in which they can be carried out properly. To take one instance, there is generally only a short period in which the soil is at its best for being made into a seed-bed and planted. If it is impossible to prepare the soil and sow the seed during this good period, the farmer will have to put in some of his seed at a time when the soil is not in the best condition to receive it. In years of particularly bad weather he may never be able to plant part of the crop at all. By being able with the right kind of machinery to make the best of the weather, the farmer is increasing the likelihood of good crops (*see* CULTIVATORS).

A problem of 'timeliness' even more urgent than the one at planting seasons comes at haymaking and harvest. Making hay or harvesting corn in climates such as that of Britain often has to be done in short spells of fine weather between long spells of wet days; and this is complicated by the fact that the total time between the grass having grown enough bulk to cut and having become woody, or between the corn being ripe and its grains having begun to shed, is short. Therefore machines which make it possible to harvest a whole crop in a very short time may make the difference between saving or losing the crop (*see* HARVESTING).

The implements and machines must, however, be used properly; for many machines can lead to bad farming if they are not used with great care. In haymaking the hay-tedder, though it may save a damp crop in bad weather, can damage a dry, ripe crop much more than hand-turning. Much of the hay's nutritive value is in the leaves, and these are easily knocked off and scattered by too vigorous harvesting methods. But by the

THE IMPLEMENTS SECTION AT THE ROYAL SHOW AT OXFORD IN 1950
Farm machinery forms an important part of agricultural shows

careful use of the proper machine the job can be done as well as ever it was done by hand, and hay can now be baled, using a stationary or a pick-up baler, in a greener condition and with less loss of leaf than if it had to wait until fit to stack (*see* HAYMAKING).

In some cases a new machine has made possible a new and genuinely better way of doing things. For example, in most crops and conditions of soil, the combine drill, which issues with each seed a little dose of artificial manure to help the seedling in its early growth, will increase yields sufficiently for the purchase of such a drill to be a good investment. At the same time, because the combine drill does two operations in one, it saves labour and tractor hours (*see* DRILLS AND DISTRIBUTORS).

Another example is the auto-recorder milking-machine, in which the milk passes through glass jars and pipes from the cow's udder to the cooler, thus saving the milk from exposure to the dust. All milking machines are considered more hygienic than milking by hand into a bucket (*see* DAIRY MACHINERY). It must be remembered, however, that the success of the newer method depends, as everything depends, upon the man who employs the method, and if he is careless over the washing and sterilizing of the complicated rubber and metal pipes, the final result will be worse than before.

It is said that machines 'save labour', and this of course is true, but is not as simple as it sounds. If the spreading of farmyard manure and other winter jobs have been mechanized so that fewer men are needed on the farm, how is the reduced staff to manage at haymaking time, unless either many casual workers are employed (which is not often practicable) or haymaking is mechanized as well? Those times of year at which most labour is needed—such as harvesting and root hoeing—are called the 'peak' periods, and mechanization should aim at levelling out the peaks so that the same number of hands are needed throughout the year (*see* FARM LABOUR).

On a mixed farm that is largely mechanized there are so many different machines, and some of them are so complicated, that a farmer nowadays has to be a skilled mechanic—or if he is not, then somebody else must be. He must know how all these machines work, how they can best be used, and how to take care of them. This makes **a well-equipped workshop a necessity.** The farmer must also be able to choose expertly when he sets out to buy some newly invented machine or to replace a worn out one, for if he is to make his farm pay he cannot afford to be out of date in his equipment, nor yet can he afford to waste money on machinery unsuitable for his particular farm.

This art and science of managing men and machines to the best advantage can be made to bring benefits to workers and manager alike. Labour-saving devices do not harm the status of the workers; instead, the increase in output per man-hour should raise the living standard of the workers, and better ways of doing things should give them a less arduous time during their working hours. In the early days of the development of the THRESHING-MACHINE (q.v.), bands of farm workers destroyed some of the newly invented machines, believing that they would imperil their livelihood (*see* LUDDITES, Vol. VII); but very few farm workers now would be willing to go back to the days when many weeks of the year were spent using a flail to thresh the grain on the barn floor.

It has been estimated that at the beginning of the 19th century three men were needed to work on the land to grow enough food to support themselves and their families and to have enough left over to send to the town to keep one town-worker with his family. In 1948, surveys made in the United States of America, where farming is highly mechanized, showed that each American farmer produced enough food to feed thirteen other American workers and their families, and also to export large quantities of food to other countries. It seems, therefore, that in 150 years the output of farm workers had increased by about ten times. This increase in production has been brought about very largely by the use of mechanical power and its application to farm implements and machines.

See also AGRICULTURAL HISTORY; FARM TOOLS, HISTORY OF; POWER FOR FARMING; RESEARCH IN AGRICULTURE.

MEDLARS AND QUINCES. These belong to the *Rosaceae* family, as do apples and pears, and are closely related to the flowering shrub 'Japonica', the fruit of which is sometimes used for making jelly. Both quinces and medlars were known to the Greeks and Romans, the quince having most probably originated in western Asia, while the medlar was a native of the continent of Europe.

Medlars will grow on most soils. They are generally grafted on to rootstocks of whitethorn, quince, or pear—the pear being suitable for a large standard tree. When the young tree has been shaped, they need no more pruning than the normal thinning of overcrowded branches. Unless there is threat of a severe autumn frost,

Amateur Gardening
MEDLARS

the fruit should not be picked until a dry November day. It is then stored in a frost-proof place for about 2 weeks, when the flesh will go soft and turn brownish-yellow. The fruit is then ready to eat.

Quinces do very much better if they are grown where there is plenty of moisture, and this is also needed for medlars grown on quince stock. They are easy to raise from cuttings, suckers, or layers—and indeed quinces are used as the

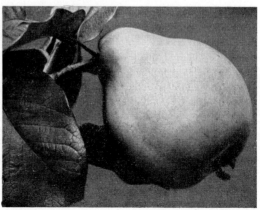
Amateur Gardening
A QUINCE OF THE PEAR-SHAPED VARIETY

principal rootstock for pears. They need little pruning after the young tree is shaped, and the bushes generally tend to grow in an umbrella-like shape. The fruit should ripen on the tree, and is not ready to pick until mid-October. When stored, it develops a very strong smell, and may taint the flavour of other fruit stored with it.

Quinces have many of the same pests and diseases as apples and pears. Both medlars and quinces suffer from leaf blotch, a fungus disease which causes black blotches to appear on the central leaf vein. The infected leaves should be picked off and burnt (*see* PLANT DISEASES, section 2).

See also FRUIT-GROWING; FRUIT PROPAGATION.

MELONS. These annual plants are closely related to CUCUMBERS (q.v.) and grow in the same way. They are natives of sub-tropical Asia, and are grown in most hot countries. They can also be grown in Britain in hothouses or on hot-beds in frames. The original melon of Asia was known as the Musk Melon—a name still used in America for all melons except Cantaloups and Water Melons. Many varieties of melons are now cultivated, and these are distinguished by their rinds, which may be thick and warted or ribbed and furrowed, cracked in a net-like pattern or smooth and thin; by their flesh which varies from green to red or yellow; and by their size which may be only 3 or 4 inches in diameter or over a foot. The Water Melon of South Carolina, U.S.A., has been known to reach a weight of 45 lb.

The Water Melon or Citrul is very popular in

R. A. Malby

CANTALOUP MELONS GROWING UNDER CLOCHES

most tropical countries. It is large, with a smooth, dark green skin and a white or pink flesh. It is less sweet but more juicy than other melons. The Kankoor Melon of India has a yellow oval fruit about 6 inches long, which is much used for curries and pickles as well as for eating raw. Its seeds are rich in oil, and are ground into a kind of meal.

Glasshouse or frame melons need a loamy soil containing about one part in four of decayed manure. The fruit will only mature satisfactorily in a warm damp atmosphere with a temperature of about 75° to 85° F. To achieve this in a frame, melons are generally planted over a HOTBED (q.v.). They need plenty of water and liquid manure during the time the fruit is swelling, and the air is kept moist by syringing twice daily. They should be shaded from hot sun. It is important to hand-pollinate the female flowers, and this is best done at midday on the day the flower first opens (*see* FERTILIZATION). The fruit should be thinned to one fruit only per shoot, and all non-fruiting shoots should be cut out. The fruiting shoots should be cut back to the first joint beyond the fruit.

MILK, *see* CATTLE, CARE OF, section 3. *See also* Vol. VII: DAIRY INDUSTRY. *See also* Vol. XI: MILK.

MILLET. 1. The name millet is applied to a large number of grasses that are grown for their grain, or as fodder, mainly in tropical and sub-tropical countries. They are not all closely related botanically, and some are annuals, others perennials. A common feature of nearly all of them, however, is that their seeds are round and very small, enclosed in a hard outer coat, and borne in large numbers on short stalks or spikes crowded at the summit of the stem. Some kinds of millet form the staple food of certain African and Asiatic peoples, but only a few kinds are exported, and in Europe they are grown only on a small scale. Most are grown by simple hand methods, though mechanized cultivation is used to a certain extent, especially in North America, South and East Africa, and Australia.

2. COMMON MILLET (*Panicum miliaceum*) has been cultivated for so long that its origin is unknown. It was grown by the ancient Egyptians; its grains have been found among prehistoric remains in south and central Europe:

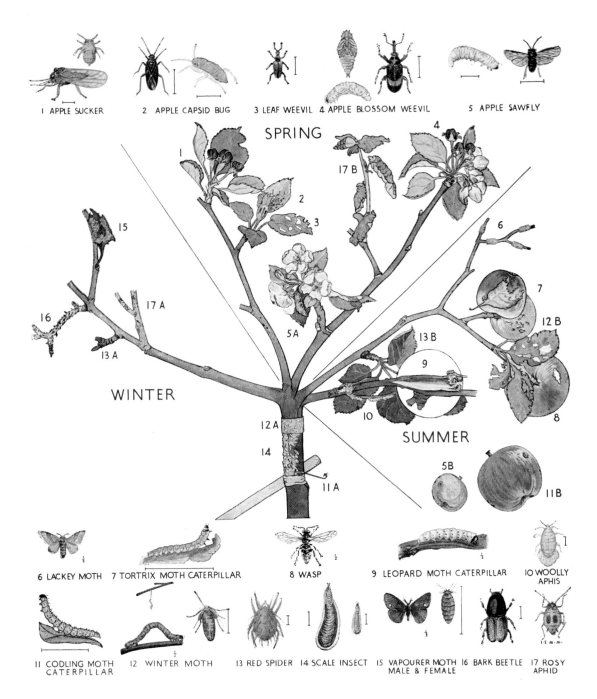

1 APPLE SUCKER   2 APPLE CAPSID BUG   3 LEAF WEEVIL   4 APPLE BLOSSOM WEEVIL   5 APPLE SAWFLY

SPRING

WINTER

SUMMER

6 LACKEY MOTH   7 TORTRIX MOTH CATERPILLAR   8 WASP   9 LEOPARD MOTH CATERPILLAR   10 WOOLLY APHIS

11 CODLING MOTH CATERPILLAR   12 WINTER MOTH   13 RED SPIDER   14 SCALE INSECT   15 VAPOURER MOTH MALE & FEMALE   16 BARK BEETLE   17 ROSY APHID

PESTS OF APPLE-TREES IN WINTER (*Left*), SPRING (*Top*), AND SUMMER (*Right*)

1. Blossoms and leaves damaged by Apple Sucker. 2. Leaf and blossom punctured by Apple Capsid Bug. 3. Leaf eaten by Leaf Weevil. 4. Discoloured blossoms caused by Apple Blossom Weevil grub. 5A. Blossoms on which Apple Sawfly lays its eggs. 5B. Hole through which Apple Sawfly grub has emerged. 6. Eggs of Lackey Moth. 7. Leaf stuck to apple by Tortrix Moth caterpillar. 8. Fruit bitten by wasp. 9. Hollow twig tunnelled by Leopard Moth caterpillar (magnified). 10. Woolly Aphid. 11A. Codling Moth caterpillar hibernating beneath sacking. 11B. Hole in apple from which Codling Moth caterpillar emerged. 12A. Winter Moth females caught on greaseband. 12B. Leaf eaten by Winter Moth caterpillars. 13A. Eggs of Red Spider. 13B. Leaves discoloured by Red Spider. 14. Scale Insects. 15. Eggs of Vapourer Moth. 16. Damage to twig by Fruit Bark Beetle. 17A. Eggs of Apple Rosy Aphid. 17B. Rolled-up leaves caused by Apple Rosy Aphid. (The actual size of the pests are given in fractions or by scale marks.)

and it was known in India a very long time ago. It is an erect annual grass, about 3½ feet high, which looks rather like a wheat plant, but bears its numerous small hard seeds in graceful drooping sprays. It is grown like a cereal crop, succeeds under dry conditions, and ripens about 5 months after sowing. It can be grown as far north as France, and stray plants that have sprung from scattered seeds are sometimes found growing wild in Britain.

3. GREAT MILLET, also known as sorghum, is a much larger annual grass (*Sorghum vulgare*) which originated in Africa, but has since been introduced into many other countries. Amongst its many names are *durra*, *dari*, and *milo* in Africa, *jawari* in India, *kaoliang* in China, and also Kaffir corn, Guinea corn, and Egyptian corn. It is a stout, erect plant, rather like maize in its general appearance, and it reaches a height of from 3 to 8 feet. Like maize, it is spaced widely apart when it is sown, and needs a well-manured soil to produce a heavy crop—though it will grow on poor soils. It is very resistant to heat and drought during its growing season.

The crop ripens in 4 to 6 months, and may yield crops of from 5 up to even 30 cwt. per acre. The small rounded grains are white, red, brown, or yellow in colour. They are made into porridge or pounded into meal, or, in Africa, fermented with water to make a kind of beer. Large quantities are also fed to livestock, particularly in North America, South Africa, and Australia, and some is imported to Britain for feeding young chickens and cage birds. Other varieties of sorghum are grown as fodder, being spaced more closely than the grain crops; others again, the sweet sorghums, are cut green and crushed to yield syrup and sugar; still others, the broom sorghums, have densely packed seed-stalks that are made into brooms or whisks after the grain has been removed.

4. FINGER MILLET, or *ragi* (*Eleusine coracana*) is an important crop in certain parts of Africa and southern India. It is a stout, tufted grass, which grows 3 feet high in 4 months, and thrives in poor soils and in warm dry climates. It is so named because the grain is borne in several short spikes or 'fingers' at the tip of the stem. As each spike ripens it has to be picked by hand, a tedious business taking several weeks to complete. The grain is extracted by pounding the cut heads with sticks, and is then either boiled whole or ground into flour. Pearl or bullrush millet, or

E. N. A.

KAFFIR CORN OR GREAT MILLET READY FOR HARVESTING IN SOUTH AFRICA

bajri, is cultivated in Egypt, India, and southeast Asia in the same way as finger millet, but is a much taller grass, up to 8 feet high.

5. ITALIAN OR FOXTAIL MILLET is grown in south Europe and North America mainly as a hay crop, and in some parts of Asia as a cereal crop; Australian millet grows wild in Australia, where its seeds are harvested by the aborigines; and Job's Tears, which is grown as a cereal in certain Asiatic countries, is a millet-like grass with big shiny grey seeds, about half an inch long, which are said to resemble tears, and are sometimes used as beads. A number of other millets, such as Guinea grass, Buffalo grass, Johnson grass, and Teff grass, are grown in tropical countries as fodder for livestock. Some yield very small seeds which are fed to cage birds.

MINISTRY OF AGRICULTURE AND FISHERIES. A government department for agriculture was first set up in 1889 when the Board of Agriculture was established. This Board took over the duties of several other government departments, and dealt with matters such as the control of PESTS AND DISEASES, TITHE Rent charges, ALLOTMENTS, DRAINAGE (qq.v.), and land improvement generally. It was also empowered to carry out certain duties in regard to agricultural education and to foster research in agriculture or forestry. The Ordnance Survey Department, which produces the official maps of Great Britain, was also transferred to the Board. In 1903 the Board took over responsibility for the Fishing Industry (q.v.) in England and Wales and thus became the Board of Agriculture and Fisheries. It also became responsible for the Royal Botanic Gardens at Kew. In 1911 the Board of Agriculture for Scotland was created, taking over responsibility for Scotland. In 1919 a newly created Forestry Commission (q.v.) became responsible for the national forests of Britain; and in the same year the Board was reorganized as the Ministry of Agriculture and Fisheries.

The purpose of the Ministry is to help the industries of agriculture and fisheries to become more efficient, and to improve the conditions of those engaged in them. Thus the Ministry is concerned with the control of pests and diseases, the improvement of standards of livestock and milk production, the encouragement of Research in Agriculture and Agricultural Training (qq.v.), and the distribution of information and advice, not only orally but by a large variety of publications issued through H.M. Stationery Office. The Ministry also sometimes gives direct financial aid to farmers, as, for example, for calf-rearing or for schemes for improving the land by liming or draining. It is the Ministry's duty to enforce good standards of farming and estate management; the Ministry may even very occasionally turn a farmer out of his farm if he has failed entirely to manage his land properly and if he refuses expert advice.

To carry out these functions the Ministry appoints a staff of technical officers who give free advice to farmers and landowners on every aspect of their work. In each county of England and Wales there is a County Agricultural Executive Committee consisting of twelve unpaid prominent agriculturists to act as the Minister's agents, and under them a staff of paid specialists appointed by the Ministry. In 1946 the National Agricultural Advisory Service was set up to help in the work of providing farmers in each county with free technical advice and instruction. As well as the county centres there are also eight main centres from which specialists in the different branches of agricultural science

can be consulted. The Ministry has also set up an Agricultural Land Service which, among other duties, gives free advice on agricultural buildings and estate management.

As well as promoting the farmer's efficiency, the Ministry gives him security by providing an assured market in which he can sell all that he produces at guaranteed prices for all the main agricultural crops and livestock products. These prices are fixed after consultations between the Ministry, the National Farmers' Union, and other interested parties, and are announced far enough ahead each year for the farmers to be able to plan their production accordingly. Minimum rates of wages for agricultural workers are fixed by an Agricultural Wages Board, consisting of representatives of employers and workers together with five independent persons appointed by the Minister.

The total staff of the Ministry exceeds 15,000, of which about 5,500 are technical officers, for the most part stationed in the country.

See also Agricultural Training; Research in Agriculture; National Farmers' Union.
See also Vol. X: Ministers of the Crown.

MINT, see Herbs, Garden.

MITE AND TICK PESTS. These are not insects, but closely related to spiders. They live by sucking, and are parasites in the adult stage when they may do great harm to both animals and plants.

One mite causes 'big bud' by damaging the tissues of the black-currant bush (see Currants and Gooseberries). The Fruit Tree Red Spider Mite is a serious pest of both fruit and vegetables, especially trees grown against walls. It should be controlled by destroying the winter eggs with a petroleum winter wash, such as the DNOC petroleum wash. Tar-oil washes not only leave the Red Spider unharmed, but destroy its own natural enemies. The Glasshouse Red Spider Mite is often found in cucumber houses or frames, and in vineries or melon houses, especially if they are dry or overheated. It is a pest on French Beans, especially if they are grown under glass, living on the undersides of the leaves and causing them to develop yellow blotches. It spins a web over itself, which to some extent acts as a protection against insecticides. It dislikes damp and cold, however, and can be discouraged by plain water sprays. It should be attacked

Harold Bastin

BLACK-CURRANT BUDS

The buds on the left are healthy and the others have 'big bud'

during the summer with derris powder, white oil (summer petroleum) wash, or Azobenzine smokes. If it is not controlled it increases extremely fast, as do all mites and ticks, for as many as seven or eight generations are produced in a season.

The human Itch-mite causes scabies; the Scab-mite attacks sheep; and other mites cause various forms of mange. Sarcoptic mange is caused by a mite of the genus *sarcoptis*, which burrows tunnels in the skin. One species of *sarcoptis* causes scabies in man, another mange in Dogs (q.v. Vol. IX), and another mange in

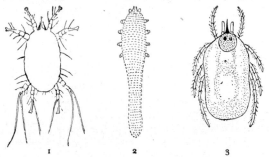

1. THE MITE WHICH CAUSES SHEEP SCAB
2. THE MITE WHICH CAUSES MANGE IN DOGS
3. SHEEP TICK GORGED WITH BLOOD
All much enlarged

horses and cattle. Psoroptic mange is caused by the mite *Psoroptes ovis*, which does not burrow but bites the surface of the skin, causing scabs, especially sheep-scab; follicular mange in dogs

is caused by a long slender mite, *Demodex folliculorum*, which enters the hair follicles (the pits in the skin out of which the hairs grow).

All these parasites cause intense, almost unbearable irritation. The mites spread from animal to animal very easily by contact, and increase rapidly in numbers on each animal they reach. They can live only for a few days in sunlight, away from their host, and even under the most favourable conditions very few survive beyond 20 days. The Scab-mite, however, spends 7 days in the egg before it hatches, and then requires a further fortnight in which to become adult and to be able to reproduce.

To kill the parasite, the skin must be dressed with a sulphur ointment (linseed oil and sulphur), which should be renewed at short intervals. A sarcoptic mange, where the insect burrows within the skin, may need prolonged treatment. Sheep-scab is controlled by SHEEP DIPPING (q.v.), the success of the treatment depending upon at least two applications, the first dipping to kill the live mites, and the second, which must take place within 7 to 10 days, to kill the mites hatched since the first dipping but not yet mature enough to lay more eggs. The infected animals should then be clean.

Ticks often feed on plants when young, but later become bloodsuckers on vertebrate animals. They swell greatly, especially the females, as they gorge themselves with blood. While they are doing this, they bury their heads in the skin of their host, and as their mouth parts are barbed, it is impossible to pull them out entire. When the female is about to lay her eggs, she drops down to the ground, and the young ticks, after crawling among the vegetation, find their way back to some warm-blooded animal. Ground which tick-infested animals have gone over is thus infected, and the infection may be carried from one kind of animal to another. Dogs, especially sheep-dogs, often carry the common Sheep-tick. The Sheep-tick, known as *Ixodes ricinus*, may carry the organism which causes red-water fever, a disease of cattle. It also carries the infective agencies which cause trembling, or 'louping-ill', and tick-borne fever in sheep in hill districts.

See also PESTS AND DISEASES; PARASITES; INSECTICIDES.

MOLE DRAIN, *see* DRAINAGE, LAND.

MOLES, *see* WILD ANIMALS ON THE FARM.

MONKEY-NUTS, *see* GROUNDNUTS.

MOTH PESTS, *see* BUTTERFLY AND MOTH PESTS.

MULBERRIES. The mulberry tree most often seen in Britain is the Black Mulberry (*Morus nigra*), a native of central Asia. This has now become almost naturalized in southern Europe. It grows very slowly into a beautiful tree with spreading branches, and it lives to a great age, one British mulberry being reported to be well over 400 years old. The fruit is purplish-black, and makes a delicious preserve. A light wine can also be made from it.

The Red Mulberry is a native of North America. It grows into a very large tree—there is one in Canada 50 feet high. It is hardier than the Black Mulberry, but its fruit is not so good. The White Mulberry, a native of China, and the Indian Mulberry are the varieties most used as food for SILKWORMS (q.v.). The White Mulberry has been grown in great numbers in southern Europe, but it will not stand as much cold as the Black Mulberry, and its whitish fruit is very inferior. The Paper Mulberry, which grows as a shrub from India to Japan, is used for making a kind of paper and also the tapa-cloth

Amateur Gardening

MULBERRIES

woven by people of eastern Asia, especially South Sea Islanders.

The mulberry needs little attention once it is established. It prefers a rich, deep, light soil in a sheltered place. It needs no pruning except a certain amount of thinning out. The flowers do not often get caught by frost, and the mulberry suffers from none of the common pests and diseases which attack other fruit trees.

See also SILKWORMS.
See also Vol. VII: SILK INDUSTRY.

MULES, *see* DONKEYS AND MULES.

MUSHROOM. This is the English name of the edible fungus *Psalliota campestris* (or *Agaricus campestris*), a wild species which is found in pastures throughout Europe, usually during the summer and autumn (*see* FUNGI, Vol. II). The cultivated mushrooms are varieties of the common mushroom and are produced in large quantities to maintain a supply throughout the year.

The culture of mushrooms in gardens is entirely artificial in character. As a rule mushrooms are grown in the dark in a specially constructed mushroom house heated with hot-water pipes; in the house are beds of suitably prepared fermenting material—composted stable manure, for instance, or a specially prepared straw compost. The mushroom spawn is inserted on the beds when the temperature of the compost is declining and is between 70° and 75° F. The surface of the beds is then covered with a thin layer of loamy soil called the 'casing'. The threads or mycelium of the fungus spread rapidly throughout the beds, and usually the mushrooms, which are the fleshy fruiting bodies of the fungus, begin to appear over the surface of the beds after 4 to 6 weeks. Although properly designed mushroom sheds are used for large-scale production, single flat beds can be made in old buildings or in a greenhouse, and ridge-shaped beds can be made in the open air.

Mushroom culture, which is one of the most skilful in horticulture, calls for the closest attention to every detail. The compost materials for the beds have to be carefully chosen and thoroughly prepared. The spawn used, known as pure culture spawn, should be of the highest quality and prepared by specialists. The right temperature and a sufficiently moist atmosphere in the mushroom house are both important

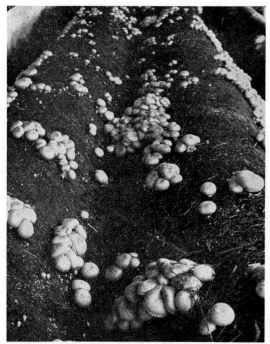

Carter's Tested Seeds Ltd.

AN INDOOR MUSHROOM BED

factors, and the highest standard of cleanliness is needed throughout. It is a type of culture where skilful practice is usually rewarded with success, but where slipshod methods lead only to failure and disappointment.

Mushroom beds remain in a cropping condition for from 3 to 4 months after the first mushrooms appear. As a rule the mushrooms appear in periodical batches called 'flushes'. A success-ful bed will yield about 18 lb. of mushrooms per sq. yard altogether. After cropping, the beds are removed, the compost used in the vegetable garden, and the shed or house disinfected with formaldehyde solution (2% formalin) before a fresh bed is made.

MUSSEL FISHING, *see* SHELL-FISH GATHERING.

MUSTARD. Two sorts of mustard are grown in Britain: white mustard, grown mainly for its foliage, and black mustard, grown for its seed from which is extracted mustard oil, used in the manufacture of table mustard. In either case deep fertile soils suit the crop best, and it is a common crop on the rich fen-lands of Lincoln-shire, Cambridgeshire, and Huntingdonshire.

The crop is usually sown in March, 4 to 5 lb. of seed per acre being needed, which is drilled in rows 15 to 18 inches apart. Occasionally the crop is thinned afterwards. Harvesting of black mustard is carried out about August, the crop being cut before it is completely ripe, so that the seed is not lost by shedding. It is tied into sheaves and stooked in the usual manner, and left to ripen and dry out completely before being carted and stacked. Later it is threshed, and some 10 to 20 cwt. of seed per acre are obtained. The straw is of no use for feeding to cattle.

White mustard is often grown with rape (2 lb. of each per acre) for forage purposes for sheep; but it may also be sown after early potatoes to be ploughed in as green manure (*see* MANURES).

MUSTARD AND CRESS, *see* SALAD CROPS.

N

NATIONAL AGRICULTURAL ADVISORY SERVICE, *see* MINISTRY OF AGRICULTURE.

NATIONAL FARMERS' UNION. In 1904, at the annual puppy show at Harmston Park, near Lincoln, nine farmers were sitting in a tent talking about the difficulties that faced farming. The little party agreed that some of the problems that faced farmers in the bad times for British agriculture at the end of the 19th century arose from the failure of farmers to act together as a body. From this discussion arose the idea of starting a farmers' organization. Each of the nine farmers paid up a pound, and Mr. E. W. Howard, one of the party, undertook to found a union.

A few days later Mr. Howard organized a general meeting of farmers at Lincoln, and there the Lincolnshire Farmers' Union was founded. Gradually the movement spread to other parts of England, and by 1908 many counties not only had their own unions but had become interested in the formation of a body to represent farmers in all parts of England. And so in December 1908 at a meeting at the Agricultural Hall at Islington, the scene of many famous farming shows, the National Farmers' Union was born, and Mr. Campbell, one of the Lincolnshire pioneers, was made President.

By 1913 membership had grown to 20,000, and the part played by the farmers during the First World War in support of the government's plans to grow more food, helped to establish the Union. Membership by 1918 had reached 100,000. In 1919 the London headquarters at 45 Bedford Square were opened. By 1951 there were about 203,000 members of the N.F.U. (about 89% of the farmers eligible to join) and branches of the union now cover every district in England and Wales. Similar unions exist in Scotland and Northern Ireland.

The N.F.U. is a body of practical farmers organized in a democratic way. To be a member a person must cultivate the land he occupies (either as owner or tenant). There is a central Council and both county and local branches. The Council is composed chiefly of delegates appointed each year by the county branches, and all the officers are elected by the members. Any individual farmer has the right and opportunity to make himself heard in his local branch, which, if it supports him, can take his case to the Council. The work of the Union, both at headquarters and in the counties, is done by committees of members chosen for their expert knowledge of a particular subject, and every branch of farming, including horticulture, is dealt with. Advice, also, is given to farmers on legal and technical matters such as income-tax, wage problems, machinery, and market prices.

The purpose of the N.F.U. (a union not of employees, but mainly of those farming land) is to do everything in its power to increase the fruits of the soil, both for the advantage of the farmer and the country as a whole, and to co-operate to this end with the MINISTRY OF AGRICULTURE AND FISHERIES (q.v.). It played a considerable part in bringing about the passing in 1932 of the Wheat Act, which guaranteed a standard price and a certain market for home-grown wheat, and the Agricultural Marketing Acts of the 1930's which made possible better marketing of other farm produce—milk, bacon pigs, potatoes, and hops, in particular. In both World Wars the Union played an important part in increasing the production of home-grown food. To gain the kind of information the Union needs to carry out these functions, a 'farm accounts scheme' is run, and facts are collected by trained accountants from some 10,000 farms, so that the Union is in the position to know what should be the prices for farm produce.

The N.F.U. publishes a monthly journal for its members, and circulates a weekly news sheet to the newspapers. It also organizes a 'Farm Week', a sort of farm exhibition, in many of the big cities. It has done much to make contact with farmers in other countries, and was largely responsible for the organization of the International Conference of Primary Producers, held in London in May 1946. This led to the establishment of the International Federation of Agricultural Producers.

See also FARM LABOUR.

NATIONAL FOREST PARKS, *see* FORESTRY COMMISSION.

NATIONAL UNION OF AGRICULTURAL WORKERS, *see* FARM LABOUR.

NECTARINES, *see* PEACHES AND NECTARINES.

NETMAKING, *see* RURAL CRAFTS.

NURSE CROPS, *see* LEYS.

NURSERY, *see* ARBORICULTURE; FRUIT PROPAGATION.

NUTS. **1.** Most nuts are very nutritious, being rich in protein and vegetable oils. There is a great variety of nut-bearing trees, some of which, botanically speaking, do not bear nuts at all (*see* FRUITS, section 2(*c*), Vol. II). Some grow in temperate climates such as Britain, while others are tropical plants. Among the most important commercially is the COCONUT (q.v.). Others are walnuts, cob nuts, and filberts, almonds and pistachio nuts, sweet chestnuts, kidney-shaped cashew nuts from Central America, the American hickory nut with its sweet kernel and hard shell, the hard-shelled Brazil nuts, peanuts which are not nuts at all but grow in pods like peas and beans to which they are related (*see* GROUNDNUTS), betel nuts or areca nuts chewed by the South Sea Islanders, the candlenut of Hawaii which is so rich in oil that it will burn like a candle, and the poison nut tree of the Far East which bears fruits about the size of a small orange, from which a medicine to treat heart disease is made.

2. WALNUTS. These have been known and valued since ancient days. Walnuts are reported, for instance, to have been grown in King Solomon's gardens, and the walnut was the sacred tree of the Greek goddess, Artemis, and was known as the Royal Nut. It is valued not only for its nuts but for its fine hard wood with a beautiful grain which has been much used for furniture-making, and is especially useful for veneering (*see* PLYWOOD AND VENEERS, Vol. VII). The English Walnut (*Juglans regia*), which originated in south-western Asia, produces better fruit than the Black Walnut of America (*Juglans nigra*), which often grows to a height of 100 feet.

A prolific walnut-tree bearing good-sized fruit can only be reproduced by grafting, since seed-

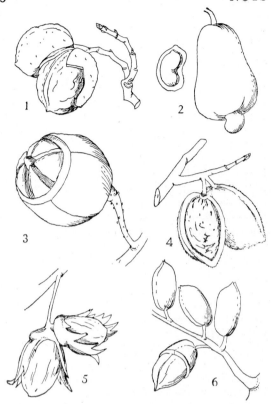

1. WALNUTS. 2. CASHEW NUT AND APPLE WITH THE NUT AT THE BOTTOM. 3. BRAZIL NUTS. 4. ALMONDS. 5. FILBERT NUTS. 6. PISTACHIO NUTS

lings grown from its nuts will not come true (*see* FRUIT PROPAGATION). Walnuts will grow on most soils so long as there is good drainage, but as the growing tips are liable to get caught and blackened by late frosts, they should not be planted in hollows where cold air collects. Also, if they are exposed to strong north and east winds, the pollen from the male catkins may not fertilize the tiny female nut buds (*see* FERTILIZATION). The worst pests of walnuts are squirrels, mice, rooks, and jackdaws (*see* VERMIN). The nuts, except for those taken in July for pickling, should mature fully on the tree, and then should be de-husked, cleaned, and dried thoroughly before they are stored.

3. COB NUTS AND FILBERTS. These are cultivated varieties of the same species as the wild hazel. They prefer a lightish soil with good drainage, and need shelter from north and east winds during February for the same reason as walnuts. The trees, if properly looked after, grow to a considerable age. A nut orchard in

Kent, Sussex, and some other districts is called a nut platt.

Cob nuts and filberts are most productive and produce the largest fruit if they are very heavily pruned and carefully shaped into a cup-shaped bush in which growth is severely restricted, and into which light and air can enter. The young plant by its third year should have grown about twelve main shoots which form the framework of the tree, and which are cut back to two-thirds or a half of their length, always to a bud growing in the required direction. When the bush is high enough, perhaps about 5 to 6 feet, these main branches are not allowed to extend farther, all the strength of the tree being thrown into forming many short twiggy side shoots, which are the fruit bearers. This annual spring pruning, however, should not be done until the catkins have shaken out all their pollen, and fertilization is completed. Winter pruning consists of thinning out that year's fruiting twigs so as to encourage the growth of more young twigs, and all unwanted strong growths and suckers from the ground should be cut out altogether. Nut-trees can be grown successfully with much less careful pruning than this, but they will not produce the best fruit (*see* PRUNING).

4. ALMONDS. These are close relatives of the PEACH and PLUM (qq.v.), but are hardier than peaches. They are natives of southern Asia and North Africa, and have now spread all over southern Europe. They are grown in Britain, not so much for their nuts as for their decorative blossom, which appears early in the spring before the leaves. The wood, which is hard and reddish, is also used by cabinet-makers. There are both bitter and sweet varieties, the bitter taste being caused by the tiny trace of prussic acid which bitter almonds contain—a trace far too small to make the almonds poisonous. In general it used to be true that the white blossomed trees produced bitter almonds and the pink blossomed the sweet almonds; but modern varieties have rather confused this simple distinction. The nuts are rich in oil which is extracted for various purposes (*see* OIL-BEARING PLANTS). Almonds are now grown commercially in France, Spain, Italy, and other Mediterranean countries, and in the U.S.A. especially in California. Almonds require no pruning apart from the shaping of the young tree and the cutting away of dead wood. They suffer from the same diseases as others of the plum and peach family—in particular, the fungus disease, peach leaf curl, for which they need an anti-fungus spray (*see* FRUIT SPRAYING).

5. BRAZIL NUTS grow on large trees in tropical South America, especially in the valleys of the Amazon and Rio Negro. About a dozen nuts are contained in a round husky fruit which, when ripe, breaks open and sheds the nuts. These are very rich in oil, but are difficult to harvest because of the height of the trees and the denseness of the tropical forests.

See also FRUIT-GROWING.
See also Vol. II; FRUITS, section 2(*c*).
See also Vol. VII: OILS, VEGETABLE.

O

OATS. This cereal crop is chiefly grown for stock feeding, though a certain amount is made into oatmeal for human consumption. The straw is a good feed for horses and cattle, especially when the crop has been cut a little unripe. There are two main sorts of oats, the winter and the spring varieties, the former being much more hardy, but the latter yielding heavier crops of grain. Apart from these distinctive features, varieties differ in minor characteristics such as length and stiffness of straw, colour of grain (white, yellow, grey, or black), and in the shape of the grain. Some varieties have short, plump grains, others long, thin grains: the flower heads in some are spreading (Common Oats), in others arranged on one side of the stalk like a banner (Tartarian Oats).

Broadly speaking, winter oats are favoured in the south of Britain, where the winters are less severe than in the north. There are several advantages in autumn sowing: it relieves the pressure of spring work; winter oats are more resistant to attacks of the frit fly (*see* FLY PESTS), which causes serious damage to spring oats in some districts; the crop is well established, with plenty of leaf to cover the ground, early in the year, so that there is less risk of weeds gaining the mastery; and earlier harvesting is possible.

Oats have no very fixed place in the ROTATION OF CROPS (q.v.). They often follow another cereal crop, but they can also follow roots or a seeds LEY (q.v.) satisfactorily, especially if a stiff-strawed variety is selected, and phosphate and potash fertilizers applied. (Too much nitrogen will make a weak strawed variety 'lodge' or fall flat.) In Scotland and northern England, where oats are more common than wheat or barley, this is their usual place in the rotation, and the crop is generally grown on the reserves of plant food left in the soil from the last crop. When it follows another cereal, however, or when the fertility of the soil is known to be low, a mixture

Eric Guy

HARVESTING OATS WITH A REAPER AND BINDER
The sheaves are being built into stooks

Plant Breeding Station, Cambridge

COMMON OATS

of sulphate of ammonia (1 cwt. per acre) and superphosphate (3 cwt. per acre) should be applied before the seed is sown.

The seed-bed is prepared in the same way as for barley, but the crop does not need quite the same attention in cultivation as does barley. For winter varieties the treatment is identical with that applied to wheat. With the exception of rye and potatoes, the oat crop is the least sensitive to soil sourness, and moderately good crops can be grown on soils short of lime where barley would fail. Therefore, the oat crop is often the first crop sown when poor permanent grassland is ploughed up. Naturally, however, the crops do better where the soil has been properly limed.

Although the seed may be broadcast by hand, it is more usual to drill it, the rate of seeding varying from 12 to 16 stones per acre, the heavier rate being used as a measure of insurance against failure when conditions are not ideal. For example, heavier seeding is given on newly ploughed turf, where wireworm may cause much damage. Winter oats should be sown before mid-November. The earlier the spring varieties can be sown in the new year the better, mid-April being the latest date for successful sowing.

Oats are often used for animal fodder. They are grown in mixtures with peas, beans, or tares (vetches), the crop being cut before the seed is formed, and fed green or made into hay or silage. For this purpose 'forage oats' varieties, which produce much more foliage and less grain than the grain-producing varieties, are used, a common type being the Potato Oat.

After drilling, the seed is harrowed in and rolled. After that, the crop is cultivated much like wheat or barley, except that oat seedlings, being more tender, must be treated less severely.

The crop is cut earlier than wheat or barley, and is not left to ripen fully for fear that the grain may shell out and be wasted. The correct time for cutting is when the grains are 'cheesy', at which stage there is still a good deal of green colour in the straw. The stooks must stand out at least 14 days (a country saying is that they 'must hear the church bells twice') so that the sheaves dry out completely, and the grain ripens further by the passage of sap from the straw. The crop is sometimes stacked around tripods, or on faggots, so that the air can penetrate the stacks, and prevent the oats from generating a natural heat, which they do easily. The commonest method, especially in the north, is to stack the crop in small, round stacks that allow the sheaves to continue drying until time for threshing. Oats, being the favourite cereal in the north and west where harvesting weather is likely to be difficult, have often to be carted before the crop is perfectly dry; so that methods of helping the sheaves to dry out in the stack are important.

In threshing, oats do not need quite as much care as do barley and wheat, for if the threshing-machine does not make a clean job of separating grain from straw, the straw is of higher feeding value. Again, if the grain is damaged by too close threshing, it has lost nothing of its feeding value. This does not, of course, apply when grain is being threshed to be used for seed. In some districts the sheaves are fed whole to the animals—indeed, nowadays the unthreshed sheaves are sometimes put through a hammer-mill, and the whole crop broken up into a coarse meal, which is then mixed with the concentrate ration (*see* FOODS, FARM ANIMALS).

About 15 cwt. of grain and 1 ton of straw are obtained from an acre of average crop, but these figures are improved upon under good conditions to give yields of 36 to 40 cwt. of grain per acre.

See also HARVESTING.

OCTOPUS, CUTTLEFISH, AND SQUID FISHING. These three 'fish' are considered great table delicacies by the people of the Mediterranean, India, and Japan. They also serve as most useful baits for hook and line fishing.

Octopuses in the Mediterranean are usually caught in narrow-mouthed traps of earthenware

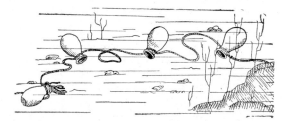

POTS USED TO CATCH OCTOPUS IN THE MEDITERRANEAN

or fine basket-work, sunk on the sea bottom. The trap is shaped like a water carafe, with a narrow neck leading into a roomy chamber with no other outlet. Several of these are strung at intervals upon a long line, and sunk in places known to be haunts of the octopus. In Palk Strait, between India and Ceylon, the large

James Hornell

A FISHERMAN WITH A SET OF OCTOPUS TRAPS, PALK STRAIT, SOUTH INDIA

The traps are conch shells fastened to lines

James Hornell

OCTOPUSES HUNG OUT TO DRY IN MAURITIUS

shells of the Five-fingered Conch take the place of pots or baskets. The 'fingers' are broken off and the shells are then tied on a line in the same way as pots in the Mediterranean. From 700 to 900 shells are often used, and the catch may number from 200 to 300 little octopuses.

In the north of Ceylon where the squid is common, the fishermen plant stout posts in the shape of a Y in shallow water, with a crossbar tied across the two limbs of the Y. The fisherman places a heap of leaves round the base, and then takes his seat on the crossbar. Hidden in the leaves he has placed a circlet of stout iron hooks fixed on the lower end of a long pole. If there are any squids about, it is not long before one comes along to inspect the leafy mass—for in such places the female squid deposits her eggs. When the fisherman sees a squid swimming over the right spot, he jerks the pole sharply upwards so that one of the jigger hooks catches in the squid's body.

In the Mediterranean, cuttlefish are often caught by a lure made in the shape of the fish. A piece of mirror fixed to one or both sides of the lure makes it so bright and attractive an object that no cuttlefish can resist it. In the South Sea Islands the bait for cuttlefish is made by tying a long imitation tail to a cowrie shell to make it look something like a rat. There is said to be constant enmity between rats and cuttlefish, so that when the cuttlefish sees something which it thinks is a rat, it seizes it and retains its hold even when hauled to the surface.

See also FISHING INDUSTRY.

See also Vol. II: CUTTLEFISH AND SQUID; OCTOPUS.

OIL-BEARING PLANTS. A great many plants are cultivated for the oils and fats which they contain. Some, such as lavender, grow in temperate countries, but many others come from tropical or sub-tropical countries. They can be divided into 'fixed' oil-bearing plants, and 'volatile' or 'essential' oil-bearing plants.

Fixed oils are so-called because they cannot be separated from the plant by distillation, but are usually extracted by pressure. The oils are nearly always in the seeds or fruit of plants. Examples of the oil crops are oil-palms, coconuts, sesame, olives, castor, and cotton seed. They are used as table or cooking oils, and in the manufacture of margarine, soap, lubricants, and sometimes illuminants. Those fixed oils, such as linseed and tung oil, which harden when exposed to air, are known as 'drying oils' and are used in making paint. The residues left after extraction are valuable cattle foods.

Volatile or 'essential' oils are essences which evaporate easily and are usually extracted by steam distillation. They are not greasy and not, therefore, 'oils' in the ordinary sense of the word. They are found in any part of the plant, the leaves, bark, roots, stem, flowers, fruit, and seed. They are used in perfume and to some extent in medicine and as flavourings.

CASTOR-OIL PLANT

SESAME PLANT

1. FIXED OIL-BEARING CROPS. These may be either annuals, which complete their life-history in one year, or perennials which persist for many years. Some of the most important oil-bearing crops, such as NUTS, COCONUTS, OIL PALMS, OLIVES, GROUNDNUTS, SOYA-BEANS, and LINSEED (qq.v.), are described in separate articles. Oils and fats are also important by-products of some crops grown mainly for other purposes, the most important being COTTON, MAIZE, and CACAO (qq.v.). A number of other oil-seed crops are described below.

(a) *Annual oil-seeds.* Sunflowers (*Helianthus annuus*), natives of Mexico, are also widely cultivated in Argentina, Russia, and east central Europe. They take from 3 to 5 months to mature from seed. The seed contains from 25% to 35% of oil, and the average yield of seed per acre is 900 to 1,200 lb. The oil, which is a clear pale yellow, is used as a salad oil and in the manufacture of margarine.

The Safflower (*Carthamus tinctorius*), a relative of the sunflower, and cultivated in many European countries and in Egypt and India, has seeds containing about 19% to 30% of an oil which is like sunflower oil and is used for similar purposes. The safflower bears orange-red flowers and is also a source of dyestuff. Niger seed oil, which comes from a related plant of tropical Africa and is cultivated to some extent in India, also resembles sunflower seed oil.

Sesame (*Sesamum indicum*), another important

oil-seed crop, yields an oil also known as simsim, benniseed, or gingelly oil. Sesame is a small annual plant taking between 3 and 4 months to mature, and grown extensively in India, Burma, and China, as well as in the Sudan, East and West Africa, Turkey, Greece, Russia, and Mexico. It has been grown in India since very early times and is believed to have been the first oil-seed cultivated. There are several varieties, bearing black, yellow, red, or white seeds; the white-seeded kinds yield the best quality oil. The crop does best on light soils with a moderate rainfall. The seeds are very small and are borne in capsules which split open when ripe. Yields range from 600 to 1,200 lb. per acre, and the seeds contain from 45% to 50% of a pale yellow oil. World production before the Second World War was estimated at 1½ million tons, mostly produced in Asia; but since then, though still very large, it has declined somewhat. Most of the oil is used in the countries where it is grown.

Rape oil or colza oil is obtained from the seeds of various species of brassica, relatives of the cabbage, which are extensively grown in India and elsewhere. The seeds contain 35% to 40% of oil, used to some extent as a cooking oil, but mainly as a lubricant and illuminant. The seed of the opium poppy also contains oil, although the plant is mainly grown for the production of NARCOTICS (q.v. Vol. XI).

Castor oil is obtained from the castor-oil plant (*Ricinus communis*), a native of Africa, where it has been cultivated since very remote times. It is grown on a large scale in India, and to a lesser extent in practically every other tropical country. The plant thrives in rich, loamy soils and needs a moderate rainfall. It grows very rapidly to a height of 5 or 6 feet, and comes into bearing about 4 months after planting, yielding over a period of about 3 months from 500 to over 1000 lb. of seed per acre. The seed consists of a brittle husk with distinctive markings which encloses a whitish, oily kernel containing 60% to 65% of a sticky, pale yellow oil. It is used in medicine as a purgative and also as a lubricating oil, for soap manufacture, and for dressing leather. As the seeds contain a poison called ricin, the residues after the oil has been extracted cannot be used as a feeding-stuff.

(*b*) *Perennial oil-seeds.* Besides coconuts, cacao, oil-palms, and olives, which are described separately, there are a large number of perennial oil-bearing shrubs and trees of importance. The

Public Relations Office, Zomba

NUTS OF THE TUNG TREE WHICH GROWS IN NYASALAND

The oil is extracted from the kernels of the nuts which are shown here with their outer skin. They are about the size of walnuts

tung-tree (*Aleurites*) yields a valuable drying oil used in the paint and varnish industry as a substitute for linseed oil. It is chiefly grown in China, but plantations exist in America, Burma, Nyasaland, and Indonesia. Besides the coconut and the oil-palm, there are many other oil-yielding palms, of which the cohune palm (*Attalea Cohune*) and the babassou palm (*Attalea funifera*), both natives of tropical America, are important. The nuts, the kernels of which contain about 65% of an oil closely resembling coconut oil, are very hard to crack; and this has so far been the main obstacle to cultivating them on a larger scale.

The Shea butternut tree (*Butyospermum Parkii*) is a large tree of tropical Africa, the seeds of which yield a stiff plastic fat, widely used for cooking by native Africans, and also commercially refined for margarine making and for cooking. Mowrah butter is obtained from Illipe (*Bassia latifolia* and *B. longifolia*) which grow in India, and the seeds of which contain 50% to 60% of fat, used as a food in India.

The seeds of certain trees and shrubs yield fixed oils which have medicinal properties. For example, the seeds of the Croton plant, a shrub with variegated leaves, yield Croton oil used in medicine as a purgative, and those of the Chaulmoogra tree contain an oil used in the treatment of leprosy.

2. ESSENTIAL OIL-BEARING CROPS. A large

E.N.A.

EUCALYPTUS TREES IN THE AUSTRALIAN BUSH

One of the oil-bearing plants most important to the perfume industry is lavender, grown in many European countries and on a large scale in England. It is a bushy shrub growing 2 to 3 feet high, and bearing dense clusters of small flowers at the end of long stalks. The perfume is distilled from the dried flowers, which yield about $1\frac{1}{2}\%$ of oil, or from 10 to 30 lb. per acre in a year. Another species, grown in France and southern Europe, produces oil of spike, used in mixing paints, especially for painting pottery and glass, and also in veterinary medicines. The oil of ylang-ylang, another perfume oil, is distilled from the flowers of the tree *Cananga odorata*, which grows in Java and the Philippines. Bay-oil, which is mixed with rum to make 'bay rum', is distilled from the leaves of the tree *Pimenta acris*, grown mainly in Dominica, West Indies.

Several tropical grasses also yield oils used in perfumery, the most important being citronella, palmarosa, and vetiver. Citronella is a coarse grass cultivated chiefly in Java and Ceylon from root divisions. The grass is cut for the first time 6 months after planting, and twice a year after that. About 110 lb. of oil per acre is obtained from its leaves in a year. Lemongrass and palmarosa are similar but less robust grasses, cultivated in the same way. Vetiver is a tropical perennial grass about 4 feet high, with stiff, erect leaves and aromatic roots. It is also propagated by root divisions, and the plants are ready for lifting after 6 months' growth. The oil, which is distilled from the roots, is used in perfumery as a fixing oil—that is, it prevents other oils in the perfume from evaporating too quickly. Patchouli is an erect, branching, hairy, tropical herb which grows from 2 to 3 feet high, and is propagated from rooted cuttings. The first crop of leaves and stalks, from which the oil is distilled, is harvested after 6 months, and two further pickings are made at 6 monthly intervals.

Many medical products are obtained from oil-bearing plants. Eucalyptus oil, for instance, is distilled from the leaves of a large Australian tree; and peppermint and menthol (or mint camphor) are obtained from a perennial herb, *Mentha piperita*, closely related to mint, and growing in temperate and tropical climates. Thymol, or thyme camphor, is distilled from a tropical plant called ajowan or from garden thyme, wild thyme, or horse mint. Oil of anise is obtained by distilling the seed of the anise plant (aniseed), a native of Egypt but also grown in Syria, Malta,

number of plants are grown partly or wholly on account of the essences which are obtained from them. The oils are mainly used in perfumery, but some, such as the thyme, eucalyptus, anise, and chenopodium oils, are used in medicine. Many SPICE CROPS (q.v.), such as cloves and cinnamon, owe their properties to the essential oils which they contain; and some essential oils give their characteristic flavour to certain LIQUEURS (q.v. Vol. XI). Some oils, bergamot oil and oil of lemon, for instance, are obtained from certain CITRUS FRUITS (q.v.). There are also some volatile solids such as camphor (obtained with camphor oil from the camphor-tree), vanillin from vanilla pods, or coumarin from Tonka beans, which belong to this group.

Shrubs and flowers which are cultivated specially to provide oils for the perfume industry include geraniums grown in Europe, some French colonies, and in Kenya, and roses, jasmine, tuberose, and violets cultivated on a large scale in the south of France, especially near the town of Grasse. Attar of roses is the fragrant essence obtained from the petals of roses, some 500,000 roses being needed to yield 1 lb. of rose oil.

and Spain. It is used in medicine, in liqueurs, and also as a flavouring Wormseed oil used in medicines is obtained in the same way from the seed of *Chenopodium anthelminticum*, a native of tropical America.

See also Vol. VII: Oils, Vegetable; Distillation; Perfumery.

See also Vol. XI: Drugs.

OLIVES. The olive-tree grows wild on the shores of the Mediterranean Sea, and it has been cultivated there for thousands of years. It is now also cultivated in many other countries including China, Australia, California, and South America. Its scientific name is *Olea europeae*. It has a slender trunk topped by a spreading crown of evergreen leaves that are small and oval in shape, dark green and shiny above, and silvery grey beneath. Its white flowers, which are small and inconspicuous, form numerous fruits like little plums, each with a hard stone at the centre and yellowish green flesh very rich in oil. The olives ripen in autumn, and though many are eaten either fresh or preserved, the bulk of the crop is sent to the oil presses. Olive oil is used in large quantities in France, Spain, Italy, and other countries as a lamp oil or fuel, for frying, and for making many kinds of dishes.

Olive-trees grow best on sloping ground with a limestone soil. They need a warm climate, and prefer to be near the sea. They are usually raised from cuttings, though the finer sorts are propagated by grafting. Some varieties bear white or blue-skinned fruits. Olive-trees often receive very little attention apart from harvesting the crop; but in France, where the olive orchards or *olivettes* are carefully tended, they yield heavier crops, and continue to bear fruit for very many years. They do not, however, come into fruit until they are several years old. Each year the trees, which bear fruit only on the wood of the previous year,

are pruned, and from time to time the orchard is manured.

The wood of the olive-tree is hard and close-grained, golden brown in colour with curious veins and streaks of black; it is used mainly for wood carving or as firewood.

See also Vol. VII: Oils, Vegetable.

ONION CROPS. This group, bearing the generic name *Allium* from the Roman word for garlic, includes the onion proper and also shallots, garlic, chives, and leeks, all of which have the same strong distinctive flavour and smell.

1. Onion. Onions have been under cultivation since very ancient times, though how the name arose is unknown. It is commonly applied to the dry or dormant bulb of the biennial plant, *Allium Cepa*, a bulb used throughout the world as a vegetable. *Allium Cepa* is not found wild in Europe, but has been located in past times in various parts of Asia. Spring or green onions may be the undeveloped thinnings of the onion crop, or a crop specially grown for salad purposes. There are other types of onion which are also used when green, such as the so-called

Paul Popper

AN OLIVE-TREE IN THE SOUTH OF FRANCE

Welsh onion (really of Asiatic origin). The Tree or Egyptian Onion is a peculiar type of plant, bearing clusters of small bulbs instead of flowers on tall stems. The Potato Onion bears clusters of bulbs beneath the soil.

There are several types and many varieties of garden onions which differ in keeping quality and the shape and colour of the bulb. Examples in general cultivation are Bedfordshire Champion, James's Long Keeping, and White Spanish.

The onion needs a rich, light, well-worked soil, containing a good deal of humus and further enriched by a dressing of a complete fertilizer several days before the seed is sown. The sowing date is usually between mid-February and mid-March, whenever the soil is dry enough for a fine seed-bed to be prepared. The seed should be sown thinly in shallow drills about 1 inch in depth, and the rows spaced 10 or 12 inches apart. Market-gardeners use mechanical drills to sow onion seed.

The crop should be kept free from weeds throughout the growing period. A modern method is to spray the beds with a 13% solution of sulphuric acid (Brown Oil of Vitriol) just before the seedlings come through, and again soon afterwards. The seedlings should be

Royal Horticultural Society

AN ONION BED WITH THE TOPS OF THE PLANTS BENT OVER TO HASTEN RIPENING

thinned out if necessary to allow the onions to develop properly. The crop is harvested during August and September, and, after being thoroughly dried, is stored in a cool, dry shed for winter use; onions are but little affected by low temperatures. They remain in a usable condition until March or April when the bulbs begin to develop flowering stems, and are then of no further use.

Onions may be grown in other ways. A common method is to sow a suitable variety, such as Reliance, in the late summer (August), and transplant the plants in March, spacing them about 8 inches apart in rows rather more than 1 foot apart. This produces large, well-ripened onions rather earlier than those grown from spring-sown seed. The seed can also be sown in seed boxes in a warm glasshouse or frame in February, and the plants transplanted in April.

Onions are sometimes seriously damaged by the maggots of the Onion Fly, which attack the plants just below the surface of the soil (*see* FLY PESTS). The fungus White Rot may attack the bases of the bulbs and destroy them. Onions in store are sometimes attacked by Neck Rot, another species of fungus disease (*see* PLANT DISEASES).

2. SHALLOTS, *Allium ascalonicum*, take the place of onions in gardens where the latter are difficult to grow, and they serve much the same purpose in the kitchen. The flavour of shallots is perhaps more delicate than that of onions. The shallot, sometimes spelt 'eschalot', has been cultivated since very early times, and is probably a native of western Asia.

This plant is unlike the onion, and the methods of cultivation differ also. Like the garlic and chive, the shallot is a perennial and develops clumps or clusters of adhering bulbs every season. Single bulbs, called cloves, are planted in February on fairly rich soil, the cloves being pushed lightly into the soil about 6 inches apart. The plants grow quickly, forming clusters of new bulbs which are usually ready for harvesting in July. Shallot bulbs need to be dried and cured in the sun before they are stored for use. While still green in early summer, shallot plants, at that stage called 'scallions', may be taken up, separated, and used as a salad.

3. GARLIC, *Allium sativum*, has a strong flavour and smell. It is used almost entirely for flavouring purposes in soups and stews, and, except in

Wales, is much more popular on the Continent than in Britain. The plant resembles the shallot in being a perennial which develops a cluster of small whitish bulbs (instead of a single large bulb like the onion). These are enclosed in a thin membrane-like skin.

Garlic is simple to grow. The cluster of bulbs is broken up, and the small bulbs, or cloves, are planted in fairly rich soil in late February or early March about 8 inches apart. The tops die down early, and the crop is ready usually by July. The bulbs are taken up and thoroughly dried in the sun, and then are usually plaited together into ropes which are hung up in a dry, airy shed to complete the curing.

4. THE CHIVE, *Allium Schoenoprasum*, is the smallest member of the onion tribe. It is a native of Europe, and is grown mainly for its delicate flavour, which is particularly useful in salads. The chive is a perennial and grows in thick clusters of plantlets, which can be taken apart for use as required. Sometimes only the leaves are used, the cutting of which makes the plant grow more vigorously.

The chive is always propagated by division, small clusters of plantlets being set in March or April about 12 inches apart. The plants are often used as an edging in the vegetable garden, for in summer they may bear pretty heads of violet-red flowers.

5. LEEKS, *Allium Porrum*, are biennials. The name comes from the Anglo-Saxon *leac*, a word meaning plant, which also had its part in garlic, charlock, and hemlock. The thickened stem of the leek plant, when blanched, provides a popular winter vegetable. There are only a few varieties of leek, the best known being Mussel-burgh, Lyon, London Flag, and Giant Carentan.

It is customary in gardens to grow leeks, like celery, in shallow trenches, so that the plants can easily be earthed up to blanch the stems. Another method, and the one used by market-gardeners, is to plant the leeks in rows with a dibber, each plant being dropped into a widish hole made several inches deep. As the plant develops, the stem lengthens and is blanched by the soil gradually filling up the hole. The plants should be about 8 inches apart in rows some $1\frac{1}{2}$ to 2 feet apart. Leeks of good quality need rich soil.

Leek seed is sown in a prepared seed-bed in March, or in seed-boxes under glass in February. The plants should be ready for transplanting

Royal Horticultural Society

PLANTING LEEKS IN HOLES MADE WITH A DIBBER
The holes are larger than the leeks to allow room for them to grow

during May and June, or in the early part of July for later crops. The vegetable is ready for use from October to March.

The only pest of leeks is the Leek Moth, the caterpillars of which tunnel into the leaves. This pest, which appeared in Britain only a few years ago, also troubles shallots and onions. There are no serious leek diseases.

OPEN FIELDS AND ENCLOSURES. 1.

MEDIEVAL OPEN FIELD SYSTEM. The DOMESDAY BOOK (q.v. Vol. X), which was a land survey made by William the Conqueror in the 11th century, shows an England consisting almost entirely of small communities, each one self-contained and largely independent of its neigh-bours. Each man in each community grew what was needed for himself and his family on the land he held from his landlord, and the necessary crops were grown in a simple rotation that had been designed partly to maintain the fertility of the land and partly to distribute the work upon

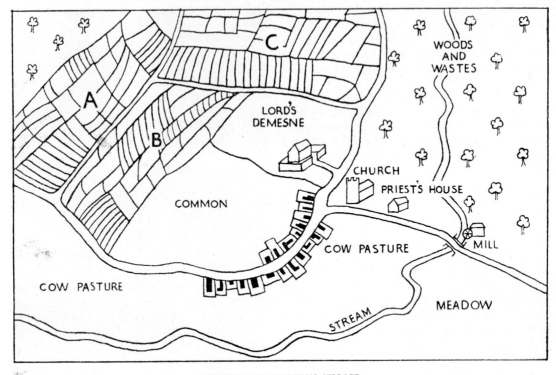

A DIAGRAM OF A MEDIEVAL VILLAGE
A, B, and C are the arable fields which were planted in a 3-year rotation

it evenly through the year. Experience had shown that the growing of crops withdrew fertility from the soil, which therefore needed a rest from time to time while Nature restored its condition; also, as some crops are slower growing than others, they must be planted earlier in the farmer's year. Thus, there was a 3-year rotation in the use of the land. One-third of it was sown in the autumn with the slow-growing wheat crop; another third was sown in the spring with quicker-growing crops such as barley, oats, or peas; and the other third was left to rest in fallow without any crop at all. In the next year this fallow portion was the one to be sown with wheat, the spring corn crop was sown in the land that had carried wheat in the previous year, while the third, which had produced two crops, rested in fallow.

Experience had shown, too, that it needed about 30 acres of land farmed in this way to provide food for a man and his family; and this was as much as any man could cultivate with the means at his disposal in medieval times. A farm as small as this, however, could not maintain the bullock team needed to draw a plough, and

so a system of communal labour had grown up, neighbours uniting to own a plough and team of oxen. As all of them farmed in the same way, this involved no great difficulty, provided that they could agree how to share the land ploughed. If one man had all his land ploughed before his neighbours', he would have an advantage in getting his corn crop sown early, while the man whose land was ploughed last might get nothing sown before the winter weather. The difficulty was solved by giving a day's ploughing to each partner in turn. A strip was ploughed today for A, the strip next to it, ploughed tomorrow, was allotted to B, the following day's work to C, and so on until A's turn came round again. The effect of this was to divide the land used by the community for food production, not into small compact fields and farms such as we see today, but into three very large open fields, in which each man's land was scattered in strips of a day's work, alternating with those of his neighbours. The three fields, of course, represented the division of the land according to the three-course rotation; and assuming that every man had his 30 acres of land, he would have 10 acres in scattered strips in each of them. In practice, of course, the system was not as clear-cut as this, and records of the time show variations in the sizes of holdings and in the distribution of the strips.

While the population of England was small, there was land and to spare for everyone; and as the village communities grew in size, more land was obtained by ploughing up the waste on the edges of the big fields. There came a time, however, when this involved too long a walk from the village to the farthest limit of cultivation, and further expansion for that community ceased.

Grazing for the livestock was provided on parts of the unploughed waste lands; but these were often not very big, and as cattle had to be kept handy, it was necessary to limit the number of animals that any one man might turn out on them. The better grasslands, such as those in the lower-lying parts or alongside streams and rivers, were reserved for haymaking, the area being allotted in alternating strips for mowing, just as the arable land was for ploughing. There was good feed for sheep and cattle on the stubbles after harvest, and when the last sheaf had been carried to the stack, the church bell was rung to make it known that the farmers could drive their livestock on to the stubble field where they could stay until ploughing for the next crop

began. There were dropped ears of corn, some grass and weeds, and in most of these big fields, which often extended to 500 acres and more, there would be rough places, such as banks or marshy spots, which had had to be left unploughed, and on these there would be some good grass. The animals helped to fertilize the ground and enrich it for the next year's crop.

The regulations controlling the use of the common grazings, hay meadows, and stubble fields, and those controlling the cropping of the big arable fields, had obviously to be very strictly enforced, since everybody's operations were so closely mixed up with those of his neighbours. The land, of course, belonged to the landlord (see Land Ownership), but the control was in the hands of the tenant farmers themselves. Regulations for the smooth working of the farming system were laid down by all the farmers in the parish, and twelve of their number were appointed every year to act as a Jury (q.v. Vol. X), to whom breaches of the regulations were reported and by whom the offenders were fined.

2. Enclosures in the 14th and 15th Centuries. The open-field system worked well until the growth of towns with non-agricultural populations began to make it possible for men to earn money by growing crops for sale on the market. The more enterprising farmers began

C. S. Orwin

OPEN FIELDS AT EPWORTH, LINCOLNSHIRE
The strips, which run in all directions, are owned by different farmers

Aerofilms

MODERN FIELDS NEAR BLANDFORD, DORSET

More variety, both in kinds of crops and types of farming, is possible in enclosed than unenclosed fields

to demand the right to control their own land and to develop their own ways of doing things to their own advantage. Bit by bit, the great open fields were divided up amongst their various owners; hedges were planted round the smaller fields thus formed; and so the landscape of farms and fields came to look much as we see it today.

This enclosure of farm-land for individual occupation was a gradual process, although it was marked by two special periods of enclosure. Apart from food, the most important product of farming has been wool, and in the 14th and 15th centuries, particularly in Britain, the WOOL INDUSTRY (q.v. Vol. VII) was expanding fast. Wool was wanted for spinning and weaving, both in England and in Flanders, and the trade was profitable alike for landlords, farmers, spinners, weavers, and merchants. Sheep-farming, too, offered special attractions, for it needed less labour, of which at this period there was a shortage throughout the country. This shortage was due to the plague, the 'Black Death', which in 1349 swept away between a third and a half of the population of Britain. Landlords enclosed the waste land in considerable quantity, so that

they could keep more and more sheep, and there is evidence, also, that many of the smaller farmers were turned off their lands in the open fields so that these might be enclosed for the same purpose. Though this boom in wool eventually came to an end, the advantages of individual farming over communal farming were so obvious that the enclosure movement continued, though more slowly. Sometimes it was carried through by agreement between landlord and tenant or neighbour and neighbour; sometimes the weaker man was forced by the stronger to agree. Over the greater part of the eastern half of England, however, farming in open fields remained the general practice up to the beginning of the 18th century.

3. ENCLOSURES IN THE 18TH CENTURY. About this time a few enterprising landlords, who had observed farming in other countries, were experimenting in the cultivation of new crops. Amongst these, TURNIPS and SWEDES, CLOVERS, and cultivated GRASSES (qq.v.) were the most important, since they provided the much needed winter keep for livestock. The simple rotation of crops practised for long centuries in the three field system left one-third of the land in fallow, without a crop. Some new crop was wanted that would occupy this unprofitable land, and the turnip filled this need. Sown in the summer, it fitted well into the organization of farm work; drilled at fairly wide distances between the rows, it enabled the farmer to hoe the weeds by hand and by horses; it matured in the autumn of the year, and could be stored through the winter, providing food both for cattle and sheep, and so making it possible for the farmer to keep more stock.

The introduction of a clover crop between the two corn crops turned the three-course rotation into a four-course one: turnips instead of bare fallow, then spring corn followed by the new clovers and grasses, and then the winter wheat (*see* ROTATION OF CROPS). Obviously, the enterprising man, anxious to alter his rotation and increase his output, would resent the restrictions of farming in the open fields. It would be useless to him to grow turnips on his strips if all his neighbours could turn their animals on to the stubbles after harvest. For reasons such as this there arose a second period of great activity in the movement towards enclosure, and it continued at ever increasing speed through the 18th century and the first half of the 19th, until open-field farming had disappeared from English agriculture altogether. At one place, however, Laxton in Nottinghamshire, it may still be seen in practice, hardly changed.

See also AGRICULTURAL HISTORY; AGRICULTURAL IMPROVERS.

ORANGES, *see* CITRUS FRUITS.

ORCHARDS, *see* FRUIT-GROWING.

ORCHIDS. There are two types of orchids, the 'terrestrial' kinds that grow on the ground, and the 'epiphytic' kinds that grow on trees or sometimes on rocks. Both kinds are grown by gardeners, but cultivation, particularly of epiphytes, is by no means easy, as they do not grow like ordinary green plants. They need special kinds of houses which are cool, intermediate, or tropical according to the kind of orchid grown.

Orchids are generally grown from seed, though the plant may be 4 to 5 years old before it begins to produce flowers. The modern method of seed raising is highly specialized. Orchids can also be grown by dividing up a well-grown plant, and in this case they flower sooner. The most suitable

Amateur Gardening

A MODERN HYBRID CYMBIDIUM

Amateur Gardening

A MODERN HYBRID CYPRIPEDIUM

A MODERN HYBRID ODONTOGLOSSUM

time for potting most kinds of orchids is early spring. Ordinary flower-pots will often do, though some epiphytal orchids are better grown in shallow orchid pots with more drainage holes, or in slatted, teak wood baskets, or on bark. The best compost consists chiefly of sphagnum moss, and the fibre of certain ferns (*Osmunda* or *Polypodium*) in variable proportions. Terrestrial orchids need some loam in addition. Potting should be firm, with the stiff fibres chopped up and placed vertically. Free drainage is essential to the welfare of orchids.

Orchids need a good deal of water when growing rapidly, but much less when resting and during cold spells in winter. Pure rain-water, at the same temperature as that of the orchid house, should be used. Syringing the atmosphere, not the plants, is helpful on sunny days as it provides the damp growing conditions to which orchids are naturally accustomed. It is a good plan to damp down the paths and under the staging in the house two or three times daily as the temperature rises. Terrestrial orchids occasionally need stimulants, and the safest way of providing this is to spray diluted cow manure over the floor once a week when growth is active. The ammonia given off will be absorbed by the plants from the atmosphere. It may very likely be necessary, on any bright days between March and September, to give the plants some shade, especially in the cool houses.

See also Vol. II: ORCHIDS (WILD).

ORNAMENTAL TREES. Trees are planted in gardens and parks for the beauty of their shape and of their flowers, fruit, and autumn tinted leaves. They also serve other purposes in the design of the garden: they may be planted to screen unsightly objects and to prevent the garden being overlooked by neighbours, or to act as valuable windbreaks protecting the garden from the prevailing wind. They can form an effective part of the design, especially of a large garden, when they are used to bring about variety, to emphasize differences of levels, and to form glades and avenues, and vistas leading towards some object of interest. Trees, both large and small, were often used in this way by the landscape gardeners of the 18th century (*see* GARDENING, HISTORY OF). Now that gardens are in general so much smaller, trees cannot be planted so freely except in public parks (*see* ARBORICULTURE).

When planting trees the gardener must be well informed about their characteristics. He must know whether the trees he is choosing are likely to grow well on the soil and in the situation intended for them; and he must take into consideration at the time of planting what will be the eventual sizes of the trees. Trees, like FLOWERING SHRUBS (q.v.), are permanent plants, and mistakes made at the time of planting cannot easily be put right later. When they come from the nursery, they are probably no more than 10 feet high, and it is difficult to allow for the space they will fill when they have grown to their full height and width. Another important thing to remember in planting trees in small gardens is that very few plants will grow under the shade, and even less under the drip, of spreading trees.

Beeches, elms, limes, horse and Spanish chestnuts, and many others have played an important part in the landscape design of big gardens; and ornamental trees such as evergreen oaks and walnuts, as well as some of the fine conifers such as cedar trees and Scots pines, are often conspicuous points of beauty in old gardens. Spanish firs, thorns, ash trees, Corsican and Australian pines, and the white and balsam poplars are well able to withstand exposed and windy conditions, and so are often planted as windbreaks; and the poplars, being very fast growers, are also useful as screens. Birches and weeping willows make attractive backgrounds to WATER GARDENS (q.v.).

In the smaller gardens it is the smaller flowering trees that are most often planted, the favour-

R. A. Malby

ORNAMENTAL TREES AT SHEFFIELD PARK

ite perhaps being the yellow-flowered laburnum of which the hybrid *Watereri* is the most handsome. The many kinds of *Prunus*, such as flowering cherries, plums, and almonds, are also popular, and so are many of the apple family, some of which are decorative both in flower, foliage, and fruit. Crab apples and some modern hybrids such as *Malus Lemoinei* are decorative from May to October. *Malus floribunda* is perhaps the most free-flowering of all spring trees, but its fruit is insignificant. The scarlet-berried mountain ash, white and crimson double hawthorn, and the decorative leaved maples, such as *Acer Negundo*, are all showy and not too large ornamental trees. Magnolias and tulip trees with their waxy flowers and deep-green evergreen leaves, and the Indian bean tree (*Catalpa bignonioides*) with white flowers and huge leaves are some of the rather larger trees often to be seen.

There are many other species, some of which, like lilacs, are sometimes grown as trees and sometimes as shrubs. Most of them have the great advantage that, once established, they need very little attention, except, perhaps, occasional cutting out of unnecessary branches to keep them a good shape.

See also ARBORICULTURE; FLOWERING SHRUBS.

OXEN, *see* CATTLE; ANIMAL FARMING, TROPICAL. *See also* Vol. IV: BEASTS OF BURDEN.

OYSTER FISHING. Dredging for oysters in Britain is a very old industry, dating from the Roman occupation. Despite intensive fishing, British oyster beds satisfied home demands until the middle of the last century. The most prolific beds were those in the Essex creeks, but the best oysters came from Whitstable in Kent on the south side of the Thames. A simple kind of oyster-culture was practised in other places on the south coast wherever there was a landlocked harbour, backwater, creek, or quiet estuary. At Emsworth, near Portsmouth, for instance, oysters used to be collected from the seaward channel and relaid in shallow oyster 'parks' on the foreshore to fatten. Bathed in the sun's rays in these 'parks', the minute organisms on which the oysters feed multiplied greatly, and so the oysters grew fat.

Most of the natural oyster-beds, however, gradually became exhausted, and today the only productive beds are in the Essex creeks near Colchester, in the Fal at Falmouth, and on the South Wales coast. These beds are dredged for brood (young) oysters, which are then protected until they are large enough to be sold. The usual oyster dredge has an iron mouth-frame 26 to 30 inches wide, to which is attached a bag made of interlocking iron rings. The oyster boat casts

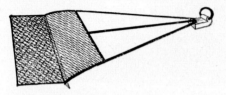

AN OYSTER DREDGE

the dredge overboard and then sails or rows backwards and forwards over the oyster-bed, hauling in the dredge from time to time to empty it of the catch. If not enough oysters are obtained by dredging, supplies are imported from France, and relaid on suitable ground. When they have grown to a fair size, they are dredged and sold as 'natives'. The years spent in English waters are considered, in spite of their birth in French waters, to entitle them to naturalization.

France is able to supply Britain with brood oysters, because oysters are cultivated there from the earliest stage. In 1848 the constant drain on the natural beds so alarmed the French oyster fishermen that the Government tried to prevent further export of brood oysters, but without success. Later, however, the scientist Coste carried out some successful experiments in Brittany, which resulted in the modern system of oyster-culture. According to Coste's system, in order to make good the loss of all the full-grown oysters which have been marketed, an adequate amount of oyster spawn must be collected during the breeding season and protected during early life. The brood oysters are then distributed on ground where there is ample food.

The two most important oyster-culture centres in France are the land-locked bay of Arcachon, near Bordeaux, and the low-tide flats at Auray in the south of Brittany.

This is the way the oysters are raised there. Quantities of curved roofing tiles are coated with a mixture of lime, sand, and water. When dry, they are put into large crates and placed in position at low water, just before the oysters are expected to spawn. If all goes well, the spat or oyster spawn will settle by the million on the limed surfaces. The tiles are left alone till the spat are about half an inch in diameter, when they are ready to be detached from the tiles. The lime coating is easily flaked off, and with it come the brood oysters, undamaged. At this stage their shells are thin and delicate, so, to protect them from boring shell-fish and other enemies, they are placed in shallow cases, covered top and bottom with fine-meshed wire netting. Later, when spread thinly on hard ground where there is plenty of food, they grow rapidly. Within a few months the shells are strong enough to defy most enemies, except the shell-boring molluscs, against which the oystermen wage continual war. The oysters remain in these centres until they reach a marketable size, and can be sold. Two species are reared at Arcachon. One is the species native to Britain, and these oysters are sold in Britain as 'natives'. The other, not so highly valued, is the Portuguese oyster, which originally came from the River Tagus. It is long and slipper-shaped, without the symmetry of form characterizing the 'native' oyster.

See also FISHING INDUSTRY; PEARL FISHING.
See also Vol. II: OYSTER.

P

PALM TREES. 1. The palm trees that grow in warm climates are very different from the common trees of temperate lands such as Europe. They belong to a large group of flowering plants called 'monocotyledons' (*see* SEEDS, Vol. II), and they build up their stems on a peculiar plan that enables them to grow steadily taller, but not much thicker. As a rule they have no side branches, and all their leaves grow in one great tuft at the top of the tree, where the flowers and fruit are also carried. The wood of their stems is a mass of interlacing fibres, without the annual rings that are found in other trees. Palm wood is not very easy to work, nor is it usually strong or durable, though some kinds are used by the natives in districts where better timbers are scarce. The flowers of palms grow in loose clusters like those of grasses, surrounded by a leafy sheath.

Many kinds of palms grow in the tropical countries throughout the world, and their fruits, leaves, and stems are put to a great many different uses. Their leaves form an excellent thatch or screening material for the walls of huts, and they may also be woven into mats, sun-hats, and baskets. Some palms are tall and slender, like the Coconut Palm; others short and squat, like the Oil Palm; and still others have slender trailing stems that thread their way through the undergrowth of the jungle. Some of these form the canes or *rattans* from which cane chairs and basketwork are made. Other kinds, such as the Fan and Sealing-wax Palms, are grown in gardens for the beauty of their leaves or stems.

2. OIL PALM (*Elaeis guineensis*). This is one of the most important of the cultivated kinds of palm tree. It grows wild in West Africa, and is cultivated there and in tropical Asia. Young palms are raised from seed and planted out about 30 feet apart on cleared jungle land with fertile soil. They grow rapidly and bear flowers and fruit 4 years after planting. Their fruits are like juicy plums, borne in huge clusters, and they ripen the whole year round. The trees grow steadily up to a height of 40 feet, and continue to bear fruit for many years. As each cluster becomes ripe, the crop is gathered by men who climb up the rough tree trunks. It is then taken by lorries or a light railway to the nearest factory, where the valuable palm oil, which is used in making soap and margarine, is extracted by machinery from both the flesh and the kernel of the fruit (*see* OILS, VEGETABLE, Vol. VII).

3. SUGAR PALMS. The sap that flows up the flowering shoots of certain palms is very rich in sugar, and some of these trees are specially grown to supply either sugar or alcohol. Two kinds so treated are the COCONUT and the DATE palms (qq.v.). Others are the Nipah Palm (*Nipa fruticans*) of Malaya, and the true Sugar Palm (*Arenga saccharifera*) of south-east Asia, the leaf-stalks of which bear a black fibre used for making rope, twine, and fishing-lines. The Palmyra Palm (*Borassus flabellifer*) is cultivated for sugar in India, Burma, and Ceylon, as well as for its edible nuts and useful fibres. All these kinds are raised from seed or offshoots.

When the trees are well-established and beginning to flower, the tapping is begun. The tapper climbs the tree, sometimes cutting shallow steps in its trunk to help him ascend, and makes a cut at the base of the flower spathe (a large, protective leaf-like sheath) which springs up amid the tuft of foliage at the top of the trunk. Beneath the cut he fixes an earthenware pot or a bamboo container to catch the sap as it flows from the wound. Each day he collects the sap, and renews the cut, often beating or shaking the flower-stalk to stimulate the flow. In this way the tapper harvests the food material that the palm would otherwise have used to develop its fruit, and consequently the tapped trees do not yield good fruit crops.

The sweet sap is poured into large iron pans and heated until the liquid becomes a thick brown syrup. When this cools, it solidifies as a brown sugar, known as *jaggery*. The sugar-making must be done within a few hours of tapping, for if the sweet sap is left it soon ferments and forms a mildly alcoholic drink called *toddy*, which is very popular in the south of India. By fermentation and distilling, a much stronger

OIL PALM

SAGO PALM   PALMYRA PALM

BUTTON NUT
PALM

BETEL-NUT   COCONUT
PALM   PALM

TYPES OF PALM TREES

spirit known as *arrack* is produced; the sap is also used as a source of industrial alcohol.

4. SAGO. Sago is obtained from the pith of the trunk of the Sago Palm, *Metroxylon sagu*, which grows in freshwater swamps and along stream sides in Malaya and the East Indies. It is an erect, unbranched tree with feathery foliage, which can be grown from seed but is more usually reproduced from the offshoots that spring up around its base. When the stems are about 10 years old and ready to flower, they are cut down and then cut across into short logs, which are sold by the growers to the merchants who extract and purify the sago. First of all the bark is cut away, leaving a core of white pith. This pith is rasped by a machine which breaks it up into a fine powder. This is thoroughly washed in running water, strained through cloth sieves to remove all fibrous matter, and then dried to yield a nutritious white flour. The pearl sago that we commonly see is made by forcing the damp flour through holes in a metal sieve, causing it to drop on to a hot metal plate, where it forms hard round lumps.

Although the sago-palm tree must be destroyed to secure the crop, its place is soon taken by off-shoots from its stump, and the yield from an established plantation is about 5 tons of flour

per acre every year. Certain other palms also yield sago, and in Ceylon an important source is the tree called *Cycas circinalis*, which looks like a palm but is botanically a much more primitive tree.

5. OTHER PALMS. The Areca-nut Palm (*Areca catechu*), in some parts called the Betel-nut, yields the nuts that many eastern people chew. 'Vegetable Ivory' is the hard kernel of the nuts of certain West African palms called *Phytelephas*, or Button Nut trees; it is hard, smooth, and white in colour, and is used in some quantity for making clothes buttons. Raffia, used in basket-making, is made from the leaves of a palm that grows in Madagascar; and *piassava*, the tough fibre used for brooms, is extracted from the leaf bases of certain palms that grow in West Africa and South America.

PARASITES. A parasite is an animal or plant which derives its nourishment from the living body of another animal or plant. It generally weakens and sometimes even kills its 'host'. Some animals are never anything but parasites at all stages of their existence; others, such as the Warble Fly, are parasites in their early stage of life but not when adult; others again, such as fleas, are parasites only when adult. Many parasites have different hosts at different stages in their lives. A parasite that lives upon the surface of its host, as does a flea, is an 'ectoparasite'; one that lives inside its host, as a tapeworm does, is an 'endoparasite'.

External or ectoparasites consist of small animals: insects, such as fleas, bugs, and lice (*see* INSECT PESTS), and mites and ticks, most of which suck the blood of the warm-blooded animals, that is, of birds and mammals. There are two kinds of lice, the biting lice or bird lice, which attack both birds and mammals, and the sucking lice, which are found only on mammals. Both kinds cling to fur, hair, or feathers by means of powerful claws, and the eggs, called 'nits', are cemented on to the hair or feathers. Domestic fowls are commonly attacked by bird lice, and if they are heavily infested, bare patches of skin show where the feathers have been destroyed. Such birds never do well, and their troubles are increased because the bird cannot help scratching the irritated places (*see* POULTRY).

Internal or endoparasites consist principally of PARASITIC WORMS and the larvae of certain FLY PESTS (qq.v.). Some microscopic forms of life, such as VIRUSES and BACTERIA (qq.v. Vol. II), which cause ANIMAL DISEASES and PLANT DISEASES (qq.v.), are also parasites, and often very deadly ones.

In all cases of both external and internal parasites, it is easier to deal with the pest in the early stages of the attack. Particular methods of control are dealt with in the articles on the

animals which they usually attack. Clean conditions will, of course, do a great deal to prevent attacks.

PARASITIC PLANTS (q.v. Vol. II) are often serious pests, especially the various kinds of FUNGI parasites (q.v. Vol. II) which cause diseases in plants, such as potato blight, rust in wheat, and vine mildew, and animal diseases such as ringworm.

See also PESTS AND DISEASES; ANIMAL DISEASES; PLANT DISEASES.

PARASITIC WORMS. 1. FLATWORMS. The Liver Fluke is a flatworm that lives in the bile

ADULT
LIVER
FLUKE
actual
size

ducts (tubes) in the liver of sheep and cattle. It pierces the walls of the ducts and feeds on the blood, thus causing the disease known as 'liver-rot', and also a condition of swollen ducts known as 'pipey-liver'. The flukes spend their early lives in small freshwater water-snails, and therefore the disease occurs in freshwater marshes where such snails live. The young flukes kill the snails by late summer or early autumn, escape from their dead bodies, and, after a short period of active swimming, settle upon blades of grass, which are then eaten by the sheep or cattle. The young fluke enters the animal's body and reaches the liver from 5 to 9 days later. As many as 200 flukes may be found in the liver of a single sheep, and such a heavy infestation probably kills the animal. Heavy losses used to be inflicted on flocks by liver-rot, but now the disease is usually cured. The flukes may be expelled by carbon tetrachloride for sheep and liquid extract of male fern for cattle. If, however, immature flukes are concentrated in the bile ducts of the liver in large numbers, carbon tetrachloride is ineffective, and the animal probably soon dies. The best way of preventing attacks is to drain the marshy land, and so get rid of the snails.

Tapeworms, which are also flatworms, are attached by suckers or hooks upon a rounded clinging organ or 'head' to the walls of the intestines of vertebrate animals. The digested food of the host is absorbed through the surface of the tapeworm's flat, ribbon-like body. The worm may set up a state of irritation at the point of attachment, and inflammation and ulcers may be caused. The parasite spends its early life as a bladderworm in a 'secondary' host—some

Harold Bastin

THE PARASITIC PLANT DODDER ON RED CLOVER
Dodder gets its nourishment from the stems of its host

animal which is eaten by the 'primary' host. The bladderworm of one human tapeworm is found in pigs, that of another in oxen; that of one dog tapeworm occurs in rabbits, that of another in sheep. The bladderworm of a cat tapeworm is found in mice. Many tapeworms infest poultry, their early life being spent in slugs and snails, in earthworms, or in insects. The harm done by the bladderworm may be very serious. A very small dog tapeworm, so small that often we never know that the dog is infested, lives as a bladderworm in the brain of a sheep, where it causes the serious trouble called 'staggers', 'sturdy', or 'gid'. Another dog tapeworm has a bladderworm that may occur in any kind of mammal, including man, usually in the liver, where it may swell to enormous size, being then known as an 'hydatid cyst'.

Tapeworms are expelled from the intestines of affected animals by the use of a strong purgative specially prepared for the purpose. The animal is not free of worms until the 'head' is ejected, and that is often difficult to dislodge.

2. ROUNDWORMS. These may be found in the digestive system of any animal, including man, and are particularly troublesome to farm live-stock. They are cylindrical in shape, and many have well-developed and extremely powerful mouth-parts through which they feed.

Most species of roundworm deposit enor-mous numbers of eggs in the stomach or intes-tines of their 'host'; but these are passed out in the ani-mal's droppings on to pasture, whence they are transferred to other animals when grazing, or through the drinking water. Almost every kind of mammal is the host of some species of roundworm, but healthy ani-mals take no harm from them unless they are present in great numbers. Some kinds migrate from the intestines to different parts of the body during the course of their development, and when fully grown may reach and damage some impor-tant organ. Some are blood-suckers, among them the Twisted Wire Worms which inhabit the stomach of sheep, cattle, and sometimes goats.

FEMALE AND MALE
ROUND WORMS
FROM HORSE
one-third size

Other roundworms cause harm by means not yet fully understood. In sheep and cattle, for example, a wasting disease develops after heavy infestation with this kind of roundworm. It has been suggested that the worms produce a poisonous substance that is absorbed into the animal's system and causes poor condition and wasting.

The Gapeworm is a lungworm (a species of roundworm) which attacks birds. A pair of Gapeworms is sometimes found, looking like one red Y-shaped worm, in the wind-pipe of a fowl. The female is the stem and thick arm of the Y; the male is the thin, threadlike arm. The two are permanently joined. It seems that the eggs are swallowed by earthworms, and that chickens become infected by eating these worms. The young Gapeworms develop in the lungs of the chicks and then travel to the throat, where they set up the condition known as 'gapes', and death results from choking. Gapes can be largely prevented by raising chickens on uninfected ground free from other birds, especially star-lings, which may be suffering from the pest, and by preventing the chicks mixing with turkeys (which alone among poultry are attacked by Gapeworms when adult). Gapes is difficult to cure. The old-fashioned remedy is to put the bird into a sack containing powdered camphor so that it sneezes or coughs the Gapeworm out of its position in the throat. This is as likely to succeed as anything else (*see* POULTRY).

FEMALE GAPE-
WORM WITH
MALE ATTACHED

Other lungworms spend at least one stage of their development in the windpipe or lungs of animals such as sheep and pigs. With sheep and calves the presence of these roundworms in the lungs causes an illness called husk. Pigs develop a cough. As with gapes, an animal once infested is very difficult to cure.

Serious infestation with roundworms can be prevented by not keeping the stock too long on the same pasture. If a great many animals of the same kind are grazed for a long time on a small acreage of land, there will be a vast accumulation of worm eggs, and the land is then said to be 'sick'. An animal in good condition is better able to withstand infestation than an underfed one. A badly infested animal can be dosed with phenothiazine, given in liquid or tablet form, or as a powder mixed with the food.

See also Vol. II: WORM, section 6.

PARSLEY, *see* HERBS, GARDEN.

PARSNIP. The large fleshy taproots of *Pastinaca sativa* have been used as an autumn and winter vegetable since early times, and are very nourishing. The English name, parsnip, is probably a corruption of the Latin name *pastinaca*, a name which the Italians still use. The common wild parsnip, a member of the carrot family, occurs throughout Europe, particularly on chalky and limestone soils. The garden parsnip has been developed by selection from the wild species, which is little different in general appearance but has a smaller taproot with a stronger flavour. The Romans first improved the wild parsnip by sowing the seed in rich garden soil and selecting the best plants for seed. Between 1847 and 1851 the well-known variety of garden parsnip, the Student, was introduced, and is still extensively grown. Other kinds are Hollow Crown, Improved Guernsey, Lisbonnais, Elcombe's Improved, and Offenham. The difference between one kind and another lies only in the shape of the tap roots, some being short and broad at the crown, others long and tapering. Market-gardeners prefer the shorter kinds as they can be packed for market more easily. The plant is a biennial, producing flowers and seed in the second year of growth.

As the parsnip needs a long season of growth to develop its large taproot, it is customary to sow the seed as early as February or early March. The crop should be grown on soil which was enriched by manuring for the previous crop and has been well prepared; fresh manure should not be applied. A complete fertilizer containing plenty of potash should be worked into the soil a week before the seed is sown. The seed should be sown in drills about ½ inch deep and spaced 15 to 18 inches apart, and then the seedlings are thinned out so that the plants

are 6 to 8 inches apart in the rows, leaving plenty of room for the roots to swell. As the roots are quite hardy, it is customary to leave them in the ground, lifting them as they are needed. If left long enough, the roots begin to make growth in March and produce flower stems during April, after which they become useless as a vegetable. Therefore, all parsnips except any needed for seed should be cleared from the ground by the middle of April at the latest.

PEACHES AND NECTARINES. These are closely related to PLUMS (q.v.), but are not nearly so hardy. Peaches probably originated in China, and were cultivated there many hundreds of years B.C. They were probably introduced to Europe from Persia, and are now grown all over southern Europe. They must have been known in medieval England, for King John is recorded as having died of 'a surfeit of peaches and ale'; but it seems likely that they were first grown in England by Henry VIII's gardener. They are now grown in enormous quantities, mainly for canning, in the U.S.A., especially in Delaware, Maryland, Virginia, Georgia, Pennsylvania, and New Jersey. In some seasons they are so prolific that they are fed to the pigs, so producing the famous 'peach-fed hams'. Peaches are grown in Britain against warm south walls, and as bushes in protected places, and they will produce very heavy crops so long as they escape the spring frosts. Nectarines are smooth-skinned peaches, and are a little less hardy.

East Malling Research Station

▲ FAN-TRAINED PEACH TREE

Peaches can be grown by being budded on to their own stock, but when so grown the trees do not generally last much longer than 25 years. In France they are often grown on almond or plum stock; English nurserymen generally prefer the common mussel plum stock, and these stocks will give the tree a much longer life. They will grow on most soils so long as there is good drainage, and they benefit from a fair amount of lime. The young tree should be planted in November, and very firmly set. Then it can be given a mulch of old manure or compost to protect it against spring droughts. If it is grown against a wall, it is not difficult to provide it with some protection against spring frosts during the critical period when the fruit is setting. Peaches flower early and so are liable to get caught by frost. They are self-fertile, but it is wise to give some assistance in pollination on a sunny day with a rabbit's tail or camel-hair paint brush (see FERTILIZATION).

Peaches are generally trained in a fan shape against walls. A single full-grown tree, covering some 24 by 10 feet of wall space, should produce 200–250 good-sized peaches in a season, if carefully and systematically pruned from the beginning to curb unnecessary growth and to throw the vigour of the tree into fruiting. Peaches are also sometimes trained into U-shaped trees, with two main branches coming from a short main stem and bearing lateral fruiting shoots (see page 320). They may also be grown as CORDONS (q.v.). If good-sized fruit is to be obtained, thinning must be carried out, preferably twice in the season. A general rule is to leave one peach per square foot of wall, but a vigorous healthy tree with fine foliage can successfully mature rather more than this.

Trees grown against a wall are liable to suffer from drought, and it is generally necessary to supply water, and a good mulch to keep in the moisture, especially during the time the fruit is swelling. The fruit needs to be harvested very carefully as it is easily damaged.

Peaches suffer from most of the diseases and pests of the plum family, such as Aphid and Red Spider, and some of these are apt to be particularly troublesome with fruit grown against a wall. Among the most serious is the fungus disease, Peach Leaf Curl, which causes the leaves to curl, to become bloated and discoloured to a reddish purple, and finally to die and fall off (see PLANT DISEASES). The disease can be controlled by an anti-fungus spray such as Bouisol or a sulphur spray (see FRUIT SPRAYING), or, if caught early, by picking off the diseased leaves and burning them.

See also FRUIT-GROWING; FRUIT PROPAGATION.

PEANUTS, see GROUNDNUTS.

PEARL FISHING. The pearls of the pearl oyster are the finest and most valuable, although other shellfish are capable of producing pearls. The pearl is formed in this way. Some minute foreign body, frequently the tiny dead body of a parasitic worm, a grain of sand, or a fragment of shell, becomes lodged inside the flesh of the mollusc. This sets up an irritation which causes the oyster to produce a secretion called nacre, which becomes deposited around the foreign body and so forms the pearl. The beautiful lustre is due to minute wavy lines which break up the light falling on the pearl's surface.

The richest fisheries for the pearl oyster are those of Ceylon, the Persian Gulf, and Australia. The Ceylon pearls, although small, are exceptionally beautiful and more valuable than the larger but less lustrous pearls of the Australian seas. The Ceylon oyster-banks lie 100 miles north of Colombo at an average depth of 8 fathoms. The fisheries are controlled by the government which, each year, fixes the date for the opening of the fishery and invites divers, boat-owners, and merchants to attend. The system of payment is that one-third of the catch

Paul Popper

A PEARL DIVER BRINGING UP OYSTERS FROM THE SEA BED

goes to the divers and two-thirds to the government.

A few days before the appointed date the divers begin to arrive from India and the Persian Gulf, bringing the boats they need. The government inspector's depot ship lies at anchor in the area to be fished, and early each morning the fishing fleet clusters around it, waiting for the signal to begin. At seven o'clock the ensign is run up the mast, and a warning shot is fired. A deafening hubbub at once breaks the stillness of the morning. The boats weigh anchor, each crew selecting its own fishing patch. The divers wear only a loin-cloth, and their equipment is equally simple. On the end of the life-line there is a net bag into which the oysters are put as they are gathered. On the end of a second line there is a heavy stone which carries the diver swiftly to the bottom. Arabs use a horn nose-clip to close their nostrils, but the Indian divers use only their fingers.

Work proceeds till one o'clock, when the cease-fishing signal is given. When the boats reach shore, the crews carry their catches into a palisaded enclosure, the *kottu*, where guards direct them to divide their oysters into three equal piles. Then the guard points to one of these piles, indicating that this is the diver's share, which he can take away with him. He may either open the oysters himself, or hawk them round the camp, where they find ready sale. In the evening the government's share of oysters is sold by auction in lots of a thousand.

Next morning the buyers have their oysters carried to fenced enclosures which they have built. The fence is double, leaving a passage between the two walls for a watchman to remain on guard. The oysters are left undisturbed for about a week, till the flesh begins to decay. Hordes of flies gather round and lay countless eggs. Out of the eggs come maggots which set to work to eat up the oysters' flesh. In about a week the maggots have passed through the chrysalis stage and emerge as yet more flies. As soon as it is judged that all the flesh of the oysters has been eaten, the merchants' servants wash and sift the shells and sandy mass which remain. This is picked over at once, for large pearls are easily found at this stage. To find the minute seed-pearls, the rubbish must be quite dry and has to be sifted grain by grain.

The pearl oysters in the Persian Gulf are fished annually by a swarm of Arab divers.

James Hornell

PICKING OUT PEARLS FROM DRIED OYSTER SHELLS IN A STOCKADED ENCLOSURE IN CEYLON

Those fished in Shark's Bay on the western coast of Australia contain pearls which, although small, are noted for their fine lustre and colouring. Elsewhere in Australian and Pacific waters, there is fishing for a pearl oyster which has a much more massive shell than the species found in Ceylon. The finest and largest is the great Gold-lip Pearl Oyster, which grows to the size of a small soup-plate. It lives in much deeper water than the small Ceylon and Shark's Bay oysters, and so has to be sought by divers wearing helmets and diving-suits. The search sometimes leads into depths which are more than a man can bear without harm; but the rewards are great, and there are always plenty of men, Japanese, Filipinos, and white men, who willingly take their lives in their hands in search for pearls of great price.

Oysters can also be made to produce pearls by artificial means, and pearls formed in this way are called cultured pearls. The most common method, perfected by the Japanese in the early 1920's, is to insert into the oyster's body a small bead of mother-of-pearl enclosed in a sac made from part of the mantle of another living oyster. The oysters into which the foreign body has been introduced are placed in wire cages and returned to the sea in their cages, where they remain, usually suspended from rafts, for 3 to 5 years. They are then reopened, and any pearls which have formed are taken out. Only a very small proportion of the original beads produce pearls of any quality, but the total yield is much greater than from untreated oysters. Although high-quality cultured pearls are very beautiful, they are not as valuable as natural pearls, and the difference can always be detected by an expert.

See also FISHING INDUSTRY.
See also Vol. II: PEARL OYSTER.

PEARS. Pears originated in the Near East, probably in Syria. They have been established in Britain for a long time, the small Perry Pear, grown particularly in the west of England, being in great demand from the 16th century onwards for making perry. Although this drink has now almost disappeared, the fine old Perry Pear trees, with their magnificent mass of white blossom, are still to be seen in western counties. During the 19th century a great many varieties were developed, and now there are varieties of cooking and dessert pears which mature from August to January, or later.

Pears can be grown as standards, as pyramids, as open bushes, as *cordons* or *espaliers*, or trained on a wall. They are raised by budding in the late summer or *grafting* in the spring (*see* FRUIT PROPAGATION). In early days they were grown on pear stock raised from pips, but now they are usually grown on quince stock, quince (Malling A or B) being used for medium-sized trees, and quince (Malling C) for cordons and small bush trees. Large standard trees are not often grown nowadays, except for some cooking pears. Pears flower earlier than apples, and are therefore rather liable to get caught by late frosts. Some varieties are self-fertile, but many are self-sterile, and all fertilize better by cross-fertilization (*see* FERTILIZATION).

Pears grow best on deep, medium loams of a type which holds plenty of moisture, and they thrive least well on sandy or shallow soils with a chalk sub-soil. They need shelter from east winds which can do a great deal of damage to the flowers in April. The sunny side of a wall or fence, well protected from late frosts, is the ideal site. The ground round the trees should always be kept well cultivated. Pears need less potash fertilizer than apples, but they benefit from about $\frac{1}{2}$ oz. to the square yard, applied in the late autumn; they need a certain amount of nitrogen, preferably in organic form (such as 'shoddy'), especially when the trees are not

R. A. Malby
PEAR TREES TRAINED ON A WALL IN U-SHAPED ESPALIERS

making enough growth. Compost or farmyard manure can be used instead of artificial fertilizers, and this is best applied as a mulch in spring or dug in during the winter (*see* MANURES).

Pears are pruned both in the winter and summer in the same way as apples, though the pruning can be more severe (*see* PRUNING). If the crop is to be thinned, this should not be done before early July, as a large proportion of the pears which have set may have been attacked by maggot and so will fall of their own accord. Healthy trees can carry a heavy crop because their leaves can hold a good supply of foodstuffs and water (*see* NUTRITION OF PLANTS, Vol. II).

Pears need to be harvested very carefully to prevent bruising the fruit. They ought to be picked while they are still green, but after they are fully grown. If picked too soon, they will shrivel; if left on the tree to ripen they will go 'mealy'. A pear ready to pick should break off easily when lifted and bent upwards. Early pears, such as Williams, ripen quickly and, unless eaten within a few days of ripening, go 'sleepy'. Later pears keep much better. They should be stored in a dark, well-ventilated, rat-proof place with a moist atmosphere, and should be brought out of store into ordinary room temperature about 12 hours before they are eaten. They are marketed while they are still hard and therefore not so likely to be spoilt by travelling. Late dessert pears are not easy to bring to perfection, especially in cold summers; they should preferably be grown on a south wall.

Pear crops are often spoilt by fungus diseases such as pear scab (black spot) and canker (*see* PLANT DISEASES), and are attacked by insect pests such as Pear Midge, Pear Leaf Blister Mite, Slug-worm (the larva of a species of saw-fly), and the caterpillars of the Lackey moth and others (*see* INSECT PESTS). Unless steps are taken, the fruit may be badly damaged by birds and wasps. This is why the fruits, as soon as they get near maturity, are often put into muslin or cellophane bags.

A well-planned pear orchard should contain varieties of both cooking and eating pears of early, late, and mid-season. The popular Williams Bon Chrêtien is not only a September dessert pear but also, under the name of Bartlett, a favourite canning pear. Other recommended varieties are:

Early (August–September): Doyenne d'Été, Laxton's Superb (Dessert).
Mid-season (October–November): Beurré Clair-geau, Pitmaston Duchess (Cookers); Conference, Durondeau, Doyenne du Comice, Beurré Hardy (Dessert).
Late (December onwards): Vicar of Winkfield, Catil-lac (Cookers): Josephine de Malines, Winter Nelis (Dessert).

See also FRUIT-GROWING; FRUIT PROPAGATION.

PEAS. These leguminous (pod-bearing) plants are grown as a garden vegetable to be used green, and as a field crop, either green or dried for human consumption, and dried for animal feeding. Field green peas, however, cannot compare in flavour with garden peas as a fresh vegetable. All the different kinds of peas are varieties of *Pisum sativum*.

1. GARDEN PEAS. With suitable management of the crops and favourable weather, green peas can be available in the garden from early June until October. They thrive best in a showery though sunny season, and a cool loamy soil gives the best crops. On sandy soil the pods are apt not to fill.

There are a great many varieties, some of dwarf and others of medium growth, and some that on a rich moist soil in a favourable season may reach a height of 5 or 6 feet. If the soil for peas, however, is too rich, the plants may produce a lot of stem and leaf and little fruit. Peas need plenty of potash and some phosphates, and a fertilizer rich in these substances should be worked thoroughly into the soil before the seed is sown. A little additional nitrogen helps the plants to develop quickly; but peas are among those plants in which the nitrogen in the air is converted by bacteria on their roots into a form usable by the plants (*see* NITROGEN SUPPLY IN PLANTS, Vol. II).

Garden peas are broadly classified into two main groups: the varieties with round and smooth or semi-smooth seeds, and the varieties with wrinkled seeds. The smooth-seeded varieties, being the hardier, are usually sown for the earliest crops. For example, Sutton's Fore-most, a variety with round seeds, can be sown as early as late February, and the crop gathered in

Royal Horticultural Society

GROWING GARDEN PEAS

Small twigs are put round the young plants on the left and taller sticks are added when the peas are about 6–8 inches high

late May or early June. Even earlier crops can be obtained, given a mild winter, by sowing a suitable kind in the open in the autumn, or by sowing either in October or in February and covering the row of seedlings with CLOCHES (q.v.) until the cold weather is past. Peas are sown in drills from 1½ to 2 inches deep. Rows of dwarf kinds are spaced 2 to 3 feet apart, and tall kinds 4 to 5 feet.

There are many varieties of peas which can be recommended for garden culture. Of the varieties suitable for early sowing, Foremost or Pilot (smooth-seeded) and Pioneer or Little Marvel (wrinkled-seeded) are reliable; for the second early crops the wrinkled-seeded varieties, Kelvedon Wonder and Onward, are suitable; for main crops the wrinkled-seeded Senator and Alderman are good varieties; and for late crops Gladstone or Late Gem will stand up to the colder weather. There are many other excellent varieties of early and late peas.

Nearly all varieties of garden peas, even the dwarf kinds, need some support, and this should be given in good time before the plants begin to fall. If the peas fall, the crop will be seriously damaged. The tall and medium climbing kinds need twiggy sticks as soon as the plants begin to produce their climbing tendrils, and then taller pea sticks soon afterwards. If sticks are hard to get, some support can be given by lengths of string fastened to sticks on each side of the row.

2. FIELD PEAS. Some crops of field peas are allowed to ripen and are then harvested and later threshed; others are picked green and marketed either as a fresh vegetable or as canned peas. Different varieties of peas are used for the different types of crops, but their cultivation and manuring are much the same. When the crop is cut green, the 'haulm' (stems and leaves) can be made into SILAGE (q.v.) or used as hay. Field peas thrive under the same conditions of climate and soil as do garden peas, these conditions being found in the east and south-east of England where the majority of field peas are grown.

Peas most often follow barley or oats in the ROTATION OF CROPS (q.v.). In very rich soils the crop is apt to produce too much haulm and too few pods, so farmyard manure and nitrogenous fertilizers are rarely used. Lime and phosphates are, however, necessary, as for all other LEGUMINOUS CROPS (q.v.). A suitable dressing for average conditions is 4 cwt. of superphosphate per acre and, on lighter soil, 1 cwt. of muriate of potash in addition (see ARTIFICIAL FERTILIZERS).

If the stubble of the previous corn crop is ploughed after harvest, the furrows may be left until the New Year, when, with suitable weather, the harrows can be used to prepare a seed-bed. Drilling in an average season takes place from January to March: 1¾ cwt. of seed per acre is sown, in rows 9 to 12 inches apart, the seed being placed about 2 inches below the surface. Given a mild winter, an autumn-sown crop may be successful, but peas cannot stand hard frosts. When the seedlings appear above ground, the crop is harrowed, and then subjected to frequent horse-hoeings (or tractor work), until the plants begin to meet in the row (see CULTIVATIONS).

A crop needed for grain is cut with a mowing-machine, and this must be done before the pods are fully ripe in order to avoid loss of grain from shedding. Good weather is needed for drying, for once the crop is cut, it damages easily, and if stacked in a damp condition it may go mouldy. The crop is threshed in the normal way, and the straw is used for feeding to stock. About 17 cwt. of grain per acre is an average yield.

Green peas are picked by hand, large gangs of men, women, and children being employed. The method is to pull up the plants and strip the pods from the stems. If the crop is for canning, it is sometimes carted away whole to the cannery, where machines strip off the pods. It is not always easy to choose a time for gathering when the majority of the pods are sufficiently well filled and yet not over-ripe. The yield of green peas varies from 70 to 120 bags an acre, each bag weighing 40 lb.

The principal pest of peas is the Pea Moth, the maggots of which infest the pods (see BUTTERFLY AND MOTH PESTS). Other pests are the Pea Midge and Pea Thrips, both of which may inflict some damage on the growing plants, the latter particularly in dry, warm weather (see INSECT PESTS).

See also LEGUMINOUS CROPS.

PEAT-LOVING PLANTS. 1. PEAT. The remains of plants which have died under exceptionally wet conditions form peat. In these conditions the bacteria, which usually cause dead plants to decay and form chemical salts useful to living plants, are almost entirely absent.

As a result the dead plants accumulate as a dark, fibrous mass, very acid, and not containing the food to satisfy most plants. Though a certain amount of decomposition takes place, the resulting chemicals are carried by water into the subsoil where plants cannot reach them—a process called 'leaching'.

Peat, therefore, is quite different from normal SOILS (q.v.), which are made up of small particles of rocks weathered in the course of time, together with the more completely decayed remains of plants (humus), and are more or less rich in chemical salts. In a few naturally fertile soils, like the black earths of the Fen district, there is so much organic matter that they are called 'peat'; but these are not acid, and must therefore be distinguished as 'fen peat'.

Horticulturists make use of peat mainly because it makes sandy soils hold together and makes clay soils less heavy and better drained. It also has the important quality of absorbing moisture and retaining it even in dry conditions. There are, however, a certain number of plants, notably those of the family *Ericaceae* (which includes the heathers and rhododendrons) that will grow on the acid peaty soils, primarily because they like acidity and cannot grow if there is lime in the soil. Most of the other plants for which peat is useful are lime haters, though they do not necessarily need acidity. Almost all these plants benefit by the abundant moisture which peat holds.

2. HEATHERS. The considerable areas of Great Britain, especially moorlands, where heathers of many species grow wild, are not limestone districts—at any rate there is no lime on the surface (*see* HEATHS AND MOORLANDS, Vol. II). Most garden heaths have been developed by selection and breeding from the various native British species. These are the widely distributed crimson-purple Scotch Heather, the pinkish-red Crossleaved or Bell Heather, the dark red Dorset Heath which is less easy to grow and is dependent on peat, the pink Cornish Heath, and the Ling, the most common of all European heathers.

Erica carnea, an Alpine heather not found growing wild in Britain, is one of the most useful heathers from the point of view of gardeners. This heath does not mind lime and also has the great virtue of flowering throughout the winter. Briar pipes are made from the tall *Erica arborea* of the Mediterranean regions. The French word

Amateur Gardening

A CULTIVATED HEATH, 'ERICA VAGANS'

for heather, *bruyère*, has become the English word 'briar'.

There are also many varieties of less-hardy, both summer and winter flowering heaths which are useful GREENHOUSE PLANTS (q.v.). They range in colour from white to crimson and purple, and many of them have been developed from plants native to South Africa. They are grown in a compost two-thirds peat and one-third silver sand. After flowering, the shoots are pruned back to 1 or 2 inches from the base. Greenhouse heaths are usually propagated by cuttings, and hardy varieties by cuttings, divisions of the plant, or layering (*see* PLANT PROPAGATION).

3. RHODODENDRONS. These are among the most magnificent of flowers. Individual blooms vary in size from those little larger than heather flowerets to great bells like tea-cups, clusters of which make huge balls of colour. Though the rhododendron has been known in Great Britain for a couple of centuries, a great many new species have recently been discovered in the Far East and have been brought to Europe. The native home of most rhododendrons is among the high mountain ranges of north-east India and western China, often right up among the Himalayan snows, in the forests, or on steep hill-sides —areas for the most part rarely visited by human beings (*see* HIMALAYAS, Vol. III). There are species from small prostrate bushes to great forest trees. They range in colour from white to yellows, and from pinks and reds to purples.

Country Life

AN AVENUE OF RHODODENDRONS AT SHEFFIELD PARK, SUSSEX

dendrons are also propagated from cuttings and by layering, and often from seed.

Many rhododendrons, being natives of one of the rainiest regions in the world, naturally do not grow as well in the eastern and drier parts of Great Britain as in the damper west. In the Royal Horticultural Society's gardens at Wisley in Surrey, the plantations of rhododendrons and azaleas have often to be watered artificially—which need not be done as a rule in Cornwall.

4. AZALEAS. The plants commonly called azaleas are classed by botanists among rhododendrons. Azaleas, however, shed their leaves in winter, whereas most rhododendrons appear evergreen.

Our garden azaleas are chiefly hybrids of Asiatic species and certain American species. These hybrids have been much inter-crossed, and azaleas in a wide variety of colours and with differing flowering seasons have as a result been produced. The florist's 'Indian azaleas' are hybrids that are winter-flowering greenhouse plants, often sold in full bloom as pot plants for the house. After flowering, they should be repotted, pruned only to remove straggly growths, and from June to September stood out of doors in partial shade. They should never be allowed to get dry.

5. OTHER PEAT-LOVERS. Among the *Ericaceae* there are several hardy evergreen shrubs, such as the Marsh Rosemary (*Andromeda*), the Strawberry-tree (*Arbutus*) with its scarlet strawberry-like fruit, and Prickly Heath (*Pernettya*) with its crimson, blue, black, and cream autumn berries.

Also thriving in peat and disliking lime are a wide range of woody evergreen plants from Australia, New Zealand, and South Africa, which are mostly rather tender in the British climate, though they are grown in the mild south-west. Magnolias, which will succeed in most parts of Britain, are best grown in peat; so are the more tender camellias.

Some, like *Rhododendron sino-grande*, have enormous leaves nearly 2 feet in length; some are sweetly scented.

There are four or five European rhododendrons, of which the commonest is the alpenrose (*R. ferrugineum*), growing in the Swiss Alps and other European mountains (*see* ALPINE PLANTS, Vol. II), and the large magenta *R. ponticum* which comes from Caucasus regions.

About a thousand rhododendron species have been brought from Asiatic regions to Europe, and plant breeders are continually producing new hybrids (offspring of mixed parents) in their attempts to find plants with the qualities most useful to gardens, such as those with larger flowers, or of a better shape, or flowering early or late in the season. Pink Pearl is a very popular hybrid, and so is *R. Loderi* which has the important quality of late flowering. The species *R. Augustinii* is among the very best of the near-blue shades; and from this lovely shrub have come charming hybrids such as Blue Tit. Another famous species is *R. Thomsonii*, a wonderful dark red, and this is the parent of many hybrids. Many of these hybrids are grafted on to the rootstock of the common *R. ponticum*. Rhodo-

All the plants so far mentioned are shrubs. Peat is often used for certain herbaceous plants such as FERNS and ORCHIDS (qq.v.), most Asiatic gentians, and the Himalayan Poppies (*Meconopsis*), all of which need ample moisture and will not stand lime.

See also SOILS.
See also Vol. II: HEATHS AND MOORLANDS.

PEPPER, *see* SPICE CROPS.

PEPPERMINT, *see* HERBS, GARDEN.

PERENNIAL PLANTS. Plants that live for many years are called by the general term perennials, as opposed to ANNUALS and BIEN-NIALS (qq.v.). They possess root systems which are persistent, and food reserves are stored in many of them (*see* ROOTS, Vol. II). Perennials are classified according to the nature and length of life of their stems. Trees and shrubs are perennials producing permanent woody stems (*see* FLOWERING SHRUBS). Some garden peren-nials, such as geraniums, tree lupins, and tree peonies, as well as most rock-plants, have stems that persist and produce new growth every year.

There are many perennial plants grown on the farm—for example, lucerne, some of the clovers, and most grasses—that last many years, but depend for their continued existence upon new growth made each year, even though the winter does not by any means destroy all their stems and leaves.

Garden perennials are classified as hardy, half-hardy, or tender, according to the degree to which they can stand the cold and damp of an English winter. Hardy perennials can live through an ordinary winter without protection. Most of the herbaceous perennials (*see* HER-BACEOUS BORDER) are hardy, as are most ROCK-PLANTS (q.v.). Most of them grow quickly from seed, and if given enough nourishment, and divided up when they grow too big, will continue at their best for many years (*see* PLANT PROPAGA-TION). Many of the half-hardy, semi-shrubby perennials, such as fuchsias and hydrangeas, are particularly useful as pot plants for cool green-houses and for out-of-doors in the summer. They propagate freely from cuttings which root easily and grow quickly.

Tender perennials are killed by the frost. Some of them, such as DAHLIAS and Geraniums, can be planted in the garden during the summer;

others, such as streptocarpus and gloxinias, are entirely GREENHOUSE PLANTS, being treated as annuals. Plants such as CHRYSANTHEMUMS, CARNATIONS (qq.v.), and cyclamen have hardy as well as half-hardy varieties, the former being as a rule rather the less showy.

See also ANNUAL PLANTS; BIENNIAL PLANTS.

PESTS AND DISEASES. Generally speaking, a pest is anything that is a nuisance or is not wanted. In farming and gardening the term is used of the animals and plants which interfere with the work of the farmer and gardener, often causing ill health or even death to his flocks, herds, and cultivated plants. It includes such creatures as flies, bugs, beetles, slugs and snails, millepedes, and mites and ticks, and might even be extended to include WEEDS (q.v.). It could also be used of larger animals, such as rats, rabbits, foxes, and pigeons, but these are usually referred to as VERMIN (q.v.). Many of the signs of ill health in plants and animals which are loosely spoken of as 'diseases' are really caused by quite large pests, such as insects or worms. Disease, however, is also caused by much smaller organisms such as FUNGI, BACTERIA, or VIRUSES (qq.v. Vol. II). These, like many of the larger pests are parasites, that is, they live upon other animals or plants and obtain their food from them (*see* ANIMAL DISEASES; PLANT DISEASES).

The harm that parasites do is very varied. (*a*) There may be actual loss of tissue, as occurs when certain fungi invade the wood of a tree or the bacillus of tuberculosis attacks a lung. (*b*) The parasite may manufacture and set free poisonous or 'toxic' substances. Thus, 'silver leaf', a disease of fruit-trees, is due to the destruc-tion of the middle tissue of the leaf by the toxins of fungi not present in the leaf at all but in the branches that bear the leaves. The poisonous toxin is carried in the sap to the leaf. (*c*) The parasite may cause wounds, sometimes very serious in themselves, like those produced by the maggot of the sheep maggot fly, sometimes serious because through these wounds other parasites may enter and cause further trouble (*see* PARASITES). (*d*) Also, in some way or another, the parasite may disturb the growth of the tissue in which it lives, perhaps by producing a tumour or gall, like 'big bud', a condition of black-currant bushes caused by mites (*see* CURRANTS AND GOOSEBERRIES).

SLUGS and SNAILS (qq.v. Vol. II) eat most

kinds of crops and are especially a danger to newly planted-out seedlings in the garden. They feed by night, taking cover by day, and are most active in warm, moist weather, generally preferring a heavy soil which holds the moisture. The great Black Slug will eat right through the stem of a large herbaceous plant such as a delphinium, and the small black Garden Slug will eat up young lettuce seedlings. Some slugs, however, the yellowish-brown Carnivorous Slug, for example, feed on other pests and are useful to the gardener. Poison bait, such as metaldehyde mixed with slightly moistened bran (1 part metaldehyde to 25 parts bran) to attract the pests, can be put out under some covering such as a piece of wood, or scattered lightly. Very precious plants in a garden are sometimes surrounded in the early stages of their growth by zinc bands which keep off the slugs who dare not touch the zinc. The WOODLOUSE or Slater (q.v. Vol. II) eats the stems, leaves, and roots of some plants, and is apt to be a particular pest in cucumber frames and greenhouses, especially if part of the wooden framework is rotten and so forms a shelter.

Millipedes belong to the class of animals called MYRIAPODA (q.v. Vol. II). These attack

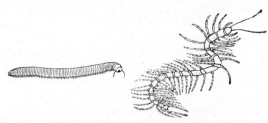

A MILLEPEDE (LEFT) AND A CENTIPEDE

the roots of most garden or field plants, especially the seeds of beans and peas, onions, carrots, potatoes, and strawberries, and are among the most serious underground pests. These hard, blackish, wire-like creatures, which coil up when disturbed, must not be confused with the orange-yellow, quick-moving centipedes, which feed upon the harmful pests and are therefore friends to the gardener and farmer. The great majority of harmful pests, however, are flies, bugs, lice, beetles, butterflies, and moths, or the larvae of these insects (see INSECT PESTS).

In controlling all kinds of pests we must remember that the more farming develops, the greater grows the danger from pests. The farmer's produce is intended for human use, but

much of it is the food of many other living things as well. In natural conditions, plants tend to spread themselves, scattering the seeds far and wide, but the farmer grows large quantities of the same kind of plant in one place: he will have a field of cabbages or turnips, for instance, or an orchard full of apple-trees. This may result in a very rapid increase in the numbers of the creatures which feed upon this particular plant, for they find a large amount of food available in one place, and the nearness of plants of the same kind to each other makes it easier for the pests to increase and to spread from plant to plant. The same applies to the pests which trouble animals: the larger the flocks and herds, the greater is the risk of infection by, say, PARASITIC WORMS (q.v.), and the more easily will the infection spread from animal to animal. A previously harmless creature may suddenly become a pest by changing its food: examples of this are the COLORADO BEETLE (q.v.) which originally fed harmlessly on an American wild plant related to the potato, and the Apple Capsid Bug, which was once found only on willows and alder. New pests have come to Britain with imported foodstuffs from other countries, among them the Leek Moth, the Fluted Scale Insect, the Woolly Aphis, and the Greenhouse White Fly.

Preventive measures must, of course, come first in the control of pests. Well-fed healthy plants and animals are more resistant to attacks by pests than starved and weakly ones, and, should they be attacked, are more likely to recover. The ROTATION OF CROPS (q.v.) and the moving of animals from field to field also help to make attacks by pests less likely. For the successful control of pests a study of their life-history is necessary; for the scientist is then able to say at what period of its life the pest is most easily destroyed, and this information is passed on to the stockman or grower. For example, in some years cereal crops grown in land freshly ploughed from grass are devastated by grubs known as leather-jackets. The scientist, studying their life history, found that these grubs of the CRANE-FLY or Daddy-long-legs (q.v. Vol. II), although they lived protected in the soil, came to the surface on mild nights in spring to feed. He was therefore able to make a poison bait which could be scattered over the field and which the grubs would eat. He also found that the crane-flies laid their eggs in the grass in the autumn, so that if the grass field were ploughed up before August, no eggs would be laid in it (*see* RESEARCH IN AGRICULTURE).

A LEATHER-JACKET

The farmer and gardener have a number of methods of control that they can use against pests, apart from the dusting, fumigating, and spraying with INSECTICIDES (q.v.) and Fumigants at the right time of year.

(*a*) CULTURAL CONTROL. This consists in creating conditions unfavourable to the pest, or so favourable to the crop that it can resist the pest, or both. For example, heavy rolling of grassland discourages cockchafer grubs (*see* BEETLE PESTS) and at the same time presses the soil particles into closer contact with the roots of the grasses. Firm, consolidated soil round carrots not only encourages growth, but helps to keep out the carrot fly (*see* INSECT PESTS). The grease-bands that are put round fruit-trees in September catch the female winter moths as they come up the trunks to lay their eggs (*see* BUTTERFLY AND MOTH PESTS). Clean land, whether farm or garden, where no litter is allowed to lie about, provides little harbourage in which pests can breed or hibernate, and at the same time lets in light and air to the crop. All refuse—piles of weeds or decaying leaves, rotting wood, or loose bark on trees—must be cleared away.

Where other means are not effective, the farmer or gardener may have to grow on a certain piece of ground crops which are immune from the particular pest infesting the ground. For example, in a field which is densely populated with wireworm it may be advisable to grow beans or peas rather than a cereal crop, until the land is cleared of the pest. Sometimes, especially in gardens, the eggs and caterpillars of the pests have to be hand-picked to get rid of them.

(*b*) BIOLOGICAL CONTROL. This is a method of destroying pests by using against them their own natural enemies. One of the first and most successful attempts to destroy pests in this way was carried out against the insect we call the Fluted Scale. This bug appeared suddenly in California in 1868, spread rapidly, and did such serious injury to the orange-trees that it was feared the industry would be ruined. Careful study of this new pest showed that it had arrived

on imported acacias from Australia, that this was its native land, and that it did no real harm there. This suggested that in Australia its own natural enemies kept it under control. A study of these was made in Australia and several kinds were sent to California. Among them was a certain species of ladybird. The ladybirds were put into a glass-house containing an orange-tree badly attacked by Fluted Scale. In about 4

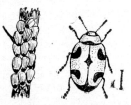

FLUTED SCALE INSECTS (HALF-SIZE) ON A PLANT STEM AND THE LADYBIRD, 'VEDALIA CARDINALIS', WHICH IS USED TO CONTROL THE PEST

months the tree was cleared, and the Ladybirds were set at liberty. They increased rapidly in numbers, spread over the orange orchards of California, and by the end of 5 years the industry was saved from a pest that had threatened its existence. This ladybird is now always used when an outbreak of Fluted Scale appears, and always with success. The story of *Cactoblastis* and the cactus plants in Australia is another dramatic example of biological control (*see* CACTUS, Vol. II); in this case an insect was used to control a pernicious plant.

The method has also been used in Britain. The Greenhouse White Fly is an incomer from America and a pest on tomatoes, cucumbers, and other plants grown under glass. A minute insect belonging to a group called CHALCID FLY

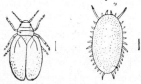

WHITE FLY ADULT AND IMMATURE 'SCALE'

(or Chalcid Wasp) (q.v. Vol. II) lays its eggs in each young White Fly, called a 'scale', that it can find. The egg hatches, and the grub that emerges feeds upon the young 'scale', which turns black and eventually dies. It is now possible to supply these black scales containing the parasitic grubs to glasshouses which are infested with White Fly, and the results have been very successful.

See also ANIMAL DISEASES; PLANT DISEASES; PARASITES; PARASITIC WORMS; INSECT PESTS; EELWORMS; TROPICAL PESTS; LOCUSTS; INSECTICIDES.

PIGEONS, *see* VERMIN, section 8.

PIGS. 1. HISTORY. The domestic pig of the present day is descended from the wild pig, which roamed the forests and lived on green food and the roots of many plants, supplemented at the right season by acorns and beech mast. So that the pig could dig for these roots, nature provided it with a very powerful snout (*see* SWINE, Vol. II). The wild pig is extremely quick on its feet; and its domestic descendant, though shorter-legged and less practised in quick movements, can turn and twist with surprising speed, as anyone knows who has tried to catch one. The domestic pig differs from its wild ancestor in build; for whereas the wild pig carries most of its weight and power in its very muscular shoulders, the domestic pig is better developed in those parts most suitable for human food—the hindquarters and the middle.

The pig was probably first domesticated in China about 5,000 years ago, and seems to have been known in Europe by about 1500 B.C. In England in medieval times, when there was still a great deal of uncleared forest land, herds of pigs were sent under the care of the swineherd to rout in the forests for food. The swineherd was so typical a character of the countryside that he figures largely in folk tales, and is the hero who marries the princess in several of the Grimms' fairy tales. These medieval pigs were, however, much more like the wild kind than the pigs of today, changes in shape and colour having been brought about mainly by the pig breeders of the 18th and 19th centuries. Pigs of both the European and the Asiatic types have been used to form our modern breeds.

2. BREEDS. The modern breeds differ in their general characteristics: some are excellent for bacon production; others are better for pork; some are noted for being good grazers; some are more prolific, that is, they produce a larger number of pigs in each litter than others. There are about a dozen breeds in Britain, and pigs from most of these breeds have been exported to other parts of the world. In very hot, sunny climates, black pigs seem able to stand the heat better than white pigs, for the same reason that the dark-skinned native gets scorched by the sun less easily than the white-skinned European. Of the pure breeds, black pigs with a white stripe round their bodies belong to one of two common breeds—the Essex Saddleback and the Wessex Saddleback. The only obvious difference in appearance between these two is that, when properly marked, the Wessex has white front feet and black hind feet, and the Essex has all four feet white and a white tip to its tail. Both breeds are popular, and may be used for either pork or bacon production. Records of a large number of herds of the Wessex breed show that the average number of pigs born per litter is 9·5, and the number reared is 8·19. A number of breeders mate sows of the Essex and Wessex breed to boars of the Large White breed for bacon production.

The Large White breed is descended from a very old Yorkshire breed known as the Large White Yorkshire. Records of its existence go back a long way. In 1774, for example, a pig of this breed is reported to have weighed 12½ cwt. at the time it was killed, a weight which seems almost unbelievable in these days when the heaviest pigs we see are only about 5 cwt. As their name implies, these pigs are white with no black markings of any sort. The pigs of this breed are long, which means that the sides of bacon are long too. The Large White is probably more popular than any other breed for bacon production, or for use as a sire for mating with sows of other breeds for bacon production.

The Middle White breed was also formed in Yorkshire, and has been improved by breeding until now it is one of the finest pork producing breeds. A good pork pig must be early maturing, that is, it must develop at an early age a high proportion of lean and fat to bone. In some bacon-producing pigs the proportion of bone would be much too high if the pigs were killed at pork age (about 6 months). Records show that the Middle White is not as prolific as the Large White; though, of course, there are exceptions. They are, in general, shorter and thicker than the Large White breed, and their colour is white, with no black markings at all. They have a snub nose (a 'dished face'), rather like that of a Pekinese dog.

The Tamworth, which belongs particularly to the West Midlands where it originated, is distinguished by its rust-red hair and its extremely

Sport & General

WESSEX SADDLEBACK GILT

Sport & General

ESSEX SADDLEBACK GILT

Sport & General

LARGE WHITE GILT

Sport & General

MIDDLE WHITE GILT

Sport & General

GLOUCESTER OLD SPOT BOAR

Farmer & Stockbreeder

TAMWORTH BOAR

Sport & General

LARGE BLACK GILT

Farmer & Stockbreeder

BERKSHIRE GILT

BREEDS OF PIG

long snout. The Tamworth is a good forager, produces a high proportion of lean meat, and is an excellent bacon pig, though not quite as prolific as some of the other breeds.

Another native of the western half of the country, and a very old breed, is the Gloucester Old Spot. It is a white pig with black spots and drooping ears that hang right forward over the face.

The most important of the black pigs is the Large Black, a breed that is fairly widely distributed. The sows are very docile and are good grazing animals. The Large Black is often crossed with the Large White for bacon production, the cross-bred pigs so produced being either black and white or 'blue' and white—a grey-blue effect being given by the white hairs on a white skin with blueish-black markings.

The Berkshire is a rusty black pig of similar shape to the Middle White. It has a short, turned-up nose, the tip of which is white, and it also has four white feet and a little white on the face. This breed is particularly popular in New Zealand and Australia, where pig breeders often combine the early maturing characteristics of the Berkshire with the length and bacon qualities of the Tamworth by crossing these two breeds together.

The Welsh breed, a white bacon pig, the Cumberland, also white, and the Lincolnshire Curly Coat, a large, white, curly coated bacon pig, are to be found chiefly in their home areas. The Long White Lop-eared is a good pig, but not often seen.

The mating of boars of one pure breed with sows of another pure breed generally produces litters vigorous in growth, uniform in shape and size, and often combining the better points of the two parent breeds. If, however, these cross-bred animals are mated together, the animals in the next generation will be of many different types, some resembling one grandparent, some resembling the other grandparent, and some resembling their cross-bred parents (see HEREDITY, Vol. II). For this reason it is not customary or wise to employ cross-bred animals as breeding stock.

3. PORK AND BACON. As has been seen, some breeds of pig are more suitable for producing pork and others for bacon. The success of the pig-keeper's business will depend on bringing his young pigs up to the required weight in the minimum time, approximately 28 weeks for a

porker and 32 to 35 weeks for a bacon pig. If he has to go on feeding them beyond that time, he may lose money. As the demand for pork is normally very small during the hot summer months, the breeder of pork pigs must so arrange his litters that they are not ready for the market during those months. Bacon pigs, however, can be killed at any time. British bacon used to be graded and sold according to its weight and the percentage of fat on it, and British-produced bacon was beginning to compete with Danish bacon, which had been for years the best. But during and after the Second World War, the pig producer had to concentrate on producing the maximum quantity of food from the limited pig food available, and so quality had to give way to quantity.

PIGS, BREEDING OF. A good sow under good management rears sixteen pigs per year in two litters. The good points for which a sow is selected are as follows. She should be typical of the breed to which she belongs (see PIGS). (The points of the breeds can be ascertained from the breed societies concerned.) No matter to which breed she belongs, she should have at least twelve sound teats to enable her to rear properly a large litter. She must be sound on her feet, her body should be long, her top-line should be straight, her hams should be well developed, and if possible she should be bred from a sow that has a record of large litters well reared. Sows that are good tempered and docile usually make better mothers and are easier to handle than bad tempered, excitable ones. As docility can be inherited, it is wise to choose the sows partly for this characteristic.

A boar during his breeding life of, say, 4 years may be responsible for the production of somewhere about 1,600 pigs, by serving 25 sows a year. It is obvious therefore that the selection of the boar is a most important matter. The purchaser should always ask to see the boar's parents, and should then select him from a large litter bred from a sow that regularly breeds good-sized litters. The boar must be a good specimen of his breed, and, like the sow, sound on his feet, long, with a straight top-line, and well-developed hams. He can first be used when he is 7 to 8 months old, and the sows (at this stage called 'gilts') can first be mated when they are 8 months old.

Throughout the boar's breeding life he must

Eric Guy

A TETHERED WESSEX SADDLEBACK SOW WITH HER PIGLETS

be kept in healthy condition and not allowed to become fat. It is illegal to keep a boar over the age of 6 months unless he has been inspected and licensed by the Ministry of Agriculture—a regulation designed to prevent the use of unsuitable boars for breeding.

A sow should have two litters a year. The gestation period (between mating and birth) is 16 weeks. The sow suckles her young for 8 weeks, so that she should have produced and reared her litter in 24 weeks. Normally she can be mated again within a few days of her litter being weaned, so that she should be mated for the second time inside 26 weeks, and so produce and rear her two litters in a year. A good and prolific sow will give birth to nine pigs in a litter, and will rear eight of them; but, of course, there are many sows which will only have a litter of about six born and rear only five. On the other hand sows commonly produce litters of eighteen to twenty pigs, and will sometimes rear fourteen. The little pigs at birth weigh about 2 lb., and their growth depends at first on the milk yield of the sow. After about a fortnight they will begin to eat solid food, and then their rate of growth depends a good deal on the skill of the person who feeds them. In New Zealand, where large quantities of separated milk and whey are fed to sows and young pigs, 40 lb. is a common weight for a weaner of 8 weeks old. Many

pig-keepers in Britain are satisfied with a weaning weight of about 30 lb. per pig.

When a litter of pigs is born, there are often one or two weak members of the litter. The smallest pig in a litter has different names in different parts of the country: reckling, Anthony, runt, and pitman are some. If the litter is a large one, it is usually the best policy to kill the weak ones, because, if left with the others, they will grow very slowly and cost too much to feed. Fed by themselves, however, they can sometimes turn into good pigs. In a large litter there are usually some losses from the sow lying on the young pigs. Some sows are rather clumsy, and in the act of lying down may lie on and kill a young pig. There are other occasional causes of death, the commonest of these being anaemia, which may occur particularly with a litter reared in the sty in winter. Anaemia is less likely to occur when the little pigs can run outside on grass after they are about a week old. Where this is not possible, they should have a few turves to root in. Usually the sty is fitted with a 'creep' —that is, a corner railed off with bars just wide enough apart to let the little pigs through. The young litter is fed in this creep, and it is important to encourage them to eat as well as suck at an early age. If they are given the right diet, and provided with clean dry beds of short straw and chaff, they should grow fast.

At the age of 4 to 6 weeks the male pigs which are not needed for breeding are castrated; that is, made incapable of breeding (*see* STOCK BREEDING). The young pigs very quickly get over the operation, and deaths are rare. The castrated male pigs (now called hogs) can then be run with the female pigs, and all can be fattened together. The young pigs are weaned at 8 weeks old, the sow being taken away from the sty rather than the little pigs away from the sow.

PIGS, CARE OF. Pigs, whether they are kept on large pig farms or in ones or twos by ordinary householders, are different in many ways from other farm stock. As they live a more artificial life and feed less naturally than most farm animals, it is essential to understand their needs.

1. PIG HOUSES AND EQUIPMENT. The pig, contrary to popular belief, is a clean animal, provided that it is properly looked after. It will usually dirty only one corner of its sty or will use an outside courtyard as a lavatory, keeping its sleeping quarters clean. Damp housing, with badly laid concrete floors, and damp, inadequate bedding are fatal to pigs, for they are subject to rheumatism and cramp. The earth should never be above floor level on any side of the buildings. All pig buildings should face south, so that they get the most sun. They need to be strong, for pigs are very destructive animals, capable of exerting great pressure with their snouts and doing much damage with their teeth, especially on woodwork which has become splashed with food. Draughts in pig buildings, particularly in farrowing (breeding) houses, should as far as possible be excluded; although, of course, fresh air is most desirable.

For permanent pig houses, concrete, brick-work, or breeze blocks faced with cement are the most suitable. Permanent housing for farrowing sows should consist of a sleeping compartment and a yard, both of which are roofed over and can be shut in during severe weather. An air space just under the roof provides for ventilation. A small 'creep' (into which the young pigs can enter and the sow cannot) is usually provided by fencing off one corner of the sleeping compartment. Both the inside and outside compartments should be about 7 feet square, the front of the house being some 7 feet high and the back 3 ft. 6 in.

But permanent buildings such as these are naturally very expensive to construct; and consequently many more temporary houses are now used. One of the most common of these is the pig ark, a triangular wooden building, easily moved, and housing a sow and litter on grass. The height at the apex of the triangle is 6 feet, and its floor is 9 by 6 feet. The sow using such a house generally wears a tethering harness, which enables her to range on grass within the radius of the chain by which she is tethered. She must be given just enough chain to enable her to enter the house but not so much that she can get round the back of the house and entangle her chain. The arks are mounted on runners so that they can be easily moved around the grassland by horse or tractor. Such huts must be very strongly constructed to stand the strain of moving. If the sows are not tethered, a permanent fence must be erected, or an electric fence used.

Fold units, consisting of a small weather-boarded house, roughly 8 feet square, with a wooden floor, are also suitable for sows and litters. A patch of grass 10 by 8 feet

A FOLD UNIT FOR PIGS
The unit can be moved as often as necessary on to fresh ground

Eric Guy

Eric Guy

A DANISH TYPE PIG HOUSE

The pigs are at bacon weight. The food troughs are inside the bars, and at the back is a dunging passage so that the
sties can be easily cleaned

beside the hut is enclosed by a timber and corrugated-iron fence, and house and run can be moved whenever a new piece of grassland is required.

Farrowing sties can also be constructed of straw bales with a roof of thatched hurdles or corrugated iron. The bales should be protected inside by wire netting to prevent the pigs pulling them to pieces.

Most of the houses described above can also be used for rearing and for fattening pigs. For keeping pigs on a big scale the Scandinavian or Danish type of house is suitable. It has a central feeding passage, with two ranges of sties covered by one roof—a layout which reduces the labour of feeding because the two rows of pigs can be fed almost as quickly as a single row in ordinary sties. A trolley to carry the buckets of food saves much labour and time.

Troughs should, if possible, be built into the front wall of the courtyard of each sty, and designed so that the food can be put into the trough from outside the sty. Movable troughs inside the courtyard are almost always thrown about by the pigs, and it is difficult to get them

into a suitable place while the pigs, hungry for their food, are pushing against the legs of the person who is feeding them. Feeding-utensils must be kept clean, and should be designed for easy cleaning. There must be enough space at the feeding-trough for each pig in the sty. Pigs are by nature greedy animals, and crowding at meal-times means that the smaller or weaker pigs do not get their fair share.

Pigs may be fenced in with pig wire, a strong type of wire netting, or with hurdles, or by means of an electric fence. The electric fence consists of a single or double plain wire which is electrified from a battery and produces a slight, harmless electric shock when touched. The first shock is usually enough to give the pigs a healthy respect for the fence, and to prevent their touching it again.

It is important to have some kind of weighing apparatus for recording the weights of litters and for gauging the exact weight of pork or bacon pigs. A weighbridge into which the pigs can be driven is the most satisfactory for large pigs, but only a big pig farm can afford this.

2. Pig Feeding. The cost of a pig's food is

three-quarters of the total cost of the production of pork or bacon. The reason for this high cost is that the pig's stomach cannot deal with large quantities of cheap, bulky, fibrous foods, such as hay and silage, which are easily digested by animals that chew the cud, such as cattle and sheep (*see* RUMINANTS, Vol. II). Although some grass or green food can be fed, and swill from private houses, hotels, restaurants, or army camps may be collected cheaply, the pig must get a proportion of the more expensive concentrated foods, such as barley meal and milling offals. The price of the swill depends upon the amount which can be collected from one place and upon the cost of boiling or steaming it before use. Swill must always be boiled in order to kill any germs which may be in it. In some towns, the authorities collect waste food from the houses and prepare it for sale to pig-keepers.

Protein, the body-building food in the pig's ration, is supplied by fish meal or meat meal from animal sources or, if they are not available, by vegetable protein from soya bean meal or from home-grown bean and pea meal. Some protein is also found in the cereal foods. The normal pig ration contains enough fats and vitamins. Fish meal or meat meal supply the necessary minerals; but if only a vegetable source of protein is available, then minerals must be added. For example, if soya bean or pea meal is being used, lime and salt should be added at the rate of about 1%. Growing pigs need certain minerals to enable them to build bone.

Before the Second World War the pig producer in this country had the choice of dozens of different foodstuffs. As the price of these varied, the farmer altered his mixtures to include as high a proportion as possible of the cheaper foods. During and after the war pig feeding was extremely difficult, since few foods were available and these were strictly rationed.

Tottenham pudding, a concentrated form of swill, first produced by a workmen's pig club in Tottenham in 1940, has been widely used as a substitute for meal; 2¾ lb. replaces 1 lb. of meal. Ordinary household swill must be cooked before use; but Tottenham pudding, having already been boiled, can be fed in the form in which it is bought. Potatoes (small or surplus ones) can be used, 4 lb. of potatoes replacing 1 lb. of meal. They are boiled or steamed, and if not needed at once can be made into silage by being lightly pressed down into a suitable container. Other root vegetables can be used in the same way.

Barley meal is made by grinding the barley that is not suitable for brewing, or that has been grown especially for stock-feeding. This is the finest pig food in existence, and if available is included in all pig rations. Breeding-stock rations should contain only about 45% of barley meal, but fattening-pig rations may contain up to 80%. Part of the barley meal in a ration can be replaced by maize meal, maize germ meal, or flaked maize. Flaked maize, made from cooked maize rolled into flakes much like those of the breakfast cereals, is very appetizing, and gives a nice texture to the ration.

When wheat is ground to make bread flour, the outer coat of the grain is separated and sold as bran. This has a limited use in pig feeding, and is included as a rule only where a laxative ration is needed, since it has a loosening effect on the bowels. The coarser parts of the wheat grain itself are also separated and sold as 'weatings' or 'middlings'; this material is used in pig rations of all kinds, about 45% being used in breeding rations and as little as 20% in the final stage of fattening. Dairy by-products, when available, are also excellent pig foods; whey (the residue after cheese has been made from whole milk) and separated milk are nowadays used in New Zealand and Denmark more than they are in Britain. From California and other states of the U.S.A. we hear of peach-fed pigs: every crop has its waste products.

Pigs are usually fed twice daily; they will grow more quickly if fed three times daily, but this may not be worth the cost of labour. The commonest method is to place the meal for each sty into a separate bucket, and mix it into a stiff porridge with water. Separate water must, of course, always be available for the pigs. Another method is to mix the food in bulk and divide the finished porridge between the pens: the rationing this way, however, is not generally so accurate.

The amount of meal eaten for each pound that a pig gains in live-weight varies from 2½ to 5 lb. according to the composition of the ration, the efficiency of the management, and the quality of the pig. Pork pigs, which are killed when they are about 29 weeks old and weigh up to 200 lb. live-weight, will be eating at the end of their time 6 to 6½ lb. of meal daily. As they increase in weight, the percentage of barley meal in their food is increased and that of 'weatings' decreased, until their mixture is 60% to 70% barley meal, 20% to 30% weatings, and 10% fish meal. The fish meal is usually omitted during the last 14 days for fear that its strong flavour may taint the flesh. Bacon pigs are usually not killed until they are 32 to 35 weeks old. After they have reached a daily ration of 6 lb. they may remain at this ration even though they could eat more (called 'restricted feeding'), or they may receive a gradually increasing ration up to 7 or 7½ lb. daily. Unrestricted feeding may not use the food to the best value, since it may produce too fat a carcass. On the other hand, restricted feeding means that the pig takes a little longer to reach bacon weight.

When a sow is in-pig (pregnant), she needs a ration of 5 to 8 lb. according to her appetite and the stage of her pregnancy, including a fair amount of laxative food, such as bran. During the few days before and after farrowing (giving birth) she should be fed lightly, and her food should be rather more sloppy than usual. After farrowing, her ration is increased gradually until she is receiving approximately as many pounds of meal, weighed dry, as she has little pigs, plus 2 lb. Thus a sow with a litter of eight will receive 10 lb. of meal.

The little pigs, by the time they are 6 weeks old, will eat about ½ lb. of meal each per day as well as the sow's milk. This should be given them in a little trough of their own behind the creep. When they are weaned at the age of 8 weeks, this ration is increased to 1½ lb. A suitable ration might consist of 50% weatings, 20% barley meal, 10% flaked maize, 10% fish meal, and 10% bran.

PINEAPPLES. These are the fruits of a plant called *Ananas comosus*, which is native to Central America but is now cultivated in many tropical countries. It is an important crop in Malaya and the Hawaiian Islands. The plant consists of clusters of long, slender, grey-green leaves that spring from the roots at ground level, and are somewhat like those of the common garden iris, with either smooth or toothed edges. In the midst of this leaf-cluster a flower-spike arises, and as the numerous tiny flowers develop, they

Central Office of Information

PICKING PINEAPPLES IN MALAYA

The fruit is stacked in clamps by the roadside to be collected and taken to the canning factory

grow together into a juicy mass made up of many separate fruits tightly packed together on the swollen stem that bears them. This fruit mass is the familiar pineapple; when ripe it is yellow in colour, and is topped by a shoot of green leaflets. The plant grows to a height of about 3 feet. The pineapple is easily raised from the leafy shoots that grow out at the base of the leaves above and below the fruits. These are planted out on fertile land, such as jungle clearings, spaced 5 feet by 2½ feet apart. In 18 months time the shoots have grown into strong clumps that bear fruit steadily for 3 or 4 years. There are two main crops each year, each yielding 2,000 or more fruits per acre. So in tropical countries pineapples are very cheap and plentiful, instead of being the luxury that they are in Britain.

A large proportion of the crop is used for canning. The coarser parts of the fruit are removed and the rest is cut up into cubes or slices, placed in tins with syrup made from cane sugar, sealed up, and then cooked. Some, however, are exported fresh: in this case they are picked before they are fully ripe. In the Philippine Islands the fibres of the pineapple leaves are used for weaving into cloth.

See also TROPICAL AGRICULTURE.

PINES, *see* TREES, CONIFEROUS.

PLANTATIONS, *see* AFFORESTATION; TROPICAL AGRICULTURE.

PLANT BREEDING. When man began to cultivate the land, he soon discovered that the yield of his crops could be increased by selecting only the best plants for seed. This method of plant improvement by 'selection' was used later on to develop other characters besides yield; for example, the shape and size of carrots and parsnips were improved in this way, and when new and better forms or varieties appeared, these were preserved. This method of plant improvement by selection served our purpose for a very long time, and it was not until comparatively recent times that the practice of hybridization, that is, the cross-breeding of plants of different varieties or species, was developed. This was made possible by the discovery that the sexes, male and female, existed in plants as well as in animals, and that the male pollen of one species could be used to fertilize the female ovum of another species (*see* REPRODUCTION IN PLANTS, Vol. II).

This fact of sexuality in plants was finally established during the 17th century, and the first record of natural cross-breeding or hybridization in plants was made by Cotton Mather (an American botanist) in 1716; he observed how different varieties of maize had bred together and produced hybrid or mixed forms. In 1717 Thomas Fairchild of London crossed a pink, *Dianthus Caryophyllus*, with the sweet william, *D. barbatus*, and found that he too had raised hybrid plants.

Towards the end of the 18th century a German biologist, Joseph Kölreuter, found that not only could species be crossed by artificial means, but that characters in the hybrid form came from both parents, and that certain characters appeared to be dominant—for example, double flowers over single flowers in *Dianthus*. From this it began to be understood that characters were inherited by plants according to an orderly plan, though the importance of this was not appreciated until later.

The great contribution to our knowledge of inheritance in plants was made by an Austrian monk named Gregor MENDEL (q.v. Vol. V) who lived in what is now Czechoslovakia from 1822 to 1884. Mendel, whose experiments with garden peas are described in the article HEREDITY in Vol. II, discovered that inheritance in plants was closely concerned with pairs of contrasting characters, such as tallness and shortness in growth and redness and whiteness in flower colour; and that the individual relationship of these pairs of characters could be described as dominant (strong) or recessive (weak). Mendel discovered that when plants possessing these contrasting characters were crossed together, the characters reappeared in the second generation in a fixed ratio according to whether a character was of the dominant or recessive type. This was the first clear evidence of the existence in plants of laws of heredity. These laws have since become known as Mendel's Laws of Heredity or Mendelian Laws.

The mechanism which operates these laws, however, could not be understood until more was known about the constitution of plant cells. Further research revealed the existence of rodlike bodies, called 'chromosomes,' which make up the nucleus of the cell. These chromosomes carry factors, called 'genes', each of which

BREEDS OF POULTRY

1. Golden spangled Hamburgh cock. 2. Houdan hen. 3. Brown Leghorn hen. 4. Black-red Game cock.
5. North Holland Blue cock. 6. Rhode Island Red hen. 7. Legbar hen. 8. Buff Rock cock.

Water-colour by C. F. Tunnicliffe

decides the inheritance of some particular character. It thus became evident that the chromosomes carrying these genes constituted the basic mechanism of heredity. The way these invisible genes behave and are passed on from one generation to another, either in plants or animals, is described in the article on HEREDITY (q.v. Vol. II).

The basis of modern methods of plant breeding is the fertilized germ or egg cell in which the genes exist in pairs, one from the male and the other from the female parent; and the character of the offspring depends on whether the members of each pair represent different or similar characters. For example, both genes might represent the character of redness in a flower, or one the character of redness and one that of whiteness. Armed with this knowledge, plant breeders nowadays aim at changing the hereditary constitution of plants, in fact, at making new plants —a very different aim from that of the old plant improvers, who were only able to select what they wished to preserve from a mixed collection of plants. The plant breeder, using the new science of chromosomes and genes, known as 'genetics', deliberately sets out to create something entirely new, whereas the selectionist picks out and encourages something which already exists. Similarly, the old-fashioned hybridist, working on the basis of chance, crossed one variety or species with another, and often produced some useful new plant; but, being a hybrid plant composed of mixed genes, it would not breed true from seed. Sometimes the desired hybrid plant could be multiplied by vegetative means (grafts, runners, and tubers, as in the plum, strawberry, and potato respectively). When, however, the desired characters of the hybrid could be handed on to successive generations only through the seed, then it was necessary to practice a system of self-fertilization for several generations in order to sort out the combinations of the genes derived from the hybrid's parents, and to 'fix' the desired character.

Usually the scientific breeder aims at producing a plant with a certain desired character, such as resistance to a certain disease (rust-resisting wheats and leaf-mould-resisting tomatoes), improved edible quality (coreless carrots), more easily handled growth (thornless blackberries), or a hardier constitution (sweet corn hardy to Britain).

It should not be thought that, because of our increased knowledge of scientific plant breeding, there is no longer any place for selection and even chance hybridization in the improvement of plants. Selection has played an all-important role in developing most of the crop plants in cultivation, and with some crops, notably the cabbage crops, it is still a valuable means of keeping the various forms true to type and preventing reversion to the original wild ancestor. With flowers hybridizations are often carried out to obtain a change or improvement of colour. Then by self-fertilizing the progeny of the hybrid the improvement may be 'fixed' in a new form or strain.

Hybridization is constantly occurring in nature, and sometimes, when the reproducing cell divides, the chromosomes fail to divide in the normal way, and an offspring results with more than the normal number, giving rise to a new kind of plant. This is called 'chromosome doubling'. For example, it has been proved that in this way the European garden plum, *Prunus domestica*, originated in nature as a result of the natural hybridization of the wild sloe and the cherry plum. The loganberry was the result of hybridization, followed by chromosome doubling, of the red raspberry and a blackberry. Recently it has been discovered that the internal or external application on plants of a chemical substance called colchicine, obtained from the roots and seeds of the autumn crocus, may induce an artificial doubling of the chromosomes in the cells of the plants, and this sometimes gives rise to larger forms. A race of giant snapdragons, for example, has already been bred by these artificial means.

Close attention to detail is needed in plant breeding. To begin with, the flowers of most plants are bisexual (male and female organs combined), and before a crossing of two parent plants can be effected, the male parts of the flower (the stamens) have to be carefully removed so that they cannot effect self-fertilization. After the female part of the flower (the pistil) has been fertilized by the pollen from the plant with which it is to be crossed, the flower or the whole plant must be covered up to prevent further cross-pollination from other plants. Cellophane or paper bags are used for individual flowers, and muslin cages for whole plants. Sometimes plants for hybridization are grown in an insect-proof greenhouse in which they are perfectly

PRODUCING HYBRID MAIZE IN AMERICA
U. S. I. S.
Pollen from a selected plant is applied to the female 'silk' of another corn plant.
The silk is then covered with a bag to prevent chance pollination

safe from contamination by other plants, since in most cases the pollen is carried by insects.

When a new form or variety of plant has been bred and an increased stock of it is needed, it must be grown in complete isolation to avoid contamination by pollen from neighbouring plants. This is particularly necessary with plants which are open-pollinated, that is, not self-pollinated. A plot of seed-producing plants may need to be a distance of 400 yards from any other related plants, and it is a general rule to separate varieties of a species by a distance of at least 50 yards. This isolation of the stock is the only way to keep it pure.

When a new type of plant has been secured, the stock of it must be frequently 'rogued': that is, the off-type or 'rogue' plants, which appear from time to time, are removed before they seed. Rogue plants are caused by reversion to the original characteristics, and also by 'accidents' to the chromosomes of the germ cells by what are known as 'gene mutations'; there is a tendency in nature for nothing to remain as it is for long.

Sometimes a naturally self-fertilized plant is found to lose vigour and productiveness when constantly in-bred (that is, self-fertilized) with the idea of keeping the stock 'pure'. This again is a natural happening, for hybridization seems to be part of nature's plan to ensure vigour in plant life. This effect may be lessened by avoiding single plant selections, and by saving seed from several selected plants which have been allowed to cross-fertilize each other. It is a natural law that hybrids are vigorous even though their offspring are hopelessly mixed in character. Sometimes advantage is taken of this fact of hybrid vigour to breed hybrid seed for the specific purpose of obtaining a vigorous crop in the first generation. It is particularly easy to raise hybrid seed of maize because of the fact that the maize plant is 'monoecious' in flowering habit (there are separate male and female flowers on the same plant); hybrid varieties of sweet corn and tomatoes are also being bred.

The plant breeder has also to face the problem of self-sterile plants, that is, plants that will not produce seed with their own pollen. This is because, after pollination, the pollen-tube fails to grow down into the ovary (*see* FERTILIZATION). Self-sterility is an inherited character and is controlled by a gene; and in order to remove this character in the plant, the gene controlling it must be destroyed. All genes occasionally mutate (change) naturally, and it has been discovered that by treating the flower buds with X-rays the rate of mutation can be considerably increased. Thus if all the pollen from the treated flowers is used, some will almost certainly have lost the controlling gene and be able to grow down the pistil and fertilize the ovum. The seed resulting from this union will have no self-sterility genes. In this way self-fertile varieties of previously self-sterile species can be bred.

Breeders are doing important work on these lines in the raising of self-fertile varieties of fruit —apples, plums, pears, and cherries. Self-sterility in fruit trees is a great disadvantage, for such trees need a 'pollinator' tree to make the fruit set, and this may be very inconvenient in a small garden (*see* FRUIT GROWING). Also, if the weather is too cold at blossom time for the insects, especially bees, to be active, cross-pollination may never take place.

See also STOCK BREEDING; PLANT PROPAGATION; FERTILIZATION.

See also Vol. II: HEREDITY; REPRODUCTION IN PLANTS.

PLANT DISEASES. 1. Plants are attacked by a large number of FUNGI, BACTERIA, and VIRUSES (qq.v. Vol. II), all of which are PARASITES (q.v.), that is, organisms or living things which attack and live on other organisms, drawing food from the living cells of their host. These cause diseases which weaken and may finally kill the plant. Epidemics of such diseases have often had very serious results: the epidemic of potato blight in 1844 and 1845, for instance, caused a severe potato famine, especially in Ireland, where the potato crop, which then provided the main food of the peasants, was destroyed in a few days. Starvation, and the emigration which followed, reduced the population by nearly one-third in 6 years (*see* FAMINE).

Parasites are of several different kinds. Some are unable to grow without their host, and are called 'obligate' parasites; these are often very delicately adjusted to their host, and can live on one species of plant only. Others, called 'facultative' parasites, can live freely on decayed plants or other organic matter in the soil, but if they come into contact with a plant which they can attack, they will do so. These are less particular about their food supply, and may attack many different kinds of plants. Parasites attack in a variety of ways: they may, like the fungi causing mildew, grow over the outside of the plant, sending minute tubes through the tough skin into the cells of the plant and sucking food out from them; or they may grow inside the tissues, having entered the plant through wounds or through the tiny breathing pores on the leaves and stems, or, like the fungi causing potato wart disease, having bored their way into the plant through soft, unprotected parts.

The symptoms of parasitic disease vary: sometimes, as in Crown Gall of fruit trees, the parasite in the tissues causes a gall or tumour; sometimes it destroys the cells, and the plant rots in parts or develops spots and patches; other parasites block the vessels which carry water from the root to the leaves, and the plant wilts and dies. Some parasites spread right through the plant, while others attack only part of it, though they generally reduce the growth and productivity of the plant.

2. FUNGUS DISEASES. Fungi are the cause of most plant diseases. Many fungi live and grow in the soil, where they may persist in the form of resistant spores until they find a suitable host. Others stay in those parts of the host plant which have remained alive through the winter, and, when the host starts growing again in the spring, the fungus grows too; it may at once produce a mass of minute thin-walled spores, and these are carried by water or wind to infect the new season's crop. More of these spores may be produced during the growing season, causing a further spread of the disease.

The following are some of the most serious fungus diseases:

(*a*) *Black Rust of Wheat.* In this disease, one of the worst dangers to WHEAT crops (q.v.), the stems and leaves of the plants are covered with reddish streaks, which blacken later in the season. The yield of grain is greatly reduced and of poor quality. The rust fungus has a complicated life-history. At the end of the wheat season, spores from diseased plants are carried on the wind to infect any bushes of the common barberry that there may be in the neighbourhood. Here they spend the winter, causing little

Plant Protection Ltd.

SMUTTED HEADS OF OATS, A FUNGUS DISEASE

yellow spots on the upper surface of the leaves. In the spring spores are produced on the barberry leaves, and these infect the new season's young wheat plants. In big wheat-growing lands such as the U.S.A., there has been a wholesale clearance of wild barberry bushes; but even so epidemics occur, because in countries such as Mexico, with warm winters, the fungus can bypass the stage on barberry and grow all the year round on wheat. The light spores are then blown up to the north, where they cause infection. In England there is little trouble with this disease, for barberry is rare and the winters are cold. The disease occurs, however, in south-west Wales, where barberry is common.

(b) *The Smuts of Cereal Crops.* Wheat, barley, oats, rye, rice, maize, and millet are all susceptible to attack by various fungi that cause these 'smuts'. In the early stages the diseases are not always visible, but as the grain develops, it becomes a mass of black spores which either remain in the ear (covered smuts) or are blown away, leaving a bare stalk (loose smuts).

Bunt, or stinking smut, of wheat is a covered smut; there is also a loose smut of wheat. Oats and barley also each suffer from a loose and a covered smut. The covered smuts of wheat and barley and both the smuts of oats can be prevented by disinfecting the seed with a powdered organic salt of mercury before sowing, as the fungi are on or very near the surface of the grain. Infection by the other smuts is inside the grain and can only be reached by a heat treatment.

(c) *Take-all of Cereal Crops.* The fungus which causes this lives in the soil for the winter months in diseased straw, ready to attack the young wheat and barley. It may kill the plants in the seedling stage ('take-all') or, if they reach maturity, the diseased plants produce empty ears known as 'white-heads'. This disease is most common on light sandy soils or when frequent cereal crops are grown on the same land. It can be controlled by planting resistant crops in rotation with susceptible ones, so that the fungus is starved out.

(d) *Club-root of Crucifers (cabbages, swedes, turnips, &c.)* The roots of infected plants become swollen and deformed (not to be confused with Turnip Gall Weevil), and the leaves and stems may wilt. Resistant spores of the fungus remain alive in the soil for up to 6 years, and, as many hedgerow weeds may be infected, the disease may spread into a clean field from the hedges.

Harold Bastin

A CABBAGE ROOT WITH THE FUNGUS DISEASE CLUB-ROOT

The trouble is more common on acid soils than on those containing plenty of lime. Some new varieties of turnip and swede show resistance to the disease, but where it is known to be present, the best protection is not to plant crucifers on the same land more than once in 5 or 6 years. In the garden the remains of all diseased plants should be burnt (see CABBAGE CROPS).

(e) *Potato Blight.* Warm wet summers are liable to bring severe attacks of potato blight. The first symptoms are brown or black marks on leaves or stem, where the fungus is killing the cells of the host and producing masses of spores. The whole top of the plant may be killed in a few weeks, and consequently the plant cannot build up foodstuffs for storage by the tubers. The tubers may also be infected, and any tubers showing dark patches of blight should be burnt (see POTATOES).

(f) *Apple Scab.* This is one of the most serious

diseases of APPLES (q.v.), and is caused by a fungus which overwinters on diseased leaves on the ground, or in the bark of the tree. Masses of spores are produced in the spring, and infect young leaves, fruits, and twigs, causing sunken black spots. As well as damaging the leaves and spoiling the appearance of the fruit, these spots provide entry points for other fungi.

(*g*) *Brown Rot of Fruit.* The fungus which causes this often enters the fruit through one of the Apple Scab spots. It may cause apples, plums, and other tree fruit to fall before ripening, or it may turn them into rotten mummified fruit, some of which remain on the trees through the winter and are sources of infection the next spring.

3. VIRUS DISEASES. Viruses are invisible agents which cause infectious diseases in many plants. They are present in all parts of infected plants except the seeds, which usually remain uninfected. Unlike most fungi and bacteria, viruses cannot live apart from their host plant, and there are no spores. The virus cannot penetrate the epidermis, or outer skin, and so infection is always through wounds; it may be transmitted by any contact which breaks the surface, such as leaves rubbing together, or the grafting of an infected plant on to an uninfected one, or it is often carried by insects such as APHIDS (q.v.), which suck the sap of an infected plant and then inject it into an uninfected one. Virus diseases can, therefore, be checked by growing new plants from seed, by propagating from uninfected plants, and by protecting them from disease-carrying insects. Otherwise, the only way is to root out and burn all infected plants. The serious swollen shoot disease of CACAO (q.v.), which is spreading through plantations in West Africa and which may be a virus disease, is being controlled by the rooting up and burning of about a million trees—the only way of preventing the destruction of the entire crop.

Among the many virus diseases common in England are the Mosaic diseases of POTATOES, TOMATOES, CUCUMBERS, SUGAR-BEET, STRAWBERRIES, RASPBERRIES, and HOPS, Reversion in BLACK CURRANTS (qq.v.), Tomato Bushy Stunt, Leaf Roll of potatoes, and Broken Flowers in wallflowers and sweet peas. The loss to the potato-grower in England and Wales through virus diseases is about £2 million a year, and the yield of glasshouse-grown tomatoes may be reduced by 20% by epidemics of Tomato Streak

and Tobacco Mosaic. In America a serious virus disease is killing many elm trees (*see* TREE PESTS AND DISEASES).

4. BACTERIAL DISEASES. Most bacteria enter through a wound, though some enter through the stomata, or breathing pores on the leaf. Many bacteria can survive, at least for a time, in the soil, and are capable of infecting a wide variety of plants.

Crown Gall is a common bacterial disease which attacks many plants, causing malformation and tumours or growths to develop, generally at, or just below, soil level. Among the plants attacked are apples, blackberries, cherries, hops, peaches, raspberries, and tomatoes.

Another bacterial disease is Soft Rot, which causes the decay of turnips, swedes, carrots, and potatoes. Plants may show signs of the disease by wilting early in the season, or the disease may not be detected until harvesting, when the root will be found to be hollow, the fleshy inside part having rotted away.

5. CONTROL OF DISEASES. The best method of control for all these diseases is prevention, by planting clean seed in uninfected land, and providing conditions suitable for healthy growth. The proper manuring of land, especially with organic MANURES such as farmyard manure, and constant CULTIVATIONS (qq.v.) stimulate strong growth which will defeat the disease.

Other methods vary with the crop. The systematic ROTATION OF CROPS (q.v.) helps to control disease, as does the use of fertilizers which build up the resistance of the crop. Plant breeders frequently produce new varieties of plants which can resist disease: the new Auchin-

Rothamsted Experimental Station
A TOBACCO PLANT INFECTED WITH TOBACCO MOSAIC VIRUS
This disease causes deformity and yellowing of the leaves

cruive varieties of strawberry remain healthy in soil infected with the fungus causing Red Core, and the Renown, Apex, and Thatcher varieties of wheat are resistant to Black Rust.

The other method of control consists, of course, in destroying the parasite; this may be done by means of SPRAYING (q.v.) at the right time of year with various kinds of fungicides, and by soil sterilization (see POTTING, section 3). The latter can be used to keep down disease in glasshouse crops such as tomatoes or chrysanthemums, but it is not practicable for most field crops.

See also ARABLE CROPS; ANIMAL DISEASES; PESTS AND DISEASES.

PLANTING MACHINES, see DRILLS AND DISTRIBUTORS.

PLANT PROPAGATION. Seed-bearing plants produce fertile seeds by a sexual process (see REPRODUCTION IN PLANTS, Vol. II). Where the seeds come from parents that are of mixed origin, they will not breed true (see PLANT BREEDING); therefore, when an exact replica is required of a hybrid plant or of one that does not produce seed, some other means, such as division, cuttings, layers, or grafting must be used. In these ways large plants, especially trees, which grow very slowly from seed, can be reproduced more quickly.

1. SEED. The commonest method of raising plants is from seed. Most seeds germinate readily in the season following their formation, but some need an after-ripening period before they are ready to germinate.

The general rule for sowing is to cover seeds with twice their depth of fine soil. Very tiny seeds, such as petunia and begonia, are best sown on the surface and just lightly pressed into the soil. Seeds of hardy plants may be sown outside in the early spring as soon as the ground is fit to work, but seeds of tender plants need a warmer soil, and should not be sown outside until late spring. Seeds sown in the greenhouse in boxes of porous, sterilized compost will germinate quicker if covered with a sheet of glass or brown paper to keep a warm, moist atmosphere immediately above them. But this cover must be removed immediately after germination or the seedlings will become 'drawn' or spindly. As soon as they are large enough to handle, seedlings should be 'pricked out'—that is, lifted

and replanted, more widely spaced, in other containers (see POTTING).

2. DIVISION. Many plants may be increased by dividing up the parent plant, in which case the new plants have the same characteristics as the parent. Most herbaceous plants may be lifted, generally in the autumn after flowering is finished, and rooted pieces split off and replanted. Clumps of perennials such as michaelmas daisies may be broken up into quite small pieces. Plants which produce suckers, rhizomes, or tuberous roots with several buds or runners can be reproduced from these so long as there is a bud attached. Rhubarb and dahlias are reproduced from tuberous roots, strawberries from runners

Imperial Bureau of Horticulture

FIG. 1. STRAWBERRY PLANT WITH RUNNERS

(see Fig. 1), raspberries and roses from suckers. With bulbs, the young bulblets or 'offsets' growing on the side of the parent may be split off.

3. CUTTINGS. Shoots may be detached from the main plant and planted in a moist sandy compost to 'strike', that is, to make their own root systems. The cuttings may be green, actively growing shoots (softwood cuttings), or woody dormant shoots (hardwood cuttings). In general, shrubs succeed best as hardwood cuttings, about 1 foot in length, inserted in the compost to a depth of about half their length. Softwood cuttings of greenhouse and outdoor perennial plants are usually 3 to 5 inches in length, and are taken in the summer when the plant is in full leaf. They must be kept in a damp atmosphere until the cutting is rooted. Root cuttings made of short sections of the thick fleshy roots are successful with plants that naturally throw up suckers readily, such as the cane fruits, and also of certain tap-rooted plants such as horse-radish and hollyhock.

Leaf-cuttings are successful with some of the ornamental-leaved begonias and gloxinias. The young plants will grow from the leaf-stalk and sometimes from the main veins when the leaf is

N.I.A.E.

FIG. 2. A THREE-FURROW PLOUGH DRAWN BY A TRACTOR

The plough is on its second bout. As it goes up and down the field it throws the furrows towards the ridge in the centre of each 'land'. Another ridge can be seen in the background

two, three, or four sets of coulter, share, and mouldboard, and there is always some automatic arrangement for raising the plough bottoms out of work when the headland is reached. The ploughman pulls a cord to operate this lifting device.

Many tractor ploughs, instead of being drawn behind, are mounted directly on the tractor and are lifted out of work by hydraulic power (oil-pressured). In some makes the depth of plough-ing is regulated by wheels. In one make, how-ever, the ploughing depth is regulated by the hydraulic mechanism itself, and can be changed from the driver's seat even while the outfit is in motion. Modern 'multi-furrow' ploughs will cut several furrows at once.

The shares of ploughs are usually of cast iron. The share wears away with use and eventually has to be replaced by a new one, but it keeps a sharp edge all through its life—the share gets shorter but its edge does not get blunter. It is self-sharpening because, when it was cast, the upper surface of the blade was made a little softer than the underside, which, therefore, wears

away less than the upper side; so the edge which is thrust against the soil tends to remain sharp. The credit for this idea and for inventing the process goes to an early Suffolk plough-maker, Robert Ransome, after a fortunate accident. One day, early in the 19th century, a moulding frame in Ransome's foundry burst, and molten iron poured on to the stone floor. When the metal had cooled and set, Ransome broke it up ready to melt it again. He noticed, however, that where the molten metal had come into contact with the cold stone floor it was harder than it was in the rest of the mass. Therefore he made up a special mould, or chilling box, to produce shares which were harder on the underside than on the top. Shares have been made in this way ever since.

Ploughing is generally carried out in 'lands'. The field is marked out with a series of ridges, with about 22 yards from one ridge to the next. The plough, which throws the furrow always to one side, usually to the ploughman's right, is taken round and round each ridge until the outermost furrow has reached nearly half-way to the next ridge. Then a 'finish' or trough is made half way between two ridges (see Fig. 2).

A plough that does work of this kind is called a run-round plough; but there are also ploughs that throw the furrow slice either to the right or to the left as desired by the ploughman. One kind of plough that works in this way has two sets of mouldboard, share, and coulter, one set throwing the slice to one side, and the other set throwing the slice to the other side. At the end of the furrow bout the plough is tipped over so that when the plough comes back down the next furrow the slice will be turned in the same direction as was the slice on the plough's upward journey. No opening ridges and no finishing troughs are needed; therefore the field is kept more smooth, and when the furrow slices have been broken down by weather or cultivator, the field is quite flat. This makes subsequent cultivations and harvesting easier.

Ploughing land which has never before been cultivated, or which has been neglected for so long that it has become overgrown with shrubs or bracken, needs very large and heavy ploughs. Some specially heavy, single furrow, tractor-drawn ploughs can cut as deep as $2\frac{1}{2}$ feet. The normal depth of ploughing of land already under cultivation is from 4 inches to 12 or 14 inches according to the soil and the crop to be grown.

The shape and curve of the mouldboard in any plough influence the condition of the slice of soil left in the wake of the plough. A plough with a long mouldboard, with the greater part of its length convex to the plough slice, leaves a smooth unbroken furrow slice (see Fig. 3 a). A plough with a short mouldboard, concave to the

FIG. 3a. LONG MOULDBOARD LEAVING UNBROKEN FURROW
SLICE

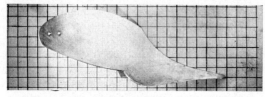

FIG. 3b. SHORT MOULDBOARD LEAVING BROKEN FURROW
SLICE

slice, leaves a broken furrow slice (see Fig. 3 b). The long mouldboard plough is called a 'lea' or 'longplate' plough; the short mouldboard plough is called a 'digger' plough. Lea ploughs were at one time used a great deal for autumn ploughing, when the furrow would lie without a crop through the winter to be crumbled by air, rain, and frost. Digger ploughs are used to give a surface more nearly ready for planting, as is wanted in the spring. Besides these two main types of plough, there were in times past many local variations. Some shapes of mouldboard were thought to keep cleaner than others in sticky soil, and some were reckoned to be particularly suitable for light, sandy soil. Now that the number of types has been reduced in order to make quantity production in factories easier, most mouldboards are of a design midway between that of the lea body and that of the digger body. This intermediate design is called a 'general purpose' plough.

It is often said that every intending ploughman ought to learn on a horse-drawn plough instead of starting with a tractor plough. There is a sound reason for this. The forces acting on a plough at work are most complex, one of them being the side draught caused by the action of the mouldboard in turning the furrow slice. Unless this side draught is properly distributed over the plough, it will make the implement run out of the straight, and a ploughman with a single-furrow horse plough cannot make a reasonably straight and well-turned furrow until the plough is correctly set. With a heavy, multi-furrow plough, however, the effects of excessive or wrongly distributed side draught are not so obvious, though they are wasting power and causing unnecessary wear. With either horses or tractors, ploughing is so skilled a craft that ploughing competitions have formed an important part of country life, and are still held in many places. The 'match plough' for horse-work is generally a refinement of the lea plough.

Plough furrows can be used as troughs for seed. The plough used to make the troughs for planting potatoes has two mouldboards to each body, and these are mounted one on each side of a single share. Usually three such bodies are carried side by side on a tool bar attached directly to a tractor. Ploughs for doing this special work are called 'bouting' or 'ridging' ploughs. Corn is sometimes broadcast directly on to ploughed land and then covered up by the use of harrows. Most corn, however, is sown by drills into a prepared seed-bed.

See also CULTIVATIONS.

PLUMS AND DAMSONS.

PLUMS AND DAMSONS. Bullaces and sloes are wild plums native to Britain, and the wild damson is also probably a native. But the ancestors of the various types of cultivated plums came from Asia Minor or southern Europe. The greengage is to be found today growing wild in the Caucasus. The blue plum, which we know when dried as a prune, came from southern Europe and was taken from there to America and Australia, where it is now grown on a large scale.

Plums will flourish in most soils where there is plenty of depth for their roots, enough moisture, and good drainage. In lime-deficient soils the trees need to be supplied with lime, and they need generous fertilization with nitrogen. This is best supplied in organic form. Short straw, dug in with a dressing of sulphate of ammonia or other quick-acting nitrogenous fertilizer, is very suitable (*see* ARTIFICIAL FERTILIZERS). The soil round plum-trees should be kept clean and well cultivated.

Plums grown for the market are best grown as bushes, half-standards, or standards; but in gardens, where quality is more important than quantity, they are often very successfully grown as fan-trained trees against a wall or fence, generally with a sunny aspect, though the excellent late dessert plum, Coe's Golden Drop, will do well on a north wall if a suitable cross-pollinator is near it (*see* FERTILIZATION). The best rootstock for vigorous-growing large trees other than the gages is Myrobalan B, though other stocks such as Brompton are used. Certain varieties of plums do better on some stocks than others. Common Mussel is a usual rootstock for small trees and for trained trees. Plums, some kinds especially, are early flowerers, and therefore, if grown in a low-lying situation, may fall victim to late frosts. The popular Victoria plum, although a later flowerer, is also often caught by frost because it flowers before it has grown any appreciable protection of leaves. If the trees are planted in an exposed, windy position, the bees may not work enough in the blossom to effect sufficient pollination. Most varieties of plums need cross-pollination. When there is a heavy crop, thinning is desirable, and

John Topham

PICKING PLUMS IN KENT

does not necessarily reduce the total weight of the crop.

When the framework of the tree has been completed, it needs little more pruning than the removal of dead wood or crossing branches. Wall trees, however, need both summer and winter pruning to curb their growth. All buds except side buds have to be rubbed out, and the shoots trained to grow sideways to make the correct fan shape. The tips of the growing shoots should be pinched out frequently throughout the summer (*see* PRUNING). Wall trees also need severe root pruning to prevent their growth becoming quite unmanageable. This should be done in the autumn after the leaves have fallen. Sometimes it is even wise to dig the plant right up so as to cut through the tap-root and cut all solid roots to half their length before replanting.

Fruit for cooking and preserving should be picked while it is still hard and not fully coloured. Even dessert plums are better picked before they are quite ripe, and in this way they can be saved from attack by wasps, flies, and birds. Plums should be picked only when they are dry. They are sent to market in light chips or cardboard containers holding 6 to 12 lb. Greengage plums, which are more easily damaged, keep their

bloom best when packed in punnets holding from
1 to 2 lb.

Plums grown in good conditions are less prone
to diseases and pests than most fruit crops. The
worst diseases are the silver leaf fungus, which
attacks certain varieties such as Czar and Victoria very badly and may eventually kill the
tree, and bacterial canker, which especially
attacks young trees (*see* PLANT DISEASES). There
is no satisfactory cure for either disease, except
enough vigorous health on the part of the tree to
resist it. The worst pests are the Leaf-curling
Plum Aphis and the Mealy Plum Aphis (*see*
APHID PESTS); the caterpillars, especially of
Winter Moths; the Red Plum Maggot which
develops inside the plum, maturing about the
same time as the plum is ripe; Plum Saw-fly
(*see* INSECT PESTS); and RED SPIDER (q.v.).

The most popular plum for dessert and cooking is the Victoria; but as has been said, this
plum may fall victim to late frosts. The delicious
Greengage and Coe's Golden Drop are neither
regular nor prolific bearers. River's Early and
Laxton's Early are useful early cooking plums,
and Czar and Giant Prune have the great
advantage that they can withstand frost and
cold, wet weather. The plum most commonly
grown commercially for preserving is the Per-
shore Yellow Egg. Several varieties of damson
are grown commercially, especially in the north
midlands, where the fruit seems to develop a
richer flavour than in the south. Farmers sometimes set damson suckers in their hedgerows or
as windbreaks, and these will bear good fruit.
The larger damson plums crop well but have
an inferior flavour. The Myrobalan or cherry
plum has a good flavour, but is only suitable for
sites well out of risk of late frosts, for it flowers
very early.

See also FRUIT-GROWING; FRUIT PROPAGATION.

POACHERS. A poacher is one who trespasses
on another's land in pursuit of game or fish. By
law wild animals are not the private property
of anyone, but it has gradually been established
in law that the occupier or owner of land has a
right to claim any game taken or killed on his
land. Animals such as rabbits, wild duck, or
snipe are included in this right, though these are
not strictly game.

The practice of forbidding the pursuit of game
on certain areas of land was established by the
Norman kings in the 12th and 13th centuries

when they enclosed the royal forests and passed
Forest Laws to preserve the deer and wild boar
—royal game—for their own use. Extremely
brutal penalties, even death, were imposed on
those caught 'poaching' in the royal forests. By
the 17th century the Forest Laws had fallen out
of use and were superseded, during the 18th
and early 19th centuries, by various game-laws
by which the sporting rights of the country were
preserved for the landed gentry; and the locally
appointed parish constables were active in laying
hands on poachers.

In 1828 the Night Poaching Act was passed,
and 3 years later the Game Act dealing with day
poaching, and the Poaching Prevention Act
followed in 1862. These Acts took much stronger
action against night poaching than day poaching,
for the traditional poacher, who is still active in
remoter parts and who mainly goes after rabbits,
employing the methods of his forefathers, usually
works by night. The Acts of 1831 and 1862 dealing with day poaching give the police no power
to arrest unless the poacher assaults them when
they stop and search him, or refuses to give his
name and address and to produce his game and
gun licence. The police can seize any poaching
implements, except dogs and ferrets, found in the
poacher's possession, and can then proceed
against him by a summons. Fines only can be
inflicted for day poaching; but, if the poacher is
convicted, his game and gun licences are can-
celled. When a poacher is seen on private
property, the police have no power to approach
him unless they are accompanied by the property owner or one of his employees; otherwise
they must wait until the poacher reaches the
highway.

The Night Poaching Act of 1828, on the other
hand, gives not only the police, but also the property owner or any of his employees the power
to arrest. They may also chase the poacher and
arrest him in any place where he may seek refuge.
The possible penalties for night poaching are 3
months' imprisonment for a first offence, double
that term for a second, and a 2 years' sentence
for any subsequent offence. For the purposes
of this Act night-time begins at the first hour
after sunset and ends at the beginning of the first
hour before sunrise.

Poachers of tradition, the old-timers, still
work in pairs, using what they call the 'long net'.
This may be up to 400 feet long, 3 feet wide, with
a 2-inch mesh to allow the smaller rabbits to pass

through. The poachers knit their nets at home, in great secrecy, on a wooden needle and a shuttle usually made from a cigar box. Then they dye them in oak-bark liquid. They choose a night when the weather is likely to encourage the rabbits to come out to grass; and then they approach the wood or warren from the down-wind side so as not to disturb the rabbits. The net is used to encircle the rabbits in different ways according to the locality. It may be laid over the holes of the warren, or held up on light stakes some yards away so that the rabbits run into it. On dark nights poachers sometimes run the net round the rabbits while they are out feeding. It may be dawn before the catch is completed. Meanwhile, the poachers wait at a distance, rarely approaching the nets, for once a rabbit becomes entangled it seldom escapes. They may catch fifty in one haul, although this depends on the length of their net and the rabbit population in the wood or warren. Within a few hours the rabbits are disposed of, being passed to an accomplice who travels daily on legitimate business to a neighbouring town. There are some poachers who have used this method all their lives without being caught. Not many use ferrets, for these animals are difficult to recover at night, when they run rabbits to a blind earth, that is, a burrow with no second exit or entrance.

In recent years, as the result of the meat shortage and its black market in the Second World War and after, a quite different kind of poacher with different methods altogether has made his appearance. Instead of nets and ferrets he uses a collapsible shotgun, almost noiseless in action; instead of passing his haul to an accomplice to dispose of, he takes it to town himself in a car which probably has false number plates. These gangs of poachers were generally habitual criminals who had switched their activities from such offences as housebreaking to assisting the black market; and therefore police action against them was intense. Towards the end of the Second World War several gangs were arrested and sentenced under the old game and poaching laws. One gang might specialize in rabbits, another in pheasants, partridges, and wood-pigeons, with a sideline of wild birds' eggs during the season.

The taking of pheasants' and partridges' eggs, and of grouse and woodcock, black or moor game, is dealt with under the Poaching Prevention Act of 1862. The taking or destroying of other wild birds' eggs is prohibited by the Wild Birds Protection acts, 1880 to 1908, and the Acts may be applied to an area if an Order is made by the Home Secretary. A copy of this Order must be produced in court when an offender is tried.

Although the art of poaching is practised

Curtis Museum, Alton

FLINT-LOCK SPRING-GUN USED BY GAMEKEEPERS AGAINST POACHERS IN ABOUT 1800

The gun was fastened to the ground by the peg underneath it. The rod was connected to the trigger at one end and at the other to trip wires. When the poacher stumbled over the trip wire the gun was turned round towards him and the trigger pulled

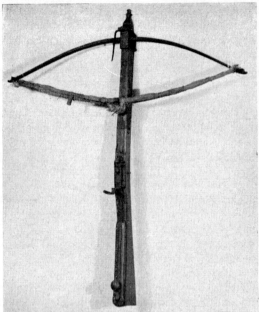

Curtis Museum, Alton

A CROSS-BOW USED BY POACHERS PROBABLY IN THE EARLY
19TH CENTURY

The bow was used instead of a gun as it was noiseless

chiefly to capture game, those who fish in the daytime in waters in which they have no right are liable to have their tackle confiscated and to a fine of from £2 to £5. Those caught fish-poaching by night can be arrested on sight by anyone and handed into police custody.

The most difficult of all poaching arts—the art of 'tickling' to catch trout or salmon—is now practised only by a few. For this the poacher does not use a rod and line, but enters the shallow stream himself, there awaiting his opportunity to take the fish unawares. When a fish comes close, he gently touches the fish's back, and then deftly raises his catch to dry land.

POISON FISHING. The capture of fish by means of poisonous material thrown into still water is so widespread a practice that it certainly must be very ancient. All the fish poisons used are, of course, harmless to human beings.

In the lagoons of many islands in the Pacific, especially in Fiji, poison fishing is common. Whenever conditions are favourable, the natives raid the forest for roots of the derris plant—the plant used in a powdered state to kill insects in Britain. The villagers pound up the roots and make the crushed mass into small balls. An hour before low water the men load their dug-out canoes with the crushed roots and, armed with fish-spears, paddle out to a selected place in the coral-reef lagoon. When the signal to begin is given, the men dive overboard with a handful of the poisonous root which they insert into any hole where fish may be hiding. After this, they wait in a surrounding circle while the poison does its work. The fish that have received a sufficient dose of poison become stupefied and float to the surface, where they are gathered in by hand or with the spear.

In Mexico the fishermen used to take the precaution of making offerings to the god or 'Master of the Fish' by way of payment for the fish which they were about to take from him. The offerings consisted of axes, blankets, pouches, and especially of knives and strings of beads.

In South America, particularly in the basin of the Amazon river, fish poison is much used. Botanists have listed nearly 100 plants in this region which are capable of stupefying fish. The majority are collected from the neighbouring forests, but a few are cultivated in small domestic clearings. In Europe the poisonous qualities of certain kinds of verbascum and cyclamen have been used. In Africa the plant preferred is a *Tephrosia*. So highly valued is this plant for poisoning fish that it is cultivated almost everywhere in and around the Cameroons region, southward of Lake Chad.

In India fish poisoning is widely practised everywhere. In Palestine, too, it was practised until after the First World War, when dynamite and gelignite were found more effective. All these fishing methods, including also the use of unslaked lime, are popular among fishermen whose only concern is to get plenty of fish to eat or sell, and who do not mind how much they waste.

See also FISHING METHODS.

POLLARDING, *see* COPPICE.

POMEGRANATES, *see* TROPICAL FRUITS.

POTATOES. The potato is a native of South America, and was cultivated in Chile and Peru for many centuries before it was introduced into Europe. Probably the Spaniards brought potatoes to Europe after their conquests in South

America in the 16th century, and it was perhaps Sir Walter Raleigh who first grew them on his estates in Ireland. From Ireland they came to England in about 1633, and it was in Lancashire that they were first grown extensively. Today they are an important field crop in many districts, and are grown in almost every vegetable garden.

The potato is propagated 'vegetatively' from a tuber or underground stem instead of from seed (see PLANT PROPAGATION). It is grown from seed only when new 'stock' is being developed. New varieties are obtained by sowing the seed of cross-fertilized flowers, and selecting promising plants from the seedlings, from the tubers of which further plants are grown.

The potato is subject to many pests and diseases, and the history of the crop in Europe is marked by the efforts of scientists to find means of prevention and cure. The series of attacks of the fungus disease, Potato Blight (see PLANT DISEASES, section 2 e), which swept the British Isles in 1845-7 and caused a devastating FAMINE (q.v.) in Ireland, stimulated the search for a cure; and control is now possible by means of a fungicide sprayed over the crops in July or later according to the locality. Potatoes are attacked by at least three types of virus diseases (see PLANT DISEASES, section 3) which are often carried from diseased to healthy crops by APHIDS (q.v.). The virus diseases do so much damage to the crops that the greatest care has to be taken to plant only disease-free tubers. The healthiest seed potatoes generally come from high-lying districts that are clear of aphids, Scottish seed having a particularly high reputation. The worst pests, apart from the aphids already mentioned, are the EELWORM, which attacks the plant's root system, and the COLORADO BEETLE (qq.v.) which devours the foliage.

Potatoes are classified according to their season of ripening into earlies, second earlies or mid-season, and maincrop or lates. The earlies and second earlies are used as they mature from April to July in Great Britain; and the late crops are lifted when mature, usually during September and October, and stored for winter use. As potatoes are easily damaged by frost, the earlies, which are naturally the first to be planted, are grown chiefly in those climates and soils which are warm and where late frosts are unlikely. Planting of the tubers, called 'sets' or 'seed', begins as early as January in such places

as the Channel Islands or Cornwall, and extends to April farther north. March and April are the main planting months for the maincrop varieties. There are a great many different varieties, many of which, such as Majestic and King Edward VII, are almost household words. Some varieties suit some soils much better than others, and some are more disease-resisting than others.

The chief potato-growing areas of Britain are in Cornwall, Norfolk, Lincolnshire, Yorkshire, Cheshire, Ayrshire, East Lothian, and parts of Ireland. Potatoes need a loose soil in which their roots can spread and the tubers swell. Heavy cultivators are, therefore, used after ploughing to break up the furrows and loosen the soil to a good depth. The crop does best on a deep, crumbly, loam soil which has been well supplied with farmyard manure and fertilizers; but potatoes do not need much lime. The general practice is to put the land into ridges and furrows, 2 to $2\frac{1}{2}$ feet apart, apply the manure in the furrow, distribute the fertilizer over all, and drop the seed tubers in the furrows, covering them in by splitting the ridges with a ridging, baulking, or double-breasted plough. Some farmers, however, prefer to spread and plough in the dung in the previous autumn, leaving the fertilizers to be applied in the furrows in the spring. The National Growmore Fertilizer is very suitable for potatoes, but the perfect balance of nitrogen, potash, and phosphate, which affects the taste and the keeping quality of the potatoes, varies with the soil, and can be found out only by experiment. The sets or seed potatoes of early varieties are planted more closely together in the row than those of the maincrop varieties, because they make less growth of haulm (foliage): earlies 12 inches, second earlies 15 inches, and maincrop 18 inches apart.

In recent years machines have been designed to do away with much of the handwork in field potato-growing. Some machines simply plant the tubers in the rows which have already been prepared; but other more complicated implements form the ridges, sow the fertilizer, plant the sets, and then cover them with soil, all in one operation (see DRILLS AND DISTRIBUTORS). Most farmers, however, stil rely on men, women, and children to do the planting, and all the work in the garden is, of course, done by hand.

In many parts of the country, especially where aphids are common, farmers use new seed each year; but where the danger of virus disease is not so great, they may purchase only a part of their seed, providing the rest from their own last year crops. Each 'set' should weigh about 2 ounces—that is, be about the size of a hen's egg. Larger sets produce a bigger total crop, but the tubers will be much smaller, a large proportion being of use only for animal food.

Many farmers and most gardeners 'sprout' their sets before planting, especially for early and second-early varieties, since sprouted sets produce a crop more quickly. The sets are placed in shallow trays or boxes in a frost-proof, well-lighted house, usually of glass, and left until the tubers begin to put out shoots from the leaf-buds or 'eyes'. In a poor light the sprouts become long, spindly, and weak, and liable to break off during planting operations; therefore the larger growers have special glasshouses, generally called 'chitting houses', for sprouting or 'chitting' their sets. These houses are often used for tomatoes or chrysanthemums after the potatoes are removed, for these will be away before the next lot of seed potatoes have to be boxed in the autumn. The great advantage of using sprouted sets is that the grower can afford to wait a week or two longer, if need be, for suitable weather before planting in the field, without getting his crop so late that it will not produce a full yield. From 12 to 20 cwt. of seed potatoes are needed to plant an acre of land.

When the plants are about 10 inches above ground, the soil is drawn up over the roots to prevent any tubers being exposed to the light and turning green. This earthing-up is done with a hoe, or in the fields with a ridging plough, and need only be done once for early varieties; but maincrop varieties often need a second earthing-up. In May or June any crops that are being grown for the production of seed, or from which seed will be saved for home use, should be 'rogued'; that is, any stray plants of another variety, diseased plants, or plants that show deterioration in type should be dug out.

Early varieties are harvested between the end of April and July, the exact time depending upon the soil and the district. The Channel Isles, the Scilly Isles, and Cornwall produce the earliest crops. At lifting time the haulm is still green and the 'new' potatoes immature, so that, in spite of closer planting, the yield is lower than that of the maincrop varieties. The latter are not lifted until they are mature, that is, when the haulm

dies back naturally about September. Blight may, however, cause a browning and wilting of the leaves from July onwards. The average yield of potatoes suitable for human consumption from a main crop is 6 to 8 tons per acre, but in a favourable soil and climate yields as great as 15 to 20 tons per acre are not uncommon.

The lifting of early varieties is usually done by hand with a fork, the crop being packed into barrels and dispatched direct to the market. The maincrops, however, when grown in large quantities, are always lifted by machinery.

The most usual kind of potato-lifter digs the potatoes out of the ground and shakes some of the soil off them, so that they are ready to be picked up by men and women with buckets or baskets. In more complete machines, the crop is lifted off the ground, cleaned, graded into sizes, and put into bags. Many of the simpler machines work on the spinner principle. Fingers, fixed to the edge of a revolving wheel, cut through the ridge in which the potatoes are lying, and throw them out sideways on to the land. Before the spinning fingers arrive, a share, fitted in front of the implement, has loosened the soil around the potatoes. In the more complicated machines, instead of spinners a much wider share, which is shovel-shaped, actually digs out the potatoes and directs them on to an elevator chain, which carries them upwards and cleans them of soil.

After they are lifted, potatoes are stored in long 'clamps' ready to be sorted later in the winter. It is best to leave the potatoes on the ground exposed to the air for 24 hours before storing them, as this dries them thoroughly and hardens their skins. The clamps are covered with a layer of straw and then a layer, 9 to 12 inches thick, of soil (see picture). Ventilation is usually provided in the ridge of the clamp. The storing of potatoes in frost-proof buildings is becoming more common: this makes sorting easier, and protection from hard frosts more certain. If potatoes get frozen, they are spoiled. The sorting of the crop into grades goes on all through the winter, the grades being (a) 'ware' or saleable, (b) 'seed', which may be sown again, and (c) 'chats', which are so small or badly damaged as to be fit only for animal food.

The garden cultivation of potatoes is much the same as on the farm, the main difference being that all the work of preparing and manuring the ground, of planting, earthing-up, spraying, and harvesting, is done by hand instead of

John Topham

UNCLAMPING, RIDDLING, WEIGHING, AND BAGGING POTATOES IN MIDWINTER

by machinery. Special, blunt-ended, digging forks are often used for lifting. As in most gardens there is not enough ground in which to grow all the potatoes needed by the family, the gardener usually grows a greater proportion of early varieties, and relies on the farmer to grow the bulk of the maincrop (*see* VEGETABLE GARDENS).

POTTING. 1. Pot plants are most usually grown in flower pots of unglazed earthenware with one or more drainage holes in the bottom. Pots are made in a range of sizes from one inch to 18 inches across, though the very big ones are seldom used. The 'pan' is merely a flower-pot of different proportions, shallow in relation to its width.

Seeds are usually sown in shallow wooden boxes. When the seedlings appear they are usually so close together that they need shifting to less cramped quarters; otherwise they become spindly and weak, and prone to a deadly fungus disease called 'damping off'. Moreover, the roots become so tangled that they suffer damage when the plants are moved, and this checks their growth. The seedlings, therefore, as soon as they are big enough to handle, are 'pricked out' at regular intervals in a deeper box, or if possible in small pots. The seedlings are usually inserted into holes pricked in the soil with a thin stick.

After this, plants are 'potted on'—shifted from one pot to another a little larger—as their roots fill the available soil. The right moment to do this may be found by examining the 'root-ball'. The pot is held upside down with the stem of the plant between two fingers and the soil surface against the palm of the hand, and the pot rim tapped gently against a solid object. This loosens the plant in the pot so that its roots can be examined. When a pot is entirely filled with roots, the plant is said to be 'pot-bound' or 'root-bound'; although certain plants flower better when pot-bound, this should, as a general rule, be avoided.

Seeds cannot be sown nor seedlings transplanted direct into a large pot, because soil that is not almost filled with roots quickly becomes stagnant—too moist and airless. In this condition roots will not enter it or may rot if they attempt to. Plants with very quick-growing roots, such as the tomato, may be grown in a large pot from the seedling stage; but these are

POTTING: 1. CROCKS IN THE BOTTOM OF THE POT   2. FIBROUS MATTER COVERS THE CROCKS

exceptions. Most plants need to be potted in succession in pots with diameters of not more than 2½, 4, 7, and 12 inches, though many greenhouse plants will flower and remain healthy in 5, 6, or 7-inch pots. Gardeners call pots by numbers according to their sizes. The 72's are the smallest pots; a 72 small has an inside top diameter of 1½ inches and an outside depth of 2 inches, and a 72 medium and 72 large are slightly larger. The next larger sizes are the 60's; then come the 54's, 48's, 40's, 32's, 28's, 24's, 16's, 12's, 8's, 6's, 4's, 2's, and the largest of all, the 1's, which have an inside diameter and outside depth of 18 inches.

Pots should always be clean, partly to avoid disease and partly because roots stick to the sides of a dirty pot and are then damaged when potted on or transplanted. New pots, before being used, should be well soaked in water so that they do not draw moisture out of the soil.

It is very important that all excess water should drain away easily from the pot. A large crock (piece of broken pot) placed over the drainage hole, with its concave side downward, holds in the soil but allows drainage. In larger pots a few smaller crocks should be added, covered by a little sphagnum moss or coarse soil to prevent the finer soil of the potting compost working its way down and clogging the drainage system.

Most plants need to be planted firmly in the pot, woody plants more firmly than soft ones. The larger the pot the more tightly should the soil be packed, and with pots over 6 inches in diameter it is wise to use a 'potting stick'—a rounded piece of broomstick will do well—to ram the soil down at the sides.

2. POTTING COMPOST. Though many gardening books, especially older ones, contain complicated 'recipes' for soil mixtures, differing for almost every plant, experiments carried out at the John Innes Horticultural Institution have shown that, in fact, the great majority of plants will grow well in a standard potting mixture, and that all seeds can be germinated similarly in a standard seed compost. These standard mixtures are balanced for texture, moisture-holding, and plant foods.

The John Innes seed compost consists of 2 parts (by bulk) of loam, 1 part peat, and 1 part sand. To each bushel is added 1½ oz. superphosphate of lime and ¾ oz. ground chalk or limestone. The basic potting compost is made up of 7 parts loam, 3 parts peat, and 2 parts sand. The fertilizers used are 2 parts (by weight) coarse hoof-and-horn meal, 2 parts superphosphate of lime, and 1 part sulphate of potash. In general, 4 oz. of this mixture per bushel of compost is used at the first potting, 8 oz. per bushel at the second potting, and 12 oz. at the third. Some delicate and hothouse plants can tolerate only the 4 oz. addition at each potting. Three-quarters of an ounce of ground chalk or limestone should be added to each 4 oz. dose of fertilizer, unless the soil is already very rich in lime or the plants dislike lime.

A standard compost for most cuttings (*see*

Amateur Gardening

3. THE PLANT IS PUT INTO THE HALF-FILLED POT

4. THE PLANT IS MADE FIRM

PLANT PROPAGATION) may be made from 1 part loam, 2 parts peat, and 1 part sand.

The loam for these mixtures should preferably be fairly rich; the best is top-soil from meadowland, for this contains a lot of fibrous roots and has been well rotted. It should not be finely sieved, except for seedlings. The purpose of the peat is to hold reserves of moisture. Ordinary horticultural grade peat is suitable so long as it is neither too dusty nor too lumpy. The sand should be coarse silver sand. This gives the mixtures their 'openness', allowing air to permeate them and excess water to drain away. John Innes mixtures can be obtained ready-made from seedsmen.

3. SOIL STERILIZATION. In SOILS (q.v.) there is a great variety of bacteria, microscopic animals, and fungi, many of which are harmful to plants. Infection can be prevented by sterilizing the soil, the pots, and the boxes. There are various ways of doing this, and curiously enough, though these destroy all the harmful organisms including weed seeds, they leave a number of beneficial ones, chiefly bacteria, unharmed. Moreover, for some reason not known, root growth is more vigorous in newly sterilized soil, particularly if steam sterilized, than in unsterilized soil.

Steam sterilization **is** the most effective method. Various systems for sterilizing whole greenhouses **at** once are used in commercial market-gardens. Small amounts of soil can be

dealt with at home in a large saucepan or a domestic 'copper'. Two gallons of dry soil can be simmered with $\frac{1}{2}$ inch of boiling water for 15 minutes, or 4 gallons can be suspended in a sack above boiling water in the copper for 30 minutes.

By another method the soil is sterilized by an electric current conducted through the damp soil.

Various chemicals can also be used, though these are not as thorough as steam, and plants cannot be grown in treated soil for at least 4 weeks. A 40% solution of formaldehyde, diluted in the proportion of 1 part in 49 of water, and applied at the rate of 5 gallons per square yard of soil, is the most effective against BACTERIA, FUNGI, and PROTOZOA (qq.v. Vol. II). Cresylic acid, a coal-tar product very like carbolic acid, is more effective against soil animals, including insects. One part of acid is diluted with 39 of water and applied at the rate of 4 gallons per square yard. Other chemicals used for specific purposes include carbon disulphide and BHC against wireworms, and chloropicrin against root eel-worm. Flaked naphthalene is useful in the garden as a deterrent to wire-worms and other large soil animals; 2 oz. per square yard may be worked into the soil around growing plants, or 4 oz. on vacant ground.

The 'damping off' disease of seedlings is usually avoided when the soil has been sterilized; should it develop, a substance known as Cheshunt Compound is watered on. This is a mixture of

2 parts fine copper sulphate and 11 parts ammonium carbonate, 1 oz. of which is dissolved in 2 gallons of water. A weak solution of potassium permanganate may also be used.

See also Pests and Diseases; Plant Diseases; Plant Propagation; Greenhouse Plants; Insecticides.

POULTRY. The term poultry includes all domestic birds kept for egg-laying or fattening for the table—chickens (or fowls), Ducks, Geese, Turkeys, and Guinea-fowls (qq.v.). Of these, fowls are the most commonly kept in Britain, on large poultry farms, on general farms, or in small numbers by domestic poultry-keepers in back yards or gardens.

The domestic fowl is a native of southern Asia, probably having evolved from the Red Jungle Fowl (see Pheasant, Vol. II) in the forests of India. Fowls were domesticated by the Ancient Greeks, and it is believed that they were first introduced to Britain about 2,000 years ago by the Phoenicians. Various types and colours developed, and from these came the breeds we know today. In the Middle Ages birds were bred for their size and fierceness, for they were kept principally for sport (see Cock-Fighting, Vol. IX) and as table birds, their egg-laying capacity being thought unimportant.

During the last hundred years varied types of fowls have been imported to Britain from different parts of the world. From China and India came such large breeds as the Cochin, Brahma, and Langshan—very handsome birds. From Spain and Italy came the much smaller breeds, Minorca, Leghorn, and Ancona. These smaller, lighter breeds, though not such good table birds, mature and come into lay more quickly than the heavier breeds, lay more eggs, and do not go broody (which stops them laying) nearly so often. They are sometimes called the Mediterranean breeds.

Nowadays it is the egg-laying capacity of a hen that is of greatest concern to most poultry-keepers, and there is an eager race between breeders to produce breeds which will lay more and yet more eggs. Perhaps the best results have come from the U.S.A., and American Rocks, Wyandottes, and Rhode Island Reds have been imported to Britain. These breeds are all a good size, and are, therefore, useful table birds as well as egg-layers. The wild Jungle Fowl lays about 30 eggs a year. If she were domesticated, housed warmly, fed well, and her eggs removed daily as she laid them, she might lay about 80 in the year. By generations of selective breeding, hens of a laying breed, or of a good cross, will today lay between 150 and 300 eggs. This has come about because the capacity to lay well is often inherited, and poultry breeders, by keeping egg-laying records, have been able to select the best laying birds for breeding. The laying-quality of ducks has been improved in the same way, and breeders have recently started similar work on turkeys; but not much has yet been attempted with geese or guinea-fowl (see Stock Breeding).

There are now a great many different breeds of fowls, some of them quite fantastic in appearance; but only a few are of practical interest to the ordinary poultry farmer (see Colour Plate, p. 336). In cold climates the heavier birds with abundant feathers are likely to do better, and the hot climates suit the lighter breeds. The Rhode Island Red is a very popular dual-purpose fowl —a good layer, carrying plenty of flesh, and hardy. If crossed with a Light Sussex an even better table bird is produced. The White, Black, and Brown Leghorns and the Ancona are excellent layers. A Leghorn crossed with a Rhode Island or with a Light Sussex produces a very useful hen for the ordinary domestic poultry-keeper.

Bantams are very small fowls that have little commercial importance, but have been bred as a hobby from exceptionally small normal birds. They lay, naturally, very small eggs and not as many, as a rule, as do birds of normal size.

Most cockerels and pullets look very much alike until they are 6 or even 10 weeks old, when the cockerels begin to show more comb and wattle on the head, with a redder colour. The cockerel's tails, too, are different—more like a round ball of feathers, whereas the pullet's tail is straight. Poultry-keepers experienced in this work, and with good eyesight can, however, sex chickens, that is, tell males from females, at a day old by differences in the vent; but after the first day this difference is not so easily distinguished. In certain crosses between one colour and another the pullet chicks are the colour of the father and the cockerels that of the mother. This fact is called 'sex-linkage' (see Stock Breeding, section 4). The most common sex-linked cross is between 'gold' males such as the Rhode Island Red or the Brown Leghorn and 'silver' females such as the Light Sussex.

A. Rice

WHITE WYANDOTTE PULLET   ·   LIGHT SUSSEX HEN   WHITE LEGHORN PULLET

Breeds have recently been developed in which the males and females are differently coloured, the cocks being lighter in colour or less distinctly marked, and it is, therefore, possible to distinguish them from the beginning. These are called auto-sex-linked breeds, and have been formed by crossing certain pure breeds: for example, Barred Rocks with one of the buff-brown breeds such as Brown Leghorns, Buff Rocks, or Buff Orpingtons. The first of these crosses was made in 1925.

For various reasons it is a help to mark the birds so that each one in the poultry yard can be identified. A coloured or numbered ring on the leg is most often used. Some breeders have a 'colour code', each colour representing a number; this is a method suited to large flocks. Sometimes small numbered or coloured bands or tabs are placed through the loose skin of the wings, or a number or letter is tattooed on this loose flap of skin; but these are not as easy to see as the leg rings. Chicks are sometimes marked when a day old by making a hole in or slitting the web between the toes. By using a code of these markings it is possible to number a great many birds, especially ducklings and goslings, which have big webs.

All animals that grow FEATHERS or HAIR (qq.v. Vol. II) change their coats at least once a year, usually in the late summer or autumn. This change of coat is known as the 'moult', and during this time of change, which lasts about 2 months with poultry, egg-laying generally ceases. A good laying hen moults later in the year (September or later) than a poor one (July or August) and, as a rule, an old bird moults earlier than a young one. It is most usual to cull (kill off) the poorer or older birds at the begin-

ning of the moult after they have ceased laying, but before they have lost condition.

A hen generally comes into lay when she is about 6 months old and lays best between the ages of 6 and 18 months. After that she lays less and less every year. Therefore her useful life is not long—generally not more than 2 laying years. Older hens also tend to lay very little in the winter, when the price of eggs is highest. A particularly good hen may be kept longer because of the value of her eggs for breeding.

In the wild state birds lay a clutch of eggs in the spring and then sit on them until they hatch. The domestic fowl, even when there has been no cock, has the same instinct in the spring to sit on and hatch eggs, and is not put off by the fact that she has no clutch to sit on. In the heavy breeds this instinct is stronger than in the light. It is called going 'broody' or going 'cluck', and the signs of it are that the hen stays on the nest all the time, except for short periods for food, and clucks and fluffs out her feathers when approached, as though she were protecting her eggs. If broodies are not needed for hatching a clutch of eggs, they should be cured of the desire to sit as quickly as possible, for they will not lay while they are broody. If a broody hen is put in a pen or hanging cage with a draughty wire or slatted floor on which she cannot sit in comfort, she will usually give up the desire to sit in 3 to 5 days, and will probably start to lay again 9 to 20 days later.

Egg-laying trials are organized in most parts of the country, usually by county or other agricultural authorities, and certificates and prizes are awarded to the winners. These tests are usually made on six to twelve pullets (hens in their first year of laying), kept separately from all the others, but fed and managed in the same way (*see* POULTRY, CARE OF).

POULTRY, CARE OF. 1. HOUSING. Domestic poultry would, if we let them, sleep out-of-doors, as their wild relations do, in trees, on the water, or on the ground. But because of foxes and other wild animals, and because a bird sleeping out lays fewer eggs in cold weather than one comfortably housed, poultry farmers provide shelter for their birds. Ducks and geese sleep on the ground or on the water, and a very simple shed will give them all the shelter that they need. Fowls, guinea-fowls, and turkeys, however, perch when they sleep, and their houses must be more elaborate.

On many poultry farms the houses are large and well lit by windows, so that in bad weather the birds can be kept indoors. Surrounding the house is a wire-netting run for use in fine weather. Sometimes the houses are lit by electricity in the winter so that the birds can have a longer day in which to eat. Such modern devices cause more eggs to be laid in the winter, when eggs fetch the highest price.

On some general farms fowls are allowed to roost in sheds attached to the farmstead, but more often they are given small portable houses that can be moved about the fields. The birds have the run of the fields, and are then said to be on 'free range'. Some farmers, however, use small houses, each with a wire-netting run attached, and large enough to hold about twenty birds. Every day the house and run are moved a few yards so that the birds get frequent changes on to clean ground, but cannot stray away. Their manure does the land good. This type of house and run is called a 'fold'.

Another method of housing laying fowls is to keep each bird in a small cage, the cages being arranged in rows and tiers in a large shed called a 'laying battery house'. The birds have food and water always before them, and in spite of this unnatural way of living without exercise, they seem to be quite content and certainly lay well.

A 'dropping board' is fitted to most chicken-houses, except fold units. This is a sort of shelf placed beneath the perches to collect the droppings so that they do not foul the floor of the house. Hens should also be provided with means of giving themselves dust baths which they need to keep themselves clear of insect pests, such as lice and fleas. The hen will sit in dry earth or sand and scuffle the dust into her feathers. Even baby chicks will 'dust' themselves if they have the chance.

A 'trap-nest' is a nest box fitted with a trap-door which closes behind the hen when she enters the nest to lay her egg, and holds her until the poultryman releases her. If the hens are all marked, the poultryman can keep a record of what each hen lays, and he then knows which are the better layers.

2. FEEDING. Geese are vegetarians, but all other types of poultry eat both meat and vegetable matter, that is, they are omnivorous. All types of poultry will, if they are on free range, find a lot of their own food—insects, seeds, and grass. If they are to lay well, however, they need more than this. Like all animals, they need enough food to provide themselves with heat and energy, to build up their bodies, and repair the worn out parts—as, for instance, to grow new feathers after the moult (*see* FEEDING (FARM ANIMALS)). But laying poultry also need food to make eggs. A first class hen may lay 300 eggs in a year. As eggs average 2 oz. each, a total of about $37\frac{1}{2}$ lb. of eggs must be formed from the hen's food. The best food consists of grain (wheat, barley, oats, and maize), miller's offals (bran or middlings), and dried waste meat or fish, ground up and mixed to form a mash—either a dry mash, or mixed with a little water to form a crumbly mash (called a wet mash). Potatoes and cooked household scraps are also suitable, and, together with fresh green food, can form the whole diet; but this sort of food takes much time and labour to prepare, and is hardly possible on a large poultry farm. Fully grown hens will eat about 4 oz. of food a day—a little more or a little less according to whether they are in full lay or not. Of this about $1\frac{3}{4}$ oz. of grain, or a good handful, is enough for each bird, and this should be scattered about to give the hens exercise in scratching for it.

The shell of an egg is largely made up of lime; therefore limestone grit or the broken shells of shell-fish must be placed in boxes where the birds can help themselves. A bird has no teeth with which to break up its food, but instead it has a 'gizzard', a strong muscular bag with a very hard inside wall, in which it stores small stones or flint grit that have been swallowed. These grind up the food as it passes slowly through, and prepare it for digestion.

Eric Guy

POULTRY ON 'FREE RANGE'

The hen houses have been put in a field of stubble so that the hens can glean the grain

Eric Guy

'FOLD UNITS' ON A POULTRY FARM

The worn ground from which the houses have been moved can be seen to the right of each house

3. BREEDING AND INCUBATION. In the wild state poultry will lay a 'clutch' of eggs, from 10 to 15 or so, and then 'incubate' them, that is, sit on them until they hatch. Domestic poultry in the springtime will also do this if they can, and if on free range often try to 'steal' a nest, that is, lay a clutch of eggs in some hidden place. The poultry-keeper, however, does not allow this because he wants to choose his own time for the hatch. Indeed, most modern poultry-keepers do not use a hen at all for incubating the eggs, but hatch them in large quantities in an incubator, a sort of heated cupboard, which is more reliable than most hens. The broody hen can then be broken of her desire to sit, and encouraged to start laying again. Some people think, however, that chicks hatched by the hen are more robust. Ducks, turkeys, guinea-fowls, and even geese do not as a rule make good mothers, and so, where an incubator is not used, their eggs are generally set under a broody hen.

If a hen is to be used, it is better to choose one of a heavy or 'sitting' breed, for such a bird will cover more eggs and will generally be more reliable. The broody hen is put on a nest in a coop in a quiet place by herself, and in the evening, when she has settled, the eggs are slipped under her. She is let off the nest once a day for food and water, and when she returns she turns each egg with her foot and beak—a necessary procedure which the poultry-keeper who uses an incubator has to do himself. The hen may often get wet when she is off the nest, and this moisture reaches the eggs and helps them to hatch.

The time taken for eggs to hatch, either under a hen or in the incubator, is:

Fowl (chicken)	21 days
Duck, turkey, and guinea-fowl .	28 ,,
Goose	30 ,,
Muscovy duck and swan . .	36 ,,

The poultry-keeper sets his eggs in the early spring, but not so early that the chicks may suffer from severely cold weather. He then hopes to get the young pullets into lay well before the following winter. Chickens for the table are hatched at various times throughout the summer and autumn.

The principle of artificial incubation is an old one. The Egyptians succeeded more than 2,000 years ago in incubating eggs in large ovens or kilns, and the Chinese still use the heat of a manure heap for this purpose. It was not until 1881, however, that a hatching-machine in which the heat could be regulated was invented by Charles Hearson, an engineer, and used in Europe. These first machines, heated by oil lamps, held from 25 to 200 eggs, and such incubators are still used; more recent incubators of the cabinet type, however, hold up to 20,000 eggs or more. Many incubators are heated by electricity, which may heat a tank of water above the eggs, or heat air which passes round the eggs; in the case of the cabinet incubator hot air is driven around the eggs by an electrically driven fan.

Some poultry-farmers do not hatch eggs from their own birds but buy day-old chicks from 'hatcheries', which are places that do nothing but incubate eggs on a very large scale. Sometimes the farmer takes fertile eggs from his own flock to the hatchery, where they are incubated for him for a small fee.

Eggs used for hatching must, of course, be fertile—that is to say, the hen must have been mated with a cock. Even then some of the eggs will be infertile: in some the chicks may be deformed and unable to break their way through the shell; in others the embryo chick may die before hatching. On an average 65% to 80% of the eggs set for hatching will actually hatch. If an egg is carefully broken open, a lighter yellow spot can be seen on the surface of the yolk. This is the 'germ spot' from which, if the egg is fertile, the embryo chick starts to grow. All the white and part of the yolk form its food while it is in the shell, and just before it hatches it takes in the remainder of the yolk as a kind of 'iron ration' to last until the bird is strong enough to run about and find food for itself. Because of this, it can live for about 48 hours after hatching without food.

4. REARING. The chick, duckling, gosling, or poult (baby turkey) is able to run about and pick up food within a few hours, but it cannot keep itself warm for very long; so the mother bird squats down and lets the little ones snuggle under her to get warm after each short run and feed. She will also let them sleep under her at night (that is, she will 'brood' them).

When young birds have been hatched in an incubator, they are either given to a broody hen who will mother them even though she has not hatched them, or, more usually, they are put into a special appliance called a 'brooder' or 'foster-mother', that has a warm compartment and an un-heated run. The chicks soon learn where to go for warmth, and a skilled poul-tryman or girl can rear the babies by these artificial means almost as well as the mother hen can. Most of these brooders are heated by a paraffin lamp, but electri-city, gas, and coal are some-times used.

'Battery brooders' are a number of brooders placed together, often one upon another, in tiers. A 'hover' is a brooder without a run; it is little more than a lamp and shelter, and is used inside a shed, which is then called a 'brooder-house'.

Chicks, baby turkeys, and guinea-fowls need some heat until they are about 5 or 6 weeks old, when their feathers will have grown enough to keep them warm; but because duck-lings and goslings are hardier and grow their feathers more quickly, they can do without heat at 3 or 4 weeks old.

All these young birds eat much the same food as do the older ones. Wheat and maize can be given if broken up (kibbled), and such small seeds as millet and canary seed are sometimes fed. Mash is also given in much the same form as to other birds.

5. HEALTH AND DISEASE. Birds can produce their best only if they are healthy, and with such short-lived stock as poultry it is particularly important to prevent disease rather than cure it. Provided the birds come from disease-free stock, cleanliness is the most important condition for health. Most poultry diseases come from para-sites picked up on dirty ground or in dirty food. Gapes is caused by a worm which gets into the windpipe of young chicks and makes them gape (see PARASITIC WORMS). It flourishes on 'fowl sick' land, that is, land on which chickens have been for too long. Scaly leg is caused by tiny mites which harbour in dirty houses (see MITE AND TICK PESTS). Coccidiosis is a disease

Sport & General

A 'LAYING BATTERY HOUSE' FOR 120 HENS

When the eggs are laid they fall to the front of the nests so that they can be easily collected

of young fowls, and Blackhead of young turkeys, and both are caused by parasites picked up from the ground. Some poultry diseases are caused by bacteria or viruses which also breed in dirt and spread more rapidly in overcrowded con-ditions. Fowl-pox is a virus disease related to human small-pox. B.W.D. (Bacillary White Diarrhoea) is a dangerous and highly infectious bacterial disease of newly hatched chickens, and is generally passed from parent to offspring through the egg. Fortunately it can be detected by blood testing; and by breeding only from those birds that pass the test, the disease is being gradually eliminated (see ANIMAL DISEASES).

See also POULTRY; DUCKS; GEESE; TURKEYS; GUINEA-FOWL; ANIMAL DISEASES.

See also Vol. VII: POULTRY AND GAME; EGG TRADE.

POWER FOR FARMING. If we include horses, tractors, stationary engines, and electric motors, there is probably some 10 million horse-power of energy available on the farms of Great Britain. Not all of it is used at the same time, but in the heavy ploughing seasons, for example, an enormous total output of power is being expended on food growing. It is this expenditure

Sport & General

A SMALL 'WALKING' 3½-5 HORSE-POWER TRACTOR PULLING
A PLOUGH

of animal and mechanical power that makes possible the great output of food per person engaged in farming.

There are occasions when horses are more economical than tractors for cultivation and cartage. Therefore, most farms have a horse or a team of horses in addition to their tractors, and these horses cannot use their 'horse-power' to the best advantage unless they are suitably harnessed (*see* HORSES, CARE OF, section 2).

Tractors range in size and purpose from miniature two-wheeled 1 horse-power tractors for garden work to tracklaying machines of 100

N.I.A.E.

A LARGE 48-HORSE-POWER TRACK-LAYING DIESEL TRACTOR
FOR HEAVY LOADS

horse-power used for laying field drains and making ditches. Between these two extremes are the 20 to 30 horse-power four-wheeled petrol or vaporizing oil (paraffin) tractors which are the most common on medium-sized farms for the ordinary day-to-day work of ploughing, cultivating, carting, harvesting, and planting. Most tractor engines work on the same principle as motor-car engines, and, just as in a motor-car, the drive from the engine is taken through a change-speed gearbox to the driving wheels at the rear (*see* GEARING, Vol. VIII). The gearing is, however, arranged so that the tractor travels slowly, since it has to develop its greatest pull when it is travelling at very slow speeds. Everything is built more sturdily than on a motor-car. There are no springs for the axles; the engine, gearbox, and back-axle are built in one rigid part. To get a grip on soft land the rear wheels have to be large. Most wheeled tractors have pneumatic tyres, but for some very slippery conditions hind wheels made of steel and fitted with long pointed lugs have to be used.

A draw-bar plate at the rear of the tractor provides a hitching place for towing various wheeled implements; but many of these medium-sized four-wheeled tractors have a bracket for the direct attachment of field implements, such as PLOUGHS and CULTIVATORS (qq.v.), to the rear of the tractor. Usually this bracket has a lifting arrangement, worked by HYDRAULIC POWER (q.v. Vol. VIII) generated by the tractor engine, which works a pump for producing the oil pressure required. Thus, by moving a small control lever, the driver can lift the implement out of work, when it can be carried anywhere, and can be used for work right up to the hedge and in corners where it would be impossible to take a trailer implement.

Tractors with very powerful engines cannot transmit all their power through wheels. Chain or 'caterpillar' tracks are, therefore, used. Each of the two endless chains goes under rollers and round two pulleys, one of the pulleys being a driving sprocket which transmits the power of the engine to the track. Most track-laying tractors are steered by driving one track faster than the other; but one type, with a short track, has pneumatic-tyred front wheels steered in the same way as those on a four-wheeled tractor.

Large tractors usually have DIESEL ENGINES (q.v. Vol. VIII) which burn heavy oil. There is no carburettor to mix fuel and air, and no

Harry Ferguson Ltd.

SAWING LOGS WITH A SAW DRIVEN BY THE POWER TAKE-OFF OF A TRACTOR

sparking-plug to ignite the mixture, as there is in the INTERNAL COMBUSTION ENGINE (q.v. Vol. VIII) of a motor-car or a petrol or paraffin tractor. Instead, a small quantity of the heavy oil fuel is squirted into each cylinder to mix with air that has been so highly compressed that it is hot enough to start the mixture burning. Diesel engines are very efficient producers of power.

Two-wheeled tractors are often called 'walking tractors' because the operator has to walk behind and control the machine by handles, much as he would control a horse-drawn plough. The smallest of these machines have tiny engines and are particularly well suited for hoeing between rows of plants, but the larger ones have engines of 5 or 6 horse-power, and can plough a single furrow and do much other useful work. The engines on most of them are air-cooled petrol engines, very much like those of motorcycles.

Petrol and paraffin engines are used on the farm for driving grinding mills, elevators, potato sorters, and many other machines. These engines are called stationary engines because they do not move from place to place under their own power, like tractors; but most of them are portable and can be moved about on trucks to do different work. They can even be taken into the field, and this is their great advantage over electric motors, which are the other great source of stationary power on farms; these must work where they can be connected with the electric mains. For driving BARN MACHINES and all other fixed installations such as DAIRY MACHINERY (qq.v.), electric motors provide easy, labour-free power. To avoid the use of shafting and belt drives, the farmer often finds it worth while to have a separate electric motor for each machine in the barn. This is a very neat and satisfactory arrangement. Electric motors need little attention and no labour in starting, and they run quietly. For these last two reasons they are used wherever possible for working milking-machines.

WATER-POWER and WIND-POWER (qq.v. Vol. VIII) are used a little on farms, but less in Britain than in countries with more mountainous streams or more powerful and regular currents of wind.

See also MECHANIZED FARMING; FARM TOOLS, HISTORY OF. See also Vol. VIII: POWER.

PRAWNING, *see* SHRIMPING AND PRAWNING.

PRIMULAS. These form a large and important genus of the family *Primulaceae*, in which there are a great many hardy garden species as well as a number of tender greenhouse plants. Horticulturists have also developed a variety of improved forms and hybrids (*see* PLANT BREEDING).

Primulas are mostly natives of Europe and temperate Asia, though a few are found in America and the mountains of Java. The Asiatic primulas in general like a rich, cool, moist soil, and positions that are more or less shady, while the European primulas prefer heavier soil and sunny positions.

The Asiatic group, which is the largest, contains many strong-growing kinds, and because of this they are sometimes referred to as 'cabbage primulas'. A good representative of this type is the crimson Japanese Primrose (*Primula japonica*), one of the easiest of the hardy primulas to grow and quite common in gardens. The popular Chinese and Star Primulas (*P. sinensis* and *P. stellata*) are not hardy, though there are many hardy Chinese primulas which are often grown in British rock gardens (*see* ROCK-GARDEN PLANTS).

In the European group there are fewer species, and they are, as a whole, less easy to cultivate. Even the common wild primrose (*P. vulgaris*), which grows abundantly in heavy, moist soils on sunny roadside or railway banks and margins of woods, refuses to grow in the London area. At Kew where bluebells thrive in their masses, hardly a single primrose is to be found. Cowslips (*P. veris*) and oxslips (*P. elatior*) are also not found very near London, and grow freely only in the open conditions of country meadows and hedgerows.

The Polyanthus (literally 'many-headed') Primrose, on the other hand, grows well in almost any type of soil and thrives fairly well under town conditions. It is of hybrid origin, having resulted from a cross between the primrose and the cowslip. There have been many developments in types and strains and many colours are now available.

Auriculas, which are not as popular as they used to be, were developed from the species *P. Auricula*, a wild flower of the European Alps. There are two main types—'Show and Fancy' and 'Alpine' auriculas. The Show type includes those varieties with green, white, and grey margins to the flowers, and in the Fancy type there is a wide range of colours. Both have a 'mealy' powder covering the foliage and flowers. Alpine auriculas have no such covering and generally have a more vigorous habit of growth.

There are now a great many varieties of primulas suitable for growing in the garden, some only 2 or 3 inches high, others from 1 to 2 feet. Some prefer cool positions, others need open, sunny positions. The majority of them range from pale mauve to rosy-lilac and crimson or purple, but there are white and yellow varieties too. The bog primulas need a peaty loam soil by the side of a pond or stream. Most of these are taller than the border primulas, some, such as the yellow *P. Florindae*, reaching a height of 3 or 4 feet.

Several species of primula, mostly coming from China and the Himalayas, are useful GREENHOUSE PLANTS (q.v.). *Primula sinensis* and *P. stellata* grow freely under quite cool conditions. The large-flowered *P. obconica* is a very handsome species, easy to grow, which is to be seen in most florists' shops. The sharp glandular-tipped hairs surrounding the margins of the leaves of this primula cause an irritating rash to the skin of some people.

P. malacoides, the 'Fairy Primrose', produces masses of dainty flowers in whorls on slender stems. Recently improved varieties in varying colour shades have been raised by seedsmen. Among other small-growing greenhouse species are *P. floribunda*, golden-yellow; *P. Forbesii*, lilac-crimson; *P. verticillata*, yellow, as well as a sweet-scented hybrid, *P. kewensis*, which is golden yellow.

The primulas are unusual in producing two different types of flower—the 'pin-eyed' in which the stigma or female part of the flower is higher than the stamens or male part, and the 'thrum-eyed' in which the stamens are higher (*see* REPRODUCTION IN PLANTS, section 5, Vol. II). Most primulas, both hardy and tender kinds, are easily raised from seed sown in spring. Some can also be increased by dividing up the plants.

Carters Tested Seeds, Ltd.

'PRIMULA MALACOIDES'

Amateur Gardening

'PRIMULA OBCONICA'

Amateur Gardening

A GROUP OF AURICULAS

R. A. Malby

HIMALAYAN PRIMROSE

PROPAGATION, *see* FRUIT PROPAGATION; PLANT PROPAGATION.

PRUNING. 1. GENERAL PRINCIPLES. Legend has it that the first pruner was a goat that broke into a vineyard and pruned the vines by eating them. The next year the vines had splendid crops, and after that, since it was clear that cutting away part of the plant stimulated its growth, pruning vines became the custom. The origin of the word is unknown, but the same word was used in English and in French in the Middle Ages to mean the cutting back of vines.

A certain amount of pruning is done to nearly all fruit trees and bushes, to some forest trees, and to most ornamental trees, shrubs, and hedges. Young trees are pruned in order to make them grow to the shape desired, and in such a way that light can get to all parts and no boughs cross and interfere with each other's growth. Growth can be stimulated or checked by the way in which a tree is pruned.

Different kinds of pruning are used for different purposes. Root pruning is sometimes needed to check too vigorous growth in rich, heavy soils. Sometimes the roots are chopped through about 18 inches from the tree, either all round or on one side. Sometimes a young tree may be lifted altogether in a ball of earth, and the main roots, including the tap root, cut through before replanting. Nicking is another form of pruning, and consists of cutting through the bark and into the sapwood just below or above a bud. A nick below prevents the bud becoming a shoot, while one above stimulates its growth (*see* Fig. 1). Disbudding, stopping, and pinching are done in spring or summer where there are too many buds, or where a particular bud is pointing in the wrong direction. These are methods used particularly for stone fruit grown on walls.

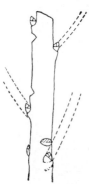

FIG. 1. NICKING ABOVE AND BELOW BUDS

The main pruning, however, is the branch pruning in winter, spring, and summer. Between all forms of winter pruning and all forms of summer pruning there is one important difference. Winter pruning generally encourages shoot growth in the following year, and if the pruning is severe, the tree is likely to produce a good deal of growth and less blossom. Summer pruning, on the other hand, checks shoot growth half-way through the growing season; and severe summer pruning makes a tree more likely to blossom freely the next year and to make less growth.

All young trees and bushes, whether fruit trees or ornamental trees and shrubs, need some pruning in winter to keep the tree a good open shape by removing unwanted branches and to strengthen those that are wanted. Let us take as an example a young apple-tree 1 year old consisting of a single stem. Having decided how high up the stem we want the 'head' or 'branch-system' to start, we cut back to a bud at that point on the stem, or a few inches above it. Three or four strong shoots will grow out the same summer, and in the winter these are all cut hard back to within a few inches of their base and to buds pointing in the right direction. The result of this is to give from six to eight shoots in the next summer. If these are shortened by one-half in winter, there should be by the end of the third season twelve to sixteen strong shoots from which to select in the fourth winter those most suitably placed. The others are cut out leaving a well-balanced 'branch-system' or 'framework' (*see* Fig. 2 A). The kind of pruning needed to develop young trees in the right way varies greatly according to the variety. When the trees have grown up, the main object of pruning is to make and keep a good balance between shoot and branch growth on the one hand, and flowering and fruiting on the other. To do this it is necessary to learn the habits of growth of different kinds and varieties. Apples and pears carry most of their fruits on short twigs or spurs, and unless the spur-bearing shoots are shortened, the trees bear too many fruits at once, and this results in very small fruits and weak growth. For this reason some parts of last year's shoots are pruned away.

Stone fruits, on the other hand, are generally allowed to keep most of the spur-bearing shoots full length, and the fruits themselves are reduced in number by 'fruit-thinning' when very small.

Methods of pruning fruit trees vary according to the space they occupy, the form or shape of the tree, and its natural vigour. Trees in orchards with plenty of space, especially when they are grafted on strong rootstocks, need very little pruning after the first few years. Trees in gardens with little space and trees trained on walls and fences need pruning both in winter and in summer.

FLOWERING SHRUBS (q.v.) are pruned according to whether they flower on last year's shoots like forsythias or prunuses, or on the tips of this season's growths like buddleias or japonicas. In the first case we cut back some of the shoots that have flowered as soon as possible after flowering. In the second case the shoots are generally pruned back behind the flowering points during the winter months. Flowering trees in parks and streets are given shaping treatment in early years, and after that can generally be left alone, except for the cutting out of dead branches.

HEDGES (q.v.) should be cut hard back for the first few years after planting in order to make them branch freely and grow thick; after that, one clipping a year, at least, is necessary. Hawthorn, holly, yew, beech, and privet can be cut several times a year without harming them.

Rambler roses should have the long rambling shoots that have already flowered cut off at the base in autumn, and the new shoots trained in their place. Of the other kinds of roses, very strong growers like Moysii are pruned as little as possible. Most of the weaker-growing roses are cut back in March to within 2 inches of the base for exhibition blooms, and to within about 5 or 6 inches of the base for ordinary flowering (*see* ROSES).

There are three useful tips for the pruning of all established fruit trees, flowering trees, and flowering shrubs:

(*a*) Trees that grow plenty of new shoots, blossom freely, and bear good crops, should be pruned lightly.

(*b*) Trees that grow very many new shoots, blossom little or not at all, or blossom without setting fruits, should be left unpruned for at least one year.

(*c*) Trees that are covered with blossom, give large crops of small fruits, and make little or no shoot growth, should be pruned severely.

2. THE TRAINING OF FRUIT TREES IN SPECIAL FORMS. The art of training fruit trees in various artificial shapes, in order to get the maximum amount of good fruit where space is limited, has been specially studied in France, and a few of these forms have been popular in England for many years. The most popular forms of trained **trees in England are as follows:**

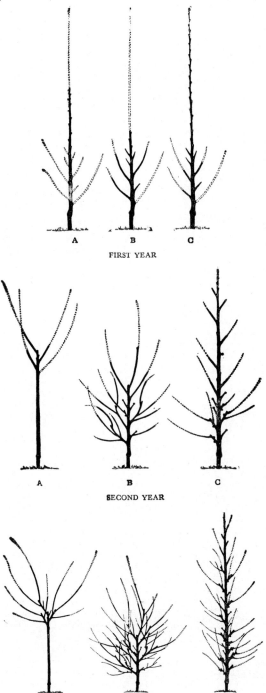

FIRST YEAR

SECOND YEAR

THIRD YEAR

East Malling Research Station

FIG. 2. METHOD OF PRUNING YOUNG APPLE-TREES TO PRODUCE (A) DWARF BUSH ON 2 FT. STEM, (B) DWARF PYRAMID AND (C) CORDON TREES

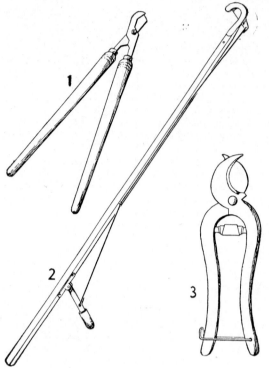

FIG. 3. PRUNING TOOLS

1. Lopping shears. **2.** Long-arm pruner. **3.** Secateurs

(*a*) *Espalier* (*see* page 320). This is a French word meaning any form of paling or fence. In France the word applies to any form of tree grown on a fence or wires; but in Britain an espalier is a fruit tree, usually apple or pear, trained on wires, having three, four, or five parallel rows of branches one above the other and extending on either side of a central stem. The fruit is borne on short spurs growing all along the main branches, and consequently such trees need careful pruning both in winter and summer.

(*b*) *Fan* (*see* page 317). In this form the tree is trained in the shape of a fan, with its main branches trained as ribs of the fan against wires on a wall or fence. The form is used most commonly for the stone fruits. Every season a certain number of young shoots are tied in beside the main branches to provide 'fruiting wood' for the next year's crop, and the tree is prevented from becoming overcrowded by disbudding, pinching, and stopping unwanted shoots during the growing season.

(*c*) *Cordon* (*see* page 29). There are various kinds of cordon, single, double, vertical, and oblique. The form most used in England is the single oblique cordon, which consists of a straight single-stemmed tree, planted at an angle of 45° from the vertical, and trained on wires. As the tree continues to extend its single stem upwards, it is periodically untied, pulled down nearer the ground, and retied. As such a tree is constantly trying to grow branches in all directions, pruning must be done both in summer and in winter. Apples and pears, and also small fruit such as gooseberries and red currants, are often grown as cordons. It is not as a rule successful to try to make a very vigorous growing tree such as a Bramley's Seedling grow as a cordon, for it cannot grow well in such a restricted way.

(*d*) *Dwarf Pyramid* (*see* page 29). In this form the tree has one central stem growing straight up, with side branches trained out in opposite pairs as nearly as possible at right angles to the stem. This form, being more natural than any of those described above, is comparatively easy to prune, but some pruning is necessary both in summer and in winter.

PUMPKINS, *see* GOURD VEGETABLES.

Fur and Feather

LOP RABBIT

Q R

QUINCES, *see* MEDLARS AND QUINCES.

RABBIT KEEPING. 1. BREEDS. The domestic rabbit, of which the earliest records are some 2,000 years old, is descended from the wild RABBIT (q.v. Vol. II), which originated in the Mediterranean countries and was introduced into England in the late 11th or early 12th century. In these early days warrens of wild rabbits were included as part of the agricultural holdings, and rabbits, which were considered a great delicacy, had a higher value than pigs. The different breeds of the modern domestic rabbit have been evolved since the 18th century. There are now several hundred different varieties throughout the world, varying in type of coat, in colour, and in size; in Great Britain alone there are over fifty different kinds. They are bred for their fur, for meat, for wool, or as pets. In Britain the breeding of rabbits for show is a very popular activity. There are over 2,500 rabbit shows held annually, varying from small local shows with perhaps 100 exhibits, to the large regional or national shows with over 2,000. In America and some continental countries they are bred for commercial purposes more than they are in Britain.

Rabbits vary in size from the large Flemish Giant rabbit which weighs up to 15 lb., to the Polish rabbit which may weigh only 3 lb. when fully grown, or the Netherland Dwarf, which weighs about 2½ lb.

There are four main types of coat, the 'normal', the 'Rex', the 'Angora', and the 'Satin', a new type recently introduced to Britain from America. The normal coat, like that of the wild rabbit, is composed of an under-coat of short hairs, and longer 'guard' hairs. In the Rex coat, which is like plush and does not fly back when stroked the wrong way, the guard hairs have been lost, leaving only the short under-coat. The Angora coat is of fluffy wool rather than fur, and consists of very long hairs, up to 3½ inches long. Rabbits with coats of this type first appeared as 'sports', that is, chance varieties from the normal. The Satin coat is smooth and shiny.

The breeds with a normal type of fur include the Beverens, which weigh at least 7 lb. and are produced in blue, white, black, or brown; the Chinchilla, with fur closely resembling real CHINCHILLA (q.v. Vol. II), which is slate blue at the base of the hair, pearl-coloured in the middle, and grey at the top; the Fox, including the Silver Fox and Blue Fox; the Havana, a rich dark chocolate; and the Sables, which are various shades of sepia. These all have very soft and dense fur.

Rabbits with fur of the Rex type are of fairly

Fur and Feather

BELGIAN HARE

J. S. Woodrow

CHINCHILLA WITH A NORMAL COAT

Fur and Feather

IVORY WITH SATIN COAT

Fur and Feather

ERMINE WITH REX COAT

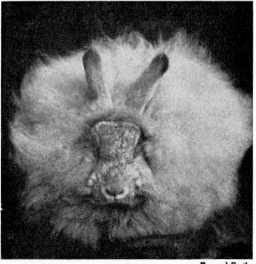

Fur and Feather

ANGORA

recent origin. In 1919 a French peasant discovered several rabbits with the Rex coat in litters from a normal-coated pair. These were given to a priest, who improved them to form the Castor-Rex ('King-Beaver') breed. The Rexes have now been produced in a large number of different colours, including pure white, black, blue, lilac, orange, dark sepia brown, and fawn.

The Angora rabbit is kept for its wool, as a sheep is, one animal yielding 6 to 8 ounces of wool a year. The rabbit is clipped or plucked every 3 months or so, when its coat is $2\frac{1}{2}$ to $3\frac{1}{2}$ inches long. There are both white and coloured varieties of Angora, the most usual colours being blue, grey, smoke, and fawn. The best quality Angora wool is expensive, especially the plucked kind.

The fancy breeds, usually kept solely for exhibition, include the belted Dutch rabbit, which is bred in a number of colours including black, blue, tortoiseshell, and grey; the spotted English rabbit of various colours; and the Belgian Hare which, although a rabbit, strongly resembles the English wild hare. There are other exhibition breeds such as the Harlequin, which has a patched black and orange coat, the Lop, which has very large ears, sometimes over 2 feet in length, and the Tans, which are black and tan or blue and tan.

All breeds may be used for meat, but those kept mainly for this purpose are often crossbreeds, as these grow quickly and are well-fleshed. They are ready for killing at about 4 months old.

The interests of each breed are looked after by a specialist club, and in addition there are over a thousand local clubs under the general control of the British Rabbit Council.

2. CARE OF RABBITS. The wild rabbit is 'herbivorous' or plant-eating, and the domestic rabbit will eat most types of green stuff and hay. Nearly all cultivated vegetables may be given, except potato and mangold tops and unripe mangolds. The leaves of many bushes and trees are safe food, but most evergreens, such as box and ivy, and also acacia, laburnum, and snowberry are poisonous to rabbits. Many kinds of wild plants are excellent food for rabbits, especially when fed in a mixture. The following are the principal poisonous plants: wild arum, bluebell, buttercup (when green, though not when dry), corn cockle, celandine, dog's mercury, foxglove, fool's parsley, hemlock, henbane, meadow saffron, poppy, the different nightshades, and toadflax. One poisonous plant in a mixture will probably not do the rabbit much harm. Before the Second World War a great deal of corn, particularly oats, was fed; but today, since corn is scarce, the domestic rabbit is fed mainly on wild plants, roots such as mangolds, swedes, and turnips, hay, and mashes made from household scraps, potatoes, and bran. Two or three ounces of hay, half a pound of greenstuff, and a handful or two of mash is enough for a medium-sized breed; though during the summer rabbits are often kept on green food only. Rabbits, particularly does who are suckling young, need plenty of water. Both food and water must be provided in a clean condition, and green food must be fresh and not frosted. Rabbits should be fed regularly, twice or three times a day.

The rabbit hutch should be light and airy and should give protection from rain, damp, and draughts. The smaller breeds need an area of at least 2 feet square, and rabbits over 10 to 12 lb. in weight need an area of 5 feet by 2 feet. Hutches, each 18 inches high, are often built in three-tiered stacks. The best and cheapest bedding is sawdust, but straw or peat are suitable. If sawdust is used, straw or hay must be given to the doe to make her nest before she 'kindles' (gives birth to her young).

Rabbits, if of medium-size, are first mated when about 7 or 8 months old, the smaller breeds slightly before this, and the larger ones later. For mating the doe is always put into the buck's cage, as otherwise they may fight. About 3 weeks later, if the mating has been successful, the doe will be seen carrying straw from her bedding in her mouth to make a nest. A nest box may be put into the hutch for her to use. She will pluck a large amount of fur from her breast and line the nest to make it warm. The gestation period (the interval between mating and giving birth to the young) is about 31 days. There are usually about five young in a litter, though sometimes as many as ten, and occasionally only one. If several does are kindling at the same time, the breeder may take some from the larger litters and give them to the does with smaller ones in order that all of them shall get enough milk. Rabbits, however, must be disturbed as little as possible during this period, for if they get scared, they may eat their whole litter. The young are born with their eyes not yet open and almost naked; but the fur grows quickly, and the eyes open in about 10 days. At 3 weeks old the rabbits are able to run about in the hutch and eat some of the doe's food. They are weaned at about 8 weeks old. It is best to take the doe away, leaving the little rabbits in the hutch in which they were born, as taking them to strange surroundings may check their growth. In 6 to 9 months from birth, if well fed, the rabbits will be fully grown.

Rabbits should always be carefully handled. When they are picked up they may be grasped by the ears, but a hand must be placed underneath the haunches to take the weight, otherwise the rabbit may be hurt and the ears damaged. A second method is to grasp the loose skin over the shoulders, taking care not to pull out any fur.

When large numbers of animals are kept, they have to be marked for identification purposes. This may be done by tattooing a number in the ear or by numbered ear tags; or a ring can be placed on the hind leg above the hock joint.

The most serious disease of rabbits is coccidiosis; this is caused by a very small parasite of which there are two types, one found in the liver and one in the intestines (see ANIMAL DISEASES). Rabbits suffer from other diseases, such as contagious catarrh or 'snuffles' and tuberculosis, but these do not cause nearly as many deaths as coccidiosis. Various types of mange caused by small external parasites (see MITE AND TICK PESTS) also attack rabbits. The tapeworms which infest the rabbit are those which at a later stage infest dogs, but the rabbits seem to take little harm from them (see PARASITIC WORMS).

The best preventions of disease are cleanliness, good ventilation, proper feeding and watering, the removal of soiled bedding at frequent intervals, and the immediate destruction of sick animals and the disinfection of their cages.

See also Vol II: RABBIT.
See also Vol. IX: PETS.

RABIES, *see* ANIMAL DISEASES, section 3.

RADISH, *see* SALAD CROPS.

RAPE, *see* CABBAGE CROPS, FIELD.

RASPBERRIES, LOGANBERRIES, AND BLACKBERRIES. These are all cane fruit, that is, they fruit on canes which were grown the year before, and will be cut off at ground level after fruiting. They all belong to the species *Rubus*. The fruit is carried in bunches on short shoots that grow out from the canes during the early summer. Raspberries are natives of Britain, and are to be found growing wild in many parts, especially Scotland, but the fruit on these wild plants is smaller and less juicy than the cultivated raspberry. Loganberries were first produced in America, and are said to be a cross between a raspberry and a blackberry. Blackberries are a very common wild fruit of which there are many different species—more than a hundred even in Britain. There are several other hybrids, such as an American fruit, the Boysenberry, which is a cross between all these three and has the colour of a deep mulberry, and the Youngberry, also American, which is a cross between a loganberry and a dewberry, as well as thornless varieties of both loganberries and blackberries.

All these fruits prefer a deep, well-drained, loamy soil, but can be grown on most soils that do not become water-logged in winter nor too dry in summer. Wild blackberries, for instance, are nearly always to be found producing the finest fruit when growing on a bank above a stream. As they all have to make a lot of new cane growth every year, as well as carrying a crop of fruit, they need generous manuring with fertilizers containing both nitrogen and potash. The ground should be given a heavy dressing of farmyard manure before the canes are planted, and then an application of potash one year and some organic nitrogenous fertilizer, such as meat meal or dried blood, the next year. These should be spread on the surface and scratched in during the winter months.

Newly planted canes should never be allowed to fruit the first year, but should be cut back in the spring—raspberries to within 9 or 12 inches of their base, and loganberries and blackberries to within about 2 feet—so that they may grow strong canes for the next year. With raspberries, each plant can support from six to twelve canes, and the rest should be cut away. In gardens these canes are usually tied to wires stretched between posts, a gap of 4 to 6 inches being left between each cane in the row (*see* FIG. 1). But as this takes a great deal of time, field raspberries, grown by the acre, are generally supported by two parallel lines of coir yarn tied to T-shaped stakes placed every 20 feet or so along the row. The canes are tipped in the spring so that they do not grow higher than about 4 feet. Loganberries and blackberries can be trained in various ways, the 'fan' method with loganberries, and the 'rope' and 'weaving' methods (*see* Fig. 2) with blackberries being popular. The plants must be kept clear of weeds, but it is very important not to disturb the roots within a foot of

Amateur Gardening

FIG. 1. 2-YEAR-OLD RASPBERRY CANES TRAINED ON WIRES

the plant. A mulch of manure, compost, or lawn mowings helps to keep in the moisture.

One of the most serious diseases which can attack raspberries is the virus disease, Mosaic, which turns the leaves yellow and mottled and soon stunts and finally kills the growth (*see* PLANT DISEASES). Infected plants should be dug out and burnt before they spread the infection, for the disease is incurable. Mosaic disease attacks the popular Lloyd George raspberry to such an extent that many growers have had to give it up. The fungus disease, Cane Spot, often attacks loganberries, and quite commonly raspberries and blackberries also. Small purple spots appear on the canes in early June, and then spread, eventually turning into cankers and producing spores. The Raspberry beetle is the most common pest, but can be easily controlled. The Raspberry moth has a little red grub which lives in the pith of shoots, which it soon kills (*see* INSECT PESTS).

The variety Lloyd George would be the most popular of all raspberries were it not so susceptible to Mosaic and Cane Spot. Norfolk Giant is a very strong grower with a large berry, as are also Preussen and Park Lane. The American variety, Newburgh, is resistant to Mosaic. New popular varieties are Malling Promise and Malling Newburgh. The varieties Yellow Antwerp and Bryne's Apricot are excellent yellow raspberries. The blackberry Himalaya Giant is a heavy cropper but needs a great deal of space. Bedford Giant is a good early variety, and John Innes an excellent late blackberry.

See also FRUIT-GROWING; FRUIT PROPAGATION.

RATS, *see* VERMIN.

REAPER AND BINDER, *see* HARVESTING (GRAIN).

RED CURRANTS, *see* CURRANTS AND GOOSEBERRIES.

RED SPIDER MITE, *see* MITE AND TICK PESTS.

East Malling Research Station

FIG. 2. LOGANBERRIES TRAINED IN A 'ONE WAY ROPE'

RESEARCH IN AGRICULTURE. Successful farming depends on the application of accurate, orderly knowledge. Under the old open-field system of farming it was not easy for an enterprising person to grow new crops for winter use, or to improve the pastures or the breeds of animals that grazed them. The period of the enclosures in the 18th century laid the foundation for individual progress, for the use of initiative, and for experiment, without finding oneself at odds with neighbours sharing the same ground (*see* OPEN FIELDS AND ENCLOSURES). Great advances were made almost immediately in the variety of crops grown, in the methods of cultivation, and in the breeding of sheep and cattle; this last was largely due to Robert Bakewell's discovery of the immense possibilities of inbreeding (*see* AGRICULTURAL IMPROVERS). It was not, however, until the first half of the 19th century that research in its modern sense was applied to agricultural problems.

New knowledge can be gained in two ways: a man may work on the system of trial and error until he thinks he has found the truth, or the best way to do something. This usually takes a long time; nevertheless, the great mass of agricultural practice in the world has been laboriously built up on a system of trial and error, of observing and acting on the dictates of experience. This way of finding out is called the 'empirical' approach to knowledge.

The research method uses observation in a different way: constantly observing certain facts, the research worker looks for the guiding principle behind, and sooner or later a theory forms in his mind as to why these facts should be. Theory, however, is not knowledge, but reasoned guessing. Therefore, the research worker must always be carrying out experiments to test his theories, and his skill consists not only in conceiving a theory that fits his observed facts, but in devising such careful experiments as will not allow of error in proving the theory. The technical advance in methods of experiment has been very great in all fields of agricultural research during the last century, especially in recent years.

Man has noticed for thousands of years that grass grew stronger where there was dung than where there was no dung. It was but a short step to apply dung to ground on which a crop was to be cultivated. Here was knowledge gained from experience—that dung would make the crops grow. There was little advance on that empirical knowledge until after A.D. 1800. Some farmers might well have said, 'That is all we need to know. All we are concerned with is getting more dung.' But inquiring men said, 'Dung makes the crop grow, but why does it? Why doesn't sawdust or brickdust do the same thing? There must be something in dung that isn't in sawdust. What is it? If we can find what it is that the plant likes in dung, we might be able to find that something somewhere else.' To find out the answers to these questions it was necessary to understand how the plant lived, how it took up water and food, how it breathed, and how it stored food. Again, it was evident that some plants nourished men and animals better than others. Why? What did they contain? The scientific inquirers of the early 19th century were eagerly asking these questions and trying to find satisfying answers.

The first agricultural research station was established by Lawes and Gilbert at Rothamsted, Hertfordshire, in 1843. This was engaged in following up the work of the Frenchman, Boussingault, who, since 1834, had been conducting experiments on soil fertilization. The main plant nutrients of the soil (nitrogen, phosphorus, potassium, and calcium) were confirmed, and it was not long before ARTIFICIAL FERTILIZERS (q.v.) containing these ingredients were found, made, and put on the market. But research did not finish there. All the mistakes of using too much, of lack of balance between the fertilizers, and of other problems which at first were not obvious, needed explanation. Pasteur's discovery of BACTERIA (q.v. Vol. II) set men to study the bacteriology of the SOIL (q.v.), a

subject found to be of tremendous importance. Advances in organic chemistry made it possible to study the science of farm animal FEEDING (q.v.), and that raised new problems in physiology. Findings in one field of research were found to have bearings on others, so that the publication of scientific journals became very necessary, and scientific conferences, at which men stated their work and argued it out, grew in number. The number of research institutes tackling the several branches of agricultural and purely scientific inquiry has grown steadily, and today farming is putting the results of research into practice on an increasing scale.

Growing a crop of wheat, for instance, in Britain today is founded on knowledge gained of soil chemistry and physics; of the chemistry of artificial manures; of plant physiology; of PLANT BREEDING which could produce suitable varieties; of the PESTS AND DISEASES (qq.v.) which may attack the crop; of engineering which designs the machinery from drill to combine harvester (see MECHANIZED FARMING); and of various sciences which are concerned with the successful storing of the grain. A dairy cow of high quality in an up-to-date byre producing disease-free milk depends upon another host of sciences. Genetics (see STOCK BREEDING) has shown how such cows can be bred with a fair degree of certainty; a knowledge of animal FOODS (q.v.) has made it possible to feed the cows in the right way by the provision of proteins, fats and carbohydrates, minerals and vitamins, in the right quantity and proportion; bacteriological technique isolated the germ of tuberculosis and later devised the test by which it is possible to know whether the cow is free of the disease or not; bacteriology also dictates the hygienic measures adopted in milking and treatment of the MILK (q.v. Vol. XI); veterinary science has contributed to an understanding of general health and the prevention of ANIMAL DISEASES (q.v.).

Research is now a corner-stone of agricultural policy, and is conducted in all civilized countries of the world. Techniques become more and more specialized, and the importance of mathematics is now fully realized. All research workers today receive some training in the use of STATISTICS (q.v. Vol. VII).

Rothamsted, the oldest agricultural research institute in the world, is now mainly concerned with soil research. Elsewhere in Britain there

Aerofilms

ROTHAMSTED EXPERIMENTAL STATION, HERTFORDSHIRE, FROM THE AIR

Different experiments in fertilizing are carried out in the various plots. The oblong plots in the lower part of the picture have been planted with barley annually since 1852. The different colours of the plots show the variety of growth due to the use of different fertilizers

are a great number of research institutes, most of them specializing in some particular aspect of research—animal nutrition, animal or plant breeding, animal or plant diseases, dairy farming, fruit-growing, horticulture, or agricultural economics. The National Institute of Agricultural Botany, for instance, is concerned with the scientific testing of crops, and the Agricultural Economics Research Institute at Oxford is concerned with the economic and social problems of the land and its use. The farmer has to know not only how to raise crops and livestock, but how to make these things profitable. The farmer must organize his farm—his machinery, livestock, and labour—to the best advantage. He must know how best to buy materials and sell his produce. The Institute sets out to help him in all these ways. It studies the various national and international systems of marketing, and has a special interest in all agricultural co-operative enterprises (*see* Co-operation in Farming).

The Ministry of Agriculture and the Agricultural Research Council not only support research at the universities and other institutions, but also have their own research stations, such as the Animal Breeding Station at Compton, Berkshire, run by the A.R.C., and financed by the state. Some business firms have their own research departments, one of which, for example, deals with the manuring and management of pasture and grass, and the preserving of grass.

The governments of the British Empire have co-operated to form a number of Imperial Agricultural Bureaux to co-ordinate and make easily available the results of research. They deal with animal health, parasites, animal nutrition, animal and plant breeding, herbage plants, fruit production, forestry, and dairying. Each is situated at a research institute concerned with the particular science.

See also Agricultural Improvers; Agricultural Training.

RHODODENDRONS,   *see*   Peat-loving Plants.

RHUBARB. The garden rhubarb is a herbaceous perennial, and is believed to be a hybrid form derived from *Rheum Rhaponticum* and *R. undulatum*. It is quite distinct from the medicinal rhubarbs, *R. palmatum* and *R. officinale*. Most of the *Rheum* species, including the garden rhubarb, came originally from the colder parts of Asia,

Royal Horticultural Society
RHUBARB WHICH HAS BEEN GROWN UNDER A BARREL
In front is a plant which has not been forced

probably Siberia. Rhubarb belongs to the same family as the docks and sorrels, common plants of the countryside. The sharp taste of the rhubarb's leaf-stalks, which form the part of the plant that is eaten, is caused by the presence of oxalic acid.

Rhubarb, being a perennial, is grown as a permanent crop in a bed set aside from other garden crops. The plant forms a large woody underground stock or rhizome, from which new growth arises each year. If not exhausted by having the stalks gathered too frequently the plants grow larger year by year, until in time the bed becomes overcrowded with growth, and it is necessary to make a new bed. Rhubarb is propagated by dividing the old roots into small pieces, each with one or two buds. New beds are made on a well-manured site by planting the divided roots 2 to 3 feet apart in rows which are spaced 4 feet apart. It is best to take no rhubarb from the new bed in the first year, for that gives the plants a chance to develop strongly. Rhubarb may also be grown from seed, but it takes longer to bring the seedling plants to the stage when a crop can be gathered. One variety, however,

Glaskins Perpetual, matures very quickly from seed. The seed is sown in the open land in the spring and the seedlings are thinned to 4 to 6 inches apart.

The rhubarb bed will yield better if given two dressings of fertilizer each year, the first when growth begins in the spring and the second after pulling is finished for the season; the second dressing can consist solely of nitrogen, such as nitrate of soda or sulphate of ammonia. Varieties of rhubarb well known in Britain are Daw's Champion, Victoria, Linnaeus, the Sutton, Prince Albert, and Hawke's Champagne.

Rhubarb can be forced to produce early supplies by covering the crowns of the plants in January with boxes or large rhubarb pots, which themselves are covered with straw or leaves. This keeps out the frost and sets up enough warmth to start growth. Also, the roots may be taken up and forced into growth in a dark, warm shed or under the stage of a warm greenhouse. After forcing, the roots may either be replanted or discarded. The same roots should not be forced 2 years running.

RICE. Rice is the principal food of millions of people in Asia. As a rule they cook the grain by boiling it in water, and then flavour it with spices or curry powder, adding pieces of meat, fish, or vegetables. It is also ground to a fine powder and used for making cakes and sweetmeats. Rice is also a source of starch for industrial purposes, and in some places the grain is fermented to make an alcoholic drink, such as the *samsu* of China.

The rice grain itself is the seed of a grass called *Oryza sativa*, of which there are well over a thousand different kinds. The largest crops are grown in China, Japan, Java, and southern India, but the enormous populations of these countries eat all that they grow—indeed, they have to import more from other lands. Most of the rice that is exported comes from Burma and Siam. Rice is also grown in Africa, especially in Egypt, in South Italy, and in the southern United

HEADS OF RICE

States. There are two main types of rice, the upland or hill kinds, which are cultivated much like any other cereal and rely upon rain for their water supply, and the aquatic or lowland kinds, which need very moist land and depend on IRRIGATION (q.v.), the artificial watering of the fields. Rice land must, therefore, always have a good natural water supply, from streams, springs, monsoons, or constant tropical rains. In order to control the depth and flow of the water, the cultivators divide the fields into sections by low mud walls. In hilly country the fields are terraced one above the other, and have curious curved outlines to follow the shape of the hillside. The season of planting depends on the local rainfall, for the weather should be wet for growing and dry for harvesting the crop.

First of all the land is flooded to a shallow depth, the weeds having been cleared by digging or by ploughs drawn by water-buffaloes. Meanwhile the rice plants have been raised in a nursery of soft mud. For raising seedlings the grains, still in their husks, are soaked in water for about 3 days and then sown thickly in the mud, the seeds often being covered with leaves to keep away the birds. After a few days they start to grow, forming tiny bright green plants like little tufts of grass. When these are 6 weeks old they are ready to be transplanted by hand. The water level in the fields is then lowered so that soft grey mud forms a damp surface in which the tiny plants can easily take root. Transplanting is slow work and is usually done by women, who work knee deep in the mud, without shoes and wearing huge sun hats. They set the seedlings in little clumps of three or four, from 6 to 12 inches apart. Later on they return to weed the crop. More and more water is gradually added so that it surrounds the growing stems of the rice plants.

Rice takes from 6 to 9 months to mature, depending on the kind and on the climate. As the plants ripen, water is slowly withdrawn from the fields by making gaps in the mud banks. Then, when ripe, the crop of brown grain is harvested, the stems being cut with knives or sickles. The seed is enclosed in a hard brown husk, and at this stage it is known as 'paddy'. After being gathered, the grain is threshed by hand by beating the sheaves against the edge of a basket. In the country districts the growers remove the outer husks by pounding the threshed grain in a hollow tree trunk, using a log as a

Paul Popper

RICE TERRACES IN BALI, INDONESIA

At the top young plants can be seen growing in irrigated terraces. In the centre the rice is being harvested. Two crops a year are harvested

saves nursery work and transplanting, and 70 lb. of seed is enough to sow 1 acre. The flat fields are flooded during the growing season, but are dried again at harvest time, so that reaping-machines can be used to harvest the crop.

See also TROPICAL AGRICULTURE.

ROCK-GARDEN. 1. A rock-garden usually attempts to imitate, as nearly as possible, a natural formation often found in mountain country, and to provide surroundings in which certain plants, known as ROCK-GARDEN PLANTS (q.v.), will thrive.

Gardens in the 18th century often had damp grottoes, built to imitate rocky caves, in which ferns and other plants would grow. The rockeries of the Victorians were mounds of earth from which upright rocky 'fangs' protruded, with no attempt at a natural arrangement. By the end of the century, largely as the result of the work of a Yorkshire garden designer, John Wood, and a nurseryman called John Stormonth from near Carlisle, the modern idea of a rock-garden had been evolved. These gardeners showed that rocks in the natural state do not jut out of the ground anywhere, but are part of a systematic rock formation, and that this pattern must be reproduced in the artificial rockery. For a time gardeners went to the other extreme, building great erections in which the stones were placed perfectly but the rock-plants played little part. Gradually, however, as more varieties of rock-plants were introduced, rock-gardens were designed to display these to the best advantage.

Nurserymen then began exhibiting rock-gardens at all the principal flower shows, and at the first great International Exhibition in 1912 the famous 'Chelsea Rock Bank' was first displayed. This rock-garden display, now shown annually at the Royal Horticultural Society's Show at Chelsea, has done as much as anything else to popularize rock-gardens (*see* AGRICULTURAL SHOWS). Another important influence on rock-gardens has been the work of Reginald Farrer, a collector of rock-plants and one of the first practical gardeners to combine artistic rock-garden construction with the provision of suitable conditions of soil, aspect, and drainage for the plants. His book, *The English Rock Garden* (1918), remains the classic work on the subject. Recently the small rock-garden has become a popular feature of a great many private gardens.

stamper. In this way they obtain 'red rice', which still keeps its outer layers and is, therefore, very nutritious. But if the paddy is sent to the towns, the husking is done in factories with steel rollers, and these take off all the outer layers, thus producing the white or polished rice that is shipped abroad. Millions of people in the cities of Asia live on this white rice, although it is not nearly as nutritious as the red rice, being largely starch.

In the south-western states of North America —Texas and California, for example—more modern methods of rice-growing are used. A variety that needs little water is selected. The land is ploughed and cultivated whilst it is still dry, and the seed is sown direct by means of DRILLS (q.v.), drawn by tractors or horses. This

2. ROCK AND SITE. Rock, in particular lime-stone, used often to be brought from a distance to make the rockery. Limestone was everywhere popular because people had seen the lovely weathered and water-worn rocks in limestone districts such as the fells of northern England. But in towns where the air is polluted by sul-phuric acid, the grey limestone rapidly bleaches to a hard and unlovely white. Some plants, also, are lime haters and will not grow near limestone. So, as knowledge of rock-gardening grew, a much wider range of rock was used. Stone from the Cheddar district, from Purbeck, from the Forest of Dean, and the wealds of Sussex and Kent; sandstone, millstone grit, granite, conglomerate, all came to be used (*see* ROCKS, Vol. III); and the present-day popularity of local stone is due to the high cost of transporting stone from a distance.

Substitutes for natural stone, such as broken masonry, concrete, and even clinkers and brick-bats, have sometimes been used for reasons of economy or convenience, and plants will grow well amongst them if they are properly arranged.

The choice of the site is important. Most rock-plants prefer an open situation, not overhung by trees or shadowed by a house or wall, and not draughty. A south-west slope is ideal, and east and north should be avoided. Some rock-plants need more shade than others, and in a properly constructed rock-garden shady places can usually be found, such as those at the foot of overshadowing rocks.

3. CONSTRUCTION. Good drainage is essential. On sites which have had to be built up artificially, or 'contoured', to obtain height and depth, the hollows must have an outlet for surplus water; otherwise they become pools in the winter. Where the rockery is built on a clay sub-soil, it is unwise to bring the clay to the surface by digging. The nature of the stone which is being used should be studied so that it can be laid in the way that is natural to it. Some rock is sharply stratified (layered), and such stone, unless laid upon its right 'bed' (that is, as it rested in the quarry), will probably split to pieces after the first severe frost. Outcropping stone, which has been weathered by centuries of exposure to wind and rain, is harder, and is usually easier for the novice to build with than quarried stone, for its natural beauty helps to hide any faults made in the building. When stratified stone is used, the strata (or layers) should always be made to tilt slightly into the earth. This tilt, incidentally, allows rain to seep towards the roots of the plants instead of away from them.

The size of the rocks must depend on the size of the garden; the addition of a few relatively large blocks much improves the effect.

The roots of even the smallest rock-garden plants are usually very long and need a consider-able depth of soil. There should be a depth of at least 2 feet of soil in small pockets and clefts among the rocks. The surrounding stones prevent the moisture from evaporating too quickly.

In the mountains in spring the melting snow produces a water-sodden subsoil, and to produce that condition in the rockery, water-pipes with small holes at regular intervals can be buried in the higher parts of the rock-garden. Reginald Farrer used this method, and it is still used by some enthusiasts; but it can easily go wrong, and the holes in the pipes become blocked. A well-drained, well-made rock-garden does not need this artificial aid to underground watering.

The rock-garden should not be built up with bricks and rubble but be of soil with the rocks embedded in it. There should be no air spaces beneath the stones, which should be well rammed in with a wooden rammer. The soil between the stones, however, should not be very tightly packed, and therefore the rockery should not be made when the soil is wet and sticky. A layer of about an inch of pure gravel or stone chippings should be put round the plants on the surface and well worked beneath their leaves and around their necks. This discourages slugs and snails, holds the moisture in the top few inches of soil,

FIG. I. THE ARRANGEMENT OF ROCKS IN A ROCK GARDEN
The stones at the base give drainage. The rocks are well set into the ground with spaces left between them for the plants

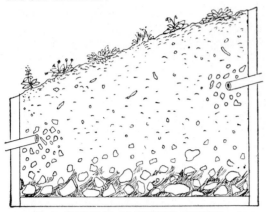

FIG. 2. SECTION OF AN ARTIFICIAL MORAINE

The moraine is encased in a concrete trough with inlet and outlet water pipes in the walls

and keeps the crowns of the plants dry during winter. It also helps to keep down weeds.

Many rock-plants normally grow in moraines or screes, the piles of mountain debris brought down by glaciers, and conditions of the same sort can be made in the rock-garden. The moraine is wet, and must be supplied with an underground water supply; the scree is dry. Small moraines can be made to sweep down between outjutting rocks, and miniature screes can fan out from the foot of little cliffs. These should be composed of at least 50% stone chippings, and should be at least 2 feet deep.

A small stream, falling in a series of pools from the highest to the lowest point, is a great addition to a rock-garden, and provides suitable homes for moisture-loving plants. If natural water does not exist, it is possible to instal a small electric pump at not too great a cost to return the water from the lowest to the highest pool.

A 'dry wall' is sometimes combined with a rock-garden, but more usually belongs to the formal part of the garden, where a show of rock-plants is wanted. The dry wall is usually a wide, hollow wall made up from more or less regular stones, so built that the two sides slope inwards towards the top. A quantity of drainage material is placed at the bottom, and the inside of the wall is filled with very porous, light soil, which is rammed into all the crevices. Sometimes the wall is made with a wide, flat top, in which irregular rocks are embedded. The top and the crevices on the side are planted with suitable rock-plants. One-sided dry walls are also often used to hold back the earth where part of the garden is terraced, or to cover a natural, dry bank that would otherwise be difficult to plant successfully.

See also ROCK-GARDEN PLANTS.
See also Vol. III: ROCK FORMATION.

ROCK-GARDEN PLANTS. 1. VARIETIES OF PLANTS. Plants grown in rock-gardens are usually described as 'alpines'; but this is an unsatisfactory name, since many plants which are commonly grown in rock-gardens are not alpine, either in their choice of environment or way of growth. Such plants are chosen because they grow well in rockery conditions and look well in such surroundings.

The majority of rock-garden plants, however, are species, or are developed from species, found growing in alpine or sub-alpine regions (*see* ALPINE PLANTS, Vol. II). They are usually PERENNIALS (q.v.), of dwarf stature, and bear flowers which are large in proportion to their size. They have developed a habit of growth which enables them to endure the conditions of their natural environment—long and severe winters, often with a great weight of snow, and short, often very hot summers. Alpine plants in their natural surroundings have to crowd their growth, flowering, and seeding into a season often no longer than a bare 3 months. Such plants have not time to grow tall and branching, and are therefore generally compressed into compact, huddled cushions, most of their growth going to the production of the flowers. They have small leaves, sometimes covered with fine hairs to protect them from loss of moisture by evaporation during the hot summer. The common thrift (*Armeria*) is a plant of this type, as are many rock-garden plants from the European Alps, the Himalayas, and other regions.

Similar habits of growth are sometimes induced by exactly opposite conditions, and many species which inhabit almost rainless districts of extreme heat, especially the Central and North American deserts, also grow as dense cushions of compressed shoots. These plants are often grown in the alpine house, where it is possible to grow plants of an alpine character which will not endure a British winter unprotected.

There are some forty important groups (genera) of rock-garden plants, most of which have several if not many species. The most

PART OF THE ROCK GARDEN AT KEW GARDENS

common are the very free-growing aubrietia, arabis, and alyssum. Among the most brilliant are the rich, vivid blue gentians and lithospernums and the many species of rock campanulas. The starry white sandwort (*Arenaria*) and the thymes grow in close mats of foliage; the saxifrages form rosettes; and the rock-roses (*Helianthemum*), St. John's Wort (*Hypericum*), potentillas, and veronicas have a shrubby growth. The great variety of stonecrops (*Sedum*) and houseleeks (*Sempervivum*) have thick, succulent growths; while the little wild cyclamens grow from tubers.

Very few of the DAISY FAMILY (q.v.) are rockplants—mainly the milfoils (*Achillea*) and alpine asters. Alpine buttercups (*Ranunculus*) and their close relations the anemones and columbines (*Aquilegia*), as well as storksbill (*Erodium*) and cranesbill (*Geranium*), with their long, beaky seed-pods, all have dwarf rock-garden varieties. Rock-penstemons and phloxes, as well as many species of IRIS (q.v.), are to be found, and there are a great many rock-pinks (*see* CARNATIONS) and PRIMULAS (q.v.).

Many bulbs, such as grape hyacinths (*Muscari*), scillas, and miniature daffodils, are well suited to the rock-garden; and a background of dwarf shrubs and miniature conifers is very effective.

2. CULTURE. Broadly speaking, it is possible to divide rock-garden plants into two main groups, the lime lovers and the lime haters. While most lime lovers will tolerate neutral or even acid soil, most lime haters will not grow at all where there is lime. The majority of heaths dislike lime, as do a considerable number of plants from the northern States of the U.S.A. (*see* PEAT-LOVING PLANTS). While most gentians either like lime or are tolerant of it, almost all Asiatic, autumn-flowering gentians will not tolerate lime at all. Amongst the few rock-plants for which lime is really necessary are almost all the pinks (*Dianthus*), all the so-called 'silver' or 'encrusted' saxifrages, and the aubrietias.

With the exception of a few rare plants, which are difficult to grow, all that is needed to produce a successful rock-garden is common sense and a little gardening skill in making the right conditions for healthy growth. The soil must be well drained and yet capable of retaining moisture during hot, dry periods. Sharp sand and grit will ensure that the drainage is good; and granulated peat or leaf-mould or even well-rotted compost mixed with the soil will make it hold the moisture. The site for the rock-garden and its construction is described in ROCK-GARDEN (q.v.).

THRIFT, 'ARMERIA HALLERII'

'CAMPANULA SAXIFRAGA'

HOUSELEEK, 'SEMPERVIVUM'

An alpine plant with succulent leaves

Amateur Gardening

'SAXIFRAGA LONGIFOLIA', A PLANT FROM THE PYRENEES

The spike is at least 12 inches long

3. ALPINE HOUSE. In the alpine house the correct use of water is important, for at certain periods in their growth the plants can easily have too little or too much. During the resting period they need very little water—just enough to prevent their becoming parched; but when they start growing, they need much more. They must have plenty of ventilation. The ideal is to have full-length ventilators along each side of the ridge of the house, and again at the staging level. These ventilators should be regulated according to the weather, but they should never be entirely closed, even in mid-winter, so that a constant movement of the air is kept up. Rock-garden plants detest stagnation, either of water or air. The staging should consist of wooden slatted benches, and on these are laid sheets of tin or corrugated iron, covered with a 2 or 3-inch layer of coarse ashes or stone grit, on which the pans and pots stand.

If the roots of a plant start to grow out through the drainage hole in the base of the pot, it is obvious that it should be repotted into a slightly larger pot or pan; but the increase in size should not be great (*see* POTTING).

Rock-garden plants should never be potted into a 'rich' mixture. Over-fed plants tend to produce too much leaf and less flower. Under hard conditions they keep healthy and flower freely. When plant foods are given, natural organic foods are much more satisfactory for rock-garden plants than artificial fertilizers (*see* MANURES).

See also ROCK-GARDEN.
See also Vol. II: ALPINE PLANTS.

ROOKS, *see* VERMIN, section 8.

ROOT CROPS. 1. These are crops in which the plant's swollen base has a store of sugar or starch and is, therefore, a source of valuable food for humans and livestock. With some such crops the foliage is also a useful fodder crop. This article is concerned only with turnips, swedes, and mangolds; other root crops, such as CARROTS, BEETROOTS, SUGAR-BEETS, and PARSNIPS (qq.v.), are described in separate articles. POTATOES (q.v.) are not, strictly speaking, root crops since the edible tuber is not a root but an underground STEM (q.v. Vol. II). Root crops take a definite place in the farmer's ROTATION OF CROPS (q.v.), usually coming between two cereal crops. Occasionally, however, patches of turnips, swedes, or mangolds are grown for a number of years on the same area of ground because it is handy to the homestead. Most root crops are also valuable garden crops.

2. FIELD CROPS. The field turnip (*Brassica napus*) and the swede (*Brassica rutabaga*) were introduced to Britain from the Continent during the 18th century. Viscount Townshend of Rainham Hall, Norfolk, introduced the turnip as a field crop in 1731, and was consequently nicknamed 'Turnip Townshend'. The swede, which has a higher food value than the turnip, was introduced later in the century from Sweden, hence the name. The mangold (or mangelwurzel) is closely related to the beetroot and has no connexion with turnips and swedes; its culture and use as a crop are, however, much the same as that of turnips and swedes. Turnips contain more water than swedes, are more easily damaged by frost, and do not store so well. They are grown a good deal in the north and west of Britain, where conditions are moist and cool. They have to be used, however, before hard frosts set in and are of little use for late-winter feeding. Swedes can be stored and used through the winter. Mangolds, which flourish best in the warmer, sunnier climates of east and south-east England, keep very well indeed, and are not in a fit condition for feeding until Christmas time. As a whole, mangolds produce the highest yield, about 20 tons an acre being an average crop, but favourable conditions and a richly manured soil may produce a crop of 50 tons an acre.

Different varieties of swedes and turnips have a white or yellow flesh and skins which may be green, purple, or mottled. The foliage leaves of turnips are grass-green and hairy and grow up from the bulb itself; those of swedes (except the first pair) are grey-green and smooth and grow from a short stem, or 'neck'. Mangolds vary in shape and colour. Globe-shaped roots vary from lemon-yellow to orange, while the oblong-shaped 'tankard' varieties are orange or crimson, and the long-rooted varieties yellow or red. There are various intermediate varieties. The choice of variety is largely determined by the type of soil and the preference of the farmer.

All these crops benefit from a rich soil with plenty of lime, dung, and a well-balanced artificial fertilizer. If possible, the ground should be given an application of farmyard manure, ploughed under in the autumn. The furrows are then left to weather over the winter, and in the

Eric Guy

SHEEP FOLDED ON A FIELD OF KALE AND SWEDES

spring a seed-bed is prepared by harrowing and rolling, during which the fertilizers are applied and worked into the surface soil. These root crops, therefore, both clean the land and leave it in good heart for the next crop in the rotation. Too much nitrogen in the fertilizer, however, may result in too much top (leaves) and small bulbs.

Mangolds are sown in April or early May, swedes about May in the south and June in the north, and turnips about a fortnight later than swedes. The seed is sometimes drilled on the flat in rows about 20 inches apart, and sometimes on the top of ridges 24 to 26 inches apart. Generally speaking, flat planting suits dry districts and ridge sowing gives good drainage where the rainfall is higher. About 4 lb. of turnip or swede seed per acre is used, and about 10 lb. of mangold seed. The seedlings appear in continuous rows which must be thinned or 'singled' to leave a plant every 10 to 14 inches. Singling is started as soon as the plants show the first pair of foliage leaves (not counting the seed-leaves), and most of it has to be done by hand. The Turnip Flea Beetle is a great danger to the young seedlings, and may clear a whole crop unless controlled by dustings with insecticide (*see* BEETLE PESTS).

Turnip and swede crops are often left in the fields in the autumn and eaten there by sheep 'folded' on them with movable fences, or lifted as required to feed in the fields or in the sheds. Swedes are also often lifted and clamped or stored under cover. The mangold crop is pulled in the autumn before severe frosts set in and is also stored. The tops are generally twisted off by hand and the roots left untrimmed, since if the skin is broken, mangolds are apt to bleed and decay. Mangolds and swedes which are clamped are heaped in long mounds and covered first with a thick layer of straw and then with soil to keep out the frost and rain and preserve the roots through the winter.

3. GARDEN CROPS. The turnip was cultivated in gardens as a vegetable long before it was taken up as a field crop; in fact, it is commonly supposed that this was one of the vegetables introduced into Britain by the Romans. The sweet, fleshy roots of turnips should be eaten while they are young, for when they get mature they acquire a strong flavour. Turnip-tops, the fresh, succulent spring growth, are used as cabbage greens at the time of year when other 'greens' may be scarce.

Early supplies of garden turnips are obtained

A MEDIEVAL FARM

Many of the methods of medieval farming have not changed; notice the wood-cutters' tools, the horses' harness, the wattle fence, and gate. The farmer and his wife are beating gongs to make the bees settle.

Illumination from a 15th century Flemish manuscript

by sowing under frames and cloches during March, the white long type such as Long Milan or Sutton's White Gem being suitable for this purpose. For later supplies, sowings are made in the open at 6-week intervals from the end of March onwards, the white round type such as Early White Milan and Early White Stone, followed by Marble Greentop and Greentop Stone being the ones generally used. One of the two latter varieties sown during May and June provides turnips for winter storage. Garden varieties of swedes, both of the white and yellow fleshed kinds, are of milder flavour than the field varieties, Laing's Garden Swede being of general use.

Turnips and swedes thrive best on a moist, loamy soil which is fairly rich and well cultivated. Early crops are sown in rows spaced 12 inches apart, and later crops 18 inches apart, and the seedlings should be thinned out to about 5 to 8 inches apart according to whether they are early or late kinds. Turnips and swedes for storage should be lifted during October, before severe frosts occur, and stored in a small clamp in the open or in ashes or sand in a cool shed. Swedes, being much hardier than turnips, are easier to store successfully. If a crop of turnip-tops is wanted for the spring, seed is sown in the previous July or August and the plants are left unthinned through the winter. As the plants have only formed small roots, they usually suffer little harm from hard weather. The turnip-tops are generally ready by March.

See also ARABLE CROPS; VEGETABLE GARDEN.

ROSES. 1. HISTORY. This large group of flowering plants belongs to the family *Rosaceae*, to which also belong the apple, cotoneaster, hawthorn, pear, plum, spiraea, strawberry, and many others. Wild ROSES (q.v. Vol. II) are found only in the northern hemisphere, in regions as far apart as North America, Mexico, Abyssinia, and Tibet. Botanists have always found it difficult to agree on the exact number of species, as wild roses cross with oné another so readily.

The name 'rose' is almost the same in many languages: in Danish, English, French, German, and Norwegian, its name is *Rose*; in Italian, Latin, Portuguese, Spanish, and Russian, it is *Rosa*.

Quite recently fossilized roses perhaps at least 35 million years old were discovered in Oregon, U.S.A., and traces of them in Stone Age deposits have been found in England, but of species not now known. The Greeks were probably the first nation to record the rose. In the *Iliad* Homer refers to the rose oils with which the goddess Aphrodite anointed the dead Hector. In the 5th century B.C. an ode was written to the rose; and rather later the historian Herodotus mentions a rose with sixty petals, exceeding all others in fragrance: this may have been *Rosa centifolia*, the Cabbage or Provence Rose.

Theophrastus, sometimes known as the Father of Botany, a pupil of Plato and Aristotle in the 4th century B.C., included the rose in his *Enquiry to Plants*. '. . . If the rose is burnt, or cut over, it bears better flowers; for then, they say, the roses are improved.' This is probably the earliest surviving reference to pruning.

The Romans induced roses and lilies to bloom in December by constructing hot-houses, heated by tubes filled with water. Roses played a prominent part in all Roman festive gatherings, couches, floors, tables, and even cups of wine being smothered in rose petals.

The rose has also religious associations in the Christian Church. It became the emblem of Christian martyrdom. Churches and cathedrals were decorated with carvings and paintings of roses—the rose window at Exeter Cathedral being one of many examples to be found in England and on the Continent. It has always been a popular heraldic emblem, as well as a favourite badge of English kings and queens. Queen Elizabeth had a Tudor Rose with the Latin motto *Rosa sine spina* (a rose without a thorn).

In the first catalogue of garden plants published by John Gerard in 1597, nine different roses, mainly summer flowering, are described; and it is probable that there were, at any rate in Britain, very few additional varieties grown until the late 18th century. In 1789 *Rosa chinensis* was brought from China. From this rose, often known as the Monthly Rose, have come most of our modern perpetual-flowering roses. In a sheltered corner, the bright pink flowers are produced without a break from May to November.

The Empress Josephine of France established a rose-garden at Malmaison in the early 19th century, where several hundred different sorts were grown. She encouraged nurserymen to raise still more varieties, and as the result of crosses between *Rosa chinensis* and other types,

N. P. Harvey

A HYBRID TEA ROSE, GORDON EDDIE

It has orange-red markings on a buff orange ground

the hybrid perpetuals were evolved. They were not, however, perpetual flowering, but bloomed spasmodically in autumn; and there were no real yellow varieties.

From another Chinese species, *Rosa odorata*, the tea-roses were developed. They are of beautiful form and soft colour, but are only half-hardy and are difficult to grow well in Britain, though in warm climates, such as that of southern California, they do well. The tea-roses crossed with the hybrid perpetuals produced the hybrid teas—the most popular class of rose today.

2. HYBRID TEAS. These vary from double flowers with plenty of petals, such as Dame Edith Helen and Red Ensign, to varieties with fewer petals, like President Herbert Hoover. Until comparatively recently the more richly coloured varieties lacked sufficient petals and were often of poor shape, but plant breeders are now overcoming these defects. The most popular type nowadays is the long, pointed flower with plenty of petals. The cup-shaped bloom, as seen in Home Sweet Home and Dickson's Perfection, is less popular.

Hybrid teas vary in height from 1½ to 4 feet,

according to variety and method of pruning. The colours include crimsons, scarlets, pinks, whites, yellows, and endless combinations of these. New varieties are always appearing. No blue roses are yet known, but Grey Pearl, raised in Ireland, is a step in this direction. Another new colour variety is the pure geranium scarlet, Independence, of German origin. The French rose Peace, a lovely yellow rose, is important because of its exceptionally vigorous growth and marked resistance to disease.

The pink hybrid teas succeed on practically any soil; the reds often prefer a fairly moist atmosphere; the yellows and whites a dry situation; the multi-colours prefer rich, well drained land.

Hybrid teas and polyantha roses are grown either as bushes or as standards—a standard being simply a bush variety on a long stem, produced by budding the variety wanted on to a long upright cane of briar or *Rosa rugosa* (*see* PLANT PROPAGATION).

3. POLYANTHA ROSES. The dwarf polyanthas or polyantha pompons were produced by crossing *Rosa multiflora* (many-flowered) with *R. chinensis*. They do not grow more than 2 feet in height and are exceptionally hardy, producing clusters of blooms very freely. They are now, however, being supplanted by the hybrid polyanthas. These are crosses between polyantha pompons and hybrid teas, and are known in America as Floribundas. They are taller than the polyantha pompons, and the individual flowers are larger. They continue to flower from June to October and are invaluable where quantity of bloom rather than quality is wanted. One of the latest additions is the American variety, Fashion, a luminous salmon pink, a shade hitherto unknown in roses. There are at present no yellow polyantha roses which hold their colour in hot weather.

4. CLIMBERS AND RAMBLERS. These are derived from various species, including *Rosa Wichuraiana* and *R. multiflora*. Climbers make a permanent framework of growth, the flowers coming from side shoots off the old canes. Ramblers, on the other hand, flower entirely on the new canes, the last year's canes being cut down to the ground after flowering in the autumn. Climbers and ramblers are suitable for pillars, arches, pergolas, and walls, though varieties of the Dorothy Perkins type must not be planted against walls or mildew will attack

N. P. Harvey

A HYBRID POLYANTHA ROSE, FRENSHAM, WITH CRIMSON
FLOWERS

N. P. Harvey

A CLIMBING ROSE, AUSTRIAN COPPER, WITH ORANGE
FLOWER

them. Certain varieties flower mainly on up-right growths, others on side-shoots; some, being only of semi-climbing habit, need a good deal of support (*see* CLIMBING PLANTS, GARDEN).

Recently some of the old-fashioned varieties of roses, such as the centifolias (hundred-flowered), pink and white damask roses, moss roses, and others, have come back into fashion. Though many are only summer flowering, they have an informal beauty distinct from modern bush roses. They need very little pruning or feeding, but often demand a good deal of space.

5. CULTIVATION. A clay soil is not necessary for roses; any land in good heart (that is, containing plenty of nourishment) will grow satisfactory roses, though perfect drainage is essential and a sunny, open position is best. Roses are planted at any time when the weather is mild from November to March, and pruning of both newly planted and established trees is done in early April. The method of PRUNING (q.v.) varies according to the class of rose and the variety; the hybrid teas are pruned comparatively hard, and reduced each year to a

specified number of buds; most other roses are cut back much less severely. Established trees may be fed with farmyard manure or artificial fertilizers in summer. Manure need never be spread on the rose beds in winter to protect the plants, as they are quite hardy enough to stand severe weather.

The chief pests are APHIDS (q.v.) and caterpillars (*see* BUTTERFLY AND MOTH PESTS). Aphids are destroyed by dusting or spraying with BHC, derris, or nicotine; DDT or nicotine is probably best for caterpillars. The fungus disease, black spot, is a serious rose disease most prevalent in a wet summer and very difficult to eradicate. Infected foliage and wood should be cut away and burned, and the beds mulched with lawn mowings during the summer. Spraying with thiram (TMT) or colloidal copper checks the disease to some extent. A humid atmosphere encourages the fungus disease, mildew, for which sulphur and thiram sprays are the best treatment (*see* INSECTICIDES). Many roses are resistant to disease attack, but no variety is absolutely immune.

THE ROSE GARDEN AT BROUGHTON CASTLE, OXFORDSHIRE

Roses are propagated by budding or by cuttings. Budding is the usual commercial method, as a shoot which provides several buds only makes a single cutting. Cuttings take longer to reach the flowering stage than budded roses, and it is doubtful whether they are as long lived (*see* PLANT PROPAGATION).

While many modern roses have very little scent, varieties such as Crimson Glory, Home Sweet Home, Polly, Red Ensign, and The Doctor are as fragrant as any of the old-fashioned sorts. Most people, in fact, remember only the best of the older varieties, yet today, if the right varieties are selected, there is a wider range of scents.

In the U.S.A., rose hedges—or, as they are called, fences—are being tried as surrounds for fields. The plants used are of the *Rosa multiflora* type. Cattle cannot push through a good rose fence, which at the same time provides welcome cover for game.

See also CLIMBING PLANTS; FLOWERING SHRUBS; PRUNING.

See also Vol. II: ROSES.

ROTATION OF CROPS. When a field does not grow the same crop every year, the order (or sequence) in which the different crops follow one another is called a 'rotation'. Thus, a rotation of crops is simply a sequence extending over several years, and planned in that order for definite reasons. Certain crops, if grown too often on the same land, become after a few years poor and unprofitable. When potatoes or sugar-beet, for example, are grown continuously in the same field, a pest called the root EEL-WORM (q.v.) will in all probability become prevalent in the soil, and the land is said to be potato or beet 'sick'. The land must then be rested from potatoes or sugar-beet for some years to allow time for the pest to die out. Corn crops, too, are likely to suffer from some of the PESTS AND DISEASES (q.v.) peculiar to cereal crops if grown frequently on the same land. To avoid such troubles, several different sorts of crops are grown, and these are arranged in such a way that no crop comes too often on the same land. Though the danger of disease is the main reason for having a rotation, it is not the only one, as will be shown later.

The need for growing crops in a rotation has

not always been appreciated. In early times, a patch of land would be cleared from the forest, and cultivated and cropped repeatedly with corn until the fertility was exhausted. Then the farmer would move to a piece of virgin land, and crop this in the same way. By the time the fertility of this was exhausted, the first piece might have recovered, through being rested, and could be cropped once more. Thus, nature forced man to adopt a simple rotation—a crop followed by a rest period. In isolated parts of Scandinavia and Scotland, as well as in many other parts of the world, this primitive form of cropping, called 'shifting cultivation', is still practised.

To have the land idle for a number of years, however, is not making best use of the soil, and even by Roman times farmers had improved upon this method. The Romans introduced into Britain a 3-year rotation (wheat, beans, bare fallow), during the third year of which the land was cultivated but not cropped. This system continued to be practised for some 1,600 years, until the introduction of turnips and clover from the Continent in the 17th century made a more elaborate and intensive rotation possible, and made the bare fallow unnecessary. Though the old three-course system still remained on some of the heavy clay land in various parts of the country, in general it gave place to the four-course rotation which, because it was first adopted to any extent in Norfolk, has always been known as the Norfolk Four-Course Rotation. Here the order is roots (turnips), barley, clover, wheat—and this illustrates the principles of most rotation systems of cropping today.

Its introduction revolutionized farming. The turnip crop is grown in widely spaced rows that makes horse and hand-hoeing possible, and this cultivation improves the condition of the soil and prevents the growth of weeds. Moreover, the turnip crop needs generous feeding with farm-yard manure and fertilizers, and some of this plant food remains in the soil for the crops that follow. Also, it is a custom, at one time very common, to allow sheep to eat the turnips where they grow, and the dung and urine from the animals enrich the land (*see* ROOT CROPS). Thus, the barley crop can follow roots without the addition of any more plant food. The barley makes a good 'nurse crop' (*see* LEYS) for the clover and grasses that follow it, and the clover, being a LEGUMINOUS CROP (q.v.), can capture

nitrogen from the air, thus preparing the way for the wheat that is the fourth course in the rotation. By now the land needs cleaning again, and the roots that follow the wheat make this possible.

The credit for this rotation is not one man's alone. There were those who, travelling abroad, were inquisitive enough to find out about the turnips and the clover; those who were enterprising and grew these 'strange' crops at home; and, not least, Jethro Tull who designed the first seed drill that really worked, and so made it possible to sow the turnips in rows.

Because there are many types of soil and many different conditions of farming, a number of other rotations are needed, however well designed the four-course rotation may be. In districts of high rainfall, for instance, less corn growing and more livestock farming will be practised. Then the four-course may be lengthened into a five or six-course by allowing the clover ley to grow on for two or more years (*see* LEYS). The rotation then becomes: roots, barley, clover, clover, clover, wheat. The clover is generally mixed with grasses, and the combination is referred to as 'seeds'. In contrast to this, in the drier parts of the country, where corn growing is favoured, the four-course is lengthened into a five-course, as follows: roots, barley, seeds, wheat, oats. Often, in place of turnips, potatoes and sugar-beet will be grown; but this does not affect the rotation, since these crops are cultivated in much the same way as turnips, swedes, and mangolds (collectively referred to as 'roots'). At all times the farmer must be ready to alter his rotation, as occasion demands, in order to suit market prices, supplies of labour, and the condition of the soil. The principles, however, must always be obeyed, if the land is to remain clean and fertile—what the farmer calls 'in good heart'.

In some rotations there is a period of several months between the harvesting of the corn crop and the sowing of the following root crop, and in some districts this time is used for growing a rapidly maturing crop, such as crimson clover (trifolium), vetches, or green turnips, to get extra fodder for sheep or cattle without interfering with the normal crops in the rotation. The snatching of a crop in this manner is known as 'catch-cropping', the crops being called 'catch crops'. In Wiltshire, Hampshire, and elsewhere the flocks of sheep that graze the Downs in summer need a great deal of winter fodder;

so catch-cropping is common, and the rotations are altered to include many such crops. The Wiltshire rotation becomes: first year, winter rye or vetches eaten off by sheep in the early spring to allow the land to be broken up in time to sow turnips and swedes, which will also be eaten on the land; second year, barley; third year, clover and grasses; fourth year, wheat; fifth year, winter rye or vetches, again eaten off by sheep, and the land sown with late turnips; sixth year (after the turnips have been eaten off), early turnips again, eaten off by sheep; seventh year, wheat; eighth year, barley. The rotation can be still further extended by leaving the seeds down for more than one year. This Wiltshire rotation, in spite of its apparent complicated structure, is founded on the basic Norfolk four-course.

The same general principles of crop rotation are carried out in the garden (*see* VEGETABLE GARDEN).

See also ARABLE CROPS; AGRICULTURE, HISTORY OF.

ROUNDWORMS, *see* PARASITIC WORMS.

ROYAL AGRICULTURAL SOCIETY, *see* AGRICULTURAL SHOWS.

ROYAL SHOW, *see* AGRICULTURAL SHOWS.

RUBBER. This is obtained from a white, milky juice called 'latex' which is found in several plants, including the ordinary dandelion, though usually in too small quantities to be of any use for industry. Nearly all the natural rubber that we use is obtained from a tree called *Hevea brasiliensis*, or the Para rubber tree, which grows wild in the jungles of Brazil, in Colombia, and in Peru and Bolivia. There is also a Central American tree from which the yield is small, and from time to time rubber has been collected from the wild trees in the Congo forests, in Africa. Another small source of rubber is the Gutta Percha tree of Malaya and the East Indies. Rubber was used for many centuries by the Indians of South and Central America before European travellers became acquainted with it during the 16th and 17th centuries. It remained scarce and costly, however, for many years, for the Para rubber trees are so scattered that only small quantities can be gathered by the natives. In 1876 an English botanist, Sir Henry Wickham, smuggled some of the seeds of the rubber tree out of Brazil, and these were sown in the

Paul Popper

TAPPING A RUBBER TREE

The cut is being opened with a special chisel so that the latex runs down into the cup

greenhouses at Kew Gardens. Twenty-two of the seeds were planted in Singapore, and a few in Ceylon, and from this small beginning sprang the millions of rubber trees that form the plantations of Ceylon, India, Burma, Malaya, and Indonesia. Finally, the production from the Far Eastern plantations became so great that it far exceeded the South American output, and only a small quantity of the world's rubber is now produced by the wild rubber trees of Brazil, which has turned its attention to growing other crops, such as coffee.

Rubber trees grow best in countries with hot, moist climates, where rain falls the whole year round. They are always grown from seed. Seeds are sown in nurseries and protected from wild animals, such as pigs and monkeys, by a screen of wire-netting. The seedlings grow very quickly, sprouting within a few days, and are transplanted to cleared jungle land when they are only a few months old. They are usually planted about 12 feet apart, though the practice varies in different places. Until recently, the highest yields of latex were obtained with trees which had been budded with wood from high yielding trees when their stems were 1 or 2 inches in diameter. Recently, however, seed from specially selected trees, called 'clonal seed', has been developed. It gives excellent yields without the labour of grafting. Between 100 and 200 trees are normally planted per acre, and as the trees grow they are thinned out until only half remain. 'Cover crops' of trailing leguminous plants between the rubber trees help to prevent the soil being carried away by rain and wind, and also help to keep the ground free from weeds. In 4 years' time the trees are often 30 feet high, and big enough to be 'tapped'.

The latex circulates in channels throughout the tree, except in the true wood. If a groove is cut into the bast of the stem, the latex flows out and can be collected. This is 'tapping' the tree. The grooves are cut with a very sharp curved chisel, gouge, or similar tool, at a height of 2 to 4 feet up the trunk, and often run half-way round the tree. They are marked out carefully so that the latex that oozes out runs freely along them to a downward channel. At the bottom of this channel a little metal spout is hammered into the bark, and below this is hung a cup of metal or smooth pottery. Every second day a tapper visits the tree and opens up the cut with his chisel. A few hours later he comes back with

a bucket and empties into it the latex that has run out of the groove, down the spout, and so into the cup. The tapping is very skilled work, and a careless tapper will damage the tree or destroy the bark faster than it grows again. Some trees continue to yield rubber for 20 or even 30 years, and on good ground the trees may become as tall as the tallest beech trees, which they somewhat resemble. About once a year each section of the rubber plantation is rested, tapping being stopped for a few months to help the trees to rebuild their stores of latex.

About half the world's rubber is grown on large estates worked by local labour, and owned by large rubber firms. But the peasants of the moist tropical countries also cultivate rubber on their small-holdings, and then prepare it for use with very simple equipment. Within a few hours of tapping a little acid is added to the latex to make it coagulate. Then, when the water is pressed out, it forms white sheets of rubber.

Several other plants besides the rubber tree contain latex, and some of these have been used as a source of rubber, especially during the Second World War when the Japanese occupied some of the Far Eastern plantations. Among these is the guayule shrub, which grows in the deserts of Mexico and Texas, and has been planted in California, Arizona, New Mexico, and Texas. A plant called *koksaghyz* or the Russian dandelion, which resembles the ordinary dandelion, has also been developed as a source of industrial rubber in Russia.

See also Tropical Agriculture.
See also Vol. VII: Rubber Manufacture.

RURAL CRAFTS. Until about 200 years ago, the villages of England were able to produce most of the things which they needed. Food was grown on the neighbouring farms; and houses, furniture, equipment, and clothes were all made by the local craftsmen. The villagers worked either in the fields or at the various country crafts. The blacksmith shod the horses and made the ironwork; the wheelwright made the carts and did other woodwork for the village; the saddler and the cobbler did the leather-work; the tiler and the thatcher covered the roofs; and a host of other craftsmen produced such things as baskets, hurdles, ladders, bricks, bowls, furniture, cloth, and so on. In most villages there was a wide choice of crafts to which boys could be apprenticed with the prospect of earning their

Paul Popper

RUBBER SPREAD TO DRY AFTER BEING FORMED INTO SHEETS

Rural Industries Bureau

MAKING THE TEETH FOR A HAY RAKE
Square pieces of wood are forced through a metal tube which cuts off their corners

living in their own neighbourhood by applying their skill to local materials: the soil, wood, leather, clay, straw, and iron.

During the 18th century this way of life, which had persisted for many hundreds of years, began to change rapidly. New methods of farming which increased the yield of the land were adopted (*see* AGRICULTURAL IMPROVERS). Landowners secured Acts of Parliament which allowed them to enclose the common lands on which the villagers used to grow much of their food (*see* OPEN FIELDS AND ENCLOSURES). At the same time the practice of producing goods in little factories in the towns gradually replaced the old system whereby the work was done by cottagers in their own homes (*see* DOMESTIC SYSTEM, Vol. VII).

These developments made it much less easy for the village craftsmen to earn their living. In many cases they had to buy food which previously they had grown on the common lands; and their families could no longer rely on their cottage industries for additional money. The result was that many people had to go to the towns to find work, which they did in the new factories, and the farmers had to sell more of their produce and buy more goods in the towns.

Although this process has continued through the last century up to the present day, neither the farmer nor his neighbours have dispensed entirely with the rural craftsmen. Farming is an industry of infinite variety, and most farmers want some implements and vehicles made to meet their own particular needs; they also want repairs done on the spot. The local craftsman has an accurate knowledge of the needs of the farmers in his neighbourhood, and he makes it his business to see that the farmer has what suits the lie of his own land or his own personal way of doing things. In an emergency the craftsman will make or mend outside normal working hours, because he understands the needs of the farmers of his own village who share his social life. The old tradition of helping each other is still strong in country life and is one that ties the craftsman to the farmer.

For generations the blacksmith in the village forge has served local farmers, shoeing their horses, making their agricultural implements, their gates, and the ironwork for their vehicles or buildings. But the modern farmer with a mechanized farm needs a modern blacksmith. Consequently the village smithy today contains far more than just a forge and anvil. The smith, in order to provide an efficient service to agriculture, has added to his traditional skill on the anvil a mastery of gas and arc WELDING (q.v. Vol. VIII). In many ways he is an example of a rural craftsman who has married his ancient craft to modern science and so continued to provide an essential service (see SHOEING).

It is true that many of the implements now used by farmers are made in factories and sold to the farmer through an agricultural engineer. But the repairs to them can often be done promptly, cheaply, and efficiently in the village workshop. When a binder breaks down in the harvest field, the farmer wants it repaired immediately and on the spot and cannot wait for a service van to come from the nearest engineer or agent. In addition to this the farmer wants metalwork for his trailers and frames for certain types of buildings.

The country woodworkers, of whom the WHEELWRIGHT (q.v.) is chief, make a number of useful things. It is the boast of the wheelwright that besides undertaking most of the carpentry and joinery which the countryman may need, he can still make or repair a wooden wheel. The traditional wagon is not in general use today; but carts of the old pattern are still occasionally built (see FARM VEHICLES), and the country wheelwright also makes modern trailers to be drawn by tractors, and he makes them, not mass produced, but designed to suit the individual needs of the farmer.

Although horses are not now used so much on farms, they still have their part to play. Horses need harness, and farmers can usually find a saddler in the village or in the nearest market town, where harness can be repaired.

The blacksmith, the wheelwright, and the saddler are the rural craftsmen most closely connected with the farmer, but there are others.

In those districts where sheep are kept, the farmer needs hurdles for keeping his flocks together in 'folds' in the fields. The hurdles are woven or cleft by craftsmen in woodlands where good COPPICE (q.v.) is grown, and sent to farmers over a wide area (see HURDLE-MAKING). In many parts of the country there are basket-makers who weave a great variety of light, strong baskets. They make baskets for carrying potatoes and grain, baskets for chickens, hampers for food, crates for pottery, lobster pots, and traps for eels and salmon (see BASKET-MAKING, Vol. VII).

Where there is suitable clay, there are often rural potters who make, in addition to domestic ware, plant-pots for market-gardeners. Pots made by hand usually absorb the moisture easily and so help to produce vigorous and healthy plants (see POTTERY, Vol. VII). In the same district there may be country tile and brickyards which also make land-drainage pipes. The thatcher (except the reed thatcher), like the saddler, depends on the farmer for his raw material. Thatched roofs are still a feature of rural England and thatchers today have more than enough work to do (see THATCHING). Another rural craft, nearly as important today as it has ever been, is the making of boundaries —HEDGING, DITCHING, AND WALLING (q.v.).

Rural Industries Bureau

A SADDLER STITCHING A BREECHING—THE PART OF THE HARNESS WHICH GOES ROUND THE THIGHS OF THE HORSE

Paul Popper

PORTUGUESE FISHERMEN MENDING THEIR NETS

Nets are used for many purposes on the farm and in the garden. Pigs or sheep taken to market in an open trailer are kept in by a strong net stretched over the top. A newly made stack can be kept compact until it is thatched or threshed by means of a net thrown over it. A hop garden is often protected from the prevailing winds by a net stretched on poles above the height of the hedges. The fruit-grower protects his soft fruit from birds with nets. Nets are used for catching rabbits, and for making haybags, or muzzles to prevent calves sucking. And nets, of course, are an essential part of the equipment of the fisherman.

These nets used to be made with hand-spun hemp yarn, and the equipment was an ash needle to hold the twine and a frame for gauging the mesh. The end of the net was fastened to a wall, and the twine passed round the frame,

knotted with the needle, and cast off. This quite difficult operation, once mastered, could be applied to all forms of netting. Such hand-made nets are still to be found in some places, but very rarely made from hand-spun yarn. Hemp and cotton are imported and spun by machine.

The country craftsmen provide the farmer with many of the things he needs, and these are generally of unrivalled quality and beauty. The crafts offer a livelihood in the country to many who otherwise might have to work in towns and cities. We can rightly be proud of the character of the rural craftsman and the pride that he takes in making, from start to finish, a fine and useful article with his own hands.

RYE. In Britain rye is not as important a cereal crop as it is in many other European countries, and its cultivation for grain is confined to poor, sandy soils that are unsuitable for growing the other and more valuable cereals. During the Second World War, when a large acreage of poor, derelict grassland was brought into cultivation for the first time, rye was often grown as the first crop. Rye not only grows where other cereals would fail, but is the hardiest of the cereals, and survives severe weather that would kill wheat seedlings. It germinates and establishes itself quickly, and is often grown as a forage crop for grazing by cattle or sheep; if sown in the autumn, it produces good grazing in the following February. After being grazed, provided the animals have not been kept on it too long, the plants recover sufficiently to come to harvest in the normal way. The crop is also grown as a catch crop (*see* ROTATION OF CROPS).

The greater part of the grain is used for livestock feeding, though a proportion is needed for making crisp bread. The long, fine, resilient straw is used for thatching roofs and for mak-

Harold Bastin

RYE

ing straw hats. It is too coarse and indigestible to be used as fodder. There are very few distinct varieties of rye, for the plants are cross-fertilized, and varieties do not, therefore, remain true to type for long.

In the rotation rye is usually grown in place of wheat or oats. Although it will grow under very poor conditions, its yields are much increased by applications of lime and fertilizers. Nitrogenous fertilizers, however, are seldom applied. The seed is sown either in September or October, or in February or March, 8 stone of seed being needed per acre for the early sowings and 12 stone for the later. The cultivation and methods of sowing are the same as for wheat. Rye is the first cereal to ripen for harvest, and is cut when dead ripe. It need not stay in the stook long, for the sheaves dry out quickly, and it is generally stacked within a week of cutting. An average crop yields 12 to 16 cwt. of grain with 30 to 40 cwt. of straw per acre.

S

SADDLER, *see* RURAL CRAFTS.

SAGE, *see* HERBS, GARDEN.

SAGO, *see* PALM TREES.

SAINFOIN, *see* LEGUMINOUS CROPS.

SALAD CROPS. 1. LETTUCE. The garden lettuce (*Lactuca sativa*) is the most important of the salad crops, and is grown throughout the world wherever the climate allows. It has been cultivated since very early times and was mentioned by writers as long ago as 500 B.C. The English name 'lettuce' came apparently from the French *laitue* (*lait* = milk), itself probably derived from the Latin *lactuca*. The name refers to the plant's milk-like juice. The garden lettuce has probably been bred from the wild lettuce (*Lactuca virosa*), for the two have many characteristics in common.

Naturally a plant that has been cultivated for so long has not only various types but a great many varieties of each type. The most commonly grown are those that form 'hearts' or blanched centres; these are the cabbage-headed types (the smooth-leaved and the crisp curled-leaved) and the Cos or Romaine type. Trocadero and All-the-Year-Round are well-known British varieties of the smooth-leaved cabbage type (often called butter lettuces), and Wonderful and Iceberg are varieties of the curled-leaved type. Typical varieties of the Cos type are Paris White, Paris Green, Giant White, and Bath Cos. American Gathering and Grand Rapids are typical varieties of the leaf or bunching lettuces, which do not form a 'heart' but have frilly leaves loosely bunched together so that the leaves of the whole plant are green. They are less popular in Britain than in America.

Lettuces are easily grown and can be made available throughout the year by the skilful management of successive crops in the open and the use of frames or cloches for protection in winter and early spring. In hot, dry weather the plants tend to run to seed quickly, so it is important to maintain a succession by sowing seed at frequent intervals. Plants raised under glass can be planted out to provide early lettuces, but for the later crops the seed is sown where the plants are to mature and the seedlings thinned to a suitable spacing, as it is thought that seedlings which are not disturbed by transplanting are less likely to 'bolt'—run to seed.

Lettuces do best in cool, moist conditions and in fertile soil which contains plenty of moisture-holding humus. In dry weather the plants need frequent watering, and they respond well to a light application of a nitrogenous fertilizer, such as nitro-chalk or nitrate of soda.

Lettuce crops are sometimes attacked by the Lettuce Aphid which not only does harm itself but also acts as a carrier of the virus disease Mosaic. Lettuces also suffer from the fungus diseases Grey Mould which rots the plants' stems and Ring Spot which makes rusty markings on the leaves (*see* PLANT DISEASES).

2. ENDIVE (*Cichorium Endivia*) is an annual plant grown as a salad vegetable. It is not very common, probably because the leaves have a

Chase Protected Cultivation
CABBAGE AND COS LETTUCES GROWING UNDER CLOCHES
Seeds were planted in October and the photograph was taken the following March

bitter taste unless they are thoroughly blanched after the plant is fully developed. The name comes from the French, though when the plant was first cultivated is not known. Wild species of plants resembling the cultivated endive are found in the eastern Mediterranean region. Two types of endive are mainly grown, the less hardy Green-curled for autumn use, and the hardier Batavian for winter use.

Endive may be grown from seed, sown in rich soil in the open from April onwards, and later thinned or transplanted; the main sowings for autumn and winter supplies are made from June to August. The leaves are blanched in various ways: the fully grown plants are covered with large pots or boards to exclude light; or the leaves are tied up like those of cos lettuce to blanch the centres; or sometimes the plants are lifted carefully and placed close together in a darkened frame or in a dark cellar. Endive is also sometimes grown under cloches which are covered completely with sacking or other material to cause blanching as the plants become fully grown.

3. CHICORY (*Cichorium Intybus*) has several forms, each used for a different purpose. It is often grown in the fields as a fodder crop, its beautiful blue flowers making it noticeable. The Large Rooted or Magdeburg chicory is grown for its roots, which are dried, roasted, and ground to provide the chicory that is mixed with coffee. The garden kinds of chicory, however, which are used both as a salad and as a vegetable, are grown in such a special way that they are quite different to look at.

The French garden chicory, called *Barbe de Capucin*, is an important ingredient of French salads. The Brussels or Witloof chicory has heads which are blanched to use as a vegetable, like seakale, mainly in the early months of the year.

Both types of chicory are grown in the same way. The seed is sown during April or May in rows 12 inches apart, and the plants, which are spaced out 6–9 inches apart, are left to grow until October when the leaves die down. For salad chicory the roots, which sometimes resemble small parsnips, are then lifted and stored in sand or soil in a cool shed until needed for forcing. They are easily forced into growth in a warm greenhouse if they are inserted in soil or sand in a large deep box covered with boards to keep out the light. Also they can be placed

Amateur Gardening
'BRUSSELS' CHICORY AFTER BLANCHING

in beds under the staging of the greenhouse near the hot-water pipes, provided the light can be excluded. Darkness is essential for blanching the leaves and shoots.

The Brussels or Witloof chicory is forced in a specially constructed bed where warmth can be maintained either by hot-water pipes or by a hot bed of fermenting stable manure. In order to obtain the compact blanched heads (*chicons*), the roots are placed close together and covered with at least 6 inches of fine light soil. Later crops of chicory (April–May period) may be grown without the use of heat by packing the roots in a trench 18 inches deep and covering them with a thick layer of fine soil and then with a layer of straw or stable litter. The chicory season extends in the main from February to April.

4. RADISH (*Raphanus sativus*) is grown for its crisp, tender root which is eaten raw. Little is known about its origin. The name comes from the Latin *radix*, a root. The plant is an annual and belongs to the cabbage family. Some varieties have round or turnip-shaped roots, others oval or olive-shaped roots, and yet others long, tapering roots. A distinct type known as winter radish has larger roots which are white, black, or red.

The ordinary spring and summer radishes, of which Scarlet Globe, French Breakfast, Scarlet Turnip-Rooted, and Icicle are representative varieties, are easily grown, provided that the soil is rich enough to enable the plants to develop quickly. Radishes are hardy and thrive best under cool, moist conditions. They are sown in the open, either broadcast or in drills, at intervals of 10 days from early March onwards. Early crops are obtained by sowing the seed in frames or glasshouses, or under cloches. They are ready for use in from 3 to 6 weeks from sowing according to weather conditions. Winter radishes are sown in June or July, and the seedlings thinned to about 2 inches apart; these can be gathered and used from September onwards, and can be stored like turnips.

5. MUSTARD AND CRESS. These are the seedlings of the white mustard (*Brassica hirta*) and the garden cress (*Lepidium sativum*), both annual plants of the cabbage family, the former a native of Europe and the latter of Asia. Excellent crops of mustard and cress can be grown so long as there is warmth, protection, and a moist rich soil. The cress, however, must be sown several days before the mustard as it is the slower to germinate. For early crops the seed is sown in rich soil in shallow boxes or seed trays in a warm greenhouse or frame with a temperature of about 60° F. After the soil has been thoroughly wetted, the seed is broadcast thickly over the surface and is not covered with soil. The boxes are covered with sacking or hessian until after the seedlings have made about 1 inch of growth. The crops are cut for use while the seedlings are still in the seed-leaf stage of growth. For later supplies during the summer the seed can be sown in an open border, but some protection is needed from heavy rain.

6. CORN SALAD. The small annual plant, *Valerianella olitoria*, sometimes known as 'lamb's lettuce' or 'fetticus', is found wild in corn fields (hence the name) and in waste places in southern Europe, including parts of Britain. It is also grown in gardens as a fresh green salad, and is useful during the autumn and early winter when other salad vegetables may be scarce. Corn salad grows very quickly in cool showery weather, but is less successful in a dry season. Two main varieties are known, one with large, light-green leaves and the other with dark-green leaves. The seed is sown on well-cultivated fertile soil at intervals during the summer, and is

sown thinly in drills spaced 6 to 9 inches apart. The seedlings are thinned to 6 inches apart. The crop is gathered by cutting the whole plant with its rosette of leaves just above soil level.

See also WATERCRESS.

SALMON FISHING. The salmon is regarded as the finest sporting fish of inland waters by all fly-fishermen, who show much ingenuity in fashioning a 'fly' which will attract it. As an alternative to the fly, some sportsmen use a spinner with an artificial minnow, or a real fish of some other species. Rod lines are made of silk with a waterproof dressing (*see* ANGLING, FRESHWATER, Vol. IX). But salmon fishing is also a big industry, especially in the U.S.A. and Canada, where the river fisheries are connected with large canning factories. American canned salmon is exported to all parts of the world. When salmon go up river to spawn, they may be caught in nets or weirs. A seine or encircling net is used wherever a suitable sandy beach comes below a rapid or anything else that obstructs the salmon's ascent. The trapped fish, once they have been encircled, are quickly hauled out of the river and brought to the bank.

In the western rivers of the U.S.A. and Canada, both seine nets and weirs are used to capture salmon in very large numbers as they fight their way upstream to the spawning-beds. One end of a seine net is dropped overboard from a motor-boat and fastened to a buoy. Then, as the boat circles round the fish, the crew let out the seine net. When the circle is complete, the ropes are hauled in, and the net closed like a purse, with great numbers of fish within. The salmon are drawn to the surface, baled out, and dropped into the boat's hold. When the hold is full, the motor-boat makes for the cannery where the fish are unloaded and fed to the machines. In some places a large revolving water-wheel lifts the struggling fish out of the river, and decants them into an open trough which carries them direct to the cannery.

In the estuaries of rivers in the south of Scotland a fence of stakes is often set in the stream to form a fishing-weir, and this drives the fish into a narrow passage or trap. A fisherman sits above this passage with his net set across it. When a fish arrives at this spot, he feels a quiver in his net, and then he quickly raises the net and takes out the fish. Another method used in the

Mrs. Nicholas Morant

LETTING OUT A SEINE NET FOR SALMON FISHING OFF VANCOUVER ISLAND

sea round the north of Scotland and in Norwegian waters is a buoyed 'leader net' which guides the fish into a bag-shaped net, from which there is little chance of escape.

On the north-east coast of England drift-nets are used a great deal to catch salmon living in the open sea. Some are used in the ordinary manner and are not anchored, but sometimes one end of the net is made fast on shore. The foot rope having been well weighted with stones, the main part of the net is set in such a way that it curves in on one side in the form of a hook. The hook greatly increases the catching power of these nets, which hold the fish as they attempt to pass through the meshes.

In rivers flowing into the lower reaches of the Severn, a funnel-shaped wicker trap called a 'putcher' or 'butt' is used. After passing through the wide mouth (about 2½ feet in diameter), the salmon becomes jammed by the head in the narrow end of the trap and dies by suffocation.

See also FISHING INDUSTRY; FISHING METHODS.
See also Vol. II: SALMON.

SALSIFY. This root vegetable has an attractive flavour, not unlike asparagus, which is sometimes compared to oyster, hence its popular name of vegetable oyster. Salsify is a hardy perennial plant, *Tragopogon porrifolius*, belonging to the daisy family; it is found wild in European fields, and occasionally in Britain where it is known as purple goat's beard. It produces long yellowish-white tap roots which are very nutritious when suitably cooked. It is not commonly grown in Britain, though some people are particularly fond of it. It is cultivated in the same way as the PARSNIP (q.v.), but usually the roots are lifted in the autumn and stored in sand under cover.

Another root vegetable, scorzonera (*Scorzonera hispanica*), sometimes called black salsify and popularly known as viper's grass, belongs to the same family as salsify, and is cultivated in the same way. It also is not often grown in gardens in Britain. The name comes from the Italian *scorza* 'bark', and *nera* 'black', referring to the long, slender tap-roots which are blackish in colour.

They have a sweetish delicate flavour when cooked.

SARDINES, *see* FISHING INDUSTRY, section 2.

SAVOYS, *see* CABBAGE CROPS, FIELD.

SAWMILLS, *see* LOGGING; LUMBER CAMPS.

SCARECROWS, *see* VERMIN, section 7.

SCYTHES, *see* HAND TOOLS.

SEAKALE (*Crambe maritima*). The use of this perennial seashore plant as a vegetable was developed in Britain, and it is still not much grown in other countries. The blanched leaf-stalks, main stem, and leaves of the plant are used in the spring. In former times it was customary to cover with sand or pebbles the dormant crowns of plants where they grew on the seashores of Devon and Dorset in order to obtain the blanched vegetable; about 2 centuries ago, however, the plant was taken into gardens for cultivation. Seakale, or sea-cole, is a member of the Brassica family; the flowers, which are white, resemble those of the cabbage.

Seakale is usually grown in a permanent bed, like rhubarb and asparagus. The plant is her-baceous in habit, developing a thick fleshy root-stock, and its growth dies down in the autumn. In the garden the crown of the plant is covered in late winter with fine earth or ashes, and then a seakale pot or a box (with a loose lid so that the plant's growth can be watched) is placed over the whole plant. The whole is then covered with leaves, stable litter, or other decaying material in order to create internal warmth which forces the plant into early growth. The seakale is cut for use from February to June by taking off the whole of the blanched growth at its base. This does not destroy the plant, for the apex of the thick rootstock develops new buds for the renewal of growth.

Market-gardeners grow seakale roots in the open field and lift them in the autumn. They force the roots into growth in specially designed, dark forcing-sheds which are heated by hot-water pipes. Darkened frames and forcing-pits also are used for forcing seakale. After forcing, the roots are discarded, a new crop of roots for the following season being grown from root cuttings taken in the autumn. Thus, commercial seakale growing is a continuous process.

In gardens, seakale may be grown from seed or propagated from root cuttings (pieces of root about 4 inches long). In the latter case the seakale may be cut for use in the second year, but when grown from seed it cannot be used until the third year. The seed is sown in shallow drills in a seed-bed and the seedlings thinned to a distance of about 6 inches. The following spring, they are replanted in the well-prepared permanent seakale bed. Three roots may be planted together at spacings of $1\frac{1}{2}$ to 2 feet in rows spaced $2\frac{1}{2}$ to 3 feet apart. When root cuttings are used, they are either planted direct in the permanent bed or grown in a propagation bed for a year and transplanted in the second year. It is possible, of course, to use the market-garden method in an ordinary garden.

SEAKALE BEET, *see* SPINACH CROPS, section 3.

SEED-GROWING. 1. Britain has always grown a large proportion of the seeds needed by her farmers and gardeners. British-grown mangold, swede, and turnip seed is famous; much of her cereal seed is grown at home; and Ayrshire ryegrass, Scottish timothy grass, and Kentish wild white clover are well-known names. On the other hand, a good deal of seed is

Sutton and Sons

SEAKALE GROWN IN A FORCING SHED

TESTING SEEDS IN A LABORATORY
On the left the seeds are being tested for purity. Under the glass covers counted samples of seed are being tested for germinating power

imported from countries where good weather at harvest time is more certain. Sugar-beet seed used to come from Germany, Holland, France, and Belgium; Canada and New Zealand export the seeds of herbage plants such as grasses, clover, and lucerne; and from the famous plant-breeding station at Svalof in Sweden come excellent varieties of all farm crops. During the Second World War Britain could not import as much seed as before, and so had to provide for herself; in consequence, the growing of home-grown seeds increased, with varieties particularly well suited to the climate and soils. Seed crops grow best in a district with a sunny climate and a not very high summer rainfall, so that the seed ripens well. In Britain these conditions are found in the eastern counties where most large seed-farms are situated.

2. ROOT-CROP SEEDS. The main centres of seed production for mangolds, swedes, turnips, sugar-beet, carrots, kale, and kohl rabi are Lincolnshire, Bedford, Kent, and Norfolk. These plants are all biennials, so that it takes two seasons to produce a crop. Seed is sown in the spring, and selected plants are either lifted in the autumn and planted out elsewhere a yard apart, or else stored in earth clamps, to be planted out in the following spring. The plants then flower and fruit. Cross-fertilization must be prevented

if the seed is to carry those qualities for which the parent plants were selected, and no other. Therefore, a crop grown for seed must not be within 400 yards of any other crop of the same family of plants. Weeds of the same family are a danger too, and must never be allowed to grow (*see* PLANT BREEDING).

When the seed is ripe, the stalks are cut by hand with a sickle, tied into bundles, stooked to dry, and then stacked until threshing time. The threshing-machine, the flail, or the flat roller passed over the plants spread on a sheet on the ground, may be used. The threshed seed from these selected plants is called 'stock' seed. This stock is sown in order to produce similar seed in much larger quantities, and farmers contract with a seedsman to do this for him. The average yields of seed from an acre are as follows: swedes 8 cwt., turnips 10 cwt., mangolds 12 cwt., kohl rabi 2 cwt., kale 7 cwt., carrots 5 cwt., and sugar-beet 12 cwt.

3. POTATO SEED. Except when new varieties are being produced, potatoes are grown from tubers and not from seed, although the tubers are always called 'seed'. Seed potatoes should be grown in districts as free as possible from APHID PESTS (q.v.), for aphids can carry virus diseases of potatoes from one plant to another, and seed infected by the virus does not yield good crops. Hence, most seed potatoes are grown in high-lying country in the north, and in Ireland. Scotch seed has a good reputation. Stock seed is given an 'SS' certificate by the Ministry of Agriculture (or other authority, according to where the seed is produced), and this seed is used to produce the commercial stocks that are distributed to potato-growers in all parts. The stocks are graded, inspected, and given certificates: A = first quality, H = healthy.

4. CEREAL SEED. This is grown in many parts of Britain, though, as with other seeds, the eastern counties have the best conditions for producing seed with the highest germinative capacity. The plant breeder supplies stock seed from selected ears to the grower, whose job it is to produce the seed in quantity. Any 'rogues' (plants that are unlike the parent stock) must be cut off before harvest. The remainder must be good specimens, well ripened, and carefully harvested and threshed. Many farmers, especially those in a district with a 'catchy' or uncertain climate, like to buy a 'change of seed': that is, seed that was grown in another part of the country.

5. GRASS AND CLOVER SEED. The stock seed is sown (usually drilled) on clean land, usually under a cereal nurse-crop. The usual harvesting implements will serve for handling grass seed crops. A seed crop of broad red clover is generally taken from the aftermath (second crop) of a hay crop; late-flowering red clover, however, can give only the one crop. The best wild white clover seed comes from old pastures, though it is sometimes grown as a LEY (q.v.). The crop is best cut with a mower, for the plants are very short, and the heads are often collected on a cloth fastened to the back of the machine.

Good weather and very careful handling is needed to harvest these herbage crops, for the seed easily knocks out of its sheath. Yields may be: ryegrass 5 to 7 cwt., cocksfoot 5 to 6 cwt., timothy 4 cwt., red clover 260 lb., and white clover 60 to 150 lb. per acre (*see* GRASSES). The straw can be used for feeding to livestock; but as so much of the nourishment in the mature plant has gone into the seed, it is not a very valuable feed.

The growing of the various crops mentioned in this article is described in separate articles.

See also PLANT BREEDING; ARABLE CROPS.

SESAME, *see* OIL-BEARING PLANTS, section 1 *a*.

SEX LINKAGE, *see* STOCK BREEDING, section 4; POULTRY.

SHALLOTS, *see* ONION CROPS.

SHARK FISHING. Sharks are worth hunting for various reasons. Shark's oil has been found a very rich source of Vitamin A. The flesh of sharks, which is nutritious and palatable, is eaten by some native peoples, especially in the Pacific Islands; in Japan it is pounded into a paste which is in great demand; in East Africa dried strips of the flesh (batons) are marketed; in China the fins are an essential ingredient of 'shark-fin soup'. The skin, especially of the Tiger Shark and the handsome Leopard Shark, may be tanned to produce an attractive hard-wearing leather. The rest of the carcase can be turned into agricultural fertilizer. When all these uses of the shark are fully exploited, shark fishing will probably be organized on a much larger scale. At present, for the most part, only small boats are used in local fisheries.

In certain of the Pacific Islands three or four men paddle out to the shark-fishing grounds in their canoe, and when they arrive there, the headman makes a speech to the shark, flattering him and inviting him to visit his friends. One of the crew stands in the bows shaking a cane-hoop strung with half-shells of coconuts, and dangles

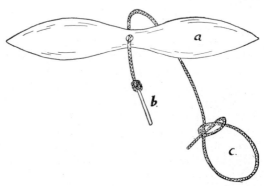

James Hornell

A SHARK NOOSE USED IN THE BISMARCK ARCHIPELAGO, NORTH OF NEW GUINEA

a. The 'retarder' which breaks the pull of the shark on the noose. *b.* The hand grip held by the fisherman. *c.* The noose which is passed over the shark's head

in the water a chunk of putrid meat. When a shark smells this 'delicacy', it swims alongside, the steersman taking care that the shark has to make its rush from astern. In the second before it reaches the bait, another man deftly slips a noose over the shark's head. A third man, standing ready with a club, strikes the shark's head a tremendous blow, which stuns it. The rest is easy: more blows are rained down on the shark, and when it struggles no longer, the crew lift it aboard.

In some islands, natives who are expert swimmers keep watch from their boat for a shark as it lies asleep with its head pushed into some large crevice in a coral-reef. When it has been sighted, one of the men slips overboard, with a rope with a noose at the end in his hands. He swims quietly down, slips the noose over the shark's tail, and returns to the surface. All hands then grasp hold of the rope and haul the great fish to the surface, where they gash its strong tail with an axe, making it easy to kill the fish with clubs.

The Arab fishers of the Kuria Muria Islands on the coast of Arabia, when they intend to catch sharks, paddle out to sea on a swimming-float made of an inflated skin. On the Malabar coast of India men go fishing in small dug-out canoes, and use a large hook baited with strong-smelling meat. When they have killed their shark, the difficulty is to get it aboard their tiny canoe. They jump overboard and cant the canoe over until it fills with water, when it is easy to slip the shark into the boat. The shark once aboard, they bail the water out of the canoe, climb aboard, and set course for home.

The natives of New Guinea use harpoons to capture the sharks found near the coast. When the fish has become exhausted by its futile struggles to get free, the fishermen paddle alongside and spear it to death (*see* HARPOONING).

See also Vol. II: SHARKS AND RAYS.

SHEARING SHEEP, *see* SHEEP SHEARING AND DIPPING.

SHEEP. 1. HISTORY AND BREEDS. Sheep have a very long history of domestication. They figure largely in biblical stories, and even today they form a considerable part of the wealth of the nomad tribes in the deserts of the Middle East and of Central Asia. There are also many sorts of wild SHEEP (q.v. Vol. II) in the world. The general opinion is that our domesticated sheep are descended from the European Moufflon which is brown in colour and grows a woolly undercoat at the base of a long hairy uppercoat. In order to produce the modern sheep with a coat almost wholly of wool, with crimped, fine, soft fibres, men have had to select, through many generations, those animals for breeding that showed this character most strongly. In Australia and South Africa sheep are bred mainly for wool, and the male sheep gives about 15 lb. at each shearing; but in Britain the emphasis is on mutton, and even the woolliest breeds do not generally yield more than 10 or 11 lb. Shetland sheep, which are nearest the Moufflon in type and still brown in colour, average only about $2\frac{1}{2}$ lb. of wool.

England has been a great sheep-breeding country since before the Norman Conquest. Through medieval times, especially in the 15th century, the wool trade formed the largest part of England's wealth (*see* WOOL INDUSTRY, MEDIE-VAL, Vol. VII). Several things led to its decline, though Britain as a whole has still a greater density of sheep than any other country in the world except New Zealand (*see* WOOL INDUSTRY, MODERN, Vol. VII). As centuries have passed, the main areas of sheep breeding have tended to move from southern England northwards into the hillier districts and westwards into Wales. The Highlands of Scotland were not colonized by sheep until the end of the 18th century. As we shall see later, sheep are important in southern England today largely because they help to keep the land fertile.

Sheep have many names, depending on sex and age and the part of the country in which they live. The most commonly used names are:

	Male	*Female*
To 6 months	Tup lamb in north Ram lamb in south Wether (castrated)	Ewe lamb
To $1\frac{1}{4}$ years and to 1st shearing	Hogg in Scotland Teg in northern England Hogget in south	Ewe hogg Ewe teg Ewe hogget
To $2\frac{1}{2}$ years	Shearling tup in north Shearling ram in south Shearling wether	Gimmer Theave (pronounced thave)
Over $2\frac{1}{2}$ years and after 2nd shearing	2-shear, 3-shear (and so on) tup or ram	Ewe

A 'cast' ewe is one sold from the flock at three or four-shear. Younger ones will be coming on to replace her, and she may at this age have lost the use of one side of her udder through disease, or if she has lived on hill ground, where the grazing is tough, her central incisor teeth may have worn down. Cast ewes which are sound in the udder are not generally sold for slaughter, but go to kinder ground where they rear one or two more crops of lambs.

There are over thirty breeds of sheep in Britain, all having special qualities adapting them to the particular area in which they live. They may be roughly divided into three main groups—the Mountain breeds, the Long-wools, and the Down and other short-woolled breeds.

Mountain breeds

Cheviot	Welsh Mountain
Scottish Blackface	Dartmoor
Rough Fell	Herdwick
Swaledale	Derbyshire Gritstone
Lonk	Shetland
Exmoor Horn	

Long-woolled breeds

Border Leicester	Lincoln Longwool
Leicester	Cotswold
Kent or Romney Marsh	South Devon
Wensleydale	Devon Longwool

Down and Short-woolled breeds

Dorset Down	Southdown
Hampshire Down	Suffolk
Oxford Down	Shropshire
Devon Closewool	Ryeland
Dorset Horn	

The original Clun Forest, Radnor, and Kerry Hill sheep are semi-upland, speckle-faced breeds of fairly close wool. The Wiltshire or Western Horn is a breed with practically no wool at all, but for crossing purposes to get early lambs it is of great value. The Penestone and the Woodlands were white-faced, mountain breeds belonging to south Yorkshire and the High Peak; they are now extinct.

The mountain breeds fall into two main groups: one of white-faced sheep, including the Cheviot, the Welsh Mountain, and the Exmoor Horn; and another of which the Scottish Blackface and its derivatives are typical. The Shetland, which came from Norway with the Vikings, is distinct from all the rest, but is classed as a mountain sheep because it lives on peaty unimproved moorlands. In their native islands the sheep come down to graze seaweed for a short time at each ebb tide.

The long-wools are all white-faced sheep, with long, fairly coarse, but very lustrous wool. Most of them carry Leicester blood in their ancestry.

The Leicester is probably of continental origin, for several early Flemish and Dutch paintings show sheep similar to them (see COLOUR PLATE opposite p. 384). The Leicester was the breed in which Robert BAKEWELL (1725-95) (q.v. Vol. V) made such remarkable improvement.

The Down breeds are dark-faced, and all carry to greater or less extent the blood of the Southdown, a small, speckly-brown-faced sheep, native to the South Downs. The breed was fixed in type and greatly improved by another far-seeing 18th-century farmer, John Ellman, of Glynde in Sussex. The Southdown and the old Norfolk Horn produced the present Suffolk, one of the most popular breeds in the whole country. At the present time the Southdown is thought to be too small for most English farms, but its wool is the finest and highest priced of all British wools except the Shetland, and the great value of the Southdown in crossing is in the early maturity of the lambs. The earliest lambs of the year are probably in Hampshire flocks, which seem to stand intensive husbandry better than any other breed. Lambs appear from Christmas time onwards.

The cross-breeding of sheep is common, and well organized. Here are two examples of popular crossing systems. (1) Scottish Blackface ewes, which can live on high exposed land, are mated to a Border Leicester tup, and the off-spring are called 'Greyfaces'. The ewes of this cross are sold on to better land where they are crossed with a Suffolk or Oxford Down tup. All the offspring from this cross are sold as fat lamb. (2) Cheviot ewes in Sutherland may be crossed with a Border Leicester tup, and the female offspring, known everywhere as 'Scotch Half-breds', are sold into the good-feeding grasslands of the southern Midlands of England. There they may be crossed with a Western Horn ram, and all the lambs will be fattened. The Hampshire Down is another famous crossing sheep. These well-organized crossing systems, starting with the hardy upland breeds, and finishing with rams of the earliest maturing breeds, are called 'stratification'. As may be imagined, the many crossing practices throughout the country mean great variety in the types of wool coming into the buyers' hands. Wool-sorting is, therefore, a skilled job (see WOOL INDUSTRY, Vol. VII).

2. HILL SHEEP. Sheep are kept on farms in many different ways and for several reasons. Take for example a sheep farm in Selkirkshire in

Farmer and Stockbreeder

BORDER LEICESTER SHEARLING TUP

Sport & General

WENSLEYDALE

Sport & General

SUFFOLK RAM LAMB

Farmer and Stockbreeder

WILTSHIRE HORN RAM

the southern uplands of Scotland: here the farmer concentrates entirely on sheep, keeping cattle for domestic use only. The uncultivated hillsides are good sheep land, carrying one ewe to 2 acres or slightly less. The breeds kept are Blackface or Cheviots, the former on 'black-top' heather hills and the latter on 'green-top' hills covered with rough grasses and sedges. The acreage of such a farm varies from 2,000 to 6,000, and the ground is divided into convenient working units, called 'hirsels', giving a shepherd from 500 to 800 sheep to manage. The divisions between the hirsels are usually those of convenience and consent between the shepherds and the farmer, who may manage the home hirsel himself. Hill sheep are noted for their ability to become 'hefted' to a particular area, that is, they

get to know the invisible boundaries. Once a stock is hefted it does not stray, so there is little difficulty in keeping the hirsels distinct. Hill sheep should spread themselves about the ground and not flock together. In this way not only do they make best use of the grazing but there is less likelihood of the soil becoming heavily infested with PARASITIC WORMS (q.v.), that in turn reinfest the sheep. It is the shepherd's daily task to get over his ground and see every sheep; he is also careful to put them up the hill each night in order to keep the lower grazing for winter, and, again, to prevent fouling of the ground. The sheep quickly learn this daily routine and tend to move upward at night of their own accord.

Lambing time is in April and the first half of

Charles Reid

CHEVIOT EWES AND LAMBS ON A SCOTTISH BORDER FARM

May, and is the shepherd's busiest time. The lambs are born on the hill, not in yards or paddocks. 'Marking' takes place in early June; this involves gathering the hirsel (that is, collecting the sheep from the hills), earmarking the lamb with the owner's own particular 'lug mark', docking the tails of the lambs, and castrating those male lambs which are not to be kept for breeding. Great care is taken to get ewes and lambs 'mothered up' again (the right ewe to the right lamb) before the flock goes back to the hill. Barren ewes and the 14-month-old hoggs are clipped at this time, but the 'milk clipping' of the ewes with lambs does not take place until July.

Hill sheep are subject to several diseases—of which braxy is one—and to attacks by the greenbottle blowfly (*see* ANIMAL DISEASES AND PARASITES). Inoculation to prevent disease, and dipping to kill the blowfly maggots, make further gatherings necessary (*see* SHEEP SHEARING AND DIPPING).

The lambs are weaned in August, and the wethers go to the sales shortly afterwards. The ewe lambs often go to some lowland farm from October to March, making the winter grazing on the hill farm less crowded.

The ewes have 2 months or more to recuperate on the hill before the tups or rams are turned out in November. 'Tupping-time' or mating time is another period of anxiety for the shepherd. The ram itself may be worth £100 (£2,000 is the record price at the Lanark Sales) and the ewes must be kept up to him so that they shall not be missed during the few hours they are 'in season', that is, ready for mating. One ram will mate with or 'serve' about 60 ewes, so a hirsel of 600 ewes will need at least 10 rams. The rams generally have their fleeces reddened with reddle (red earth mixed with mutton fat) so that when they service a ewe they mark her rump with red, and the shepherd can tell that mating has taken place. The rams stay on the hill for a month and are then brought back to a paddock on their own. The ewes have their lambs 20 to 22 weeks after mating.

Hill sheep have a good understanding of the dangers of deep snow, but the shepherd and his collies have to work exceptionally hard when there are heavy falls. Buried sheep have to be dug out, hay must be carried up to the sheep, and frequent counts made to prevent loss.

3. LOWLAND SHEEP. Low-ground flocks of Down and cross-bred types are often kept by farmers of light land for the purpose of eating off a crop on the ground, and thus treading and manuring the soil to bring it into condition for growing a crop of winter wheat or oats. The sheep are 'folded' or fenced in closely on the ground with hazel or chestnut hurdles. The danger of worm infestation is not great because the sheep will soon be moved on to a fresh patch, and the ground is not permanently under sheep as it is on the hill farm. A full-grown sheep eats about 1 cwt. of greenstuff in a week; at this rate 200 sheep will clear a half-acre of thousand-headed kale or swedes in a week.

Lambing begins in January on these southern arable sheep farms, and all the lambs not kept for breeding will be sold, either to the butcher or to other farmers wishing to buy new stock. Obviously, the ewes have to receive special feeding of hay, roots, and concentrates such as beans, crushed oats, or sugar-beet pulp. Lambing often takes place in special yards, built by the shepherd, of hurdles laced with straw. The ground itself is littered with straw to keep it as clean as possible. On hill-farms about 80 to 90 lambs from 100 ewes is considered a satisfactory result, and the lambs will weigh about 7 lb. at birth. On southern arable sheep farms, however,

Eric Guy

LAMBING FOLDS FOR HAMPSHIRE DOWN SHEEP

The lambs are born in the thatched cubicles surrounding the folds. After a few days several lambs and sheep are put into a small fold to learn to recognize each other before they are allowed to go into the large fold. Outside the folds are the sheep which have not yet lambed and the hut where the shepherd lives all through the lambing season

there may be 150 or more lambs from 100 ewes, and these will weigh 16 to 19 lb. at birth. Many sheep will produce twins and some triplets. In the case of triplets, the shepherd will remove immediately the strongest of the three and coax a ewe who has lost her lamb, or who has only a singleton, to take it. Much patience and ingenuity has often to be exercised in persuading the ewe to accept it.

Some low-ground farmers are not really sheep breeders at all but keep a 'flying flock' or a 'walking flock'. In the first case cast ewes are bought in autumn, put to a ram of an early maturing breed, and lambs and ewes are fattened off in the following spring and summer. A walking flock is one where the ewes are bought at a younger age and remain on the farm for a few seasons, the lambs being sold each year.

Neither of these types of flock provides the farmer with the interest of a continuous breeding policy.

See also Foods (Farm Animals); Animal Diseases; Agricultural Improvers; Shepherd.

See also Vol. II: Sheep (Wild).

SHEEP DOGS. The term sheep dog is a broad one. A sheep dog in the Carpathian Mountains is a different creature altogether from a collie on the Welsh or Scottish hills or in the north of England, and the work each does is also entirely different.

Dogs have been used by shepherds for a long time. The Roman writer on husbandry, Columella, mentions them, saying that they should be white or at least light in colour to enable the shepherd to tell which is dog and which wolf

A SHEPHERD WITH HIS COLLIE IN THE NORTH-WEST HIGH-
LANDS OF SCOTLAND

The sheep are Cheviots

when the flock is being threatened by wolves and the dog is defending the flock. This point shows the main difference between the two kinds of sheep dogs: the one that herds the flock, and the one that defends it. Even now, nearly 2,000 years after Columella wrote, the sheep dogs of the Carpathians are cream-coloured animals of large size whose main job is to keep marauders away from the flocks. The mastiff of the Pyrenees is also white or cream and serves the same purpose.

But in Britain, where there are no longer any wolves, the herding faculty of sheep dogs has been developed to a higher degree than anywhere else in the world. Since wolves had finally disappeared, even from the Highlands, by 1743, it was no longer necessary to have a big, heavy dog, and the shepherd was able to concentrate the dog's mental and physical energies on helping him to control the sheep rather than guard them. British sheep dogs, therefore, are much smaller than those in wolf-infested countries, and instead of being white they are dark. It is a curious fact—on hill farms anyway—that the sheep are not so easily moved and controlled by a light-coloured dog as by one predominantly black.

British sheep dogs are of several types: there is the Old English bob-tailed sheep dog which is naturally short-tailed, and has a profuse blue

and white woolly coat which has to be stripped (cut and thinned) each year, as it does not shed naturally. The bob-tail is used with quiet kinds of sheep that naturally keep together in a flock. It helps the shepherd move the sheep in and out of the folds and from place to place, when the work is all at close quarters. The bob-tail has a sweet, steady nature which may have been one reason for its having become a popular show variety; but these show specimens are no good to a shepherd in the field or on the hill, for they are too big, and have been bred for coat and appearance rather than for work. In Wales, northern England, and Scotland the collie is used instead of the bob-tail. There are three varieties of collie: the flat-coated, the smooth-coated, and the beardie. The beardie is most like the bob-tail, with the same sort of rough coat, with plenty of hair on the lower jaw, and often of a similar blue or grizzled colour; but it is much smaller and has a tail of normal length. The smooth-coated collie has a short coat and tends to be longer on the leg than the flat-coated collie, which is by far the commonest kind in the hill districts. The show breeders, however, during the course of nearly a century have produced a collie that is quite unlike a working dog and quite useless in the field. It has a long snipy nose, a very heavy coat, and is ginger and white in colour.

The working collie has a clean-cut head, and a muzzle of average length. Its eyes are alert and forward-looking, not placed far round to each side of the head in wolfish fashion. The ears are pricked so that the cups face forwards, but the tips of the ears should fall forwards and not stand upright as do some of the present-day trials-bred strains. Its head is well domed with plenty of width between the ears. Its chest is deep, its back strong with well-coupled loins, its shoulders well but not too steeply sloped, its legs straight, and feet short and round. Its tail should fall gracefully and turn upwards at the tip at about the level of the hocks. Collies are mostly black on top with white on the chest and legs, but there are often tan spots over the eyes. Their coats are of moderate length, silky, and carrying a good woolly undercoat.

The collie is not a big dog or heavy in the bone. It must be extremely active, and the eagerness that goes with it makes the collie a highly sensitive, nervous animal. It will not endure harsh treatment or being shouted at. It is excitable, but has a very sweet and kindly nature. Training begins at about 8 months old and takes possibly 6 months to complete. There is a saying of the hill collie: 'Three years to grow, three to run, and three to go': in other words a collie is at its best at 3 to 6 years.

Hill sheep do not flock but scatter themselves about the ground. Many hill farms are steep and full of rough, awkward places, and the sheep themselves are very active. A man alone has little chance of gathering a flock or of catching individuals; so were it not for the collie, hill sheep farming would be impossible. The

The Times

SHEEP DOG TRIALS AT BARBON, WESTMORLAND

The dog on the right is working the sheep towards the mouth of the pen

shepherd has developed the natural instinct of the wild dog to gather small hoofed animals into a restricted space. Wild dogs do this in packs; the collie dog does it with his master and possibly with another collie.

Let us imagine that we have to gather a hundred sheep from a hillside of 300 acres. There may be fifty sheep in sight, and when the shepherd whistles a few times another twenty-five may show up. He will put the dog out to one side of him, and the collie will run not towards the sheep but in a wide curve, climbing fast and eventually getting above the sheep. He will work along above the sheep, watching them as they tend to bunch downhill, and at the same time watching the shepherd. The shepherd may be able to see a sheep in a place invisible to the dog; and if so he will sign to the dog from perhaps half a mile away, and the dog will go back, hunt the sheep, and work it towards the main bunch. Sometimes he may be out of sight of the shepherd altogether, hunting the gullies and hidden places himself. Then, having made a semicircle behind the sheep, he will work back again in a smaller semicircle, bringing the sheep together and nearer to the shepherd. If the shepherd has two collies, he may slip them both, one to either side, and they will keep their own sides and work in harmony, waiting on each other when one is faced with a difficult bit.

Driving is the opposite to gathering and less

natural to the dog. He has to restrain himself from overrunning the wings of the flock, for that might turn the sheep and lose time, as well as upsetting them.

In work closer at hand, the collie has to show his qualities of 'eye'. The sheep may be stationary and undecided whether to 'break' or not. If they do break away it means time lost, more running for the dog, and more fatigue for the sheep. The collie crouches and gazes intently at the sheep, especially at the leader of them, and in this silent battle of wills the collie with the strongest 'eye' usually manages to prevent the breakaway. At short work with two or three sheep (a more difficult number to handle than a hundred) the collie's movements are for the most part extremely slow and calculated, but he can act with lightning speed if necessary.

Sheep-dog trials have become very popular functions in the last half century, and especially since 1918. They give the general public a chance to see what the collie can do. A trials course includes a variety of situations for man and dog to manage in a period of 10 to 12 minutes. Three sheep are liberated half a mile away from the shepherd, who is confined to a ring a few feet across by a string looped on his left arm and fastened to a peg in the ground. The collie is slipped, makes its detour at great speed, gets behind the sheep and, following the whistles of the shepherd, brings them through

SHEARING SHEEP WITH ELECTRIC SHEARS IN WILTSHIRE

Eric Guy

a variety of hurdle obstacles and to the mouth of the 'maltese cross' made of hurdles. The shepherd can now leave his ring to go and work with his dog. Together they must pass the sheep through one way of the maltese cross, then gather them to the mouth of the other arm and pass them through that. Finally the sheep must be penned in a small enclosure of hurdles. If the class is for double dogs, six sheep are gathered and are later shed into two threes for penning in separate pens. There is no finer day's entertainment than sheep-dog trials, though the best trials' dogs are not necessarily the best under the hard and varied conditions of the hill.

A shepherd's collie is not a pet and should not be treated as a pet. No person other than its owner should pet it or speak to it. Shepherds between themselves always ignore the other man's dog or ask its owner to speak to it if necessary. Also, if collies are not left loose when not at work, they are more obedient and immediately responsive when on the job.

See also SHEPHERD.
See also Vol. II: INTELLIGENCE.
See also Vol. IX: DOGS, CARE OF.

SHEEP SHEARING AND DIPPING. 1. SHEARING (clipping). The wool is taken from the sheep once a year at the time of the 'rise of the wool', that is, when the heavy winter coat is about ready for a natural fall and is only held to the skin by comparatively few hairs through which the shears or machine clippers can cut easily. In Britain, lowland sheep are ready for shearing by May, but the northern hill sheep are not sheared till July. It is important to shear the sheep as soon as the fleeces are ready, as the long fleeces in hot weather encourage the fly and other parasites.

Sheep are not now generally prepared for shearing by being put through a washing dip, especially if they come off grass; but 'tagging' is an important preparation for shearing. The shepherd rounds up the sheep and picks out any animal that needs attention. He catches it round the neck with his hooked stick and holds it by the upper part of the hind leg. He then clips off all dirty matted locks of wool round the tail, and trims the tail square. These 'tag locks' are dried and bagged separately.

On hill farms the shearing is still done largely

by hand. The clipper sits astride the narrow end of a clipping form, a long-topped stool wider at one end than the other. His helpers bring him the sheep, take them away when finished, and roll up the shorn fleeces. The sheep is laid on its back on the form, and the clipper starts at its throat. He clears the neck and shoulders, cuts along the belly and down the ribs, thighs, and rump. Then he turns the sheep over and clears the back. The fleece, which should come off in one piece, is then rolled up and secured with a twisted rope of its own wool, and stored in a dry place until it goes to the wool merchant (*see* WOOL INDUSTRY, Vol. VII). The sheep can only be sheared when they are dry, so fine weather is essential. The clippers have to work as fast as possible, as the ewes, which are still suckling the lambs, must not be kept separated from their lambs for long. In hill districts the sheep shearing means a gathering of all the neighbourhood, and used in olden times to be accompanied by much feasting and merriment.

On farms in southern England machine shearing has almost entirely replaced hand shearing. Sometimes hand-driven machine clippers are used; sometimes the clippers are driven by a petrol engine or electric motor. The sheep are clipped on the ground on a large board or tarpaulin. In the north the shearers purposely leave a good inch of wool on the sheep, but the machine-clipped southern sheep are cut much closer. If a shearer can, with a machine, take the wool off a sheep in 5 to 10 minutes without injuring the animal, he is thought in Britain to be making good speed. In Australia and New Zealand the specialist shearers are much faster. Speed depends upon the size and condition of the sheep, and whether the shearer has to catch his own sheep and wind each fleece afterwards. Any accidental cuts made during shearing must be treated to disinfect and heal them; they are often smeared with tar.

2. DIPPING. The law demands that all sheep should be dipped as a precaution against sheep-scab, a mange infection caused by a parasitic MITE (q.v.). The dipping must take place between certain dates as laid down for the county (for example, between 1 July and 31 August). In counties where sheep-scab is particularly common, there must be two dippings at an interval of 10 to 14 days, or a special 'single-dipping' type of dip, approved by the Ministry, must be used. Lambs and sheep are generally

Eric Guy

DIPPING SHEEP IN MID-WALES
The dipping is supervised by a policeman

dipped a week or so after the ewes have been sheared.

The dipper is a long trough, sheer at one end and deep enough to swim a sheep, and sloping at the other end to enable the sheep to walk out. Pens are so arranged that the sheep can be kept going in a continuous stream through the dipper. Each sheep is in the bath for 1 or 2 minutes, and is made to swim through by a man with a dipping pole. It has its head ducked once. The sheep-dip is made up of carbolic and coal-tar products and arsenic compounds. The local policeman is informed by the farmers when they are going to dip, so that he can be present if he wants to.

In districts where the bacterial disease, footrot, is a danger, the sheep are put through a footbath, perhaps once a week, in which a 10% solution of copper sulphate acts as a preventive.

See also SHEEP; ANIMAL DISEASES; PARASITES.

SHELL-FISH GATHERING. The molluscs and crustaceans found near the British coast are very important to the fishing industry. Some are valued solely as table delicacies, whereas others

Graphic Photo. Union

WOMEN GOING TO COLLECT COCKLES ON LLANRHIDIAN SANDS, SOUTH WALES

called the 'byssus', by which they are firmly anchored.

WHELKS (q.v. Vol. II) are also much in demand as bait, and many are also sold as a cheap delicacy in parts of London. They are caught in baited traps or on long lines called 'whelk trots'. Instead of a baited hook, half a dozen small crabs are strung on each branch-line (snood) of the whelk trot.

SCALLOPS (q.v. Vol. II) are dredged in winter from banks in the English Channel and Irish Sea. Although intensive fishing has caused a greatly decreased catch, there is no cultivation of scallops.

are also in great demand as bait. OYSTER FISHING, CRAB AND LOBSTER FISHING, and SHRIMPING AND PRAWNING (qq.v.) are described in separate articles.

MUSSELS (q.v. Vol. II) are found in closely packed colonies attached to rocks on the sea-shore; mussels breed so freely in British waters that very little restriction need be imposed on gathering them. There is a great demand for mussel bait by fishermen who fish with lines for haddock, cod, and halibut. Where possible the mussels are collected by means of a special kind of rake armed with long prongs which are curved at the point. When mussels are found growing on rocks above low-tide level, a special kind of knife is used to cut the tuft of tough threads,

Periwinkles (see SNAIL, section 4, Vol. II) are collected on rocky coasts in large numbers. The only restrictions laid down are that they must not be collected during the breeding season, nor from places where there is danger of pollution by sewage. In the west of Ireland they are sometimes kept in net-walled enclosures until enough are in stock to dispatch by steamer to Billingsgate, the London fish market.

COCKLES, LIMPETS, and the ormers or sea-ears of Jersey are usually collected by hand at low tide. CLAMS and RAZOR-SHELLS are dug out of the sand or mud (qq.v. Vol. II).

See also Vol. II: MOLLUSCS; CRUSTACEANS.

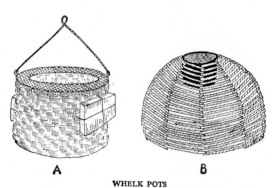

WHELK POTS

A is used in the Wash. It is made of basket-work with a net at the top to prevent the whelks from crawling out. *B* is used in Norfolk. It has a wire frame strung with thin rope

SHEPHERD. The shepherd is the most independent member of a farm staff. The farmer does not dictate to the shepherd but allows him to do most things in his own way, and is usually ready to hear the shepherd's opinion and carefully weigh his advice. There are no set hours of work for the shepherd, for he does the job whatever the hour. It is the boast of many shepherds that during the lambing month they never take their clothes off or sleep in a bed. Such men are devoted to their work.

It is an almost invariable rule that a shepherd does not do any other farm work. In the north, where his house may be far away from any others, he is allowed to keep two or three cows of his own and ten to twenty ewes; and ground

Gwyneth Pennethorne

A SHEPHERD GIVING A LAMB TO A FOSTER MOTHER

is also set aside for him to grow potatoes, oats, and hay for his stock.

The success of the work of the shepherd depends very largely on close observation. If he has 600 ewes in his flock he will almost certainly know every one and its history. This in itself is a feat of memory, for the flock changes to some extent each year as young stock comes in and 'cast' ewes go out. Then, in the day-to-day work, the shepherd must be able to see any trouble almost before it begins. Footrot, or decomposition of the hoof, should be prevented before it has time to get started. Sheep struck by blowfly should be identified as soon as the maggots hatch, when the sheep shows their presence by shaking its tail, nipping round at its flank, and keeping away from the rest of the flock (*see* FLY PESTS).

Many sheep diseases are now preventable by inoculation and vaccination (*see* ANIMAL DISEASES); internal parasites such as liver flukes (*see* PARASITIC WORMS) can be kept in check by 'drenching' the sheep (that is, giving it a dose) with particular chemicals. The shepherd knows about these things, and makes good use of what science can offer.

The south-country shepherd, who may be running his sheep over a succession of arable crops grown specially for them, has to work to a close time-table, for he has to make the crops last and yet to get them eaten at the right stage of growth. The hill shepherd knows the succession of natural plants and will herd his sheep at the right times to the areas where these grow. The shepherd's busiest times are lambing, marking, shearing, dipping, the lamb sales, tupping time (when the rams are put out to the ewes), and when heavy snow falls and drifts.

The life of the shepherd is very different in different parts of the world: for example, the half-nomadic sheep husbandry of the Bible and of some primitive peoples today is largely one of leading the sheep to the best pastures and protecting them from predatory wild animals. There is no attempt to improve the ground or conduct the careful cross-breeding and fattening processes that concern the shepherd of progressive countries. Again, in a ranching country such as Australia, where men of British stock and their dogs have gone, the shepherd is a horseman for much of his time. The sheep, mainly Merinos of Spanish extraction and kept largely for their wool, are herded in 'paddocks', which may be several square miles in extent.

See also SHEEP; SHEEP DOGS; SHEEP SHEARING AND DIPPING.

SHIFTING CULTIVATION, *see* AGRICULTURAL HISTORY; ROTATION OF CROPS.

SHOEING. A horse is shod in order that its hoofs may stand the wear and tear of work on hard surfaces. In some countries other hoofed animals, such as oxen, are also shod. A horseshoe is made in a smithy, the blacksmith's or farrier's workshop. This generally consists of an inner forge, fitted with a fire blown red hot by big bellows, a wooden block topped with iron called the anvil, and a tank of cold water for cooling the tools and tempering the iron shoe; and an outer shoeing shed where the horse stands.

A horse's foot consists of a sensitive inner part and an insensitive outer envelope of horny matter (the wall) through which nails can pass, if driven properly, without injury or pain to the animal. Only the wall of the hoof is pierced by the shoe nails, which are specially shaped to reduce the danger of their touching the sensitive part. In preparing the hoof for shoeing, the farrier will pare away overgrown or uneven wall, but will not touch the 'sole', the 'frog', or the 'bars', nor will he file away with his rasp any

Eric Guy

SHOEING A HORSE

The nails are driven into the wall of the hoof and do not touch the sensitive parts. The smith works with his left hand when shoeing a right-hand hoof

of the outer surface of the wall because this tends to remove the protective layers and results in a brittle hoof.

The shoe is made from a length of bar iron varying in breadth and thickness according to the size of the horse and the type of shoe to be made. The good smith, or farrier, shapes the shoe for the individual horse's foot; he does not cut the hoof to fit the shoe. A good fit is very important to the comfort of the horse. The smith takes the bar of iron in long iron tongs and holds it in the fire until it is red hot and soft. Then he puts it on the anvil and hammers it into shape with a steel hammer, making the sparks fly as he works. He uses a special tool called a 'fuller' to make a groove round the shoe, and through this he stamps the nail holes. Then he draws out a 'clip' (or with shoes for heavy horses more than one clip) to fit against the outer surface of the hoof to hold the shoe in place. While the shoe is still hot, it is quickly fitted on the horse's hoof, making a sizzle and a burning smell as it touches the insensitive horny part of the foot. If it does not fit, it must be reheated and reshaped.

When the shoe is ready, the smith lifts the horse's hoof, rests it on his leather-aproned knee, and holds it firmly while he nails on the shoe. Horses soon get to know what is required of them and stand patiently during the operation; but some horses will lean heavily on the smith, demanding considerable strength from him, while young, nervous horses need to be held steadily and talked to quietly all the time while the smith is working.

Since the shoes prevent wear, the hoof, which grows somewhat like a human finger nail, soon grows too long, so that, even if the shoes themselves are not worn out, the horse must go to the smithy every 4 or 5 weeks to have the shoes removed, the walls pared down, and the shoes replaced. The amount of wall to be pared down depends upon the rate of growth of the hoof, and this is not the same in all horses.

We do not know when the practice of putting iron plates or 'rim-shoes' on horses' hoofs began, but probably not earlier than the 2nd century B.C. Earlier than that, socks or sandals were sometimes tied on to the animals' hoofs to protect them from hard surfaces. Iron horse-shoes were not commonly used in Europe till the end of the 5th century A.D., or even later. It is said that they were introduced to Britain at the time of William the Conqueror. In Japan, iron horse-shoes were not used until the 19th century, the horses wearing instead slippers of straw.

See also HORSES, CARE OF.
See also Vol. II: HOOF.

SHOWS, AGRICULTURAL, *see* AGRICULTURAL SHOWS.

SHRIMPING AND PRAWNING. The common shrimp is usually to be found in large numbers wherever there are sandy beaches or shallow water sand-banks. Prawns usually prefer deeper water, or rock pools which seldom go dry at low tide. In England the usual way to catch shrimps and prawns is to wade in the shallows, pushing forwards a broad hand-net called a 'push-net'.

At Southport horses and carts are often used. A net is suspended from a boom on each side of the cart, which is driven along the sands, often in water up to the horse's girth. When, however, these crustaceans are specially abundant and the water deeper, a small-sized trawl (bag-net) is towed by a sailing-boat. The shrimps are boiled on board the boat immediately they are caught. On shore the shelling and the potting of shrimps forms a minor industry.

In India, where large numbers of prawns are found in certain of the salty backwaters and lagoons, traps are set at the apex of two converging rows of stakes. The stakes direct the shoals of fish into the entrances to the traps, which are closely woven of thin strips of palm leaves. At each entrance (there are generally two) is a sleeve-like funnel, armed at the inner

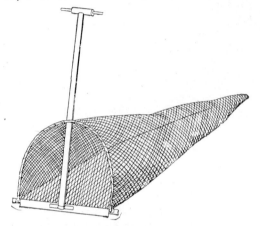

A PUSH NET USED FOR SHRIMPING

end with numerous fine splints, which prevents the fish from escaping. When the catch is more than is needed locally the prawns are often sun-dried, and then shelled by the simple process of beating them with sticks or trampling them under foot.

In Burma, where prawns abound in every tidal creek of the Irrawaddy at certain times of the year, vast quantities are caught to make the highly flavoured condiment known as *balachong*. To produce this, the prawns and some of the small fish caught with them are fermented.

See also Vol. II: PRAWNS AND SHRIMPS.

SHRUBS, *see* FLOWERING SHRUBS.

SILAGE. Drying a crop in the sun (as in haymaking) or by means of a machine (as dried grass is made) are not the only ways of preserving green crops for feeding to livestock during the winter. Grass or other green fodder crops can be cut at an early stage in their growth, when they are at their richest in protein, and converted by a process of controlled FERMENTATION (q.v. Vol. II), without any drying, into silage. They then retain about 80% of their original food value.

The green crop may be packed into a pit in the ground or built into a stack, or stored in a container called a 'silo', which is a tower usually made of wood or concrete. In the U.S.A., and sometimes in this country, a special machine is often used to slice the green crop into small pieces before it is put in the silo. As the material collects it is compressed either by trampling it in the silo or by driving the tractor and trailers over it. The temperature rises—but should not be allowed to exceed 100° F.—and fermentation sets in. At the same time a solution of molasses and water is generally sprinkled over successive layers, or a weak solution of acid may be used instead. The sugars in the plant juices, and the molasses when used, are converted by bacterial action into lactic and acetic acids, and these act as preservatives. When the silo has been completely filled, it is sealed with a layer of soil and, perhaps, thatch, to make it air-tight and water-proof. The silage will then keep in good condition until used during the autumn and winter. The finished product is moist, yellowish brown in colour, has a sharp, acid smell, and retains many of the physical characteristics of the original plants.

Silage making is independent of weather conditions, and this is a great advantage; but to offset this the carting of the crop in the green state is both slow and laborious, and special equipment is necessary. Thus, when fine weather is reasonably assured, most farmers preserve their grass by the older method of haymaking. Many, however, regularly convert the aftermath (second growth) into silage, because by the time the second crop of grass is ready for cutting, the weather in most districts has become too uncertain and the days too short to make good hay.

In dry areas grass does not make a great deal of growth, and hay crops are frequently poor. Other provision must, therefore, be made for winter fodder, and a mixed crop of oats, tares, peas, and beans, which is much more bulky, may be grown and cut in summer for drying as hay or converting in the green state into silage. Sun-loving crops such as maize and lucerne are also grown for silage making, maize being used a great deal in the U.S.A. In wet districts where the rainfall exceeds 40 inches a year, grass and mixed forage crops often grow so well that there

Eric Guy

ENSILING A GREEN CROP IN A TEMPORARY SILO

is a superabundance of summer keep for the stock. In this case it is a good plan to preserve the surplus in the form of silage.

See also GRASSLAND; GRASSES; LEYS; HAYMAKING; GRASS-DRYING.

SILKWORMS. Silk is made from the thread which forms the cocoon of the silkworm, the larva of the SILK MOTH (q.v. Vol. II), which passes through the usual stages of egg, larva (silkworm), pupa (chrysalis in cocoon), and moth (*see* METAMORPHOSIS, Vol. II). Silkworms have been bred for their silk for thousands of years. They are bred on a large scale in China, Japan, and other eastern countries, Italy and France, and to some extent in Russia, though Russia does not export silk, and on a small scale in Britain. For example, some British-produced silk was used in making the wedding dress of Princess Elizabeth in 1947.

The Latin name of the silkworm is *Bombyx mori*, the last word meaning 'mulberry-eating', for the silkworm, though it will eat other kinds of leaf, does not produce silk that can be reeled unless it is fed on mulberry leaves. The main kinds of MULBERRY-trees (q.v.) are the black and the white—the latter producing a rather finer silk. Other kinds of mulberry-tree have been specially bred for silkworm-rearing. The mulberry can be grown either as a tree or as a bush. Trees are useful only where there is plenty

of space, and they take a long time to bear sufficient leaves. In goat-keeping countries, such as Greece and Cyprus, trees have to be used, as otherwise the goats would eat the leaves. In Europe generally the Japanese custom of planting dwarf mulberry trees has been adopted. These are planted 2 feet apart, in rows from 3 ft. to 3 ft. 6 in. apart, so that about 6,000 bushes can be grown on an acre of ground. The bushes can also be formed into a hedge.

When the female silk moth is about to lay her eggs, the silkworm farmer encloses her in a cotton bag, where she lays about 300 to 450 eggs, fixing them to the cotton with a gum which she produces. After laying her eggs, she dies. The eggs are a clear yellow colour when laid, and, if fertile, change to slate-grey after about 4 weeks. The farmer then turns the bags inside out, damping them with cold water so that the gum is softened, and gently rubbing off the eggs into the water so that they are washed, and any dirt or infertile eggs float to the surface. The eggs are then dried on a cotton sheet in the shade, weighed, put into boxes, and kept for about 6 weeks at a temperature of 31° to 32° F. before they are incubated.

When large numbers of worms are being reared, an incubator is used for hatching. Usually the temperature in the incubator starts at about 62° F. and is raised gradually every 24 hours until it reaches 72° F., when the eggs hatch. The silkworms, or 'ants', as they are called when they first hatch, bite their way out of the eggs after about a week or 10 days in the incubator. They are about $\frac{1}{12}$ inch long, dark, and covered with long hairs, which disappear after the fourth day. The farmer then puts them on to strips of mulberry leaves, usually placing a layer of thinly perforated paper or coarse muslin between the worms and the mulberry leaves, so that they crawl through this and leave behind any empty shells or unhatched eggs that may be stuck to them. Then he puts the mulberry strips and worms in the rearing-rooms on

RICE FIELDS IN MALAYA

Men are working in a field flooded from the irrigation channel in the centre. Behind are fields of young rice.

Water-colour by A. B. Ibrahim

large wooden trays stacked in tiers. These rooms are kept at a temperature not below 70° F. The worms are fed five times a day, at first with strips of mulberry leaf, but eventually with whole leaves. The leaves must always be kept quite dry. Six days after hatching, the silkworm sheds its skin: it generally moults about four times during its life.

The silkworm lives, as a larva, for about 35 to 42 days. During the last week of its life it eats continually, but gradually its appetite lessens until it finally stops eating, and begins to look transparent, and its body shrinks. It then climbs, or 'rises', on to a truss of straw placed ready, 'empties' itself by emitting a soft excreta and a yellow fluid, and then begins to spin its cocoon. (In Japan silkworms have been made to spin on a flat surface, thus producing sheets of silk instead of cocoons.) The silk comes from the two sacs which lie along each side of the body of the worm. It consists of a thick, sticky solution which on contact with the air hardens into a thread of silk. Each sac opens at a little cone, the 'spinerette', under the lower lip of the worm, and the two threads come together and are stuck by a natural gum. The separate threads are called 'brins', and the two threads when cemented together make the silk fibre or 'bave'. Before it spins the cocoon, the worm emits a coarse thread which it attaches to supports, making a kind of hammock of tangled fibres called the 'floss', and in the middle of this it spins its cocoon. The first wrapper of the cocoon, the 'blaze', is made of thick threads woven into little bundles; the later threads are finer. After about 3 days the cocoon is complete, and consists of about 2,500 yards of unbroken thread.

Most of the cocoons are collected before the moths have time to develop, leaving only those which are to be used for breeding. The chrysalids in the cocoons which are collected are killed by placing the cocoons in an oven at a temperature of about 168° to 174° F. They are then cooled, the 'floss' is removed by machinery,

Silk and Rayon Users Association
SILKWORMS FEEDING ON MULBERRY LEAVES

and the cocoons are sorted into the various sizes and qualities. The dried cocoons are placed in boiling water to soften the gum, and then the threads are wound off and twisted together into a single thread—the 'raw' or 'net' silk. Four or or five threads are twisted together into yarn, which can then be woven into material (*see* SILK INDUSTRY, section 2, Vol. VII).

The cocoons left for breeding are collected 10 days after spinning, the rough floss is stripped off, and they are strung together in long chains, hanging from hooks in a dry, warm room. In 10 to 16 days the moths hatch, and, as soon as their wings are dry, the males fly to the females for mating. As they unite, the silkworm farmer removes them in pairs on to trays, and places them in a dark quiet room. Mating takes from 3 to 6 hours, at the end of which time the farmer destroys the male moths, and places each female in a cotton bag, as described, to lay her eggs.

See also MULBERRIES.
See also Vol. II: SILK MOTH.
See also Vol. VII: SILK INDUSTRY.

SISAL, *see* FIBRE CROPS.

SLUGS, *see* PESTS AND DISEASES.

SNARES, *see* TRAPS AND SNARES.

SNAILS, *see* PESTS AND DISEASES.

SOILLESS CULTURE. This is a method of growing plants without any soil, the plants getting all the food they need from water to which certain mineral salts have been added. Normally these salts are in the soil, and when dissolved in water can be absorbed by the roots. Altogether about forty different chemical elements have been discovered in plants, but most plants seem to grow satisfactorily with twelve of these—carbon, hydrogen, oxygen, nitrogen, sulphur, phosphorus, potassium, calcium, magnesium, manganese, borum, and iron. Of these, all but carbon, hydrogen, and oxygen are obtained as minerals from the soil, hydrogen from the water in the soil, and oxygen and carbon (the latter in the form of carbon dioxide) from the atmosphere.

For some time experiments in soil culture have been carried out, whereby given quantities of certain mineral salts have been added to the soil before the crops are planted, and the effect on the plants noted. As a result a great deal of knowledge has been built up about ARTIFICIAL FERTILIZERS (q.v.). Even more accurate experiments can be carried out in the laboratory, however, if the plants are grown in water to which given quantities of the chemical salts have been added. In this way it was shown that almost all plants up to small shrubs could be grown in water without soil so long as the right proportions of the necessary mineral salts were added to the water. This has been tried out on a commercial scale; and in America growing plants, such as tomatoes, without soil seems to have been established as a successful industry. During the Second World War green vegetables for the American troops stationed on volcanic Pacific Islands were grown on this system. In Britain and elsewhere people without gardens have grown plants successfully in tanks of solution on flat roofs or balconies. Certain soil-borne diseases can be avoided this way, and the method has proved particularly successful with carnations.

Soilless culture is generally carried out by one of two methods. A wire netting tray covered with vegetable litter is placed above a trough of water containing the mineral salts, and the plants are held by the wire netting so that the roots dip into the water. Alternatively the plants are grown in a tray of coarse sand or gravel, and fed continually with water containing the salts, the quantity given depending on the stage of growth of the plants. Enough liquid must be given at a time to soak the sand and begin to drain through—too much will suffocate the roots. Every 3 or 4 weeks the sand must be rinsed through with clear water, partly dried, and then replanted and fed again. For both methods the nutrient solution must be very accurately made up, and this is perhaps easier to do by the sand or gravel method.

The following formula provides a solution containing the major elements needed by most plants: 14 oz. sodium nitrate; 2 oz. potassium sulphate; $4\frac{1}{2}$ oz. magnesium sulphate; $7\frac{1}{4}$ oz. superphosphate of lime; 50 gallons of water. To this must be added, just before use, a concentrated solution of essential 'trace elements', or elements of which the minutest traces have astonishing effects on plant growth. This consists of $\frac{1}{4}$ oz. boric acid; $\frac{1}{4}$ oz. manganese sulphate; 3 oz. iron sulphate; 1 pint of water. One teaspoonful of this solution to every 10 gallons of the main solution should be used.

See also ARTIFICIAL FERTILIZERS.

SOILS. To the farmer the soil is the layer of 'earthy' material that lies upon the surface of the earth, which he cultivates in order to grow plants. This layer consists of particles of minerals of varying sizes with some dark material coating each one. Between the particles there are spaces, called 'pore spaces', containing both air and water, and in the natural state the particles and their coatings are damp. In addition, there are many living things in the soil—worms, insects, fungi, and millions upon millions of microbes, some of which are helpful, others harmful. All this applies more to the top few inches of soil than to the lower layers which form the 'subsoil', this being generally lighter in colour, with fewer bacteria, and not usually disturbed by cultivation. The subsoil is, however, if not too wet, penetrated by the roots of many plants.

Where the soil and subsoil have been exposed, as in a quarry or a railway cutting, the change from one layer to the next can be seen. An exposed face of soil such as this is called a 'profile'. Sometimes a hard layer of rock or earthy material is discovered in a profile. Farmers call it a soil 'pan', and if it is at all near the surface it prevents the roots of plants growing downwards as they should, and it must be broken up before the soil can grow good crops.

The mineral particles which make up the soil

The Controller, H.M.S.O.

A CLAY VALE: VALE OF MARSHWOOD, DORSET

Clay soil gives good pasturage but, as water drains slowly through clay, it often lies wet in winter. In rainy districts, therefore, it is not suitable for arable crops. Oak and elm are the chief natural trees.

The Controller, H.M.S.O.

PEAT SOIL: THE FENS NEAR WISBECH

The fens are flat and low lying, and the land consists of several feet of peat which has been drained by canals and pumping stations. It is very fertile and is intensively farmed with arable crops. In the foreground is a crop of sugar-beet with corn stubble beyond

were all, at one time, part of the rocks that form the great mass of the earth. Weathering agents, such as frost, rain, sun, and wind, big changes in temperature, running water, glaciers, and the chemical action of air and water, have all played their part in splitting up these rocks and wearing down the fragments into particles of small sizes. Living things in the soil have also helped in this great work. Plants push their roots into and extend the cracks in the rocks, earthworms swallow the tinier particles in their search for food and grind them to a still smaller size, and almost all living things breathe out a gas, carbon dioxide, which, when dissolved in the soil water, helps to disintegrate (break up) the rocks (*see* DENUDATION, Vol. III).

Sometimes the soil lies directly on top of rocks like those from which it was made. This is called a 'sedentary' soil. Other soils have been moved from their original situation by running water, glaciers, or the wind, and these are called 'transported' soils, or, where the soil has been transported by water, 'alluvial' soils. The soil in the bottom of a valley is often of such a type. The manufacture and movement of soil is going on day by day, but progress is so slow that it can hardly be observed. The movement accounts, in part, for the mixture of different types of soil that we find on a farm, or even in one field.

The largest mineral particles in the soil are called stones and gravel, and the smallest (too small to be seen even with a strong microscope) are called clay. In between these are coarse sand, fine sand, and silt. Every normal soil contains some of each of these particles, the character of a soil largely depending upon the proportions in which the different particles are mixed together. For example, if a soil contains a large proportion of the bigger particles, water drains out of it easily, and it dries so quickly that crops grown on it may suffer severely during a drought. Manure quickly decays in such a soil, and plant food washes easily out of it. A soil of this type is called a gravel or a sand, and farmers describe it as a light, hungry soil. A heavy soil, on the other hand, which contains a large proportion of the small silt and clay particles, is able to hold a great deal of water, drains slowly, and if cultivated when wet becomes sticky and unmanageable. It becomes, as the farmer says, 'puddled' or 'poached', and then will not drain at all. When such a soil dries, it shrinks and cracks, and is liable to form big, hard clods. It is called a silt or a clay soil, according to which type of particle is more numerous. A soil containing a fair amount of both the larger and smaller particles is called a loam. There are light, medium, and heavy loams, and the names sandy loam and clay loam are also used.

The dark material which, as we said, coats the mineral particles is called 'humus', and is largely composed of decayed and decaying vegetable matter and the droppings of animals, their decay being brought about by the action of bacteria and fungi in the soil (*see* SAPROPHYTES, Vol. II). Humus is rich in plant food; its addition to a clay soil improves the drainage; a sandy soil is held together and is less likely to dry out if it contains plenty of humus. It is impossible to cultivate and crop any soil that is without humus.

In the pore spaces between the particles of soil the roots of plants travel and water and air circulate. These spaces vary in the different soils. Coarse sandy soils have larger but fewer spaces between the particles than clay soils, and the total pore space is less than in the finer soils. When rain falls upon the surface of the earth, some of it enters the pore spaces. Part passes down into the subsoil, carrying air down with it; the rest is absorbed either by the roots of plants or by the tiny clay and humus particles, which then become jelly-like. It is this that makes a clay soil sticky after rain, and a clay soil or one rich in humus is able to hold a lot of water by absorption.

The farmer and gardener try by DRAINAGE, IRRIGATION, and CULTIVATIONS (qq.v.) to control the amount of water in the top soil so that the crops get enough but not too much water. If the ground is always full of water, with little or no air in the pore space, it is said to be 'water-logged', and drains must be put in to carry the water away.

In a properly cultivated soil the particles cling together in loose crumbs, and the way in which they are arranged together is called the soil 'structure'. The structure of a soil containing much clay or fine silt can be destroyed by working it when wet. This is why a much-used gateway on clay soil becomes a quagmire in wet weather, and in dry weather hardens into ruts and clods. Humus and LIME (q.v.) are both needed to keep the structure right.

Crops begin to grow earlier in the spring and

The Controller, H.M.S.O.

CHALK SOIL: THE SOUTH DOWNS

Chalk land usually consists of rolling downlands and dry valleys, for chalk drains quickly. The soil on chalk hills is thin, and much of the land is under grass. In the foreground is a corn stubble ready for ploughing

The Controller, H.M.S.O.

SANDY SOIL: HEATH AND WOODLAND NEAR SANDRINGHAM, NORFOLK

Heather, bracken, and coniferous trees grow on this barren soil. The sand allows the water to drain away, carrying the lime with it and making the soil acid. On the surface is a layer of peat which is very different from the deep fertile peat of the fens

continue their growth later in the autumn on some soils than on others. Such soils, which are dry and warm, are called early soils. A wet soil gets warmed by the sun more slowly than a dry one, and therefore clay soils are generally colder than sandy ones. Also, clay soils cannot be cultivated so early in the year because they are still too wet, and a seed-bed cannot be prepared in a really wet soil.

In the Northern Hemisphere land facing towards the south gets more heat from the sun than land with a northern aspect. Shelter and the height above the sea (altitude) also influence the temperature of the soil, for cool dry winds increase the rate of evaporation of water from the soil, and as the water evaporates it takes heat from the soil. If two soils, one darker than the other, are equally wet, the darker one will warm up more quickly, because its colour enables it to absorb heat more quickly from the sun. Many dark soils, however, owe their colour to the presence of larger quantities of humus, and humus has a great capacity for holding water.

Green plants obtain their food partly from the carbon dioxide gas in the air and partly from materials dissolved in the soil water. Food obtained from the soil is taken in through delicate hollow hairs on the tips of the ROOTS (q.v. Vol. II). It passes in as a very weak solution, the dissolved materials being known as 'available foods'. These are obtained from the mineral particles, from the humus, and from any manures that the farmer may have applied to the land. As the mineral particles of the different types of soils are generally broken-up rocks with different chemical compositions, so the plant food available differs in kind and in amount from soil to soil. In most soils there is not enough plant food to grow continuous big crops; therefore the farmer and the gardener put MANURES (q.v.) and fertilizers on the land.

The soil also contains millions of different kinds of living things, microscopic bacteria and fungi. Most of these feed by breaking up organic matter (bits of dead plants and animals) to make humus—a very valuable service. Others are able to absorb nitrogen gas out of the air, with which they enrich the soil in which they live (see NITROGEN SUPPLY IN PLANTS, Vol. II). These are called 'nitrogen-fixing' bacteria; some of them live freely in the soil, whereas others live inside the tiny swellings on the roots of legumes (clovers, peas, beans, and others). There may

also be in the soil living things that do harm to the farmer's crops and animals—the bacteria and fungi that cause disease, and various kinds of pests (see PESTS AND DISEASES). These, however, are less numerous than the living organisms that are helpful.

Sandy soils, silts, clay soils, and loams can be identified by the feel of them when rubbed moist between finger and thumb. A sandy soil feels extremely gritty, and many of the individual particles are visible to the naked eye. A clay feels sticky, and the rubbed surface is smooth and 'soapy'. A silt also feels smooth, but 'silky' rather than soapy. A loam, as would be expected, combines these characteristics, the sand making it gritty and the clay making it somewhat sticky. When judging a soil by touch in this way, we are judging its 'texture'.

Chalky soils generally lie on top of a chalk subsoil. Where the top soil is only a very few inches deep, it will be, when cultivated, almost white in colour. Limestone is a similar material to chalk, but much harder. Soils which come from either a chalk or limestone rock are usually, but not always, rich in lime, a necessary part of any fertile soil. If a soil is short of lime it is said to be acid or sour, and the farmer must remedy this by spreading lime on the fields. There will be very few earthworms in a sour soil, and sour grassland grows less nourishing varieties of grasses. There may even be a layer of peat, which is vegetable matter that has not fully decayed to form humus.

A 'fen' soil is one in which there is a great deal of humus, well rotted, and not sour like a peat. The colour of such a soil is often almost black, due to the presence of so much humus.

We can tell something about the nature of the soil by the kinds of wild plants growing there. Oaks and primroses, for example, grow best on clay soils; silver birch and ragwort flourish on sandy soils; alder and rushes indicate that the land lies wet; beech and traveller's joy are most common on chalky soils; and sheep sorrel and foxglove grow where the soil is sour (see ECOLOGY OF PLANTS, Vol. II).

See also CULTIVATIONS; DRAINAGE, LAND; IRRIGATION; LIME; MANURES.
See also Vol. III: ROCKS.

SORGHUM, see MILLET, section 3.

SOYA BEANS. These are produced by the

plant *Glycine hispida*, an erect annual LEGUMINOUS CROP (q.v.) from 2 to 4 feet high, which bears short hairy pods, each containing from two to four seeds. These vary in colour according to the kind: they may be black, brown, green, or yellow. The crop, of which there are several varieties, needs a moderate rainfall and a crumbly soil. It is sown in rows about 2 feet by 1 foot, some 20 lb. of seed being needed for every acre. The crop matures in about 3 months. A good average yield is about 1,000 lb. of seed per acre.

Soya beans are native to China and Japan, and used to be considered suitable only for subtropical climates. They can thrive, however, under fully tropical conditions, in suitable soil, and can also be grown as a summer crop in temperate regions, such as the U.S.A. and parts of Britain. In recent years production has greatly increased, especially in the U.S.A., the total world production being now about 14 million tons, some 5 million of which are grown in the U.S.A. and 5 million in China and Manchuria.

The beans are a valuable food, as they are rich in protein. They may be eaten boiled, or made into various food preparations such as 'tofu cheese' and 'soy sauce', which are eaten in Japan and China, and soya bean flour, which is used in Europe and America. A milk substitute is prepared from the protein of the bean. Mainly, however, the crop is of importance as oil seed (*see* OIL-BEARING PLANTS). It produces a brownish-yellow oil which is used in the manufacture of margarine, soap, and paint (*see* OILS, VEGETABLE, Vol. VII). The residue left after the oil has been extracted is made into cattle cake.

SPICE CROPS.

Most of our SPICES (q.v. Vol. XI) are obtained from tropical plants, and have been imported from the East for hundreds of years.

Chillies are the bright red pods of shrubby perennial plants called capsicums, grown in tropical and sub-tropical countries including the Far East, East and West Africa, and Central America. The dried pods and seeds, which are very sharp-tasting, are used in sauces and pickles and, when ground, make red pepper, the chief ingredient of cayenne pepper and paprika.

Cinnamon is the dried bark gathered from the

E. O. Hoppé
PEELING GINGER ROOTS

young shoots of a tree called *Cinnamomum zeylanicum*, which is cultivated in Ceylon and southern India. The shoots are cut back in order to harvest the crop, but grow again freely the next year.

Cloves are the flower buds of an evergreen tree called *Eugenia caryophyllata*, which is cultivated mainly in the East African island of Zanzibar. It is grown from seed in nurseries and transplanted to orchards, where the trees produce flower buds 4 years after planting, and continue to do so for many years. The buds are picked as they appear, and are then dried in the sun.

Ginger (*Zingiber officinale*) comes from the underground stems of a plant that rather resembles the garden iris, and is grown in south China and the eastern tropics. Portions of the stem and root are planted in well-cultivated and manured soil, and the crop is lifted about 10 months later, parts kept for next year's crop, and the rest is cleaned and dried.

Mace and nutmegs are both obtained from the nutmeg-tree (*Myristica fragrans*), grown in the East Indies. It is raised from seeds and transplanted, and bears fruit after 7 years' growth. Mace is the outer flesh of the fruit, whilst nutmegs are the kernels obtained by cracking the hard shells.

CLOVE BUDS   *E. O. Hoppé*

The buds are pinkish-green in colour and are ready for picking

NUTMEGS AND MACE   *E. N. A.*

The fruit is split showing the outer flesh (mace) and the kernel (nutmeg)

Pepper is obtained from the seed of an ever-green climbing plant called *Piper nigrum*, which is cultivated in Malaya and the East Indies, and is as a rule trained up living trees, such as kapok, that themselves yield useful fruits. The plant is propagated from cuttings. It bears little black berries in long clusters, like strings of beads, and continues to fruit for several years. The seeds are known as peppercorns, and are dried and cleaned before being ground to produce the familiar powder.

Turmeric, important in the East as a flavouring for curry, is prepared from the roots of a plant called *Curcuma domestica*, which belongs to the same family as ginger; it is bright yellow in colour (*see* TROPICAL ROOT CROPS, section 6).

Vanilla is the fruit of a tall, fragrant Mexican orchid named *Vanilla planifolia*, which grows also in Central America and the West Indies.

See also SPICES, Vol. XI.

SPINACH CROPS. 1. SPINACH, because of its high content of mineral salts and vitamins, is the most important green vegetable outside the *Brassica* or cabbage group. *Spinacia oleracea*, which is an annual plant, is believed to be a native of western Asia. There are several types of this spinach, differing mainly in leaf and seed characters; they may be grouped as Norfolk or Bloomsdale, Round-leafed, Thick-leafed, and Prickly-seeded. Varieties in general cultivation have changed very little during the last 50 years and are mainly of the types just mentioned. Summer crops grow most satisfactorily on cool,

loamy soils which hold moisture; on dry, sandy soils the crop tends to run to seed quickly in hot weather. Autumn and winter crops, however, usually do well on lighter soils which have better drainage than the loams. The seed is usually sown in drills spaced 12 to 15 inches apart. The seedlings are seldom thinned on market-gardens, but in the home garden the plants are generally thinned to about 4 to 6 inches apart in the rows. The spinach plant develops a large rosette of leaves, the largest leaves being gathered for use as required, until the plants begin to run to seed; then the whole plant is pulled up and used.

2. SPINACH BEET (*Beta vulgaris*) is of the same species as BEETROOT and SUGAR-BEET (qq.v.), but is a special variety producing many edible light-green leaves, which are used as ordinary spinach is used. Spinach-beet is a biennial and can be grown both as a summer crop and as a crop to last through the winter and provide spinach in the early spring. For a summer supply, the seed is sown thinly in April on fairly rich soil in the same way as spinach, except that the plants should be spaced rather more widely. The leaves are gathered as they develop throughout the summer and autumn, and then the plants are discarded. For crops which are to grow through the winter the seed is sown in July, but usually the leaves are not gathered until the following spring, when fresh leaves begin to grow, producing an abundant crop of useful early spinach. A little fertilizer in the early spring helps the growth.

3. SEAKALE BEET OR CHARD is another

variety of the beetroot species *Beta vulgaris*, and is grown mainly for the sake of its thick, white or yellow leaf-stalks and leaf-ribs, which are cooked after the manner of SEAKALE (q.v.). The leaves of some forms are also used as a kind of spinach. Seakale beet is not difficult to grow, though the plants are not very hardy. Well-known and useful varieties are Fordhook Giant, Lucullus, and Lyon. The seed is sown in the open ground, like that of beetroot, in April or May, or the plants are raised under glass and transplanted after the risk of frost is past. Rich soil is needed to produce large succulent stalks. The rows should be 18 inches apart and the plants 10 to 12 inches apart—some varieties needing even more space.

4. NEW ZEALAND SPINACH (*Tetragonia expansa*), a native of New Zealand, has no connexion with the true spinach, but is an excellent substitute for ordinary spinach and can be grown on poorer, drier soil and in the warmer months of the year which normally are not so suitable for spinach. The plant is a tender annual which is easily injured by frost.

The seeds of New Zealand spinach are sown in the open in May and thinned out as the seedlings appear. To obtain earlier crops, plants may be raised in pots or boxes in a glasshouse or frame and transplanted in May. The plants need as much as 18 inches square of space for development, for they quickly spread along the ground. They continue to give a supply of leaves and shoots throughout the summer months.

SPRAYING AND DUSTING MACHINES.
Chemicals for killing weeds and insects (*see* IN-SECTICIDES) and for controlling plant diseases need accurate machinery for their distribution over the crop. The chemicals may be used as wet sprays or as dusts, wet spraying being the more usual process. Sprayers for liquid and dusters for powder are of different kinds, varying according to the nature of the spray material and to the degree of concentration at which the crop is to be covered.

In some of the sprayers the liquid is pumped under pressure through jet nozzles. In other kinds air is pumped into the tank containing the liquid, and the pressure of air forces the liquid out of the tank through spray nozzles. The first of these principles is the one most used on the small sprayers which the operator carries strapped on his back like a knapsack for spraying fruit trees. There is a hand-lever pump for pumping the liquid out of the container. Usually the pump lever also works a paddle for stirring the liquid to keep it well mixed. Both types of sprayer are used on field machines which spray ground crops against WEEDS (q.v.). For field work the outfit is mounted on a frame and either towed by a tractor or carried directly on the tractor itself. The pump for the liquid, or for compressing the air to drive out the liquid, is driven either by an engine carried on the frame or is operated through gearing from the engine of the tractor. There are also some horse-drawn machines in which the pump is driven through gearing from the land wheels. In some cases crops are sprayed from the air by aeroplanes fitted with the necessary pumps, spray-bars, and tanks.

Large spraying outfits are made for use in commercial orchards. The pumps of these are powerful enough to send the spray to the tops of the largest trees (*see* FRUIT SPRAYING).

Powders are spread as a dust by air pressure. In small hand-carried outfits a bellows worked by hand provides the draught to disperse the powder. In tractor outfits there is usually a rotary fan driven by a separate engine or, through gearing, from the tractor engine. Some hand-carried outfits are, however, made with small rotary fans driven by a tiny petrol engine

E. Allman and Co.

A SMALL ENGINE-DRIVEN DUSTER FOR FRUIT TREES
The powder is carried in the container on the man's back

A SPRAYER FOR FRUIT TREES

John Bean Div., Food Mchy. and Chem. Corp.

The pump is driven through a power take-off shaft of the tractor

or by an electric motor worked from an accumulator.

The difficulty in designing satisfactory spraying and dusting machinery has been to produce a spray of liquid or a dust of powder so finely divided and so evenly distributed that some of the liquid or powder reaches every part of every plant in the field, and to do that without using extravagant quantities of liquid or powder. Unless the fluid is kept very well mixed by constant stirring, it tends to block the fine jets. Another difficulty is that the materials used, particularly the liquids, are often damaging to the metals normally used in making farm machinery. Special non-corroding metals have had to be used for the pumps and pipes and other parts.

All these difficulties have now been overcome, but the machines have to be used skilfully to get the best out of them and out of the many chemicals available for farm work. These include selective weed killers which can destroy weeds and yet leave unharmed the crop in which they are growing, and liquids and powders that kill insect pests which could not be tackled by any other means. Sprayers and dusters have other uses too. Harvesting the potato crop can be made much easier if first the haulm is sprayed with sulphuric acid to burn it and hasten its dying. The yields of crops can sometimes be improved by chemicals applied by sprayer or duster, as, for example, the application of manganese to the leaves of growing crops.

See also INSECTICIDES; WEEDS.

SQUASHES, *see* GOURD VEGETABLES.

SQUID FISHING, *see* OCTOPUS, CUTTLEFISH, AND SQUID FISHING.

SQUIRRELS, *see* VERMIN; FUR FARMING.

STOCK BREEDING. 1. REPRODUCTION. Adult male and female animals, including human beings, produce inside their bodies certain reproductive or 'germ' cells, called 'gametes'. In the male these are called 'sperms' and in the female, 'ova' (sing. 'ovum'). A new animal is formed by a union of a sperm and an ovum, the sperm being introduced into the body of the female at the time of mating. The introduction of sperm is 'insemination' of the female; the union is called 'fertilization of the ovum', and if this is successful the female has conceived.

In mammals the fertilized ovum begins its life inside the womb of the dam, who is thus pregnant, and she carries her young in her body until it is sufficiently developed for birth or 'parturition'. The length of time between fertilization (or conception) and parturition is called the 'period of gestation', and it differs from one species of animal to another. With a mouse, for example, it is 3 weeks, and with an elephant about 18 months. After birth the young mammal depends for its nourishment on the milk of its dam, at first entirely and then to a less extent as it learns to eat other food. When it ceases to suck its mother's milk it is said to be 'weaned'.

In birds the ovum, instead of developing inside the female's body, is enclosed with a supply of food in a protective shell, and is at once passed out of her body as an egg—that is, it is 'laid'. If the ovum has been fertilized, and the egg is kept warm, a chick develops inside the shell, and after a period of 'incubation' it hatches from the egg and starts a free life. The length of the period of incubation differs from one species of bird to another. With the domestic fowl it is 3 weeks.

2. SELECTIVE BREEDING. In the wild state the animals choose their own mates, but on the farm the stockman decides which animals shall be the parents of the next generation, and by selecting only the best for breeding, he tries to improve the quality or change the characters of his stock. For example, whereas the wild jungle fowl produces relatively few eggs in a year, and lays these only in the spring in one batch or clutch, the domestic fowl, although descended from the same ancestry, produces eggs regularly and almost continuously. When animals are selectively bred for such things as better egg production, more milk or beef, to win races, to grow fine or coarse wool, and so on, the breeder is concerned with 'performance' or 'production' characters—things of direct use to the farmer. He may also, however, breed for such things as points of colour and markings, which are called 'breed characters or 'fancy points' and need have no real connexions with the animals' use-

fulness. Very often both kinds of character—production and fancy—are bred for together, and selection for the one may not help selection for the other.

With domestic mammals both reproduction and lactation (giving milk) are of importance. For example: the number, size, and quality of young pigs depend both upon the fertility (number of young born) of the sow and upon her ability to produce milk to feed her litter; and although the value of a dairy cow is due directly to the amount and quality of the milk she gives, she does not give milk until she has produced a calf. Differences in characters may exist between animals of the same species. For example, beef animals of high quality have, very often, poor milk yields, the qualities of beef and milk not being closely related in one animal. In consequence, beef calves often cannot get enough milk from their own dams to make good early growth and have in consequence to be reared on 'nurse-cows' of a milk (or dairy) strain (*see* CATTLE, CARE OF).

On the average, about the same numbers of male and female young are born. But one adult male can successfully be used to mate with many females, so that the breeder is able to select from among the males those of the best quality and to use only these as sires for mating. The surplus males are castrated, that is, they are prevented from breeding by removal of the sperm-producing organs, and are then usually fattened for meat (bullocks, hogs, and wethers) or used for work (geldings and draught oxen).

In recent years as the result of artificial insemination, greater numbers of offspring can be sired by one male than is possible with natural mating. The sperm is collected from, say, some particularly good bull, and, with suitable precautions, diluted and then distributed to many distant farms, where it is used for the artificial insemination of many cows. This method not only makes possible the wider use of better sires, but also helps to prevent the spread of certain diseases. The females do not have to be moved from their home farms to be served (mated).

3. INHERITANCE. The characters of an animal depend upon what it inherits from its parents, though its performance characters depend as well upon the conditions in which it lives, that is upon such matters as feeding, care, and management that make up its environment.

The inherited characters depend upon some things called 'genes' in the male and female reproductive cells. These cells differ in the genes they contain, so that differences in inherited characters are due to differences in genes, or, as it is called, in 'genetic constitution'.

In some cases a gene is related to or governs the development of a single character. Thus, for example, a real albino rabbit (that is, one with white fur and pink eyes) owes its albino character to the presence of a particular gene that prevents the formation of pigment (colouring matter) in the animal's body. Or, again, polled (hornless) cattle are produced because of a 'polled' gene which has been passed to the offspring by one or both the parents. Such genes affect only one character; others affect more than one character: the 'pink eye' gene in mice, for example, influences not only the colour of the eye but the colour of the coat and the size of the mouse as well.

In order to understand how the genes pass from parent to offspring we must understand what happens when the germ cells are formed. In each cell of an animal's body (and of a plant, too) there is a 'nucleus' that contains a number of thread-like or rod-like bodies called 'chromosomes', and each chromosome is in effect a string of genes (see HEREDITY, Vol. II). Every species of animal has cells with a characteristic number of chromosomes: for example, man has 48 to each cell, the pig and cat have 38, the dog 78, and horses and cattle 60. These chromosomes occur in pairs within the cells.

As an animal grows, the cells that compose its body divide and become more numerous, and whenever a body cell divides, each chromosome divides too, each half carrying to each new cell the full number of genes. But during the formation of the germ or reproductive cells, instead of splitting in half, the pairs of chromosomes separate, so that only one chromosome of each pair gets into each new germ cell; therefore a germ cell contains only half the number of chromosomes that the ordinary body cells contain. For example: each bull sperm carries only 30 chromosomes instead of 60, and each cow ovum also only 30, so that when a sperm fertilizes an ovum the 30 from the sire are added to the 30 from the dam to give the offspring, the new calf, the characteristic 30 pairs, that is, 60 chromosomes.

Each gene has a definite position on its

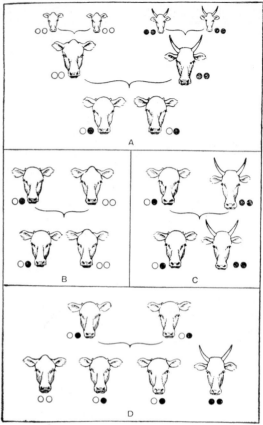

From J. E. Nichols: 'Livestock Improvement', Oliver and Boyd.

FIG. I.   INHERITANCE OF POLLED AND HORNED CHARACTERS
○ = polled gene   ● = horned gene
A. Pure polled and pure horned cattle mated
B. Impure and pure polled cattle mated
C. Impure polled and pure horned cattle mated
D. Impure polled cattle mated

chromosome, so that in a pair of chromosomes there are corresponding pairs of genes. These pairs may consist of similar genes (for example, two 'polled' genes) or of contrasting genes (for example, one 'polled' and one 'horned' gene). In the first case, every germ cell produced must carry a 'polled' gene, and the animal so bred is said to be 'pure' in its polled character; whereas, in the second case, a germ cell will receive either a 'polled' or a 'horned' gene, and the animal is said to be 'impure'.

It has, however, been discovered that when an animal carries genes of both kinds in its body cells, if the two meet in a new individual the effect of the 'polled' gene is dominant to (overrides) the effect of the 'horned' gene, and the 'horned' gene is recessive to (hidden by) the 'polled' one. In other words, the animal is

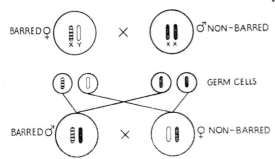

FIG. 2. ARRANGEMENT OF CHROMOSOMES WHEN BARRED
FEMALE AND NON-BARRED MALE POULTRY ARE MATED

polled, and looks no different from an animal that carries two 'polled' genes. Yet, when it breeds, it does not pass on the same inheritance as a pure polled animal, for its germ cells are of two kinds ('polled' and 'horned') and it may therefore produce horned calves. Horned animals must always be pure for hornedness; otherwise the recessive 'horned' gene could not produce this effect. The different possibilities are shown in Fig. 1.

This diagram shows, of course, only the results of a small number of matings: only enough, in fact, to show the possibilities. But when a large number of matings are taken into account, we find that the different results occur in definite proportions. For example, a large number of matings between impure polled and pure horned beasts (case C) gives approximately equal numbers of polled and horned calves, and a large number of matings between impure polled beasts (case D) gives a ratio in calves of 1 pure polled, 2 impure polled, and 1 pure horned, which, if we judge only by appearances, are 3 polled and 1 horned.

In these examples only one pair of genes with contrasting effects is considered. When more than one pair are concerned, the ratios become more complicated, though they can generally be calculated in the same way.

It is clear, therefore, that the appearance of an animal is not always a guide to its real character, and that only by the appearance of their offspring can we discover the genetic constitutions of the parents. The real breeding worth of a sire or a dam can be determined, therefore, only by breeding from it and thus seeing what characters it passes on. This is especially true of the performance characters, such as meat qualities and milk yield, which are each affected by many genes and the inheri-

tance of which is very complicated. The record of an animal's ancestors (its pedigree) is no absolute guarantee of its genetic constitution and, therefore, its breeding worth, although a pedigree gives some guide to the genes that an animal is likely to have inherited from its parents.

4. SEX LINKAGE. The male and the female animal differ from one another in respect of one pair of chromosomes, the sex chromosomes. In mammals the female has a pair of sex chromosomes that consists, like all normal pairs, of two identical chromosomes, usually represented on paper as XX; but the male has a pair of sex chromosomes which are not alike, and are shown as XY. Therefore, every ovum produced by a female carries an X chromosome, but the sperms of a male are X-bearing or Y-bearing in equal numbers. Thus, it is clear that over a large number of matings, males (XY) and females (XX) are produced in equal proportions. In other words, the sex ratio is 1 : 1.

A knowledge of this form of inheritance can be turned to practical use in cases where the sex chromosome is known to carry genes that control other characters. These are called 'sex-linked' characters, and we know most about them where poultry are concerned.

In the fowl, unlike the mammal, it is the male that is XX in sex chromosome constitution and the female that is XY. The barred feather colour, characteristic of the Barred Rock breed of fowls, is due to a gene carried on the X chromosome. Fowls of a breed in which the

J. S. Woodrow

MALE (LEFT) AND FEMALE (RIGHT) SEX-LINKED WELBAR
CHICKS

The male has lighter patches on its head and less-defined markings than the female

feathers are not barred carry non-barring genes, also on the X chromosome. The barred character is dominant to the non-barred. A barred hen (XY) passes her Y sex chromosome to her daughters (otherwise they would not be females), and her X sex chromosome to her sons. A non-barred cock (XX) transmits one X to his sons, the other to his daughters. Thus, in matings between barred hens and non-barred cocks the sons (cockerels) are barred like their mothers and the daughters (pullets) are non-barred like their fathers (Fig. 2). As the effect of the barred gene shows up in the down of the young chicks as lighter patches around the head, it is possible to separate pullets and cockerels (that is, to sex them) at the day-old chick stage, a great convenience to poultry breeders (*see* POULTRY).

See also PLANT BREEDING.
See also Vol. II: HEREDITY; REPRODUCTION IN ANIMALS.

STRAWBERRIES. This fruit grows well in most countries with a temperate climate, though in few countries do strawberries have such a good flavour as in Britain. They can be grown on any well-drained soil, but prefer a medium to heavy deep loam, into the top 2 feet of which a generous supply of manure—preferably farmyard manure—has been dug. The strawberry bed also needs a great deal of humus in the form of well-rotted leaf-mould and garden compost. If farmyard manure is scarce, other forms of organic nitrogenous fertilizers, such as hop manure, shoddy, or meat or fish meal, can be used instead, as well as sulphate of potash at the rate of 2 cwt. per acre. Strawberries do not like much lime.

As strawberries grow so low on the ground, they are vulnerable to late spring frosts which blacken the centre of the flower from which the future fruit develops. It is important, therefore, to place the strawberry bed in a high and protected part of the garden. The ground, having been deeply dug, should be allowed to settle so that the surface is firm before planting in late July, August, or September. Only really good runners should be planted, and these should be spaced 18 inches apart in rows 2 ft. 6 in. apart. The roots should be well spread out in the planting hole, the plants very firmly set, and the soil trodden tight. Although the bed needs cultivating with a hoe between the rows to keep it clear of weeds, the hoe should not disturb the soil immediately round the plants. It is wise to

go over the bed after the first winter, treading round the plants which may have been loosened and lifted by frosts.

The normal custom is to keep strawberry plants for 3 years; the second year generally produces the heaviest crop, though the finest individual berries are often produced on first-year plants. Plants grown for the market are often prevented from fruiting the first summer, so that all their strength is directed into developing size and vigour for the second year crop. When the fruit is swelling, towards the end of May, a thick layer of clean straw is laid round the plants to keep the berries clear of the ground. It is best to pick strawberries in the morning while it is still cool, but they must never be picked wet. For market some growers sort the fruit by size into two grades, putting the extra large and choice fruits into small 1 or 2 lb. chip-baskets or punnets, and the rest into 3 or 4 lb. chips.

When the strawberries are over, the straw litter is cleared off, the plants cleaned of dead leaves and all runners, and the bed weeded and

GROWING STRAWBERRIES IN A BARREL

John Topham

PICKING STRAWBERRIES IN KENT

hoed before the spreading of the autumn mulch of manure and compost. With garden strawberry beds it is the usual custom to replace a third of the bed each year with new plants. Strawberries are propagated by runners taken from good plants (*see* FRUIT PROPAGATION).

Various ways have been devised for growing strawberries in very confined spaces. They can be grown in pots on window-sills or in window boxes, or terraced in a series of 'steps' made of bricks which hold in the soil. The most spectacular is the barrel method of cultivation, by which as many as twenty-four plants can be grown on a square yard's space. Eighteen holes, $2\frac{1}{2}$ inches in diameter, through which the plants are to grow, are bored at suitable places in the sides of a large barrel. Smaller drainage holes as well as a layer of broken brick are put at the bottom of the barrel. The barrel is then filled with a rich mixture of loam, cow manure, and sharp sand, the plants being set as each line of holes is reached. A shaft of broken brick for drainage and aeration is built up the centre of the barrel. Then a further six plants are set on the top (*see* sketch).

Virus diseases, such as Yellow Edge and Crinkle, do more harm to strawberries than any other disease or pest (*see* PLANT DISEASES). These diseases are often carried from infected to healthy plants by the Strawberry Aphis and the Tarsonemid Mite, which also do harm to the plants on their own account by sucking the sap. There is no cure for diseased plants, so they should be rooted out and burnt. A fungus disease, Strawberry Mildew, can be very troublesome, but can be checked by dustings of sulphur. Various other pests such as wireworm and leatherjackets, the grubs of crane-flies, attack the plants, and slugs, ants, and birds devour the fruit if they can (*see* PESTS AND DISEASES).

Royal Sovereign is a very popular early strawberry of excellent appearance and flavour, which does well on a medium or light soil; but it is very subject to disease, and a sound, healthy strain must, therefore, be secured. It is self-fertile and so can be grown alone, while Tardive de Leopold, a strong later strawberry with a good flavour, is self-sterile and must be planted with another variety. Oberschlesien is a good self-fertile berry, but is also very subject to disease. Huxley is a strong grower which crops heavily, especially in heavy soils, but its flavour is less good. Though a carrier of disease, it does not suffer itself. Perle de Prague, Western Queen, and Climax are all suitable for gardens.

See FRUIT-GROWING; FRUIT PROPAGATION.

SUGAR-BEET. The sugar-beet plant has been developed from the wild beet found on the shores of the Mediterranean. It was developed on the Continent as a farm crop during the Napoleonic wars, when the British blockade prevented the importing of cane-sugar from the West Indies. Its cultivation on any large scale in Britain, however, did not begin until about 1920, but now it is firmly established as one of the most important crops.

The plant has a conical root, rather like a parsnip, and it contains on the average about 15% to 16% of sugar. This is extracted at the sugar-beet factories, the pulp being returned to the farmer for feeding to livestock. Farmers living near a factory may take the pulp in its natural, wet condition; but for the most part, the pulp is dried, for the greater convenience of transporting and storing, and sold as 'dried beet pulp'.

The leaves and crowns are cut off when the roots are 'lifted' (that is, pulled out of the ground) and these are generally left in the field for sheep or cattle to eat. These 'tops' have a feeding value about equal to swedes. When there are more tops than can be eaten fresh, they are usually made into SILAGE (q.v.). Thus, a farmer gets a fodder crop as well as a cash crop (one to sell) when he grows sugar-beet. The roots are sold to the factory for an agreed price per ton of washed roots having an agreed content of sugar—the richer the sugar content, the higher the price. Samples, therefore, must be taken from each load sent to the factory, and the amount of soil sticking to the roots (dirt tare) and the sugar content measured.

Sugar-beet does well on soils of many different types, so long as there is plenty of lime present and the soil is well manured with dung and fertilizers. It is a greedy crop and takes a good deal out of the soil. The seed of varieties grown in Britain has been bred from foreign stocks imported before 1939. This accounts for such names as Kleinwanzleben, Dobrovice, and Kuhn, though these are all nowadays produced in Britain.

When sugar-beet is grown, its place is that of roots in the ROTATION OF CROPS (q.v.). Its cultivation is very like that of mangolds (see ROOT CROPS), to which it is related botanically. The seed is sown from March to May in a fine, firm, deep, and moist seed-bed, at the rate of 15 lb. of seed per acre, in rows spaced 20 to 22 inches apart. Like mangolds the seedlings are thinned out into single plants as soon as the first pair of true leaves appears, leaving 10-inch spacings between plants in the row. This should allow for not less than 30,000 plants per acre. Sometimes the seed may be sown on ridges, but is more often drilled on the flat. Recently beet

Eric Guy

TOPPING SUGAR-BEET BY HAND

The Times

UNLOADING BARGES OF SUGAR-BEET AT A FACTORY AT ELY

seed, which is really a fruit containing 2 to 5 seeds, has been 'sheared' or split by machinery before sowing to separate the individual seeds, and these not only germinate more quickly, but give fewer plants in a row, and this makes thinning easier.

During the growing season, horse-hoeing or tractor-hoeing between the rows is carried out to keep the weeds in check; but the crop receives no other attention until the roots are ready for pulling from September onwards. The roots are first loosened with a beet plough, and then pulled by hand, 'knocked' to free them from soil, and 'topped' with a knife to sever top and crown from the root proper. Lifting continues until December, and during these months the sugar-beet factory works night and day.

For many years engineers have tried to invent a machine that will lift the sugar-beet roots, clean and top them, and load them into a cart or wagon ready for transport to the factory. Though these machines are not yet perfect, many are in use, and they save much hand labour. Complete sugar-beet harvesters have a

topping-knife, as well as digging-shares, incorporated in their mechanism. Usually the tops are cut, while the beets are still in the ground, by revolving horizontal knives attached to the front part of the machine. The severed tops are thrown to one side of the machine. Then, behind the revolving knife comes the lifting-share, which digs out the root of the beet and puts it on to an elevator, to be conveyed upwards and cleaned.

The average yield is about 9 tons of washed beet an acre, with the sugar content about 16%. The same weight of tops as of roots is usually obtained.

SUGAR-CANE. The sap of many plants contains sugar, but nearly all the sugar we eat comes from only two of them: the SUGAR-BEET (q.v.) which is grown in Britain, and the sugar-cane which can be grown only in tropical and sub-tropical countries with a warm, moist climate.

The sugar-cane, *Saccharum officinarum*, is a giant grass about 10 feet high, with a stout, round, much jointed stem, long narrow leaves, and grows in great tufts from an underground rootstock. It will persist for many years if left undisturbed, but when cultivated, is usually grubbed up and replanted every few years. It is no longer found wild, though it is probably a native of the Pacific Islands. It was widely grown in China, India, Persia, and Egypt before the 1st century A.D. Sugar was known in Europe from Roman times, but only as a rare spice obtained at great cost and difficulty from the East; the Venetian merchants were prominent in this trade. During the Crusades the plant was taken to Cyprus and Sicily, and its cultivation begun in those islands. In the 15th century it was taken to the Canary Islands and in the 16th century to Central America and the West Indies, and it has since been introduced into nearly every tropical country. It is now extensively grown in the southern United States of America, Jamaica, Cuba, Brazil, Natal, Fiji, Hawaii, and Queensland.

Sugar-cane grows very rapidly from any portion of the stem that includes two or more joints, the new shoot arising from a little bud in the axil of a leaf. Such shoots, known on the plantations as 'seed', are planted by almost burying them in moist ground, where they soon give rise to new plants of the same variety of cane. Feathery tufts of flowers are borne at the tips of the tall shoots of most, but not all, varieties. The cane, however, is rarely allowed to seed, as that would use up the valuable reserves of sugar in the sap. So cane is only grown from seed when a new variety is being raised. When the crop is cut, the plant grows again from the roots, such crops being called 'ratoons'. After two or three crops have been harvested the roots are generally dug up, the land cleaned and cultivated, and a fresh supply of 'seed' set. This 'seed' cane is usually cut from the tips of a previous crop, as that part of the stem contains least sugar.

Many Indian peasants grow the sugar-cane simply as a sweet vegetable in their gardens, from time to time cutting a piece of cane which they suck as a sweetmeat. For centuries, however, sugar-cane has been grown on a larger scale to produce sugar crystals and syrup, all the work being done by hand or with animal power. The crop is harvested some 10 months after planting, when the cane has reached its full height, is hard in texture, and is beginning to flower. The stems are cut through at the base with a short, sharp knife, called a 'cutlass', the leaves cleaned off, and the cane loaded on to ox-carts to be carried to the primitive sugar-mill. There the cane is cut into short lengths which are ground between rollers turned by hand, by animals, or even by wind or water power, to extract the sweet juice. This juice is at once concentrated in great iron pans over wood fires, until it forms a thick syrup, which, when cool, crystallizes into a coarse brown sugar. These were the simple methods used on the West Indian plantations; they needed a great deal of labour, about one man per acre, and it was largely to grow sugar that the slaves were brought over from Africa. For a long time there was keen rivalry between English, French, Dutch, Spanish, and Portuguese growers, who all developed sugar plantations in various parts of America and the West Indies.

Nowadays the bulk of the cane-sugar grown for export is raised by more modern methods on large plantations where every stage of the work is highly organized. Fertile, well-drained land is selected, manured, and thoroughly tilled by tractor-drawn ploughs or gyro-tillers. Before the seed shoots are planted, the soil is thrown into ridges about 5 feet apart; the shoots are then set in pairs, about 4 feet apart, in the furrows between the ridges, and they are afterwards earthed up. Sometimes a planting plough is used to set the seed mechanically, and machinery is used for cultivation and weeding. The crop is usually still cut by hand because of the difficulty of handling the tangled mass and removing the leaves. In Hawaii, however, a light fire is run through the plantations, which burns off the leaves but does not damage the cane stems. Then an enormous crane, moving on crawler tracks and carrying a great grab, the jaws of which cut through the cane stems, gathers the crop and loads it into lorries. Modern means of transport, such as light railways, aerial ropeways, barges on narrow canals, and motor lorries are used to convey the heavy and bulky crop to the factory. The harvest of cane is from 30 to 40 tons per acre, yielding 3 or 4 tons of actual sugar. Once cut, the cane must be treated within 48 hours, or its sugar content will fall; hence the growing and cutting must be carefully planned so that the crop is gathered over a long season, keeping the factory working steadily. Ample rainfall is essential, and in some countries

CUTTING SUGAR-CANE IN HONDURAS

the plantations are irrigated. In a suitable climate cane grows all the year round, and crops are ripening every month in one or other of the many countries where it is grown.

An elaborate modern plantation factory for extracting sugar works on the same main principles as the primitive mill, crushing the cane to get the juice, and then concentrating the juice until the sugar crystals form (*see* SUGAR-REFINING, Vol. VII). Besides solid sugar, the cane yields syrup, treacle, rum, molasses for animal feeding, and industrial alcohol; the fibrous matter of the stalks, called 'bagasse', is either burned to provide power for the factory or is made into wallboard.

See also TROPICAL AGRICULTURE.
See also Vol. VII: SUGAR-REFINING.

SUNFLOWERS, *see* OIL-BEARING PLANTS.

SWEDES, *see* ROOT CROPS.

SWEET CORN. This is a special type of MAIZE (q.v.), the unripe ears of which, known as 'corn cobs' or 'corn on the cob', are often used as a vegetable. During recent years sweet corn has become more popular in Britain and is now often grown, particularly in the south of England where the climate is more suitable than in the north. There are many kinds of sweet corn, but the specially produced hybrid seed is considered to be the most productive. Varieties and hybrids particularly suited to the climate of Britain are the *John Innes Hybrids Nos. 1* and *2*, *Northern Cross, Early Golden Market, Extra Early Bantam, Canada Gold*, and *Golden Cross Bantam*.

As sweet corn is very sensitive to cold weather, the seed should not be sown in the open until May, though it may be sown earlier under cloches, which are removed when the risk of frost is past, or it may be sown under glass in pots or boxes during April, the plants being put out in May.

To ensure that the pollen is well distributed, sweet corn should preferably be grown in blocks of several rows rather than in single rows. The rows should be from 2 to 3 feet apart with the plants spaced from 12 to 18 inches in the row. When sown in the open, the seed is placed in shallow drills from 1 to $1\frac{1}{2}$ inches deep, two or three seeds being sown together to ensure an evenly spaced block of plants, and the surplus seedlings removed while they are quite small.

Sweet corn must have an open sunny position and a rich soil. If necessary, farmyard manure may be dug in when the ground is prepared. Before the seed is sown a complete fertilizer should be well cultivated into the surface soil at the rate of 2 oz. per square yard. As sweet corn roots remain near the surface, all cultivations of the growing crops should be of a shallow kind, so that the roots are not harmed. During dry weather the plants need watering, and the soil between the rows may be mulched, that is, covered with some vegetable matter such as grass mowings to help it retain the moisture.

The ears are ready for gathering when they reach the so-called 'milk stage' (the grains are then of a soft-cheese consistency). They are picked by hand, together with the husks or sheaths. Sweet corn should always be used in as fresh a condition as possible.

See also MAIZE.

SWEET PEAS. This very popular annual flower (*Lathyrus odoratus*) belongs to the family *Leguminosae*, as do clovers and all other LEGUMINOUS CROPS (q.v.). It is a native of Sicily, and was introduced into this country in 1699 by a priest named Francis Cupani. Cupani's sweet peas were all of the same colours, the standards (the upper petals) being purple-maroon and the wings (the two side petals) mid-blue. The blooms were hooded and not much bigger than those of green peas. Two and occasionally three flowers grew on a stem.

The modern sweet pea has a large range of colours, and the flower is big and frilly, often carrying double and triple standards. There are usually four blooms to a stem, modern varieties sometimes having up to seven. The development of the modern sweet pea was largely the work of Henry Eckford at the end of the 19th century, and during the 20th century many breeders have produced new varieties in colour and shape.

At present there are three distinct races of sweet peas: winter-flowering, largely grown under glass for early marketing; spring-flowering, originated by Frank G. Cuthbertson, and increasingly popular in the U.S.A.; and the summer-flowering, or Spencer variety, most commonly grown out of doors in Britain.

Those who want early flowers or seed crops sow their seeds in the autumn, in late September or October, and bring them on slowly through the winter in FRAMES (q.v.). In southern counties they are even sown in the open ground, some-times under CLOCHES (q.v.), and in a mild winter come safely through to give a magnificent display from early June onwards. Sweet peas are often sown in a warm temperature in January, then hardened off slowly in a frame, and transplanted outside in March or April. Or they may be sown directly in the flowering quarters in March or April, according to the weather, to flower in the late summer.

If the seeds are sown in boxes or pots, a good compost is 3 parts clean loam, 1 part leaf-mould, and 1 part sand, though any sweet garden soil will do instead. No manures or fertilizers are needed at this stage, though later fertilizers can be used to encourage growth, vigour, and colour. The planting site should be prepared in the autumn and allowed to settle during the winter. It should be dug to a depth of 2 feet, and the bottom forked to secure good drainage. Then old decayed farmyard manure or garden compost should be mixed with the soil in the bottom foot or so.

A heavy sprinkling of bone meal and a good dusting of superphosphate of lime in the soil helps the plants to form good roots. The surface should be left rough through the winter, and in the spring the soil will break down easily to a fine tilth. Plenty of dry wood ash or a light dusting of sulphate of potash forked in on top will help to keep the young plants healthy and bring out their full colour later.

When the young plant is about 3 inches high, the growing tip is pinched out to induce it to make several side growths. For exhibition work the plants are limited to one or two main

J. E. Downward

SWEET PEA, 'ELIZABETH TAYLOR'

growths, which are trained up bamboo canes, all side-shoots and tendrils being pinched off. Greenfly is the worst danger at all stages (*see* APHID PESTS), and the plants should be sprayed regularly with a good INSECTICIDE (q.v.). The sweet peas continue to produce flowers for a long time so long as they are kept picked.

SWEET POTATOES, *see* TROPICAL ROOT CROPS.

T

TAPEWORM, *see* Parasitic Worms, section 1.

TAPIOCA, *see* Tropical Root Crops, section 2.

TEA. The tea from which our everyday drink is made consists of the dried leaves of a bush that is grown in parts of Asia and Africa. Its scientific name is *Camellia sinensis*, and it has been cultivated for thousands of years in China and Japan. When tea was first introduced into Europe in the 17th century it was so scarce and costly that tea caddies were fitted with locks and keys. China continued to be the main tea-producing country until the 19th century, when it was discovered that tea grew also in Assam, a district of north-east India. In 1839 the first India Tea Company was formed for the cultivation of Indian tea, and, in 1870, when blight destroyed the coffee crop in Ceylon, tea was planted there. Later it was introduced to the East Indies and also into Africa where, especially in East Africa, there are large plantations. In the middle of the 19th century fast-sailing ships called CLIPPERS (q.v. Vol. IV) raced all the way from Foochow on the coast of south China to London, to bring the first tea crops of each season. Nowadays the biggest plantations are in Ceylon and Assam, and tea is so cheap and plentiful that it is found on everyone's table. In China and Japan tea is grown on peasant holdings, and there are no large plantations such as those of India and the East Indies.

Fertile soil, a warm climate, and ample rainfall are needed for growing tea crops, and the best teas are usually produced in the hills. Tea is sometimes grown on ploughed-up grassland, but more often on cleared jungle land. The seeds of the tea plants are sown in a nursery bed, and when the seedlings are about 18 months old, they are carefully lifted from the ground and planted on the cleared land at about 4 feet apart each way. Here, in a very hot climate they grow for about 3 years before leaf-plucking can be begun, though in a colder region it may be as much as 10 years. During this time they are pruned at intervals to make them grow into bushy shrubs. If allowed to grow freely they would form small evergreen trees with pretty flowers like the garden camellia, to which they are related. The ground around them is kept free from weeds, and sometimes a tree is planted to provide shade.

When the bushes are about 3 feet high and big enough for plucking, the young and tender leaves are picked by hand, often by women. This is done at intervals of 10 days or a fortnight, so that a heavy crop is gathered, from 500 to 1,000 pounds of prepared tea being obtained from each acre every year. This yield continues for many years before it is necessary to replant the crop; but frequent manuring is needed to prevent the soil from becom-

Tea Bureau

PLANTING TEA SEED IN NURSERY BEDS IN SOUTH INDIA
Holes for the seeds are made through the wooden frame

PLUCKING TEA IN SOUTH INDIA

Tea Bureau

hairs lie one way. Each flower in the flower-head has a sharply hooked bract, and it is with these hooks that the cloth is combed (*see* WOOL WEAVING, Vol. VII).

The crop has been grown in Britain since the 14th century, at one time in many counties, but nowadays only in one small district in Somerset. The plants grow best on a heavy soil, from seed broadcast, though sometimes drilled, in March at the rate of 2 pecks to the acre. Farmyard manure is sometimes applied the preceding autumn when the land is ploughed, but not usually again, as on too rich soil the plants tend to produce more leaf and less flower. In the November following sowing the plants are transplanted by hand, being set out about 18 in. apart. The plants start to flower in the following July, and the first heads, having dropped their petals, are ready for harvesting early in August. From then onwards the ripe heads are cut as they are ready, a few inches of stalk being left on each. They are tied up in bundles and hung to dry, preferably outdoors, though as wet spoils the quality of the heads, indoor drying may be necessary. Once dry, the heads can be stored almost indefinitely.

Wireworms and leather-jackets sometimes damage the plants in the seed-bed, and greenfly may attack the growing crop in a hot summer. Plants attacked by a fungus disease, called 'cabbage disease', produce a great deal of leaf and very few heads. A good crop is 7 to 10 'packs' per acre, a pack being 20,000 teazles. Higher yields do not usually produce such good-quality heads. Nowadays the teasels are marketed loose in sacks, and are no longer graded by size.

ing exhausted. The bushes are pruned each year to keep them in shape, and the prunings are dug into the soil.

During harvest time the plucked leaves are taken each day to the estate factory where the tea is prepared by being dried under carefully controlled conditions. Green China tea is the kind preferred in China and Japan, but it comes from plants of the same kind as the darker teas of India and Ceylon, though it is treated differently after plucking. The Chinese growers wither the freshly plucked leaves on an iron pan heated by a wood fire, then roll them by hand, and finally dry them in the sun.

See also TROPICAL AGRICULTURE; TROPICAL PESTS.
See also Vol. VII: TEA TRADE.

TEASELS, The dried flower-heads of the cultivated, biennial plant, the Fuller's teasel (*Dipsacus fullonum*), are used by cloth-manufacturers in machines designed to 'raise the nap' on cloth, that is, comb it so that nearly all the surface

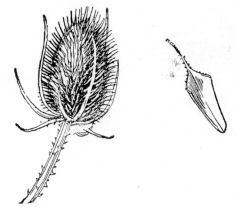

A TEASEL HEAD AND ONE OF THE SPINES (ENLARGED)

TENANCY, *see* LAND OWNERSHIP.

THATCHING. Thatching was adopted as a method of roofing a home long before slates or tiles were known (*see* HOUSES, HISTORY OF, Vol. XI). Today thatch can be seen on houses, farm buildings, stacks of corn and hay, and even silos. It has the advantage that the material of which it is most often made, the straw, is grown on the farm.

As a roofing for a house, thatch has the great advantage that it is a good insulator, helping to keep a house warm in winter and cool in summer. Also, a thatched roof needs less costly timbering than a tile or slate roof; but this initial saving of expense is offset in the long run by the fact that, whereas slates and tiles may last for several generations, a thatch must be renewed periodically—the frequency depending on the materials used and their condition at the time of thatching, as well as on the thoroughness with which the thatcher did his work. A well-bedded thatch of Norfolk reed, for instance, has been known to

Norman Wymer

SECURING THE THATCH WITH SPARS AT THE BASE OF A CHIMNEY

To the left of the ladder is a 'dog' (forked stick) in which the straw is carried up to the roof, and beneath it is the beginning of the 'bed' or under layer of thatch

last as long as 50 years, whereas the normal life of wheat straw may be only about 10 to 20 years.

Although Norfolk reed is by far the most durable, it is also the most expensive, and thatching, as a rule, is carried out with local materials. These are usually the straw of wheat or rye, but in parts of Essex rushes are often introduced, and in moorland areas heather may also be used. This wide variety of materials, as well as the fact that even the straw itself varies according to local soil, has helped to make thatching one of the most individual of crafts. For instance, whereas the East Anglian craftsmen usually made their gables sharp-edged, those in the West Country tend to round theirs. So, too, do they differ in their treatment of dormer windows, the way they cap their ridges, and in their general trimming and finishing.

Though no two craftsmen ever work exactly alike, yet in main essentials, all thatchers follow the same principle. As a rule they work in pairs, the master thatcher laying the thatch, and his labourer or mate preparing the straw. This initial preparation is very important. To begin with, the straw (or whatever material is to be used) must be tossed again and again into the air with a pitchfork to allow the wind to carry away any loose strands. Then buckets of water are thrown on the pile to damp it down. Then, working from the bottom of this heap, the labourer draws the straw away in handfuls and lays it on the ground beside him to form a series of neat, straight bundles, or 'yelms', of more or less uniform length, a process known as 'knocking up'. As each yelm is completed, it is placed in a fork-shaped stick, or 'dog', ready to be carried up the ladder to the master thatcher as he wants it.

The thatching begins at the eaves of the roof and finishes at the ridge, and the thatcher works from right to left. He places his ladder just to the left of the section he is thatching. Thus, suppose that the roof to be covered is a simple structure of but two spans—one at the front of the house and the other at the back—the first yelm is placed over the bottom right-hand corner of one of the spans, and securely tied to the rafters with yarn or wire. The next yelm is then laid to the left of the first and similarly bound. As soon as the small section of the eaves within reach of the ladder has been covered, the thatcher climbs a further rung or two, and lays more yelms so that the lower ends of these

Norman Wymer

BEATING DOWN THE SPARS WITH A THATCHING RAKE
The lower edge of the thatch is secured and decorated
by the pattern of spars

surface. Then, while the straw is wet, he proceeds to 'dress it down' with the flat face of his rake-head in a combined beating and smoothing movement designed to remove all ridges that might catch the wind or rain.

When both spans of the roof are covered, an extra 'capping' of straw is laid across the ridge, to give added protection to a naturally vulnerable point; and this is then 'sewn up' with a series of spars. This 'sparring' gives a particularly neat finish, and thatchers have their own individual patterns for sparring; a favourite one is two parallel lines of sticks at a distance of 2 feet or so from one another, secured to the straw by spars, and linked with further sticks, set in criss-cross fashion to form a kind of diamond or lacing pattern.

This description is of thatching at its simplest and most straightforward. Thatchers often have infinitely more complicated roofs to cover, and are faced with many problems that need considerable skill and initiative. A good deal of thatching of a less skilled kind is also done on most farms in making more temporary roofings to corn and hay stacks.

See also RURAL CRAFTS.
See also Vol. XI: ROOFS.

overlap the upper ends of those he has just set. And so he works his way to the ridge until one end of the roof is filled in. Then he moves his ladder a few feet to the left, and sets to work as before, laying a second series of yelms to the left of the first. In this way his thatch gradually spreads across the entire roof.

So far, however, he has done no more than lay the 'bed' for his main thatch. Where a roof has been covered before, the thatcher lays his fresh straw on top of an old 'bed'; but when thatching a new roof he must provide the under layer, and then bring his ladder back to the starting-point and lay a whole new series of yelms on top of the first. This time, however, instead of binding his straw to the bare rafters, he now secures the yelms to the 'bed' with 'spars' or 'spicks', hazel sticks twisted to the shape of a V. By inserting the points and driving them home into the straw, he secures the yelms to the 'bed' in much the same way as a strand of wire may be attached to a wooden post with a staple.

As each section of his roof is finished, the thatcher rakes the straw with a special rake with 4-inch teeth and tosses buckets of water over the

THRESHING-MACHINE. The purpose of the thresher is to beat out and thus separate the grain from the ears of corn. The essential part of the most common type of machine is a revolving drum which has beater bars fixed round its circumference, and rotates very near to a concave grid which partly encircles it. The corn is fed into the space between the drum and the grid, and the bars on the drum knock the grain out of the ears. The peg drum, which is less common and has been introduced to Britain from America, has upstanding pegs instead of beaters on the drum.

The straw passes over shakers which toss it out of the machine. The grain and the chaff (the empty shells of the grain) fall through the bars of the shakers, and then blasts of wind from power-driven fans winnow the grain free from the chaff. The grain is graded into various sizes by means of a rotary screen, and leaves the machine through two or three separate spouts to which sacks are hooked. Weed seeds are mechanically separated from the grain and come out of an opening low down to one side of the machine. Broken pieces of straw and other rubbish

A THRESHING-MACHINE

The corn is put into the top of the machine. The straw is
ejected at the back on to the elevator and the corn into
sacks in front. The machine is driven by power from a
tractor transmitted to it by the belt on the left

accumulate underneath the thresher as 'cavings'.
The process within the threshing-machine needs
several elevators to carry the grain from the
bottom to the top of the machine so that it can
fall again into cleaners and separators. The
elevators consist of endless belts bearing little
buckets. The threshed straw is either built into
a stack again, or bundled mechanically into
trusses, or compressed into bales.

The threshing-machine, and any other machine
such as the elevator or baler, is towed to its
place of work against the stacks of corn by the
tractor which will drive the machines when the
outfit has been set up for work. Some smaller
machines are stationary in buildings near the
farmhouse (*see* BARN MACHINES), such threshers
being more used in Scotland than in other parts
of Britain.

Some crops grown for seed are threshed in
more simple ways: for example, with the flail,
or with a roller passed over the gathered crop
which is spread on a sheet on the ground.

See also HARVESTING.

THRIPS, *see* INSECT PESTS.

THYME, *see* HERBS, GARDEN.

TIED COTTAGES, *see* FARM COTTAGES; LAND
OWNERSHIP.

TIMBER. The wood that forms the trunks and
branches of trees is made up, like other parts of
trees and smaller plants, of tiny box-like units
called 'cells' (*see* FLOWERING PLANTS, Vol. II).
In leaves and flowers the cells are often square
or rounded in outline, but in timber they are
mostly long and narrow, for they have to serve
as tubes to carry sap from the roots up the tree
trunk. Their walls are very strong and fibrous,
because they have to support the weight of the
branches and leaves above them. They interlock to form that wonderfully strong and supple
substance, wood, for which we have found so
many uses (*see* STEMS, Vol. II).

The important growing parts of the trunk and
branches of a tree are the outer layers. These
layers may be no more than an inch or two in
thickness in a big trunk, or a fraction of an inch
in a thin twig. Between the bark and the true
wood inside is a vital layer of cells which forms
a kind of skin or sheath, and which is so thin that
it can be seen only with a microscope. This
layer, called the 'cambium', creates year by year
the cells which form the wood. The cambium
creates cells both on its outer and inner surface.
Those on its outer surface, that is, between the
cambium and the bark, are called 'bast'; this is
a soft, weak layer, usually less than an inch thick,
which carries the sugar sap, formed by the leaves,
downwards to feed the roots. No matter how
big the tree grows, the bast seldom gets much
thicker, but in spite of this it is an essential part
of the tree, and if it were broken all round the
stem, the roots would starve and the tree would
die.

The cambium layer also builds up a series of
wood cells from its inner surface, the main work
of which is to carry the root sap upwards from
the roots to feed the leaves and to keep them
supplied with water. As the tree grows, it needs
more and more root sap, so every year a new
layer of wood cells is formed, and the trunk gets
steadily bigger.

These wood cells do not continue to carry sap
for the whole lifetime of the tree, because the

trunk and boughs grow steadily stouter, and soon contain more cells than are needed for the sap. So the inner part of each trunk and branch ceases to carry sap, while the outer layers continue to do so. The cells of the inner part become gradually closed up with substances, such as gums and resins, which make them stronger, harder, and better able to resist decay. This hardened inner part of the wood, which has the main burden of supporting the weight of the trunk and branches, is called 'heartwood'. The outer, much softer part, through which the sap is still passing, is called 'sapwood'. In young trees and small branches this sapwood extends right to the centre, but as soon as the wood is a few inches thick, most trees begin to form heartwood at the centre. In large and old treetrunks most of the timber is heartwood, which is more useful and valuable than sapwood. When a tree is cut, the sapwood is generally seen to be light in colour and the heartwood dark.

At the very centre of every trunk or branch of our common trees lies a soft core called 'pith'. This is the remains of the weak cells of the thin green shoot which grew before the wood formed.

The rate of growth of a tree varies with the seasons. In the spring, when the leaves open and the tree grows most quickly, much soft and porous wood is needed to carry the increased amount of sap. In the summer, stronger cells of hard wood are needed to support the growing weight of leaves and new branches at the top of the tree trunk. So we find alternate bands of soft and hard wood right through the tree trunk. As each pair of bands was formed in one year (soft, large cells in the spring, and harder, smaller cells in the summer) they make up an annual ring. By counting these rings on a stump at ground level, one can find out the age of the tree that grew there. No wood is formed in winter, as growth ceases with the colder weather.

In close-grained wood, which has grown slowly, the annual rings are narrow and packed closely together. In coarse-grained wood, which has grown more quickly, they are broader and spaced more widely apart. Either type of grain can be formed by most kinds of trees, according to the circumstances in which they grow. Each type has its uses, but close-grained wood is usually the heavier, harder, and stronger.

The annual rings look like circles only when the tree trunk is cut across. When it is cut lengthwise, they show as bands or lines; these patterns can be seen on most pieces of wood. When the trunks of many kinds of trees are cut across, narrow bands of cells can be seen spreading out from the central pith like the rays of the sun. These are the pith rays, which store the tree's food and help to strengthen its trunk. In some timbers, such as oak, they form a beautiful pattern called 'silver grain', which is revealed by skilful sawing. When the wood is sawn lengthwise, the pith rays show up as smooth plates or dark streaks.

As the tree trunk expands, it encloses the ends of the small side branches, and these then become preserved in the timber in the form of 'knots'. If the side shoot was dead when enclosed, the side shoot knot is usually hard and black, and it may fall from a thin plank, leaving a round hole. If it was still alive when it was enclosed in the trunk, it will be softer and browner and firmly attached to the true timber. Knots, which are seen as dark rods, bands, or circles according to how the trunk is sawn, weaken the timber and make it harder to work. By pruning off side branches as they appear, the forester can grow clean, strong, knot-free wood.

Many much finer details are seen when wood is examined under the microscope, and experts can tell the various timbers apart by looking at the intricate patterns of their cells. No two timbers have the same pattern, and so we get a

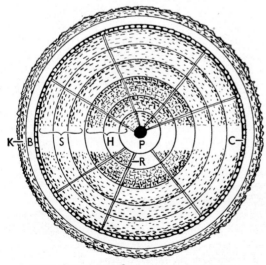

CROSS-SECTION OF A 6-YEAR-OLD TREE TRUNK

The alternating zones of paler spring wood and darker summer wood make up the annual rings. *K.* bark. *B.* bast. *C.* cambium. *S.* sapwood. *H.* heartwood. *P.* central pith. *R.* pith rays

STRIPPING THE BARK FOR TELEGRAPH POLES IN THE NEW FOREST
The timber will season in the open air, and later it will be preserved with creosote

wonderful range of woods, with varying qualities of hardness, lightness, strength, colour, and appearance, each valued for some special use.

When a tree is felled, even in winter, the little tubular cells are full of watery sap, and the timber must, therefore, be dried by 'seasoning'. The wood, after being sawn up, is stacked in the open air for several months; or else it is heated in a special drying-room, called a kiln, for several days. Seasoned wood is lighter, harder, stronger, and less liable to shrink or twist than green wood, that is, freshly cut wood.

Timber, one of the most widely used of raw materials, is very strong in comparison with its weight, nearly all timbers being lighter than water. It lasts well, and those kinds that decay if exposed to damp or to insect attack can be preserved by chemicals such as creosote. The beautiful grains of some woods can be preserved and shown up by polishing. Besides being sawn into planks, timber is now often 'peeled' into sheets and used for PLYWOOD AND VENEERS, or it is turned into pulp for PAPER-MAKING The cellulose (that is, a compound of carbon, hydrogen, and oxygen) in wood is converted into wood alcohol, which is used as a fuel. It is also converted into RAYON, and into some forms of sugar and PLASTICS (qq.v. Vol. VII). These are only some of the uses of timber.

The forester must know the various uses of timber so that he may grow the most profitable kinds in the best way. If his trees are required for pit-props or wood pulp, when quantity is more important than quality, he may try to grow a large volume of timber in a short time, planting many small trees fairly close together. But if he is growing timber mainly for sawing, or making into plywood, he will aim at growing tall, straight trees with large, well-shaped trunks, which he will prune to keep free from knots. These big trunks will probably sell at a better price; they are cheaper to handle weight for weight, and there is less waste in cutting them up. No two timbers can be handled in the same way, for each has its special qualities, and a skilful sawyer who understands how wood is formed can saw up the logs so that they form strong beams and boards, or show beautifully grained and figured surfaces.

See also FORESTRY; TREES, BROADLEAVED; TREES, CONIFEROUS.
See also Vol. VII: TIMBER INDUSTRY.

TIMBER FELLING. Timber is obtained from forests either by 'clear felling', that is, felling all the trees standing on the chosen area, or by 'selection felling', in which certain trees only are marked for felling. Selection felling is generally for the purpose of 'thinning', a proportion of the trees being cut out to give the remainder more room in which to grow. The selection of trees for felling is a skilled task. If the selection were left to the merchant who is buying the timber, he would naturally choose the best and leave the worst; but the forester must be content to leave many of the better trees to mature into bigger timber. Clear fellings are usually left until the crop is mature.

In countries where timber is still cheap and plentiful, the trees are often felled with the axe alone, being generally cut so that a stump 2 or 3 feet high is left. This is a very wasteful method. In Britain, where timber is valuable, the timber fellers, who are amongst the most skilful in the world, cut the tree as near as possible to ground level, and use axes, cross-cut saws, and wedges. They usually work in pairs, and are paid according to the size of the tree they fell.

First of all, the tree fellers inspect the tree and decide in which direction to fell it. Other things being equal, they plan to bring it down in the direction in which its weight is greatest, either because the trunk is leaning or because the crown of foliage is heavier on one side than on the other.

Next they 'lay-in' the trunk at the base with their axes. With alternate vertical and horizontal strokes, they cut away the thicker base of the trunk, forming a level ledge; this is done most deeply on the side to which the tree is to fall, and so lessens the work for the saw, without wasting useful timber. Then the felling saw is brought into action. Crouching or kneeling upon the ground, each man takes one handle, and they draw the long blade to and fro, working towards the direction in which they wish the tree to fall. After the saw has cut a few inches into the trunk, steel wedges are driven in behind it in order to keep the weight of the tree off the saw blade. They also tilt the tree slightly in the direction in which the fellers want it to fall. Then the sawing is resumed to complete the cut, and at length, with a tearing and rending sound, the trunk finally breaks away from its stump, and the great tree swings over to fall amidst the crashing of its branch-wood.

The next step is to trim out the trunk by cutting off or 'snedding' the side branches. The smaller branches are burned, but the larger ones, suitable for firewood, are stacked in piles called 'cords'. The top of the tree is sawn off at a convenient place, called the 'timber-point'. Forked or bent trunks are generally cross-cut into sections. The timber lengths are then measured, so that the fellers' pay can be calculated, and the merchant can find out exactly how much material he has obtained. Then the fellers move on to their next tree, and the timber hauliers take charge of the logs, which are now ready for removal from the forest.

In Britain the first stage of a log's journey from the forest to the sawmill is known as 'tushing'. A strong chain is secured to the butt or bottom end of the log, which is then hauled over the ground to the nearest road by a tractor or a team of horses. There, it is loaded on to a timber carriage, usually a pole wagon—two two-wheeled axles connected by a long pole. The logs rest on cross-bars above the axles, and are held in place by upright iron bars and secured by chains. Pole wagons may be drawn by tractors, horses, or specially designed lorries.

Forestry Commission

FELLING A SCOTS PINE IN THE NEW FOREST

When the saw cut was nearly through the trunk, the man in the centre gave the two wedges a blow with his mallet. This tilted the tree so that it fell

The usual method of loading is called 'parbuckling'. Wire ropes are led from the wagon under and around the log, which has previously been brought to lie parallel with the wagon on the ground beside it. The free or running ends of these ropes are carried over the pole wagon, and hitched to horse or tractor on the side farther from the log. Wooden ramps are set in place between the log at ground level and the bed of the wagon a few feet above it. Then the horse or tractor hauls away. As the ropes tighten, the log is rolled up the ramp and comes to rest on top of the wagon. When the load is completed, it goes on its way to the mill (see picture, p. 241).

See also FORESTRY; LOGGING; LUMBER CAMPS.

TIMBER MEASUREMENTS. Squared or sawn timber is measured by its volume in cubic feet. This is found in the usual way, by multiplying its length by its breadth, and the result by its thickness. For convenience, it is often bought and sold by the 'foot run', or by its superficial area; but in such cases the breadth and thickness are stated, so that the actual volume can be found by calculation.

MEASURING THE GIRTH AND LENGTH OF A LOG

The customary unit for importing softwood timber from northern Europe is the 'standard' of 165 cubic feet. Each actual standard is made up of many small pieces of timber to make up this total volume; the actual number varies with the dimensions to which they are cut. In America the unit of measurement is the 'board foot', which is equal to one-twelfth part of the English cubic foot.

Round timber in the log is measured throughout Britain in special units called 'Hoppus cubic feet'. To measure a log, its girth at the midpoint is first measured in inches with a measuring tape. This figure is divided by 4 in order to give the 'quarter girth', also in inches. This quarter girth is multiplied by itself to give the square of the quarter girth, which corresponds to the area of the cross-section of the log, in square inches.

The length of the log is then measured in feet, and the result multiplied by the square of the quarter girth. The result is divided by 144 to give the volume in Hoppus cubic feet. These Hoppus feet are larger than the true cubic feet, so that the volume of the log is understated. But the difference disappears (in the form of waste wood) when the log is sawn to a squared shape, and so the Hoppus measurement gives a good indication of the amount of useful timber that can actually be cut from the round log.

In practice, the calculations are done with simple tables known as Hoppus calculators. As only two measurements of the log are needed (length and quarter girth), the forester can measure the volume of his timber quickly and easily, as soon as it has been felled. The same method can be applied to estimating the volume of a standing tree, and can therefore be used for finding out the amount of timber in a whole forest.

See also FORESTRY; LOGGING; AGRICULTURAL MEASUREMENTS.
See also Vol. VII: TIMBER INDUSTRY.

TITHES. These were at one time gifts made to the Church. They are of very ancient origin, and were supposed to amount to one-tenth of the produce of the soil, that is to say, of corn, hay, wood, fruit, calves, lambs, pigs, eggs, milk, and wool. Such gifts or payments were enjoined by the Law of Moses, and the Christian Church also required them of its members from early times. In Britain, they existed in Anglo-Saxon days, and were at first voluntary payments,

A 14TH-CENTURY TITHE BARN AT HARMONDSWORTH, MIDDLESEX

Topical Press

which gradually became customary, and later, from the end of the 8th century until 1836, they were a legal charge upon the land.

In principle, tithes were paid to the parish priest. In practice, the living was sometimes held by an abbey or monastery, which took the bulk of the tithes, paying only a small part to the vicar, or curate, appointed to serve the parish. It was the duty of the farmer to notify the parson when he was going to carry hay or corn, or when his flock had finished lambing and his sows had their litters of pigs, so that he might collect every tenth swath of hay or sheaf of corn, and every tenth lamb or little pig. Great barns were built, called tithe barns, to hold the parson's corn; many of these can still be seen. The tenth child in a family was also often dedicated to the service of the Church, probably entering the monastery at a very early age for that purpose.

In the days when money was little used and most of the people lived by the land, the practice of tithing the land to support the Church worked well enough. But with the growth of towns and industry, and the more general use of money as a medium of exchange, the system became very inconvenient for both farmer and parson. So whenever the enclosure of parishes took place by Act of Parliament (*see* OPEN FIELDS AND ENCLOSURES), the opportunity was taken to change the basis of payment, the parson's rights being satisfied either by awarding him a piece of land able to produce a return equivalent in value to the tithe, or by paying him annually an equivalent sum of money. In 1836 the Tithe Commutation Act abolished all tithes in kind, converting them into tithe rent charge—an annual money payment to be calculated, year by year, on the average prices of wheat, barley, and oats of the seven preceding years. This protected the farmers from having to hand over more money than the value of the produce formerly surrendered, while at the same time the parson received payment which increased if prices rose. These money payments were still called 'tithes'.

BRINGING THE TITHES TO THE PARSON
The tithes include the tenth baby of the family. 18th-century Staffordshire pottery group

After the First World War, however, when market-prices were fluctuating violently, the tithe rent charge was fixed for a period of 8 years. Then, in 1925, the level of tithe payment was lowered, and part of the money was paid into a sinking fund to make it possible to get rid of the rent charge altogether in $81\frac{1}{2}$ years. Agricultural prices, however, continued to fall, and farmers complained that the tithe payments were an unfair tax on agriculture. So in 1936, a Tithe Act was passed abolishing tithe rent charges and substituting an annual payment at a still lower rate, enough of which would be paid into the sinking fund to bring all payments to an end in 60 years. This tithe annuity is a legal charge upon the owner of the land, and if payments fall in arrears, they can be recovered by order of the courts.

Tithes, and the various charges upon land for which they have been changed in modern times, have the longest consecutive history of any land tax. Under the sinking fund provisions of the Act of 1936, they will be abolished, finally, by the end of the present century.

TOBACCO. The tobacco used for smoking consists of the prepared leaves of an annual plant called *Nicotiana tabacum*, native to Central America, and was introduced into England in the reign of Queen Elizabeth (*see* TOBACCO INDUSTRY, Vol. VII). Although it can be grown in a temperate climate like Britain's, its cultivation as a crop is mainly carried out in tropical and sub-tropical countries. Important tobacco-growing countries are the southern States of North America, the West Indies, Turkey, and parts of Africa such as Rhodesia and Nyasaland. There are several different varieties of tobacco to suit different conditions, the most widely cultivated being the type which produces the various kinds of Virginia tobacco. Turkish tobacco is produced from a dwarf plant descended from this but grown and cured under different conditions. Much of the high-grade tobacco used for cigars comes from Cuba.

A tobacco crop needs light, loamy, fertile soil, which must be thoroughly cleared and cultivated before being planted. The higher the grade of tobacco the more attention it needs. Tobacco is an annual crop and cannot stand frost. The seeds are so fine that they are often sown mixed with sand, and one teaspoonful of seed is enough to plant out about $\frac{1}{2}$ acre of land. Seed is sown first in a separate nursery bed, usually shaded from the heat of the sun. Before sowing, the seed-beds are often sterilized either by applying steam or by burning brushwood on the surface. When the plants are between 1 and 2 months old, they are carefully transplanted to the cultivated fields, where they are spaced about 3 feet apart, using some 5,000 plants to each acre. As they grow, the soil between the rows is frequently hoed to keep down weeds. In America both the transplanting and the hoeing are usually done by machines drawn by horses or tractors. To produce the 'wrapper' leaves used in the manufacture of cigars, the crop is sometimes grown under shade.

The tobacco plant itself is green and soft in texture, with wide, oblong leaves spreading out at intervals from an upright stem. If left alone, this stem reaches a height of 4 to 5 feet, and bears handsome, pink, tube-shaped blossoms; but except for seed the tobacco planter does not want these flowers, and so he 'tops' the stems of nearly all plants by cutting back the main shoots when the plants are about 3 feet high to get a heavier crop of leaves. For high-grade tobacco, the plants are 'primed', that is, the lowest small leaves are removed.

Office of the High Commissioner for Southern Rhodesia

WEEDING TOBACCO SEEDLINGS

Dept. of Agriculture, Uganda

PICKING TOBACCO LEAVES IN UGANDA

Tobacco is grown in Uganda by African smallholders. It
is supervised and marketed by the government

The crop is ready for harvesting about 6
months after it has been planted out. The
method of harvesting varies with the kind of
tobacco: if the tobacco is to be cured in the open
air, the whole plant is cut down when the leaves
are ripe; but for tobacco cured by artificial heat,
each leaf is picked separately as it turns yellow.
For Turkish tobacco, leaves from different parts
of the plant are kept separate, as their position
on the plant determines their quality. After
being picked, the leaves are taken to the curing
sheds, where they are dried for shipment to the
factories.

See also Vol. VII: Tobacco Industry.

TOMATOES (*Lycopersicon esculentum*). The fruit
of the tomato plant is used for various purposes,
but mainly as a salad. The tomato is grown
throughout the world. The plant is an annual,
being raised from seed each year; though when
grown in the open in warm countries it may live
longer than a year. It is a member of the same
family, *Solanaceae*, as the potato and the tobacco
plant, and is a native of South America, the
English name being derived from the Spanish
tomate, which in turn came from the Mexican
tomatyl.

The tomato is used to a warm climate, and
though it can be grown in the open in Britain, it
is commonly grown under glass where the
warmth of the glasshouse gives a longer season of
growth and a more abundant crop. The plants
cannot be planted in the open with safety until
June, and an early frost in September is likely
to prevent further ripening of the fruit. Under
glass the plants are usually planted out in March
and continue to flourish until late autumn or
early winter. A winter crop of tomatoes can be
grown under glass with the aid of artificial heat.

There are a great many varieties or forms of
the tomato. Among those commonly grown in
the open and also under glass in Britain are Best
of All, Market King, Potentate, Harbinger,
Earliest of All, and E.S.I. The dwarf bush type
of tomato, which was developed from the
Canadian wild bush tomato, is now often grown,
especially out of doors, as it is hardier than the
standard tomato, and can therefore be sown and
planted earlier. Such established varieties as
Bakers' Rosebush and Stonor's Dwarf Gem make
a dense bush about 2 feet high.

In order to raise tomato plants, seed is sown
under glass usually during March for outdoor

Amateur Gardening

TOMATOES GROWING IN A LOW GREENHOUSE

crops and during December or January for indoor crops. The seed needs a fairly high temperature, from 65° to 70° F., to germinate. If it has been sown in a suitable compost such as the John Innes seed-sowing compost (*see* POT-TING), the seedlings should be ready to be pricked out in about 14 days, and after that should have a temperature of 65°, dropping later to 60°. After a fortnight the good seedlings should be transplanted to 3-inch pots, the weaklings being thrown away. These potted plants should be hardened off in a cold frame before being planted out of doors; they are then about 9 inches high and showing the first truss of flowers.

The tomato plant is of a branching habit, but under culture it is customary to prune it to a single stem which is tied to a stake or supported on string fastened to overhead wires. Side shoots as they appear are removed. In the open, the plants are spaced 1½ or 2 feet apart in rows 3 feet apart. The soil should be well manured in advance of planting; and during the season, growth and fruiting are sustained by the application at intervals of a suitable complete fertilizer. In cold districts the plants flourish better out of doors if they are planted in front of a wall or fence; they should always have a sunny position. When the weather becomes warm, the soil

needs the protection of a mulch of strawy stable manure or grass mowings to keep in the moisture, and the plants should be well watered.

Fruit forms and develops better if the plants make only moderate growth, and this depends on the use of suitable manures and fertilizers. Too much nitrogen in the early stages, for example, may lead to rank growth which tends to make the plants less fruitful. Out of doors the weather is not likely to allow for the ripening of more than four trusses of fruit, and therefore it is best to cut off the tops of the plants a little way above the fourth spray. Under glass many more trusses can develop. Towards the end of the season some growers cut off all the lower leaves to let the sun in to the fruit; but this should never be done before fruit development is complete. When the nights begin to get cold, outdoor ripening can be extended a little by the arrangement of some sort of covering that can be placed over the plants at night and lifted by day.

The tomato, being a relative of the potato, suffers from potato blight (*see* PLANT DISEASES, section 2 *e*); indeed, it is the only serious trouble common with outdoor plants. Therefore the plants, like potatoes, should be sprayed with a suitable fungicide, usually in July or August. Tomatoes under glass suffer from attacks of several glasshouse pests and diseases. Serious attacks of the Tomato Moth can be checked by sprayings of arsenate of lead; and Tomato Leaf Mould, often a serious menace in tomato houses, can be checked by spraying with a suitable fungicide. A virus disease which attacks tobacco plants can be spread to tomatoes by the tobacco-stained fingers of cigarette smokers. Too damp or too dry an atmosphere in the house and too much or too little watering can produce conditions which result in uneven ripening or splitting of the fruit.

See also GLASSHOUSES.

TOOL-SHED, *see* HAND TOOLS.

TOPIARY. This is the art of clipping trees and shrubs into formal and fanciful shapes, and is very much like the making of GARDEN HEDGES (q.v.). Yew and box, which have the necessary small leaves and compact growth, are the plants most commonly used; bay is occasionally used, and juniper was used in the past. These are plants that grow slowly, and great patience is therefore needed.

In the formal gardens of Tudor times (*see* GARDENING, HISTORY OF), the popular shapes were the simple symmetrical ones: cones, pyramids, and spheres. Fashions change, however, and by the end of Queen Anne's reign, topiary had become much more elaborate, and all manner of fantastic shapes, including those of animals, birds, and heraldic beasts, decorated the formal gardens. There were also spirals, arches, tunnels, crowns, and battlements, all produced by the clipping and training of suitable shrubs and trees.

It is usual to start with young pyramid-shaped trees, about 3 feet high, and these must be well established on their roots before clipping or training starts. The shape of the young tree must be suited to the final shape that is wanted; thus, if a bird is to be fashioned, there must be twigs on the young tree in the right places to make head and tail. Some shapes, of which the 'cone and button' is one, can be produced by trimming only (*see* picture, p. 191); but to get others, especially the more complicated ones, such as birds or crowns, training also is needed. For the trimming, ordinary shears or electric clippers can be used, and stout fencing-wire serves for the training. The wire is bent to form the desired outline, fastened firmly to the trunk, and the growing shoots are tied to it (Fig. 1). Sometimes a curve can be formed by bending over and tying down a long springy shoot (Fig. 2). To make a spiral, the trunk is trained round a central stake, which is removed when the shape is 'fixed' (Fig. 3). Arches and tunnels are made by training growths of two trees inwards from either side over wires. All wires and string ties must be examined from time to time to ensure that they do not bite into the stems.

Amateur Gardening

YEWS CLIPPED INTO ELABORATE SHAPES

There are plenty of examples of topiary in English gardens. Among the oldest, dating from the 16th and 17th centuries, is Chastleton House, Oxfordshire, where a great circle of unusually large box trees have been clipped into the shapes of animals, birds, teapots, and purely fantastic figures. Hutton John, Cumberland, has very massive, simple yew topiary; Levens Hall, Westmorland, demonstrates the variety of designs into which yew can be clipped; and at Packwood House, Warwickshire, there is a great concourse of yews of different shapes representing a grotesque 'Sermon on the Mount'.

See also GARDENING, HISTORY OF; GARDEN HEDGES.

TRACE ELEMENTS, *see* ARTIFICIAL FERTILIZERS.

TRACTORS, *see* POWER FOR FARMING.

TRAILERS, *see* FARM VEHICLES.

TRANSPLANTERS, *see* DRILLS AND DISTRIBUTORS.

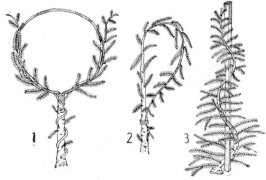

1. TRAINING YEW SHOOTS ROUND A WIRE. 2. BENDING DOWN A SHOOT TO FORM A LOOP. 3. TRAINING A SPIRAL

TRAPS AND SNARES

TRAPS AND SNARES. The Old English word *treppe*, probably the origin of the word trap, meant a step; so that it may be said that a trap is something that is stepped on or into. Animals and birds have been trapped and snared from very early times; and at the present day, we find among the most primitive tribes great skill in devising and setting various types of trap and snare. Trapping has played an important part in the story of FUR HUNTING (q.v.). It is the traps and snares connected with the supply of fur that will be dealt with here.

There are two main types: the holders and the killers. Holding traps seize or enclose the animal until the arrival of the trapper. Good examples are the pitfall, the cage trap, the net (into which hunted animals may be driven), and the steel trap. The snare or noose may belong to this group, but it is frequently set, as in rabbit catching, to strangle the caught animal. The killing traps are fewer; the breakback mousetrap is the best known. In this class is also the gun trap, used for dangerous game such as lions and leopards, and the widely used deadfall.

The simplest of all traps, and no doubt the

THE HUMANE RABBIT SNARE

The knot prevents the snare from tightening sufficiently to strangle the rabbit

oldest, are those without mechanism, such as the pitfall. This is a pit dug in the game trails and skilfully disguised in some way. Often the sides are made with a moderate inward slope, the bottom of the pit being narrower than the top; the effect of this is to jam the feet of a large animal together, so that its efforts to escape are hindered. Sometimes a spiked stake or a spear is set in a pit, thus converting it into a killing trap.

The snare or noose in many forms has been used all over the world, and is still relied on by many native trappers to take animals up to the size of deer. Until wire took their place, local materials such as *lianas* (the stems of some climbing tropical plants), or in northern lands strips of whalebone, were used. In the British Isles snares are used almost solely for the capture of rabbits. The art of setting a rabbit wire is quickly learnt by the country boy, but it needs a good eye to detect the best place to ensure success. For most animals, particularly those in the habit of using regular trails, snares are set unbaited: many native tribes make long fences in forest or bush, in which they leave a few gaps, and in the gaps they set snares.

The snare may be combined with a natural spring in the form of a bent sapling fastened in such a way that, on a trigger being released, the sapling springs back and jerks the animal clear of the ground. The advantage of this method is that the captive is held beyond the reach of other animals, thus possibly saving a valuable fur.

Before the white man introduced the steel trap to North America, the deadfall was the mainstay of the Indian trapper. Animals as large as bears could be killed by this method, although normally it was used for the smaller fur bearers. The trap is simple. Over the narrow

Curtis Museum, Alton

AN OLD DEADFALL MOUSE TRAP

The trap is shown set. A strip of wood attached to the string is fixed in notches, one in the block of wood and the other in the stick projecting in front, which is joined to a baited platform inside the trap. When the mouse stands on the platform the strip is thrown out of the notches, and the block falls and crushes it

entrance to the baited pen or enclosure, a heavy log or stone is laid on a lighter one, which is itself balanced on a spindle so finely that it is easily displaced by any animal attempting to pass. This lets the heavy log fall and crush the victim to death. Where timber is scarce, the deadfall may be constructed of slabs of stone. The chief difference between the deadfall and the common breakback rat or mouse trap is that in the latter the killing blow is struck by the operation of a spring instead of by gravity. For destroying the larger carnivorous animals such as lions, leopards, and hyenas, particularly in Africa, the gun trap is widely employed. Any type of gun or rifle may be used; it is fixed either alongside or over the entrance to a baited pen, with the muzzle directed at the entrance. A line attached to the trigger is stretched across the entrance or attached to the bait in such a way that any movement fires the gun. Such traps are very effective, but, as may well be imagined, the skin of an animal shot at such close quarters is likely to be very much damaged.

By far the most effective trap today for most purposes is the steel trap or gin. Types of gin traps have been known since the Middle Ages, but the modern steel trap dates from the latter part of the 19th century. A movable flat pan or treadle, set centrally between a pair of opposing steel jaws, with or without teeth, is held by a catch connected with a powerful spring. An animal treading on the pan releases the catch, and the jaws spring together, seizing it by the leg. Since the bone is usually broken, and muscles and ligaments torn, the steel trap undoubtedly inflicts much suffering; many trapped animals pull or gnaw the trapped foot off in their struggles to escape. The steel trap has the advantage that it is durable and simple, and is adaptable enough to be set under water for beaver, musk-rat, and otter, on branches and stumps for martens and squirrels, or buried in the ground, baited or unbaited, for other animals. As in all forms of trapping, success depends upon a sound knowledge of the habits of the animal sought, and a proper concealment of the trap. Many trappers wear gloves or smoke the traps to obliterate their own scent, and it is quite a common practice to scatter a few drops of a strong natural scent around the trap to attract the animals and hide the human scent. Castor (from the scent-gland of the beaver), musk, aniseed oil, or fish oil may be used for this

Canadian National Film Board
INDIAN TRAPPERS SETTING A BEAVER GIN IN CANADA
The gin is placed in the beaver's hole

purpose. The common mole trap is a variety of the steel trap in which the animal is crushed by the jaws closing on its body, instead of holding it by the leg.

For many years humane people have sought for ways of taking wild animals without the prolonged sufferings which are inflicted by the snare and steel trap. The first practical result of their efforts was the knotted snare, so constructed that the noose holds a rabbit by the neck without tightening to strangulation point. Recently the Royal Society for the Prevention of Cruelty to Animals has adopted a humane steel trap, designed to kill rabbits instantly. This model, known as the R.S.P.C.A. Sawyer trap, earned for its inventor, Mr. F. E. Sawyer, the reward offered by the Society. It has a rectangular base frame incorporating a pan or tread, a powerful coil spring, and two strong steel arms, which lie apart and flat when the trap is set. When the rabbit treads on the pan, releasing the catch, the two arms fly together and interlock in a killing grip round the neck. The trap is designed to be set inside the entrance of the burrow, being concealed in the loose soil in

Fox Photos

THE SAWYER TRAP. THIS KILLS THE ANIMAL INSTANTLY BY
BREAKING ITS BACK

the same way as the gin. Although designed to catch rabbits, the R.S.P.C.A. Sawyer trap may prove to be of great use in trapping many of the main fur-bearing animals.

See also FUR HUNTING; POACHERS.

TRAWLING. This is the dragging of a bag-net over the sea bottom to catch whatever fish may be lurking there: soles, plaice, rayfish, dog-fish, cod, dabs, and turbot, for instance. This method of fishing is very old and has changed little until quite recent times. In a tomb dating from about 2000 B.C., situated in the hills behind Qûrna in Upper Egypt, a model was discovered of two canoes towing between them a big bag-net (*see* FISHING, HISTORY OF). Today, in the Mediterranean, pairs of trawlers from Spain or Italy fish in very much the same way. The boats of each

pair are exactly the same size, so that they can sail abreast and exert an equal hauling power upon the net.

In Britain trawling is the most important method of commercial fishing. Using either the beam trawl or the otter trawl, British fishermen are able, with a single vessel, to do the same work as the pairs of Mediterranean trawlers. Beam trawls are bag-nets with wide mouths (18 to 48 feet wide), which are kept open by the upper lip (the head-rope) being laced to a wooden beam (*see* Fig. 1). The beam is kept 12 to 20 inches off the bottom of the sea by two iron runners (called trawl-heads). The weight of the trawl-heads prevents the net rising too easily off the bottom. The lower lip of the net, the ground rope, is heavily weighted, very often with an iron chain. The weighted rope churns up the sandy bottom and drives out any fish hiding there. When disturbed in this way, the fish rise and are swept into the hinder or cod-end of the net. British fishermen first used the beam trawl from their sailing-boats in the 19th century. It is still used today, but the otter trawl has largely taken its place. (The name 'otter' comes from the name of a piece of fishing tackle formerly used on Irish lakes to capture trout and carp.) The otter trawl is a net in which the beam is replaced by two large boards fitted to each corner of the net (*see* Fig. 2). By careful adjustment the boards are kept in a slanting position across the direction of the pull, and so keep the net's mouth stretched wide open.

If a trawl is towed at more than a moderate speed, it tends to rise from the bottom, and it is therefore sometimes used in this way to catch fish, particularly herrings, which swim in shoals some distance above the bottom. An electrical device, the echometer, tells the fishermen where the fish are. Then the depth of the trawl-net can be adjusted by regulating the speed of the

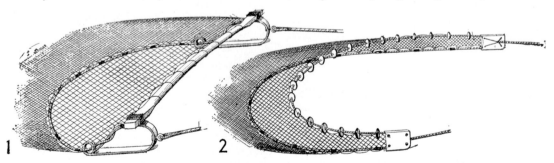

1. THE MOUTH OF A BEAM TRAWL.   2. THE MOUTH OF AN OTTER TRAWL

trawler. Most herring fishing, however, is done with drift nets worked from vessels called drifters (*see* HERRING FISHERY).

See also DOGGER BANK; FISHING METHODS.

TREE GROWING, *see* AFFORESTATION; FORESTRY.

TREE PESTS AND DISEASES. Trees form the home of many kinds of tiny insects that feed on their leaves, flowers, fruits, bark, timber, and roots. But they seldom do serious harm, because birds such as woodpeckers, nuthatches, and tits eat great numbers of them, and they are also attacked and kept in check by insects of other kinds. Only a few, therefore, are serious pests of forest trees, but as these attack the trees at a tender stage, they may, if numerous, kill them outright.

One of the worst is the Pine Weevil, a little grey beetle that lays an egg on the stump of a felled pine tree. A soft white grub hatches out of the egg and feeds on the soft bast just below the bark for one or sometimes two years. Then the grub pupates, and when the adult insect emerges, thus completing the life cycle, it flies to young conifers and eats patches of their bark. In great numbers the weevils may kill the young trees. The forester cannot, therefore, safely replant infested coniferous woods after felling until the weevils have swarmed and disappeared, as they usually do in a few years' time (*see* WEEVIL PESTS).

Bark Beetles, which are also serious pests, lay eggs beneath the bark of a dead or dying trunk or log where their larvae feed, and their pupae are formed. When the adult beetles emerge, they fly to the tops of tall trees and feed on their shoots, sometimes stripping whole branches of their leaves. Many kinds of bark beetles are known, each preferring one particular kind of tree. One of the worst of them spreads Dutch Elm Disease, by carrying the spores of this harmful fungus from tree to tree. Some kinds can be checked by removing felled timber from the woods, or by stripping its bark so that the insects have no breeding home. A picture showing the galleries formed by Bark Beetles in the soft bast tissues beneath the bark of an elm log can be seen on page 39 of Volume II. The behaviour of the Bark Beetles is described in the article WEEVIL to be found in Volume II.

Forest Products Research Laboratory

HONEY FUNGUS AT THE BASE OF A YOUNG LARCH TREE

Most of the diseases of trees are caused by fungi (*see* PLANT DISEASES, section 2). The tiny threads of the fungus growth spread over the surface of the tree or sink deeply into its timber. After a time the fruiting fungus bodies appear on the surface as brackets or toadstools. These are called 'sporophores' or 'sporebearers', and they scatter tiny spores which carry the disease to another tree. Fortunately, however, they can seldom penetrate the tree's bark unless they can gain entry at some weak point in the tree, such as a wound. A fungal thread or 'hypha', spreading from a rotting log, may work its way, for example, into the trunk of a growing tree through a damaged root or a broken branch. Where these diseases of the tree trunk are common, the tree crops may have to be cut at an early age, and certain kinds cannot be grown at all.

Another tree disease, caused by the Honey Fungus, may spread from a decaying stump by means of a black thread or 'rhizomorph' to a young coniferous tree. From this, tiny white threads (hyphae) grow out and encircle the stem of the young tree, finally killing it. Then the fungus bears little toadstool-shaped sporophores which scatter spores to infect other decaying stumps. Where the Honey Fungus is common in old woods, some kinds of young conifers cannot safely be planted.

See also PESTS AND DISEASES; PLANT DISEASES.

TREES, BROADLEAVED. 1. These are the trees with broad-bladed leaves which in temperate or cold climates drop off in winter, that is, they are deciduous, though in the tropics they often remain evergreen. At one time most of the timbers used in Britain were HARDWOODS cut from broadleaved trees, but nowadays far more SOFTWOODS (qq.v. Vol. VII) from conifers are used. Foresters, however, still plant large areas of the better soils with certain broadleaved trees, and others are grown for shelter or ornament. The most important of these are described below.

(a) Alder (*Alnus*). This common riverside tree is seldom planted; but the trees that grow wild in marshy places are cut for poles and timber which is easily carved. New shoots grow from the stumps, so it is not necessary to replant them.

(b) Ash (*Fraxinus*). This graceful tree yields valuable timber. It needs rich soil and often grows well in limestone country, but it does not succeed in large plantations or on bare open ground. It may reach a height of 80 feet in as many years, and is often cut down at about that age.

(c) Beech (*Fagus*). Although it grows on many soils, the beech is usually chosen for planting on chalk downs, where it thrives better than any other timber tree. Conifers are used to shelter the young beeches on exposed hillsides, but later the beech outgrows them. When 100 years old it may be 100 feet high and ready for cutting, but it will live for twice as long.

(d) Birch (*Betula*). This tree is seldom planted because it grows wild very freely from its little wind-borne seeds. Self-sown birches are often looked after by the forester, for they yield soft, easily-worked timber when only 60 years old. Most of the birchwoods used for making plywood are imported

(e) Chestnut. The horse-chestnut (*Aesculus hippocastanum*) was originally introduced from Asia Minor, and is often grown for the sake of its beautiful blossoms. But its timber is soft and weak, so it is not planted in our forests. The sweet chestnut (*Castanea sativa*) was introduced from Italy by the Romans about 2,000 years ago, and now grows wild in southern England. When grown as a timber tree it is ready for

cutting at an age of 100 years, but the logs are seldom really sound. Coppice-grown poles which are cut every 14 years are valued because they last a long time (*see* COPPICE).

(f) Elm (*Ulmus*). Elm trees need fertile soil and are trees of the hedgerows and farmlands rather than of the forests. They are grown from root shoots or suckers, usually for ornamental planting. Cornish elms, which grow in a spire-like form, have the advantage that they have no heavy side branches which are liable to fall and cause damage—a serious danger with the commoner kinds. The wych elm of Scotland is grown from seed and is sometimes planted in the woods.

(g) Hazel (*Corylus*) and Hornbeam (*Carpinus betulus*). Though not a timber tree, the shrubby hazel is grown in southern coppices to produce hurdle material, thatching spars, bean rods, stakes, and pea sticks for use on farms and in gardens. The bushes are cut about once every 7 years, and soon shoot again. Hornbeams are not often planted because there is not much demand for their hard timber, which is very difficult to work. In some places a great many grow wild, and they are sometimes coppiced for firewood, stakes, and pea sticks.

(h) Oak (*Quercus*). This is the most important of British broadleaved timber trees, but it needs better soil and takes longer to grow than any other. Oaks are easily raised from acorns in the nursery. The young tree needs the shelter of other kinds, and so it is often planted with larches, which nurse it up and are cut out later when the oak is big enough to grow by itself. It does not reach timber size until it is 120 years old, and it may live to an age of 500 years. Poor oaks grown on infertile soils and oak coppice are of little value as timber. Most of the oaks grown in other countries, such as the Red Oaks of North America, do not produce such hard timber.

(i) Sycamore (*Acer pseudoplatanus*), Lime (*Tilia*), and Plane (*Platanus*). These are grown more as ornamental trees than for their timber, though the easily worked lime timber is in some demand for WOODWORK (q.v. Vol. VII), and sycamores grown on fertile soil produce a very useful timber. The flowers of limes are very fragrant and attract the bees, who make a delicious and very white honey from their nectar. Self-sown sycamores are common, and the trees make good shelter belts round hillside farms and along the

LEAVES AND FRUITS OF BROADLEAVED TREES

1. Alder.   2. Ash.   3. Beech.   4. Birch.   5. Sweet chestnut.   6. Horse-chestnut.   7. Elm.   8. Hazel.
9. Hornbeam.   10. Oak.   11. Sycamore.   12. Lime.   13. Plane.   14. Walnut.   15. Willow.   16. Poplar

sea coast. Planes thrive well in smoky towns; they are the characteristic trees of London.

(*j*) Walnut (*Juglans*). As a forest tree the walnut is not easily grown, and so it is only planted on the best of soil, often in groups amongst trees of other kinds. It was introduced from Asia Minor. Most of the walnut used in the FURNITURE INDUSTRY and for CABINET-MAKING (qq.v. Vol. VII) is imported from abroad.

(*k*) Willow (*Salix*) and Poplar (*Populus*). These are usually grown from cuttings instead of seed, and they need fertile soil, well drained and well watered, and plenty of light and air. Therefore they are not good forest trees. They grow very quickly. Black poplars after 50 years growth may reach 110 feet in height, with a great bulk of timber. The tall and slender Lombardy Poplar, which is planted to form an ornamental screen of foliage and not for its timber, grows a considerable height in a few years. The Cricket Bat Willow, the kind most often cultivated, is famous for the strong, supple wood it provides for bat making. Other kinds are grown as coppice for basketry materials.

(*l*) Trees of the Rose (*Rosa*) family. Several wild trees of the rose family, which have beautiful blossoms, mostly white in colour, and large, soft, juicy, and brightly coloured fruits, are planted as ornamental trees in parks and gardens. These include crab apple and wild pear, the rowan of the northern hills, the whitebeam of the chalk downs, and the hawthorn and blackthorn grown as hedging shrubs. The wild cherry sometimes grows to timber size.

2. TROPICAL BROADLEAVED TREES. Broadleaved trees make up the bulk of the dense forests and jungles that grow in the moister countries of the tropical zone (*see* FORESTS, Vol. III). With them are found PALMS (q.v.) of many kinds, and sometimes a few conifers. Where rain and warmth are spread evenly over the year the broadleaved trees are, on the whole, evergreen. Some of them may lose all their leaves for short spells of a month or less, but the jungle as a whole remains green all the year round (*see* LEAVES, section 4, Vol. II).

Very many kinds of broadleaved trees grow in the jungle. Some reach to great heights, up to 200 feet or more, so that their flowers are seldom seen. Others never rise to the topmost leafy layer, but grow in the partial shade below. The finest timber trees, such as teak, grow scattered amidst many less valuable kinds. All alike grow rapidly, often several feet each year, for the climate is warm all the year round, and there is no pause for winter rest. Indian foresters have begun to form pure plantations of teak in order to increase production.

The industrial use of the timbers mentioned in this article is dealt with in Vol. VII under the title HARDWOODS.

See also FORESTRY; AFFORESTATION; TIMBER; COPPICE.

TREES, CONIFEROUS. Most of these evergreen trees have narrow, needle-shaped leaves, and bear their seeds on the open scales of woody cones. They are therefore called CONIFERS (q.v. Vol. II) or cone-bearers. They belong to a very ancient class of plants, and their wood is soft and easily worked. This wood, and other parts of the tree, contain resin, a clear, gummy substance with a peculiar smell, which helps to heal the wound if the stems are cut.

Nine-tenths of the timber used in Britain is SOFTWOOD (q.v. Vol. VII) from coniferous trees, which are grown in forests in Britain, North America, and northern Europe on a very large scale. At first sight all the coniferous trees look very much alike, and are often grouped together as 'pines' or 'firs'. But the forester has to know the different varieties.

(*a*) Cedar (*Cedrus*). True cedar trees are often found in old gardens; in their native forests they can live for more than 500 years. Cedars have widespreading branches, which bear evergreen needles in clusters on short shoots. They flower in autumn, and bear large cones shaped like little barrels. Originally they were brought to Britain from North Africa, Palestine, and northern India. Cedar wood has a distinctive aromatic scent, and is much prized in the East. Wood from the Cedars of Lebanon was used to build King Solomon's temple.

(*b*) Cypress (*Cupressus*). These are tall, slender trees, with leaves pressed so tightly against their stems that both twigs and buds are hidden. Their cones look like small balls, and often carry little knobs. Lawson Cypress, which has its leaves and twigs flattened like the shape of a fan, is a hardy tree from British Columbia, often planted in gardens and woodlands. Monterey Cypress, or *C. macrocarpa*, has leaves set squarely around its stem; it comes from California, and is only hardy in southern Britain, where it is grown for hedges and windbreaks.

(*c*) Douglas Fir (*Pseudotsuga*). Great forests in

LEAVES AND CONES OF CONIFEROUS TREES

1. Cedar of Lebanon.   2. Lawson Cypress.   3. Douglas Fir.   4. European Larch.   5. Scots Pine.   6. Wellingtonia (Sequoia).   7. Noble Silver Fir.   8. Norway Spruce.   9. Yew

British Columbia are composed of Douglas firs which are named after the Scottish explorer who first sent seeds to Britain. The tree thrives on good soil and gives big crops of timber. It will grow 110 feet in 50 years, the tallest British Douglas Fir being 175 feet high. Its needles are borne singly, and it is distinguished by its thin brown buds with papery scales, and the three-pointed bracts on its cones.

(d) Larch (*Larix*). Unlike the other common conifers, larches are deciduous, that is, they lose their leaves each winter. In spring their needles reappear as bright green tufts on little knobs called 'short shoots'. At the same time the pink 'larch roses', or female flowers, come out. Larch cones are small and barrel-shaped. One kind, brought to Britain from Europe, has yellow twigs and green needles; the other, from Japan, has red-brown twigs and blue-green needles. Both grow quickly in plantations, up to 100 feet high in 80 years, but they give only a light crop of timber.

(e) Pine (*Pinus*). True pines always bear needles in clusters of two, three, or five, held together at the base by a little sheath. They form great forests in Europe, Asia, and America. The Scots Pine is known by its pairs of short, blue-green needles, its oval, pointed cones, cylindrical buds, and the beautiful red upper bark of old trees. It grows wild in the Highlands of Scotland, and is often planted elsewhere because it will thrive on poor soil—even on heathery moorlands Scots Pines reach a height of 100 feet in 80 years, and give good crops of useful timber. Another quick-growing pine comes from Corsica, and has long, twisted needles and pointed buds.

Pines grown for ornament or as shelter belts include the Italian Maritime Pine, with long, leathery, paired needles and huge cones; the Californian Monterey Pine, very quick-growing, with bright green needles in threes; and the Weymouth Pine from the east of North America, which has needles in fives and long cones shaped like bananas.

(f) Sequoia or Redwood (*Sequoia*). These Bigwoods, as they are often called, grow wild in California, and are the biggest and oldest trees in the world. The tallest known is 364 feet high, and the oldest on record was reputed to be over 3,000 years old when it was cut down. Seeds have been brought to Britain, and trees over 150 feet high have already been grown.

(g) Silver Fir (*Abies*). These conifers have their needles set singly but arranged in two rows, and if they are pulled away a circular scar is left on the twig. The cones are very large and upright, and fall to pieces as soon as they ripen. European and North American kinds are planted in Britain for their white, easily worked timber.

(h) Spruce (*Picea*). The needles of these trees resemble those of the Silver Firs, but if they are pulled away they leave little woody pegs on the twigs. The cones hang downwards, and remain on the tree after the seeds have fallen.

The commonest spruce comes from Norway, and is the familiar Christmas Tree. Another well-known spruce is the Sitka Spruce from Alaska, with its characteristic sharply-pointed blue-green needles. Both thrive on poor soil on grassy moors high in the hills, and give heavy crops of timber. The Norway Spruce grows 100 feet high in 70 years, and the Sitka Spruce is an even faster grower.

(i) Thuya (*Thuja*). This tree resembles the Lawson Cypress except for its slender cones. It is planted to produce straight poles, which are extremely light and very durable. It is also grown in gardens, usually as a hedge. Thuya is native to British Columbia, where it is called 'Red Cedar', and its light wood is used by the Indians for their canoes.

(j) Yew (*Taxus*). This tree, which grows wild in Britain, bears juicy red fruits instead of cones, and its leaves are poisonous. Yew timber is very durable, and was formerly valued for making longbows for archers. The tree reaches a great age, up to 1,000 years, but grows so slowly that it is never planted for its timber.

See also: FORESTRY; AFFORESTATION; TIMBER.
See also Vol. VII: SOFTWOODS.

TROPICAL AGRICULTURE. Agricultural methods are largely governed by climate, which itself influences the nature of the soil. The climate varies in different regions of the tropics, but everywhere the most important factor is sunshine; for not only is the sun intensely hot, but the hours of daylight are approximately the same throughout the year, the seasons being marked by periods of rain.

Tropical areas may be divided roughly into three kinds, each with its own particular agricultural problems. First, there are the arid, or dry, regions, where there is scant rainfall. Here

PLOUGHING RICE FIELDS WITH BUFFALO IN BALI, INDONESIA

agriculture depends entirely on IRRIGATION (q.v.), that is, the provision of an artificial water supply, which makes it possible to produce many crops on land which would otherwise be desert. Secondly, there are the areas where there is heavy rainfall at certain seasons, as in countries such as India, where the MONSOONS (q.v. Vol. III) produce a rainy season from about June to November, and irrigation is needed only in the hot, dry season from about March to June. In Ceylon, for instance, there were artificial reservoirs over 2,000 years ago, storing water mainly for rice cultivation. Without irrigation agriculture would be restricted to annual crops that mature in a short time, and to perennial crops (including tree crops) which can withstand long periods of drought. Thirdly, there are regions where the rainfall is heavy and fairly evenly distributed throughout the year: here vegetation is luxuriant, and a great number of crops can be grown. The serious danger in clearing the ground for cultivation in all regions of heavy rainfall, however, is soil erosion. Clearing exposes the ground to rain and wind; under the tropical sun the organic matter in the soil quickly decays, and cultivation loosens the soil, making it very liable to be washed away during

the torrential storms of the tropics. Methods of cultivation have now been devised to prevent the land being lost in this way, and steps have been taken to reclaim the land in many eroded areas (see SOIL EROSION, Vol. III).

Different tropical regions are suited to different crops: the date palm, for instance, is an important crop in dry tropical regions, but is unsuited to the wet tropics, which in their turn are particularly suitable for the culture of many of the TROPICAL ROOT CROPS (q.v.). Heavy foliage and broad-leaved plants grow in the wet tropics (see TROPICAL JUNGLES, Vol. II); narrow-leaved, spiny plants are more suited to dry regions (see DESERT PLANTS, Vol. II).

The primitive methods still practised on millions of small holdings throughout tropical Asia have changed very little in the course of centuries. The number of crops has increased, and their quality has been improved by cultivation and selection; but crude implements and much hand-labour are still used as they have been since the very earliest days of farming. In most Asiatic countries the local law of inheritance insists that all property shall be equally divided amongst the immediate descendants. Thus the unit of land cultivated tends to become smaller and more scattered in successive generations. This farming of very small holdings, more than anything else, is responsible for the fact that primitive methods of farming have survived for so long, and also largely explains the poverty of the Asiatic peasant, for it hinders the introduction of more productive methods.

In the main, the staple crop in any region is generally one which is indigenous, that is, it grows there in a wild state. Successful crops, however, are taken from one place to another, so that, even before the era of easy transport, crops were spreading over a wide area and were successfully established in countries far from their original home.

When the demand for Eastern tropical products, such as rice and tea, increased in Europe, the primitive Asiatic methods of agriculture were unable to meet it. Europeans, and later Americans, therefore began to establish plantations for producing crops on a large scale, side by side with the primitive farming. They began with spices, gradually extending to sugar, tea, coffee, cocoa, and later to rubber, palm oil, tobacco, coconuts, and other crops for which there continued to be a large demand in Europe, America, and other civilized countries. European and American capital has been poured into tropical Asia for this large-scale agriculture, which uses modern methods of cultivation and is aided by the work of scientific research institutions and stations and government departments of agriculture. In spite of this, however, the great bulk of the crops both for home consumption and for export are still grown on small holdings by peasants.

Developments of this kind have also taken place in the tropical regions of Africa and in America, where there are vast areas suitable for tropical agriculture. South America has helped to meet the demand for such products as sugar, cotton, indigo, cocoa, and coffee. Some of these crops are now grown very little, but Brazil, Ecuador, and Venezuela still produce about one-third of the world's cocoa, while coffee is still one of the most important crops of South America, most of it coming from Brazil, Colombia, and Venezuela. Among the new developments in tropical regions are the extensive rubber plantations in Malay, Indonesia, and Ceylon; the sugar industry in Indonesia, Cuba, Porto Rico, and elsewhere; the pineapple industry in Hawaii and Malaya; bananas in the Caribbean; ground-nuts in East Africa; tea in India and Ceylon; tobacco in Sumatra; and coconuts in many tropical countries. Great improvements in production have been made by selection and by breeding new varieties, and greater control of pests and diseases has been achieved (*see* TROPICAL PESTS). Advances have also been made in the technique of treating the crops, in processing, and in preparation for market. Livestock has also been improved, and the native cattle have been crossed with imported breeds to produce types suitable for the tropics. In many countries cattle are beasts of burden as well as a source of food (*see* ANIMAL FARMING, TROPICAL). The work of improvement has therefore been somewhat complex, and much scientific research yet remains to be done.

These large-scale developments have enabled the small-holder to grow the better crops introduced by Europeans and Americans, and have provided a ready market for his produce. But more than this, they have enabled social services, such as education and medical services, to be developed within the areas, and have raised the standard of life of the peasant.

Large-scale tropical agriculture has developed in tropical Asia more than elsewhere, not only because the land is suitable for these crops but also because there is an almost inexhaustible supply of labour, especially in India and China. But the south Asian countries have enormous and steadily increasing populations for whom food must be grown. The rice-eating population of the world is increasing so fast that the production of rice in these countries has to be continually expanded. This can be done in two ways: by increasing the total area cultivated, and by increasing the yield per acre. The area under cultivation obviously cannot be increased beyond a certain point, but there is still plenty of room for expansion, especially in large-scale production with the use of modern farm implements. The yield per acre may be increased by the use of better seed, and improvements in methods of cultivation and fertilization, in the supply and control of water, in the control of pests and diseases, and by better methods of harvesting and storage. Education is very largely the answer to this problem, and great advances are being made in teaching more productive methods to native farmers. The importance of education amongst them, therefore, cannot be exaggerated, for on it depends the ultimate success or failure of tropical agriculture to feed its own population and to increase its wealth by exports.

The culture of the different crops mentioned in this article is described in separate articles on each crop.

See also AGRICULTURAL HISTORY.

TROPICAL FRUITS. Many fruits grown in tropical or sub-tropical countries, for example BANANAS, DATES, COCONUTS, MELONS, PINE-APPLES, and the CITRUS FRUITS (qq.v.), are to be seen commonly in European shops. There are many others which are rarely, if ever, exported, though they may be important food crops in the country where they are grown. This article covers a few of the best known of them. Many of them are still like the ones that grow wild, though in the course of centuries growers have selected for cultivation those of the best types (*see* PLANT BREEDING).

1. GUAVA (*Psidium Guajava* and other species). This pear-shaped fruit grows on a small tree, native to tropical America and the West Indies, but is now grown also in Southern Asia and the warmer parts of the U.S.A. The fruit has a yellow skin beneath which is a soft yellowish pulp. It is very perishable, and is usually, therefore, exported only in the form of guava jelly.

2. AVOCADO PEAR, or Alligator Pear (*Persea gratissima* and *P. americana*), also a native of tropical America, is now widely cultivated. The pear-shaped, green-skinned fruit grows on a tree that reaches a height of 25 to 30 feet. The flesh of the fruit, which is firm and greenish-yellow in colour, encloses a single large round seed. The flesh is scooped out with a spoon and eaten as a salad with pepper, salt, and vinegar.

3. POMEGRANATE (*Punica granatum*). Pome-granates grow best in the hot, arid regions of Persia, Arabia, Afghanistan, and India, where they have been grown for centuries. The tree grows 15 to 20 feet high. The fruit is about the size of an orange, with a smooth skin, brownish-yellow to red, containing a great many seeds surrounded by a reddish, juicy pulp.

4. MANGO (*Mangifera indica*). The Indian mango tree, which may reach a great age, grows to a height of about 50 feet. The fruit, which varies in size, texture, and flavour according to the variety, may weigh up to 5 lb., and is green, yellow, or red in colour. It contains a single seed enclosed in a very juicy flesh, yellow or orange in colour.

5. MANGOSTEEN (*Garcinia mangostana*). This is one of the best and most sought-after fruits of the Malay Peninsula, but it is almost unknown outside this region, as it is very perishable. The mangosteen tree reaches a height of 15 to 20 feet. The fruit is about 2½ inches in diameter, and consists of a thick, reddish-brown rind containing 5 to 7 soft white parts of delicate flavour

E. N. A.

GUAVAS FROM HAWAII   POMEGRANATES FROM UZBEKISTAN, U.S.S.R.   MANGOES FROM NIGERIA

E. N. A.

DURIAN FRUIT FROM CEYLON

Artocarpus produce large, edible fruits, the most important being the breadfruit, a staple food of the south Pacific. This roundish, green fruit, weighing several pounds, has a white, fibrous pulp. It is borne on a handsome tree, some 40 to 60 feet high, with a heavy canopy of large, deep green leaves. The fruit is eaten before it is fully ripe, and is cooked in several ways.

9. OTHER FRUITS. The Soursop (*Anona muricata*), which probably originated in tropical America but is now grown in most wet tropical countries, is a soft, kidney-shaped, green fruit, weighing 2 or 3 lb., with a rough skin covered with a number of short, soft spines. The pulp is white, resembling cotton-wool, juicy, and somewhat acid, and makes an ideal flavouring for ices and cooling drinks. The Papaya-tree (*Carica papaya*), also of wet tropical regions, has soft-fleshed fruit of orange colour, sometimes as large as rugby footballs, with a thick skin, inside which are attached numerous black seeds. Papaya leaves are said to make meat tender if it is wrapped in them for several hours before use. A milky juice, called papain, is extracted from the unripe fruit, dried, and sold as a digestive. The papaya is often called 'pawpaw', but the true

which may contain seed, although a large proportion of these are sterile.

6. DURIAN (*Durio zibethinus*). A writer describes this fruit in these words: 'It is a fruit for which Asiatics pay a high price willingly, a fruit which the tiger disputes with the pig and the bear snatches from the deer, a fruit which all domesticated animals, including horses, eat greedily, and a fruit which has charms only known to those who venture upon it boldly.' The durian-tree, which flourishes in the Malay archipelago, may reach a height of 100 feet and live for a century. The fruit, which may weigh up to 15 lb., has a hard, greenish-yellow husk armed with sharp spines, and a strong smell, considered very offensive by many people. Inside, the seeds are enclosed in a cream-coloured rich pulp which is the edible portion, although the seeds may be eaten roasted.

7. LITCHI (*Litchi chinensis*). This tree, native to China but now grown also in India, is longer lived even than the oak, and reaches a height of about 40 feet. The full beauty of the tree is seen during fruiting, when it is covered with clusters of red fruits somewhat resembling strawberries. These have a rough red skin, a white flesh, and a single seed. Preserved litchi are exported from China in cans and as a dried fruit.

8. BREADFRUIT. Various species of the tree

Paul Popper

BREADFRUIT FROM JAMAICA

pawpaw is *Asimina triloba*, a North American shrub of the custard apple family, bearing fleshy fruit, from 2 to 3 inches long, with an orange-coloured pulp. The Sapodilla (*Achras Sapota*), a large evergreen tree of tropical America, bears fruit about the size of a hen's egg, which looks like a potato, and contains a pleasantly sweet brown pulp. The Rambutan (*Nephelium lappaceum*), a Malayan tree, bears a yellowish-red, hairy fruit about the size of a plum, with a sweet fleshy interior enclosing a seed. The Cat's Eye (*Nephelium malaiense*) is a smooth brown fruit which grows in Asiatic countries, and is so called because when pressed between the fingers the skin splits, revealing an interior which resembles a cat's eye.

There are also many tropical Nuts (q.v.), such as Brazil nuts and Cashew nuts, grown near the seaboard in many tropical countries. These are often important articles of diet in the countries where they grow, as well as valuable exports.

See also Tropical Agriculture.

TROPICAL OIL-SEEDS, *see* Oil-bearing Plants.

TROPICAL PESTS. For the most part, pests belong to the group of animals we call insects, and insect life is particularly abundant in the tropics. In the tropics, as elsewhere, the majority of insects are either beneficial or at the least harmless; but those that are harmful are able to cause great damage resulting even in Famines (q.v.), if not kept in check. As examples of this there are the huge swarms of Locusts (q.v.) and the ravages of the white ants, or Termites (q.v.Vol. II).

The tropical countries supply a number of very important crops, such as Sugar, Tea, Coffee, Cacao, Rubber, Cotton, and Rice (qq.v.). These crops are apt to be attacked by particular pests, all of which cannot be dealt with here; but a few examples will help to explain the problem as a whole.

Tea is grown in several different parts of the tropical world, and in each place there is something to attack the tea-plants—by sucking their juices, eating leaves or stems, or boring through the stems. The Tea Tortrix, a small moth $\frac{1}{2}$ to 1 inch across, with brownish fore-wings and pale hind wings, is a serious pest of tea in Ceylon, Assam, and southern India, where it is known as the 'Flushworm'. The pale green eggs are

Paul Popper

PAPAYA TREES IN TANGANYIKA

Papain is being collected on cloth trays. It drips from cuts in the skin of the fruit

laid in flat clusters on the leaves, and the caterpillars, when they hatch, spin two leaves together to enclose a green shoot, on which they feed (*see* Leaf-Rollers, Vol. II). The Tea 'Mosquito' is a bug with long legs that looks superficially like a mosquito. It is found in Ceylon, India, Assam, and Java, and both young and adults puncture the leaves of the tea-shrub with the proboscis and suck the sap. Plants attacked by the bug develop brown patches on the leaves and finally shrivel. The Shot-hole Borer, a beetle $\frac{1}{12}$ inch long, bores into the stems and interferes with the flow of the sap. The Orange Beetle, so called from its colour, and $\frac{3}{8}$ inch long, eats through the stems.

Sugar-cane is attacked by a similar series of pests. In the West Indies, one of the chief areas for the supply of sugar, the Frog-hopper Blight, closely-related to our own Cuckoo Spit (*see* Frog-hopper, Vol. II), attacks the roots when a larva and the stems when adult, in both stages living in a mass of froth. The larva of the Sugar-cane Borer weevil, a handsome green beetle an inch or more long, bores into the roots. It also attacks banana crops and several kinds of palms (*see* WEEVIL PESTS). The sugar-cane is also attacked by a variety of BEETLE PESTS (q.v.). The Hard-back beetles of the West Indies have larvae $1\frac{1}{2}$ inches long that bore into the canes. In Hawaii the Japanese Sugar-cane Beetles, about $\frac{1}{2}$ inch long, have grubs which feed on the roots; but this pest is kept in check by a wasp imported from the Philippines.

The leaves of the cacao-tree, the source of cocoa and chocolate and grown principally in the West Indies, West Africa, and Central America, are attacked by thrips, very small insects that rasp away the undersides of the leaves and pods; by Longicorn beetles, known as Cacao Borers, which tunnel the stems; and by the Cacao Bark Louse, a night feeder, which attacks the young shoots and stems, making them discoloured. There is also a Cacao 'Mosquito', a long-legged mosquito-like bug which feeds on the pods, causing them to turn colour and shrivel.

The pests of coffee are much like those of tea and cacao. The Coffee Bug, $\frac{3}{8}$ inch long, sucks the juices; the Coffee Cherry Borer, a beetle $\frac{1}{4}$ inch long, found in India, Java, Africa, and South America, feeds on the berries; and several species of Longicorn beetles, from $\frac{1}{2}$ inch to $1\frac{1}{2}$ inches long, bore through the stems. The Coffee Mealy Bug of East Africa and southern Asia and the Green Scale belong to that curious group of bugs in which the adult insects form scales (*see* SCALE INSECT, Vol. II). Both live by sucking the juices of the plant, and the Green Scale, up to $\frac{1}{12}$ inch long, accumulates in enormous numbers over the shoots to form a scaly kind of crust.

Rubber-trees are by no means free from disease and pests, but a careful watch is kept and no great damage is done. Cotton, on the other hand, suffers a great deal. The Pink Boll-worm, which feeds on the cotton seeds, is a pest of cotton wherever it is grown. It is the larva, $\frac{3}{4}$ inch long, of a small brownish moth. As a result of its attacks the boll may fail to open, or it may become deformed and the cotton fibre discoloured and poor in quality. The Spiny Bollworm of India and Africa, also the larva of a moth, likewise feeds in the bolls. The Cotton Stainers of the West Indies and elsewhere are black and brown bugs, 1 inch long, which both as young and adults pierce the cotton seeds and suck the juices. They release oil from the seeds

which stains the fibres, as also do the insects when crushed in the gins as the cotton is processed in factories. Finally, in Africa, large crickets, $2\frac{1}{2}$ inches long, feed on the roots of the cotton plants.

Much has been done to find ways of controlling the pests on these and other crops, both by INSECTICIDES (q.v.) and by biological control, that is, a control based on a knowledge of the biology or life-history of the pest, and often consisting of setting one insect to kill another. The most successful story of tropical pest-control is perhaps that of the Fluted-scale or Cottony Cushion-scale, accidentally introduced into California from Australia in 1868. This scale-insect became a serious menace to orange and other citrus-fruit growers. By 1886 it had increased so much that it threatened to wipe out the fruit trees. An entomologist went to Australia and returned with the knowledge that a small ladybird beetle, *Vedalia cardinalis*, fed on the Cottony Cushion-scale in that country. The ladybird was imported into California and has now practically wiped out the scale pest.

Insect pests also affect forest trees (*see* TREE PESTS), and stored products and manufactured goods, domestic animals, and even man himself; although the most spectacular and obvious of their ravages are among cultivated crops. Carriers of disease, however, such as the malaria-mosquito and the TSETSE FLY (q.v. Vol. II), are spectacular enough. The African tsetse fly, besides causing SLEEPING SICKNESS (q.v. Vol. XI) in humans, also causes illnesses in horses, dogs,

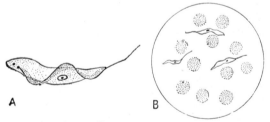

A. TRYPANOSOME. B. TRYPANOSOMES SWIMMING BETWEEN BLOOD CORPUSCLES (GREATLY MAGNIFIED)

and cattle—in particular the cattle disease, nagana; and this has prevented the development of vast areas of otherwise suitable and productive country in Africa. The fly is responsible for transmitting a microscopic flagellate protozoon called a 'trypanosome' (*see* PROTOZOA, Vol. II). It pierces the skin of an animal infected with these parasites and sucks up blood containing them. The trypanosomes then undergo changes in the body of the fly, and finally reappear in the salivary glands of the fly, ready to be injected into the next animal the fly pierces.

No really effective preventive or curative treatment for the disease is known; the only hope is to destroy the flies. Tsetse flies live in forest and bushy areas where there is warmth, damp, and shade; they do not inhabit open grassland. In some districts in Africa, therefore, the woodland and bush where the pests breed have been cleared; but Africa is too large a country for this to be a practical method for exterminating the tsetse fly. Another difficulty is that certain wild animals, such as antelopes, sometimes act as reservoirs for trypanosomes: although immune themselves from the disease they carry the parasites in their blood, and from them they are transmitted by the fly to cattle or to man.

Until the discovery of DDT and BHC (benzene hexachloride) as INSECTICIDES (q.v.), the use of chemicals against tsetses was very limited. Work with these insecticides is now progressing, and they are proving more successful against some species of the fly than against others. In certain districts the coats of the cattle have been treated with DDT, and this has so far proved the most successful method. Experiments have also been made in spraying districts with DDT from aeroplanes. Cost, however, is the chief argument against the general adoption of this method.

There are other harmful animals besides insects, but their numbers and habits do not make them pests as serious as the teeming insect populations.

See also PESTS AND DISEASES; INSECTICIDES.

TROPICAL ROOT CROPS. Most of these are not, strictly speaking, roots at all, but UNDERGROUND STEMS (q.v. Vol. II). Almost all tropical root vegetables require a rich and well-watered soil capable of deep cultivation—conditions generally to be found in the wet tropical regions. Many of these crops, such as the sweet potato, are important foods in the countries in which they are grown; only tapioca, arrowroot, and ginger (see SPICE CROPS) are important as exports.

1. TAPIOCA or cassava (*Manihot utilissima*) is native to South America, but is now grown throughout the tropics. It is cultivated from stem cuttings and will grow to a height of from 10 to 15 feet. The tubers, which are like thickened roots, are fully developed in about 15 to 18 months. There are many varieties, but the two main divisions are the sweet and the bitter, the latter containing a certain amount of prussic acid which, however, dissolves in the water when the tubers are cooked.

The tapioca which we use in puddings is the starch extracted from the tubers. The tubers are grated in water, when the starch, being heavy, falls to the bottom. The water is then drained off and the starch purified by repeated washings. Tapioca is sometimes confused with sago, which is, in fact, obtained from an entirely different plant, being extracted from the pith of a PALM TREE (q.v.).

2. ARROWROOT. Various starch products are loosely known as arrowroot, but real arrowroot is obtained from the tubers of a plant, *Maranta arundinacea*, cultivated chiefly in the West Indies, but also found in most tropical countries. It is a fleshy and scaly cylindrical tuber obtained from a herbaceous perennial (a plant with a non-woody stem which flowers every year) with a creeping root-stock. It grows to a height of from 2 to 3 feet.

3. YAMS. There are many varieties of yams, both wild and cultivated, which vary greatly in habit, growth, size, shape of the tubers, as well as in pleasantness of taste. Some of the wild varieties bear leaves on long stalks and produce huge tubers which can be eaten only after careful

Uganda Government

TAPIOCA PLANT DUG UP TO SHOW THE TUBERS

NATIVE METHOD OF STORING YAMS IN WEST AFRICA
The yams are tied to poles and protected by leaves

trolled conditions, the tubers are cured and kept in good edible condition for from 6 to 7 months. The crop is propagated from stem cuttings planted in well-cultivated soil. It takes from 2 to 6 months to mature, according to the kind. The tubers are usually boiled when freshly lifted from the ground, but in Asiatic countries and the U.S.A. they are often sliced and dried, in which condition they may be stored for a long time.

5. *Colocasia esculenta* is a root for which there are many names, such as 'dasheen', 'taro', 'eddoe', 'keladi', for the crop is grown in almost all tropical countries with sufficient rainfall. It is an erect, herbaceous perennial, with underground tubers from 6 to 12 inches long. It is propagated from the young tubers, which must be planted in moist, heavy clay soil, or in peaty soil. The tubers are valuable food in many countries, and the young leaves and leaf-stalks may also be cooked as a green vegetable.

6. TURMERIC. The shoots of this erect perennial plant spring from a mass of rhizomes or underground stems which are yellowish-orange within. In the many countries in which the plant flourishes, both the leaves and fresh rhizomes are used in cooking. The crop is propagated from portions of the growing rhizomes, and takes about 9 months to mature. Dried turmeric is one of the main ingredients of curry powder (*see* SPICE CROPS). The yellow-coloured water obtained from cooking fresh turmeric is used in Asia for colouring rice, cakes, and other confections, especially for use on ceremonial occasions.

See also TROPICAL AGRICULTURE.

TSETSE FLY, *see* TROPICAL PESTS.
See also VOL. II: TSETSE FLY.

TUNNY FISHING, *see* BONITO FISHING.

TURKEYS. Turkeys are native to Mexico and the southern parts of the U.S.A., where they are still to be found wild in the woods. When the Spanish General, Cortes, came to Mexico he is said to have found 'several millions' of these birds in Montezuma's palace (*see* AZTECS, Vol. I). They were, apparently, the cheapest form of meat in Mexico, and the Spaniards are reported to have purchased the first ones for only four beads each. They were introduced into England about 1524, and the family of the man who first brought them in has a turkey cock

preparation, as they contain needle-like crystals of oxalate of lime which irritate the stomach and cause digestive troubles. The two important cultivated varieties are the Greater Yam (*Dioscorea alata*) and the Lesser Yam (*D. esculenta*). Both are climbing plants, and tubers may be harvested from 4 to 12 months after planting, according to the variety. The Greater Yam is a large unshapely tuber, and the Lesser Yam bears a bunch of elongated tubers, which are considered to be superior in flavour. In many tropical countries yams form an important article of diet amongst the inhabitants, who prepare and cook the tubers in various ways— roasted, baked, boiled, or steamed.

4. SWEET POTATO (*Ipomoea Batatas*) is a trailing herbaceous perennial, producing round or cylindrical 'edible' starchy tubers weighing up to 1 lb. each. There are many varieties, the skins varying in colour from white to deep pink and the flesh of the tuber from white to purplish-yellow. The vegetable is grown throughout the wet tropics and is an important article of diet. Large areas are cultivated in the United States, where, by storing them under carefully con-

'in pride', that is, with his tail fanned out, on his coat of arms. This habit of the turkey cock, or 'stag', of displaying his tail and wings has led to the term 'turkey cock' being used for a pompous or self-important person. The turkey is now the most highly prized of table poultry, especially in America, where it is the traditional dish for Thanksgiving Day in November.

There are three main breeds: the American Bronze, which is most like the wild bird; the White, sometimes called the White Holland; and the Norfolk Black. There are several new colours, for example buff; but they are not often seen in England. Most turkeys in Britain are kept on farms in small numbers on free range, and find a good deal of their food for themselves, especially in the stubble fields after harvest. In America, however, there are often flocks of several thousand birds. Turkeys are also often kept intensively, in which case an area of 6 square feet of floor space per bird must be allowed.

In a breeding-pen the proportion is one stag to from four to ten hens. Turkey hens usually lay from 40 to 60 eggs in a season in clutches of from 12 to 20; but some have laid as many as 150. The eggs can be hatched in an incubator, under a broody hen, who will cover about 10 eggs, or under the turkey herself, who will cover about 20 eggs. Turkeys make good mothers. The eggs take 28 days to hatch.

Turkey chicks are often said to be difficult to rear. This is because of a serious disease known as blackhead, which can be passed on from one bird to another in the soil. New drugs, and improved knowledge of feeding which enables young birds to be reared without contact with the soil, have nowadays much reduced the risks. Well-drained, sandy soil is least likely to become infected, and for this reason the dry, light lands of Norfolk became famous for turkey rearing. The business is now, however, much more general. Turkey chicks need a little more training than chicks do to use the brooders, but with good food and good conditions they are now almost equally easy to rear (*see* POULTRY, CARE OF, section 4).

Young turkeys must be well fed, for they grow rapidly. Their principal foods are grain, a mixed mash, and a great deal of green food. Birds kept intensively should have in addition certain minerals and about 2% of cod-liver oil added to the mash and, if possible, a little dried

A. Rice

AMERICAN BRONZE TURKEY HEN

A. Rice

NORFOLK BLACK TURKEY COCKEREL

A. Rice

WHITE TURKEY COCKEREL

skimmed milk. The constituents of the mash must depend to some extent on what foods are available. With birds on free range the mash can contain cooked potatoes at the rate of one part in four. Roughly speaking, turkeys should have the following amounts of food per bird per day:

Age	Grain and Meal	Green food
4 weeks	2 oz.	3 oz.
14 weeks	5 oz.	14 oz.
22 weeks	9 oz.	24 oz.

When green food is difficult to obtain, swedes or turnips chopped in half can be used instead.

See also POULTRY.
See also Vol. II: TURKEYS (WILD).

TURNIPS, *see* ROOT CROPS.

TURTLE-FISHING. Turtles living in tropical seas are often caught in large numbers when they go ashore to lay their eggs in a hole in the sand. While they are busy digging holes the turtle-hunters, who have been lying in wait, come out of their hiding-places and turn the turtles on their backs. The turtles, now helpless, are easily collected.

For hundreds of years in many parts of the world turtles have also been hunted with remoras (sucker-fishes). This strange method of fishing was mentioned by Columbus when he sent home an account of his discoveries in the West Indies. It is used today by the natives of Australia, the Somali fishermen of Zanzibar, and the Chinese.

The REMORA (q.v. Vol. II) has an oblong sucker consisting of a number of transverse plates on the top of its head—hence its name 'sucker-fish'. A full-grown remora is about 2 feet long. If it is held up by its tail it can support, by means of its sucker, a weight of about 20 lb. After having caught a remora, the natives first tame it, so that it will not struggle when it is being handled. Then, when they go turtle-fishing, they fasten a line round its tail, and if they sight a turtle dozing on the surface of the water, put the remora overboard and chase it away from the boat. As the turtle is the only solid body in sight, the remora swims to it and anchors itself to the underside of its shell by means of its sucker. It would be willing to let the turtle carry it wherever it went, but as soon as the fishermen see that the remora has fixed itself securely to the turtle, they begin to haul in the line tied to the remora's tail. Held fast by the remora's sucker, the turtle is slowly drawn alongside the boat and taken aboard.

See also Vol. II: TURTLE.

James Hornell

CATCHING A TURTLE WITH A REMORA

V

VEGETABLE. The word means, in its wider sense, any form of plant; but it is usually given only to certain plants grown for human food. The name 'vegetable' derives from Latin words meaning 'to quicken', which seems sensible, as vegetables contain materials that are essential to the health of human beings (*see* NUTRITION, Vol. XI). The SALAD CROPS (q.v.) such as lettuce, mustard and cress, and chicory, are especially valuable because, since they are eaten raw, their vitamins and minerals are not altered by cooking. In order to preserve as much of this value as possible, all vegetables that are normally cooked before they are eaten should be very carefully handled (*see* VEGETABLE COOKING, Vol. XI).

With some plants, such as cabbage, lettuce, and spinach, the whole of the above-ground part is eaten; with some, such as carrot, beetroot, and parsnip, the large taproot only is eaten; with others, such as celery, seakale, and rhubarb, the leaf-stalk only is eaten. With some other plants a particular organ of the plant is the part eaten, as for example the tuber of the potato, the bulb of the onion, the green pod of the runner bean, the seed of the pea, and the flower-bud of the artichoke. Also, in one instance (asparagus) the plant's young succulent shoots that spring up from the perennial rootstock in the springtime are gathered and eaten.

Many plants that are cultivated as vegetables have been derived from species that can be found growing wild in Europe. The wild parsnip, carrot, and watercress can be found throughout the English countryside, and the wild cabbage, which has given rise to all the different kinds of garden cabbages, can be found growing on rocky cliffs near the sea. Seakale, beet, celery, and asparagus are other wild plants found by the sea coast in various parts of England, and all of them

have produced garden varieties. Other vegetable plants are exotics (from overseas), having been introduced into Europe either from Asia or the New World; the potato, sweet corn, kidney bean, and runner bean, for example, were introduced from Central and South America. It is believed that the onion and the rhubarb came originally from Asia. A few vegetables seem to have no wild ancestors and to have come into existence as hybrids or to have been derived from existing species. For example, the origin of the garden pea and the lettuce is unexplained.

Some vegetable plants—lettuce, peas, and beans, for example—are ANNUAL PLANTS, raised afresh from seed every year. Others, such as carrots, parsnips, beetroot, and onions, are BIENNIAL PLANTS, raised from seed and making vegetative growth in the first year and developing flowers and seed in the second year. A few, such as rhubarb, asparagus, and globe artichokes are herbaceous PERENNIAL PLANTS (qq.v.), going on from year to year by means of a persistent rootstock, and propagated mainly by vegetative means instead of by seed (*see* PLANT PROPAGATION).

A vegetable garden maintained for supplying the home is often called a kitchen garden; a market-garden is a vegetable garden in which vegetables are grown for sale (*see* VEGETABLE GARDEN). The particular problems of cultivating each type of vegetable are discussed in articles on the vegetables themselves.

VEGETABLE GARDEN. 1. There are two main types of vegetable garden: the market-garden, in which vegetables are grown for sale, and the kitchen or home garden, in which vegetables are grown to supply the family table. The market-gardener needs to grow some kinds of vegetables out of season when prices are high (*see* MARKET-GARDENING), and the home garden ought to provide a succession of many varieties of vegetables throughout the year. In order to do this both market-gardener and home-gardener make use of FRAMES, CLOCHES, and GLASSHOUSES (qq.v.). A great variety of vegetables can be grown in the temperate climate of Britain, and these are described in separate articles. Some of them—potatoes, cabbages, and peas, for example—are also ARABLE CROPS (q.v.) of the farm. Other vegetables, such as sweet potatoes and yams, depend on a warm or tropical climate (*see* TROPICAL ROOT CROPS).

2. SITE. Frost, mist, fog, and low temperatures are apt to be worst on low-lying land. In valley bottoms spring and autumn frosts are more likely to be severe. High land, on the other hand, is often exposed to cold winds and gales. Exposed situations are not suitable for gardens unless hedges and shelter-belts of shrubs and trees can be planted to give protection. Many old kitchen gardens have brick or stone walls around them, and these not only give protection from cold winds but help to retain the sun's warmth, and so help the growth of early crops. Another drawback to low-lying land is that it is often not well drained, and plants cannot make healthy root-growth in waterlogged soil (*see* DRAINAGE). On steeply sloping land, however, water may drain away too quickly, and heavy rains may wash away the valuable top soil. This 'water erosion' is a serious cause of trouble in some countries, and gardeners prevent it as much as possible by keeping land on a slope covered with crops, to hold both the water and the soil (*see* SOIL EROSION, Vol. III).

3. PLANNING AND PLANTING. Both the market and the home garden must be planned. The plots of land under cultivation are easier to work if they are regular in shape and as level as possible. The garden should be intersected by well-made paths, and the market-garden needs roads to take implements and vehicles from one part of the garden to another. A well-planned modern market-garden has washing, packing, storage, and tool sheds, and an irrigation plant, all conveniently placed so that time, power, and labour are not wasted. The unit of frames or Dutch lights for growing early crops and the glasshouses for propagation and for the culture of indoor crops are placed in sheltered positions where the most can be made of the available sunlight during the winter and early spring months. Manure or compost heaps are situated, if possible, near the cropping areas, so that time is not wasted in carting. Trees and tall hedges, unless needed as wind-breaks, should be taken out, for they rob the surrounding land of moisture and plant food, shade the crops, and in wet weather cause drip on the soil below.

The layout of the home vegetable garden follows the same general principles. Fruit trees are better not grown in the vegetable garden, for their branches shade the land and their roots draw valuable materials from the soil; also, the manuring and spraying they need are not likely to suit the vegetables. The ideal home garden has frames, cloches, greenhouse, tool and store sheds, a water supply and watering equipment, and if there is a potting-shed, the gardener can work in wet weather (*see* POTTING). There should be permanent site for the compost heap and manure store, and a place where the garden rubbish can be burnt. In many gardens there is, of course, not room for all this.

It is as important to follow a ROTATION OF CROPS (q.v.) in the garden as it is on the farm. A useful rule is to allow an interval of at least 2 years before any crop is grown again on the same site; this rule applies especially to potatoes.

A suitable cropping system to give a 3-year rotation is as follows:

1st year—Onions, leeks, and potatoes on manured land.
2nd year—Brassica and salad crops on land dressed with fertilizer and lime.
3rd year—Legumes (peas and beans) and root crops on land dressed with fertilizer.

In this type of rotation the land receives a dressing of manure or compost at least every third year. By applying the manure or compost to a third of the area each year, and making full use of lime and fertilizers, the soil gets enough humus and is kept fertile.

4. WATERING (irrigation). A supply of water properly laid on is a great help in any garden, for vegetables need a lot of water. Most market-gardens are provided with pumping machinery and hoses and sprayers. Sometimes the water is stored in large tanks or reservoirs from which it is drawn off. Sometimes it is pumped from a lake, pond, or river direct on to the crops through the pipes which feed the spray-lines and sprinklers. To a certain extent plants can absorb nutrients (foods) through the leaves as well as through the roots, and nutrient solutions can be passed into the irrigation water so that the crops are both watered and fertilized at the same time. Crop irrigation on a large scale, however, needs special knowledge (*see* IRRIGATION).

5. SOIL AND FERTILITY. All types of soil are used for growing vegetables, but sandy loam and medium loam soils are the most suitable. The clay and silt in them helps them to hold moisture, and the sand makes them warm and easy to cultivate and lets air and water through. Market-gardeners prefer a sandy loam because it is an 'early' soil, that is, it warms up quickly in

A VEGETABLE GARDEN IN SUMMER   *Amateur Gardening*

the spring and so encourages early growth. If the soil is too sandy, however, the crops may suffer from the effects of drought more quickly than those on heavier soils.

Often, however, a garden soil which is of low quality to begin with gradually becomes much improved by the regular addition of large amounts of organic matter. Most market-garden soils are 'built up' in this way, and finally become richer and more productive than the soils of the surrounding fields. Market-garden land often fetches a higher price. In the old days market-gardens generally absorbed large amounts of horse manure from the stables of towns and cities; but nowadays such supplies of dung are no longer obtainable in quantity, and the vegetable grower has to make use of COMPOST (q.v.) and other organic manures such as guano, sewage sludge, or shoddy—waste material from the wool mills (*see* MANURES). Often the soil of the vegetable garden, though well supplied with humus, is deficient in plant foods, in particular nitrogen, phosphate, and potash. Commercial fertilizers, usually of a compound type (that is, a mixture containing all three), are applied over the surface of the soil and well worked in, and these will make good the deficiency. Often, however, certain vegetables require a further supply of food, nitrogen in particular, in order to maintain or stimulate growth. This fertilizer is applied to the surface as a 'top-dressing', and is hoed or cultivated into the soil. Many crops respond to the use of a top-dressing in the spring. The leafy members of the cabbage group can use much more nitrogen than peas and beans and the root crops, which instead need larger amounts of potash and phosphates (*see* ARTIFICIAL FERTILIZERS).

Several other elements, such as boron, iron, magnesium, manganese, and calcium, are needed also in very small quantities, but usually the soil contains enough of these to satisfy most plants. A regular application of LIME (q.v.), however, keeps the soil from becoming sour and helps in the decomposition of organic matter, and also checks club-root disease in brassica crops.

6. SEEDS. Most vegetables are grown from seeds, though a few, such as rhubarb, seakale, potato, and globe artichoke are usually propagated vegetatively (*see* PLANT PROPAGATION). In at least one instance (sweet corn) hybrid seed **is** generally used, because the first-generation progeny of cross-breeding (the hybrid race) are found to be more vigorous and productive than those of an in-bred stock. The cross has, of course, to be made every time a supply of hybrid seed is needed (*see* PLANT BREEDING).

It does not pay the vegetable grower to sow anything but high-grade seeds since he does not wish to waste his labour, land, and manures on producing inferior crops. The Seeds Regulations made under the Seeds Act, 1920, require that nearly all garden seeds shall be tested for purity and fertility before they are put on sale, and that a statement of the percentage of germination, which must reach a certain standard, shall be supplied. The quality of crop, however, cannot be ascertained by a seed test, for that depends upon 'strain'. Strain in vegetable seeds is so important that the vegetable gardener should always obtain seeds of good strains (*see* PLANT PROPAGATION).

Seeds, which are living organisms, have varied periods of life: some die quickly after about a year from harvest, while others live for several years. Seeds of onion, parsnip, and sweet corn are stale after one year, but seeds of peas and beans and most of the other vegetables are good for 3 years if properly stored.

7. TOOLS AND OTHER IMPLEMENTS. The larger market-gardeners nowadays use many kinds of machines and implements—tractor ploughs, rotary hoes, roto-tillers, rowcrop cultivators, seed drills, transplanters, mechanical washers. Several types of mechanical tools and CULTIVATORS (q.v.) are available for use also in big home gardens; but on the whole the private gardener relies upon HAND TOOLS (q.v.).

SPRAYING AND DUSTING MACHINES (q.v.) to control pests and disease are an essential part of the market-garden's equipment. Weeds in onions and some other vegetable crops may now be controlled by spraying at appropriate times with a suitable weed-killer. The flame gun or torch is another serviceable modern device for controlling weeds without hoeing the soil. The hoe, however, is still a valuable tool for controlling weeds, aerating the soil, and keeping the surface soil in a loose condition (*see* WEEDS).

8. PESTS AND DISEASES. Garden crops may suffer, as field crops do, from PESTS AND DISEASES (q.v.). These can be dealt with in the garden

in ways that would hardly be practicable on a large scale: the hand picking of the eggs of the Large White Butterfly, for example. Sprays and dusts are also used in the garden, though the machinery used (as, for example, knapsack sprayers) is less elaborate.

See also FLOWER GARDEN; MARKET-GARDENING.

VERMIN. 1. This word may be used of any animal that is harmful to human beings, including even the many INSECT PESTS (q.v.). Generally, however, 'vermin' in the farmer's and gardener's sense means pests such as rats, weasels, rabbits, foxes, moles, mice, and grey squirrels, and the few wild birds, such as woodpigeons, that are a serious nuisance. It is not possible to draw a strict dividing line between animals which are harmful and those which are useful: many pests feed upon other pests, and to exterminate them would upset the balance of nature and be definitely harmful to agriculture. The MINISTRY OF AGRICULTURE (q.v.), however, has listed certain animals as pests, and occupiers of land may be ordered to destroy such animals on their property, and be fined if they fail to do so. Animals which are friends of the farmer, or at least do good as well as harm, are described in the article WILD ANIMALS ON THE FARM (q.v.).

2. RATS. The common or brown rat is a most serious pest. It does enormous damage to human and animal food, as well as to farm and other buildings. It eats and spoils grain, kills young chickens and steals eggs, makes holes in floors and walls, and spreads disease. It is to be found in places where food is kept: in the animal houses, in store places, in corn ricks, and so on. The smaller black rat is equally harmful, but is rarer than the brown rat, being found mainly in London and the other big sea-ports (*see* RAT, Vol. II).

In the past there was usually a local rat-catcher in every country district who specialized in this work. Nowadays the local agricultural committee appoint 'rodent officers', or 'pest officers', who will give advice and help in the destruction of rats. The usual methods of control are by the use of poisoned baits, traps, gas, and ferrets. Where possible, buildings should be made proof against rats by the stopping-up of holes and other places through which they can pass, and food should be kept in galvanized iron bins with tightly fitting lids. Empty food bags should be hung up and not left lying on the

Harold Bastin

A FRUIT TREE BARKED BY RABBITS

ground. When full sacks are stored and leant against a wall, it is wise to leave spaces behind and between them so that the cat can get in to catch the rats.

3. MICE. The house mouse, being smaller than the rat, is a less serious pest, but it still does a great deal of harm. It eats and spoils the farmer's stores of grain and other foods, and causes loss by gnawing holes in bags and sacks. The long-tailed field mouse, or wood mouse, destroys grain and other seeds, vegetables, roots, and bulbs, and disturbs seed-beds (*see* MOUSE, Vol. II). Mice will eat the pea and bean seeds sown in the ground.

4. RABBITS. When allowed to become plentiful, which they quickly do if not kept down, RABBITS (q.v. Vol. II) do great harm to growing corn, vegetables, and other farm and garden crops. One rabbit in a garden can do a great deal of damage in a short time. When introduced by the white colonists into Australia, rabbits increased so rapidly that they threatened disaster to the farmer, and it was some time before they were brought under control.

The usual methods of controlling them are by

TRAPS AND SNARES (q.v.), by FERRETING (q.v. Vol. IX), and by shooting, gassing, digging out the burrows, or long-netting, a method of netting rabbits at night much used by POACHERS (q.v.).

5. SQUIRRELS. The red squirrel, which is rare, is not a serious threat to agriculture, but the grey squirrel is one of the worst of the pests, for it damages corn, roots, fruit, bulbs, trees, thatch, and many other things, often taking the eggs and young of wild birds. As with the rat and rabbit, special measures are being taken to destroy it: the Ministry of Agriculture has a special campaign against it, and grey squirrel clubs have been formed all over the country. The North American gopher, which is a kind of squirrel, is extremely destructive to wheat (*see* SQUIRREL, Vol. II).

6. FOXES. The fox, though it kills other vermin such as rabbits, hares, rats, mice, moles, and sometimes even frogs and beetles, does more harm than good. It kills a great many fowls, geese, and other kinds of poultry, usually at night, and it quite often kills young lambs in hill sheep country (*see* FOX, Vol. II). It is, however, protected by public opinion in some areas because of the demands of FOX HUNTING (q.v. Vol. IX).

7. BIRDS. The woodpigeon, except that it eats the seeds of various kinds of weeds, is almost entirely harmful. It attacks most cultivated crops, especially corn, peas, beans, turnips, and greens. The stock-dove, closely related to the woodpigeon, is nearly as harmful (*see* PIGEON, Vol. II).

Another very harmful bird is the carrion crow, which often steals young chicks, and has even been known to kill very young lambs. The rook, another member of the CROW family (q.v. Vol. II) is harmful in that it eats great quantities of corn seed, but, on the other hand, it destroys a great many insect pests. The great majority of wild birds present this kind of problem: sparrows, starlings, tits, bullfinches, and others all do damage to the crops, but cannot really be regarded as vermin since they do so much good by destroying harmful insects.

Scarecrows are used to scare other birds besides crows, especially from newly sown corn fields, orchards of soft fruit or cherries, and fields of ripening peas. Some 50 or more years ago, boys were still being regularly employed as 'bird-scarers' or 'bird-starvers' to walk about the fields shaking a tin of stones or some other

Fox Photos

A SCARECROW BEING MADE BY MEMBERS OF A YOUNG
FARMERS' CLUB

rattle, shouting, and sometimes singing a song
which went like this:

> You're harlock, you're harlock!
> O'er hedges and ditches
> You little brown witches!
> You're harlock, you're harlock!
> You stole your master's charlock.
> There is but a little,
> And that's in the middle.
> You're harlock, you're harlock!

A scarecrow is still often to be seen set up in
a field where corn has been sown, but the difficulty is to prevent the birds getting used to him.
He can be made more alarming if he is decorated
with pieces of tin or mirror which swing in the
breeze and reflect the light; or the dead body
of a bird may be hung from his outstretched arm.
Scarecrows, like the one in the picture, are
sometimes called 'tattie-bogles'. There is a
modern mechanical scarecrow that explodes a
cartridge every few minutes.

In cherry orchards at harvest time all devices
have to be used. Bird-scarers, camping in the
orchard, get up with the early birds and drive
them away with shots and rattles. Tins or pieces
of iron hung in the trees are fastened to a string
which runs to some convenient place such as a
gate or kitchen window; any passer-by can pull
the string and set the tins jangling.

8. OTHER PESTS. The red DEER (q.v. Vol. II)
in Somerset and other parts, the roe-deer, and
fallow deer all do harm to growing corn and
other crops at times. The HARE (q.v. Vol. II),
though less common than the rabbit, is quite
plentiful in some parts of the country, where it
eats the corn, roots, and vegetable crops and
strips the bark from the stems of young fruit
and forest trees. The MOLE (q.v. Vol. II) can
be a great nuisance, making its tunnels among
the plants in the garden. The bank vole and the
field vole are harmful in much the same way as
field mice; they make underground runs and
tunnels, which sometimes cause damage to implements at work in the fields. The musk-rat of
North America does great damage by under-
mining the banks of rivers, canals, and lakes (*see*
VOLE, Vol. II); and the woodchuck, an
American MARMOT (q.v. Vol. II), does much
harm in the forests.

See also WILD ANIMALS ON THE FARM; PESTS AND
DISEASES; TRAPS AND SNARES.

VETCHES, *see* LEGUMINOUS CROPS.

VETERINARY SURGEON, *see* AGRICULTURAL
TRAINING; ANIMAL DISEASES.

VINES, *see* GRAPES.

VOLES, *see* VERMIN, section 8.

Cress, and the Brown or Winter Cress, the latter being a hybrid form derived from the Green Cress and a wild species.

Watercress is a valuable SALAD CROP (q.v.), very rich in minerals and vitamins, and yielding many crops in a season. The wild plant has been eaten as a medicinal plant since early times, and has for long been used as an ingredient of salads. It has been a cultivated crop for only about a century. It can be successfully cultivated only in specially constructed beds, as it requires a constant supply of running water and is, therefore, seldom grown in private or in market gardens but usually by special watercress-growers, who devote their time the whole year round to the routine management of the beds.

A watercress bed is made near a stream or spring, or where artesian wells have been sunk, so that a steady supply of clean water containing plenty of lime is available throughout the year. Usually the retaining walls of the beds are concreted and the bottoms covered with clean sand or gravel. No soil is needed as watercress, being a true WATER-PLANT (q.v. Vol. II), gets all its foods out of the water. Some waters, however, do not contain enough of some of the

WAGONS AND CARTS, *see* FARM VEHICLES.

WALLING, *see* HEDGING, DITCHING, AND WALLING.

WALNUT, *see* NUTS; TREES, BROADLEAVED.

WATERCRESS. The common watercress (*Nasturtium officinale*) is a creeping perennial plant, which grows in ditches and streams throughout Europe. It is a member of the family of plants, *Cruciferae*, to which all the cabbage family belong. Two forms of watercress are cultivated, the Green or Summer

The Times

WATERCRESS BEDS IN HAMPSHIRE

necessary minerals, and so superphosphate of lime and sometimes also nitrate of soda are added to the water to supply phosphorus and nitrogen. When new watercress beds are being formed, the water is often analysed in order to find out what it lacks.

Usually watercress is propagated by cuttings taken from established beds, though the Green Cress can be grown successfully from seed. It is customary to clean out the beds and replant them every year, though sometimes they are allowed to stand for 2 years. Old stocks, which have stood for a year or more, are hardier and give a better yield than freshly planted ones, but replanting is necessary to keep down the weeds and to prevent the floor of the bed being choked with silt.

The Brown Cress, which is a winter crop, is best grown in water from springs or from artesian wells, for this is warmer in winter than water from open streams. It is important to keep the watercress fully submerged during cold weather. On the other hand, stream water, which is warmer in summer than spring water, is used for growing the Green Cress. Watercress beds are found usually in the neighbourhood of chalk and greensand formations, which give rise to reliable springs of the most suitable type of water.

See also SALAD CROPS.
See also Vol. II: WATER PLANTS.

WATER GARDENS. WATER PLANTS (q.v. Vol. II), and in particular the water lily, have been thought by many ancient peoples to possess mystical qualities. Their annual resurrection from the mud and slime of pond or river symbolized immortality and purification. The water garden, however, as a special form of gardening, has really only developed since cement for making the pools became available in the 20th century. Concrete is durable, easy to mould, reasonably cheap, and can be successfully handled by the amateur.

1. BUILDING THE POOL. Nearly all water plants need full sunshine, and therefore the pond should be in the open. The best time for building it is in the autumn, and square or oblong shapes are likely to be the most successful. The soil should be excavated 2 ft. 6 in. deep and the bottom made quite firm. Only the best materials should be used, for poor materials may result in leaks from the pool later on. One part by

bulk of best Portland cement, 2 parts good-quality building sand, and 3 parts clean shingle or a similar substance should be used. When the materials have been mixed well together, enough water is added to make the consistency soft without being sloppy. Then a layer of concrete

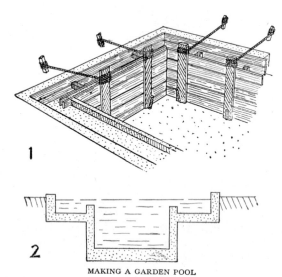

MAKING A GARDEN POOL
1. The wooden frame in position for the concrete walls
2. Section of pool with a shallow portion round the edge

6 inches thick is put on the floor of the pool, and allowed to dry; then the walls are built, also 6 inches thick. The walls are made with the help of a wooden frame (*see* Fig. 1) which is placed against the side of the pool, forming a false wall 6 inches from the side. Fresh concrete is packed into the space between earth and frame; and when it is set, the boards of the frame are removed. If they have been oiled beforehand, they will come away from the concrete quite easily. Bricks or concrete slabs can be used for this frame, but wood is the most satisfactory.

All aquatic plants do not need so deep a pool as this: some need only very shallow water. They can be provided for by excavating a shallow addition to the pool 10 inches deep round part or the whole of the deeper pool, an addition which helps to break the formal lines of the water garden (*see* Fig. 2).

When the concreting is finished, the floor and walls must be waterproofed, either with a proprietary compound or with several coats of waterglass (sodium silicate) diluted with water. Plants must not be put into the pool until the

A WATER GARDEN

Humphrey and Vera Joel

toxic alkalis, which always seep from new concrete, have been neutralized. The pond should be filled with water, and sufficient crystals of permanganate of potash added to colour it wine red. After a week it may be emptied, rinsed, and a layer of heavy loam, free from fibrous roots, put on the bottom. Then it is ready for planting.

2. PLANTING. Water lilies (*Nymphaea*) and other aquatics are best planted in early spring. Plants with tuberous roots, such as water lilies and water hawthorns, benefit from a small quantity of bone meal in the soil. Water lilies can be set straight into the soil at the bottom of the pond, or they can be planted in baskets and later dropped into the water. In either case it is very important that the crowns, immediately after transplanting, should be covered by only a very small depth of water, and that this is increased gradually as the plants grow; otherwise they will not bloom the first season. There are varieties of water lilies for pools of all depths.

Some water plants live with all or part of their leaves submerged, and a few of these, perhaps twelve in a pond 6 feet square, should be included, as they help to purify the water and form suitable cover and nesting-places for fish.

In the shallow parts many types of water plants will grow, but those with scrambling roots should be planted with caution as they soon crowd out the others. Attractive varieties with compact growth are *Iris laevigata*, which has purple-blue flowers about 18 inches tall; the Arrowhead (*Sagittaria japonica plena*) with double white flowers about 2 feet high and arrow-shaped leaves; and the Bog Arum (*Calla palustris*) which has glossy foliage and miniature white arum flowers about 6 inches high, followed by scarlet berries. The double and single Marsh Marigolds and Water Forget-Me-Nots are very attractive in shallow water, and the Pickerel Weed (*Pontederia cordata*) is a fine water plant with dark-green heart-shaped leaves and spikes of soft blue flowers, growing about 2 feet high.

When the plants have become established, usually 6 to 8 weeks after planting, some fresh-water fish may be introduced to the pond. Golden Orfe and Goldfish (*see* CARP, Vol. II) are undoubtedly the best, since they are hardy, brightly coloured, and keep near the surface.

See also Vol. II: WATER PLANTS.

WATER SUPPLY, FARM, *see* FARMSTEAD; IRRIGATION.

WEASEL, *see* WILD ANIMALS ON THE FARM.

WEEDS. On arable land weeds are easily recognized, for they include all plants except the crop that has been sown. On GRASSLANDS (q.v.), however, the 'crop' is already a mixture of different plants, some of which are more valuable than others for feeding the livestock. Plants, therefore, that are poisonous or that crowd out those more nourishing than themselves can be reckoned as weeds in pasture or in hay.

1. VARIETIES OF WEEDS. Many weeds flourish on soils of different types, and do well even under poor conditions. This is one reason why weeds are so successful. Some, however, prefer one soil to another, and the presence of a number of weeds with the same preference growing together may be a reliable indication of soil conditions (*see* SOILS). For example: although a few plants of horse-tail are no guide as to the nature of the soil, a number of them growing with rushes and sedges shows that the drainage is bad. An association of knawel, sheep sorrel, and foxglove clearly indicates that the soil is sour (needs lime), though the presence of knawel by itself only suggests it. Isolated plants of gorse may be found in many places, but if plentiful and in the company of broom or ragwort, the soil is certainly dry and either sandy or gravelly. Mignonette flourishes on chalk, but is more reliable as an indicator of this kind of soil if found in the same neighbourhood as old-man's beard and chicory (*see* ECOLOGY OF PLANTS, Vol. II).

The kinds of weeds that appear in arable fields depend also on the time of year at which the crop is prepared for and sown. Black bent, for example, is specially troublesome in autumn-sown cereals, since it starts to grow at the same time as the crop and cannot easily be distinguished until it flowers. Thus, the selection of weeds that grow in any one field is due to a combination of circumstances rather than to any direct and simple effect of the crop itself.

2. DAMAGE DUE TO WEEDS. Weeds growing amongst the crop reduce the yield by competing for water and food in the soil and for the light above ground. Some weeds are parasitic, and absorb food directly from their host, the crop, by means of sucking organs (*see* PARASITIC PLANTS, Vol. II). Red bartsia that grows on wheat, and dodder and broomrape that attack clover are parasitic weeds. Poisonous plants are fortunately rare in England, but autumn crocus is dangerous and fool's parsley may be harmful if eaten in large quantities. In other and unexpected ways weeds may be a nuisance: for example, wild onion, when eaten by a cow, can taint the flavour of milk, and weeds with burred or hooked fruits that cling to the sheep's wool spoil the value of a fleece. The harvesting of grain crops is more difficult in a dirty field, for a tangle of weeds hinders the drying of the straw, and a mixture of weed seeds in a crop grown specially for its seed is a serious matter. Weeds also harbour plant pests and even act as carriers of disease from one crop to the next (*see* PESTS AND DISEASES).

3. CONTROL METHODS. Though the farmer cannot entirely prevent weeds he can do much to control them. The most important ways of doing this are by crop rotation, cultivation, and by the use of chemicals.

(*a*) *Crop rotation and cultivation.* All fertile soils contain a large number of dormant weed seeds ready to germinate when conditions are favourable—that is, when they are near the surface and when the soil is well broken down and moist. In order to clear the soil of weeds these dormant seeds must be encouraged to grow into plants that can be killed before they have had time to produce fresh seed. This can be done by cultivation, a term which includes all mechanical methods of working the soil, such as ploughing and harrowing. It is essential that the cultivation takes place at the right time of year. Many weeds will germinate in the autumn, but they cannot be easily eradicated from the growing crop. Weedy land, instead of being planted with an autumn-sown crop, should therefore be worked at intervals through the autumn and winter to kill the successive germinations of weed seeds, and not be planted till the spring.

The choice of the spring crop is also important. Roots, such as turnips and sugar-beet, are specially suitable, for they give the farmer a chance to continue his cleaning operations while the crop grows. Potatoes or clover are also useful since they tend to smother any weeds by their thick, leafy growth. If none of these methods is successful, the land may be put down to grass in the hope that the weeds will be crowded out by the close-growing herbage or eaten by the grazing animals, or even that the weed seeds, by being buried very deeply, will rot in the ground. The seeds of some species, such as charlock, can live a very long time, however, and may germinate freely when the land is again ploughed, even though they have been buried for a number of years. Some weeds, such as knot-grass and red bartsia, germinate mainly, or even solely, in the spring, and no amount of cultivation will make them alter this habit.

By growing a succession of different crops on the same land (crop rotation) the farmer can usually prevent any one weed getting established, since the times of cultivation will vary each year, and the weeds that escape one season can be got rid of the next.

(b) *Chemical methods.* Chemicals in the form of liquid sprays or dusts are used to control weeds in the same way as they are used to control pests (*see* INSECTICIDES). They are generally applied by means of special machines. They act in one of several different ways. Some, like sodium chlorate, are strong plant poisons, and though they kill the weeds they make the land temporarily unfit for a crop. This method is useful, however, for clearing bare ground or when time can be allowed for the poison to wash out of the soil before sowing.

Other chemicals are applied directly on the growing crop, for they will scorch the weeds without harming the plant provided that these are of a different habit of growth. For example, grasses and cereals have upright, narrow, slightly waxy leaves, and the growing-point of the shoot is protected by the leaf sheaths; but charlock and many others have broad, hairy leaves and an exposed growing-point. When a chemical solution is sprayed on to a mixture of these two types of plants, it tends to run off those with long, narrow leaves and protected growing-points, leaving them unharmed, while it collects on the broad leaves of the weeds, injuring them and killing their exposed tips. These sprays cannot, therefore, be safely used for broad-leaved crops such as peas, clover, or cabbage.

Sometimes a 'wetter' or 'spreader' is added to the spray to help it cover the leaf surface. Much the same result is obtained with dry materials dusted on to the plants when they are wet with

Harold Bastin
POPPIES AND OTHER WEEDS IN CORN

dew. Sprays and dusts are generally best applied when the crop and weeds are small, for, if the crop is accidentally damaged, it has then more chance to recover before the weeds have time to offer much serious competition. Spraying or dusting is only fully effective if there is a dry spell during which the poison can penetrate the plant. The chemicals most commonly used are sulphuric acid, copper sulphate, copper chloride, and some yellow dye-stuffs such as DNOC. These dye-stuffs must be handled with care. Sometimes it is possible to use substances as weed-killers that will afterwards have a fertilizing action on the crop. Calcium cyanamide and kainit are good examples of such compounds, the former supplying nitrogen and calcium, while the latter contains potassium.

Some substances, first used to encourage cuttings to root quickly (and for this reason known as plant-growth substances), were accidentally discovered to be good weed-killers. They are usually known by an abbreviation of their chemical formula, such as MCPA, DCPA, or 2-4D. They can be absorbed either by the leaf or root of the plant; and as some plants, grasses and cereals for example, are unharmed by them, they are very useful for LAWNS (q.v.). Some weeds are also resistant to them, but the reason for this is not yet understood. The time at which spraying is carried out is important, since plants vary greatly in susceptibility with age. Most weeds are more readily killed as seedlings, and by careful timing it is possible to spray even a non-cereal crop, such as flax, without doing it any damage. This type of weed-killer is also useful for getting rid of perennials such as thistles and creeping buttercup.

These compounds have several advantages over the other chemicals mentioned—they are not injurious to men and animals, do not corrode the machines or spoil the worker's clothes, and are, therefore, less unpleasant to use. The action of these plant-growth substances and of the other sprays is called 'selective', since the effect is not the same upon all plants.

4. PERENNIAL WEEDS. Annual weeds are, of course, more easily controlled, whether by cultivation or chemical methods, than perennials with their deep roots or underground stems stored with reserves of food. The roots of some such weeds, if cut into small pieces during soil cultivation, may only spread farther, each piece growing into a new plant. For that reason the disk harrow is rather a dangerous implement to use on land that is full of twitch (or couch). It is better to work their underground stems and roots to the surface with tined cultivator and harrow (*see* CULTIVATORS), for then the sun and wind will shrivel them up, or they can be raked into heaps and burnt. Repeated cutting of the tops helps to weaken such plants as bracken, thistle, docks, or ragwort by exhausting their food reserves, and 'spudding' (cutting through at ground level) is a common and important practice on the farm.

Thus, in order to keep the land clean and to get the best possible yields from his crops, the farmer has to use all his skill and ingenuity, basing his methods on a thorough understanding of the habits of the different weeds and the effect of the various chemical sprays on each species.

5. INJURIOUS WEEDS AND WEED SEEDS. By Act of Parliament a farmer (or anyone else who occupies land) can be compelled to cut certain weeds before they seed. These weeds are: ragwort, spear thistle, creeping thistle, broad-leaved dock, and curled dock. A seller of seed must also declare the presence of certain weed seeds in a sample of seed, if more than 5% by weight of the seed is composed of these weeds. The species concerned are docks and sorrels, cranesbills, wild carrot, Yorkshire fog, and soft brome grass.

See also CULTIVATIONS.

WEEVIL PESTS. The WEEVIL (q.v. Vol. II) is a kind of beetle several species of which are very destructive to crops. Damage may be done by both the adult insects and by their grubs, which are soft, white, footless creatures.

1. THE APPLE BLOSSOM WEEVIL. This weevil lays an egg in a hole bored into the immature bud of an apple blossom. The grub hatches out in the spring, preventing the blossom from expanding, and turning the petals brown. These are known as 'capped blossoms'. The weevils emerge in June, feed on the foliage of the apple-trees for a few weeks, and then disappear into cracks in the bark, into hedge-bottoms, and among rubbish until the following spring, when they return to the apple trees. To control the pest the buds should be sprayed or dusted in March with DDT.

2. PEA AND BEAN WEEVIL. These are usually about ¼ inch long, and brownish with a few darker lines running down the back. They appear in the spring and feed on the leaves of the young plants. They are very active in sunshine and can be seen moving over leaves and stems of beans, peas, clover, and other leguminous crops. In dry weather their attacks on seedlings may cause complete failure of a crop. The females lay their eggs on the ground, and the

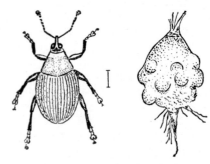

TURNIP GALL WEEVIL AND GALLED TURNIP

larvae, which are white and crescent-shaped, feed on the roots of the plants, and, unless action is taken against them, may eat through the stems of tiny seedlings. A sprinkling on the ground of BHC or DDT dusts is the best protection.

3. THE TURNIP GALL WEEVIL. The larvae of this beetle cause the hard round swellings often to be found upon turnips and the roots of cabbages and related plants, including wall-flowers and charlock. If one of the swellings is cut across, the yellowish-white, curved bodies of the grubs can be seen inside.

4. NUT WEEVILS. These beetles eat the leaves of the nut. In May the female beetle, with

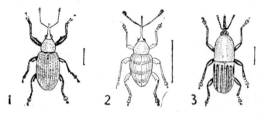

1. APPLE BLOSSOM WEEVIL. 2. NUT WEEVIL. 3. GRAIN WEEVIL.

her gimlet-like mouth and jaws, pierces the nutlet and inserts an egg. This hatches within the nut and the larva grows fat and white. Then about the end of July it comes out through the original hole, falls to the ground, and pupates. Next spring the adult weevil returns to the tree. Nut weevils are not easy to control; a spray of arsenate of lead which poisons the leaves on which the beetle is feeding, or even better of DDT, is effective.

There are several other weevils which attack fruit-trees, in particular the Raspberry Weevil and the Vine Weevil, both of which bore into shoots and fruit. The best deterrent is the removal of all winter harbourage, such as litter in ditches, piles of unburnt raspberry canes and other rubbish, or stumps of old canes not cut off to the ground.

5. GRAIN AND RICE WEEVILS. These are pests of stored produce, and are found in barns, granaries, mills, and similar buildings. They are slender, brown in colour, and quite small, but the damage they do is considerable. The grub lives in the kernel of the grain which it eats out entirely, leaving only the husk. In the empty husk it pupates, and later the adult beetle eats its way out and itself attacks the grain. These weevils have been brought from warmer coun-tries, and although they breed, when conditions are warm, so freely and rapidly that a granary may at times be 'alive' with them, they cannot live in the open. An infested storehouse may be cleared by leaving it empty, cleaned, and out of use for some months, or it may be fumigated with DDT or BHC smokes.

In tropical and sub-tropical countries there are many other types of weevils, such as the large Palm Weevils, which attack and even kill coconut palms, or the Cotton Boll Weevils (*see* TROPICAL PESTS).

See also BEETLE PESTS; PESTS AND DISEASES; SPRAYING AND DUSTING MACHINES.
See also Vol. II: WEEVIL.

WHALING. For more than a thousand years men have hunted WHALES (q.v. Vol. II), at first from near the coasts, but, as the supply of local whales diminished about the end of the 14th century, the whaling gradually spread farther afield until the pursuit ranged over all the seas of the world. At the present time 90% of the world's whale-oil comes from whales caught in the Antarctic, but whale-hunting is also carried out in the Atlantic, the Pacific, and off the coasts of Africa, South America, and Japan.

1. WHALES. Although all kinds of Whales are not fish, but mammals, they are born, live, and die in the water, and never come to land deliberately. All whales, from the 100-foot blue whale (the largest creature that has ever lived on land or sea, which may weigh up to 115 tons) down to the 5-foot porpoise and dolphin, are members of the same natural order of mammals, the *Cetacea*. They are not aggressive animals, with the exception of the ferocious killer whale, which hunts in packs and attacks the larger whales (*see* picture, p. 468, Vol. II).

There are two main groups of whales, the toothed whales and the whalebone or baleen whales. So far as whaling is concerned, the only important toothed whale is the sperm whale— by far the largest of this group, reaching a length of 65 feet. The baleen whales have no teeth; but instead the immense mouth is equipped with a sieve in the form of a system of vertical plates of baleen, a horny fibrous material frayed at its lower end, which is the 'whalebone' of commerce— although there is nothing bone-like about it. The great bulk and richness in oil of the baleen whales, especially the enormous blue whale, make them the most important to the whaler, and they are now the chief source of the world's whale-oil supply. They include the 'right' whale, so named because it combines numbers with large size, slow speed, high quality of whalebone and oil, and, not least, buoyancy

A WHALE BEING TOWED TO THE FACTORY SHIP

lb., and since one big right whale (these yield the best whalebone) might furnish anything from 1,500 to 3,300 lb., as well as up to 30 tons of oil, the capture of one such animal might well repay the entire cost of fitting out a vessel. Whalebone is now of much less value, though it is still used for making brushes.

(c) *Ambergris*, by far the most valuable, but also the most scarce, of all whale products, is believed to be the result of a diseased or irritated condition of the intestine of the sperm whale. This greyish, greasy substance, with an offensive smell when fresh and a sweet earthy odour after exposure to the air, is of great value to the PERFUMERY Industry (q.v. Vol. VII) because of its power to fix the finer perfumes. It is sometimes found floating at sea or washed up on the shore in lumps weighing from a few ounces to a few pounds; but in 1716 a 400 lb. piece was found at St. Helena, and more recently some Norwegian whalers found a mass weighing 924 lb., valued at £27,000.

(d) *Other Products*. Whale meat, which has always formed part of the diet of whaling crews, and is popular in Japan, became, after the Second World War, an important addition to British meat supplies. The refrigerator vessels that accompany the factory-ships bring the meat to market. A product of the sperm whale is spermaceti—a kind of oily wax, which was much used for candles in the 19th century, but has now lost its importance. Those parts of the carcass which are unfit for human food are used as a constituent of cattle and poultry foods, and the intestines are made into manure.

3. WHALING METHODS. In early times, when men in small boats pitted their skill, courage, and primitive weapons against the huge bulk and strength of the whale, risks and hardship were involved, but great profits were to be made from a successful hunt.

Early records suggest that the Vikings of north-west Europe organized whale-hunts in the

when dead, all of which make it the ideal or 'right' whale from the point of view of the whaler.

2. WHALE PRODUCTS. Whales are hunted first and foremost for whale-oil, but also for whalebone, ambergris, and of recent years for whale meat.

(a) *Whale-oil*. This oil is obtained by rendering down ('trying-out' is the old whaling term) the thick layer of blubber found under the smooth skin of the whale. This blubber, which varies from 6 to 14 inches in thickness, is the animal's natural protection against the coldness of the sea, for it is not cold-blooded like fish. Some oil is also obtained by treatment of other parts of the carcase. A large whale will yield up to 30 tons of oil. The oil is used in the manufacture of SOAP, in the CURRYING of leather (qq.v. Vol. VII), and for many other industrial purposes; and since the processes for extracting glycerine for EXPLOSIVES (q.v. Vol. VIII) and for producing hard oils for MARGARINE (q.v. Vol. VII) were perfected, the demands for whale-oil have much increased.

(b) *Whalebone*. Until the end of the 19th century, when whalebone was the essential foundation for corsets, bustles, and other women's garments, this whale product was often more valuable than the oil. In 1890 first quality whalebone sold in America at 5 to 7 dollars per

9th century, and in the 13th century there was hunting by the Basques of right whales in the Bay of Biscay. The hunt was in the first place conducted on 'off shore' methods, and men in look-out towers gave the signal for the small boats to put out when a whale was sighted. Often the first indication of a whale's presence in the water is the 'spout', which is not a column of sea-water, but the condensation in the cold air of the warm moist breath expelled forcibly through the blowhole, or holes, in the top of the whale's head.

Paul Popper

FLENSING A WHALE AT A WHALING STATION IN SOUTH GEORGIA

From the earliest times baited harpoons, to which a length of line was attached, lances, spears, and knives were the weapons used. The equipment of the early whalers was simple. After the whale had been killed from small boats it was towed ashore for 'flensing', as the stripping of the blubber was called. At the shore stations there were 'try-works' where the blubber was converted to oil. As it became necessary to go farther afield to find whales, the small hunting-boats operated from larger sailing-vessels with a look-out man in the 'crow's nest' to spot the whales. These vessels were fitted out for long voyages and equipped for oil-refining on board. In this deep-sea whaling the carcass was brought alongside the ship to be stripped, and men descended on to it with their flensing knives. The work was arduous and risky, but the rewards were so great that there was never any lack of crews to man the ships.

These attempts to work from what were, in effect, early examples of the modern 'factory-ship', were for a time given up, largely because in the middle of the 16th century the seas around the island of Spitsbergen, in the Arctic Ocean, were found to be regularly visited by whales. Spitsbergen became for many years a busy centre of the whaling industry. Both British and Dutch ships were engaged. Their methods were a mixture of the 'off-shore' and 'factory-ship' methods. Flensing was done alongside the ships, to which the captured whales were towed; but the blubber was cut up and put into barrels or tanks, and trying-out was done ashore.

By the end of the 17th century, however, this industry declined, and the whales were again pursued in distant waters. In the 18th century the sperm whale industry was almost entirely in the hands of the American whalers, and whaling was the mainstay of many American east coast towns. Here ships were built and fitted out for voyages into the Atlantic and Pacific lasting 2 or 3 years. So long as the sperm whales were easy to find, the profits were great; but hunting this whale was often a risky business. Frequently boats were smashed or overturned in the whale's death struggles. Hermann Melville's famous book, *Moby Dick*, was founded on the author's own experiences of sperm whaling.

As long as whalers depended on harpooning the whale by hand from rowing or sailing boats, they had to confine themselves to the slower right whales and sperm whales, since the bigger and faster rorquals or fin whales could rarely be approached. A fin whale swims normally at 12 knots, and when frightened is much faster. Also its body sinks when it is killed, so that its pursuit was altogether too troublesome to be worth while. But in the 19th century the introduction of the steamship and, even more, the invention of the gun harpoon (*see* HARPOONING) led to a rapid growth in fin whaling in northern waters, mainly conducted from Norway; and by pumping air into the carcass it was possible to keep it afloat. About the beginning of the present century news of immense numbers of fin and blue whales in Antarctic waters, particularly around the island groups of South Georgia, South Orkneys, and South Shetlands, led to the rapid development by the Norwegians of whaling in those seas.

At first these whales were towed to shore bases; but by 1923 new developments of factory ships made the whalers quite independent of shore stations, and made intensive hunting in the most remote seas a practical possibility. The modern factory-ship is a specially designed and equipped ship of 20,000 to 30,000 tons, with a slipway in the stern for hauling the whale on to the deck. It burns oil fuel, and is refuelled at sea by tankers from the shore base. It is accompanied by a refrigerator-ship, about ten whale-catchers (about the size of a trawler), four buoy-boats or towing-boats for towing whales to the factory-ship, and a store and supply ship. The captains of the ships are usually Norwegian, and the deck officers and crews British and Norwegian. The harpooner-gunners who work on the whale catchers are almost invariably Norwegian, the trade usually descending from father to son. When the whale is killed, it is brought alongside the catcher and pumped up with compressed air. It is then either taken in tow towards the factory-ship by one of the buoy-boats, or buoyed to mark its location until it can be towed away later. In the southern summer work goes on throughout the 24 hours of daylight.

In the 1937–8 season in the Antarctic no less than 46,000 whales were killed. In the following season, with 34 factory-ships, 2 shore stations, and 281 catchers operating in the same area, the catch dropped to 38,356 whales, which suggests that stocks were beginning to diminish. After the Second World War, radar and sea-planes for whale-spotting and weather reconnaissance have been added to the modern whale hunting equipment, and it seems likely that in the future a combination of helicopter aircraft and electrical harpooning equipment may transform existing methods of whale-hunting.

Altogether, since 1900 over three-quarters of a million whales have been killed, and until 1937 no serious attempt was made to control this indiscriminate slaughter in the interests of maintaining a breeding stock for the future. Since 1937, however, the nations most concerned in whaling have agreed on measures limiting the open season in the Antarctic, protecting sperm and right whales, and female whales with calves, fixing minimum size limits for all species, and limiting the total annual catch permitted. In 1946 fresh restrictions were introduced; but the limits were often exceeded, and by 1951 there was evidence that the numbers of whales were still decreasing. Moreover, whales reproduce themselves slowly (the gestation period varies from 10 to 12 months in most species, with only one young at a birth) and blue whales, for example, take 7 years to reach maturity. It seems likely, therefore, that further measures of conservation will be necessary, or the source of some of the world's most valuable raw materials may vanish altogether.

See also HARPOONING.
See also Vol. II: WHALES.

WHEAT. This cereal is grown in all countries with temperate climates, the grain being used not only for bread but also for making macaroni, biscuits, and confectionery, and for livestock feeding. Some of the great wheat-growing areas

Plant Breeding Institute, Cambridge
YEOMAN WHEAT

High Commissioner for Canada

FOUR COMBINES HARVESTING WHEAT ON THE CANADIAN PRAIRIES

of the world are in North America, in the Caucasus in Russia, in the central European countries, and in Australia.

As with most farm crops, there are many varieties of wheat, the best for bread-making having a grain that looks steely and translucent when cut across. Such grain is said to be 'strong', and the flour made from it gives a loaf that is spongy and light. The 'weak' varieties, with a white, mealy grain, are used for biscuit-making and livestock feeding. Generally speaking, the varieties that can be grown in Canada, America, and Australia are stronger and give more loaves from a given quantity of grain than do most of the varieties that can be grown in the United Kingdom, though some of the newer varieties grown in Britain, such as Yeoman, Warden, Redman, and Holdfast, are almost as good. Unfortunately, it is the weak English wheats that yield best.

Wheat needs a warm, sunny climate and a moderate rainfall, so the crop grows best in the eastern and midland counties of England and on the heavier types of soil. Light, sandy soils are liable to get too dry, and then the yield is never so good. On peaty and fen soils the plant is liable to grow too much straw and to give inferior grain.

In farm rotations wheat usually follows a LEY (q.v.), a bare fallow, beans, or potatoes, its cultivation and manuring naturally depending upon the condition of the land and the treatment given to the preceding crop. After a ley, farm-yard manure is spread on the land and ploughed in; but after the other crops there is seldom any need for additional fertilizing. Wheat is a plant

that develops at ground level a large number of side shoots (tillers), which, if they develop before mid-March, probably produce ears at harvest. Thus, the seed should be sown early, and the cultivations and manuring should be the sort to encourage early tillering. 'Blind' tillers, that is, those that fail to produce ears, are useless to the farmer except for the production of straw. At about mid-May 1 to 2 cwt. per acre of sulphate of ammonia, or some other nitrogenous fertilizer, should be applied to the growing crop as a top dressing, to increase the size of the ears (upon which the yield largely depends) without increasing the amount of straw. A very long straw is likely to be weak, and to bend over, or 'lodge', when the ears get heavy, adding considerably to the labour of harvesting.

The majority of the hundred or so varieties of wheat are suited to autumn sowing, that is, October–November, and for them a rather rough seed-bed is prepared by ploughing, cultivating, and harrowing. Small clods give some protection from the cold winds of winter. If the seed-bed is too fine, the soil tends to run together, or 'pan', drying into a cement-like hardness which checks the growth of the seedlings. These difficulties do not arise with spring sowing in February to April, for which a fine tilth can be prepared, free from weeds and retentive of moisture.

The seed is usually sown with a corn DRILL (q.v.), the coulters or corn spouts being 4 to 7 inches apart. Twelve stone of seed per acre is common; the later the date of sowing in either the autumn or spring, the more seed is needed. For the spring varieties, which do not tiller as much as the winter ones, up to 16 stone per acre may be sown. Sometimes the complete operation of ploughing, harrowing, seeding, and covering is carried out with one gang of implements (one behind the other) pulled by a tractor. Sometimes the seed is broadcast by hand on the furrows after ploughing, in which case it falls into the depressions, or 'seams', between the crests of the furrows, and needs only a stroke or two of the harrows to cover it.

On fertile land, and often following a mild winter, the crop grows so well that in the spring it has made too much growth; if allowed to proceed unchecked, it might become too tall, and be in danger of 'lodging' or bending over before ripening. It is then said to be 'winter proud', and to reduce the danger of lodging it is usual to remove the excess of leaf by grazing it with sheep or cattle. Provided that this is carried out before the end of April, the yield is not likely to suffer, and the straw will be shorter by several inches. After a severe winter, frost will probably have lifted the surface of the soil, and many seedlings will be lying with their roots exposed. Rolling is then necessary to press them back into position. On the other hand, a wet winter may have made the surface soil run together to form a crust or pan, and a good harrowing is needed to break the crust and give the seedlings a chance to continue growth. This harrowing also encourages tillering. Later in the season, if necessary, the crop should be sprayed with chemicals to kill annual weeds, and any thistles or docks got rid of by hand-hoeing.

When a combine harvester is used, the crop is left until it is dead ripe; but when cut with the self-binder, the crop must be tackled before this stage is reached, otherwise much of the corn would be shaken out during cutting, tying, and stooking. The unripe crop must, therefore, finish ripening in stooks in the field, a process which may take from 7 to 14 days, according to weather conditions. When thoroughly ripe the crop is carted and stacked, either in the open to be thatched later, or in a barn to await threshing. Provided that the sap has dried from the straw, a little surface moisture in the form of dew or rain does not prevent the carting of wheat, for it has an open straw that allows the wind to drive through the stack and complete the drying. If the sheaves are in poor condition when carted, as, for instance, after prolonged wet weather, it may be necessary to leave the crop unthreshed in the stack until the spring. On an average, about 17 cwt. of grain and 25 cwt. of straw per acre are obtained, but up to 2 tons of grain per acre is not uncommon. The winter varieties yield better than the spring varieties.

The extraction of the flour in a mill for human food leaves by-products called 'miller's offals', and these brans and pollards are used for feeding to pigs and poultry. The straw is too coarse to feed livestock and is used chiefly for bedding and THATCHING (q.v.). When food for cattle is scarce, however, as in war-time, wheat straw can be softened and so made digestible for cattle by being soaked in caustic soda. The straw is first cut up into chaff, and the whole process is known as the 'straw pulp process'.

See also ARABLE CROPS; HARVESTING.

WHEELWRIGHT. Although many of the country woodworkers call themselves wheelwrights, their skill is not confined to building old-fashioned carts with high wooden wheels. Most of them now make modern trailers to be drawn by tractors, and do all the various woodwork repair jobs wanted by the farmer and countryman. The wheelwright knows a very great deal about wood, some of this knowledge having been handed down from generation to generation, and some added by recent research and a study of new methods.

When building a cart the wheelwright is concerned with making as light a vehicle as possible consistent with strength. He chooses his wood and uses his well-tried methods of construction to make the cart as strong as possible, while by chamfering away all unnecessary material he both lightens the vehicle and gives it graceful, curved lines. His wood must be well-seasoned—indeed, he will carry stocks for several years while the wood dries out; for example, elm for the hub or for the felloes (or rim) of the wheel may lie in the shop 7 years or more.

A practiced wheelwright often works without drawings; he knows the precise proportions of a tip cart, or just how to lay the floor of a dung-cart so that the edge of the boards do not obstruct the shovel. He knows how to design his carts for particular jobs and to build his wheels to suit particular soils. Unlike the factory, he does not have to produce hundreds to the same pattern in order to pay his way; in fact, he often adapts

Rural Industries Bureau

A WHEELWRIGHT SHAVING THE SPOKES OF A CART WHEEL

The spokes are shaped to give the maximum strength combined with lightness

a standardized product to suit a particular purpose.

On his bench new power-driven tools take their place alongside the traditional adze and draw-knife. In the old days the hub or felloes had to be roughed out laboriously by hand, whereas now they are cut out in a matter of minutes by the power lathe and band saw. Power tools give the craftsman the opportunity to make the greatest use of the traditional skill of his hand. An example of this skill is the way in which a wooden wheel is 'dished' (made slightly concave) to make it stronger and more manœuvrable.

The wheelwright frequently works with the blacksmith, who makes the ironwork for carts and the welded frame for a trailer, and helps in the exciting task of fitting a red-hot iron tire to a wooden wheel.

See also FARM VEHICLES; RURAL CRAFTS.

WHELK FISHING, *see* SHELLFISH GATHERING.

WILD ANIMALS ON THE FARM. Many wild creatures influence the work of the farmer and the gardener. Some are harmful and destroy the crops, but still more do good in various ways, mainly by preying upon other pests. The same animal may do good at one season of the year and harm at another, and it is impossible to say what would be the result of exterminating any animal, even the most obvious pests, such as wood pigeons, rats, or the cabbage white butterfly. Insects, harmful as many of them are, carry out much of the work of pollination (*see* FERTILIZATION), without which the fruit would not develop. This article deals with those animals that on the whole do good; the most harmful of the birds and mammals are dealt with under VERMIN, and the harmful insects under INSECT PESTS (qq.v.).

There are several wild mammals which, like the MOLE (q.v. Vol. II), do both good and harm. The mole, spending most of its life underground, does harm when it eats EARTHWORMS (q.v.), but good when it eats such pests as wireworms (*see* BEETLE PESTS). Its underground tunnels help to drain and aerate the soil, but at the same time they do great damage to seed-beds and to growing crops by loosening the soil round them. On a farm damage may be done if an implement breaks through the thin crust of earth into a mole's tunnel, or a mower knife hits a hidden molehill. The BADGER and members of the WEASEL family such as the stoat (qq.v. Vol. II) are often regarded as pests because they occasionally steal young chickens, and, in the case of the weasel, eggs from the farmyard. The badger also sometimes eats cultivated vegetables. But they all do more good than harm, for they destroy many much more serious pests—rabbits, rats, mice, and harmful insects. Indeed, the stoat is one of the most effective 'mousers' among four-footed animals. The OTTER (q.v. Vol. II), though it kills a great many fish, also destroys many 'cannibal' trout, which are themselves harmful.

Many insect-eating animals such as the HEDGEHOG, the SHREW, and the BAT (qq.v. Vol. II) are extremely useful in destroying insect pests. Hedgehogs, though they occasionally steal eggs, eat large numbers of slugs, snails, and

Eric Hosking

A KESTREL WITH A FIELD-VOLE IN ITS CLAWS

insects. Bats feed entirely on insects; and the shrew is a greedy little animal that eats three times its own weight of insects, slugs, and worms in 24 hours.

Birds, on the whole, do much good, though many of them certainly do harm at certain seasons of the year. Owls (q.v. Vol. II) feed largely upon rats and mice, as well as on harmful insects, though they occasionally also take chicks and small wild birds. The kestrel, a kind of Falcon (q.v. Vol. II), does by day the same kind of work that the owl does by night.

Starlings, Tits, Bullfinches, Nightjars, and Thrushes (qq.v. Vol. II) do valuable work in destroying insects and grubs, even though at times they may damage the crops. Starlings, when they get short of food, turn to grain crops, fruit, and other cultivated crops; but their work on the ploughed fields in winter and spring in destroying wireworms is very important. The bullfinch and the blue tit do a good deal of damage by pulling off the buds from fruit-trees, but generally it is the grub inside the bud they are searching for. The nightjar, which flies and feeds by night, resting by day, destroys large numbers of cockchafers and moths. The lapwing, or peewit, not only eats many insect pests and slugs, but also destroys a certain kind of water snail that acts as the host of the larvae of liver flukes, parasites which attack sheep (*see*

Parasitic Worms). The thrush is particularly useful in killing snails, which it can often be seen cracking on a stone, or thrush's 'anvil'. Swallows, swifts, house-martins, robins, wrens, hedgesparrows, wrynecks, spotted flycatchers, treecreepers, the wagtails, and black-headed gulls all serve the farmer and gardener well in destroying insect pests.

See also Pests and Diseases; Insect Pests; Vermin.

WILLOW, *see* Trees, Broadleaved.

WINDOW-BOXES. These are placed on the ledge outside the window, and give those people who have no garden a chance to grow a few flowers. This helps to brighten up the fronts of houses and flats.

The smallest useful size for a window-box is 6 inches wide and 8 inches deep; its length will be the width of the window. If the boxes are of wood, only well-seasoned planks, at least $\frac{3}{4}$ inch thick, should be used, and fixed together by brass screws. The best woods are teak and oak, but deal, elm, and ash are suitable. Whether made of wood or of metal, the box should have at least two coats of oil paint—not creosote. Unless the window ledge is very wide, the box needs to be fixed in position for safety, and it should be tilted inwards slightly with small wooden wedges. Boxes are sometimes fixed away from the windows for decorative effects, but they must be within reach for watering.

Drainage is very important. The boxes should have several large drainage holes in the bottom, covered with crocks (bits of broken pot) or wire mesh; and then an inch or two of small crocks, medium gravel, or pebbles should be put beneath the soil.

The soil must be rich and pest-free, the best being the balanced, sterilized John Innes compost, as for Potting (q.v.). An inch layer of peat on the surface after the plants are in place is valuable for keeping in the moisture. The soil should be firmly packed in, and changed twice a year. It is sometimes more convenient to fill the boxes with damp peat and to plunge the plants, still in their pots, into the peat. In any case the soil should never be allowed to get dry, and watering every other day may be necessary in hot weather. Some thought must be given to where the water will go when it has drained through the soil and out of the box.

Plants are not usually grown from seed in

window boxes as they tend to grow spindly and weak, and one must wait a long time before the flowers appear. They should be grown elsewhere and put into the boxes just as they are about to flower.

During the spring and summer most of the usual BEDDING PLANTS (q.v.) are suitable for window-boxes, those which flower for a long period with little attention being the best. In the autumn the boxes may be planted up with BULBS (q.v.), especially hyacinths, tulips, and daffodils, with wallflowers, or with small evergreen shrubs, such as winter-flowering heaths (*Erica carnea*), *Veronica Traversii*, or dwarf conifers. Bulbs interplanted with spring-flowering plants such as polyanthus, pansies, or forget-me-nots, make a good display.

Plants which hang down over the side of the box, and others which climb up stakes or wires arranged at the ends, make a good variety. In fact, it is possible to 'frame' the whole window in this way.

SUITABLE PLANTS FOR WINDOW-BOXES.

(*a*) Plants for sunny or shady (but not dark) positions.

Upright	Trailing
Begonias	Creeping Jenny
Calceolarias	Ground Ivy
Fuchsias	Periwinkle
Pansies	
Mignonettes	
Pelargoniums (Geraniums)	*Climbing*
Petunias	Ivy
Violas	

(*b*) Plants for sunny positions only.

Upright	Trailing
Antirrhinums	*Campanula isophylla*
China Asters	Trailing Lantanas
Heliotropes	Trailing Lobelias
Lobelias	Ivy-leaf Pelargoniums
Marigolds	
Nasturtiums	
Phlox Drummondii	*Climbing*
Salvia splendens	Canary Creeper
Stocks	Hop
Tobacco Plant	Morning Glory
Verbenas	Climbing Nasturtiums
Zinnias	

See also HOUSE-PLANTS.

WINTER-FLOWERING PLANTS. In the British Isles, especially in the warmer south and west, there are various plants which will flower freely out of doors during the winter months from November till the end of March, whenever there is a mild spell of weather. Winter flowers are not normally as large or as brilliant as those of spring and summer, but they are often delicately attractive and have a strong sweet scent. There are few summer flowers so strongly scented as Daphne or Winter Sweet.

The winter garden should, if possible, be near the house, and in blocks small enough for all the plants to be easily seen from the paths. An open, sunny position is needed, if possible sheltered from the north and east. The ideal position is in front of a brick wall facing south, with a group of dark evergreens providing protection from the east. Against the wall the winter jasmine (*Jasminum nudiflorum*) will grow well and produce great spurs of brilliant yellow, star-like flowers, flushed red in the bud, throughout the winter. This jasmine, unlike the summer jasmine, has no scent; but if picked in bud the flowers will open in the house, and the plant is all the better for this pruning. It will grow very nearly as well on a north or east wall, or cascading over a steep bank.

Also against the wall should be placed clumps of *Iris unguicularis* (*stylosa*), natives of the pine woods of Algeria and the islands of the Mediterranean. They grow best in a light sandy soil, and frequently throw up their first delicate mauve flowers, marked with gold, early in November. There is a later variety with narrow leaves and deeper blue flowers, which comes from Crete. *Iris alata*, another beautiful

Amateur Gardening

CHRISTMAS ROSE

Amateur Gardening

WINTER SWEET

native of Algeria, may flower about the same time if the tubers have been well baked and dried during the summer. *Iris reticulata* and *I. histrioides* are very early spring-flowering irises particularly resistant to cold weather (*see* IRISES).

The basis of the winter garden should be the winter-flowering shrubs. Among the best of these is the Japanese winter cherry (*Prunus subhirtella autumnalis*) which produces its many little pale pink flowers during every mild spell. The yellow-flowered Witch Hazel (*Hamamelis mollis*), with curious narrow twisted petals, is even more resistant to frost. The fragrant *Daphne Mezereum*, with both purple and white forms, the pinkish-white *Viburnum fragrans*, and the yellow and red Winter Sweet (*Chimonanthus praecox*), of which the best variety is *luteus*, are all remarkable for their sweet scent. These shrubs can be underplanted with the autumn-flowering cyclamen (*C. neapoli-*

tanum) whose decorative leaves are beautiful in themselves, or with the winter-flowering heath (*Erica carnea*) which will continue to flower from November till March.

In a protected situation in a mild district, where the soil has no lime, varieties of the ever-green *Camellia* will provide flowers from February onwards, as will also the early flowering rhododendrons such as the rosy-purple *R. mucronulatum* and *R. praecox*.

Species of crocus, snowdrops, and cyclamen, if carefully chosen, can provide flowers from October till April. The lilac *Crocus laevigatus* and *Crocus Imperati* should flower at Christmas time, and are followed in January and February by the pale lavender *C. Tomasinianus*, the orange-yellow *C. chrysanthus*, the little golden *C. susianus* streaked with mahogany, and finally the well-established brilliant Dutch Yellow, a sterile form of unknown origin. The large-flowered snowdrop *Galanthus Elwesii* is one of the best of the snowdrops. Anemones and scillas will flower very early in the spring if the weather is mild.

The waxy white Christmas Rose (*Helleborus niger*) and the later purple Lenten Rose (*H. orientalis*) will flower very freely in well-manured soil in a partly shaded site, once the plants are well established and so long as they are left undisturbed. If possible, they should be given some protection, such as CLOCHES (q.v.) or a lightly constructed frame, during the flowering period.

See also FLOWERING SHRUBS.

WIREWORM, *see* BEETLE PESTS.

WOOD, *see* TIMBER.

WOOLLY APHIS, *see* APHID PESTS.

WORMS, *see* EARTHWORMS; PARASITIC WORMS.

Y

YAMS, *see* TROPICAL ROOT CROPS.

YOUNG FARMERS' CLUBS. 1. ENGLAND AND WALES. Anyone over 10 years and under 26, wherever he lives or whatever his job, can be elected a member of a Y.F.C. Members must be ready to take on certain responsibilities, such as attending club meetings regularly, carrying out their share of the work of organization and management, taking part in club activities, and paying their club subscriptions. New members are elected by those already in the club.

There are about 50,000 Young Farmers in England and Wales, organized in some 1,300 clubs. Most of these are 'open' clubs, that is, they are open to all the young people in the district; but there are also 'school' clubs, each formed from the pupils of a particular school. The management of the club is in the hands of the members. Their aim is to make themselves 'Good farmers, good countrymen, and good citizens': this is their unofficial motto.

A well run Young Farmers' Club gives its members a chance to see, to enjoy in their own way, and to understand the countryside. They also learn to do many of the things that farmers, farmers' wives, and other country people do. Young Farmers, therefore, pay visits to farms, factories, research stations, and so on, and they invite experienced people to talk and give demonstrations at the club meetings—held, probably, once a fortnight.

The Club Leader and the members of the Club Advisory Committee, all older people, help the members to learn farm and other country crafts, such as thatching, ploughing, hedging, walling, poultry trussing, and canning. Competitions in these are often held, and in some crafts certificates of proficiency are awarded.

Members sometimes keep their own livestock (calves, pigs, sheep, poultry, or rabbits) or cultivate their own plots of land, and groups of members occasionally join together to do this. Sometimes members carry out surveys of their districts—indeed there are national competitions for such projects. In addition they take part in such church festivities as harvest festivals, and organize many recreative club activities—concerts and dances, for example. Many Young Farmers also take training in and practise public speaking, so that they are able to express themselves at meetings with confidence and clarity. Competitions in this are organized both by clubs and by counties.

There are inter-club meetings, and all the clubs in a county assemble once a year for an Annual General Meeting. On other occasions they meet for a 'field contest' or 'rally', held on a farm, when competitions in and demonstrations of farm and domestic work are staged, together with exhibitions of club work. Judging livestock is popular on these occasions. In nearly every county there is a County Federation, employing an organizer who helps to form new clubs, advises

F. G. Oliver

A YOUNG FARMERS' CLUB VISIT TO A FARM
The members are being shown young shorthorn cattle

F. G. Oliver

A YOUNG FARMERS' CLUB PUBLIC SPEAKING COMPETITION

existing ones, and organizes county events. Each County Federation is managed by a council on which the clubs are represented.

All well-established and active Young Farmers' Clubs are affiliated to the National Federation of Young Farmers' Clubs, the members of whose council represent the County Federations and other bodies specially interested in the work, such as the Royal Agricultural Society and the Ministries of Agriculture and Education. Every club in the country is entitled to send representatives to the Annual General Meeting of the National Federation, when a report and the accounts for the year are presented, and all kinds of questions are discussed and decisions are taken. Thus, both the County Federations and the National Federation are answerable to the club members. The National Federation employs eight advisers, called liaison officers, one in each area of England and Wales, as well as a small staff at the central office in London.

The clubs are financed by their members' subscriptions, which vary from about 2s. 6d. to about 10s. a year. The clubs send subscriptions to the County Federation which usually also receives a grant from the County Education Authority. The National Federation receives dues from the affiliated clubs, a number of donations, grants from the Ministries of Agri-culture and Education, and some profits from the sale of its publications.

2. SCOTLAND AND IRELAND. The Scottish Association of Y.F.C.s, with headquarters in Edinburgh, is run on similar lines to the National Federation. It is organized in five areas instead of in counties, the members of the headquarters staff serving as organizers. Many of the clubs in the Highlands and in the outlying islands have a very isolated existence. The membership is approximately 10,000, between the age-limits of 14 and 26. There are no junior members. There are also separate associations of Young Farmers' Clubs in Eire and Ulster.

3. OTHER COUNTRIES. There are Y.F.C.s, or similar organizations with different names, in many other countries, such as the U.S.A., Canada, Australia, New Zealand, South Africa, France, Holland, Belgium, Luxembourg, Switzerland, Denmark, Norway, Sweden, Finland, and Jamaica. A good deal of international visiting goes on, and parties of members from Great Britain have been to most countries in Europe, to Canada, Australia, New Zealand, and the U.S.A. In return they have received guests from abroad, and some of these have represented their countries in the competitions held each year at the Royal Show.

See also Vol. IX: CLUBS, BOYS' AND GIRLS'.